UNWITTING TRAVELERS:

A HISTORY OF PRIMATE REINTRODUCTION

Benjamin B. Beck

Copyright © 2018 by Benjamin B. Beck

All rights reserved.

ISBN 978-1-62806-208-3   (print | paperback)
ISBN 978-1-62806-209-0   (ebook)
ISBN 978-1-62806-210-6   (ebook)

Library of Congress Control Number 2019934192

Published by Salt Water Media
29 Broad Street, Suite 104
Berlin, MD 21811
www.saltwatermedia.com

No part of this book may be reprinted or reproduced without the written permission of the author and publisher.

Cover Images & Design: PPG gorilla in pirogue by Tony King and golden lion tamarins by Andreia Martins are used with permission. Design by Salt Water Media.

TABLE OF CONTENTS

Foreword and Summary i

Chapter 1: Definitions 1

Chapter 2: Reintroductions of Chimpanzees and Bonobos 11

Chapter 3: Reintroductions of Gorillas 61

Chapter 4: Reintroductions of Orangutans 86

Chapter 5: Reintroductions of Gibbons and a Siamang 128

Chapter 6: Reintroductions of Asian Monkeys (and Barbary Macaques) 147

Chapter 7: Reintroductions of African Monkeys 203

Chapter 8: Reintroductions of New World Monkeys 232

Chapter 9: Reintroductions of Lorises and Lemurs 275

Chapter 10: Tabular Summary of Primate Reintroduction Programs 297

Bibliography 324

Index 368

FOREWORD AND SUMMARY

A History of Primate Reintroduction was first published in 2017 on my website (www.drbenjaminbeck.com) for broad, rapid, and free distribution and review. The site got 6,000 unique views from 98 different countries in the first six months. I don't know how many people read all or parts of the book, but I like to think that the first edition had thousands of reviewers. I received many suggestions, corrections, additions, and even a few compliments. The book is popular. Time will tell if it is useful and influential. This second edition is completely updated and refreshed as of 10 September 2018. This second edition is intended to be a "real book", whatever that means these days.

The title of the first edition, *A History of Primate Reintroduction*, was deadly boring. My editor and my writer's intuition told me that I needed something more inviting.

When humans began traveling long distances – crossing rivers and island-hopping, and later ocean-hopping in boats, and traveling overland by wheeled vehicles and later airplanes – we began taking stuff with us. Some of this stuff included wild primates that we liberated at our destinations, i.e. we reintroduced them. Sometimes the primates just hitchhiked, without any human intent. But mostly we took them intentionally, enabled by technology and human agency, fueled by human arrogance, and replete with the full range of noble to crassly self-serving motivations with which we treat our fellow primates. The primates themselves (with one exception) did not consent to the journeys and had no idea where they were going or why, hence the new title: *Unwitting Travelers: A History of Primate Reintroduction*.

Sailors took the smaller, more tractable species along as living food, to be killed and eaten at sea. Some of the survivors somehow made it to dry land when the ship arrived. Sometimes the primates served as exotic living gifts and trophies. In some cases we took them as our own pets and dumped them (or they escaped) far from home when we tired of them. Later, primates were taken and reintroduced as seed stock for island breeding colonies, whose offspring could be harvested and lucratively sold as research animals to laboratories in temperate climes. Sometimes we moved monkeys because they were harassing their human neighbors and stealing food, and moving them to somebody else's backyard was preferable to tolerating or killing them. Some reintroduced primates had outlived their value as laboratory research subjects and were reintroduced as an alternative to killing them. Some have been reintroduced so that we could study how they adapted to a new environment. Our recent intentions have been more noble. We reintroduce them to give them a "second life" in the wild after they have been captured as babies and mistreated by humans, or when their natural homes are imminently threatened by fire or bulldozers. We have rescued and rehabilitated more than 2,500 orangutans for these reasons alone. In a few cases we have reintroduced captive- or wild-born primates to increase the numbers and genetic diversity of their wild species-mates. Some reintroduce primates because they believe it is God's intention, or an ethical imperative, that they live in the wild.

I like to think of *Unwitting Travelers* as a tool for colleagues and students (and anybody else who is interested), present and future, to increase the efficiency and success of future reintroductions and to improve the wellbeing of reintroduced primates. The text provides as much descriptive information about each reintroduction program as I could find. For some programs I've added some subjective impressions of the human and nonhuman primates involved and about the program's context. These stories make up the Narrative section, which comprises chapters 2 through 9. The Table, which is Chapter 10, summarizes this descriptive information for each program. I also included some "text boxes" among the narratives for information that I found to be instructive, compelling, and/or historically significant.

The term Reintroduction is used in *Unwitting Travelers* as a generic term that includes Translocation, Reintroduction (*sensu strictu*), and Introduction (please see Definitions, Chapter 1).

I was able to document 234 primate reintroduction programs (see Definitions) that involved 24,212 individual prosimians, monkeys, and apes. The precision of that number is misleading because some sources do not state how many primates were actually reintroduced, and at least one program probably exaggerated the number that were released.

I had been invited by Serge Wich and Andy Marshall in 2014 to write a chapter on primate reintroduction as a conservation strategy for their book *An Introduction to Primate Conservation* (Beck 2017). I quickly began to suspect that for primates, reintroduction was less a conservation strategy for primate populations than a strategy for enhancing welfare of individual primates. I wrote the chapter knowing that I was aware of only a small proportion, perhaps 25%, of all primate reintroduction projects. I decided to write a complete history of primate reintroduction, which has taken about four years. I was completely unprepared for the magnitude of the history, never imagining that I would find 234 programs and more than 24,000 reintroduced primates.

I sensed that more wild-born primates had been reintroduced than captive-borns, and that welfare-based reintroductions were more frequent than conservation-based reintroductions. These became "hypotheses".

Of the total of 24,212 reintroduced primates, 23,219 (95.9%) were wild-born and 993 (4.1%) were captive-born (Figure 1). Zoos, aquaria, arboreta, and other captive breeding institutions can justly be proud of providing captive-born animals and plants for conservation-based reintroductions, but, with regard to primates, the claims should be moderated.

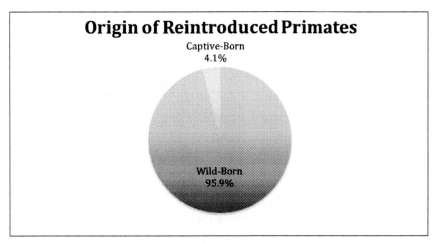

I attributed, where possible, a primary and secondary purpose for each of the 234 programs (see Definitions). A primary purpose could be attributed for 217 of the 234 programs and a secondary purpose could be attributed for 112 of the 234 programs. I calculated the percentages of the different purposes of the 329 purposes combined. Conservation was a primary or secondary purpose of 50 (15.2%) of the programs, and Welfare was a primary or secondary purpose of 151 (45.9%) of the programs. The breakdown of the most common purposes is shown in Figure 2.

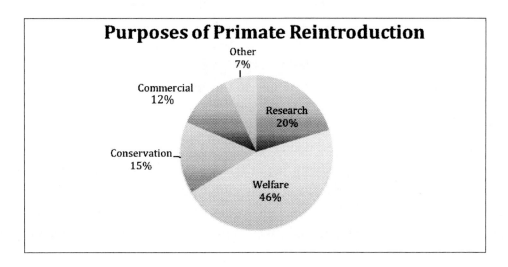

There is a major and disconcerting disconnect between this outcome and IUCN guidance on reintroduction. The IUCN guidelines on reintroductions of all plants and animals (IUCN/SSC 2013) state unequivocally that a reintroduction "must be intended to yield a measurable (sic) conservation benefit at the levels of a population, species or ecosystem, and not only provide benefit to ….. individuals" (IUCN 2013, pg. VIII). There are also IUCN guidelines targeted specifically to the reintroduction of nonhuman primates (Baker, 2002). These also exclude welfare reintroductions: "The main goal of any re-introduction effort should be to re-establish self-sustaining populations of primates in the wild and to maintain the viability of those populations. Although exceptions to this, such as trial re-introduction of common species and rescue/welfare releases, should also adhere to these guidelines as much as possible, such projects are not considered true re-introductions or conservation approaches and are not specifically covered in these guidelines" (pg. 6). Welfare reintroductions were not only excluded but were deemed to be not "true" reintroductions.

Yet 46% of the primary and secondary purposes of all primate reintroductions are Welfare. Indeed the *primary* purpose of 60% of all primate reintroductions (for which the primary purpose is known) is the Welfare of individual animals, and the primary purpose of only 12% is Conservation. Only rarely can Welfare reintroductions credibly be claimed to serve Conservation as well as the welfare of individuals.

Practitioners of primate welfare-based reintroductions and primate conservationists are largely different sorts of people with largely different interests. Their techniques differ, they seek largely different outcomes, and they produce different products. Primate welfare reintroduction programs appear to have different funding sources, and donor motivations and interests. One would hope that a common goal is the conservation of primate species and native habitats. Some conservationists claim that welfare reintroductions actually impede attainment of these conservation goals. There is legitimate debate about the overall value of welfare reintroductions, and of their conservation value, but offhanded denial of the legitimacy of welfare reintroductions does little to advance the debate, and actually excludes many primate reintroduction practitioners from the stakeholders' table. It also leaves many of them without guidance, and isolated from a pool of international expertise.

I first became aware of this simmering divide in 2006, at an "African Primate Reintroduction Workshop", organized by the Pan African Sanctuary Alliance in conjunction with the IUCN Re-introduction Specialist Group, the Captive Breeding Specialist Group, and the Apenheul Primate Park. I had just been asked by IUCN to author a set of guidelines specifically for the reintroduction of great apes, and used my talk as an opportunity to seek input from the directors of a number of ape sanctuaries who were keenly interested in reintroduction. The first interruption of my talk came in 30 seconds, and was followed by a seemingly endless string of jeers and hostile comments. I made it through the talk but the effect was devastating. It took several days, many helpful conversations, some long walks with colleagues, and a few beers to realize that the criticism was not personal, but was rather an expression of pent-up suspicions, frustrations, and exclusions toward IUCN restrictions on welfare-based reintroductions. How could struggling sanctuaries afford to do guidelines-mandated comprehensive pre-release habitat surveys, extensive pre-release training, and systematic post-release monitoring with radiotelemetry? The directors of African sanctuaries had to feed hundreds of hungry mouths every morning, enlist the support of sometimes-angry local neighbors, soothe avaricious government regulators, provide shelter and love to an endlessly growing number of physically and psychologically damaged ape orphans, and try to raise funds to keep their operations going. I was implored by many conference attendees, from both the conservation and welfare communities, to drop the guidelines project, which actually increased my determination to produce a set of guidelines that would be pertinent, helpful, and respectful to managers of welfare-based ape reintroduction while upholding the highest conservation and scientific standards. My co-authors and I specifically acknowledged the existence and legitimacy of welfare-based reintroductions. "[Rescue-welfare releases] should adhere to these guidelines as closely as possible. Projects that address the welfare of individual apes must also consider the conservation of the species as a whole" (Beck et al 2009, pg. 6).

Many commonly ask if reintroduction is successful. The answer depends on one's definition of success. I used two criteria for success. The first (Success A in the table) is a lower bar (survival of some of the released individuals for at least one year, and integration with wild conspecifics or post-release reproduction, and ability to survive without provisioning or human support. The second (Success B) is a higher bar (contributed to the establishment of a self-sustaining wild population). I was pleasantly surprised that 101 of the 234 (43.2%) programs attained the less demanding criterion of success (Success A) and, of these, 31 (14% of total programs) also reached the more demanding criterion (Success B).

To be clear, 43.2% pertains to the percentage of *programs* that are successful, not the percentage of animals that lived for a specific period after release.

The Bornean Orangutan Survival Foundation has recently included long-term post-release monitoring. Two resultant presentations (Husson et al 2018, Sulistyo et al 2018) use survival for one year after release as a criterion of success for individual animals within a program. However, in calculations of the percentages of success, these authors exclude orangutans that have been reintroduced but for whom one-year outcomes are unknown. This dramatically inflates success rates.

It should be noted that lack of evidence for success does not equate with failure. It should also be noted that reintroduction managers who claim success should provide their definition of success.

Many programs do not conduct sufficient post-release monitoring to report any outcomes. Many report only "happy" outcomes, such as survival of one individual for a decade, or a birth. Few rigorously account for deaths or disappearances. Popular accounts, e.g. "news stories" on websites and Facebook posts, are frequently used in lieu of rigorous, systematic reporting. The lack of post-release monitoring and credible reporting of outcomes is a violation of IUCN reintroduction guidelines. Of course, many programs lack the expertise, time, and money to conduct post-release monitoring under difficult field conditions. The real question is whether a program's management really wants to know the outcomes, and really wants to report the outcomes, but lacks the resources to do so, or whether the managers don't really want to know what happened to the animals. Even worse, managers may censor reporting unpleasant outcomes for fear of disillusionment by followers, financial supporters, and government regulators. We owe more to the nonhuman primates that we reintroduce.

A major question about outcomes is whether Welfare-based reintroductions actually increase the health and wellbeing of individual animals. I acknowledge a bias here. I believe in what I call the "Bahati Principle": In terms of health and wellbeing of many orphaned, rescued, or long-term captive primates, life in a supportive, well managed, captive environment is preferable to life in the wild. This *History* shows that reintroduction, even when well planned and executed, is rarely beneficial for the wellbeing of an individual primate. Hunger, aggression, pain and suffering, or at least discomfort, and conflict with humans are common after reintroduction. Freedom comes at a price.

There are few data that bear on the issue. Indeed, there is no consensus about what relevant data would look like. It's difficult to measure welfare, even in captive primates. Woodruff et al (2016) measured fecal glucocorticoids (FGCMs) of 15 mandrills during a reintroduction process. FGCMs are considered to be an indicator of stress. The FGCMs increased after the move from a sanctuary to an acclimation cage at the release site and then again after actual release to the wild. In each case, however, the FGCM levels returned to sanctuary levels within a month of being placed in the new environment. This is one of only a few studies of stress during the reintroduction process, and suggests that the animals' welfare was not permanently harmed by release to the wild. Without such data, program managers should be reserved in claiming that the welfare of reintroduced primates is actually enhanced by reintroduction. Intuition and philosophical predispositions are not data.

Many reintroductions that were motivated by Commercial purposes appear to have been successful, as judged by profits. Again, data are scarce because most private commercial enterprises do not publicize financial information. Monkey "farming", harvesting the descendants of reintroduced monkeys and selling them to biomedical and pharmaceutical research laboratories, appears to be immensely profitable. As an example, between 8,000 and 10,000 crab-eating macaques are exported annually from the island of Mauritius to North America and Europe. At a per-monkey price of US$1,500, gross proceeds would be US$10,000,000 per year (Wadman 2017). Many thousands of descendants of reintroduced vervets from Barbados, St Kitts, and Nevis; crab-eating macaques from Tinjil Island; and rhesus macaques from Silver Springs, the Florida Keys, Cayo Santiago, and Morgan Island have been harvested and sold as laboratory research subjects.

A measure of success for those reintroduction projects in which Research is a goal is publication of results in a peer-reviewed scientific journal or book and/or presentation at a peer-reviewed scientific conference. Of the 67 primate reintroduction projects for which research is a primary or secondary goal, 62 (92.5%) satisfied the publication criterion.

The *History* will support an almost endless supply of other questions, conclusions, relationships, and comparisons. Please share your findings with me and others. Publication of the first edition of this History coincided with the publication of the first edition of *Primate Conservation; Global Evidence for the Effects of Interventions* (Junker et al 2017), which is an ambitious project aimed at collating the effects of interventions to conserve primate biodiversity. A major portion of the work evaluates correlational evidence for the effects of animal histories and various forms of pre- and post-release management on the success of primate reintroductions. Sample size is small (approximately 20 primate reintroductions), but the results are suggestive if not definitive.

Please leave your additions, corrections, suggestions, updates, and other thoughts in the "Forum" section on my website (www.drbenjaminbeck.com) and/or send them to me directly (benbeck21@gmail.com). Please try to follow the Definitions (Chapter 1) and include pdfs of source articles. This book has been published with no photos to make it less costly. I would be happy to maintain a primate reintroduction photo archive. Readers could contribute photos, but their copyright can no longer be guaranteed in reprintings and there can be no restrictions on use.

Thanks in advance to those who have provided information for the first and second editions. I also wish to thank Sian Evans of the DuMond Conservancy for bringing some projects to my attention and for making her libraries available. Others who provided historical details and data, or linked me to additional contacts, are Jim Anderson, Claudine Andre, Walter Angst, Paul Beaver, Kaitlyn Bock, Janis Carter, Arnold Chamove, Leif Cocks, Debbie Cox, Larry Curtis, Tim

Davenport, Tom Defler, Andrea Donaldson, Brian Hare, Chris Herzfeld, Satoshi Hirata, Rob Horwich, Cecilia Kierulff, Tony King, Bill McGrew, Russ Mittermeier, Dominique Morel, Carlos Ruiz-Miranda, Nadezda Msindai, Anthony Rylands, Rob Shumaker, Tara Stoinski, Caroline Tutin, Missy Williams, and Liz Williamson. Alexandra Palmer and Anne Russon reviewed the section on orangutan reintroductions, providing additional references, updates, and corrections.

The Reptile Database, managed by Peter Uetz, though far more ambitious than this *History*, provides a model for the future of this project that includes the addition of photographs and additional references, and processes by which trained volunteers can curate the information, ensuring that it stays comprehensive and timely. Peter provided much-needed advice and encouragement.

Stephanie Fowler and Patty Gregorio of Salt Water Media in Berlin, Maryland helped with the format and layout.

My wife Beate, always a supporter, has put up with years of long mental absence as I tracked and wrote about primate reintroductions.

Finally, I am grateful to the 24,212 primates who were, as *Unwitting Travelers*, compelled to participate in these endeavors. Their individual health and wellbeing were not always foremost in our intentions.

Benjamin B. Beck, 30 October 2018

REFERENCES FOR THE FOREWORD AND SUMMARY

Baker, L.R. 2002. IUCN/SSC Re-introduction Specialist Group: Guidelines for nonhuman primate re-introductions. *Re-introduction News* 21: 29-57. (Cross-listed as IUCN/SSC 2002).

Beck, B.B. 2016. The role of translocation in primate conservation. In S.A. Wich and A.J. Marshall, eds. *An Introduction to Primate Conservation* pp. 241-255. Oxford, UK, Oxford University Press.

Beck, B.B. 2017. *A History of Primate Reintroduction*. Accessed at www.drbenjaminbeck.com

Beck, B.B., Walkup, K., Rodrigues, M., Unwin, S., Travis, D., and T. Stoinski. 2007. *Best Practice Guidelines for the Re-introduction of Great Apes*. Gland, IUCN/SSC Primate Specialist Group.

Bock, K. 2018. Personal communication (e-mail, 26 June).

Faust, L.J., Cress, D., Farmer, K.H., Ross, S.R., and B.B. Beck. 2011. Predicting capacity demand on sanctuaries for African chimpanzees. *International Journal of Primatology* 32(4): 849-864.

Husson, S.J., Suyoko, A., Kurnianwan, D., Sunderland-Groves, J., and J. Sihite. 2018. Factors affecting the successful reintroduction of Bornean orangutans (*Pongo pygmaeus*). Abstract of a paper presented at the 27th Congress of the International Primatological Society, Nairobi, Kenya.

IUCN/SSC. 2013. *Guidelines for Reintroductions and Other Conservation Translocations. Version 1.0*. Gland, IUCN Species Survival Commission.

Junker, J., Kühl, H.S., Orth, L., Smith, K., Petrovan, S.O., and W.J. Sutherland. 2017. *Primate Conservation: Global Evidence for the Effects of Interventions*. Cambridge, UK, University of Cambridge.

Stiles, D., Redmond, I., Cress, D., Nellemann, C., and R.K. Formo. 2013. *Stolen Apes: The illicit Trade in Chimpanzees, Gorillas, Bonobos and Orangutans*. GRID-Arendal.

Sulistyo, F., Fahroni, A., Sriningsih, A.P., Sunderland-Groves, J. and J. Sihite. 2018. Overview of medical interventions in Bornean orangutan reintroduction sites in Kalimantan, Indonesia. Abstract of a paper presented at the 27th Congress of the International Primatological Society, Nairobi, Kenya.

Uetz, P., Freed, P., and J. Hošek, eds. *The Reptile Database*. http://www.reptile-database.org.),

Voigt, M., Wich, S.A., Ancrenaz, M., Meijaard, E., Abram, N., Banes, G.L., Campbell-Smith, G., d'Arcy, L.J., Delgado, R.A., Erman, A., Gaveau, D., Goossens, B., Heinicke, S., Houghton, M., Husson, S.J., Leiman, A., Sanchez, K.L., Makinuddin, N., Marshall, A.J., Meididit, A., Miettinen, J., Mundry, R., Nardiyono, M., Nurcahyo, A., Odom, K., Panda, A., Prasetyo, D., Priadjati, A., Purnomo, Rafiastanto, A., Russon, A.E., Santika, T., Sihite, J., Spehar, S., Struebig, M., Sulbaran-Romero, E., Tjiu, A., Wells, J.,

Wilson, K.A., and H. S. Kühl. 2018. Global demand for natural resources eliminated more than 100,000 Bornean orangutans. *Current Biology* 28(5): 761-769.

Wadman, M. 2017. Mauritius invites primate research labs to set up shop. *Science* 356(6337): 472-473.

Woodruff, M. C., Lavin, S. R., Atencia, R., Woodruff, G. T., Lambert, F. N., Hill, R. A., Wheaton, C. J., and J. M. Setchell. 2016. Measuring fecal glucocorticoid metabolites during a reintroduction of mandrills (*Mandrillus sphinx*) in the Republic of Congo. Abstract of a paper presented at the joint meeting of the 26th Congress of the International Primatological Society and the 39th Meeting of the American Society of Primatologists, Chicago, IL, USA.

CHAPTER 1
DEFINITIONS

Reintroduction: I define "Reintroduction" as humans moving a wild nonhuman primate (henceforth primate) from one place in the wild (origin site) and releasing it in another place in the wild (destination or release site), or from an origin site in captivity to a destination site in the wild, for purposes of conservation and/or for other non-conservation reasons (see below). "Moving" implies some form of captivity for some duration before the release, even if it's just a few hours in a shipping crate.

The term "Reintroduction" is used herein as the generic term for moving animals or plants from captivity to the wild or from one place in the wild to another place in the wild. The term "Reintroduction" is also used as a particular type of conservation release (see below), in which case it will be clearly differentiated as "Reintroduction *sensu strictu*". The term "Translocation" will be used for moving animals from one place in the wild to another place in the wild. The term "Release" is used to describe setting animals free at a destination site. But "Reintroduction *sensu strictu*", "Translocation", and "Release" are all subsumed under "Reintroduction".

According to IUCN guidelines (IUCN/SSC 2013), the generic term for moving animals or plants is "Translocation". The guidelines reserve the term "Reintroduction" for a particular type of translocation (which I term "Reintroduction *sensu strictu*"), but this technical distinction has been confusing to many readers and has not been adopted by most scientists and authors. It does not conform to common usage of "Reintroduction".

As used herein, "Reintroduction" is synonymous with "Rewilding" and "Restocking".

Reintroduction Program: Each row in the database table and each "story" in the text is a program. A program can consist of a single release or a series of releases of one or more animals of the same species that is (are) conducted by a single organization or person(s) in the same general geographical area. A program can also be a series of releases of the same species that are conducted by different organizations or practitioners but are documented in a single source. If an organization or person(s) reintroduces a single primate species in different countries, states, or areas, each is considered to be a different program. If an organization or person(s) reintroduces two or more primate species in the same geographical area, each is considered to be a different program.

If an organization changes its name, or if there is an uninterrupted succession of organizations or persons reintroducing a single primate species in the same geographical area over time, the work is regarded as one program. However, if a different organization or person(s) assumes responsibility for the management of the reintroduction of a single primate species in a given geographical area, the releases before and after the change are regarded as different programs. Primates that escaped or were abandoned are included as programs.

Names of Primates: Scientific and common genus and species names follow the Appendix of Primate Names in Streier, K. B. 2007. *Primate Behavioral Ecology*, Boston, Allyn and Bacon. Pp 376-387. Synonyms for both common and scientific genus and species names are given in this history if the sources used different names than Streier used. The order in which species are listed in the database and narratives also follows Streier, but is reversed (apes first, prosimians last). Programs for each species are arranged in chronological order, from the earliest to the most recent. There are some exceptions to these ordering conventions. The African great apes are treated first. Grauer's gorillas and mountain gorillas are of the same species and are treated together, chronologically, (from the earliest to the most recent), although the text differentiates them by subspecies. Reintroductions within the range of eastern chimpanzees are treated before those of western chimpanzees. Orangutans are listed after chimpanzees and gorillas (Bornean preceding Sumatran), and gibbons are listed after the great apes. Bornean loris programs are also listed before Sumatran and Javan programs. Barbary macaques are listed with the Asian macaques. Five reintroductions of squirrel monkeys in Florida, USA are listed sequentially (not chronologically) for historical clarity. Three reintroductions of rhesus macaques and several reintroductions of chimpanzees and vervets are also listed sequentially for historical clarity

Country: The present name of the country in which reintroduced primates were released. For analysis, the names of protectorates and territories, e.g. Gibraltar, Puerto Rico, are used rather than the name of the governing nation.

Destination (Release) Site: Name and size (in ha) of the release site(s) for each program. The destination site can be unbounded, or it can be an island on which the animals are intentionally or unintentionally confined by water. It can also be a large, naturalistic fenced enclosure that is not part of a facility that is surrounded by a second, perimeter fence. Reintroductions onto islands or into large enclosures are included when the intent is to provide the animals with a larger, more naturalistic habitat with less dependence on and control by humans than would otherwise be available. Islands or large enclosures that are expressly used as pre-release training or acclimation sites (see below) for future reintroductions are not included as reintroduction destination sites. For example, seven New World monkey species have been released on the Ecuadorian island of

Sumak Allpa (114 ha), but managers of this program state that this is merely pre-release preparation for eventual reintroduction to the wild (e.g. Banerjee 2015, Walder 2014). Thus the program is not (yet) included in this history. Zoo exhibits (even "free ranging exhibits") or research center enclosures (e.g. Oregon Regional Primate Research Center) are not included.

The type of destination site that is included in this history is informed by the argument advanced by the British Union for the Abolition of Vivisection (now Cruelty Free International) (Anon. undated c) and by the definition of "captive-bred" by the Convention on International Trade in Endangered Species (CITES).

I include as reintroduction destination sites those enclosures and islands in (on) which primates have "constant interaction with other native fauna and flora". Water or fences may serve as boundaries that prevent the primates from entering or leaving, and food, water, shelter, and some health care might be provided, but the primates are "subjected to the same conditions as other wild animals and they directly contribute to and are part of the ecosystem involving the other wild animals and plants [in these enclosures or] on these islands. They do not live in a vacuum; rather they are part of the biodiversity of that ecosystem. They are logically and biologically wild animals and any change in their numbers or activity will have an impact on the other species of animals and plants that inhabit the islands." (Anon. undated d). The primates in these enclosures or on islands are free to eat whatever is available and may encounter potential predators and dangerous animals and plants without human intervention. They may disappear and their fate might remain unknown. Animal waste and dead bodies might not be removed. Mate choice is uncontrolled by humans.

For purposes of this history, primates that are born in such enclosures or on such islands are considered wild-born.

Note: The 2013 IUCN guidelines recommend that the destination sites for translocations of living plants and animals 1) be large enough to support a self-sustaining population of the species in question, or be connected to other areas where the species occurs, 2) contain sufficient resources to meet all of the needs of a self-sustaining population of the species, 3) have a climate that is appropriate for the species, 4) be securely protected and free of anthropomorphic threats to the species, 5) be part of a landscape that meets the needs of surrounding human communities, and 6) have land-use regulations that allow reintroduction of the species in question.

Year(s) in which release(s) was (were) conducted: Where possible, the years of actual releases in a program are specified (separated by commas in the table). A span of years is given when releases of separate cohorts occurred in different, unspecified years within a specified period (start and end dates separated by a hyphen in the table). The designation of years includes only years during which actual releases occurred, and does not include the years of captivity, pre-release preparation, or post-release monitoring in which actual releases did not occur.

Number of Animals: The number of animals released is specified when it is provided or can be inferred from the source(s). The number is often stated in sources as the minimum number. In these cases, we use the term "at least" in the text but show only the minimum number in the table. If no number of released primates is specified or can be inferred for a program in the source(s), "unspecified number" is used in the text, and "1" (in bold) is used in the table. This will cause an underestimate of the numbers actually reintroduced and some confusion with programs in which only one individual was actually released, which are also noted as "1" but in standard black font. When known, the number that were wild-born (WB) or captive-born (CB) is given. This is not always known or specified for each program, in which case all are considered WB for a translocation from a wild population of origin, and all are considered CB for a reintroduction from a captive population of origin.

Primary and Secondary Purpose: These describe the reasons the reintroduction was conducted. A program can have more than one purpose. The primary and secondary purposes are given. The authors' stated purposes are usually used. In some cases these are inferred or assumed. However, an author's (authors') stated purpose of conservation is not used if the numbers of animals involved is too small to be realistically conservation-relevant.

1) Conservation Releases, including:

Reinforcement (within historic range, existing population).

Reintroduction *sensu strictu* (within historic range, no existing population).

Introduction or Assisted Colonization (outside of historic range, to save population from extinction).

Ecological Replacement (outside of historic range, to restore critical ecosystem function).

2) Welfare Releases, including:

Rehabilitation: Release of sanctuary primates, zoo primates, or orphan primates when the intent is to improve the physical or psychological wellbeing of the released primates. The animals involved must have been held in a sanctuary, research center, or zoo long enough to have received at least some observation of their condition, provisioned food, and care intended to bring them to a state of health that is sufficient for release. Some form of social integration with conspecifics, and pre-release behavioral training in survival-critical skills may have been offered (see pre-release preparation).

Rescue: Capture of wild animals in imminent danger and translocating them to a safer area after a minimal time in captivity. This would include translocations to mitigate threats to primates caused by human activities (such as dam construction).

Non-lethal Control (including unwanted pets): Release is undertaken as an alternative to killing the animals because they are "problems", are overpopulated, or are unwanted by their owners.

3) Commercial Releases: Includes reintroductions and translocations that are intended to start breeding colonies to produce colony-born offspring for biomedical research, or to stimulate tourism.

4) Research/Scientific Releases: This may be basic scientific research, e.g. study of activity patterns before and after release, or applied research, e.g. comparing "hard" and "soft" release strategies or testing new telemetry technologies.

5) Recreational/Aesthetic

6) Religious

7) Accidental/Escape

8) Unspecified

Pre-release Preparation: Yes ("1") in the table indicates that IUCN guidelines were followed, at least partially. No, indicated by a blank cell in the table, is assumed unless pre-release preparation is specified in the source. If some of the animals in the program received pre-release preparation and others did not, Yes is assumed if the majority did receive pre-release preparation and No is assumed if the majority did not.

Preparation should involve quarantine, veterinary examination and screening, and perhaps immunization.

Preparation could also involve training of the release candidates. Training involves active, purposeful exposure to natural foods, model or surrogate caregivers, predators (or predator models), natural substrates and nesting materials, anthropogenic threats (e.g. cars, power lines, people themselves) and other significant features of the post-release physical or social environments. Training can consist of simply placing the animal(s) into naturalistic, free-ranging environments that support undirected learning in locomotion and/or foraging. Training may involve classical or respondent conditioning to establish survival-critical behaviors through reinforcement. Training may also involve exposure to skilled conspecifics (human models were used in a few cases as well) on the assumption that survival-critical information can be acquired by social learning. Training may also involve early imprinting to encourage normal adult social and sexual behaviors.

Acclimation: There are three categories of acclimation: Less Than One Month, One to Six Months, and Greater Than Six Months. Acclimation for one of these duration categories is indicated in the table by "1" in the appropriate cell. If acclimation is not indicated in the source, or if the source states that there was no acclimation, these cells are left blank. If the source states that there was acclimation but the duration is not specified, it is assumed that the duration was Less Than One Month. If some of the animals in the program were acclimated and others were not, Yes is assumed in the table if the majority were acclimated, and No is assumed if the majority were not. If the durations of acclimation differed for different animals in the program, the shortest duration experienced by the animals is used.

Acclimation usually takes place at or near the release site in some type of enclosure. It involves passive exposure to local climate; day length; landscape views; night sky; sights, sounds, and smells; water quality; and/or a subsample of natural foods. It may allow the animals to recover from the stresses of transportation from their former captive homes. The cage might be left open after release to provide temporary refuge and other forms of post-release support (see below).

Post-release Support: There are three categories of post-release support: Less Than One Month, One to Six Months, and Greater Than Six Months. Post-release support for one of these duration categories is indicated in the table by "1" in the appropriate cell. If post-release support is not indicated in the source, or if the source states that there was no post-release support, these cells are left blank. If the source states that there was post-release support but the duration is not specified, it is assumed that the duration was Less Than One Month. If some of the animals in the program received post-release support and others did not, Yes is assumed in the table if the majority did receive post release support and No is assumed if the majority did not. If the durations of post-release support differed for different animals in the program, the shortest duration experienced by the animals is used.

Post-release support includes provisioning with supplementary food and water, providing veterinary care, warding off predators or aggressive conspecifics, capture and re-release to avoid life threatening situations, capture and re-release of lost animals, guidance in navigation, providing artificial sleeping, roosting or nesting sites, and/or continued training.

Post-release Monitoring: There are three categories of post-release monitoring: Less Than One Month, One to Six Months, and Greater Than Six Months. Post-release monitoring for one of these duration categories is indicated in the table by "1" in the appropriate cell. If post-release monitoring is not indicated in the source, or if the source states that there was no post-release monitoring, these cells are left blank. If the source states that there was post-release monitoring but the duration is not specified, it is assumed that the duration was Less Than One Month. If some of the animals in the program were monitored post-release and others were not, Yes is assumed in the table if the majority were monitored and No is assumed if the majority were not. If the durations of post-release monitoring differed for different animals in the program, the shortest duration for living animals is used.

Post-release monitoring can include ad lib visual observation of the animals for physical condition, death, disappearance, and reproduction. It can include rescue of animals that are not adjusting well or who are injured or ill. It can include ad lib observation or some form of sampling of their vocalizations, social behavior, home range and activity cycles, and feeding behavior. Tracking by radiotelemetry might be used and, less frequently, transect surveys of occurrence and abundance, and/or scat or nest counts.

Success: I use two definitions of success.

Success A = Evidence that there was:

Survival of some of the released individuals for at least one year, *and*
Integration with wild conspecifics or Post-release reproduction, *and*
Ability to survive without provisioning or human support.

Yes is indicated by the digit "1" in the appropriate cell. No, unspecified, or unknown is indicated by an empty cell. An empty cell is not synonymous with Failure.

Criteria for Success A do not include enhanced environmental protection or increased public awareness or support for conservation.

Success B = Contribution to establishment of a self-sustaining population. Yes is indicated by the digit "1" in the appropriate cell. No, unspecified, or unknown is indicated by an empty cell.

"Self-sustaining" is defined as having at least 250 individuals living and reproducing in the wild, independent of provisioning or other forms of post-release support, or where a formal genetic/demographic analysis, e.g. Population and Habitat Viability Analysis, predicts that the population is likely to survive for 100 years. The reintroduction need not have been the sole or most instrumental factor contributing to the population being self-sustaining. The program must have met the criteria for Success A to be evaluated for Success B. Note: Releasing a small number of individual primates successfully (A) to a wild population of hundreds that is already self-sustaining can be counted as successful according to the criteria for Success B; this will inflate the number of programs attaining Success B.

REFERENCES FOR CHAPTER 1: DEFINITIONS

Anon. undated c. BUAV (The British Union for the Abolition of Vivisection) Briefing on Environment Protection and Biodiversity Conservation Amendment (Prohibition of Live Imports of Primates for Research), Bill 2015, Submission 48 - Attachment 3.

Anon. 1998. *IUCN Guidelines for Re-introductions*. Gland, IUCN/SSC Re-introduction Specialist Group.

Anon. 2002a. *Guidelines for the Placement of Confiscated Live Animals*. Gland, International Union for the Conservation of Nature and Natural Resources.

Baker, L.R. 2002. IUCN/SSC Re-introduction Specialist Group: Guidelines for nonhuman primate re-introductions. *Re-introduction News* 21: 29-57.

Banerjee, D.P. 2015. *Population Assessment of the Common Squirrel Monkey* (Saimiri sciureus) *on Sumak Allpa, Ecuador*. Undergraduate thesis, Environmental Studies, University of Delaware.

Beck, B.B. 2016. The role of translocation in primate conservation. In S.A. Wich and A.J. Marshall, eds. *An Introduction to Primate Conservation*, pp. 241-255. Oxford, UK, Oxford University Press.

Beck, B.B., Rapaport, L.G., Stanley Price, M.R., and A.C. Wilson. 1994. Reintroduction of captive-born mammals. In: P.J.S. Olney, G.M. Mace, and A.T.C. Feistner, eds. *Creative Conservation: Interactive Management of Wild and Captive Animals*, pp. 265-286. London, Chapman and Hall.

Beck, B.B., Walkup, K., Rodrigues, M., Unwin, S., Travis, D., and T. Stoinski. 2007. *Best Practice Guidelines for the Re-introduction of Great Apes*. Gland, IUCN/SSC Primate Specialist Group.

Campbell, C.O., Cheyne, S.M., and B.M. Rawson. 2015. *Best Practice Guidelines for the Rehabilitation and Translocation of Gibbons*. Gland, IUCN/SSC Primate Specialist Group.

Cheyne, S.M. 2009. The role of reintroduction in gibbon conservation: Opportunities and challenges. In S. Lappan and D.J. Whittaker, eds. *The Gibbons, Developments in Primatology: Progress and Prospects*, pp. 477-496. New York, Springer.

Ewen, J.G., Armstrong, D.P., Parker, K.A., and P.J. Seddon. 2013. *Reintroduction Biology: Integrating Science and Management*. London, Wiley-Blackwell.

Fischer, J. and D.B. Lindenmeyer. 2000. An assessment of the published results of animal relocations. *Biological Conservation* 96: 1-11.

Germano, J.M., Field, K.J., Griffiths, R.A., Clulow, S., Foster, J., Harding, G., and R.R. Swaisgood. 2015.

Mitigation-driven translocations: are we moving wildlife in the right direction? *Frontiers in Ecology and the Environment* 13(2): 100-105.

Griffith, B., Scott, M., Carpenter, J.W., and C. Reed. 1989 Translocation as a species conservation tool: Status and strategy. Science 24: 477-80.

Guy, A.J., Curnoe, D., and P.B. Banks. 2014 Welfare based primate rehabilitation as a potential conservation strategy: Does it measure up? *Primates* 55: 139-147.

Harcourt, A.H. 1987. Options for unwanted or confiscated primates. *Primate Conservation* 8: 111-113.

Harrington, L.A., Moehrenschlager, A., Gelling, M., Atkinson, R.P.D., Hughes, J., and D.W. Macdonald. 2013. Conflicting and complementary ethics of animal welfare considerations in reintroductions. *Conservation Biology* 27(3): 486-500.

Hockings, K., and T. Humle. (2009) *Best Practice Guidelines for the Prevention and Mitigation of Conflict Between Humans and Great Apes*. Gland, IUCN/SSC Primate Specialist Group.

IUCN/SSC. 2013. *Guidelines for Reintroductions and Other Conservation Translocations*. Version 1.0. Gland, IUCN Species Survival Commission.

Kavanagh, M. and J.O. Caldecott. 2013. Strategic guidelines for the translocation of primates and other animals. *The Raffles Bulletin of Zoology*, Supplement 29: 203-209.

Walder, C. 2014. *Rehabilitation Assessment of a Juvenile Woolly Monkey* (Lagothrix lagotricha poeppigii) *Troop on Sumak Allpa Island, Ecuador*. Report submitted for Bowdoin College's Comparative Ecology and Conservation SIT Study Abroad Program.

CHAPTER 2
REINTRODUCTIONS OF CHIMPANZEES AND BONOBOS

Chimpanzee (*Pan troglodytes*). The Frankfurt Zoological Society released 17 chimpanzees in four cohorts on 24,000-ha Rubondo Island, in Lake Victoria (Tanzania) between 1966 and 1969. There were eight males and nine females. Msindai et al (2015), on the basis of mtDNA evidence, concluded that the founder population had been a mixture of two subspecies, the west African *P. verus* and the central African *P. troglodytes*. They had lived between three months and nine years in German and Dutch zoos and circuses. They were between four and 12 years of age when released. Some had been socially housed under good zoo conditions and some had been caged alone. Some were healthy and behaved normally but others were judged in retrospect to have been physically and/or psychologically unfit for release. Some of the chimpanzees knew each other and others were socially deprived. One male was known to be aggressive toward humans while in captivity and attacked humans after release. He was shot. Another male may have met the same fate.

There were no other chimpanzees on Rubondo at the time of the release although the island is within the range of eastern chimpanzees. However, as noted, the reintroduced chimpanzees were of the western and central subspecies.

There was no pre-release preparation or acclimation. Post-release support and monitoring were intermittent, but the chimpanzees were provisioned with food for two months. They were eating natural foods and building nests within a few months. At least two of the released chimpanzees were known to be alive in 1985. As noted above, one or perhaps two of the males was shot shortly after release because of aggressiveness toward humans. Some of the others continued to harass people and invade homes (with decreasing frequency) at least through 1985. Two island-born infants were first observed in 1968, and by 1985 the population numbered approximately 20 (Borner 1985). Some of these must have been among the original reintroductees because one female was seen stealing a blanket and wrapping herself in it in 1998, and a male was later observed to steal and drink a bottle of whiskey from a tourist camp. They could only have learned about blankets and whiskey in captivity. Moscovice et al (2007) estimated that there were between 27 and 35 chimpanzees on Rubondo in 2004. Moscovice et al also found that the chimpanzees subsisted entirely on natural foods in 2002. These authors also provide data on party size and nesting group size.

This was the first documented reintroduction of any African ape. The number of chimpanzees that were reintroduced in this program is small compared to the total population of eastern chimpanzees. However, the reintroduction may have contributed to Rubondo later being designated as a national park. This reintroduction may in part have been motivated by zoo and circus officials who were seeking a humane way of disposing of some chimpanzees that were not adapting well to zoo life (Non-lethal Control). However, the reintroduction was also intended to serve conservation, and it succeeded.

But there was a lost opportunity. There was abbreviated post-release monitoring by observers who did not know most of the chimpanzees individually. Except for the few observations and inferences described above, we do not know which of the chimpanzees survived and reproduced, the causes of most losses, how social groups were formed and changed, and the processes involved in beginning to eat natural foods and build nests. The variable histories of the chimpanzees provided a natural experimental population for investigating post-release adaptation. This reintroduction did show that at least some chimpanzees that had been captured as juveniles and subadults in the wild and held in captivity could be reintroduced successfully and establish a self-sustaining population, even with minimal post-release support. Importantly, natural foods were plentiful on Rubondo, and the reintroduced apes had no competition from a resident chimpanzee population.

Conservation (Introduction), Welfare (Non-lethal Control)

References

Borner, M. 1985. The rehabilitated chimpanzees of Rubondo Island. *Oryx* 19: 151–154.

Matsumoto-Oda, A. 2004. Chimpanzees in the Rubondo National Park, Tanzania. http://mahale.web.infoseek.co.jp/PAN/7_2/7(2)-02.html

Moscovice, L. R., Issa, M.H., Petrzelkova, K.J., Keuler, N.S., Snowdon, C.T., and M.A. Huffman. 2007. Fruit availability, chimpanzee diet, and grouping patterns on Rubondo Island, Tanzania. *American Journal of Primatology* 69: 487–502.

Msindai, N.J., Sommer, V., and C. Roos. 2015. The chimpanzees of Rubondo Island: Genetic data reveal their origin. *Folia Primatologica* 86(4): 327.

Chimpanzee (*Pan troglodytes*). The Ugandan Wildlife Authority and members of the research staff of the Kibale Forest Chimpanzee Project reintroduced a single orphaned and partially rehabilitated eastern chimpanzee in 1994. The reintroduced chimpanzee was a female, named "Bahati", who had been captured at approximately four years of age and had been kept in a home near the Kibale National Park (76,600 ha) in Uganda for between three and six months before being confiscated. Bahati's mother had probably been killed by poachers in the southern portion of the national park. The purpose of the reintroduction was stated to be research on Bahati's pre- and post-reintroduction behavior and her social integration into a community of wild chimpanzees. I think at least some wanted also to improve Bahati's welfare by returning her to the wild.

Bahati still had the white tail tuft that is indicative of chimpanzee infancy at the time she was confiscated. She was said to have been "remarkably healthy" and well nourished. She weighed 10.5 kg, climbed and walked competently, built nests, ate foods that are eaten by wild chimpanzees, and refused to be carried by humans. These observations suggest that she had gained considerable independence before her capture. Bahati was taken to the northern portion of Kibale National Park where she lived with caretakers at remote sites in the forest for three weeks.

During this time, she was examined by a veterinarian and given a tuberculosis skin test, which proved to be negative. Her caretakers took her for long walks in the forest and gave her the opportunity to hear wild chimpanzees. She was induced to avoid unfamiliar humans and taught to remove snares from herself. Provisioning with human foods was cut to one time per week, and she was induced to eat one kind of natural fruit that was preferred by wild chimpanzees.

Bahati was described as having an "attraction to human males", although she showed no signs of sexual cycling.

After three weeks of this pre-release preparation, Bahati was led by her caretakers to a party of 16 chimpanzees. This chimpanzee community (Kanyawara) had been habituated to the presence of rangers, scientists, and tourists, but of course it was not Bahati's natal community. The party approached immediately, led by males. Bahati observed quietly as the males displayed, and then she approached and embraced an eight year-old male. She returned to her caretakers when a dominant male displayed, but then left the humans and approached another dominant male who embraced and groomed her. The caretakers then left Bahati with the chimpanzees.

Ten days later Bahati was found looking for food in a village on the park border. She was retrieved by the caretakers and taken back to the forest, and then spent ten more days interacting with and traveling normally with wild chimpanzees. But she began to travel alone more frequently and entered villages five times in the next three weeks. She was returned to the forest each time but finally would not go back. She was taken to the Entebbe Zoo 45 days after her reintroduction, and then to the Ngamba Island Chimpanzee Sanctuary (see below), where she was living at least through 2018 (www.ngambaisland.org, accessed 29 June 2018).

When reintroduced, Bahati approached and was accepted by wild chimpanzees. This would be predicted for a young wild-born female chimpanzee who had spent only five months in captivity. The observers left her for several days after her reintroduction to decrease the likelihood that she would return to humans. There is therefore no information about her social integration and feeding behavior during a critical period in the reintroduction, and no information about what prompted her to return to a village. It appears that, understandably, concerns for her long-term welfare took precedence over the research agenda.

Upon being returned to the forest after her first venture to a village, Bahati was observed for ten days with wild chimpanzees. She interacted with 28 different members (approximately half) of the Kanyawara chimpanzees, groomed or was groomed by ten (mostly adult males), and played with four immatures. Bahati was the subject of aggression only four times, none serious. She stayed away from human observers, climbed high into trees, and ate fruit, leaves, and insects. Despite these indications of success, Bahati began to spend less time with the wild chimpanzees and to enter villages to "beg for food". Unlike some reintroduced chimpanzees and gorillas, she did not harass or attack people. The source suggests that she entered villages because fruit became scarce but the authors do not discount the possibility that her inability to keep up with the wild chimpanzees, unobserved aggression from females, and/or an unspecified psychological "depression" contributed. Richard Wrangham, co-director of the Kibale Chimpanzee Project suggested that "she came back to us because it was safe" (Morell 1994, p 312).

Research, Welfare (Rehabilitation)

References

Morell, V. 1994. Orphan chimps won't go back to nature. *Science* 265: 312.

Treves, A. and L. Naughton-Treves. 1997. Case study of a chimpanzee recovered from poachers and temporarily released with wild conspecifics. *Primates* 38(3): 315-324.

www.ngambaisland.org

THE BAHATI PRINCIPLE

The Bahati Principle is that: In terms of health and wellbeing of an orphaned, rescued, or long-term captive primate, life in a supportive, well managed captive environment is preferable to life in the wild.

Bahati was a four-year old chimpanzee who lived in the Kibale Forest in Uganda (see above). Her mother was presumably shot, and Bahati was taken captive by poachers. She was confiscated, found to be healthy, and prepared for reintroduction to the wild.

She was accepted by a group of wild chimpanzees. She groomed and was groomed by them, played with them, climbed trees, traveled with them, and ate the same wild foods as they did. She was rarely the subject of their aggression. However, she left the wild chimpanzees five times during a month and entered villages. She was sent to the Entebbe Zoo and finally to the Ngamba Island Chimpanzee Sanctuary, one of the best in Africa (see above).

Richard Wrangham said that "she came back to us because it was safe". This deceptively simple statement suggests a profound truth. "Freedom" in "the wild", is the goal of reintroduction, but for primates it comes with food shortages, weather extremes, predators, biting insects, venomous snakes, aggression, sometimes violent, from group mates and strangers, painful and debilitating injuries, untreated illnesses, and conflict with people. Further, as Russon (personal communication 2018) says, "having no relatives or friends in the forest community into which [apes] are released can be a serious problem".

"Shirley", an adult female chimpanzee who escaped from the Pandrillus center in Nigeria in 2018 (see below), also chose a life in human care over life in the wild.

In exchange for surrendering pure freedom and the chance to have and raise offspring, a primate in a good sanctuary is buffered from all of these unpleasantries. If I were a chimpanzee, I would make the same choice as Bahati.

There are two premises to the Bahati Principle:

1) This *History* shows that reintroduction, even when well planned and executed, is rarely beneficial for the wellbeing of an individual primate. Hunger, aggression, pain, and suffering, or at least discomfort, and conflict with humans are common. Freedom comes at a price.

2) The wellbeing of individual primates, especially of captive-born primates, is compromised in almost all cases of conservation-based reintroductions.

I am not arguing against reintroduction, but there may be other ways to achieve our conservation and welfare goals, and the Bahati Principle suggests that we should explore them. Lifetime care in a sanctuary is more expensive. At the very least, primates in sanctuaries and primates reintroduced on small islands should be permanently contracepted so that lifetime care is limited to one generation.

A group of experts in primate reintroduction (Sherman et al 2018) have also concluded that the decision not to reintroduce primates is underutilized.

Palmer (in press) has provided what promises to be an influential and widely cited analysis of the values and ethics of orangutan rehabilitation and reintroduction (Disclosure: I am cited in the article). She makes us aware that there are theological positions that oppose the Bahati Principle. She cites Muslim and Christian interviewees saying "all God's creations" "have their own path" and "belong to [God's] forest garden". "The forest needs them" and "they should do their duty there". "God put orangutans in the forest for a reason", and all rehabilitated orangutans, whether they are regarded as releaseable or not, should be reintroduced. Palmer also notes that indigenous cultures may regard orangutan reintroduction as "restoring the world to its natural order". These views (the quotes are a composite of quotes from three of Palmer's interviewees, in press, pg. 9) value "wildness over welfare" and the Bahati Principle values "welfare over wildness". I respect but don't share these theological and cultural arguments, and stick by the Bahati Principle.

References

Morell, V. 1994. Orphan chimps won't go back to nature. *Science* 265: 312.

Palmer, A. In press. Kill, incarcerate, or liberate? Ethics and alternatives to orangutan rehabilitation. *Biological Conservation*.

Sherman, J., Farmer, K.H., Williamson, E.A., Unwin, S., Kahlenberg, S.M., Russon, A.E., Cheyne, S.M., Humle, T., Mylniczenko, N., Macfie, E., and S. Wich. 2018. Methodology and technical advisory resources for ape reintroductions to natural habitats. Abstract of a paper presented at the 27th Congress of the International Primatological Society, Nairobi, Kenya.

Treves, A. and L. Naughton-Treves. 1997. Case study of a chimpanzee recovered from poachers and temporarily released with wild conspecifics. *Primates* 38(3): 315-324.

www.ngambaisland.org

Chimpanzee (*Pan troglodytes*). The Entebbe Zoo (now the Uganda Wildlife Research and Education Center) cared for orphaned chimpanzees from the 1960s to the 1990s despite inadequate facilities and support. The Jane Goodall Institute-Uganda, with additional support from the Sheraton Kampala hotel and the US Agency for International Development, moved 11 chimpanzees from the Entebbe Zoo to 5-ha Isinga Island in Lake Edward in 1995. The 11 were introduced in two cohorts, the first comprising eight subadults and adults (two males and six females) and the second comprising three infants (two males and one female). An orphaned infant male was added later in the same year. The purposes of this reintroduction were to relieve overcrowding at the zoo, and to rehabilitate the chimpanzees so that they might be reintroduced to a larger area.

Three of the released chimpanzees had been confiscated from a European circus and returned to Uganda. The others were orphans that had been confiscated in Uganda. I think all had been born in the wild although there is no information about where in Africa they had been born. A veterinarian accompanied the chimpanzees when they were moved by truck to Lake Edward, but there is no record of their medical condition or screening. The adult males were said by ecotourism guides to have been vasectomized (personal communication).

A jetty for a support boat and sleeping platforms for the chimpanzees had been constructed on Isinga, and a small logistics camp had been established on a nearby islet. There were no other primates on the island, but hippopotami were present. The first cohort of eight was released in the late afternoon of 3 March, the day they had travelled from the zoo. They fed immediately on provisioned market foods. The three infants stayed on the islet with caretakers and were gradually introduced to the other eight on the island over a week.

The first cohort explored the island on the day after release and returned to the jetty when they heard the supply boat arrive. A young male named "Sunday" began to dangle from tree branches over the water, and actually dropped onto the supply boat several times. The food was thereafter thrown to shore from a distance. Caretakers began bringing the three infants to the island while the other chimpanzees were being fed. The older chimpanzees behaved protectively and affiliatively toward the infants, and the infants were left permanently on the island after several days. Two of the infants, both males, were found in the water, dead, a few mornings later. There was no sign of aggression. They had drowned but the reason they fell into or entered the water is unknown.

A vasectomized one year-old male orphan was later introduced to the group and was adopted by one of the adult females.

The chimpanzees were provisioned heavily and observed daily throughout their whole stay on the island. Isinga was opened to ecotourism in May 1995. Visitors were able to view the chimpanzees at the feeding area from a floating platform. As an ecotourist, I saw ten chimpanzees on Isinga Island in February 1996. I have no further information on their status until late 1997/early 1998 when at least eight chimpanzees were removed and returned to the Uganda Wildlife Research and Education Center in Entebbe. Most were later moved to the Ngamba Island Chimpanzee Sanctuary (see below). The Isinga reintroduction was terminated.

During our 1996 visit, one of the adult males (Sunday) was able to jump onto the small boat being used by caretakers to feed the chimpanzees. The boat drifted toward the floating observation platform and Sunday came onboard. He sniffed every one of the 12 tourists and our backpacks, and touched a few of us nonaggressively. I had prepared the tourists for interactions with apes, and they remained quiet and still during the encounter. Caretakers finally induced Sunday to reboard their boat for return to the island. None of the tourists was injured or became ill. I don't know if Sunday became ill.

Given their unknown medical histories and their unknown provenance, it is best that these chimpanzees were never truly reintroduced to the wild. Vasectomizing the males was wise. The Isinga case confirms that chimpanzees can be introduced to and maintained successfully on islands. Provisioning, of course, is necessary on islands that are too small to provide sufficient natural foods. The welfare of the Isinga chimpanzees was definitely enhanced during their two years on the island.

Welfare (Non-lethal Control, Rehabilitation)

REFERENCES

Manning, C. 1996. The Lake Edward Chimpanzee Sanctuary. *IPPL News* 23(2): 25-28.

A CHIMPANZEE SANCTUARY THAT IS ALMOST A REINTRODUCTION

The Ngamba Island Chimpanzee Sanctuary is similar to a reintroduction in many ways, but because the chimpanzees are induced to enter a modern holding facility nightly for feeding and sleeping, they cannot be said to have "constant interaction with other native flora and fauna" at the destination site (See Definitions).

Information on thesanctuary is provided here for those readers who disagree and wish to have it included in this history.

Chimpanzee (*Pan troglodytes*). The Chimpanzee Sanctuary and Wildlife Conservation Trust, a collaborative effort originally involving the Ugandan Wildlife Authority, the Ugandan Wildlife Education Center, the Zoological Parks Board of New South Wales, the Jane Goodall Institute, the International Fund for Animal Welfare, and Born Free, brought 15 chimpanzees to Ngamba Island in Lake Victoria in 1998. Ngamba, which was described as a 32-ha forested "cork bobbing on the vastness of Africa's Lake Victoria" (Ward and Nelving 1999, pg. 56), is approximately 30 km from the mainland at Entebbe, Uganda.

The initial cohort of 15 had all been kept at the Ugandan Wildlife Education Center (the Entebbe Zoo) for varying periods of time. There were eight mature females but I have no other information on the ages, sexes, and histories of these chimpanzees except that at least some the eight chimpanzees who were removed from Isinga Island (see above) were among this cohort. All of the chimpanzees were moved in one day, and on the next day they were released in an electrically fenced-off forested portion of the island. They explored the forest and ate wild figs. They were and continue to be heavily provisioned with market foods, although they do forage on natural foods as well. As noted, they are induced to enter a holding facility each night. The move of the chimpanzees was attended by veterinarians, but I have no information about what sort of veterinary screening was used or whether all of the males were vasectomized. The chimpanzees currently receive state-of-the-art veterinary care at the Ngamba Sanctuary.

The chimpanzees were forming a community (for chimpanzees, a social group) and had learned how to orient in the entire forested area within six months. Some were eating enough wild food and refused the provisioned food that was distributed in the forest and in the holding area.

Ecotourism began in 1999. Ngamba has been a gateway experience for many who wish to see chimpanzees in the wild. Proceeds help to support the facility and to improve the local economy. Fishers who used to live and hunt on the island have voluntarily relocated in response to educational efforts, compensation, and employment opportunities. There has been some poaching on the island and some chimpanzees were injured in snares in the early days of the project's existence. Rising lake levels have now begun to inundate low-lying parts of the island.

The Ngamba Island Sanctuary anchored a Uganda-wide survey of wild chimpanzee populations and field research and conservation programs. The sanctuary chimpanzees also participate in noninvasive research projects, e.g. cognitive testing. Although the Ngamba chimpanzees are contracepted, there have been at least three births due to contraception failure. There were 49 chimpanzees in the sanctuary in 2018. Most were wild-borns who have been have been confiscated after having been poached elsewhere in Uganda.

REFERENCES

Ward, M. and A. Nelving. 1999. Island home for chimps. *Sanctuary* 1(1): 56-61.

www.ngambaisland.org

Chimpanzee (*Pan troglodytes*). Eight chimpanzees were reintroduced to the 65-ha Ipassa Island in the Ivindo River in what is now the 15,000-ha Ipassa Makokou Biosphere Reserve in Gabon in 1968. The purpose of the reintroduction is unknown, but it may have been to facilitate research because wild apes on the mainland were difficult to observe. The chimpanzees were wild-born and had been captured and had lived in a medical research facility for several months to several years before reintroduction. Their ages at capture and release were not provided. Their geographic origins and medical histories were unspecified, but they were described (in a French-to-English translation) as "semitame". There were no other apes or large predators on the island.

The chimpanzees were provisioned but ate natural fruits, leaves, ants, small mammals, and birds and bird eggs. They built sleeping nests nightly.

The chimpanzees began to wade from the island to the mainland in 1978, and were therefore captured and returned to a laboratory. However, several chimpanzees evaded capture and escaped to the mainland. Wild chimpanzees did occur on the mainland; the escapees may have interacted with them, raising questions of disease transmission and subspecific hybridization. One source says the escapees were never seen again but Hannah (1989) cites a personal communication that one of the escaped adult females was later seen with an infant.

Unspecified

REFERENCES

Hannah, A.C. 1989. *Rehabilitation of Captive Chimpanzees* (*Pan troglodytes verus*). PhD Dissertation, University of Stirling.

Hannah, A.C. and W.C. McGrew. 1991. Rehabilitation of captive chimpanzees. In: H.O. Box, ed. *Primate Response to Environmental Change*, pp 167-86. London, Chapman and Hall.

Hladik, C.M. 1978. Adaptive strategies of primates in relation to leaf-eating. In G.G. Montgomery, ed. *The Ecology of Arboreal Folivores*, pp. 373-395. Washington, DC, Smithsonian Institution Press.

PREVIOUS REVIEWS OF CHIMPANZEE REINTRODUCTION

Alison Hannah and William McGrew published a comprehensive and oft-cited review of five chimpanzee reintroductions that took place between 1966 and 1975, and an extensive discussion of a sixth reintroduction, the ViLab program in Liberia, that took place between 1978 and 1985. Readers should assume that I consulted Hannah and McGrew's paper when writing the accounts of the former five programs, even if it is not cited. The paper is cited in the discussion of the ViLab reintroduction, which continues today, four decades later. This reminds us to think of long-term outcomes when managing reintroductions.

The Hannah and McGrew paper framed primate reintroduction as an adaptation to environmental change, and emphasized the importance of individual developmental history and behavioral and social competence in post-release adaptation.

Their paper has also influenced the format that I have used for this history and for other reintroduction reviews, e.g. Beck et al 1994.

Janis Carter also published a review of chimpanzee reintroductions in western Africa. Her work updated the information in the Hannah and McGrew paper and provided me with information that supplemented what was already in my files. Readers should assume that I consulted Carter's paper when writing the following accounts. It is cited in the accounts of chimpanzee reintroduction efforts in The Gambia in which Carter played a major role.

Hannah and Farmer both provided reviews of primate reintroductions in their doctoral theses. I had been unfamiliar with some of these events and drew on the theses to include those programs here.

References

Beck, B.B., Rapaport, L.G., Stanley Price, M.R., and A.C. Wilson. 1994. Reintroduction of captive-born mammals. In: P.J.S. Olney, G.M. Mace, and A.T.C. Feistner, eds. *Creative Conservation: Interactive Management of Wild and Captive Animals*, pp. 265-286. London, Chapman and Hall.

Carter, J. 2003b. Orphan chimpanzees in West Africa: Experiences and prospects for viability in chimpanzee rehabilitation. In R. Kormos, C. Boesch, M.I. Bakarr, and T.M. Butynski, eds. *West African Chimpanzees. Status Survey and Conservation Action Plan*, pp. 157-167. Gland, IUCN.

Farmer, K.H. 2002. *The Behaviour and Adapation of Reintroduced Chimpanzees (Pan troglodytes troglodytes) in the Republic of Congo*. PhD Dissertation, University of Stirling.

Hannah, A.C. 1989. *Rehabilitation of Captive Chimpanzees (Pan troglodytes verus)*. PhD Dissertation, University of Stirling.

Hannah, A.C. and W.C. McGrew. 1991. Rehabilitation of captive chimpanzees. In: H.O. Box, ed. *Primate Response to Environmental Change*, pp. 167-86. London, Chapman and Hall.

Chimpanzee (*Pan troglodytes*). Stella Brewer, with support of Senegal's Direction de Parcs Nationaux (DPN), released 14 chimpanzees in eight cohorts into the 913,000-ha Niokolo Koba National Park in Senegal between 1972 and 1977. There were 12 wild-born and two captive-born rehabilitants, all less than 11 years old. Nine were males and five were females. The captive-borns came from the London Zoo, where they had been hand-reared. The wild-borns had been kept variously as pets in houses, zoos, research colonies, and tourist resorts in Africa. Another was contributed by an Italian pet owner. Two of the 12 wild-borns had lived at the Twycross Zoo in the UK.

Some accounts say that 15 chimpanzees were released in this program, and other accounts say 16. I think the discrepancy in the total number who were reintroduced in this program is due to double-counting one individual who was released, rescued, and re-released, and to counting an additional chimpanzee in the Twycross Zoo cohort that died at the release site before she could actually be released (see below).

Eddie Brewer, then director of The Gambia's Wildlife Conservation Department, and his daughter Stella Brewer (later Stella Brewer Marsden) had begun a rehabilitation and release program for confiscated chimpanzees in the Abuko Nature Reserve in The Gambia in 1969. S. Brewer began the pre-release training for the chimpanzees in the earliest cohorts by leading them into the forest at Abuko and teaching them how to select appropriate foods, how to use stones as hammers to open hard fruits, and how to use sticks to extract termites. She encouraged them to sleep in trees and showed them how to build nests. The first four chimpanzees were moved to Senegal and actually reintroduced in Niokolo Koba National Park in Senegal in 1972.

The release was soft. The chimpanzees could stay near the release site or move into the neighboring forest at will. S. Brewer monitored them, provided supplemental food, and continued to train them in survival-critical skills after their release. They were slow to leave camp, and they imitated many human behaviors. The youngest male was not adapting well and was returned to Abuko for more preparation.

Subsequent cohorts were released at Mount Asserik, also in Niokolo Koba National Park, in early 1974 (one, plus the re-released male), late 1974 (one), April 1975 (two), July 1975 (one), 1976 (one), and 1977 (two). All of these had had pre-release preparation at Abuko. Post-release management was more intensive and frequent than it had been for the first cohort. There were wild resident chimpanzees in Niokolo Koba, who ultimately attacked the rehabilitants at Mount Asserik when they left the release site and were separated from Brewer or her staff. These attacks resulted in serious wounding. One infant was born to reintroduced parents at Mount Asserik. His mother had disappeared from the main reintroduced group and returned with the newborn infant four days later. One of the males ("William"), who had been destructive and sometimes aggressive toward the other reintroduced chimpanzees and toward female caretakers, was gentle with this baby, who was presumed to be his son.

Cohort 8 comprised the Twycross Zoo chimpanzees, who were shipped in 1975 or 1976 to Senegal to join those who had already been released at Niokolo Koba. They were three, five, and seven years old; I infer that they were wild-born. They were to be taken first to Abuko, but a last-minute change in plans resulted in their being driven directly to Mount Asserik, a long drive in blistering heat. The three year-old died of heat exhaustion in the truck that was transporting them from the airport to Niokolo Koba. She is therefore not counted here as having been reintroduced, but other accounts do include her. The other two, a male and a female, were released directly from their transport crates because the crates were too heavy to unload from the truck. They ran to Brewer's released chimpanzees in the forest and were found dead the next morning of exhaustion and dehydration.

Of the 14 chimpanzees who were reintroduced at Niokolo Koba, seven survived and were moved ultimately to a different reintroduction site (see below), two were known to have died, four disappeared, and the outcome for another (William) is unspecified. This is curious because William's behavior was described so richly and extensively in Brewer's book. The infant who had been born to reintroduced parents survived, and was moved to the second reintroduction site.

The Niokolo Koba program is unique because it was the first that did not involve releasing chimpanzees on an island. However, aggression ("hostile territoriality", Brewer Marsden 2006, pg. 392) by wild chimpanzees caused them to be moved ultimately from Niokolo Koba to an island in the River Gambia National Park in The Gambia in 1979. Because this destination site is in another country, the River Gambia reintroduction is listed as a separate program (see below).

Welfare (Rehabilitation)

References

Badham, M. 1979. *Chimps with Everything*. London, W.H. Allen/Virgin Books.

Brewer, S. 1976. Chimpanzee rehabilitation. *International Primate Protection League Special Report*, December 1976: 1-10.

Brewer, S. 1978. *The Chimps of Mt. Asserik*. New York, Alfred A. Knopf.

Brewer, S. 1980. Chimpanzee rehabilitation, why and how? *International Primate Protection League Newsletter* 7(2): 1-5.

Brewer Marsden, S., Marsden, D., and M.E. Thompson. 2006. Demographic and female life history parameters of free-ranging chimpanzees at the Chimpanzee Rehabilitation Project, River Gambia National Park. *International Journal of Primatology* 27(2): 391-410.

Carter, J. 2003b. Orphan chimpanzees in West Africa: Experiences and prospects for viability in chimpanzee rehabilitation. In R. Kormos, C. Boesch, M.I. Bakarr, and T.M. Butynski, eds. *West African Chimpanzees. Status Survey and Conservation Action Plan*, pp. 157-167. Gland, IUCN.

Carter, J. 2003c. The Gambia. In R. Kormos, C. Boesch, M.I. Bakarr, and T.M. Butynski, eds. *West African Chimpanzees. Status Survey and Conservation Action Plan*, pp. 51-53. Gland, IUCN.

Carter, J. 2017. Personal communication (e-mails, 10-17 May, 4-5 June).

Carter, J., Ndiaye, S., Preutz, J., and W.C. McGrew. 2003. Senegal. In R. Kormos, C. Boesch, M.I. Bakarr, and T.M. Butynski, eds. *West African Chimpanzees. Status Survey and Conservation Action Plan*, pp. 31-39. Gland, IUCN.

Lemmon, T. 1987. The long way back to nature. *BBC Wildlife* 5(2): 172-175.

Chimpanzee (*Pan troglodytes*). Stella Brewer's Chimpanzee Rehabilitation Project reintroduced the eight surviving chimpanzees (seven of the original 14 plus one wild-born offspring) from the Niokolo Koba reintroduction (see above) to an island in the River Gambia, which is in the River Gambia National Park, in early 1979. In a different program, another group was also being released by Janis Carter on a neighboring island in the River Gambia National Park in 1979 (see below). Both reintroductions were conducted in collaboration with The Gambia's Wildlife Conservation Department (now Department of Parks and Wildlife Management).

There were no wild chimpanzees on the islands at the time, and there is no record that there ever were. Chimpanzees had become extinct in the country in the early twentieth century. Moving this group to the island was intended to be a temporary measure, until a new, larger reintroduction site without wild chimpanzees could be found. However, the search was unsuccessful and the chimpanzees were never moved off this group of islands.

The River Gambia National Park comprises 600 ha. There are five islands, of which three have now been populated with chimpanzees. The five islands are known in English as the Baboon Islands. The largest, Island 1, also known as Baboon Island, is 435 ha in area. Island 2 is 77, and Island 3 is 53 ha in area. The islands consisted of savanna, swamps, woodland, and dense riverine forest. There were no human settlements on the islands. There was "a virtually complete spectrum of the Gambia's mammal fauna" (Carter 2003c, pg. 52) on the islands: hippopotamuses, baboons, vervet and colobus monkeys, hyenas, genets, otters, porcupines, antelopes, warthogs, leopards and other unspecified feline species, manatees, reptiles (including crocodiles, pythons, monitor lizards, and venomous snakes), and a rich bird fauna. The baboons occurred only on Islands 1 and 2.

Brewer originally released her eight chimpanzees on the 77-ha Island 2. The chimpanzees were provisioned on the island and monitored daily. Because these chimpanzees had already learned to survive in the wild at Niokolo Koba before their release on this island, we would not expect the high initial mortality that occurs in many reintroduction programs.

I could find no specific published data on births, deaths, and transfers between 1979 and 1985 for Brewer's group. According to Carter (pers. comm.), at least three of the original Island 2 chimpanzees died or disappeared during this period. One of the Island 2 chimpanzees was moved to Island 1 and two were moved to Island 3. Brewer also released 16 additional rehabilitants on the northern end of Island 1 and on Island 2 during this period.

Brewer's group was merged with Carter's rehabilitants on island 1 in 1985 (see below). At that time, Brewer's community (group) consisted of one adult male, four adult females, five subadults, and four infants (who apparently were born on Island 2). Only two from the original Niokolo Koba group remained among them.

I will return to the merged groups after describing Carter's program.

Welfare (Rehabilitation)

REFERENCES

Brewer, S. 1976. Chimpanzee rehabilitation. *International Primate Protection League Special Report*, December 1976: 1-10.

Brewer, S. 1980. Chimpanzee rehabilitation, why and how? *International Primate Protection League Newsletter* 7(2): 1-5.

Brewer Marsden, S., Marsden, D., and M.E. Thompson. 2006. Demographic and female life history parameters of free-ranging chimpanzees at the Chimpanzee Rehabilitation Project, River Gambia National Park. *International Journal of Primatology* 27(2): 391-410.

Carter, J. 1988. Freed from keepers and cages, chimps come of age on Baboon Island. *Smithsonian* 19(3): 36-49.

Carter, J. 2003b. Orphan chimpanzees in West Africa: Experiences and prospects for viability in chimpanzee rehabilitation. In R. Kormos, C. Boesch, M.I. Bakarr, and T.M. Butynski, eds. *West African Chimpanzees. Status Survey and Conservation Action Plan*, pp. 157-167. Gland, IUCN.

Carter, J. 2003c. The Gambia. In R. Kormos, C. Boesch, M.I. Bakarr, and T.M. Butynski, eds. *West African Chimpanzees. Status Survey and Conservation Action Plan*, pp. 51-53. Gland, IUCN.

Carter, J. 2017. Personal communication (e-mails, 9-17 May, 4-5 June).

Chimpanzee (*Pan troglodytes*). Janis Carter reintroduced nine chimpanzees in a series of releases on Baboon Island (Island 1) in the Gambia River in the River Gambia National Park in 1979 and 1980. Baboon Island was only a few hundred meters from Island 2 on which Brewer reintroduced her group of chimpanzees at about the same time. Baboon Island is described above in the description of the Brewer Gambian reintroduction. Of note, it was the largest of the islands (435 ha). Baboons lived on Baboon Island and competed with Carter's chimpanzees for food.

Like Brewer (above), Carter searched for a larger, mainland reintroduction site for these chimpanzees but could not find one.

There were three wild-born orphaned males, four wild-born orphaned females, and two captive-born females in Carter's original chimpanzee group. Two of the wild-borns had been confiscated in The Gambia. Another had been surrendered by a pet owner in Zaire. Four had been confiscated from smugglers in the Netherlands. All were younger than six years old. One of the captive-borns in the group was "Lucy", who was 13 years old when she arrived in Africa. She had been born in Anna Mae and Bob Noell's Chimp Farm in Florida in January 1964, separated from her mother within 48 hours, taken to Oklahoma, USA, and raised as a human in a human household environment. She was considered by her foster parents to be a daughter, not a pet. Her behavioral development was compared with that of a one year-old boy in the family. She was taught American Sign Language. As a subadult chimpanzee, she is remembered by Larry Curtis, then the director of the Oklahoma City Zoo, as a "frequent, effective but self-indulgent, bartender; heavy on the Scotch, light on the water" (personal communication, 13 July 2017). As an adolescent, Lucy became "difficult to control, destructive, sexually restless, unpredictable, and potentially dangerous" (Herzfeld, 2017, pg 248). The language project had ended, and Lucy's release to "freedom in the wild" was seen as preferable, in terms of her wellbeing, to a lifetime in captivity or euthanasia. Lucy had been provided with a chimpanzee companion, "Marianne", a captive-born hand-reared four year-old female chimpanzee. She too was included in the reintroduction.

Carter had first acclimated these nine chimpanzees, much like those reintroduced at Niokolo Koba by Brewer, in a large naturalistic enclosure within the Abuko Nature Reserve for up to 18 months, tutoring them in selection of appropriate foods, nest building, tool use, and predator avoidance. The younger animals were taken on forest walks. The chimpanzees were tutored further after their release on Baboon Island, and were given supplemental food and medical treatment. The chimpanzees were regularly screened and treated for endoparasites and routinely given antihelminthics. There was no genetic screening, but there were probably at least two different subspecies in the group.

Carter lived with her chimpanzees on Baboon Island, providing emotional support and continued tutelage in survival-critical skills. She was largely isolated from contact with other humans and lived in extremely primitive conditions. The chimpanzees gradually acquired normal feeding, nesting, and social behavior. They learned to use tools and to recognize predators and emit appropriate alarm calls. The older wild-borns needed less time and instruction than the captive-borns. Each of the captive-born females adopted one of the 3 year-old males, and showed good maternal-like behavior. Lucy's adopted son died of endoparasitism. Marianne later gave birth, but needed assistance from Carter in rearing her baby. Marianne also captured, killed, and ate a colobus monkey (now known to be a common chimpanzee behavior), and learned to detect venomous snakes and give the appropriate alarm call.

Carter's and Brewer's projects are distinctive in successfully rehabilitating two captive-born, hand-reared chimpanzees from the United States and another who was born at a UK zoo. Their adaptation took a long time and a lot of tutoring, and they might not have survived without provisioning and emotional support, but they did finally show many normal behaviors. However, they appeared to be dependent on provisioned food.

There were eight chimpanzees in Carter's Baboon Island community when it was merged with Brewer's community in 1985.

Welfare (Rehabilitation, Non-lethal Control)

REFERENCES

Carter, J. 1981a. A journey to freedom. *Smithsonian* 12(1): 90-101.

Carter, J. 1981b. Free again. *International Primate Protection League Newsletter* 8(1): 2-4.

Carter, J. 1988. Freed from keepers and cages, chimps come of age on Baboon Island. *Smithsonian* 19(3): 36-49.

Carter, J. 2003b. Orphan chimpanzees in West Africa: Experiences and prospects for viability in chimpanzee rehabilitation. In R. Kormos, C. Boesch, M.I. Bakarr, and T.M. Butynski, eds. *West African Chimpanzees. Status Survey and Conservation Action Plan*, pp. 157-167. Gland, IUCN.

Carter, J. 2003c. The Gambia. In R. Kormos, C. Boesch, M.I. Bakarr, and T.M. Butynski, eds. *West African Chimpanzees. Status Survey and Conservation Action Plan*, pp. 51-53. Gland, IUCN.

Carter, J. 2017. Personal communication (e-mails, 9-17 May, 4-5 June).

Curtis, L. 2017. Personal communication (letter, 13 July).

Herzfeld, C. 2017. *The Great Apes*. New Haven, Yale University Press (originally published in French in 2012 by Editions du Seuil).

Chimpanzee (*Pan troglodytes*). Brewer and Carter, in cooperation with the Department of Parks and Wildlife Management, merged their projects administratively and geographically in 1985, under the name of the Chimpanzee Rehabilitation Project. There were eight reintroduced chimpanzees in Carter's community on Island 1, and approximately 14 in Brewer's community on Island 2 at the time. Brewer had also placed some chimpanzees on the northern end of Island 1 prior to the 1985 integration.

Brewer's and Carter's chimpanzee communities were merged on Island 1, Baboon Island, following construction of several large cages on the southern end of the island that would be used for social integration and subsequent post-release management. Carter relocated her personal camp to the mainland.

To begin the integration, Carter trapped her largest adult male and her two oldest females and one of their adopted sons in one of the cages. Then, five of the subadults from Brewer's group were brought to Baboon Island and released on the southern end of the island in proximity to the remaining uncaged four of Carter's group.

An additional adult male, four females, their four infants from Brewer's Island 2 community were then brought to Baboon Island. Three of the females and their infants were released at the northern end of the island. Carter's five caged chimpanzees were freed, and Brewer's adult male, and the fourth female and her infant were anesthetized and placed in the integration cage at the southern end. They were released a few days later.

There were dispersals and returns, but the chimpanzees from both ends of Baboon Island sorted themselves out into two or three groups within a week with no serious wounding. The whole process was very well managed and is described in detail by Carter (1988). Brewer was not present and did not participate in the merger of the groups. However, her two field assistants, Rene Bonang and Bruno Boubane, who had originally been employed by Brewer at Niokolo Koba in the mid-1970s, did participate.

As noted above, one of Carter's hand-reared females, Lucy's companion Marianne, had a female infant in 1987. She raised it with Carter's help, which is nonetheless remarkable since the female had herself been reared by humans and had never seen a chimpanzee mother with a newborn infant. Lucy signed "baby" repeatedly.

I have gone into such detail here to emphasize Hannah and McGrew's conclusion that reintroduction is really an exercise in cognitive adaptation. Hannah and McGrew and I (Beck 2010, 2016) agree that chimpanzees who are young, wild-born, mother-reared for a least a year, and who have spent a short time in captivity predispose them (and probably other primates) to reintroduction success. However, the Baboon Islands programs demonstrate that even older, captive-born, hand-reared chimpanzees who have spent years in captivity can be reintroduced successfully with enough post-release support. Herzfeld (2017) poignantly points out that humans first asked Lucy to be human, and then expected her to become a chimpanzee, and she tried her best to comply, a willingness that Herzfeld describes as "consilience". Indeed, the reintroduction plan had been described to Lucy, and she may have been the only primate among the 24,212 who was not an "unwitting" traveler.

I do not include the survivors of Brewer's original eight Island 2 chimpanzees and Carter's original nine Island 1 chimpanzees as having been released in this "merger" program. They were simply moved to a different island and regrouped in what is essentially the same destination site.

However, thirty-three wild-born orphans were added to the program between 1979 and 2003, 16 before and 17 after the 1985 merger. These 33 are counted as having been released in this "merger" program. Most of these had spent time at Abuko before their release, presumably with some pre-release preparation. I do not know the number of cohorts and the precise details of their reintroduction and post-release management. They were released on Islands 1, 2, and 3, which caused some social disruption to established groups. A number of chimpanzees died or disappeared, and some had to be moved to different islands/groups as a result of the conflicts.

Two major publications provide snapshots of population dynamics.

Carter (2003b) states that the total River Gambia population numbered 62 at the time she prepared her paper. They were living in four groups on Islands 1, 2, and 3. A total of 47 of the 62 had been reintroduced (including the original 17), of which 18 were still alive. There had been 55 births on the three islands (five of which were second-generation), of which 11 died in their first nine years of life.

Brewer Marsden coauthored her account of the River Gambia program in 2006. When she submitted her manuscript, the total population had grown to 69, still living in four social groups on Islands 1, 2, and 3. The number of reintroduced chimpanzees had grown to 50, presumably through the reintroduction of three more after Carter had written her paper. There had been 63 births, eight of which were second-generation. The chimpanzees were still being provisioned.

They were wormed periodically, and given antibiotics when necessary. The staff provided food and medicine from boats, and could target provisions to individual animals. There was no contraception. Because the genetic provenance of the founders of the River Gambia program is not completely known, and because at least two subspecies are likely to have been represented, there has very likely been subspecific hybridization in this population.

Brewer Marsden et al's paper provides a detailed treatment of the River Gambia chimpanzee population's demographics. Female reproductive parameters resembled those of other wild chimpanzee populations. Births were seasonal. Life expectancy was greater than that of other wild populations, and resembled that of captive chimpanzee populations.

Carter (personal communication, 2017) provides a current snapshot. There were 116 chimpanzees living on the three islands at the end of 2016. In the 38 years since the original 1979 reintroductions of Brewer's eight and Carter's nine chimpanzees, 33 more had been reintroduced to the islands. Fourteen of these 50 reintroduced chimpanzees still survived on the islands. Lucy was found dead in 1987. There has been much speculaton about the cause of her death, but the cause remains unknown. At least one of the reintroductees was estimated to have been more than 45 years old at death. There have been no reintroductions since 2003.

There had been a total of 145 births on the islands (some third generation) by the end of 2016, of which 102 were alive at that time.

The merged River Gambia reintroduction is clearly successful in terms of survival and reproduction. The chimpanzees are provisioned, sometimes heavily, and probably would not be able to survive on these islands without human support. The provisioning also prevents the growing population from destroying the islands' vegetation, and allows observers to see and monitor the chimpanzees.

Behavioral monitoring and veterinary surveillance continue. Attempts at oral contraception have been unsuccessful. There are no cages on the islands from which caretakers and veterinarians could have safe protected contact with the chimpanzees. Successful contraception is unlikely in the absence of such a facility.

There is now a modest ecotourism program in which visitors can see chimpanzees from a boat on the river. The program has for many years supported improvements in health care, water supplies, and education for residents of local communities, and has provided local employment opportunities.

The Gambian government assumed responsibility for the Chimpanzee Rehabilitation Program in 2008 and delegated management responsibility to Carter. Friends of Animals has provided financial support since 2008.

Carter and Brewer had a strained, sometimes acrimonious, and sometime litigious relationship over the years. Carter was not consulted on or offered co-authorship of the Brewer Marsden et al (2006) paper, although data that she had contributed to the merged project records were used. Carter's publications are not cited in the paper, and she is not mentioned except as a staff member/volunteer in the acknowledgements (she was legally co-director of the project).

I mention this because such professional disengagement by two talented and dedicated people with such similar goals and shared concern for chimpanzees is unexplainable and counterinstructive.

Stella Brewer Marsden died in 2008, having been awarded the Order of the British Empire for her conservation work.

Welfare (Rehabilitation)

REFERENCES

Beck, B.B. 2010. Chimpanzee orphans: Sanctuaries, reintroduction, and cognition. In E.V. Lonsdorf, S.R. Ross, and T. Matsuzawa, eds. *The Mind of the Chimpanzee*, pp. 332-346. Chicago, University of Chicago Press.

Beck, B.B. 2016. The role of translocation in primate conservation. In S.A. Wich and A.J. Marshall, eds. *An Introduction to Primate Conservation*, pp. 241-255. Oxford, UK, Oxford University Press.

Brewer Marsden, S., Marsden, D., and M.E. Thompson. 2006. Demographic and female life history parameters of free-ranging chimpanzees at the Chimpanzee Rehabilitation Project, River Gambia National Park. *International Journal of Primatology* 27(2): 391-410.

Carter, J. 1988. Freed from keepers and cages, chimps come of age on Baboon Island. *Smithsonian* 19(3): 36-49.

Carter, J. 2003b. Orphan chimpanzees in West Africa: Experiences and prospects for viability in chimpanzee rehabilitation. In R. Kormos, C. Boesch, M.I. Bakarr, and T.M. Butynski, eds. *West African Chimpanzees. Status Survey and Conservation Action Plan*, pp. 157-167. Gland, IUCN.

Carter, J. 2003c. The Gambia. In R. Kormos, C. Boesch, M.I. Bakarr, and T.M. Butynski, eds. *West African Chimpanzees. Status Survey and Conservation Action Plan*, pp. 51-53. Gland, IUCN.

Carter, J. 2017. Personal communication (e-mails, 9-17 May, 4-5 June).

Hannah, A.C. and W.C. McGrew. 1991. Rehabilitation of captive chimpanzees. In: H.O. Box, ed. *Primate Response to Environmental Change*, pp. 167-86. London, Chapman and Hall.

Herzfeld, C. 2017. *The Great Apes*. New Haven, Yale University Press (originally published in French in 2012 by Editions du Seuil).

www.friendsofanimals.org

Chimpanzee (*Pan troglodytes*). The New York Blood Center (NYBC) released approximately 125 chimpanzees in six cohorts from a biomedical research colony on five (or six, sources vary) small islands (5.5 10, 17, and 35 ha have been specified for four of the islands) in the Little Bassa River in Liberia between 1978 and 2006. The purposes of the releases were to relieve overcrowding at the research facility, improve the welfare of the captives, and perhaps to prepare the chimpanzees for ultimate reintroduction to the wild. The number of individual chimpanzees who were released may actually be fewer because some were released, rescued, and returned to the laboratory, and later re-released on the islands a second or even third time. On the other hand, between 15 and 30 who may have been reintroduced in 2006 are not included in the total because I could find no documentation of their release.

NYBC, a not-for-profit organization, has collected and supplied human blood and blood products for treating people in the northeastern United States and beyond since 1964. NYBC also conducts research on communicable blood-borne diseases. In 1974, NYBC acquired a closed facility in Robertsfield, Liberia that was owned by the Liberian Institute for Biomedical Research, and converted it into a new chimpanzee research colony known as VILAB (later as VILAB II). The purpose of the research was to develop vaccines against hepatitis B and C, river blindness, and other communicable diseases that affect people. Chimpanzees can be infected with hepatitis but do not develop disease symptoms. Between 200 and 400 chimpanzees are said to have served as research subjects at VILAB in Liberia. NYBC chose Liberia as the location for VILAB because there were already many confiscated pet and orphaned chimpanzees available in Liberia, and others could easily be acquired from the wild. Dr. Alfred Prince, NYBC's senior scientist, also believed that the welfare of the research chimpanzees would be improved if they could be kept outdoors in large enclosures in a tropical environment rather than in small laboratory cages. Betsy Brotman, a secretary at NYBC in New York, was selected by Prince to manage VILAB in 1975. By all accounts, Brotman cared deeply for the welfare of the chimpanzees.

Because chimpanzees live for more than 20 years but can only serve briefly in hepatitis research, the VILAB facility rapidly became overcrowded. Prince and Brotman decided to release former research chimpanzees on the islands in the Little Bassa River, near the VILAB facility.

The first cohort, (Hannah's Group A), was released in 1978 on the 5.5-ha island, which was bordered by mangrove swamp. Canals had been dug and deepened to prevent escape from the island, and a water supply was established for the chimpanzees. A small holding cage was built on the island. There were no wild chimpanzees on the island (chimpanzees had been driven to near-extinction in Liberia). There were initially 18 chimpanzees in Cohort 1. All were wild-born. Some had been kept as pets for as many as four years before being placed in the laboratory.

At the VILAB facility, the chimpanzees had lived in cages and/or a large outdoor enclosure. They had been housed in various social combinations to familiarize them with others. Most could be kept in pairs or small groups, which constituted affinity-based subgroups of between two and 12 for the reintroductions. The subgroups were released sequentially, not all at one time.

Some of the released chimpanzees wore radiocollars. The released chimpanzees were provisioned with food and water, and were monitored. Five more chimpanzees were added to Cohort 1 in 1980. Four of these, all males, died: two were killed by the other chimpanzees and two drowned (probably driven into the river in aggressive encounters). Some chimpanzees were removed and returned to captivity between 1978 and 1980 to treat illnesses and to decrease aggression. I could not follow these many interventions but it appeared that approximately 60% of the chimpanzees survived on the island for a year or more.

Cohort 2 (Hannah's Group B), comprising 24 chimpanzees, was released during a one-month period in 1983. The destination site consisted of two of the islands that were said to total nearly 100 ha (including mangroves between them). These were near the island that was the destination site of the first cohort. The backgrounds, preparation, and post-release management of the Cohort 2 chimpanzees were presumably like those of Cohort 1. Eight of the Cohort 2 chimpanzees died or disappeared in the first post-release year. Again, approximately 60% survived on the islands after the first year.

Cohort 3 (Hannah's Group D) was released over a period of several months in 1985. There is more detailed information about the post-release behavior of these chimpanzees because they were the subjects of Hannah's PhD dissertation.

There were 22 chimpanzees (10 males, 12 females) in Cohort 3. Most were between five and ten years old. One female was more than 20 years old. Six of the 22 released chimpanzees wore radiocollars. The chimpanzees were released in four successive affinity-based subgroups. All were wild-born. They had lived in the laboratory for as long as 15 years. Before being placed in the laboratory, some had been kept as pets without contact with other chimpanzees for up to seven years.

The released chimpanzees of Cohort 3 were heavily provisioned with food and water and were monitored intensively for two years. Three disappeared on the day of release. Another died within four months. Five others fell ill and were removed within seven months. One adolescent male and two females waded at low tide to another island that was occupied by 15 chimpanzees from a previously released cohort. The male was killed by the chimpanzees who were living on the other island. The females returned unhurt. The surviving Cohort 3 chimpanzees began to eat natural plant foods and ants. Most eventually built nests and used stones to crack open palm nuts. Observation of competent chimpanzees is said to have helped others learn these behaviors. Normal social behavior emerged. From the day of release, two individuals showed dramatic decreases in abnormal stereotypic behaviors that had been prominent at the laboratory. Approximately 55% survived after one year. One infant was born shortly after release.

Some of the surviving members of Cohort 3 were captured from the islands and returned to the laboratory in 1986. They were re-released, and some were captured a second time and returned to the laboratory where they were socially introduced to members of Cohort 4.

Cohort 4 (Hannah's Group E) was released during June 1987. There were 18 chimpanzees (eight males, ten females). They were introduced in three successive affinity-based subgroups. Many (44%) had to be returned to the laboratory because of aggression from those members of Cohort 3 who remained on the islands at the time of release of Cohort 4. One male of Cohort 4 was killed by chimpanzees, and another drowned. Approximately 45% survived after one year.

Cohort 5, documented by Agoramoorthy and Hsu (1999) but not in Hannah, Hannah and McGrew, or Carter, consisted of 30 chimpanzees who were released on the 9.7-ha Little Bassa island in July 1987. There were 19 females and 11 males, between three and 20 years of age. At least six had been in Cohorts 3 and 4. Pre-release methodology was the same as it was for previous cohorts, although the Cohort 5 chimpanzees were specifically said to have been acclimated in a holding cage on the island for several days prior to release. Agoramoorthy and Hsu also state specifically that the Cohort 5 chimpanzees were screened for hepatitis A, B, and C as well as for tuberculosis and endoparasites, and that only disease-free chimpanzees were released. Twenty-four of the 30 chimpanzees wore radiocollars. The reintroduction consisted of successive releases of small social groups.

The chimpanzees of Cohort 5, like those of Cohorts 3 and 4, were provisioned with food but quickly began to eat natural plant foods and insects. They used stone tools to open palm nuts and most made night nests. The quick adaptation is not surprising because some of these Cohort 5 chimpanzees had been exposed to or had mastered these behaviors when they had been released previously in earlier cohorts. Some of the Cohort 5 chimpanzees stopped performing the stereotypic behaviors that they had exhibited in the laboratory. Seven Cohort 5 chimpanzees, all former pets, were returned to the laboratory because they did not adjust to group living. Three other Cohort 5 chimpanzees who were injured in aggressive encounters were returned to the laboratory, treated, and re-released. Some Cohort 5 chimpanzees attacked humans; a young fisher was seriously injured. Four infants were born in 1987 but two did not survive. Monitoring of Cohort 5 ended in 1989.

Hannah and McGrew state that there were 58 reintroduced chimpanzees living on three islands "at present", i.e. 1988 or 1989.

An era of violent political instability and actual civil war began in Liberia in 1989. The VILAB II laboratory was frequently threatened, and some chimpanzees died of starvation and thirst when employees could not get to work. These may have included survivors of the chimpanzees from Cohorts 1, 2, 3, 4, and 5, who had all been removed from the islands and returned to the laboratory during the violence. Brotman's husband, who worked at VILAB II, was shot to death by rebels in the Brotman family's Liberian home in 1993. She and her children were evacuated but she returned to continue VILAB's work in Liberia. Work resumed but the cycle of violence was repeated in 1996. Brotman and her family once again fled.

Carter states that all of the surviving reintroduced chimpanzees were recaptured and returned to the laboratory in 1995, but she did not know how many there were at the time. This appears to have been the second time that chimpanzees were evacuated from the islands due to violence.

Prince states that there were 33 chimpanzees living on three of the islands in 2005. I do not know when and how many of the rescued chimpanzees from Cohorts 1, 2, 3, 4, and 5 were re-released onto the Liberian islands between 1996 and 2005.

Cohort 6 was reintroduced to some of the islands in 2005 and 2006, when political stability had returned to Liberia. There were more than 15 chimpanzees in Cohort 6, but I have been unable to find details of the releases. The number of chimpanzees in Cohort 6 were in addition to the 33 cited above.

VILAB II closed in 2007. The NYBC turned over ownership of the islands to the Liberian Institute for Biomedical Research, which took over management of the chimpanzees and the islands. Both Prince (now deceased) and Brotman affirmed that NYBC committed to funding lifetime care ("retirement") for the chimpanzees. NYBC has denied the lifetime-care commitment, but continued to fund the Liberian Institute to care for the chimpanzees from 2007 to 2015. Maintenance costs are said to be US$25,000 per month. However, NYBC withdrew support for the chimpanzees in 2015. Local volunteers continued to feed the chimpanzees at their own expense until a consortium of not-for-profit welfare agencies, led by the Humane Society of the United States, and many individual private donors, assumed the costs in 2016. There were 66 chimpanzees on the islands in 2016. The former employees who had been providing food on a volunteer basis have been rehired, and a holding facility and a functioning fresh water supply have been constructed on the island. New orphan chimpanzees are once again showing up at the mainland facility, which has been reopened as a sanctuary. On 30 May 2017, the New York Blood Center contributed US$6,000,000 to the Humane Society of the United States, which then committed to lifetime care of the VILAB chimpanzees in Liberia and Ivory Coast (see below).

I do not know if the reintroduced VILAB chimpanzees were contracepted, but some recent photos show very young individuals, and there are reports of births over the years. Apparently there were some (largely unsuccessful) attempts at contraception after 2000, and new attempts are underway. Had they been consistently contracepted, this population could have been humanely managed to extinction. There was never a realistic hope that they could have been self-supporting on the islands or reintroduced to a larger mainland forest. This suggests that contraception should be considered when introducing chimpanzees and other apes to small islands where there would be lifetime dependence on human support.

Welfare (Non-lethal Control, Rehabilitation), Conservation (Reintroduction)

References

Agoramoorthy, G. and M.J. Hsu. 1999. Rehabilitation and release of chimpanzees on a natural island. *Journal of Wildlife Rehabilitation* 22(1): 3-7.

Carter, J. 2003b. Orphan chimpanzees in West Africa: Experiences and prospects for viability in chimpanzee rehabilitation. In R. Kormos, C. Boesch, M.I. Bakarr, and T.M. Butynski, eds. *West African Chimpanzees. Status Survey and Conservation Action Plan*, pp 157-167. Gland, IUCN.

Clifton, M. 2015. Abandoning ViLab II chimps in Liberia, New York Blood Center did it before in Ivory Coast, SAEN charges. *Animals 24-7*. 12 August 2015. www.animals24-7.org

Conlee, K. and J.A.Z. Desmond. 2015. Liberian chimpanzees abandoned by New York Blood Center. *African Primates* 10: 57-58.

Hannah, A.C. 1989. *Rehabilitation of Captive Chimpanzees* (Pan troglodytes verus). PhD Dissertation, University of Stirling.

Hannah, A.C. and W.C. McGrew. 1991. Rehabilitation of captive chimpanzees. In: H.O. Box, ed. *Primate Response to Environmental Change*, pp. 167-86. London, Chapman and Hall.

Prince, A.M. 1985. Rehabilitation and release program for chimpanzees. *Primate Conservation* 5: 33.

Prince, A.M. 2005. Leadership sought for chimpanzee sanctuary in Liberia. *ASP Bulletin* 29(4): 15.

Revkin, A. C. 1996. A life's work disrupted in Liberia; Newark native hopes to return to her study of chimps. *The New York Times*, 1 May 1996.

www.humanesociety.org

Chimpanzee (*Pan troglodytes*). The New York Blood Center (NYBC) released 20 chimpanzees from a biomedical research colony, VILAB in Liberia, on a 169-ha island in the Bandama River in the Azagny (Assagny) National Park in Côte d'Ivoire (Ivory Coast) in 1983. The purposes of the release were to relieve overcrowding at the research facility, improve the welfare of the captives, and perhaps to prepare the chimpanzees for ultimate reintroduction to the wild. NYBC also reintroduced laboratory chimpanzees on islands in neighboring Liberia between 1978 and 2006 (see above), but the Ivory Coast reintroduction is regarded as a distinct program in this history because it took place in a different country.

The Ivory Coast reintroduction involved ten males and ten females, between seven and 11 years of age. I assume that their backgrounds and pre-release preparation were like those in the Liberian reintroductions. It is not clear if they had been reintroduced previously on Liberian islands or if they came directly from the laboratory colony. The Ivory Coast chimpanzees have been provisioned and monitored at least periodically for 30 years. Volunteers have been largely responsible for monitoring during the past decade (see below). There were no wild chimpanzees on the island but they did occur on the Ivory Coast mainland.

Six of the 20 chimpanzees died and five disappeared in the first year. The cause of death (and probably of many of the disappearances) was a bacterial gastrointestinal disease that could have been treated if veterinary support had been available. The nine survivors were transferred to a smaller island. VILAB hired a local villager to provide food to the chimpanzees, and a veterinarian (apparently paid) visited several times a year. Nonetheless, five more of the chimpanzees died by the end of 1984. This left an adult male, "Ponso" and an adult female. They had two surviving offspring over the next several decades.

VILAB discontinued its support of the Bandama River chimpanzees in approximately 2003. Germain Djenemaya Koidja, the son of the formerly employed local caretaker, began to visit and provide food and water to the remaining four chimpanzees on the island. The adult female and the two offspring died by 2013, leaving Ponso alone. Actually, he was not totally alone. Germain, a minimally educated son of a local farmer, defied and defined the concept of chimpanzee personhood that was being debated by Western scientists and lawyers by offering simple, selfless friendship to a lonely 40 year-old chimpanzee who had barely enough to eat. Germain, on a voluntary basis and at his own expense, regularly visited and fed Ponso. He also managed to alert the world, and individual donors and not-for-profit welfare organizations have raised enough money to provide funding for Germain and his son Junior to continue to feed and visit with Ponso until a more enduring future for him can be identified. A not-for-profit named Les Amis de Ponso (Friends of Ponso), also known as SOS PONSO, began raising funds for Ponso's care in 2015. The government of the Ivory Coast refused a proposal to move Ponso to an out-of-country sanctuary, declaring that "Ponso was a non-transferable Ivorian citizen".

The videos of Germain and Junior visiting Ponso are at once anguishing and inspiring to watch and remind us of our affinity to these apes.

Welfare (Non-lethal Control, Rehabilitation), Conservation (Reinforcement)

References

Carter, J. 2003b. Orphan chimpanzees in West Africa: Experiences and prospects for viability in chimpanzee rehabilitation. In R. Kormos, C. Boesch, M.I. Bakarr, and T.M. Butynski, eds. *West African Chimpanzees. Status Survey and Conservation Action Plan*, pp. 157-167. Gland, IUCN.

Clifton, M. 2015. Abandoning ViLab II chimps in Liberia, New York Blood Center did it before in Ivory Coast, SAEN charges. *Animals* 24-7. 12 August 2015. www.animals24-7.org

Hannah, A.C. 1989. *Rehabilitation of Captive Chimpanzees (Pan troglodytes verus)*. PhD Dissertation, University of Stirling.

Koffi, C. 2017. Helping Ponso, sole survivor of 'Chimapnzee Island', I. Coast. www.phys.org 24 September.

Prince, A.M. 1985. Rehabilitation and release program for chimpanzees. *Primate Conservation* 5: 33.

Wanshel, E. 2016. "World's loneliest chimp, Abandoned on a small island, gets cuddly teddy bear". *Huffington Post*, 9 March 2016.

Chimpanzee (*Pan troglodytes*). The Yerkes Regional Primate Research Center (YRPC) released eight chimpanzees in two cohorts on 9.6-ha Bear Island, Georgia, USA in 1972 and 1973. Bear Island is separated by marsh and a tidal creek from the larger and better-known Ossabaw Island. Cohort 1, comprising four adult chimpanzees (one male and three females) was released in June 1972. Two of these were wild-born and two had been born at YRPC and raised there without early social experience with other chimpanzees. All four had been introduced to each other before release. Cohort 2 (four females) was released in September 1973. Three were wild-born and one had been born at YRPC. Two were experienced mothers. These four chimpanzees had also been socially introduced to each other while at Yerkes.

The purpose of this reintroduction was to explore the possibility of establishing free-ranging chimpanzee colonies to provide biomedical research subjects.

A short survey of flora and fauna was conducted on Bear Island prior to the release. The island was uninhabited by humans. A holding cage and two small, enclosed shelters for the chimpanzees and a working area for caretakers were built before the release. The shelters were unheated but (belatedly) bedded with straw during cold weather. The chimpanzees received a thorough veterinary examination before release and were judged to have been in good health. They were provisioned with monkey chow, fresh fruits, and water after release, and were monitored almost every day until the end of 1973. Veterinary care was available.

Three of the Cohort 1 chimpanzees climbed trees and built nests and ate natural foods. One of the deprivation-reared females stayed in or around the shelters and never climbed trees. She later died of pneumonia and dehydration. Two of the females became pregnant but miscarried; one died subsequently of infection and hemorrhage.

The four Cohort 2 chimpanzees joined the two surviving Cohort 1 chimpanzees with no overt aggression. They climbed trees, roamed over the entire island, and ate natural foods. They were quickly infested with ticks, which the chimpanzees removed by grooming. The surviving Cohort 1 female gave birth in November 1973; the infant did not nurse, was removed from the mother, and taken to YRPC for nursery-rearing.

The (presumably six) chimpanzees were removed from the island, and the project was "abandoned" sometime after 1974.

The release of laboratory chimpanzees into a "mild temperate" climate with occasional subfreezing temperatures created detrimental cold stress for the chimpanzees. In retrospect, the deprivation-reared Cohort 1 female who was not adapting well to the island should probably have been removed.

Soave concludes that the "published attempts at rehabilitating apes have not been eminently successful with respect to the numbers of animals placed in groups in the wild or in captivity" (pg. 5). McGrew (1983) disagreed, citing inaccuracies and omissions in Soave's review of ape rehabilitation and reintroduction, and his utilitarian definition of success. Soave's intent was to establish small captive breeding colonies of uncaged chimpanzees in accessible locations for scientific research. In contrast, the intent of many ape rehabilitation programs is to improve the health and wellbeing of the animals, restore their physical and behavioral competencies, and release them to the wild or to tropical or subtropical, semi-naturalistic environments.

Commercial, Research

References

McGrew, W.C. 1983. Chimpanzees can be rehabilitated. *Laboratory Primate Newsletter* 22(2): 2-3.

Soave, O. 1982. The rehabilitation of chimpanzees and other apes. *Laboratory Primate Newsletter* 21(4): 3-8.

Wilson, M.L. and J.G. Elicker. 1976. Establishment, maintenance, and behavior of free-ranging chimpanzees on Ossabaw Island, Georgia, U.S.A. *Primates* 17(4): 451-473.

Chimpanzee (*Pan troglodytes*). Habitat Ecologique et Liberté des Primates (HELP), founded in 1991 by Aliette Jamart, reintroduced 53 chimpanzees in three cohorts in the 145,000-ha Conkouati Reserve (since 1999, the 505,000-ha Conkouati-Douli National Park) in Republic of Congo between 1996 and 2012. The chimpanzees were all wild-born rescued or confiscated orphans.

Jamart, a French expatriate, founded a sanctuary for confiscated chimpanzees in Pointe Noire, Republic of Congo (Congo-Brazzaville) in 1989. For many years she provided much of the funding and animal care herself. In 1992, having founded HELP, a private not-for-profit organization, Jamart began to move the chimpanzees from her sanctuary and the Pointe Noire Zoo to a new sanctuary on the shore of the Conkouati Lagoon, 180 km north of Pointe Noire. The new sanctuary included three forested offshore islands in the lagoon, the largest of which is 50 ha (or 100 ha, sources vary) in area; the islands could be connected with pontoon bridges to enable group formation with individuals from different islands. The general strategy has been to move the orphans from the onshore sanctuary facility to the islands and then, as possible, reintroduce them to the wild.

The chimpanzees who were reintroduced in the first two cohorts had lived for four to ten years on the islands. While on the islands, the chimpanzees had the opportunity to acquire skills in locomotion, navigation, nest building, and foraging. They were kept in large social groups where they could develop normal intragroup social behaviors and relationships, and could reproduce. They also experienced natural weather conditions on the islands. Although they found some natural food on the islands, they had to be fed by caretakers each day. The chimpanzees were given routine preventive veterinary care at the sanctuary, including tuberculosis tests, examination of fecal samples for endoparasites, and vaccination against polio and tetanus. In addition, hematological and blood chemistry analyses; serological screening for retroviruses, filoviruses, hepatitis A and B viruses, and blood parasites; vaccination boosters; and antibiotic and vitamin injections were administered before reintroduction. DNA samples from hair were analyzed to verify the chimpanzees' geographic origin and to ensure that there were no close relatives among them. At least 16 chimpanzees were deemed physically or psychologically unfit for reintroduction and were retained on the islands or in the onshore facility.

The destination site was known as the Triangle. The Triangle, which had a small wild chimpanzee population, is a 2,100-ha area that is bounded by the lagoon and two rivers. Four of the 37 chimpanzees in Cohorts 1 and/or 2 were actually released just across one of the rivers that bound the Triangle. The Triangle is connected to this area and to the rest of the national park by natural bridges. An elaborate trail system had been installed to facilitate monitoring. The national park had a large chimpanzee population as well as gorillas.

A total of 37 chimpanzees were reintroduced in two cohorts between 1996 and 2001. These chimpanzees probably originated from different areas, and thus different wild communities, within the Republic of Congo.

Each cohort included successive releases of small groups, pairs, or single individuals. There were four groups of three or more (19 individuals), seven pairs, and three singles. There were 27 females and 10 males. The groups consisted of animals who already knew each other from their time on the islands.

This sex ratio (fewer males) was thought to favor reintroduction success because resident adult male chimpanzees are intensely xenophobic toward unfamiliar males, but they generally accept unfamiliar females. Additionally, Tutin (personal communication) notes that "male orphans [chimpanzees] tend to form excessively strong bonds with human caretakers which can hinder the independent spirit essential for successful adaptation to return to the wild."

All of the released individuals, except an infant and two large males, carried collar-mounted radio transmitters and were monitored closely on a daily basis. The GPS-mapped trail system facilitated monitoring. Systematic observations were made of social, ranging, nesting, and feeding behavior. Supplemental feeding was minimal, although observers attempted to lead the chimpanzees to fruit trees. As of early 2004, there had been five confirmed deaths, nine disappearances, and 23 survivors. Some of the individuals who disappeared may well have been alive and assimilated into the wild population. The chimpanzees ate a wide variety of wild plant and animal foods, had a diet and activity budget resembling that of wild chimpanzees, made night nests, and appeared healthy. They ranged widely, and most made excursions into neighboring forests. They also had many interactions with the resident wild chimpanzees.

As of 2009, including the 2004 figures cited above, there had been nine confirmed deaths, 14 disappearances (all females), and one (male) had been rescued and returned to the islands. Thirteen of the original 37 were known to be alive and were nutritionally and behaviorally self-sufficient. This is doubtlessly an underestimate of survival because many of the missing females had probably joined wild groups that were living outside the monitoring area. Seventeen infants were known to have born to reintroduced females; six of these infants were known to have been alive in 2009. Approximately half of the infant deaths were due to infanticide, which is known to occur in wild chimpanzees as well. Some of the released chimpanzees encountered a group of gorillas for the first time in 1997. They approached the gorillas. Neither the chimpanzees nor the gorillas were aggressive. The chimpanzees were described as being curious.

Nine of the ten released chimpanzee males were attacked by wild chimpanzees, some repeatedly. Four died or disappeared following attacks, and one male was captured, treated at the sanctuary facility, and returned to the release site. At least three of the others required veterinary intervention at the release site. This supports the growing consensus that reintroduced male chimpanzees will be at high risk of attack at sites where there is a resident wild population. Nine females were also attacked by wild chimpanzees; two died and the dependent infant of another was killed.

Many of the serious and fatal wounds to both males and females have been to the anogenital area. It should be noted that some reintroduced chimpanzees were attacked by other, previously reintroduced, chimpanzees, but these attacks did not result in wounds that were as serious as those inflicted by wild chimpanzees on reintroduced chimpanzees.

Some of the reintroduced females formed sexual consorts with wild males, disappearing for days at a time. Several of these females were integrated into wild groups for extended periods, and then returned to the release zone pregnant and gave birth in their released group. However, at least one infant was born to reintroduced male and female parents.

A long-term study of eight of the Cohort 1 and 2 chimpanzees found that their consumption of fruit, seeds, leaves, stems, and insects was typical for wild chimpanzees. They spent less time traveling and more time engaged in social behavior by 2006 than they did initially.

The surviving chimpanzees of Cohorts 1 and 2 settled into a typical chimpanzee fission-fusion social organization by 2007. They formed a community (social group) consisting of males and females who associated in various subgroups of different individuals for different durations. Chimpanzees that had known each other on the islands and chimpanzees that were released at the same time tended to associate more closely and for longer periods.

There were apparently 16 more chimpanzees released in the third cohort (between 2005 and 2012), but I could not find details of these releases. Some were quarantined and then taken directly to the release area in the Triangle and allowed to range in the forest under close human supervision and support. This was considered to be pre-release acclimation and training.

As of 2012, 17 of the total of 53 released chimpanzees were known to be alive, 15 were known to be dead, 20 had disappeared, and one had been returned to the islands (these figure include those given above for 2004 and 2009).

The Conkouati reintroduction effort has from the outset adhered closely to the then-current guidelines for reintroduction published by the IUCN Re-introduction Specialist Group (the Conkouati program strongly influenced later versions of the guidelines). The rationale for decision-making is clearly explicated, and is rooted in a scientific understanding of chimpanzee natural history and a careful review of other reintroduction efforts. Tutin et al's paper should serve as a planning guide for all reintroduction managers. Individual chimpanzees underwent veterinary and genetic screening and were behaviorally assessed before reintroduction. They experienced a long period of pre-release preparation in a nearby naturalistic environment (the islands), and their release site was carefully chosen and exhaustively surveyed. There has also been intensive post-release monitoring of the reintroduced chimpanzees, and peer-reviewed scientific documentation of their outcomes (at least for the first 37 released chimpanzees). There has been an associated community education program with participatory management, and local people have been employed by the project; these factors have been shown by Beck et al (1994) to be correlated with reintroduction success. Not only has the survival rate of reintroduced individuals been relatively high, but reductions in poaching and deforestation in the release area have been suggested to have been an additional benefit. Farmer et al (2010) provide an excellent set of recommendations for chimpanzee reintroduction.

Welfare (Rehabilitation), Conservation (Reinforcement)

References

Aczel, P. 1993. Pointe-Noire zoo chimpanzees rescued. *International Primate Protection League News* 20(2): 15-16.

Aczel, P. 1997. Encounter between a group of ex-captive chimpanzees and a group of lowland gorillas in the forest of the Conkouati Reserve, Congo. *Gorilla Gazette* 11(1): 5-6.

Beck, B.B., Rapaport, L.G., Stanley Price, M.R., and A.C. Wilson. 1994. Reintroduction of captive-born animals. In P.J.S. Olney, G.M. Mace, and A.T.C. Feistner, eds. *Creative Conservation: Interactive Management of Wild and Captive Animals*, pp. 265-286. London, Chapman & Hall.

Farmer, K.H. 2000. The final step to freedom. Conkouati chimpanzees returned to the wild. *International Primate Protection League News* 27(2): 17-20.

Farmer, K.H. 2002. *The Behaviour and Adapation of Reintroduced Chimpanzees (Pan troglodytes troglodytes) in the Republic of Congo*. PhD Dissertation, University of Stirling.

Farmer, K.H., and A. Jamart. 2002. Habitat Ecologique et Liberté des Primates: A case study of chimpanzee re-introduction in the Republic of Congo. *Re-introduction News* 21: 16-18.

Farmer, K.H., Buchanan-Smith, H.M., and A. Jamart. 2006. Behavioural adaptation of *Pan troglodytes troglodytes*. *International Journal of Primatology* 27(3): 747-765.

Farmer, K.H., Honig, N., Goossens, B., and A. Jamart. 2010. Habitat Ecologique et Liberté des Primates: re-introduction of central chimpanzees to the Conkouati-Douli National Park, Republic of Congo. In

P.S. Soorae, ed. *Global Re-introduction Perspectives 2010: Additional Case-Studies from Around the Globe*, pp. 231-237. Abu Dhabi, UAE, IUCN/SSC Re-introduction Specialist Group.

Goossens, B., Funk, S.M., Vidal, C., Latour, S., Jamart, A., Ancrenaz, M., Wickings, E.J., Tutin, C.E.G., and M.W. Bruford. 2002. Measuring genetic diversity in translocation programmes: principles and application to a chimpanzee release project. *Animal Conservation* 5: 225-236.

Goossens, B., Setchell, J.M., Vidal, C., Dilambaka, E., and A. Jamart. 2003. Successful reproduction in wild released orphan chimpanzees (*Pan troglodytes troglodytes*). *Primates* 44: 67-69.

Goossens, B., Setchell, J.M., Tchidongo, E., Dilambaka, E. Vidal, C., Ancrenaz, M., and A. Jamart. 2005. Survival, interactions with con-specifics and reproduction in 37 chimpanzees released into the wild. *Biological Conservation* 123: 461–475.

IUCN. 1998. *Re-introduction Specialist Group: Guidelines for Reintroduction*. Gland, International Union for the Conservation of Nature.

Karlowski, U. 1996. The Conkouati Chimpanzee Refuge – a new chance for orphans. *Gorilla Journal* 12(June): 20.

Le Hallaye, Y., Goossens, B., Jamart, A., and D.J. Curtis. 2010. Acquisition of fission-fusion social organization in a chimpanzee (*Pan troglodytes troglodytes*) community released into the wild. *Behavioral Ecology and Sociobiology* 64(3): 349-360.

Renaud, A., Jamart, A., Goossens, B., and C. Ross. 2013. A longitudinal study on feeding behavior and activity patterns of released chimpanzees in Conkouati-Douli National Park, Republic of Congo. *Animals* 3(2): 532-550.

Tutin, C., Ancrenaz, M., Paredes, J., Vacher-Vallas, M., Vidal, C., Goosens, B., Bruford, M., and A. Jamart. 2001. Conservation biology framework for the release of wild-born orphaned chimpanzees into the Conkouati Reserve, Congo. *Conservation Biology* 15(5): 1247–1257.

Chimpanzee (*Pan troglodytes*). The non-governmental organization "Help Guinea", established by European expatriate Helen Dorkenoo, released 12 rescued and confiscated chimpanzees on the 1-ha Kerfalya Island in the Republic of Guinea's Konkoure River in 1992. There were six males and six females. Twelve additional chimpanzees remained in Dorkenoo's house until she abandoned the project and fled the country with one of the chimpanzees from her house. The island chimpanzees continued to be provisioned by a salaried caretaker, but ten died or disappeared within two years. The other two continued to be provisioned and died in 1999 and 2000. Janis Carter (see above) personally arranged for the care, housing, and ultimate rescue of these chimpanzees. They became some of the first residents of the Projet de Conservation des Chimpanzés en Guinée, Guinea (see below).

Welfare (Rehabilitation)

REFERENCES

Carter, J. 2003b. Orphan chimpanzees in West Africa: Experiences and prospects for viability in chimpanzee rehabilitation. In R. Kormos, C. Boesch, M.I. Bakarr, and T.M. Butynski, eds. *West African Chimpanzees. Status Survey and Conservation Action Plan*, pp. 157-167. Gland, IUCN.

Teleki, G. 2001. Sanctuaries for ape refugees. In B.B. Beck, T.S. Stoinski, M. Hutchins, T.L. Maple, B. Norton, A. Rowan, E.F. Stevens, and A. Arluke, eds. *Great Apes and Humans: The Ethics of Coexistence*, pp. 133-149. Washington, DC, Smithsonian Institution Press.

Chimpanzee (*Pan troglodytes*). The primary focus of Pandrillus, the Drill Rehabilitation and Breeding Center, is to care for, rehabilitate, and reintroduce drills (*Mandrillus leucopheus*). Over the years the Center's managers, Liza Gadsby and Peter Jenkins, have also accepted more than 30 confiscated and rescued chimpanzees. The Center is located in Nigeria's 10,400-ha Afi Mountain Wildlife Sanctuary, in which wild populations of drills, chimpanzees, and gorillas survive despite considerable hunting pressure. The site would probably support chimpanzee reintroduction, but the center's chimpanzees are of at least two subspecies. The hunting, and the possibility of subspecific hybridization have impeded chimpanzee reintroduction (drills have been reintroduced, see below). The chimpanzees live in a large forested enclosure at Pandrillus' field station in the Sanctuary.

According to Carter, two chimpanzees escaped into the Sanctuary and were not seen again. Farmer states that four chimpanzees escaped, but one was recaptured the day after the escape and another was recaptured, in good health, after three months. The other two, both males, were able to survive, without crop-raiding or other conflict with people, for at least three months. They were never recaptured. One might have been killed by hunters. It is likely that Carter and Farmer described the same escape event, and that it took place in the late 1990s.

Two uncommonly strong storms downed trees and fences at the Pandrillus center in March and April, 2017. No chimpanzees died, but five drills were killed. However, another tree fell on the fence of the chimpanzee enclosure on 29 March, 2018. Facebook posts of a local community organization (Boki Blog, dated 4 and 7 May 2018) described the discovery of an adult female chimpanzee in the field of a local farmer, who lived 10 km from Pandrillus, on "the other side of Afi Mountain". The farmer welcomed the friendly but hungry chimpanzee into his village, and fed and protected her until Pandrillus staff could recover her. The chimpanzee, named "Shirley", had been confiscated from the parking lot of a restaurant in Cameroon in 1992, where she had been chained as an attraction. Shirley was approximately 4 years of age at the time. She had been rehabilitated at Pandrillus and had been living in a social group of chimpanzees for 20 years when the tree came down on the enclosure fence. Shirley escaped and had survived in the forest for more than a month when she showed up in the farmer's field, essentially opting for a life under human care.

Accidental (Escape)

REFERENCES

Boki Blog Facebook page, 4 and 7 May 2018.

Carter, J. 2003b. Orphan chimpanzees in West Africa: Experiences and prospects for viability in chimpanzee rehabilitation. In R. Kormos, C. Boesch, M.I. Bakarr, and T.M. Butynski, eds. *West African Chimpanzees. Status Survey and Conservation Action Plan*, pp. 157-167. Gland, IUCN.

Farmer, K.H. 2002. *The Behaviour and Adapation of Reintroduced Chimpanzees (Pan troglodytes troglodytes) in the Republic of Congo*. PhD Dissertation, University of Stirling.

Gadsby, E.L. 2002. Planning for re-introduction: 10 years of planning for drills in Nigeria. *Re-introduction News* 21: 20-23.

Pandrillus Facebook page, 1 and 3 May 2017, 30 May 2018.

Chimpanzee (*Pan troglodytes*). The Tacugama Chimpanzee Sanctuary is located in the 17,688 ha Western Area Peninsula National Park in Sierra Leone. Its purpose is to care for, rehabilitate, and reintroduce confiscated and rescued chimpanzees. The chimpanzees live in large forested enclosures with indoor night quarters. Very young chimpanzees were in the past taken for walks in the adjacent forest. There have been no intentional reintroduction attempts by the Center to date, perhaps because the national park's wild chimpanzees would be a threat to newly introduced ex-captives. However, Farmer provides a personal communication from the Center's director that five chimpanzees escaped during a forest walk, probably in the late 1990s. Three of the chimpanzees were recaptured, all in good health, within 12 months of their escape. At least one was seen in good health more than one year after escape. A wild female may have acted as a surrogate mother to some of the escaped chimpanzees.

An additional 31 chimpanzees escaped in 2006, after a juvenile used a combination of tools to open a locking mechanism on their enclosure. The escapees comprised 16 males and 15 females, between 2.5 and 20 years of age. Twenty-seven were wild-born and four had been born in the sanctuary.

A human visitor to the sanctuary was severely injured and the taxi driver who had brought the visitors to the sanctuary was killed by these chimpanzees shortly after their escape. By the end of 2006, 21 of the chimpanzees had returned to the sanctuary voluntarily and six had been captured and returned from as far as 10 km from the sanctuary. Four (all males) were unaccounted for by 2007.

Kabasawa et al is a remarkably frank and constructive account of this most unfortunate accidental reintroduction.

Accidental (Escape)

References

Carter, J. 2003b. Orphan chimpanzees in West Africa: Experiences and prospects for viability in chimpanzee rehabilitation. In R. Kormos, C. Boesch, M.I. Bakarr, and T.M. Butynski, eds. *West African Chimpanzees. Status Survey and Conservation Action Plan*, pp. 157-167. Gland, IUCN.

Farmer, K.H. 2002. *The Behaviour and Adapation of Reintroduced Chimpanzees (Pan troglodytes troglodytes) in the Republic of Congo*. PhD Dissertation, University of Stirling.

Kabasawa, A., Garriga, R.M., and B. Amarasekeran. 2008. Human fatality by escaped Pan troglodytes in Sierra Leone. *International Journal of Primatology* 29: 1671-1685.

Chimpanzee (*Pan troglodytes*). Janis Carter released an 18 to 24 month-old male orphan chimpanzee to its natal group along the Diarra River in Senegal in 2002. A local farmer had found the infant near the body of a dead female, presumably the infant's mother. It took a month for Carter and the farmer to get official permission to reintroduce the infant. They then returned the infant, whom they had named "Boubane", to its natal group by simply letting it out of a bag that they had used to carry him to the group. The infant was observed to be accepted initially by the group and was seen with the group on several subsequent occasions.

This is an obscure reference with limited information but is important for decision-making by those who will face the dilemma of reintroducing individual young chimpanzees.

Welfare (Rescue)

References

Carter, J. 2003a. Tama and the baby. *Friends of Animal Action Line*, Autumn 2003: 5-7.

Carter, J. 2013-14. Toto orphaned chimpanzee. *Friends of Animals Action Line*, Winter 2013-14: 1-3.

Chimpanzee (*Pan troglodytes*). Janis Carter released two orphaned infant chimpanzees in separate events at an unspecified location(s) in Guinea on unspecified dates. Both infants were at least 18 months old. They had been in captivity for less than six months and were released near the sites of their capture. They were accepted by the chimpanzee group(s) "after a great deal of screaming and histrionics".

As noted above, this is an obscure reference with limited information but these cases are important for decision-making by those who will face the dilemma of reintroducing individual young chimpanzees.

Welfare (Rescue)

References

Carter, J. 2013-14. Toto orphaned chimpanzee. *Friends of Animals Action Line*, Winter 2013-14: 1-3.

Chimpanzee (*Pan troglodytes*). The Chimpanzee Conservation Centre (CCC, formerly the Projet de Conservation des Chimpanzés) in Guinea reintroduced six male and six female chimpanzees into the 55,400-ha Mafour core area of the Haut Niger National Park in Guinea in 2008. The chimpanzees were between eight and 20 years old. A second cohort of five (two adult males, two adult females, and one infant) was released in 2011. One of the Cohort 2 males had been released with Cohort 1 but had been returned to captivity and then re-released. Thus a total of 16 chimpanzees were reintroduced in this program. Two of the Cohort 2 female chimpanzees may have been those who voluntarily returned to the sanctuary after their release in Cohort 1 (see below), but the sources do not state this specifically.

There was a viable population of chimpanzees already living in the park, but the purposes of this reintroduction were said to be reinforcement of the wild population, increasing its genetic diversity, and enhancing protection of the park. The reintroduction also served to reduce the population in the Centre's overcrowded sanctuary.

Ten of the Cohort 1 chimpanzees were wild-born rescued or confiscated orphans. Two had been born at the sanctuary due to contraception failure. They all had lived at CCC for seven to 11 years and had known each other for at least seven years. While at CCC, the chimpanzees had been taken on guided forest walks until they were ten years old, and then they lived in social groups in large forested enclosures that gave them opportunities to discover and eat natural foods and locomote on natural vegetation. Before release, the 12 chimpanzees had learned to eat a variety of natural plant and animal foods, exhibited normal social behavior, and built nests. They were given wild forest fruits in the year prior to release. The chimpanzees were screened for endoparasites, viruses, including hepatitis A, B, and C, blood parasites, and tuberculosis. They were dewormed and given antibiotics in the two weeks prior to release. Blood samples were used for genetic analysis that showed that they were all from the local *verus* subspecies. The chimpanzees who were to be released were fitted with "dummy" collars in 2006 so that they could acclimate to wearing them. The planning and preparation for this release closely followed then-current IUCN guidelines. Some of the chimpanzees had learned to escape from their CCC enclosures by placing branches on the electrical fencing, but these escapes are not treated here as separate reintroduction events because all of those who escaped were eventually released intentionally.

Five of the males of Cohort 1 were acclimated in a cage at the release site for three months. The others were brought to the release site on the day of release, and all 12 were released simultaneously. Provisioned food was offered for several years but the chimpanzees rarely returned to the provisioning site. They dispersed widely. Most males traveled farther from the release site than the females. They all preferred forested areas to open and wooded savannas. A reintroduced male suffered only minor injuries in the only known case of aggression by wild chimpanzees.

There were seven cases in which released chimpanzees traveled far from the release site and appeared lost; they were retrieved by CCC staff and brought back to an area near the release site. One male died under anesthesia during a retrieval. In another of these retrievals, local villagers alerted CCC staff to a large collarless male chimpanzee who was far from the release site. His collar had become detached and, being motionless, was emitting a "mortality signal". Estelle Raballand, then CCC's director, found the male, named "Robert", alive, sitting near his collar. In a remarkable display of friendship and endurance, Raballand escorted Robert on a five-day hike back to the release area.

As of 2009, six of the 12 chimpanzees were known to be alive and nutritionally independent in the wild. Two males and three females of these six had coalesced into a single group. Two of the females in this group gave birth to healthy infants. Both infants disappeared, and were presumed to have been killed by baboons. One other reintroduced female joined a wild group. One of the captive-born females voluntarily returned to the sanctuary with a wild female (a "reverse reintroduction"), and a male was returned to the sanctuary for treatment of wounds inflicted by other released males. Three (without collars) disappeared in 2009 but were thought to still be alive. One adult male was known to be dead (see above). I could find no specific information on outcomes for the five chimpanzees who were released in 2011, although Vanlangendonck et al claim that the reintroduction of at least two was successful. The coalesced "core group" was reported to have eight members in 2013. Two of the 2011 female chimpanzees may have been those who voluntarily returned to the sanctuary shortly after the 2008 release.

Colin reports that as of 2017, there was a small released group "of seven chimpanzees with four babies" in the wild. It's not clear to me if the four infants were included in, or in addition to, the count of seven. At least two of the infants were born in the wild after their mothers were reintroduced. Colin also repeats that an unspecified number of the released chimpanzees have been integrated into wild groups.

Although their paper does not bear directly on these reintroductions, Ongman et al studied the pre-release behavior of other orphans at CCC, and hypothesized that orphaned or rescued chimpanzees who spent part of their lives in different natal populations can bring different survival-critical skills, e.g. specific forms of tool use or specific dietary preferences, to a release group that, when imitatively copied by other members of the release group, would provide a broader, and therefore more adaptive, set of behaviors for adapting after reintroduction. Of course, all reintroduced chimpanzees should be of the subspecies that is native to the destination site.

Conservation (Reinforcement), Welfare (Rehabilitation)

References

Colin, C. 2017. Saving chimps in Guinea. *International Primate Protection League News* 44(3): 10-11.

Humle, T., Colin, C., Laurans, M., and E. Raballand. 2011. Group release of sanctuary chimpanzees (*Pan troglodytes*) in the Haut Niger National Park, Guinea, West Africa: Ranging patterns and lessons so far. *International Journal of Primatology* 32(2): 456-473.

Humle, T., Colin, C., Laurans, M., Danaud, C., and E. Raballand. 2013. Release of the western subspecies of chimpanzees in Guinea, West Africa. In P. S. Soorae, ed. *Global Re-introduction Perspectives: 2013. Further Case Studies from Around the Globe*, pp. 222-228. Gland, IUCN/SSC Re-introduction Specialist Group and Abu Dhabi, UAE, Environment Agency.

Humle, T., Legras, J., Kalyongo, P.S., Raballand, E., and C. Colin. 2018. Releasing chimpanzees back to the wild: Lesson learnt and challenges ahead. Abstract of a paper presented at the 27th Congress of the International Primatological Society, Nairobi, Kenya.

Ongman, L., Colin, C., Raballand, E., and T. Humle. 2013. The "super chimpanzee": The ecological dimensions of rehabilitation of orphan chimpanzees in Guinea, West Africa. *Animals* 3: 109-126.

Raballand, E. 2008. Annual Report, Chimpanzee Conservation Center, 2008.

Vanlangendonck, N., Colin, C., Laurans, M., Raballand, E., and T. Humle. 2013. The socio-ecological adaptation of released chimpanzees in Guinea, West Africa. Abstract of a paper presented at the 5th Congress of the European Federation of Primatology, Antwerp, 10-13 September 2013. *Folia Primatologica* 84: 341.

Chimpanzee (*Pan troglodytes*). Professor Jill Preutz, then of Iowa State University, and Senegal's Department of Eaux and Forets, returned a poached nine month-old female chimpanzee to its native group in 2009. Preutz was (and still is) conducting a long-term field study of chimpanzees in Senegal at a site known as Fongoli, although she was not present at Fongoli when this event began. A villager alerted Preutz's field team that local hunters had captured an infant chimpanzee and were keeping her in a nearby private home. A staff member confiscated the chimpanzee and brought her to his own home. The infant, whom researchers had named "Aimee" at birth, was fed milk and bits of fruit. Contact with humans was minimized and good sanitary conditions were maintained during feedings and treatments of Aimee's eye, which had become infected.

The hunters had found Aimee on the ground after their dogs had attacked and wounded her mother, "Tia", who was a member of Preutz's study group. Tia had escaped and fled, but Aimee had fallen off or had been pulled off by the dogs during the attack. The hunters had hoped to sell the infant.

Preutz flew immediately to Senegal from the USA. On the fifth day after confiscation, she and her team carried Aimee in a sack to within 15 meters of Tia and her group. They opened the sack and retreated. An adolescent male (not a close genetic relative of Tia's) climbed down a tree and approached. Aimee climbed on him. He then carried Aimee up the tree and returned her to Tia. Aimee was seen nursing on Tia the same day. Tia was weakened by wounds and had difficulty carrying Aimee and keeping up with the group during the next several weeks. The same male assisted Tia by carrying Aimee twice during the two days following the reunion. Tia recovered. Aimee survived.

To my knowledge, Aimee is the youngest chimpanzee orphan to be successfully reintroduced to the wild. Her natal group was known, and she was returned within a week of her capture. Tia was still lactating. Aimee was in good health (her eye had healed), and there was little chance of her introducing disease to the wild population. The decision to restrict human access after Aimee was confiscated doubtlessly deprived her of the comfort of bodily contact but prevented her from becoming overly attached to humans.

As a footnote to this reintroduction, Tia was killed by a venomous snake in 2012. She had a two month-old infant, "Toto", at the time. Toto was found lying on the ground next to Tia's body. The chimpanzee group had left the area but Aimee had remained near Toto. Toto was rescued, raised by Janis Carter (see below), and was being integrated with other orphans and taken for forest walks at the Chimpanzee Conservation Centre in Guinea as of April 2017.

Aimee served as a model for chimpanzee "Bee's" reintroduction to her natal group in the novel *Ape* (Beck 2015).

Welfare (Rescue)

References

Beck, B. 2015. *Ape*. Berlin, MD USA, Salt Water Media Press.

Carter, J. 2013-14. Toto orphaned chimpanzee. *Friends of Animals Action Line*, Winter 2013-14: 1-3.

Preutz, J.D. 2011. Targeted helping by a wild adolescent male chimpanzee (*Pan troglodytes*): evidence for empathy? *Journal of Ethology* 29(2): 365-368.

Preutz, J.D. and D. Kante. 2010. Successful return of an infant chimpanzee to its natal group after a poaching incident. *African Primates* 7: 35-41.

ANOTHER CHIMPANZEE SANCTUARY THAT IS ALMOST A REINTRODUCTION

Chimpanzee (*Pan troglodytes*). The Jane Goodall Institute's Tchimpounga Chimpanzee Rehabilitation Centre acquired three forested islands in the Kouilou River, Republic of Congo, in 2011. The intent was to release 100 of the 160 orphaned and rescued chimpanzees who were living at the Centre's mainland sanctuary near Point Noire to the islands. The largest of the three islands, Tchindzoulou, is about 100 ha in area. The other two islands, Tchibebe and Ngombe, appear to be approximately 40 and 60 ha respectively from unscaled maps on the Jane Goodall Institute website. Each island has fences that separate chimpanzee-accessible forest areas from chimpanzee housing facilities and staff access areas. There are a veterinary facility, staff and visitor housing facilities, an office, and food storage areas on the mainland. Ecotourists can view the chimpanzees from pontoon boats on the river. The chimpanzees are provisioned with food and monitored daily. Some are shown in various videos wearing radiocollars. Approximately 60 had been put on the islands by 2016.

It is not clear to me whether placing these chimpanzees on these islands is considered a form of pre-release training and acclimation for a later reintroduction into the Conkouati-Douli National Park, or if placing the chimpanzees on the islands is intended to improve their welfare by housing them in a large, naturally forested sanctuary environment. If the intent is the latter, these islands are comparable to the Ngamba Island Sanctuary in Uganda (see above). The Tchimpounga Centre has actually released mandrills to the wild in the past (see mandrills, below). The mandrills had been placed on islands as a form of pre-release training and acclimation, but are said to have been reintroduced only when they were moved from the islands to unbounded mainland forest. Thus, whatever the ultimate intent and despite the large size of the islands, the definitions used in this history do not allow us to consider these Tchimpounga chimpanzees as having been reintroduced.

References

www.janegoodallinstitute.org

Bonobo (*Pan paniscus*). Gen'ichi Idani of Kyoto University attempted to rehabilitate two bonobo orphans in 1991, during the long-running field study of wild bonobos in Democratic Republic of Congo (at that time Zaire). Both were females whose mothers had been killed by poachers. They had been cared for in a mission for more than eight months. One was three years old and the other was two. Idani took the bonobos to the field every day and exposed them to two of his study groups. He left the two year-old with one of the groups after two months of this supervised exposure. She was observed two days later clinging to an adolescent male in his nest, and became a member of the group. The three year-old could not be reintroduced "because of her extreme dependence on people". These bonobo groups were provisioned and studied for many years before and after this reintroduction, but the English summary of the source did not mention post-release support or monitoring of the released individual.

Welfare (Rehabilitation)

References

Idani, G. 1993. (A bonobo orphan who became a member of the wild group). *Primate Research* 9(2): 97-106. Note: This account and the title of the article are from an English summary that was attached to this longer article, which was published in Japanese.

Bonobo (*Pan paniscus*). The Lola ya Bonobo Sanctuary, in collaboration with the Ministry of the Environment of Democratic Republic of Congo, the Ilonga-Pôo community, and Les Amis des Bonobos du Congo (ABC), released 16 bonobos in three cohorts in 2009 and 2011 at a site named Ekolo Ya Bonobo in the Maringa-Lopori-Wamba forest landscape. This reintroduction is notable for its strict adherence to all IUCN guidelines despite considerable logistical challenges. The site, which is 16,200 ha in area, was carefully chosen based on stakeholder consultations and surveys of flora and fauna. There was swampy forest, some dry land, and abundant bonobo food. There was no permanent human presence, and the traditional owners of the site, the Ilonga-Pôo community, committed to support the reintroduction and agreed not to hunt the bonobos. Bonobos had occurred at Ekolo but none had been seen for a decade. Wild bonobos lived nearby but were separated from Ekolo by a river. Trails were built and marked at the release site.

The released bonobos included 14 bonobo orphans who had been rescued from the bushmeat and wildlife trade and rehabilitated at Lola ya Bonobo sanctuary, and two offspring born at the sanctuary in the years prior to the release. Each released bonobo had been under careful veterinary observation for at least 18 months prior to release. They were screened for viruses, bacteria, and parasites. Each individual was genotyped. They were immunized against polio and tetanus, and quarantined before release. Bonobos at the sanctuary were taken on forest walks and lived in forest enclosures to provide opportunities for exploration and for foraging and locomoting on natural vegetation. The 14 bonobos to be released were grouped in the sanctuary's largest forested enclosure (15 ha) prior to release. There was behavioral and cognitive testing to ensure that the bonobos had a behavioral repertoire that would support post-release survival. There was gradual reduction of contact with humans before the bonobos were sent to the release site.

The first release cohort consisted of an established group of nine (four females, five males, including an infant). They were taken from the sanctuary to the release site by truck, airplane, and canoe, over a distance of 1,000 km, in one day. They spent three days in an acclimation enclosure at the release site (two escaped on the first day but stayed near the enclosure).

Three of the first nine released bonobos were returned to the sanctuary within three months because of aggressive displays toward humans that interfered with post-release monitoring. Two infants were born in 2009 and 2010, of which one died (of snake bite). The second cohort, comprising one male and two females, was released in 2011. They integrated quickly into the original group. The third cohort included four bonobos (three males, one female, including an infant) who were released a few months later, also in 2011. This resulted in the fission of three bonobos from the group that had formed from the first two cohorts. Another infant was born in 2011, and three more were born in 2013, 2014, and 2016. At the end of 2016, there were 18 bonobos in two groups at the release site. There was one group of 15 and another of three, although these three had not been seen for some time. There were reports by locals to the trackers that one of these may have been shot.

The first release cohort was initially provided with drinking water and supplementary food. Most began eating natural fruit and building nests on the first day of release. The bonobos expanded their range significantly over time, although they revisited the acclimation enclosure almost every day for food. There was systematic post-release veterinary and behavioral monitoring by trackers for more than 18 months, at which time some of the bonobos suddenly and severely attacked three male trackers (the female monitoring staff was not threatened). Out of concern for the safety of the local population, the bonobos were provisioned thereafter at the edge of the river, and monitoring was done from boats. Direct contact between staff and bonobos was prohibited. Provisioning was discontinued in 2013, although food is sometimes provided to facilitate observation.

Radiotelemetry had not been used because radiocollars were judged to be too heavy and because there was poor satellite coverage in the area. A new generation of collars was tested in 2015 and will be used in the next release, of 13 bonobos, which is planned for 2018.

Animal biodiversity has increased at the release site as a result of anti-poaching patrols. This has ironically attracted poachers. There are some temporary human settlements, seasonal eel fishing, and wood collection in the reserve. ABC has implemented conservation education activities in schools and villages and with river travelers. Public awareness and support for conservation are said to have increased. The release project has generated local employment opportunities and various local socio-economic community development projects.

The attack on the trackers was quickly and frankly acknowledged to all stakeholders, and the injured men were given state-of-the-art medical care. The program's director, Claudine André, is to be complimented for excellent incident management and her overall planning and coordination of this reintroduction.

Conservation (Reintroduction, Reinforcement), Welfare (Rehabilitation)

REFERENCES

Clay, Z., Garai, C., André, C., Minesi-André, F., and R. Belais. 2018. Reintroducing bonobos (*Pan paniscus*) into the wild – insights and outlooks from the Ekolo Ya Bonobo Project. Abstract of a paper presented at the 27th Congress of the International Primatological Society, Nairobi, Kenya.

Morel, D. 2017. Personal communication (e-mail 11 January, with numerous attachments of unpublished quarterly reports to the World Society for the Protection of Animals in 2009, 2010, and 2011, proposals and reports to the Great Ape Conservation Fund of the US Fish and Wildlife Service, and presentations to the Pan African Sanctuary Alliance in 2009 and 2013 by Claudine André).

CHAPTER 3
REINTRODUCTIONS OF GORILLAS

Western Lowland Gorilla (*Gorilla gorilla*). An unknown number of gorillas were reintroduced to an island in the Ivindo River in what is now the 15,000-ha Ipassa Makokou Biosphere Reserve in Gabon in the early 1970s. The gorillas may have been kept or even born at a medical research facility. I could not find any further information about the purpose of this reintroduction, or about the gorillas or the techniques. Hladik, who studied the composition of foods eaten by these gorillas and by chimpanzees who were reintroduced on other nearby islands (see above), stated that the gorillas' island was too small to sustain the gorillas and that they destroyed most of the edible trees and lianas. I could find no further information on the outcome of this reintroduction.

Unspecified

References

Hladik, C.M. 1978. Adaptive strategies of primates in relation to leaf-eating. In G.G. Montgomery, ed. *The Ecology of Arboreal Folivores*, pp. 373-395. Washington, DC, Smithsonian Institution Press.

Western Lowland Gorilla (*Gorilla gorilla*). The Brazzaville Zoo, in the capital of what is now the Republic of Congo, has cared for orphaned lowland gorillas and chimpanzees since the 1970s. Yvette Leroy, a French expatriate, began rescuing and rehabilitating gorillas in her own garden and then volunteered to manage this early African ape sanctuary at the zoo in 1981. The zoo and the ape sanctuary were handicapped by insufficient funding and the lack of trained staff. A flood of baby apes who were orphaned by the bushmeat trade made the situation dire in the mid-1980s. Leroy was even willing to export gorillas to North American and European zoos, an idea that was abandoned because it would have created a perception of successful commerce in orphaned wild apes, even if legal permits could have been acquired.

John Aspinall, owner of the Howletts and Port Lympne Animal Parks in England, came to the rescue in 1986, sowing the seeds of gorilla reintroductions that would not occur until years later and would eventually involve his son Damian, then in his 20s, his then-teenage stepson Amos Courage, and his then-unborn granddaughter Tansy. Howletts was and still is famous for one of, if not the most successful *ex situ* captive breeding programs for lowland gorillas. Pictures of Damian as a baby playing with the zoos' gorillas were powerfully instrumental in converting the public's image of gorillas as ferocious beasts to recognition of their gentleness and social affinity.

Aspinall went to the Congo in 1986 and contracted with the Congolese Ministry of Economics and Forestry to open a gorilla conservation program that would be called the Projet de Protection des Gorilles (PPG) and would be funded by the John Aspinall Foundation (then the Howletts and Port Lympne Foundation). The primary goal of PPG was to rescue, rehabilitate, and reintroduce orphan gorillas (and rescuing bonobos as well). Management and protection of the Congo's biodiversity was also a goal. This led to the reintroduction of more than 60 gorillas by 2015. Some were born at the Howletts and Port Lympne wildlife parks in the UK. Because the destination sites were in two different countries (Republic of Congo and Republic of Gabon), and because some of the Gabon reintroductions were conservation-driven and some were welfare-driven, I have divided PPG's efforts into three different programs in this history.

The PPG Congo Program began by establishing a well equipped and well staffed gorilla orphanage on the grounds of the Brazzaville Zoo in 1989. Mark and Helen Attwater were hired to succeed Madame Leroy in managing the orphanage. The orphanage took in 65 gorillas and nine bonobos between 1989 and 1996, although it had been designed for only 30 apes. The gorillas were initially treated for dehydration, gastrointestinal disorders, and emotional stress and trauma, but mortality was nonetheless high. Foster mothering of infants by humans became an important component of the apes' regaining emotional health. Socialization with other gorillas was also a crucial step. The orphans who survived and regained health were organized into age-based groups (less than one year of age, one to three years, and older than three). Human attendants oversaw all daytime activities. The gorillas were given supervised access to a 25-ha forest tract on the zoo grounds, in which they could sample natural foods and locomote on natural vegetation. Most of the gorillas quickly expressed a wide range of affiliative and competitive behaviors, nest-building, and foraging. Gorillas who had been orphaned after the age of two years appeared to retain a normal gorilla behavioral repertoire and were said to serve as models for observation learning by those who had been orphaned at earlier ages. The gorillas were immunized for many communicable diseases and continued to be treated for diseases and injuries.

Chapter 3: Reintroduction of Gorillas

In 1993, PPG and the Congolese government agreed to found the Lesio-Louna Sanctuary, within the 44,000-ha Lesio-Louna Reserve, which is adjacent to the Lefini Faunal Reserve. The Lesio-Louna Sanctuary was approximately 140 km north of Brazzaville. The Aspinall Foundation built, fenced, and staffed a simple veterinary isolation facility and caging for young gorillas in the sanctuary. The intent was to move healthy and partially rehabilitated orphans from the Brazzaville sanctuary to the Lesio-Louna sanctuary for more pre-release preparation and then release into the reserve.

The Foundation funded surveys of the Lesio-Louna and Lefini Reserves that showed that there were sufficient and appropriate foods for a large number of gorillas, that gorillas had been absent from the protected areas for at least two decades, that there was heavy hunting pressure (which explained the absence of gorillas), and that a combination of natural features such as escarpments and rivers would separate reintroduced gorillas from human settlements. Local people, including hunters, were hired as trackers and protection was enhanced.

The first gorillas were moved from Brazzaville to Lesio-Louna in 1996. After a short period of medical observation, two groups of three gorillas each began the reintroduction process. The gorillas were between six and nine years old. The gorilla groups were escorted by caretakers into the forest surrounding the sanctuary, and were provisioned with food and led back to cages for the night. Their vaccination schedules were continued and their health was monitored closely. The intensive immunization and disease surveillance program is remarkable because there were no gorillas (but there were chimpanzees and people) at the release sites.

Civil war broke out in the Republic of Congo in 1997. The gorillas and bonobos at the Brazzaville orphanage were heroically evacuated under fire to the Jane Goodall Institute's Tchimpounga sanctuary in the Congolese city of Point Noire. Seven (another source says 11) of the gorillas continued their supervised forest walks at Tchimpounga. When hostilities waned in 1998, the apes were transferred to the Lesio-Louna sanctuary. Reintroduction of the gorillas at Lesio-Louna resumed. The bonobos were later relocated to the Lola ya Bonobo Sanctuary in the Democratic Republic of Congo. It should be noted that there had been a plan to introduce the bonobos to an isolated forest tract in Lesio-Louna, but this plan was abandoned because bonobos had never occurred naturally in Republic of Congo.

A total of 25 gorillas (24 wild-borns and one born in captivity during the rehabilitation process) in five groups (or 26 in four groups, the sources vary) were reintroduced in Lesio-Louna and Lefini between 1996 and 2006. The process began for the last three groups as described above for the first two groups. Then, when the gorillas stopped returning to the cages at night, their caretakers began to decrease supplemental feeding and to escort them deeper into the forest, toward the final release sites. The duration of pre-release training/acclimation and supplemental provisioning of the later two or three groups was reduced during the course of the reintroductions, and the duration and intensity of contact and supervision by human caretakers were also reduced.

Some of the gorillas had to be taken to the final release site by truck or boat. There was no acclimation at the release sites. There was daily post-release monitoring, some supplemental feeding, and occasional medical treatment for up to three years, and periodic monitoring for a longer period. Post release survival was unusually high (greater than 90% over five years). There were 30 surviving gorillas in the reintroduced Congolese population in 2009, including 22 of the reintroduced wild-born former orphans, the captive-born individual, and seven that were born in the wild after reintroduction. Three of the 25 reintroduced gorillas had died and three had disappeared. The same authors stated in another article that in 2009 there were 23 surviving gorillas in the reintroduced Congolese population, including 15 wild-born reintroduced orphans, the captive-born individual, and the seven first-generation offspring. Apparently there had been two additional deaths or disappearances, and the bachelor group (see below) was not included in this count. Ikoli (2012) stated that there were 15 surviving reintroduced gorillas and 11 wild-born offspring in 2012. Ikoli stresses the importance of ecotourism to the conservation of Lesio-Louna (see below).

Despite the expectation that natural barriers would separate the gorillas from people, four of the reintroduced young adult male gorillas did enter villages, raid crops, and threaten people. They had to be captured and placed in cages and later on a 25-ha (or 130-ha, sources vary) island in the Louna River. The island gorillas were provisioned with food every day. There is apparently no intention to reintroduce them again. They are counted by King et al (2012) as being among the 30 survivors, but not in King et al (2014). There was a fifth member of this bachelor group, who had never been reintroduced or who had been reintroduced and accounts for the difference between a total of 25 or 26 gorillas having been reintroduced.

The last three reintroduced groups were released in more remote areas of the Lefini Reserve to further decease the likelihood of conflict with people. Surviving members of the first two reintroduced groups were also recaptured from the Lesio-Louna Reserve and re-released in Lefini. There were some limited tourism opportunities offered during this reintroduction program, which the program managers saw as interfering with program success.

Population modelling suggests that this Congo gorilla population has a probability of greater than 90% of surviving for 200 years, although the small size of the existing population creates considerable sensitivity to small changes in birth rates, female mortality, additional reintroductions, and catastrophe.

A media article (Leclere 2017) states that the Aspinall Foundation was preparing to send four captive-born gorilla brothers (presumably half-brothers) to Lesio Louna, where they would be placed on (reintroduced to?) the 17-ha Ndouna Island, which is in the Congo River, near Brazzavlle. The gorillas were between 13 and 17 years of age. All four gorillas had been born at the Aspinall Foundation's Howletts Zoo in the UK, but have been living at the park's sister park, Port Lympne. They are said to have been prepared for their new life by undergoing "subtle changes to their diet and daily routine". It is not clear from the article if the island is to serve as a temporary preparation and acclimation facility, or if it is to be a permanent home. Tourists will be able to view the gorillas. If and when these gorillas are reintroduced, the purposes would be Commercial and Welfare (Non-lethal Control) for surplus adult male gorillas.

Conservation (Reintroduction), Welfare (Rehabilitation)

REFERENCES

Anon undated b. Draft Project Proposal, Lesio-Louna Site, Lefini Reserve, Republic of Congo. Unpublished.

Attwater, H. 1999. *My Gorilla Journey: Living With the Orphans of the Rainforest*. London, Sidgwick & Jackson.

Attwater, M. 2001. Challenging developments in primate rehabilitation programs, Africa. *Re-introduction News* 20: 12-13.

Courage, A., Henderson, I., and J. Watkin. 2001. Orphan gorilla reintroduction: Lesio-Louna and Mpassa. *Gorilla Journal* 22: 33-35.

Farmer, K.H., and A. Courage. 2008. Sanctuaries and reintroduction: A role in gorilla conservation? In T.S. Stoinski, H.D. Steklis, and P. Mehlman, eds. *Conservation in the 21st century: Gorillas as a case study*, pp. 79–106. New York: Springer.

Hanlon, M. 2007. ASBO gorillas: How delinquent gorillas were given a second chance. www.dailymail.co.uk

Ikoli, P.F. 2012. Reintroduction des Gorilles orphelins dans la Rserve de Lesio-Louna en Republique du Congo. *Proceedings of the Africa-Asia Ape Conservation and Poverty Alleviation Learning Exchange*, Bogor, Indonesia, 11-15 January. Retrieved from www.povertyandconservation.info/node/7916

King, T. 2004. Reintroduced western gorillas reproduce for the first time. *Oryx* 38(3): 251-252.

King, T. and C. Chamberlan. 2007. Orphan gorilla management and reintroduction: Progress and perspectives. *Gorilla Journal* 34: 21-25.

King, T. and A. Courage. 2008. Western gorilla re-introduction to the Batéké Plateau region of Congo and Gabon. In P.S. Soorae, ed. *Global Re-introduction Perspectives: Re-introduction Case-Studies from Around the Globe*, pp. 217-210. Abu Dhabi, UAE IUCN/SSC Re-introduction Specialist Group,

King, T., Chamberlan, C., and A. Courage. 2005a. Rehabilitation of orphan gorillas and bonobos in the Congo. *Oryx* 52(4): 198-209.

King, T., Chamberlan, C., and A. Courage. 2005b. Reintroduced gorillas: Reproduction, ranging and unresolved issues. *Gorilla Journal* 32: 30-32.

King, T., Chamberlan, C., and A. Courage. 2012. Assessing initial reintroduction success in long-lived primates by quantifying survival, reproduction, and dispersal parameters: Western lowland gorillas (*Gorilla gorilla gorilla*) in Congo and Gabon. *International Journal of Primatology* 33: 134-149.

King, T., Chamberlan, C., and A. Courage. 2014. Assessing reintroduction success in long-lived primates through population viability analysis: western lowland gorillas *Gorilla gorilla gorilla* in Central Africa. *Oryx* 48: 294-303.

Leclere, M. 2017. Port Lympne gorilla brothers heading to Congo in Back to the Wild initiative. *KentOnline*, 6 October 2017.

McRae, M. 2000. Central Africa's orphan gorillas. *National Geographic*, February 2000: 84-97.

Wells, K. 1993. This mom teaches her young to walk on the wild side. *The Wall Street Journal*, 22 March 1993: A1, A6.

Western Lowland Gorilla (*Gorilla gorilla*). The Gabon program of the Projet de Protection des Gorilles (PPG) began in 1998 when, under contract with the Gabonese Department of Eaux and Forêts, PPG established a sanctuary in the Mpassa Reserve. The Mpassa Reserve was later incorporated into the 204,400-ha Batéké Plateau National Park (BPNP), which was created in 2002. As in the PPG Congo program, the primary purpose of the PPG Gabon program was to reintroduce lowland gorillas to establish a viable wild population within their former range.

The Batéké Plateau is the same vast geologic formation in which the Lefini Reserve is situated in Republic of Congo (see above). The PPG reintroduction sites in Gabon and Congo are separated by about 200 km. There were 60,600 ha of forests within BPNP, of which 6,200 ha were within the Mpassa site. Chimpanzees, but not gorillas were present when the program began at Mpassa/BPNP. The nearest villages were 30 km away. Pearson et al (2007) present extensive lists of mammals, birds, reptiles, and amphibians that lived in the park. Hunting pressure was moderate but is said to have decreased after 2000, in part due to the PPG camp and activities. The Mpassa area was judged to have the resources to support a population of 500 wild gorillas.

A total of 23 wild-born orphan gorillas were brought to the PPG sanctuary in the BPNP between 1998 and 2003. All had been confiscated or surrendered within Gabon. Nine young gorillas, in two separate cohorts (two in 1999 and seven in 2003), who had been born at the Howletts and Port Lympne Wild Animal Parks in the UK were also exported to the PPG sanctuary in BPNP. The youngsters had been hand-reared at the zoo because they had been rejected by their mothers. These infants were ex situ captive-born orphans. PPG managers thought that these gorillas would be well suited for export and reintroduction because the gorillas had confidence in human support. The managers thought it would have been unethical to separate mother-reared gorillas from their mothers, and they thought that older gorillas from the zoos would not adapt well to such a drastic environmental change.

The objection to the reintroduction of *ex situ* captive-born apes is treated at length in the account of the Sumatran Orangutan Conservation Programme (see below). The *IUCN Best Practice Guidelines for the Re-introduction of Great Apes* states that "Currently there is little scientific justification for re-introducing captive-born ... great apes. There are usually enough great apes in sanctuaries ...within the country of origin that can be re-introduced, as well as threatened wild apes that need to be relocated". (Beck et al 2007, pg. 13). The PPG managers noted but challenged this guideline, noting that there were no wild gorillas in Gabon that needed to be relocated, and that there were not enough suitable wild-born orphans in Gabonese sanctuaries to establish a wild population. This issue will be revisited in the discussion of the third PPG program (see below).

All of the Gabon gorillas were included in an extensive health management plan that included screening for communicable diseases, immunizations, and preventive and curative disease treatment. Staff were also included in a health management plan. Details of the reintroductions varied but were similar to the "ultra-soft" PPG reintroductions in the Congo. The gorillas were first "stabilized" and medically monitored for two months at the base facility. They were then taken for supervised walks into the forest near the base facility, where they had access to natural foods and natural locomotor substrates. They were led back to the base facility at night for supplemental feeding and to sleep. The daily walks were gradually extended, and some gorillas chose not to return to the base facility at night. They began to sleep in the forest, but were still offered supplemental food, although in decreasing amounts. In some cases the gorillas walked themselves to the final release site, and in some cases they had to be transported to the release site. In some of the latter cases, small acclimation cages were provided for a period. The whole pre-release process took 18 months or more. The presence of captive-borns lengthened the process.

There was first daily and then periodic post-release monitoring over several years. Some supplemental feeding was offered, and medical support was provided as needed. This even included a dramatic case of surgery to treat a brain injury and another case of amputation of a hand that had been injured in a snare.

A total of 29 gorillas began the actual reintroduction process at PPG Gabon (one had died during the stabilization period). They were coalesced into two groups, one of 19 and one of ten. The first, which initially included 17 wild-borns and two captive-borns, began the "supervised liberty" phase in 2001. However, two of these nineteen died (one of an intestinal tumor and one of appendicitis) during the pre-release preparation. Thus only 17 were actually reintroduced in the first group. The second group, which initially comprised three wild-borns and seven captive-borns, began supervised liberty in 2004. However, one gorilla died (of peritonitis) during pre-release preparation. Thus only nine were actually released in the second group. In all, PPG Gabon reintroduced 26 gorillas to the wild.

Two of these 26 gorillas died and two disappeared within 2.2 years after reintroduction. Four infants had been born by 2011, and more have apparently been born subsequently. Extensive data on ranging, social behavior, dispersal, activity budgets, and foraging were collected.

The uncommonly high survival rate in this reintroduction program is probably related to the uncommonly intensive and extended pre-release preparation, post-release monitoring, and post-release support.

More gorillas may have been reintroduced in this program. Le Flohic et al (2015) describe aspects of the pre-release training of a group five young gorillas that took place after the reintroduction of the 26. The 2015 study examines the effects of seasonality and food availability on the social and play behavior of the group of five during a seven-month period in their rehabilitation, when they were being taken by caretakers on forest walks during the day and returned to cages at night. The group comprised a four year-old male and four females, who were one to three years old. The male and two of the females had been born at the Aspinall Foundation's Howletts and Port Lympne Wild Animal Parks in the UK. The other two had been confiscated in Gabon. The gorillas played more, fed less, and spent more time together during the fruiting season than they did when fruit was less available. The one year-old was killed brutally by a wild chimpanzee during the study. Caretakers tried unsuccessfuly to interrupt the attack. Group cohesion and social behavior decreased after the attack, and the group shifted their range away from area of highest chimpanzee density. These observations were made in 2010. The last reintroductions recorded for this program were conducted in 2004. I don't know if the surviving four young gorillas of this study group were ever reintroduced to the wild, were reintroduced in this program sometime after 2010, or were included among those reintroduced in the following program (see below) in 2014.

Like the the PPG Congo program, modeling of the Gabon gorilla population suggests that it has a probability of greater than 90% of surviving for 200 years, although the small size of the existing population creates considerable sensitivity to small changes in birth rates, female mortality, additional reintroductions, and catastrophe.

Conservation (Reintroduction), Welfare (Rehabilitation)

References

Beck, B.B., Walkup, K., Rodrigues, M., Unwin, S., Travis, D., and T. Stoinski. 2007. *Best Practice Guidelines for the Re-introduction of Great Apes*. Gland, IUCN/SSC Primate Specialist Group.

King, T., Chamberlan, C., and A. Courage. 2012. Assessing initial reintroduction success in long-lived primates by quantifying survival, reproduction, and dispersal parameters: Western lowland gorillas (*Gorilla gorilla gorilla*) in Congo and Gabon. *International Journal of Primatology* 33: 134-149.

King, T., Chamberlan, C., and A. Courage. 2014. Assessing reintroduction success in long-lived primates through population viability analysis: western lowland gorillas *Gorilla gorilla gorilla* in Central Africa. *Oryx* 48: 294-303.

Le Flohic, G., Motsch, P., DeNys, H., Childs, S., Courage, A. and T. King. 2015. Behavioural ecology and group cohesion of juvenile western lowland gorillas (*Gorilla g. gorilla*) during rehabilitation in the Batéké Plateaux National Park, Gabon. *PLoS ONE* 10(3): e0119609.

Pearson, L., Aczel, P., Mahé, S., Courage, A., and T. King. 2007. Gorilla reintroduction to the Batéké Plateau National Park, Gabon: An analysis of the preparations and initial results with reference to the IUCN guidelines for the re-introduction of Great Apes. Franceville, Gabon, PPG-Gabon/The Aspinall Foundation.

Western Lowland Gorilla (*Gorilla gorilla*). The Aspinall Foundation reintroduced an established family group of lowland gorillas into the Batéké Plateau National Park (BPNP), Gabon, in 2014. The group comprised one wild-born adult male gorilla ("Djala"), four females and their four offspring who had been sired by Djala, and an additional adult female. Djala had lived at the Howletts and Port Lympne Animal Parks in the UK for more than 25 years, and the females and infants had been born there. This is listed as a separate program in this history because the primary reason for the reintroduction was starkly different from that of the PPG Congo and PPG Gabon programs (see above). The Congo and Gabon programs were motivated primarily by conservation; they aimed to restore wild gorilla populations by reintroduction and to manage and protect large expanses of forest. The rehabilitation of orphaned gorillas was a secondary goal. However, the 2014 release in Gabon was motivated by Damian Aspinall's belief that "(t)hat's where they belong". After decades of his and his father's owning and operating two of the most highly regarded zoos in the world, Damian decided that "(i)f I could extinguish all zoos over the next 30 years, including my own, I would. I wouldn't hesitate". (Stahl 2015). He felt that it was morally wrong to keep wild animals in zoos, even in the zoos that were managed by the Foundation.

To my knowledge there is no scientific documentation of this reintroduction. I have had to rely on popular sources. There was some pre-release training of the gorillas in their zoo enclosures before they were sent to Gabon. High standards of quarantine, veterinary support, and immunization appear to have been maintained throughout the reintroduction process. After arrival in Gabon, the gorillas were acclimated for one year on a large island near the release site, where they had the opportunity to feed on and locomote in natural vegetation. They were also given supplementary food daily. Actual release consisted of building a bridge from the island to the mainland forest. They entered the forest on the first day. Within three weeks, five of the ten gorillas were found dead and another had disappeared. The losses may have involved conflict with a wild (previously reintroduced) gorilla(s). The remaining four were returned to the island. The Aspinall Foundation website noted that Djala, at least one other male, and one of the surviving females were still on the island in 2015. That female was later relocated to a newly created private wildlife sanctuary in Gabon, Le Parc de la Lékédi, where she was to be housed with another male.

By our definitions, this was not a conservation-motivated reintroduction. The Foundation's staff in Gabon may have considered the primary purpose to have been conservation (T. King, personal communication, 5 May 2015), but Aspinall, in his own words, did not. He considered the primary motive for the reintroduction of these ten gorillas to have been one step in an idealistic, romanticized commitment to closing zoos and returning the animals to the wild. Of course, his continued funding for the management and protection of BPNP is certainly a major conservation commitment. At one point I considered the primary purpose of this reintroduction to be welfare, but I no longer think that it was reasonable to think that the welfare of these gorillas would have been improved by reintroduction. I now consider it to have been an indulgence, which in our terms would be an aesthetic purpose.

Aesthetic, Conservation (Reinforcement)

References

Beck, B.B. 2016. The role of translocation in primate conservation. In S.A. Wich and A.J. Marshall, eds. *An Introduction to Primate Conservation*, pp. 241-255. Oxford, UK, Oxford University Press.

Jones, D. 2014. Who murdered my gorillas? Heartache for the man who returned his family of primates to African jungle as his experiment ends in a bloodbath – and the prime suspect is a jealous ape. www.KentOnline.co.uk, 6 September 2014.

Stahl, L. 2015. Back to the wild. http://www.cbsnews.com/news/zoo-gorilla-family-freed-to-wild-60-minutes 15 March 2015.

www.aspinallfoundation.org

Western Lowland Gorilla (*Gorilla gorilla*). In 2001, Operation Loango, a consortium comprising the Conseil National des Parcs Nationaux du Gabon, the Société pour la Conservation et le Development, and a tourism company, Africa's Eden, reintroduced a family of four western lowland gorillas on the 200-ha Petit Evengue island in what is now the Loango National Park in Gabon. The family was made up of a wild-born adult male, a wild-born adult female, their three year-old captive-born daughter and their one year-old captive-born son. The gorilla family had lived previously at the Centre International de Recherches Médicales Franceville, but had never been used in biomedical research. The young gorillas had been born at the center.

The purposes of the reintroduction were to give the gorillas an opportunity to live a more natural life, to conduct research, and to found an ecotourism program. The gorillas were initially acclimated for three months in a small fenced enclosure on the island in which they had access to natural foods and trees to climb. They were then given access to the whole island, except for a small fenced base camp. The infant male died the first night after release, and the three survivors were confined again in the acclimation enclosure. The gorillas were re-released a few months later but had to be confined again because of the adult male's aggression toward people. The female gave birth to a male infant a year later in their enclosure. The gorillas were to be given access to newly constructed larger enclosures, and at least one confiscated orphan was added to the group.

Sometime later, the project, renamed the Fernan-Vaz Gorilla Project released six (three male and three female) lowland gorillas on a "lagoon island", near Orique island, which is near the Loango National Park in Gabon. The six orphaned gorillas had spent more than two years in "forest rehabilitation" on Petit Evengue, where thay had been quarantined and socialized. Although they are described as being free, and have been observed building nests, project managers consider this to be the gorillas' second stage of rehabilitation, and I therefore have not counted them as having been reintroduced.

A Projet Gorille Fernan-Vaz Facebook post, dated 8 June 2018, refers to nine gorillas on the island who are "destined for release into the wild".

Welfare (Rehabilitation), Research, Commercial (Tourism)

References

Keizer, F. and M. Keizer. 2004. The gorillas of "Petit Evengue". *Gorilla Journal* 29: 28-30.

Projet Gorille Fernan-Vaz Facebook page, 8 June 2018.

www.gorillasgabon.org

Grauer's Gorilla (*Gorilla beringei [graueri]*). An infant female Grauer's gorilla was bought by a miner (Lyon 1976) or a farmer (Anon undated b) in 1973 or 1974, after her mother was shot by poachers in or near the Kahuzi-Biega National Park in the Democratic Republic of Congo (DRC, at that time Zaire). The charismatic and fiercely protectionist Belgian warden of Kahuzi-Biega, Adrian Deschryver, confiscated the gorilla. He named the gorilla "Julie" and raised her with his family in his home in the national park. She was about six months old when confiscated. Descrhyver chose not to send Julie to a zoo, intending instead to reintroduce her to a habituated wild gorilla group within the park after she reached 18 months of age. Julie was first bottle-fed milk and given soft solid food, bathed, and allowed to play with human toys.

Deschryver began taking Julie into the forest, first carrying her and then inducing her to walk quadrupedally, and introducing her to a variety of plants that were eaten by wild gorillas, and to small forest animals. Although the exact timing is not clear, Julie appeared to have been about 8 months old when Deschryver decided to take her to the 19-member habituated group that was led by the equally charismatic silverback male "Casimir" (or "Kasimer"). Deschryver wanted Julie to see and hear wild gorillas. Deschryver and Casimir knew each other well and had had many peaceful and friendly interactions. Upon hearing the gorillas, Julie vocalized ("cried") and Casimir charged Deschryver. Deschryver was convinced that Casimir was about to attack him and dropped Julie to the ground. Casimir immediately picked Julie up, dropped her, picked her up again, and carried her back to the group. The gorillas appeared to be interested and did not appear to be aggressive toward Julie. The group moved off with her (or she with the group). She is said to have lived for ten days although it is not clear if she was observed in the meantime. She may have starved (there was no lactating female in the group at the time), died of exposure (the weather was unusually cold and rainy at the time), been killed by the gorillas, or been killed by a predator.

There are many unanswered questions about this reintroduction. Was Julie's "cry" upon first hearing gorillas evidence of recognition, despite being only eight months old and having been in captivity for at least two months during which she became completely habituated? Did Julie cling to one of the wild gorillas or simply struggle to keep up with the group as it moved. In the video cited below, Julie is seen to be carried *by* humans rather than clinging *to* them before the reintroduction; she may have forgotten how, or lost the ability, to cling. Was there any form of veterinary examination or even consideration of the health risks of exposing wild gorillas to a conspecific orphan who had had extensive contact with humans? Had Julie even originated in the Kahuzi-Biega population? As Deschryver had to fly his plane to the point where he confiscated her, Julie probably had not come from Deschryver's study population and may not even have come from Kahuzi-Biega. Had she survived, there may have been some interpopulational hybridization (see Banes et al. 2016 for an analogous concern for Bornean orangutans).

Although Deschryver had intended to reintroduce Julie and had initiated pre-release training, this reintroduction was accidental.

Accidental

References

Banes, G.L., Galdikas, B.M.F., and L. Vigilant. 2016. Reintroduction of confiscated and displaced mammals risks outbreeding and introgression in natural populations, as evidenced by orang-utans of divergent subspecies. *Scientific Reports* 6, 22026; doi: 10.1038/srep22026.

Buxton, A. (producer) and C. Willock (writer). 1974. *Gorilla* (documentary film). UK: Survival Anglia Ltd.

Heminway, J. 1972. A walk with the gorillas. *Africana* 4(11): 11, 22-23, 26.

Lyon, L. 1976. The saving of the gorilla. *Africana* 5(9): 11-13, 23.

Williamson, E.A. 2017. Personal communication, e-mail 23 July.

Mountain Gorilla (*Gorilla beringei*). Gorilla researcher and conservationist Dian Fossey, working with permission of the Office Rwandais du Tourisme et des Parc Nationaux, reintroduced a three year-old orphaned female mountain gorilla into Rwanda's Parc National des Volcans in 1980. The following account is based on Fossey, 1983, pp 222-229, from which the quotes are taken.

The gorilla had been confiscated by Jean-Pierre von der Becke, a conservationist and the first director of the then newly founded Mountain Gorilla Project. Von der Becke gave the gorilla to one of Fossey's porters, who brought the young gorilla to Kariosoke, Fossey's mountainous research camp, on New Year's Day of 1980. She was soon named "Bonne Année". Fossey presumed that the infant's mother had been shot by poachers. Before confiscation, Bonne Année had been kept in a dark shed and fed bread and fruit for approximately six weeks. She was badly dehydrated, had severe lung congestion, and was terrified of people. Once at Kariosoke, she became habituated to humans, played and rested with the camp's dog, and her "health was completely restored". Fossey provided foods of the types that were eaten by wild gorillas, which Bonne Année ate, and nest-building materials. Bonne Année used nests built by humans but we are not told if she built nests herself. In March 1980, Bonne Année was taken to a remote camp without heat, special (human) foods, her dog companion, or many attentive humans. Fossey first attempted to reintroduce Bonne Année into Group 5, which was a large group with an established silverback male and many related females, juveniles, and infants. All of the adult females were raising infants at the time (Weber and Vedder 2001).

Bonne Année immediately approached the gorillas. Two adult females began to pull, drag, and bite her. Fossey rescued Bonne Année, but the infant returned to the group. The same females resumed their aggressive behavior. The silverback broke up the interaction but otherwise ignored

Bonne Année. However, younger group members approached her, and she began to feed in their proximity. Then a young silverback male began to drag Bonne Année, and was soon joined by the two original aggressive females. The old silverback intervened again, but he soon departed, and the young silverback and one of the females resumed their "torture". Bonne Année finally stopped screaming and resisting. The young male again grabbed, dragged, and threw her, but she was able to crawl back to Fossey, who rescued her. Bonne Année was not seriously injured (even though the gorillas could easily have killed her). In April, apparently after Fossey had temporarily left Kariosoke, von der Becke reintroduced Bonne Année to Group 4, a newly formed group whose six members were not related and which had no infants. She was playing with a young adult male within an hour. Bonne Année traveled with Group 4 for up to a year, "protected and cuddled" by all of the members. She died of pneumonia between six and 12 months after the April release (the sources vary) during a long, cold, rainy period.

At three years of age, Bonne Année had been weaned and had acquired sufficient social and subsistence skills before being poached to allow her to survive in the wild without a mother. These behaviors endured despite the trauma of her mother's being killed, being held for six weeks under deplorable circumstances, and being held for 12 to 16 weeks under supportive circumstances in a human environment, during which she lost her fear of humans. At the first opportunity, she returned without hesitation to the company of wild gorillas, and persisted despite being treated aggressively.

Again, there are intriguing and important questions. Why did some members of an established wild group treat Bonne Année aggressively rather than welcome her as a female immigrant? Why did the older silverback intervene to stop the aggression, but then ignore Bonne Année's approach? Why did the younger silverback treat her so aggressively? Fossey notes that the younger silverback was becoming dominant. At the time, Fossey was not yet aware that newly dominant silverback mountain gorillas often kill infants when they take over a group, although, at three years of age, Bonne Année might have been spared. Were the aggressive adult females fighting to possess Bonne Année, as Fossey initially suggested, or would they have killed her in "xenophobic brutality", as a potential competitor of their own offspring and kin?

Fossey had originally thought that Group 4 would have been the best choice for the reintroduction, but the Group 4 gorillas were involved in inter-group conflict on the day that Bonne Année was scheduled to be reintroduced. Indeed, Group 4 readily accepted Bonne Année on the second reintroduction attempt. Group 4 was newly formed and had no infants; the silverback appeared to treat her as an immigrating young female rather than as the offspring of a rival male. And Bonne Année would not have been a competitor of any member's offspring or kin. Fossey hypothesized that the group's "lack of strong kinship bonds permitted instant acceptance". Of course, Bonne Année would probably have also been accepted readily by her natal group, with which she would have had strong kinship bonds.

Fossey assumed that Bonne Année had been captured in the Virungas, and thus was from the same genetic subpopulation as the goups to which she was introduced. Had she survived and reproduced, her offspring would not have been specific or sub-specific hybrids. Fossey also assumed that Bonne Année was free of communicable disease at the time of release, even though there was no veterinary examination or testing. Bonne Année's death of pneumonia, with her history of respiratory congestion, would later reinforce Harcourt's major concern about Julie's reintroduction (see above).

Of course this reintroduction preceded Harcourt's classic "reintroduction options" paper (see below), but Fossey did explicitly consider and reject the option of sending Bonne Année to a zoo abroad. She understood that Bonne Année may have lived longer in a zoo, but questioned the value of the "trauma of captivity only to gain a few more years of sterile existence". Fossey emphasized that "Bonne Année, at least, died free". (Note that her position is directly counter to the Bahati Principle, see above). As Harcourt later repeated, Fossey said that Bonne Année's case "proved that it is possible to reintroduce captive gorillas to their natural habitat if a receptive free-living gorilla group is available". Fossey did not seem to recognize the importance of the reintroductee's age or the health threats to the wild population.

Fossey's experience with reintroduction was similar in many ways to Galdikas' and Rijksen's earliest experiences with orangutan reintroduction (see above). All were field scientists that were thrust by their own compassion into becoming ape rehabilitators with inadequate facilities, support, or expertise.

Welfare (Rehabilitation)

REFERENCES

Fossey, D. 1983. *Gorillas in the Mist*. Boston, Houghton Mifflin.

Weber, B. and A. Vedder. 2001. *In the Kingdom of Gorillas*. New York, Simon & Schuster.

AN INFLUENTIAL NON-REINTRODUCTION

Grauer's Gorilla (Gorilla beringei [graueri]). "Amahoro", a Grauer's gorilla, was confiscated in the Kigali (Rwanda) airport in July 1992. She was estimated to have been 18 months old at the time. She was presumed to have been captured in the Kahuzi-Biega National Park in the Democratic Republic of Congo (DRC, at the time Zaire). Amahoro was kept in Rwanda for approximately eight months under unspecified circumstances, and then at the Goodall Institute's primate sanctuary in Burundi for about eight months. In the end, Amahoro was not reintroduced, but her case is examined here because her plight stimulated an unprecedented discussion among international experts of options for the future of one individual orphaned ape.

These discussions of Amahoro's options, and their advantages and disadvantages, were strongly influenced by a concise, objective paper, aptly and succinctly titled "Options for unwanted or confiscated primates" that had been published by Alexander Harcourt in 1987.

Harcourt had identified five options for rehabilitated or rescued primates. We can expect that, as an expert on the behavioral ecology of gorillas, he may have been thinking especially about apes. The options are 1) euthanasia; 2) euthanasia with use of the body or its parts for educational or research purposes; 3) export (outside of the range countries) to captivity in a zoo, research institution, or the pet trade; 4) captivity in a zoo or a sanctuary within range countries; or 5) release to the wild. Advantages and disadvantages are weighed in terms of the welfare of the orphan, benefits and risks to wild populations, public awareness and support for biodiversity conservation, encouragement or discouragement of wildlife trade, overall ethical considerations, and costs (not in order of importance). Each option has different advantages and disadvantages; the reader is directed to the original Harcourt paper or to Beck (2010), Harcourt (1993), and/or Kalpers (1993) for more detail.

After Amahoro's confiscation, the Zairois government asked the International Gorilla Conservation Programme to develop a recommendation for placing Amahoro. The organization's director, José Kalpers, developed a working paper to facilitate the discussion. He carefully reviewed the options that were provided in Harcourt's paper and recommended that Amahoro be placed in captivity, either at an ape orphanage in Africa or a western zoo. He rejected reintroduction because he felt that Amahoro would not survive and that there would be health risks to the wild gorilla population. Significantly, Kalpers identified questions for which more information was needed before a decision could be made.

The Programme then contracted Harcourt to review Kalpers' working paper, solicit opinions from experts, and make a recommendation. Harcourt recommended that Amahoro be reintroduced to a small and isolated subpopulation of Grauer's gorillas within Zaire with little delay. He favored a hard release, with little or no training and acclimation, and extensive post-release monitoring. Harcourt was deeply concerned about the possibility of transmission of an undetected communicable disease from Amahoro to the wild population, especially the wild population of an endangered species, and recommended establishment of a veterinary team that could deploy quickly to deal with any medical issues that might be caused by the reintroduction. He recognized that reintroduction posed a risk to Amahoro, but cited Dian Fossey's quote about another reintroduced gorilla, "Bonne Année" (see above), who "at least, died free". He noted that the reintroduction, whether successful or unsuccessful, would have virtually no impact on the genetics, demography, or conservation of wild Grauer's gorillas. However, the reintroduction could enhance public awareness of and support for the conservation of wild apes. Harcourt also noted that the reintroduction would be expensive, but not as expensive as a lifetime in captivity.

The Zairois government decided to place Amahoro at the Antwerp (Belgium) Zoo on indefinite loan. Antwerp Zoo was the only zoo that had mountain gorillas at the time. Amahoro was still alive in 2017. She was living with an adult male and an adult female lowland gorilla.

Harcourt and others involved in this process had actually overlooked a precedent paper (Mensink 1986), in which options were discussed for the placement of another orphan gorilla, named "Julia" (not to be confused with "Julie", see above). Julia was a western lowland gorilla (*Gorilla g. gorilla*) who had been born somewhere in Africa in 1982. She was poached, probably in 1984, and exported to Belgium. A well-meaning individual purchased her from the Belgian importer so that she could be "returned to Africa". Mensink, a veterinarian, was hired as her caregiver and tutor. Julia was sent to the Gambia. There are no natural gorilla populations in the Gambia, but there was a large rehabilitation program for chimpanzees (see above). Mensink identified euthanasia, use in scientific research, participation in a captive breeding and education program within or outside of a range country, and reintroduction to the wild as options for Julia. Mensink also identified the threat of communicable disease and the behavioral disruption and competition of wild populations that are created by reintroduction. She also noted that an orphan ape's dependence on and lack of fear of people could be dangerous to people living near a destination site. Julia was eventually sent to a European zoo, transferred several times, reproduced, and died in the Melbourne (Australia) zoo in 2015.

The critical point here is that Amahoro led the scientific and conservation world to the then-obscure but seminal paper by Harcourt, and stimulated two classical, though unpublished, reports and a wide-ranging discussion of a difficult topic.

Consensus has not yet been reached. Harcourt articulated five options, and no new options have been identified in nearly 30 years. Details have changed, e.g. the quality of ape care in most western zoos and most range country sanctuaries has improved, costs have escalated dramatically, most feel that tourism involving potentially releaseable apes at sanctuaries is ill-advised, and the number of unreleaseable ape orphans has risen sharply. But despite earnest and agonizing efforts to identify a sixth option, we have still not found the perfect one that would have no disadvantageous consequences. Any option that has or will be chosen by rehabilitation and reintroduction managers has been/will be criticized. I feel that those who would criticize the choice of any one of Harcourt's options in a particular case should be willing to identify their option of choice for that case.

Amahoro's case also led to a broader set of guidelines from the International Union for the Conservation of Nature and Natural Resources (World Conservation Union, IUCN) that is titled "Guidelines for the Placement of Confiscated Live Animals" (Anon. 2002a), which brought clarity, consistency, and guidance for those struggling with these difficult issues with increasing frequency for all animals.

Harcourt's 1987 paper is cited in dozens of the references used for this history. Many have reinvented his work, some giving him credit and, unfortunately, some without acknowledging his pioneering contribution. For example, Kavanagh and Caldecott's (2013) failure to acknowledge of Harcourt's 1987 paper is incomprehensible.

REFERENCES

Anon. 2002a. *Guidelines for the Placement of Confiscated Live Animals*. Gland, International Union for the Conservation of Nature and Natural Resources.

Beck, B.B. 2010. Chimpanzee orphans: Sanctuaries, reintroduction, and cognition. In E.V. Lonsdorf, S.R. Ross, and T. Matsuzawa, eds. *The Mind of the Chimpanzee*, pp. 332-346. Chicago, University of Chicago Press.

Harcourt, A.H. 1987. Options for unwanted or confiscated primates. *Primate Conservation* 8: 111-113.

Harcourt, A.H. 1993. Options for confiscated infant gorilla, Amahoro. Unpublished report to the International Gorilla Conservation Programme.

Kalpers, J. 1993. Long-term future for Amahoro: Summary of possible options. Unpublished working paper, International Gorilla Conservation Programme.

Kavanagh, K. and J.O. Caldecott. 2013. Strategic guidelines for the translocation of primates and other animals. *The Raffles Bulletin of Zoology*, Supplement 29: 203-209.

Mensink, M. 1986. Julia: A gorilla with an identity crisis. *New Scientist* 19 June: 68-69.

Grauer's Gorilla (*Gorilla beringei [graueri]*). An adult male and female mountain gorilla were shot to death by poachers in the Democratic Republic of the Congo (then Zaire), hours after tourists visited their group, in 1995. A 2.5 year-old male mountain gorilla was found wandering in cultivated fields several days later. The Institut Zairois pour la Conservation de la Nature (IZCN) confiscated the young gorilla and, in collaboration with the International Gorilla Conservation Programme (IGCP), reintroduced him to the same group. The young male was assumed to have been captured by poachers after the killings, and later abandoned. The young male was taken to the group, released, and was immediately accepted. There is no mention of veterinary examination or post-release monitoring.

The success of this reintroduction was doubtless due to the gorilla's being reintroduced to its natal group, within days of being poached.

Welfare (Rehabilitation), Conservation (Reinforcement)

References

Morris, J. 1995. Gorilla conservation program suffers setback. *Oryx* 29(4): 219.

Grauer's Gorilla (*Gorilla beringei [graueri]*). There was a noticeable uptick in gorilla poaching in Rwanda and the Democratic Republic of Congo between 1995 and 2005. The poachers generally shot females with young infants, fended off the silverback male and the rest of the group (sometimes shooting them too), and then stealing the infants. The Rwandan and DRC governments confiscated between ten and 15 of these orphans, some in DRC and some in Rwanda, during this period. Most of the infants were between one and two years old. Coordination and cooperation between Rwanda's Office Rwandais du Tourisme et des Parc Nationaux (ORTPN) and DRC's Institut Congolais pour la Conservation de la Nature (ICCN) slowly emerged to respond to gorilla poaching. Many of the orphans were confiscated in Rwanda and DRC before the gorillas could be exported out of Africa. There was initially strong interest in reintroducing these infants to the wild. One of the first of this era was "Bitorwa", a two year-old male who was confiscated in DRC in 2000. His family had been killed in Kahuzi-Biega National Park. He had been fed fruit during his brief time in captivity but had also been fed leaves of plants that were normally eaten by wild gorillas. Approximately ten days after his capture, he was introduced to a wild group comprising six gorillas. It was not Bitorwa's natal group. The silverback behaved aggressively three times toward Bitorwa. The infant rushed back to the humans that were conducting the reintroduction, but they apparently retreated, leaving him alone in the forest, where he died several days later. There was no veterinary examination, quarantine, pre-release preparation, acclimation, or post-release support. Bitorwa could not have been completely weaned before he was orphaned.

This was a hard release by a team that lacked the expertise, experience, and knowledge of the Harcourt options. Bitorwa's reintroduction is treated as a different program than that of "Julie" (see above) because of the different methods. The purpose(s) of this reintroduction are unstated but assumed to have been welfare and conservation.

Welfare (Rehabilitation), Conservation (Reinforcement)

References

Morris, J. 1995. Gorilla conservation program suffers setback. *Oryx* 29(4): 219.

Shalukoma, C. 2000. Attempt to re-introduce a young gorilla to the Kahuzi-Biega forest. *Gorilla Journal* 21: 3-4.

Mountain Gorilla (*Gorilla beringei*). Rwanda's Office Rwandais du Tourisme et des Parc Nationaux (ORTPN), in collaboration with the Dian Fossey Gorilla Fund International (DFGFI), the Mountain Gorilla Veterinary Project (MGVP), and the International Gorilla Conservation Program released a confiscated orphan mountain gorilla into the Volcanoes National Park in Rwanda in 2002 and another in 2003.

After nearly two decades of no gorilla poaching in Rwanda, a group of mountain gorillas was attacked by poachers in 2002. The carnage was found on a routine DFGFI patrol. Two mothers had been shot to death. One infant was missing and another, called "Ubuzima", was found alive alongside the body of her dead mother. Ubuzima, a female, was one year old and was not completely weaned. Ubuzima was examined and treated by MGVP veterinarians. She was reintroduced to her natal group, apparently within a few days of the poaching event. Each of the surviving adult females in the group was nursing her own infant at the time, leaving no candidate for a foster mother. Upon reintroduction, Ubuzima was surrounded by the group and inspected by the dominant male. She was then picked up and adopted by her brother, a young adult male. He was subsequently seen carrying Ubuzima, and she slept between him and the silverback. She was seen eating natural vegetation. Ubuzima disappeared after approximately seven months. As a footnote, the "missing infant" in this poaching incident may have been the gorilla that was successfully exported from Rwanda, seized at the Cairo airport, and euthanized by Egyptian authorities in 2003 (F. Launay, personal communication).

"Mvuyekure", a female, was confiscated in 2003. She was estimated to have been between two and three years old. She was examined, medically evaluated, and quarantined in a makeshift facility in Rwanda. A team of experts was formed to monitor her care, much of which is documented in detail in an unpublished report. Mvuyekure was fed natural gorilla foods and given access to a large outdoor enclosure. She was cared for by a small group of people who were judged to be free of communicable disease. The care team thought that she was of an age that she could be in close contact with a few humans to provide emotional support without losing her ability to recognize other gorillas, although there was apparently some disagreement about this. According to another unpublished report that documents the choice of a group for reintroduction, her natal group was determined to have been an unhabituated group that lived in a remote location on the Democratic Republic of Congo side of the park. The group could not even be located at the time. She was therefore reintroduced to a group that had been habituated previously for tourism on the Rwandan side. This group was selected because it had a relatively high ratio of males to females. I could not access any detailed accounts of the reintroduction itself. Mvuyekure is said to have been "rejected by the new group, suffering injuries from bites inflicted by one of the group's silverbacks" (Anon. 2003, p 42). A knowledgeable expert who did not want to be identified informed me by e-mail that Mvuyekure was reintroduced a second time (probably to a different group) and was again attacked and seriously injured. She required surgery. During her recovery she was being taken on walks into the forest, where she died, supposedly due to hyperthermia. A published source said that she "died after multiple failed attempts to re-introduce her to non-natal groups" (Whittier and Fawcett 2006, p 40).

These were two early cases of growing collaboration and coordination between governmental and non-governmental stakeholders for dealing with orphan gorillas. The options of euthanasia and export to a foreign institution were explicitly rejected for Ubuzima and Mvuyekure. There was no established sanctuary for mountain gorillas (or Grauer's gorillas) at the time, which made long-term captivity in Rwanda untenable. Euthanasia and captivity were also thought to carry a negative conservation message. Reintroduction was favored because these two mountain gorillas were known to have originated in the Virunga mountains, each was a potential breeding female for a small, endangered population, and each could be reintroduced after only a short period of human care after confiscation (Whittier and Fawcett 2006). ORTPN made the final decision to reintroduce these infants.

The short-term success of Ubuzima's reintroduction was attributed to her being reintroduced quickly to her natal group. I have inferred the purposes of the reintroductions.

The program that comprises these two reintroductions is treated separately from Bonne Année's reintroduction (see above) because Dian Fossey made the decision to reintroduce Bonne Année, at least the first time, and ORTPN made the decision to reintroduce Ubuzima and Mvuyekure.

I could find mention of a total of 18 additional Grauer's, and mountain gorillas that were confiscated in DRC and Rwanda between 2003 and 2015. Two were in advanced stages of planning and preparation for reintroduction in Rwanda in 2004, but were not reintroduced. The ICCN, IUCN, DFGFI, MGVP, and IGCP steering committee decided in 2005 that reintroduction of orphaned gorillas should be suspended until a new reintroduction strategy could be developed (Childs 2006, Spelman 2007, Whittier and Fawcett 2006). There were also renewed concerns about transmission of communicable diseases that were contracted by the orphans while in captivity. Planning began in 2007 to enlarge the orphanage in Rwanda and to construct a permanent orphanage in DRC. The latter, called the Gorilla Rehabilitation and Conservation Education Center (GRACE), opened in 2010, with funding from the Disney Conservation Fund and the US Fish and Wildlife Service, and currently holds 14 Grauer's gorillas. The Humane Society International and the International Fund for Animal Welfare have become additional supporters of GRACE.

Reintroduction is still stated as a goal (Cress 2010, www.gracegorillas.org), and the possibility of reintroducing some or all of the 14 gorillas to the Virunga national park careful is being carefully considered (Kahlenberg et al 2018, Sherman et al 2018, Smiley Evans et al 2018).

Conservation (Reinforcement), Welfare (Rehabilitation)

References

Anon. 2002b. Poachers kill mountain gorilla and steal a baby. *Gorilla Journal* 24: 11.

Anon. 2003. First attempt made at mountain gorilla reintroduction. *Communique, Newsletter of the American Zoo and Aquarium Association*, February, 2003: 42.

Childs, S. 2006. Caring for confiscated gorillas: Making decisions, learning, teaching. *The Gorilla Journal*, Fall 2006: 2-4.

Cress, D. 2010. Gorilla Rehabilitation and Conservation Education (GRACE) Center. *Gorilla Journal* 40: 7-9.

Kahlenberg, S.M., Williamson, E.A., Mbeke, J.K., Syahula, E.K., Cranfield, M., de Merode, E., Caillaud, D., Farmer, K.H., Iyer, N., Kyungu, J., and J. Sherman. 2018. Reinforcement for imperiled Grauer's gorilla population in Democratic Republic of Congo: Prospects, preparation, and remaining obstacles. Abstract of a paper presented at the 27th Congress of the International Primatological Society, Nairobi, Kenya.

Mudakikwa, A. 2002. Ubuzima, a 13-month-old re-introduced to her group. *Gorilla Journal* 25: 8.

Sherman, J., Farmer, K.H., Williamson, E.A., Unwin, S., Kahlenberg, S.M., Russon, A.E., Cheyne, S.M., Humle, T., Mylniczenko, N., Macfie, E., and S. Wich. 2018. Methodology and technical advisory resources for ape reintroductions to natural habitats. Abstract of a paper presented at the 27th Congress of the International Primatological Society, Nairobi, Kenya.

Smiley Evans, T., Gilardi, K., Lowenstine, L., Ssebide, B., Nizeyimana, F., Noheri, J., Kinani, J., Syahula, E., Cranfield, M., Mazet, J., and C. Johnson. 2018. Human herpes simplex virus 1 (HSV-1) and reintroduction risks for free-ranging mountain gorillas in the Virunga Massif. Abstract of a paper presented at the 27th Congress of the International Primatological Society, Nairobi, Kenya.

Spelman, L. 2007. Eastern gorilla orphans: Update. *Gorilla Journal* 35: 8.

Whittier, C. and K. Fawcett. 2006. Application of the RSG Guidelines in the case of confiscated mountain gorillas, Virunga Massif: Rwanda, Uganda & DRC. *Re-introduction News* 25: 40-41.

www.gracegorillas.org

> **NOTE:** *Gorilla Journal* and *The Gorilla Journal* are two different publications. The former is published by the German NGO Berggorilla & Regenwald Direkthilfe, and has been a source of objective information about gorillas for decades. The latter is (or was) published by the Dian Fossey Gorilla Fund International.

CHAPTER 4
REINTRODUCTIONS OF ORANGUTANS

Bornean Orangutan (*Pongo pygmaeus*). Tom Harrisson was Curator of the Sarawak Museum of Natural History in the 1950s and 1960s. He and his wife Barbara lived in a house in a gardened section in the capital city of Kuching. Tom Harrisson's Christmas present to Barbara in 1956 was an infant male orangutan that had been confiscated by a forest guard and turned over to the Museum. The Harrissons named the infant "Bob". Bob was ultimately sent to the San Diego Zoo, but first he and Barbara invented the strategy of rehabilitating and releasing confiscated or rescued orangutans. Sadly, more than 2,000 have had to be rehabilitated in Borneo and Sumatra in the succeeding 60 years. Barbara Harrisson's procedure, which she used with at least 12 orangutans, began with a veterinary evaluation, and treatment as necessary. A newly arrived orangutan lived in a small outdoor cage and was nourished and nurtured to health. Then the orangutan would be taken on supervised trips and play sessions in the Harrissons' back yard. The apes were allowed slowly to climb in tall trees and sleep outside of the cage overnight. After Harrison observed wild orangutans, she realized that her apes were spoiled and got too much human support and attention. She then took a "toughened" approach, forcing the animals to stay up in trees for longer periods, rather than playing with them on the ground.

But as the apes grew they became difficult to control, and the back yard clearly could not accommodate a full repertoire of locomotor and foraging behavior. Some of the 12 young apes were sent to selected zoos in North America and Europe. Harrison now knew that rehabilitation would require a larger forested area, and she took her three remaining orphans to Bako National Park in 1962. Her goals were to devise ways, under controlled conditions, by which young orphaned orangutans could be rehabilitated so as to be self-sufficient in the wild, and to observe orangutans under semi-wild conditions to contribute to our knowledge of the species. She was an astute and thorough observer, and had a good grasp of the natural history of orangutans.

The Bako releases were milestones in the history of reintroduction because Barabara Harrisson was truly the first to conceptualize, indeed to invent, the process of primate rehabilitation and reintroduction.

Bako is a small island (less than 15 km²) near Kuching. There was a visitor center and beaches that were used by many people for swimming. It was the only national park in Malaysian Borneo at the time. The orangutans were taken first to a 20-foot (6.1 meters) by 40-foot (12.2 meters) by 13-19-foot (4–5.8 meters) (high) mesh cage. The cage had been built on a slope for drainage, and had sleeping and feeding platforms, ropes, and a few small trees (which did not last long). There were monkeys in the surrounding forests, but there were no wild orangutans on the island. Barbara Harrisson considered the absence of a wild orangutan population to be detrimental to the rehabilitation process because she thought that wild orangutans could serve as models from which the rehabilitant orangutans could learn the skills that are necessary to survive in the forest. She and the caretakers minimized their contact with the orangutans in the cage, and she decided that they would not try to intentionally teach the apes any skills. Instead they would allow the orangutans to acclimate to the sounds, sights, and smells of the forest. The first orangutan, a juvenile male named "Arthur", was released from the cage after ten days, but stayed in the area, paying more attention to his caged companions and their caretakers than to the forest. The staff reversed their decision and began to tutor him by taking him on walks in the forest. He slowly became more comfortable, locomoting in the trees, eating a variety of natural foods (including insects), drinking from natural water sources, building nests, and using tools. He ultimately ranged over 4 square miles (10 km²) of the island, but eagerly approached the human tourists he encountered. Another cage and base of operations had to be built farther from the visitor center and beaches. The second orangutan, a younger female named "Cynthia", was released from the cage after a month. She was reluctant to leave the area of the cage, did not build nests, and slept on the ground. The youngest animal, a one year-old male, was taken into the forest at the same time, and the three orangutans spent considerable time together in the forest. But the youngest was returned to the cage each evening for six months. All three animals remained healthy.

Harrisson concluded that young orphaned orangutans can be rehabilitated with some tutoring by humans; that the process is slow; and that individual differences in history, age, and temperament will affect the speed and success of the process. She urged that protected areas with wild orangutan populations be established, and include well-financed and well-staffed rehabilitation centers for orphaned and rescued orangutans. After two years, Arthur's affinity for people and his increasing strength prompted Harrisson to find a larger, more remote area for a rehabilitation center. The Sabah government responded by establishing a center at Sepilok, in Malaysian Borneo.

Welfare (Rehabilitation), Research

References

Harrisson, B. 1963. Education to wild living of young orangutans at Bako National Park. *Sarawak Museum Journal* 11: 222-258.

Harrisson, B. 1987. *Orang-Utan*. New York, Oxford University Press.

Bornean Orangutan (*Pongo pygmaeus*). The Fauna Conservation Ordinance of 1963 outlawed capturing, keeping, or killing orangutans within the Malaysian state of Sabah, but authorities had few good options for placing a confiscated orangutan and thus did little to enforce the law. At least 20 confiscated orangutans had been sent from Sabah to European and Australian zoos by 1963. The Game Branch of the Forestry Department of Sabah decided in 1964 to discontinue export to foreign zoos, and founded a state-supported experimental release site of 4,050 ha (later expanded to 4,294 ha) in the Sepilok Forest Reserve. Thus the Sepilok Orangutan Rehabilitation Centre, the first real center for the rehabilitation and release of orangutans, was founded, not to promote conservation of biodiversity, but as a well-intended attempt to find a humane and ethical way to deal with confiscated orangutans. But, to the degree that this promoted enforcement, and to the degree that enhanced enforcement discouraged killing or capturing wild orangutans, rehabilitation did indeed serve conservation.

According to de Silva, the specific aims of the Sepilok project were "to rehabilitate orang-utan [sic] into the wild by gradually giving them more freedom in their natural surroundings, to restore their survival instincts and encourage self-reliance in the forest, so that they may return to the wild or form a semi-wild breeding colony to enhance the depleted stock in the State. As and when they are able to survive on their own they will be released in batches in forests remote from habitation and timber operations". Note that the goal had come to include the replenishment of depleted wild populations. There are key assumptions in this statement: that rehabilitation had to be gradual, that it should include some form of transitional acclimation between captivity and true release to the wild, that at least some normal survival-critical orangutan behavior was innate, that these innate behaviors were unexpressed in captivity but could be reactivated under appropriate environmental conditions, that rehabilitated orangutans would reproduce, and that releasing groups of orangutans was preferred. Also noted by de Silva was that captive orangutans had learned behavior in captivity that was undesirable, e.g. smoking cigarettes, or that could compromise adaptation to life in the wild, e.g. having to be chained to be able to fall asleep. Harrisson and her work were familiar to de Silva, and he clearly built on her assumptions and adopted much of her methodology. All of these issues are pertinent today.

Of note is that de Silva had a good understanding of the natural history of orangutans, and was acquainted with scientists such as Barbara Harrisson, Kenji Yoshiba, John MacKinnon, R.K. Davenport, and David Horr, who were conducting some of the earliest studies of wild orangutans, and with their findings on the behavioral ecology of the species. He kept and published detailed records of outcomes for each of the first 41 orangutans who were released at Sepilok. He also was a keen observer of the behavior of captive orangutans, and was among the first to note their predilection for imitating the behavior of humans.

Arthur and Cynthia (see above) were among the first orangutans to be released at Sepilok. Most of the Sepilok orangutans had been in captivity for months or years, and most arrived in poor condition. When an orangutan was confiscated or surrendered, it received a veterinary examination and treatment, and was then quarantined for one to six months. At first this was done at a veterinary station in the nearby town of Sandakan, but the project has had its own veterinary and quarantine facilities since 1987. After quarantine and screening, the orangutans were housed with like-aged orangutans, and were gradually allowed to leave cages, climb trees, and travel to more distant feeding platforms. They were provisioned with fortified milk and other types of food. The amount of provisioned food was decreased when natural fruits were abundant, and ultimately the orangutans could choose to live entirely on natural foods or return to a feeding platform. The orangutans were tutored in survival-critical skills by project staff, and they also learned by observing more proficient orangutans. Post-release veterinary assistance was provided to ill or injured orangutans. As Harrisson would have recommended, there were initially wild orangutans in the Sepilok Reserve, but de Silva documented only one interaction between a rehabilitant and a wild orangutan: each was a female with an infant and the two females shared a nest. Later, newly released orangutans could interact with previously released orangutans. Some, including Cynthia, were taken to areas several miles from the initial release site to encourage independence and dispersal.

The Sepilok project took in 41 orangutans between 1964 and 1969, ten more between 1969 and 1973, and more than 600 since (not all of these have been released; many did not survive and many were unsuitable for release). Palmer (personal communication) has told me that a sign she saw at Sepilok in 2017 states that 760 have been taken in. A few Sumatran orangutans may have been among the arrivals but it is unknown if these were ever released.

As of 2002, 226 orangutans had been released at Sepilok since its founding. Ten of the first 41 released orangutans are reported to have died. Arthur was shot because of his destructiveness around the project headquarters and his aggressiveness toward people. Another rehabilitant, a mother with an infant, attacked a ranger who was feeding her.

The number of releases must be greater. Palmer says that the sign she saw at Sepilok in 2017 that states that Sepilok has taken in 760 confiscated or surrendered orangutans also states that 81.6% of these have been rehabilitated and 66% have been "successfully" released to the wild. Palmer (in press) concludes that the total number released may have been between 409 and 620. I will use 409 as the number released because it seems reasonable given that between 650 and 760 have been taken in, and is consistent with our practice of using the lowest estimate of the number of primates that were reintroduced by a program when a more definitive number can not be determined.

Many of the released orangutans disappeared. Because there has been little systematic post-release monitoring, there is no sure way to know if they went off into the forest and survived and reproduced, or died. Several females of the initial 51 (and more of those released subsequently) have given birth and raised infants in the forest. An analysis of Sepilok reproduction records (Kuze et al 2008) revealed that 14 reintroduced female orangutans produced 28 infants between 1967 and 2004. Infant mortality was high (57%), and the age at first reproduction was earlier and interbirth intervals were shorter than those of wild orangutans. The sex ratio at birth was heavily biased toward females. Second-generation births have been recorded. A distance sampling survey conducted during 2002 indicated that there were approximately 105 orangutans living in the forest. Some returned to feeding platforms at the rehabilitation station, but it can be assumed that many could survive on natural foods without any human support. The area is probably too small to sustain a genetically and demographically viable wild population.

Of historical interest is that Sepilok was opened to visitors in the early 1990's, (perhaps even earlier) and the rehabilitation project became an ecotourism destination. Tourists were allowed to come into close proximity with and to feed the rehabilitant orangutans, although this was later discontinued. Tourism was said to add conservation education as a purpose for rehabilitation, and to generate revenue for reserve management. The Sepilok Orang Utan Rehabilitation Centre remains open today but apparently has ceased releasing orangutans into the forest reserve, although a rescued and rehabilitated male was released there in 2017, and had to be recaptured due to injuries sustained in a fight with another male. He was later released in the Tabin Wildlife Reserve (Anon 2017). This male is not counted among those released at Sepilok but rather is counted among those released at Tabin (see below).

In a unique but controversial public/private partnership, the Sabah Wildlife Department and the Shangri-La Rasa Ria Resort and Spa arranged in 1996 for orphaned orangutans "in the first stage of their rehabilitation" to live in a 27-ha area of the resort's grounds, near the rehabilitation center. Presumably, this reduced crowding at the Sepilok center and provided entertainment and educational opportunities for resort visitors and local schoolchildren. The partnership ended in 2016, during which a total 43 orangutans lived at the resort (Anon 2016). An organization known as Friends of Orangutans Malaysia alleged that orangutans at the resort were neglected and cared for inadequately, and that three orangutans had been stabbed by a resort employee (www.cleanmalaysia.com).

Palmer was informed that between 30 and 40 orangutans still lived at Sepilok in 2017. Most had access to the forest that surrounds the center, which is now known as the Kabili Sepilok Forest Reserve.

Welfare (Rehabilitation)

REFERENCES

Anon. 2016. Orangutan care program nearly completed at Rasa Ria Resort. *BorneoPostonline*. 1 February 2016.

Anon. 2017. Tiger release. *Orangutan Appeal* UK News 33: 3.

Agoramoorthy, G. and M.J. Hsu. 2006. Rehabilitation and release of orangutans in northern Borneo. *Journal of Wildlife Rehabilitation* 28(3): 10-17.

Aveling, R. and A. Mitchell. 1981. Is rehabilitating orang utans worthwhile? *Oryx* 16: 263-271.

de Silva, G.S. 1971. Notes on the orang-utan rehabilitation project in Sabah. *Malayan Nature Journal* 24: 50-77.

Fernando, R. 2000/2001. Rehabilitating orphaned orang-utans in North Borneo. *Asian Primates* 7(3/4): 20-21.

Kuze, N., Sipangkui, S., Malim, T.P., Bernard, H., Ambu, L.N., and S. Kohshima. 2008. Reproductive parameters over a 37-year period of free-ranging Borneo orangutans at Sepilok Orangutan Rehabilitation Centre. *Primates* 49: 126-134.

MacKinnon, J. 1977. The future of orang-utans. *New Scientist* 74: 697-699.

Mydans, C. 1973. Orangutans can return to the wild with some help. *Smithsonian* 4(8): 26-33.

Palmer, A. 2017. Personal communication; e-mail 4 November.

Palmer, A. In press. Kill, incarcerate, or liberate? Ethics and alternatives to orangutan rehabilitation. *Biological Conservation*.

Russon, A. 2018. Personal communication; e-mail 7 March.

www.cleanmalaysia.com

www.orangutan-appeal.org.uk

AN IMPORTANT SOURCE

Dr Anne E. Russon has written the definitive chapter on orangutan reintroduction. It is titled "Orangutan rehabilitation and reintroduction" and appeared in *Orangutans: Geographic Variation in Behavioural Ecology and Conservation*, which was published in 2009. Russon herself has been involved with orangutan conservation for decades, has been a steady advocate for consistent, scientific documentation of all stages of rehabilitation and reintroduction/translocation, and has published pioneering work on the cognition of wild and rehabilitant orangutans. I have attempted to consult as many of the primary sources on orangutan reintroduction and translocation as I could find, but have relied on Russon's chapter for some of the information that appears below. Readers should assume that I have consulted Russon's chapter in addition to the listed references for all of the orangutan programs that follow.

Additionally, Dr. Russon reviewed the narratives for the orangutan reintroduction programs in the first edition of this book and provided many useful additions, corrections, and suggestions for the second edition.

References

Russon, A.E. 2009. Orangutan rehabilitation and reintroduction. In S.A. Wich, S.S. Utami Atmoko, T. Mitra Setia, and C.P. van Schaik, eds. *Orangutans: Geographic Variation in Behavioural Ecology and Conservation*, pp. 327-350. Oxford, UK, Oxford University Press.

Bornean Orangutan (*Pongo pygmaeus*). The National Parks and Wildlife Office of the Sarawak Forest Department's Wildlife Rehabilitation Centre in the Semenggoh (Semenggok, Semengok) Forest Reserve released 27 (12 males, 15 females) rescued and rehabilitated orangutans into the forested area around the center within the 640-ha Semenggoh Forest Reserve between 1975 and 1997, and five more between 1997 and 2000.

Orangutans who were confiscated or surrendered were given medical examinations upon intake. Staff then took young orangutans into the forest and allowed them to climb in natural vegetation and eat normal foods. They were released after two to four years. Released orangutans could return to the center for supplemental feeding. Some were moved from the Semenggoh Forest Reserve and released into other national parks or wildlife sanctuaries in Sarawak. Semenggoh officially ceased rehabilitation and release of orangutans in 2013, but 11 of the previously released orangutans still live in the forest. At least 16 infants have been born to the released orangutans (Chong, in Commitante et al 2015). The center is now a tourist destination with a variety of captive wildlife, including orangutans. Some of the "wild" orangutans that still live in the forest return to the center for food, where they can be observed by tourists. The orangutan rehabilitation program has been relocated to the Matang Wildlife Centre (see below).

Welfare (Rehabilitation)

References

Commitante, R., Unwin, S., Jaya, R., Saraswati, Y., Sulistyo, F., and C. Nente (eds.). 2015. *Orangutan Conservancy 2015 Orangutan Veterinary Advisory Group Workshop Report.* wwww.orangutan.com

Mail, R. 2013. Orangutan population looking good but wildlife centre runs out of space. *The Star, Malaysia* 26 July 2013,

www.sarawakforestry.com

Bornean Orangutan (*Pongo pygmaeus*). The Sabah Wildlife Department captured 177 wild orangutans and translocated them to the 120,000-ha Tabin Wildlife Reserve in 1993 and 1994. The orangutans were moved from unprotected areas in which habitat was being rapidly converted for industrial agriculture and logging. The surviving orangutans had little to eat and were raiding crops and coming into conflict with humans. Translocation was seen as a feasible and humane alternative to killing the orangutans. Tabin, which was 40 to 70 km from the capture sites, had a small wild orangutan population at the time. The translocated and resident orangutans were assumed by the authors to be from the same genetic population.

The orangutans were chemically immobilized and/or manually caught, and placed in individual cages. Blood, fecal, and hair samples were taken, and the orangutans were given a physical examination at the release site. They were moved by truck during the cool late afternoon, and were fed and given drinking water during the trip. They were released individually at sites that were at least 1 km from each other. There was no acclimation, pre- or post-release support, or post-release monitoring, but the report states that "So far there are no disquieting signs and the animals appear to have settled well into their new environment" (Sale et al, pg 12).

Welfare (Non-lethal control)

References

Andau, P.M., Hiong, L.K., and J.B. Sale. 1994. Translocation of pocketed orang-utans in Sabah. *Oryx* 28: 263-268.

Sale, J.B., Andau, P.M., and L.K. Hiong. 1995. The capture and translocation of orang-utans in Sabah, Malaysia. *Re-introduction News* 10: 12-14.

Bornean Orangutan (*Pongo pygmaeus*). The Orangutan Appeal UK and the Sabah Wildlife Department released three ex-captive, rehabilitated orangutans into the 120,000-ha Tabin Wildlife Reserve in 2010, another five into the same reserve in 2012 and three more in 2016. Tabin was estimated to have had 1,400 wild orangutans at the time of the first releases. The reserve was surveyed to find suitable release sites. The chosen sites were far from the nearest human settlements, but there is no mention of whether resident orangutans visited the sites.

The orangutans were taken from the free-ranging forest at the Sepilok Orangutan Rehabilitation Centre (see above). Although these orangutans had been living in a free-ranging controlled forest environment at the center, they were returning daily to food platforms for supplemental feeding in view of tourists. The medical records of the orangutans were reviewed to ensure that they had had no serious health problems, and they were given extensive veterinary screenings and were treated for endoparasites shortly before the Tabin releases. The first three were equipped with newly developed subcutaneous radiotelemetry transmitters. There is no mention of acclimation at the release site.

The 2010 release was a hard release, with no supplemental feeding. The orangutans released in 2012 and 2016 received supplemental food for an unstipulated period and were checked by veterinarians periodically after release. The orangutans were monitored for at least a year after release. The surviving orangutans are said to have "integrated adequately", with wild orangutans, and at least two of the females gave birth in the wild.

The authors note that the Sabah Wildlife Department had previously released "many" rehabilitated orangutans from Sepilok into Tabin, but provide no further information. These previous releases of Sepilok orangutans into Tabin are not captured in this history; some of those orangutans might be among the 502 that were released by the Sepilok center (see above). Robins et al (2013) do not even acknowledge the 177 rescued orangutans that had been translocated into Tabin by the Sabah Wildlife Department in 1993 and 1994 (see above). Incomprehensibly, they also claim that in their study "(L)arge amounts of intensive behavioural data have for the first time been collected on the fate of individual rehabilitated orangutans" (pg 220).

The Tabin population appears to be self-sustaining

Research, Welfare (Rehabilitation)

REFERENCES

Robins, J. 2016. Post release monitoring project. *Orangutan Appeal* UK News 31: unpaginated.

Robins, J.G., Ancrenz, M., Parker, J., Goossens, B., Ambu, L., and C. Walzer. 2013. The release of northeast Bornean orangutans to Tabin Wildlife Reserve, Sabah, Malaysia. In: P.S. Soorae, ed. *Global Re-introduction Perspectives: 2013. Further Case Studies from Around the Globe*, pp. 215-221. Gland, IUCN/SSC Re-introduction Specialist Group and Abu Dhabi, UAE, Environment Agency – Abu Dhabi.

Singleton, I., Wich, S., Husson, S., Stephens, S., Utami Atmoko, S., Leighton, M., Rosen, N., Traylor-Holzer, K., Lacy, R., and O. Byers. 2004. *Orangutan Population and Habitat Viability Assessment: Final Report*. Apple Valley, MN, IUCN/SSC Conservation Breeding Specialist Group.

Bornean Orangutan (*Pongo pygmaeus*). The Sarawak Forestry Department/Sarawak Forestry Corporation transferred responsibility for the rehabilitation and release of orangutans from the Semenggoh Wildlife Rehabilitation Centre to the Matang Wildlife Centre, which is in the 2,230-ha Kubah National Park (or Batang Ai National Park; sources differ) in the late 1990s. Russon states that three orangutans had been released into the national park by 2000. Mail notes that there were 18 orangutans at the center in 2013, and Siali (in Commitante et al 2015) notes that there were 30 at the center in 2015, of which 12 were "semi-wild". The rehabilitation and release methodology is presumably similar to that used at Semenggoh but this is not assumed in the table. Palmer (personal communication) was told that there were 21 orangutans at Matang in 2017, of which 10 were spending most or part of their time in the forest

Welfare (Rehabilitation)

References

Commitante, R., Unwin, S., Jaya, R., Saraswati, Y., Sulistyo, F., and C. Nente (eds.). 2015. *Orangutan Conservancy 2015 Orangutan Veterinary Advisory Group Workshop Report*. wwww.orangutan.com

Mail, R. 2013. Orangutan population looking good but wildlife centre runs out of space. *The Star, Malaysia* 26 July 2013.

Palmer, A. 2017. Personal communication; e-mail 4 November.

Russon, A.E. 2009. Orangutan rehabilitation and reintroduction. In S.A. Wich, S.S. Utami Atmoko, T. Mitra Setia, and C.P. van Schaik, eds. *Orangutans: Geographic Variation in Behavioural Ecology and Conservation*, pp. 327-350. Oxford, UK, Oxford University Press.

www.sarawakforestry.com

Bornean Orangutan (*Pongo pygmaeus*). Birute Galdikas and Rod Brindamour began a field study of wild orangutans in the 415,040-ha Tanjung Puting Wildlife Reserve in the southern part of Central Kalimantan in Indonesian Borneo in 1971. Galdikas, as well as Jane Goodall and Dian Fossey (see above), were protégés of the renowned archeologist Louis Leakey. The "trimates", as they were called, brought the study of wild apes into the scientific and popular mainstream.

Galdikas and Brindamour had not intended to rescue, rehabilitate, and release orangutans but, as so often happens at research field sites, government officials and well-intended citizens brought confiscated and donated captive orangutans to Camp Leakey, Galdikas' and Brindamour's research field station. At the request of the Nature Protection and Wildlife Management Agency of the Indonesian Forestry Service, Galdikas and Brindamour founded the Orangutan Research and Conservation Program and the Orangutan Rehabilitation Center in Tanjung Puting. Recall that Barbara Harrisson had only started releasing rehabilitated orangutans in Bako National Park in 1962 (see above). Galdikas and Brindamour had, for the most part, to reinvent the technique.

They took in six young ex-pet orangutans in the first year. They understandably did not have a quarantine facility or even adequate caging for the orangutans. The apes required nearly constant attention. Galdikas took some of the infants into the forest as she studied the wild orangutans, and noted that the presence of an infant seemed to make the wild apes more tolerant of her presence. She tried to identify techniques by which wild mothers facilitated their infants in learning survival-critical skills. Galdikas, Brindamour, and their staff tried to wean the youngsters and get them to eat natural foods, and to induce them to climb and locomote on natural vegetation. The humans were constantly challenged by the cleverness, persistence, and destructiveness of the rescued infants. They confirmed de Silva's observations of the imitative abilities of orangutans. In 1974, the researchers built a food platform that was several hundred meters from the field station to encourage the orangutans to leave Camp Leakey. At least four began to stay and sleep in the forest. One had left on his own before any rehabilitation process. The source did not mention the outcome for the sixth. At some later point, there was an attempt to keep the rehabilitants on one side of the river that ran near Camp Leakey and the wild population on the other, to keep the two populations separated until the rehabilitation process was complete. Tourism began at Camp Leakey in the 1980s, and many expatriate volunteers were invited to help care for the rehabilitants. When Camp Leakey became overwhelmed with orangutans and tourists, several other orangutan rehabilitation sites were established in Tanjung Puting (see below).

The sources do not always agree on the names of the organizational stakeholders, the numbers of orangutans released, descriptions of their pre-and post-release management, and the descriptions of outcomes in the ensuing 45 years. Indeed, many of these factors may have changed over time. The most recent collaborating government agency is the Nature Conservation and Forest Protection branch of the Indonesian Forestry Department. Tanjung Puting has been upgraded to a national park. Galdikas' nongovernmental support organization changed from the Orangutan Research and Conservation program to the US-based Orangutan Foundation International (OFI) in 1986. OFI has affiliates in several other countries. The release sites expanded from Camp Leakey to other sites, e.g. Tanjung Harapan, Pondok Tanggui, both within Tanjung Puting, and then to sites outside of but connected to the park, e.g. Camp Kerantungan, Camp Seluang, and the 54,000-ha Lamandau Wildlife Reserve. Palmer (personal communication) cites sources written in Indonesian that a third release site, Camp Filomena, has been established more recently within Tanjung Puting. The OFI website notes additional sites. Orangutans were released in 2017 in the 64,977-ha Rimba Raya Biodiversity Reserve, which is managed by Infinite EARTH. Rimba Raya is adjacent to Tanjung Puting (OFI website news story, 7 March 2017). Orangutans are also being rehabilitated and released by OFI at Camp Rendell, whose location is unspecified (OFI website news story, 9 May 2017). All rehabilitation and release operations were supposed to have been moved out of Tanjung Puting in 1995 at the direction of the Indonesian Forestry Department, which assumed responsibility for orangutan rehabilitation and release. OFI built a large intake and quarantine center, the Orangutan Care Centre and Quarantine, near the park in 1998.

I consider all of this work in and around Tanjung Puting to be a single program under Galdikas' scientific and managerial leadership. An affiliate, the Orangutan Foundation of the United Kingdom (OFI-UK), which manages orangutan rescue, rehabilitation, and release in Lamandau, appears to be an administratively distinct organization, in which case the Lamandau reintroductions would be a separate project in this *History*. However, OFI began reintroductions at Lamandau, and the orangutans who live at all of these sites are part of one wild population.

The Orangutan Foundation International website states that more than 450 individual ex-captive orangutans have been rescued, rehabilitated, and released, or wild orangutans have been rescued and translocated, between 1971 and 2016. There were more than 325 orangutans at the intake and quarantine center in 2015, many of which are unreleaseable. Of the 450 that were released, more than 200 ex-captives are said to have been released within Tanjung Puting between 1971 and 1995 (OFI website, "Former Release Site" tab), presumably from Camp Leakey, Tanjung Harapan, and Pondok Tanggui. There have been a few additional releases within Tanjung Puting since 1995. Four rehabilitated orangutans had been released from Camp Filomena by mid-2017. More than 20 ex-captives were released from Camp Kerantungan between 2008 and 2013, and at least 32 ex-captives were released from Camp Seluang since it was opened in 2012. Two wild orangutans were rescued and translocated to Camp Seluang as well. These are all included in the total of 450. The OFI website (news story, 15 July 2017) states that 27 additional rehabilitated or rescued orangutans were released in 2017. This would include the four released from Camp Filomena, and the ten who were released at Rimba Raya (OFI website news story, 7 March 2017). I was unable to identify the release sites for the other 13.

The Orangutan Foundation International and the Orangutan Foundation of the United Kingdom (OFI-UK), with the approval of the Indonesian Forestry Department, released 150 ex-captives from the Orangutan Care Centre and Quarantine to the Lamandau Wildlife Reserve between 1998 and 2008. They also translocated ten rescued wild orangutans into Lamandau during the same period. The number of orangutans released in Lamandau by OFI and/or OFI-UK between 2008 and 2013 is not published. The OFI-UK website, in 27 different news stories (blogs), describes the release of 37 orangutans in Lamandau between 2013 and April, 2018. Some of these were rescues and immediate translocations of imperiled wild orangutans and some involved releases of longer-term rehabilitants. There were doubtlessly more releases than those described on the website, but I could find no inclusive systematic report. Palmer (2017) found that 22 have been rehabilitated and released and 49 have been rescued and released in Lamandau between 2013 and 2017. I am using Palmer's count (71), plus two that were rescued and released in 2018 (OFI-UK website, newstories dated 19 January and 28 April 2018), which brings the Lamandau total to 233 between 1998 and April 2018. However, 160 of these were released from the OFI Orangutan Care and Quarantine Center between 1998 and 2008, and are included in the OFI total of 450 (see above).

Thus I was able to document the release of a total of 550 (450 plus 27 plus 73) orangutans in this program. I'm aware that these numbers may not actually be as precise as I make them to appear. Published sources lack detail and records were not maintained continuously or consistently.

Pre- and post-release methodologies for orangutan reintroduction and translocation have evolved at Tanjung Puting, as they have generally in Indonesia. Quarantine, medical screening, and treatment have become far more extensive and standardized. After quarantine, young orangutans are placed in social groups during the rehabilitation process, and it is the group, rather than individuals, that is released. Contact with human caretakers is reduced during the process. The orangutans are more systematically and gradually exposed to natural foods and to forest sites that provide opportunities for arboreal locomotion, although they are initially given the option to return to cages and feeding platforms at night. Descovich et al (2011) concluded that forest walks were somewhat effective for developing survival-critical locomotor and feeding skills in Tanjung Puting orangutans, but arboreal proclivities, nest-building, and social skills require additional experience. These authors also conclude that orangutans who are new to the rehabilitation process, and individuals of lighter body weight, are most likely to benefit from the forest walk staregy.

Many of the Tanjung Puting orangutans determine their own "release" by not returning to the base camp after daily forays into the forest. Thus there is no distinction in such cases between acclimation and pre-release training. There is an attempt to conduct releases in suitable forests that do not have wild or previously released ex-captives, although this is not always possible.

Tourism is supposed to be tightly controlled in the base camps and prohibited at the release sites. Supplemental food is provided after the orangutans have been released, and individuals that come into conflict with humans are captured and released again in more remote locations. There has been greater emphasis on the importance of post-release monitoring, pre- and post-release record-keeping, and reporting of outcomes, although this is still not common practice at Tanjung Puting (or most primate reintroduction programs).

Yeager (1997) criticized the Tanjung Puting rehabilitation and release program in particular, and orangutan reintroduction in general. Yeager cites a 1994 Tanjung Puting park management plan as stating that more than 180 ex-captive orangutans had been released in the park between 1974 and 1994, and focuses on a subsample of 27 that were released between 1980 and 1982. Of these 27, 11 were known to have survived for two years. Two are known to have died and three had to be captured and relocated because of aggression toward humans. Males dispersed farther than females. Yeager felt that some individuals had been reintroduced before they were self-sufficient. Yeager reported that 29 infants had been born (presumably between 1974 and 1994), of which ten are known to have died. The released orangutans interacted, reproduced, and presumably competed with wild orangutans and influenced the wild orangutans' movements and behavior. Yeager notes that at least one Sumatran orangutan as well as Bornean orangutans from western and eastern Borneo had been released at Tanjung Puting, making outbreeding depression a possibility. Yeager acknowledges the difficulties involved in placing or releasing confiscated orangutans, and concedes that the Tanjung Puting work had been undertaken with the "best intentions".

Banes et al confirmed Yeager's predictions about the likelihood of outbreeding depression. Genetic evidence shows that individuals of several historically separated populations (subspecies, or, some would say, species) of Bornean orangutans, as well as at least one Sumatran orangutan, were released and reproduced with each other and with truly wild orangutans at Tanjung Puting. Outbreeding depression can produce "(d)evelopmental, genetic and other abnormalities" (Banes et al, p 4), but none have been documented among the Tanjung Puting orangutans. Galdikas asserts that most of the released orangutans came from areas near Tanjung Puting, but many doubtlessly were of undocumented provenance. Some of the animals had lived in captivity in Java and perhaps other nations before being repatriated; their origins are especially obscured. There are now 60 wild orangutans at Camp Leakey, including fourth-generation infants, some of which resulted from interbreeding with the wild population.

OFI-UK has managed a "soft-release" rehabilitation program at five different locations within Lamandau since 2013 (OFI-UK website, news stories dated 2, 12 May and 9 June 2017). All of the orphans, and some of the rescued adults, are included in the soft-release program. The orangutans are taken on supervised forest walks during the day, and led back to night quarters. The orangutans are allowed to wander off into the forest, by which time most are eating natural foods and building tree nests. There appears to be ample feeding and other post-release support, and systematic post-release monitoring for at least two weeks. All of the OFI-UK orangutans receive comprehensive veterinary screenings and treatments. Heroic attempts were made to restore the sight of a female orangutan who had 104 air rifle pellets in her body (37 in her head) when she was rescued. She remains blind and will receive lifetime care at Lamandau. Second-generation births have been observed among the orangutans who have been reintroduced at Lamandau. The website provides several references to reintroductions of gibbons and slow lorises in Lamandau, but there are too few details to include these as separate programs.

For all of its faults and attendant contentiousness, the Tanjung Puting orangutan reintroduction program meets both of our criteria for success. There were an estimated 6,000 orangutans in and around the park in 2004, and statistical models suggested that the population will survive for more than 100 years unless there is a dramatic decrease in habitat or some other catastrophe. Released ex-captives, translocated wild orangutans, and their offspring probably constitute only a small portion of the 6,000, but dozens of released orangutans have survived, are free of dependency on humans, and have reproduced in the wild.

Galdikas and many visiting colleagues and students have studied the behavior and cognition of the rehabilitant orangutans and produced scientific articles, books, and book chapters. OFI-UK is sponsoring research in Lamandau and Tanjung Puting.

Welfare (Rehabilitation), Research

REFERENCES

Aveling, R. and A. Mitchell. 1982. Is rehabilitating orang utans worthwhile? *Oryx* 16: 263-271.

Banes, G.L., Galdikas, B.M.F., and L. Vigilant. 2016. Reintroduction of confiscated and displaced mammals risks outbreeding and introgression in natural populations, as evidenced by orang-utans of divergent subspecies. *Scientific Reports* 6, 22026; doi: 10.1038/srep22026.

Descovich, K.A., Galdikas, B.M., Tribe, A., Lisle, A. and C.J. Phillips. 2011. Fostering appropriate behavior in rehabilitant orangutans (*Pongo pygmaeus*). *International Journal of Primatology* 32(3): 616-633.

Galdikas-Brindamour, B. 1975. Orangutans, Indonesia's "People of the Forest". *National Geographic* 148: 444-473.

Palmer, A. 2017. Personal communication; e-mail 4 November.

Russon, A.E. 2004. *Orangutans: Wizards of the Rainforest*. Firefly Books, Buffalo, NY.

Singleton, I., Wich, S., Husson, S., Stephens, S., Utami Atmoko, S., Leighton, M., Rosen, N., Traylor-Holzer, K., Lacy, R., and O. Byers. 2004. *Orangutan Population and Habitat Viability Assessment: Final Report*. Apple Valley, MN, IUCN/SSC Conservation Breeding Specialist Group.

Warren, K.S. and R.A. Swan. 2002. Re-introduction of orang-utans in Indonesia. *Re-introduction News* 21: 24-26.

www.orangutan.org

www.orangutan.org.uk

Yeager, C.P. 1997. Orangutan rehabilitation in Tanjung Puting National Park, Indonesia. *Conservation Biology* 11(3): 802-805.

Bornean Orangutan (*Pongo pygmaeus*). The Wanariset Orangutan Reintroduction Project, which was established in 1991 and which became the Balikpapan Orangutan Survival Foundation (BOS or BOSF) in 1994, the East Kalimantan Natural Resources Conservation Agency (BKSDA), and the Indonesian Forestry Department, released at least 566 Bornean orangutans into the 9,783-ha Sungai Wain Protection Forest (88) and the 28,261-ha Meratus (Beratus) Protection Forest (345) between 1991 and 2008 (releases were terminated in Meratus in 2002), and into the 86,450-ha Kehje Sewen Forest (97) between 2012 and early September, 2018. Each of these forests is located in East Kalimantan, Borneo, Indonesia. There were no wild orangutans in Meratus and Sungai Wain when the reintroductions began in 1991. A habitat survey had indicated that the forests would support orangutans, although Meratus' elevation was greater than that preferred by Bornean orangutans. There was a small wild population at Kehje Sewen in 2012, and a phenological survey had shown that there was sufficient food to support a larger orangutan population.

Most of these orangutans (467) were confiscated or surrendered wild-born ex-captives who had undergone rehabilitation (or their offspring who were born during the rehabilitation process). But 63 of the 345 reintroduced at Meratus and Sungai Wain were wild orangutans who had been rescued from imminent threat, e.g. fire, and then translocated, in some cases after a short stay in the care center. An additional 36 rescued wild orangutans were specifically noted to have been translocated in this way to unspecified locations in 2015, which brings my total of reintroduced orangutans to 566 for BOS's East Kalimantan program.

The releases were conducted initially from the Wanariset intake, quarantine, and rehabilitation center, and then, after 2006, from the more modern and extensive Samboja Lestari Center.

As at Tanjung Puting, many of the orangutans at Wanariset and Samboja Lestari had originally been captured in East Kalimantan, but others probably came from other areas in Borneo. Some were confiscated in Taiwan, Japan, Java, and Bali; the origins of these individuals are especially difficult to determine.

BOS also manages a Bornean orangutan rehabilitation and release program at Mentang in Central Kalimantan, but this is treated as a separate program because it is in Central Kalimantan, a different state (see below). BOS, which is sometimes known as the Bornean Orangutan Survival Foundation (BOSF), has affiliates in several nations.

Because Wanariset opened in 1991, it was informed from its inception by the history of orangutan rehabilitation and release, and by a commitment to enlightened pre- and post-release management. Willie Smits, the director of the programs, built on the recommendations of Herman Rijksen to revise techniques for the rehabilitation and release of orangutans that were promulgated in the late 1980s. Waniriset can be said to have been the first orangutan reintroduction program to have instituted these new reintroduction techniques. As in the revised pre-release protocol at Tanjung Puting, orangutans at Wanariset and Samboja Lestari were strictly quarantined, medically screened, and tested and treated for communicable diseases. Many of the orangutans who were released in Sungai Wain and Meratus were implanted with a microchip for long-term positive identification.

After quarantine, young orangutans were placed in age-graded social groups in cages to reduce dependence on humans and foster social interactions with other orangutans. The orangutans were exposed to some natural foods and natural nest-building materials while in the cages. The groups were then moved to larger cages and in some cases even later to a block of forest to acquire more social and ecological skills, especially more opportunity for climbing and arboreal locomotion, and more exposure to natural foods. Contact with human caretakers was reduced during the later stages of the process. A group that was deemed ready for release was taken by foot, vehicle, and/or helicopter to the release site, and placed in an acclimation cage for one to seven days. In general, it was the group, rather than individuals, that was released. Groups were sometimes combined for release into what are termed "phases" by Siregar et al (2010). Some adults and translocated wild orangutans may have been released individually. It is notable that the release sites were far from the care centers. There was an attempt to conduct releases at sites at which there were no previously released orangutans. This was not always possible, and, of course, there would be previously released orangutans at a destination site after some years. Tourism was tightly controlled at the care centers and prohibited at the release sites.

The orangutans were said to have been released at the beginning of the fruiting season to ensure a supply of recognizable natural foods. Supplemental food was also provided after the orangutans had been released, until they no longer returned to the acclimation cage. Individuals that came into conflict with humans were captured and released again in more remote locations. Injured orangutans were recaptured, treated, and, if indicated, re-released. Most of the released orangutans were monitored by field staff for two to four weeks. In some cases, scientists provided more extensive observations (see below). Post-release monitoring, pre- and post-release record keeping, and reporting of outcomes were emphasized, although this has at times been sporadic in this program.

Visiting scientists and students have documented the behavioral ecology and cognition of some of the released orangutans and the cognition of some of those undergoing rehabilitation. Scientific observation of released orangutans provided snapshots of the numbers released and of outcomes. For example, Grundman provided data on the numbers released and outcomes at Meratus, although her paper is confusing. First she says that more than 100 orangutans had been released at Meratus between 1997 and 2005, of which she was able to identify 25 in 1999. Later she says that 191 orangutans had been released at Meratus between 1997 and 1999, of which she found only 11 in 1999.

Grundman studied a sample of 20 released individuals at Meratus for 14 months in 1999. Six of these, the most recently released of the 20, continued for several years to be reliant on provisioned food, did not build or use nests, and initiated contact with humans. The others were self-sufficient, although some seemed to be more capable than others. Siregar et al were able to identify 14 previously released orangutans at Meratus in a 2002 survey, 20 in a 2004 survey, and 16 to 18 in a 2009 survey (these were not necessarily the same individuals). In 2001, they documented that three infants had been born to released females in Sungai Wain, and in 2002 and 2009 they observed that two more infants had been born in Meratus (one of these infants later died). The Siregar et al paper includes frank assessments of the Wanariset program and cogent, experience-based recommendations for improvement.

Peters (1995) and Fredrikson (1995) studied a subsample of 61 orangutans who had been released in Sungai Wain between 1992 and 1995. Their studies began in October 1994. Fredrikson's study ended in November 1994, and Peters' ended in May 1995. Some of the same information appears in both publications; I used Peters' more extensive work for the following account. All of the studied orangutans were ex-captive wild-born Bornean orangutans that had been rehabilitated at Wanariset. They had been released in five groups at four different sites in Sungai Wain. Some had to be recaptured due to injury and then re-released. Fifteen of the 61 orangutans were seen regularly at the end of Peters' study, and some of these had become completely self-sufficient. Many of the 61 had disappeared in the first month after release. Peters and Fredrikson provide detailed data on activity, ranging, feeding, nest building, locomotion, and social behavior. No births are mentioned by these observers, although we know from other sources that infants have been born to released females in Sungai Wain. Russon (2002b) studied the cognitive processes that support food processing in a subsample of ten of these same released orangutans at Sungai Wain for several years. She stresses that survival-critical skills are acquired slowly by orangutans, and that social learning through observation of skilled orangutans is important to the process.

Some of these observers state or imply that actual pre- and post-release methodology did not always meet the program's high standards, e.g. some released orangutans spent most of their time on the ground and/or did not make nests. At least one ex-captive was released only a month after arrival at the care center. Russon (2002) concluded that "Critics [of orangutan rehabilitation] often focus on behavioral deficiencies of ex-captives and attribute them to ineptitude. From a cognitive viewpoint, it is equally likely that deficiencies owe to poor programing and unreasonable expectations, e.g., low management of human contact, low appreciation of the social, ecological, and developmental conditions that foster readaptation and of the learning problems caused by human contact, and underestimation of the time needed to acquire feral skills." (pg. 475).

BOS opened a new destination site in East Kalimantan, the 86,450-ha Kehje Sewen Forest, in 2012. Orangutan reintroduction in East and Central Kalimantan had largely been halted between 2002 and 2012 because of lack of suitable destination forests. In 2009, BOS founded a private entity, Restorasi Habitat Orangutan Indonesia (PT RHOI), to identify and acquire forests that were suitable for reintroduction. PT ROHI acquired Kehje Sewen from a private lumber concession in 2012, and reintroduction appears to have begun in that year. As noted above, a total of 97 rescued or confiscated orangutans who had been rehabilitated at the Samboja Lestari center had been reintroduced in several cohorts into Kehje Sewen as of early September, 2018. At least four had been been born at the center. Most of the 97 were between seven and 12 years old at the time of reintroduction and had spent five to eight years at the rehabilitation center. Many carried implanted radio transmitters when they were released. The orangutans had received all of the veterinary oversight and pre-release training that is now typical for orangutans at BOS rehabilitation centers. Some orangutans who were reintroduced in Kehje Sewen in 2018 had spent the final phase of their rehabilitation on a man-made 83-ha forest island named Juq Kehje Sewen Island (see www.orangutan.or.id news stories dated 27 and 29 August 2018). The BOS staff transported the orangutans from Samboja Lestari to Kehje Sewen in an arduous 17-hour journey by truck, boat, and the backs of humans. There has been no acclimation at the release site and little post-release support at Kehje Sewen, although injured orangutans and those who come into conflict with humans are relocated. There has been systematic post-release monitoring. Orangutans released in 2018 were monitored for 30 days after release. At least two females have given birth to healthy infants.

Basalamah et al (2018) studied the post-release behavior of six orangutans (four females, two males) who were reintroduced by PT RHOI and BOS in the Kehje Sewen forest in 2012. The orangutans had been rehabilitated at Samboja Lestari, and were among the first to have been released in Kehje Sewen. They were between eight and 13 years old. They were released in three cohorts within a three-week period. All had passed through Samboja Lestari's soft pre-release preparation. Each was fitted with a radio transmitter. They were acclimated in cages at the release sites for an unspecified period. There was no post-release support except that one orangutan was given food for a few days after release. They were followed extensively (344 follow-days) for more than a year. Some of the released individuals returned to the base camp to scavenge food during the first two post-release weeks. One of the males returned to the base camp during the second post-release month. His damaged radio transmitter was replaced, and he was re-released.

Five of these six orangutans were known to be alive after 34 months. One disappeared after eight months. In general, the orangutans spent more time feeding and less time resting than wild counterparts. They built nests competently but preferred to reuse nests. They preferred fruit but ate a wide variety of plant foods and insects. They established overlapping home ranges, and spent time in association with each other, especially in co-feeding. They spent more time on the ground than wild orangutans of the same age.

None of the studies cited above allows calculation of post-release survival rates, but some of the Meratus, Sungai Wain, and Kehje Sewen individuals have become self-sufficient, interacted with previously released orangutans, and reproduced. The two BOSF websites post news stories about opportunistic sightings of orangutans who had been released years before. One male was seen at Sungai Wain almost ten years after release.

Sulistyo et al 2018 have finally provided quantitative data on post-release outcomes for BOS orangutan rehabilitation programs. Their report states that BOS has reintroduced 326 Bornean orangutans into "three remote forest sites in Kalimantan" between 2012 and 2017. These may have been in East and/or Central Kalimantan. They may have been rehabilitants or rescued wild orangutans (I was able to access only the abstract of this presentation and thus lack details). Their study pertains to a subsample of 254 of the 326 reintroduced individuals. Post-release outcomes are known for 181. Of the 181, 160 are known to have survived for at least one year, which is the authors' criterion of reintroduction success. Thus they claim a success rate of 88%. However, many reintroduction practitioners believe that animals that disappear should be considered to have been unsuccessfully reintroduced. If we include the disappearances as losses (73), then 160 of 254 orangutans (63%) are *known* to have survived for one year. Even this lesser figure is impressive and attests to the effectiveness of the BOS programs.

Sulistyo et al also provide details of post-release medical interventions, of which there were 55 in their study. Mediating human-orangutan conflict was the most common cause for intervention (22 cases). "Reintroduction failure" that resulted in death was the cause of 12 interventions. The remainder were injuries and illnesses, and infant deaths.

These efforts to systematically monitor and document post-release survival and behavior are unique and welcome. The work suggests that rehabilitation does foster survival of reintroduced orangutans and, while the effects of early captivity are evident, that the behavior of rehabilitants supports successful adaptation to the wild.

I am unaware of any modeling of long-term survival of the orangutan populations at Sungai Wain or Meratus. Russon (2009) thinks that Sungai Wain is too small and has too few orangutans to be self-sustaining. Meratus is large enough and may have enough orangutans, but much of the area is high elevation habitat (above 1,200 m) that tends not to be preferred by Bornean orangutans. It's still to early to judge the long-term success of the Kehje Sewen population.

Significantly, the Samboja Lestari Center is designed to provide lifetime care and accommodation in forest cages and on islands for orangutans (and some other species) who are unsuitable for release for medical or behavioral reasons. Palmer (2017) shared that there were 202 orangutans at Samboja Lestari in 2016, many of whom were not suitable for release. The number at Samboja Lestari was reported to have decreased to 140 in 2018 (news stories dated 27 and 29 August 2018, www.orangutan.or.id)

Welfare (Rehabilitation), Research

REFERENCES

Anon. 2015b. Indonesia: Rescued orangutans returned to the forest. *AP Archive*, 21 July 2015. (Accessed on Youtube.com).

Basalamah, F., Atmoto, S.S.U., Perwitasari-Farajallah, D., Qayim, I., Sihite, J., Van Noordwijk, M., Willems, E., and Van Schaik, C.P. 2018. Monitoring orangutan reintroduction: Results of activity budgets, diets, vertical use and associations during the first year post-release in Kehje Sewen forest, East Kalimantan, Indonesia. *Biodiversitas* 19(2): 609-620.

Commitante, R., Unwin, S., Jaya, R., Saraswati, Y., Sulistyo, F. and C. Nente (eds.). 2015. Orangutan Conservancy 2015 *Orangutan Veterinary Advisory Group Workshop Report*. wwww.orangutan.com

Grundmann, E. 2005. Will re-introduction and rehabilitation help the long-term conservation of orangutans in Indonesia? *Re-introduction News* 24: 26-27.

Palmer, A. 2017. Personal communication; e-mail 4 November.

Peters, H.H. 1995. *Orangutan reintroduction? Development, use and evaluation of a new method: reintroduction*. M.Sc. dissertation, University of Groningen, The Netherlands.

Russon, A. 2002a. Activities in Kalimantan focus on orangutan reintroduction & environmental protection. *Voices from the Wilderness* (Newsletter of the Balikpapan Orangutan Society/USA) 5(1): 1-2.

Russon, A.E. 2002b. Return of the native: Cognition and site-specific expertise in orangutan rehabilitation. *International Journal of Primatology* 23(3): 461-477.

Russon, A.E. 2004. *Orangutans: Wizards of the Rainforest*. Firefly Books, Buffalo, NY.

Russon, A.E. 2009. Orangutan rehabilitation and reintroduction. In S.A. Wich, S.S. Utami Atmoko, T. Mitra Setia, and C.P. van Schaik, eds. *Orangutans: Geographic Variation in Behavioural Ecology and Conservation*, pp 327-350. Oxford, UK, Oxford University Press.

Russon, A. 2018. Personal communication; e-mail 7 March.

Siregar, R. S. E., Farmer, K.H., Chivers, D.J., and B. Saragih. 2010. Re-introduction of Bornean orangutans to Meratus protected forest, East Kalimantan, Indonesia. In: P.S. Soorae, ed. *Global Re-introduction Perspectives 2010: Additional Case-Studies from Around the Globe*, pp. 243-248. Abu Dhabi, UAE, IUCN/SSC Re-introduction Specialist Group.

Smits, W. 2001. From the desk of Dr. Willic Smits. *Voices from the Wilderness* (Newsletter of the Balikpapan Orangutan Society/USA) 4(1): 12-15.

Smits, W.T.M., Heriyanto, and W. Ramono. 1995. A new method for rehabilitation of orang-utans in Indonesia: A first overview. In: R.D. Nadler, B.M.F. Galdikas, L.K. Sheeran, and N. Rosen, eds. *The Neglected Ape*, pp. 23-27. New York and London, Plenum Press.

Sulistyo, F., Fahroni, A., Sriningsih, A.P., Sunderland-Groves, J. and J. Sihite. 2018. Overview of medical interventions in Bornean orangutan reintroduction sites in Kalimantan, Indonesia. Abstract of a paper presented at the 27th Congress of the International Primatological Society, Nairobi, Kenya.

Warren, K.S. and R.A. Swan. 2002. Re-introduction of orang-utans in Indonesia. *Re-introduction News* 21: 24-26.

www.orangutan.or.id

www.redapes.org

www.yorku.ca/arusson/rehab_sites.htm

Bornean Orangutan (*Pongo pygmaeus*). The Wanariset Orangutan Reintroduction Project/Balikpapan (Bornean) Orangutan Survival Foundation (BOS or BOSF) judged that the Samboja Lestari center and the Meratus and Sungai Wain forests in East Kalimantan were at capacity in 1999 and initiated the Nyaru Mentang Orangutan Reintroduction Project in Central Kalimantan. The Nyaru Mentang program, in collaboration with the Indonesian Forestry Department and the Central Kalimantan Conservation and Natural Resources Authority, released 175 confiscated and rehabilitated orangutans from the Nyaru Mentang rescue center into the 35,000-ha Bukit Batikap Bukit Raya Conservation Forest between 2012 and May 2018, and an additional 102 rehabilitated orangutans into the 27,472-ha Bukit Baka Bukit Raya National Park between 2016 and May 2018.

BOS also rescues wild orangutans who are in peril and moves them to other, relatively safe forests without rehabilitation. Fires raged through Central Kalimantan in 2015, killing and displacing many wild orangutans. The Nyaru Mentang staff rescued a total of 87 wild orangutans in imminent danger of starvation and human conflict from an area known as Mangkutub, and released them after only a short delay in areas named Bagantung and the Mantangi River. The first 76 were rescued in 24 days in 2016, and an additional 11, including a fully adult male and two mother/infants pairs, were rescued in 2017. These were heroic, logistically demanding operations. One adult male was deemed to be too badly injured to be released and was sent to Nyaru Mentang for lifetime care.

Thus the total number of orangutans reintroduced by BOS in Central Kalimantan is 364 through early September 2018.

Husson et al (2014, 2016) provided comprehensive accounts of reintroduction at the Batikap Conservation Forest for the years 2012 to 2015. The 2014 report is remarkable for its detailed treatment of reintroduction outcomes, with detailed data on survivorship, recaptures and re-releases, and on the behavioral ecology of released orangutans. It sets a welcome standard for the reintroduction and translocation of not only orangutans but of all primates. Husson et al (2014) reported that 131 orangutans had been released in Batikap by the end of 2014, which is consistent with the figure of 155 by 2016 that is provided by Husson et al (2016). The 131 had been released in nine separate cohorts, and included 30 orangutans that had been born during the rehabilitation process. At least 82 of the 131 (63%) survived, independent of human support, for at least 15 months, and there were two births in the wild. Eleven are known to have died in the first year. At least two of these had been shot. Four released orangutans (one with a dependent infant) who were not getting enough to eat were provided with supplementary food and medication in the field until they recovered. Three other orangutans were recaptured and brought into captivity for treatment; two of these were re-released and one died. Five "nuisance" orangutans (one with a dependent infant) were translocated to other forested areas. BOS has reimbursed people for property that was lost to or damaged by orangutans. Husson et al (2014) also provide detailed data on the activity budgets and diet of the released orangutans.

Angus (in Commitante et al 2015) reported that there were 136 released orangutans (including three infants that had been born in the wild) living in Batikap in 2014. Husson et al (2016), in an abstract of a scientific conference presentation, stated that BOS had released 155 ex-captive orangutans into Batikap between 2012 and 2016. This total includes the 131 discussed above. They confirm that the first 119 of these had been monitored extensively using radiotelemetry, and that 82 were living independently in the forest after one year and seven were confirmed to have died. A BOSF website news story dated 17 February 2017 stated that 167 orangutans had been released into Bukit Betikap between 2012 and 2017, and the website home page stated that a total of 175 had been released by May 2018. Various stories on the website state that at least seven infants had been born to reintroduced orangutans in the Batikap Conservation Forest.

BOS opened an additional destination site in Central Kalimantan in 2016 in the 27,472 -ha Bukit Baka Bukit Raya National Park. Again, in cooperation with the Central Kalimantan Natural Resources Agency, a total of 102 confiscated or rescued, rehabilitated orangutans had been released in at least 24 different cohorts at this site by early September, 2018. One had been confiscated in Thailand and returned to Nyaru Mentang, and at least six had been born at Nyaru

Mentang. The released orangutans were between nine and 17 years old at release and had been at the rehabilitation center for between four and 14 years. Some of the orangutans carried radio-transmitters. There was systematic post-release monitoring for 30 days in the most recent releases (www.redapes.com, news stories dated 17 July and 14 August, 2018).

The Nyaru Mentang care and quarantine center (rescue center) is located in a 62.5-ha arboretum, which, in addition to a modern medical/quarantine space and caging, provides space for large cages with naturalistic vegetation, small forest tracts, and five forested islands in the Rungan River (totalling 876 ha in area) for orangutans to be exposed to authentic natural vegetation and natural foods. The center had taken in 1,182 rescued and confiscated orangutans between 1999 and 2015 (about 40% had been rescued directly from the wild and 60% had been confiscated from captivity).

Angus, and Husson et al (2016) say that there were still approximately 500 orangutans at Nyaru Mentang in 2016, and more than 1,500 in rehabilitation centers in Borneo and Sumatra. There appear to be insufficient suitable forests to comply with the Indonesian Orangutan Action Plan and Conservation Strategy 2007-2017, which dictated that all eligible orangutans in rehabilitation centers should have been released by 2015. Significantly, many of the Nyaru Mentang (and Samboja Lestari) orangutans are unsuitable for release and will spend the rest of their lives receiving expert and compassionate care in these and other sanctuaries.

The pre-release methodology at Nyaru Mentang was similar to that of Samboja Lestari. Newly arrived orangutans received an extensive medical examination and treatment for communicable diseases and injuries (one rescued orangutan had been shot with more than 100 air rifle pellets, and had been blinded). Genetic samples were taken to identify subspecies (at least three individuals have been sent to other care centers in Indonesia to avoid subspecific mixing). After the initial examination, the orangutans were quarantined and then, depending on their age, were either caged alone or in compatible age-graded groups. They moved through a series of larger and more naturalistic enclosures and forested islands until they were locomoting consistently and competently in trees, eating natural foods, and building nests. The final months of pre-release training, which took place on the 108.5 ha Kaja Island, were regarded as a form of soft-release (I would call it a different form of pre-release training).

The orangutans were quarantined again before release. Radiotransmitters were surgically implanted. To qualify for release, an orangutan must have been at least seven years of age, demonstrated survival-critical skills, and been free of diseases that don't exist among wild orangutans. Once qualified, they were then trucked, flown, and/or carried by boat to the release sites in what appear to have been cohorts of five to 13. I could find no mention of acclimation at the release site or of routine post-release supplemental feeding of the rehabilitated orangutans, and I am unaware if there was any post-release support or monitoring of those who were rescued and translocated

Field staff and scientists monitored the orangutans for up to three years after release. The BOS websites began posting informational news stories about these reintroductions in 2016.

Sulistyo et al (2018) provided an account of post-release outcomes for 254 reintroduced orangutans at three of BOS' orangutan rehabilitation sites (see the above account of the BOS program in East Kalimantan for a more detailed description of this presentation). Depending on the formula for calculation, the reintroduction success rate for Sulistyo et al's large sample was 63% or 88%. Note that Husson et al (2016) also found a survival rate of 63% in their Batikap sample.

Husson et al (2018) state that BOS has reintroduced 246 ex-captive orangutans into natural habitat in Central Kalimantan since 2012 (presumably between 2012 and late 2017/early 2018). Of the 246, 112 were known by the authors to have been alive or dead after one year. They calculated a survival rate of 90% for their sample, which is similar to Sulistyo et al's 88%. (Some the same animals were probably included in both studies.) Husson et al's reintroduced orangutans spent significantly less time feeding during their first post-relase month than wild orangutans. Survivors spent more tme feeding in the second and third post-release months, but those who died never increased their feeding time, which the authors assumed led to "malnutrition, disorientation, poor decision-making and the eventual death or illness". The authors conclude that rehabilitant orangutans should be exposed to "rainforest habitat during the critical developmental age (2-4 years)" and that supplemental food should be provided to "at-risk" orangutans after they are released. I was able to access only to abstract of this presentation and thus lack some details.

Marzec et al (2018) provided an account of post-release behaviors of a sample of ten rehabilitated orangutans who BOS had reintroduced to Bukit Batikap. I was again able to access only the abstract of this presentation and thus am unaware of critical details, such as how long after release the subjects were observed. The ex-captives showed higher rates of exploration of environmental objects, more time in same-sex association, higher peering rates (looking at other orangutans), and a more diverse diet than a matched sample of wild Bornean orangutans. They conclude that reintroduced orangutans use a mix of individual and social learning to survive in the wild. One wonders why the reintroduced orangutans who died in Husson et al's 2018 study did not learn more about feeding by watching more skilled conspecifics.

Russon et al (2005) provide a clue. Studying leaf-carrying, a component of nest-building, they concluded that "Reintroduction has better chances of success if ex-captives are released to forest life as juveniles, because of their optimal potential for learning ecological skills, and if rehabilitant communities are managed to develop strong adolescent networks and to provide juvenile learners with access to older, more experienced members" (pg. 199). In brief, rehabilitant and reintroduced orangutans need to learn survival-critical skills and knowledge, and they have no mothers to help them learn. Juveniles are optimally predisposed to learn socially if they are exposed to experienced models. But can they learn in semi-natural environments during rehabilitation (Marzec et al seem to think they can't), and can they continue to perfect these skills as they get older and after they are reintroduced (Russon et al think they can)?

Welfare (Rehabilitation, Rescue), Research

References

Commitante, R., Unwin, S., Jaya, R., Saraswati, Y., Sulistyo, F. and C. Nente (eds.). 2015. *Orangutan Conservancy 2015 Orangutan Veterinary Advisory Group Workshop Report.* wwww.orangutan.com

Husson, S., Nayasilana, I., Maruly, A., Purnomo, Suyoko, A., and D. Kurniawan. 2014. *Progress Report #4. Orangutan Reintroduction and Post-release Monitoring in Bukit Batikap Conservation Forest, Murung Raya.* BOS Foundation.

Husson, S.J., Kurniawan, D., Purnomo, P., Boyd, N., Suyoko, A., Sunderland-Groves, J., and J. Sihite. 2016. The survival and adaptation of reintroduced ex-captive orangutans in Central Kalimantan, Indonesia. Abstract of a paper presented at the joint meeting of the 26th Congress of the International Primatological Society and the 39th Meeting of the American Society of Primatologists, Chicago, IL, USA.

Husson, S.J., Suyoko, A., Kurnianwan, D., Sunderland-Groves, J., and J. Sihite. 2018. Factors affecting the successful reintroduction of Bornean orangutans (*Pongo pygmaeus*). Abstract of a paper presented at the 27th Congress of the International Primatological Society, Nairobi, Kenya.

Marzec, A., Laubi, B., Kurniawan, D., Utami-Atmoko, S., van Noordwijk, M., Willems, E., and C. van Schaik. 2018. Can necessity be the mother of invention? How do Bornean orangutans (*Pongo pygmaeus*) adjust to a new environment? Abstract of a paper presented at the 27th Congress of the International Primatological Society, Nairobi, Kenya.

Nugraha, I. and P. Jacobson. 2016. 10 orangutans released into the wild in Borneo. www.news.mongabey.com 15 August.

Russon, A.E., Handayani, D.P., Kuncoro, P., and A. Ferisa. 2007. Orangutan leaf-carrying for nest-building: Toward unraveling cultural processes. *Animal Cognition* 10: 189-202.

Sulistyo, F., Fahroni, A., Sriningsih, A.P., Sunderland-Groves, J. and J. Sihite. 2018. Overview of medical interventions in Bornean orangutan reintroduction sites in Kalimantan, Indonesia. Abstract of a paper presented at the 27th Congress of the International Primatological Society, Nairobi, Kenya.

www.redapes.com

www.orangutan.or.id

Bornean Orangutan (*Pongo pygmaeus*). International Animal Rescue opened a rehabilitation center in Ketapang, West Kalimantan in 2009, and released one rescued and rehabilitated orangutan in the 32,000-ha Gunung Tarak (Protected Forest), which is southeast of and continguous with Gunung Palung National Park, in 2010 and another in the same area in 2013. Both had to be rescued after release because of malnutrition. They were treated at the rescue center and re-released in 2014 with a third rescued and rehabilitated orangutan and an additional translocated wild orangutan. There were wild orangutans in Gunung Tarak. Pre- and post-release methodology seems to have been similar to that of Nyaru Mentang and Samboja Lestari. Radiotelemetry and ground follows were used for post-release monitoring.

Campbell-Smith et al (2016) monitored the three rehabilitated orangutans (the translocated orangutan disappeared immediately upon release and was apparently not wearing a transmitter) with the intent of comparing the time they spent in human interaction, their home ranges, and their activity and feeding time budgets with those of wild Gunung Palung orangutans. They specifically examined the effect of releasing rehabilitated orangutans in areas with existing wild populations. The abstract did not include outcomes for these three orangutans.

Dasgupta's 2016 video noted that IAR had also released a total of 11 orangutans who had been rehabilitated at Ketapang in the 3,500-ha Bukit Baka Bukit Raya National Park through the end of 2016. An additional 19 (at least one of which was born at the sanctuary during rehabilitation) were released in Bukit Baka Bukit Raya and in and around the Gunung Palung National Park in 2017 and in the first eight months of 2018 (IAR website, news stories dated 3, 7 March, 25 May, 20 June, 20 July, 19 September, 12 December 2017, 28 January, 27 March, 23 April, 25 July 2018). Some of these had been rehabilitated at Ketapang, and others had been rescued in very small patches of forest in which they could not find enough to eat and were being harassed (and shot) by humans. The rescued individuals were skillfully captured under difficult conditions, given veterinary screenings and, in some cases, treatment, and carried to the destination sites, having spent very little time in captivity. Those that had been rehabilitated at Ketapang had been exposed to natural vegetation for feeding, locomotion, and nest-building in a cage and later on a large island prior to release. One released subadult male had spent eight years in rehabilitation at Ketapang. Some of the rehabilitated orangutans from Ketapang had to be driven for 20 hours, transported by boat for an hour, and then carried in heavy metal cages for eight hours to get to release sites in Bukit Baka Bukit Raya.

There appears to have been no acclimation at the release sites, and there is no mention of post-release support. Post-release monitoring does not appear to have been systematic, although some previously released orangutans were observed opportunistically.

There were 86 orangutans at the Ketapang center in 2015. (Adi in Commitante et al 2015). A news story on the International Animal Rescue website (27 May 2016) states that were 106 in mid-2016. Dasgupta's video says that there were more than 100 rescued orangutans at the Ketapang center at the end of 2016.

Welfare (Rehabilitation)

REFERENCES

Campbell-Smith, G., Sanchez, K.L., and A.A. Jabbar. 2016. Long-term post-release monitoring of three female orangutans (*Pongo pygmaeus*) in Gunung Tarak Nature Reserve, West Kalimantan, Indonesia. Abstract of a paper presented at the joint meeting of the 26th Congress of the International Primatological Society and the 39th Meeting of the American Society of Primatologists, Chicago, IL, USA.

Commitante, R., Unwin, S., Jaya, R., Saraswati,, Y., Sulistyo, F. and C. Nente (eds.). 2015. *Orangutan Conservancy 2015 Orangutan Veterinary Advisory Group Workshop Report.*

Dasgupta, S. 2016. Video: Two rescued pet orangutans return to the wild. *Mongabay* 21 December 2016.

www.internationalanimalrescue.org

www.orangutan.com

Sumatran Orangutan (*Pongo abelii*). The rescue and release of Sumatran orangutans began approximately a decade after Barbara Harrisson's pioneering work in Malaysian Borneo. The first Sumatran rehabilitation center was at Ketambe, which opened in 1971 in the approximately 8,000-km² Gunung Leuser Reserve. Gunung Leuser was upgraded to national park status in 1980 and was designated a UN Biosphere Reserve and part of a World Heritage site in 1981. Gunung Leuser had a rich fauna, including orangutans, gibbons, and several monkey species. The Ketambe rehabilitation center was founded by Herman Rijksen and Ans Rijksen-Graatsma, who had intended only to conduct a field study of the behavioral ecology of Ketambe's wild orangutans. The center was funded and managed by the World Wildlife Fund and the Nature Conservation and Wildlife Management Service of the Indonesian Directorate-General of Forestry. A Dutch scientific committee provided technical advice, and the University of Wageningen (with which Herman Rijksen was and is still affiliated) assumed responsibility for organizing research in the reserve.

Despite legal restrictions, there was a brisk export trade in orangutans at the time, but ratification of the Convention on International Trade in Endangered Species in 1973 and increased government resolve resulted in locating and confiscating many orangutans that were being held in captivity in Sumatra. This created a need for orangutan rehabilitation and reintroduction. As at Tanjung Puting (see above) confiscated orangutans were brought to the Rijksens' research camp. Rijksen and Rijksen-Graatsma were familiar with Harrisson's and de Silva's work (see above) and patterned the Ketambe reintroduction/translocation facilities and methods after their work.

Confiscated orangutans that were brought to Ketambe were isolated in an enclosure and observed for two to five weeks. Sick animals were treated. They were then moved to one of four compartments in a large wood and mesh cage that was elevated off the ground to allow feces and food waste to fall through the poles that formed the floor of the cage. They would be grouped with like-age individuals, and fed fruits, vegetables, vitamin supplements, milk, and leafy branches. The older orangutans were moved to a larger cage after this quarantine; infants were bottle-fed, carried, and supervised by human attendants until they were more independent. Because Ketambe is within the reserve, it was possible to simply open the doors of the larger cage and allow the orangutans to explore the forest and interact socially with the others. Contact with humans was minimized for these older orangutans. There was no release or acclimation per se. The adolescent and older orangutans were allowed to sleep where they chose, including in the cage. Food was provided twice a day. The food given to the older adolescents was monotonous and reduced in quantity to encourage them to forage for natural foods. The orangutans were checked and treated for parasites after "release". There was no systematic post-release monitoring but many were seen during Rijksen's field work. There were 12 wild orangutans living near Ketambe during the time that rehabilitants were being released.

Rijksen stressed that the orangutans that were released at Ketambe appeared to learn quickly how to identify and process local foods, and appeared to learn quickly to interact effectively with other orangutans, including wild individuals. He echoed de Silva's observations of the rehabilitants' manipulative and tool-using abilities and their ability to learn from others by observation. He initially favored releasing rehabilitated orangutans in protected areas that were already inhabited by wild orangutans, provided that there was sufficient food, to foster social learning of survival-critical skills. He suggested long-term provisioning of the mixed wild and rehabilitant population. Wild orangutans frequently visited the center, and even remained there for several days. Rehabilitants often accompanied wild orangutans into the forest and remained there for some time. Rijksen and Rijksen-Graatsma (1975) did caution against the possible spread of communicable diseases from rehabilitants to the wild population.

As of 1974, Ketambe had taken in 28 infant, juvenile, and adolescent orangutans. Two died shortly after arrival due to malnutrition and disease. Of the 26 that were later released, seven were killed by a leopard that frequented the cage and feeding area. Three returned to the forest and became completely self-sufficient. Nine died of unspecified causes. Russon (2009), citing Rijksen (1978), states that the number released at Ketambe between 1971 and 1974 was 31. I was unable to access this original Rijksen source to determine the outcomes for these additional orangutans.

MacKinnon (1977), an expert in the behavioral ecology of wild orangutans, was among the first to question the release of rehabilitated ex-captive orangutans in areas with wild orangutans, citing overcrowding, competition, and the potential of spreading communicable disease. "The return of captive [orangutans] to healthy wild populations can no longer be justified." (MacKinnon 1977, pg. 698). Recall that the desirability of releasing ex-captives with wild orangutans had previously been assumed by all orangutan reintroduction practitioners since Harrisson (see above). Ketambe's orangutan rehabilitation and release program for confiscated orangutans ended in 1979, in part because Rijksen himself recognized the potential for the spread of communicable, human-born diseases to the wild population. The six orangutans that remained at Ketambe were transferred to the Bohorok center (see below).

The Gunung Leuser orangutan population is self-sustaining. Reintroduction at Ketambe and at other sites (see below) probably contributed little in terms of numbers or genetic diversity, but by our definitions, the Ketambe work was successful. The behavioral ecology field study of the wild Ketambe orangutans that was begun by Rijksen and continued by many scientific successors is one of the longest running studies of wild apes.

Welfare (Rehabilitation), Research

References

MacKinnon, J. 1977. The future of orang-utans. *New Scientist*, 74: 697-699.

Rijksen, H.D. 1974. Orang-utan conservation and rehabilitation in Sumatra. *Biological Conservation* 6(1): 20-25.

Rijksen, H.D. 1978. *A Field Study of Sumatran Orang Utans (Pongo pygmaeus abelli, Lesson 1872), Ecology, Behavior and Conservation*. Wageningen, the Netherlands. Mededlingen Landbouwhogeschool: H. Veerman and B.V. Zonen.

Rijksen, H.D. and A.G. Rijksen-Graatsma. 1975. Orang Utan rescue work In North Sumatra. *Oryx*, 13: 63-73.

Russon, A.E. 2009. Orangutan rehabilitation and reintroduction. In S.A. Wich, S.S. Utami Atmoko, T. Mitra Setia, and C.P. van Schaik, eds. *Orangutans: Geographic Variation in Behavioural Ecology and Conservation*, pp 327-350. Oxford, UK. Oxford University Press.

Sumatran Orangutan (*Pongo abelii*). The Bohorok (later Bukit Lawang) orangutan rehabilitation program was founded in 1973 by Regina Frey and Monica Boerner, with funding from the Frankfurt Zoological Society (disclosure: Frankfurt Zoological Society supported my work on reintroduction of golden lion tamarins in Brazil) and later from the World Wildlife Fund. Like Ketambe, Bohorok was located in the Gunung Leuser Reserve, but was approximately 20 km east of Ketambe. Rosalind and Conrad Aveling managed Bohorok from 1975 to 1980, at which time the Indonesian Directorate of Wildlife Conservation took over. This coincided with the closure of Ketambe. Orangutan reintroduction at Bohorok was officially terminated in 1991 (or 1995 or 1996, sources vary), although it appears that there have been some subsequent reintroductions there. The center had become (and still is) a major tourist attraction. Close contact of rehabilitant orangutans with humans and the potential for the spread of communicable diseases to the wild primate populations of Gunung Leuser were the reasons for the rehabilitation program's termination. Singleton wrote a comprehensive history of the Bohorok/Bukit Lawang orangutan reintroduction program, but I did not see it until I was revising the first edition of this *History*.

Bohorok received 74 orangutans between 1973 and 1978, 56 of which were infants or juveniles. Ten of these died before release, and 46 were released. (Frey 1978). Dellatore's much more recent search of official center records revealed that, as of 2007, 229 orangutans had been received into the Bohorok/Bukit Lawang reintroduction program, of which 51 were confirmed to have died "during the reintroduction process". Singleton (2012) states that 226 orangutans were received at Bukit Lawang, and that at least 49 died during the rehabilitation process. It appears that 226 (or 229) arrived at the center, and 177 were actually released. Another source (www.orangutan-republik.org) states that that 218 had been released between 1973 and 2000 (but I can no longer document this source). Six are said to have been relocated to other areas or returned to quarantine after release. Dellatore stresses that some of the unaccounted individuals might have successfully integrated into the wild population and lived (are living?) independently, farther from the center. He notes that as of 2007, there were nine reintroduced ex-captives and three of their adolescent offspring living in the forest in close proximity to the center. A "semi-wild" (ex-captive?) male was also seen occasionally in the area. Singleton states that as of 2012, there were only two caged orangutans at the center, and fewer than ten were showing up for scheduled feedings at the platforms.

Tourists regularly visit the center's animals, as well as previously reintroduced and truly wild orangutans in the area, and sometimes feed them. This makes it difficult to judge if these individuals could live independently with no provisioned food. (Feeding the free-ranging orangutans by tourists is said to have been stopped in 2015 [www.bukitlawang.com]). Dellatore confirmed that the home range of these reintroduced orangutans, their offspring, and the wild orangutans living near the center is smaller than that of wild orangutans, and that they spend less time foraging on natural foods. Infant mortality is also greater (56% compared to approximately 5% for wild orangutans). This compares with infant mortality at Sepilok, which was found to be 57% (Kuze et al 2008). Singleton reviews factors that could account for the high infant mortality at these rehabilitation centers. Singleton's review also includes an excellent account of the dangers and drawbacks of tourism, close proximity, and daily feedings at orangutan rehabilitation centers. Some orangutans have been killed at Bukit Lawang because they attacked people. Singleton also provides an account of the dangers and stresses of releasing rehabilitated orangutans into forests that already have wild orangutan populations.

Pre- and post-release methodology at Bohorok appears to have been very similar to that of its predecessor at Ketambe. Confiscated orangutans that arrived at Bohorok were quarantined for at least two months, received thorough veterinary screenings, and were vaccinated (Frey 1978). Singleton notes that the quarantine was "rudimentary" and ineffective. After quarantine, infants and juveniles were fed by attendants and given free nighttime access to caging at the center. Juvenile, adolescent, and adult individuals were encouraged to visit and remain around an elevated feeding platform that was 500 m from the main part of the center. Wild orangutans visited the platform and some rehabilitants returned to the cages, but some used this as a point from which to move permanently into the forest. Some were moved deeper into the forest by helicopter. Monitoring was even less systematic at Bohorok because it initially lacked the strong scientific presence that Rijksen brought to Ketambe. Dellatore's work shows the importance of systematic research for understanding post-release outcomes.

I was unable to access any original source that confirmed that orangutans who had been released at Bohorok survived at least a year, interacted with wild orangutans, and were independent of human support. However, two secondary reports, by authors (Husson et al 2014, Russon 2009) who presumably had access to more detailed published and unpublished information, provide survival rates that would imply that some of these released orangutans had met these criteria.

Welfare (Rehabilitation)

References

Aveling, R. and A. Mitchell. 1981. Is rehabilitating orang utans worthwhile? Oryx, 16: 263-271.

Dellatore, D.F. 2007. *Behavioural Health of Reintroduced Orangutans (Pongo abelii) in Bukit Lawang, Sumatra, Indonesia.* Master's Thesis, Oxford Brookes University.

Frey, R. 1978. Management of orangutans. In J.A. McNeely, D.S. Rabor, and E.A. Sumardja, eds. *Wildlife Management in Southeast Asia*, pp 199-215. Bogor, SEAMO Regional Center for Tropical Biology.

Husson, S., Nayasilana, I., Maruly, A., Purnomo, Suyoko, A., and D. Kurniawan. 2014. *Progress Report #4. Orangutan Reintroduction and Post-release Monitoring in Bukit Batikap Conservation Forest, Murung Raya.* BOS Foundation.

Kuze, N., Sipangkui, S., Malim, T.P., Bernard, H., Ambu, L.N. and S. Kohshima. 2008. Reproductive parameters over a 37-year period of free-ranging Borneo orangutans at Sepilok Orangutan Rehabilitation Centre. *Primates* 49: 126-134.

Singleton, I. 2012. Stasiun pengamatan orangutan semi liar dan tantanganya: Orangutan tourism case study. *Proceedings of the Africa-Asia Ape Conservation and Poverty Alleviation Learning Exchange*, Bogor, Indonesia, 11-15 January. Retrieved from www.povertyandconservation.info/node/7916

www.bukitlawang.com

www.orangutanrepublik.org

Sumatran Orangutan (*Pongo abelii*). The Sumatran Orangutan Conservation Programme (Program), in collaboration with the Frankfurt Zoological Society (see disclosure above), the Indonesian Department of Forest Protection and Nature Conservation, The Natural Resources Conservation Office of Aceh (BKSDAAceh), the Sustainable Ecosystem Foundation (YEL), and the PanEco Foundation has released at least 290 rehabilitated, wild-born, confiscated, orphan Sumatran orangutans and three subadults who had been born in the Perth Zoo in Australia. Releases have occurred between 2003 and August, 2018, and are ongoing. The orangutans were quarantined and given thorough veterinary screening, and then then moved to either the Jambi Reintroduction Station or the Jantho Reintroduction Station for rehabilitation and preparation for release.

The Sumatran Orangutan Conservation Program also translocated wild orangutans who were stranded in tiny patches of converted habitat and were under imminent threat. These animals were taken to suitable forest, sometimes including Jantho and Jambi (see, for example, Sumatran Orangutan Conservation Programme website, news item dated 10 October 2017 and Sumatran Orangutan Conservation Programme Facebook post dated 31 August 2018). They are usually released without being taken to the quarantine center. Some of these are included in the numbers that are provided above.

One of the release sites for the rehabilitated orangutans is at the edge of the Bukit Tigapuluh National Park in the Jambi province of Sumatra, into which 180 orangutans had been released by 2016 (J. Siregar in Commitante et al 2015, Singleton website), and another is the Pinus Jantho Nature Reserve in Aceh province of Sumatra, into which 80 had been released by 2016 (Mukhlisin in Commitante 2015; Singleton website), 100 by November 2017 (Sumatran Orangutan Conservation Programme website, news item dated 10 November 2017), and 109 by March 2018 (Sumatran Orangutan Conservation Programme website, news items dated 5 February and 5 March 2018). Orangutans had been absent in these areas since the late 19th century. Bukit Tigapuluh and surrounding buffer zones have about 35,000 ha of lowland forest (Trayford et al. 2010), and Jantho and surrounding areas have an additional 7,500 ha. There has been some post-release monitoring at both release sites (eight infants are known to have been born), and survival was estimated to be 70% (Riedler et al. 2010, www.orangutan.org.au). A rehabilitated female who was released in 2011 was opportunistically seen with an infant at Jantho in 2017 (Sumatran Orangutan Conservation Programme website, news item dated 17 November 2017).

Newly arrived orangutans, most of which have been confiscated by Indonesian authorities, have for several years been quarantined at Batu Mbelin Quarantine Station outside of Medan, North Sumatra. (Some arrivals had been confiscated in Borneo and Java. When genetic testing revealed that they were Sumatran orangutans, they were sent to SOCP.) Each arrival at Batu Mbelin received a throrough veterinary screening, vaccinations, and treatment if necessary. Each individual was tattooed with a distinctive number and a transponder was implanted. Batu Mbelin is closed to visitation.

As of 2018, SOCP has received 360 ex-captives since 2011; some will never be able to be reintroduced back into the wild due to physical disabilities, e.g. total blindness. PanEco and YEL are funding the construction of "Orangutan Haven", comprising forested islands and night houses, at Batu Mbelin, primarily to provide lifetime accommodation for unreleaseable orangutans. Orangutan Haven will be open to public visitation.

After quarantine, releaseable orangutans were gradually given the opportunity for visual and then physical contact with other orangutans in socialization cages at the quarantine station. Some arrivals have been given the opportunity for social contact with other orangutans even during quarantine and early treatment. Most young arrivals were able to be placed in social groups. They were then moved to larger cages at either Jambi or Jantho. Young, friendly individuals were taken into the forest each day and directed toward natural foods. They were shown how to build nests and given opportunities to climb and locomote on natural vegetation. Less handleable individuals were given a variety of natural foods in their cages. More recently, operant conditioning and tutoring by skilled orangutans were used at Jantho to instruct young orangutans that had specific behavioral deficiencies.

The younger, nonaggressive orangutans were "released" by simply by allowing them to wander away from the cage area into the forest. Older or aggressive animals were taken to distant release sites. Both destination forests had been surveyed intensively before being chosen as release areas. Food was plentiful, but supplemental food was provided in some cases. As noted, there were no wild orangutans in these forests when the program began, but both Jambo and Jantho connect to other forested areas in the Gunung Leuser Reserve where there are wild orangutans. Outcomes are rarely reported for most of the SOCP reintroduced orangutans, but a few were monitored closely after release; data were collected on range use, diet, activity, social behavior, mortality, and reproduction. Riedler et al systematically monitored the post-release activity, habitat use, foraging, nesting, and social behavior of eight orangutans that had been reintroduced in Bukit Tigapuluh. They concluded that social contact with humans before and during the rehabilitation process slowed post-release adaptation and independence, and that contact with conspecifics facilitated post-release adaptation. Nonetheless, all eight were adapting successfully.

Three orangutans that were born in Australia's Perth Zoo have been reintroduced in this program. The first, a 13 year-old adolescent female, was reintroduced in 2006 and was thought to still be alive in 2016. The second, a seven year-old male, was reintroduced in 2011. He died due to snakebite after having lived for 17 months in the forest. The third, an eight year-old male, was reintroduced in 2016. All three had been reared by their mothers at the zoo, and had been prepared for reintroduction at the zoo by having opportunities for locomoting and building nests in live trees, socializing with other orangutans, and being presented with varying quantities of food to simulate the seasonal variation in food availability that occurs in the wild. Zoo caretakers even spoke some Indonesian words to at least the first of the orangutans to prepare her for communication by Indonesian trackers. These orangutans were strictly quarantined and immunized while still at the zoo, and they were quarantined and given further training after arrival in Sumatra. Supplemental food was provided.

I have argued that, from a conservation perspective, there is little need to reintroduce captive-born primates to the wild at this time (Beck 2016). Most suitable primate habitat is already at carrying capacity, and most primate rescue centers are already overcrowded with ex-captive or rescued individuals that could be reintroduced if habitat were available. This is especially true for orangutans. Also, wild-born primates generally have a better chance of survival than captive-borns.

In an e-mail exchange, Perth Zoo curator Leif Cocks noted that the reintroductions of these captive-born orangutans conformed strictly to the IUCN guidelines for the reintroduction of great apes, and that extra staff would be supported to specifically monitor the zoo-born orangutans and intervene if necessary. Further, the reintroductions allowed Perth Zoo to provide financial support for the Sumatran Orangutan Conservation Programme in general, in addition to the actual costs of releasing the zoo-born orangutans, and allowed the zoo to present the conservation status of orangutans to a broad general audience. Further, the "wild space" that is occupied by these three orangutans is not a truly significant part of the habitat that is available for rehabilitated wild-born orangutans.

Perth Zoo advertises itself as "the only zoo in the world breeding orangutans for reintroduction to the wild". This claim is probably true, but most zoos acknowledge that there is no need to reintroduce captive-born orangutans to the wild at this time. Instead they collaborate with other zoos to maintain genetically, demographically, medically, and behaviorally healthy populations of Bornean and Sumatran orangutans for public education and entertainment, and as a back-up if wild orangutans become extinct.

The sources appear to place about equal emphasis on two purposes for this program. One is to reestablish wild orangutan populations in areas in which orangutans have not lived for approximately 150 years. Another is to release confiscated, rehabilitated Sumatran orangutans and zoo-born orangutans to improve their welfare.

Conservation (Reintroduction, *sensu strictu*), Welfare (Rehabilitation)

References

Beck, B.B. 2016. The role of translocation in primate conservation. In S.A. Wich and A.J. Marshall, eds. *An Introduction to Primate Conservation*, pp. 241-255. Oxford, UK, Oxford University Press.

Cocks, L. and K. Bullo. 2008. The processes of releasing a zoo-bred Sumatran orang-utan (*Pongo abelli*) at Bukit Tigapuluh National Park, Jambi, Sumatra. *International Zoo Yearbook* 42: 183-189.

Commitante, R., Unwin, S., Jaya, R., Saraswati, Y., Sulistyo, F. and C. Nente (eds.). 2015. *Orangutan Conservancy 2015 Orangutan Veterinary Advisory Group Workshop Report*. wwww.orangutan.com

McKelson, J., UNU, M., and I. Singleton. 2016. Training ex-captive orangutans within the Jantho Reintroduction Station Aceh, Indonesia. Abstract of a paper presented at the joint meeting of the 26th Congress of the International Primatological Society and the 39th Meeting of the American Society of Primatologists, Chicago, IL, USA.

Riedler, B., Millesi, E., and P. H. Pratje. 2010. Adaptation to forest life during the reintroduction process of immature *Pongo abelii*. *International Journal of Primatology* 31, 647-63.

Sumatran Orangutan Conservation Programme Facebook page.

Trayford, H., Pratje, P., and I. Singleton. 2010. Re-introduction of the Sumatran orangutan in Sumatra, Indonesia. In P.S. Soorae, ed. *Global Re-introduction Perspectives 2010: Additional Case-Studies from Around the Globe,* pp. 238-242. Abu Dhabi, UAE, IUCN/SSC Re-introduction Specialist Group.

www.iansingletonsocp.com

www.orangutan.org.au

www.paneco.ch

www.sumatranorangutan.org

WHY SO MANY ORANGUTANS?

There is a stark and perplexing difference between the reintroduction of orangutans in Borneo and Sumatra, and gorillas, bonobos, and chimpanzees in equatorial Africa. Between 1962 and the present, 2,647 orangutans have been reintroduced, in 13 programs. (Palmer's estimate [in press] is 2,394, but her end date was 2016.) Between 1974 and the present, a total of 470 gorillas, bonobos, and chimpanzees have been reintroduced, in 31 programs. That's more than a five-fold difference! Why?

a) The additional ten years of orangutan data are not the reason; if we looked only at orangutan reintroductions since 1974, the number would be approximately 2,500.

b) If Palmer's count is more accurate, there is still a five-fold difference.

c) It's not sampling error; I used the same methods for all taxa. Two experts on African ape reintroduction who reviewed the first edition found no significant omissions. Two experts on orangutan reintroduction found no inflated numbers, and indeed suggested that my orangutan numbers might be low due to unreported reintroductions.

c) It's not an effect of the total sizes of the ape populations. African ape and orangutan abundance are both declining, but the number of wild African apes is at least five times that of orangutans.

d) The only plausible explanation is that more orangutans are being orphaned and arriving at sanctuaries for rehabilitation, and more orangutans have to be rescued and relocated. Between 2000 and 2006, 56 chimpanzees per year were taken in to eleven sanctuaries that were members of the Pan African Sanctuary Alliance (Faust et al 2011). Few if any were rescued and relocated without a stop at a sanctuary. This average does not include gorillas or bonobos, of which there may have been an additional 20. Bock (personal communication 2018) reported that all of the PASA sanctuaries combined took in only 30 African apes between 2016 and 2017. I don't have any firm figures on orangutan sanctuary intakes and rescues, but the number appears to have been greater than 200 per year. This would be consistent with Stiles et al's (2017) calculation of the numbers of orangutans lost in in-country trade, which was based largely on sanctuary intakes.

Further, Indonesian law has required that sanctuaries reintroduce their orangutans. I am unaware of any such laws in the affected African countries.

It is possible (but I think unlikely) that equal numbers of African apes and orangutans are being orphaned or rendered homeless by habitat conversion, but fewer of the African apes are taken to or rescued by sanctuaries, perhaps because they are killed, eaten, or exported.

Thus there have been significantly more orphaned, abused, injured, and disfigured orangutans entering sanctuaries or being rescued and relocated by sanctuary staff than there have African apes, and there has been greater pressure to reintroduce the orangutans.

The different numbers of sanctuary arrivals and rescues itself raises another "Why" question. I would propose that habitat conversion, selective logging, and hunting have been more more extensive, rapid, and more visible on Borneo and Sumatra than they have been in equatorial Africa. The population of Bornean orangutans alone declined by 100,000 between 1999 and 2015 (Voight et al 2018). But this is not simply a recent trend: Spehar et al (2018) demonstrate that the abundance, distribution, and behavior of orangutans have been strongly influenced by human hunting and other human activities for 70,000 years.

Thus the disproportionately high number of orangutans who have been reintroduced over the past 65 years is the culmination of an unusually tight association between orangutans and humans that has existed for millennia.

References

Bock, K. 2018. Personal communication (e-mail, 26 June).

Faust, L.J., Cress, D., Farmer, K.H., Ross, S.R., and B.B. Beck. 2011. Predicting capacity demand on sanctuaries for African chimpanzees. *International Journal of Primatology* 32(4): 849-864.

Palmer, A. In press. Kill, incarcerate, or liberate? Ethics and alternatives to orangutan rehabilitation. *Biological Conservation*.

Spehar, S.N., Sheil, D., Harrison, T., Louys, J., Ancrenaz, M., Marshall, A.J., Wich, S.A., Bruford, M.W., and E. Meijaard. 2018. Orangutans venture out of the rainforest and into the Anthropocene. *Science Advances* 4: e1701422.

Stiles, D., Redmond, I., Cress, D., Nellemann, C., and R.K. Formo. 2013. *Stolen Apes: The illicit Trade in Chimpanzees, Gorillas, Bonobos and Orangutans*. GRID-Arendal.

Voigt, M., Wich, S.A., Ancrenaz, M., Meijaard, E., Abram, N., Banes, G.L., Campbell-Smith, G., d'Arcy, L.J., Delgado, R.A., Erman, A., Gaveau, D., Goossens, B., Heinicke, S., Houghton, M., Husson, S.J., Leiman, A., Sanchez, K.L., Makinuddin, N., Marshall, A.J., Meididit, A., Miettinen, J., Mundry, R., Nardiyono, M., Nurcahyo, A., Odom, K., Panda, A., Prasetyo, D., Priadjati, A., Purnomo, Rafiastanto, A., Russon, A.E., Santika, T., Sihite, J., Spehar, S., Struebig, M., Sulbaran-Romero, E., Tjiu, A., Wells, J., Wilson, K.A., and H. S. Kühl. 2018. Global demand for natural resources eliminated more than 100,000 Bornean orangutans. *Current Biology* 28(5): 761-769.

CHAPTER 5
REINTRODUCTIONS OF GIBBONS AND A SIAMANG

Siamang (*Symphalangus syndactylus*). The Kalaweit Gibbon Reintroduction Program released an adult pair of siamangs onto the 1,000-ha Marak Island off the western coast of Sumatra in 2006. Pre- and post-release methodology can be assumed to be similar to that of the Kalaweit Program's release of rehabilitated agile gibbons in Borneo (see below). This source specifies that there was no provisioning and that the pair was alive but had not reproduced in 2007. No further details are provided.

The Fondation Le Pal Nature website states that another rehabilitated siamang pair had been released at an unspecified site in Sumatra in 2014. Chanee's blog states that this pair gave birth to an infant in late 2016 and that the infant was alive as of May 2017.

The Kalaweit Gibbon Reintroduction Project released three pairs of siamangs in an isolated tract of forest of unspecified size in western Sumatra in 2015. I am assuming that this is a different site than those of the 2006 and 2014 reintroductions, but near enough to be included in the same program. Siamangs had been hunted to extinction in the 2015 release area. Each reintroduced pair spent six months in pre-release enclosures at the release sites, which were between 1 and 2 kilometers apart. Two infants had been born by 2017, but only one survived. Supplemental food was provided at the pre-release enclosures "when needed". The siamangs were monitored daily. Nine siamangs were said to be living in this forest in 2018; the source of the additional two individuals is not specified. There were plans to reintroduce an additional five pairs of siamangs in the same area in 2018.

Welfare (Rehabilitation)

REFERENCES

Brulé, A. 2017. Kalaweit – The Founder's Dream. *IPPL News* 44(2): 22-23

Cheyne, S.M. 2009b. The role of reintroduction in gibbon conservation: Opportunities and challenges. In S. Lappan and D.J. Whittaker, eds. *The Gibbons, Developments in Primatology: Progress and Prospects*, pp. 477-496. New York, Springer Science+Business Media.

www.chaneekalaweit.com

www.fondationlepalnature.org

Yellow- (Golden-) Cheeked Crested Gibbon (*Nomascus gabriellae*). The Endangered Asian Species Trust's Dao Tien Endangered Primate Species Centre, in collaboration with the Vietnam Forestry Protection Department, rescued, rehabilitated, and released six yellow-cheeked crested gibbons into Vietnam's Vinh Cuu Nature Reserve in 2011. The Centre is within the 970,000-ha Cat Tien National Park, which already had a large gibbon population. Vinh Cuu, which is adjacent to Cat Tien, was chosen for the release because it had fewer gibbons than Cat Tien. The Centre is distinctive in having a 57-ha forested island that has large enclosures in which the gibbons get pre-release exposure to natural vegetation and natural foods. Release into these enclosures was not considered to be a reintroduction, but releases to the national parks were. Two families, each with an adult pair and an immature captive-born offspring, were released in Vinh Cuu. The adults had been illegally captured for the pet trade, confiscated, and rehabilitated. An additional adult pair was released in Cat Tien National Park in 2012. The paper (Kenyon et al 2015) that documents this release focuses on the design, deployment, and performance of radio collars for post-release monitoring, and provides little information on the history and pre- and post-release management of the gibbons. I assume that it is similar to those of the other six.

All gibbons at the center were quarantined and got complete veterinary screenings. They were treated for injuries or illness, and some individuals were disqualified from release for medical reasons. The large forested enclosures provided an opportunity for passive training in locomotion and feeding. Each gibbon family, and the adult pair, was placed in an acclimation cage at the release sites for up to two days before their releases. The adult males of the families, and each member of the adult pair were fitted with radiocollars and there was extensive post-release monitoring and supplemental feeding for up to one year. Research on radiotelemetry was a secondary goal of the releases of the families and a primary goal of the release of the adult pair. Three types of collars were tested and all seemed to perform satisfactorily, although territorial vocalizations ("singing") were absent with some types.

Cronin (2011) provided only short-term information on post-release outcomes of the families. I could find no further information, even though the males of each family wore radio collars. The 2012 adult pair was recaptured and returned to the rescue center.

Welfare (Rehabilitation), Research

References

Cronin, A. 2011. Rescued, rehabilitated, and released. *Ape Rescue Chronicle*, Summer, 2011: 2-3. (Retrieved from www.go-east.org).

Kenyon, M., Streicher, U., Jai-Chyu Peil, K., Cronin, A., van Dien, N., van Mui, T., and L. van Hien. 2015. Experiences using VHF and VHF/GPS-GSM radio transmitters on released southern yellow-cheeked gibbons (*Nomascus gabriellae*) in South Vietnam. *Vietnamese Journal of Primatology* 2(3): 15-27.

Pileated Gibbon (*Hylobates pileatus*). Mahidol University and the Krabok Koo Wildlife Breeding Center released three adult pairs of pileated gibbons into the 14,500-ha Khao Kheio-Khao Chompoo Wildlife Sanctuary in southeast Thailand between 2004 and 2006. The gibbons were presumably wild-born and had been captured illegally for the pet trade, and then confiscated and placed in the sanctuary. Details of this program are unknown because I was able to access only the abstract of this source. There was extensive post-release monitoring and systematic data collection. There was some post-release food supplementation, and several of the released gibbons were captured and re-released at other sites in the sanctuary.

Welfare (Rehabilitation), Research

References

Yatbantoong, N. 2007. Reintroduction of pileated gibbons (*Hylobates pileatus*): A study in southeastern Thailand. MSc Thesis, Department of Environmental Biology, Mahidol University.

Pileated Gibbon (*Hylobates pileatus*). Wildlife Alliance, in collaboration with the Cambodian Forestry Administration and the Apsara Authority, released an adult pair of gibbons in 2012 and another adult pair in 2015. The gibbons were presumably wild-borns that had been captured illegally and then confiscated and rehabilitated. The release site is an extensive forest surrounding the 40,000-ha Angkor Temple complex. Gibbons have lived in this forest in the past but had been extirpated by hunters. The first pair was acclimated in a large cage at the release site for seven months, and the second pair was likewise acclimated for 11 months. The source does not mention medical examinations or other forms of pre-release preparation, but the long acclimation periods in large cages imply some passive pre-release learning. They were monitored and given post-release food supplementation for more than one year. The first pair gave birth to an infant in 2014, and all five are thriving as of 2016.

Welfare (Rehabilitation)

REFERENCES

www.wildlifealliance.org

MERCY RELEASES

The destination sites of several of the reintroductions that are described in this history have been the grounds of Buddhist temples. Some of these may have been "mercy releases" (*fang sheng*), which in the Budddhist tradition is a compassionate act of freeing and providing a safe home to an animal. Some of these reintroductions may therefore have been religious releases. Some were commercial in that they were intended to increase tourism at the temples. Others were welfare releases, in which temples provided protected forest habitat into which rehabilitated primates could be reintroduced.

REFERENCES

Actman, J. 2017. A Buddhist tradition to save animals has taken an ugly turn. news.nationalgeogrpahic.com 23 January 2017.

Mueller's (Grey) Gibbon (*Hylobates muelleri*). The National Parks and Wildlife Office of the Sarawak Forest Department's Wildlife Rehabilitation Centre in the Semengok (Semenggok, Semenggoh) Forest Reserve released 87 confiscated or surrendered ex-pet Mueller's gibbons (66 males, 21 females) into the 650-ha Reserve between 1976 and 1988. There were no gibbons in the reserve at the time the program began, but Mueller's gibbons may have occurred there historically. There were "veterinary checks" but no other information on pre-release management is available. Some of the gibbons had not been weaned at the time of release. The period of "rehabilitation" in captivity was very brief in many cases. However, some of the adults were paired and held for longer periods. The gibbons were not provisioned or otherwise supported after release. They were released in close proximity to one another, which probably resulted in aggression. A 1988 survey located fewer than ten of the released gibbons living in at least three groups. "The results of the gibbon rehabilitation project at Semengok to date show that releasing confiscated gibbons to the forest can be highly ineffective, potentially inhumane, and has not contributed significantly to their conservation." (Bennett, pg. 163). The candidness in this short scientific paper appears to have helped stimulate the production of IUCN guidelines for gibbon reintroduction, and there have been improvements in gibbon rehabilitation and reintroduction throughout southeast Asia.

Reintroduction of gibbons and other endangered animals was discontinued at Semenggok in 1998, but a six month-old female Mueller's gibbon was surrendered at the center in 2000, and permission was given to begin a program for her rehabilitation and eventual release to the wild. She was quarantined and underwent a veterinary screening. She was taken out of her cage and allowed to explore natural trees almost every day. She gradually improved in locomotor ability, expanded the range in which she moved, and began to eat natural foods. She spent less time with humans and played with a wild long-tailed macaque that had also been released in the area. The description of this rehabilitation (Ramlee 2006) ended after 11 months, by which time the gibbon had not yet been truly reintroduced.

Welfare (Rehabilitation)

References

Bennett, J. 1992. A glut of gibbons in Sarawak – Is rehabilitation the answer? *Oryx* 26: 157-164.

Campbell, C.O., Cheyne, S.M., and B.M. Rawson. 2015. *Best Practice Guidelines for the Rehabilitation and Translocation of Gibbons*. Gland, IUCN/SSC Primate Specialist Group, Gland.

Ramlee, H. 2006. Re-introduction of gibbons in Sarawak, Malaysia. *Re-introduction News* 25: 41-43.

Javan Silvery Gibbon (*Hylobates moloch*). The Silvery Gibbon Project and its Javan Gibbon Centre in the Gunung Gede-Pangrango National Park in West Java released 12 silvery gibbons between 2009 and 2015. An adult pair was released in a small forested patch, called Patiwel, in 2009, another adult pair was released in a 9,000-ha forested area, called Mount Puntang of Malabar (owned by a state plantation company) in 2013, an adult pair and two captive-born offspring were released in the same area in 2014, and two additional pairs were released in the same area in 2015 (with the President of Indonesia in attendance). The 2009 reintroduction was actually conducted by the Javan Gibbon Foundation, which merged with the Silvery Gibbon Project in 2010. Both organizations have collaborated throughout with the Indonesian Department of Forestry.

The adult gibbons were all wild-born and had been captured illegally for the pet trade, confiscated, and rehabilitated at the center. All gibbons arriving at the center were given thorough physical examinations and were quarantined; only gibbons that were free of communicable disease were deemed suitable for reintroduction. The gibbons were held in a large cage in a forested area. They were fed some natural foods, and the cage was tall and large enough to allow brachiation. They were moved to acclimation cages at the release site for an unspecified period before release. The gibbons were monitored for up to two years after release, and the 2009 pair was studied intensively before and after release by Smith. All of the gibbons survived as of 2016. Smith provides thoughtful, data-based recommendations for criteria for reintroducing rehabilitated gibbons.

Welfare (Rehabilitation), Research

References

Smith, J.H. 2011. *Reintroducing Javan Gibbons (Hylobates moloch): An Assessment of Behavior Preparedness*. M.A. Thesis, Department of Anthropology, San Diego State University.

www.ekuatorial.com

www.silvery.org.au

Javan Silvery Gibbon (*Hylobates moloch*). The Aspinall Foundation Indonesia Programme and the Javan Primate Rehabilitation Centre released 12 silvery gibbons in six cohorts into the 8,000-ha Mount Tilu Nature Reserve in West Java, Indonesia between 2014 and 2017 (Javan Primate Conservation Project Facebook pages 28 February, 9 May, 10 November, 2015, 12 February, 21 April, 7 December 2016, 24 May, 12 December 2017). Ten of these gibbons had been born in the wild, captured illegally, confiscated, and rehabilitated. One had been born in the rehabilitation center and another, a female, had been born at the Perth, Australia Zoo, shipped to the Aspinall Foundation's Howlett's Wild Animal Park, and returned to Java for reintroduction. This individual rivals the Cayo Santiago rhesus macaques for being the most travelled reintroduced primate in history.

All of the gibbons were quarantined and had a veterinary screening. They were held in large cages at the center and were fed some wild foods. They were then moved to acclimation cages at the release site for several weeks. Some had implanted radio transmitters. They were monitored intensively for as long as four years after release, and were provided with some supplemental food. One of the females (apparently the captive-born) disappeared four months after release, thus necessitating the 2016 reintroduction of a single female as a mate for the surviving male. At least two infants have been born after release.

Although most of these gibbons were rehabilitated, confiscated individuals, these reintroductions are said to have been attempts to reinforce the silvery gibbon population in the Mount Tilu Nature Reserve. Research was also a purpose of the reintroduction.

A brief post on the Javan Primate Conservation Project's Facebook page, dated 13 August 2018, noted the reintroduction of one additional gibbon. No further details are provided. The accompanying photo appears to be of a silvery gibbon, but there is too little information to yet include this individual in the total number of gibbons reintroduced in Java by the Aspinall Foundation program.

Conservation (Reinforcement), Research

References

Adiputra, M.W. and S. Jeffery. 2016. Reinforcing the Javan silvery gibbon population in the Mount Tilu Nature Reserve, West Java Indonesia. Abstract of a paper presented at the joint meeting of the 26th

Congress of the International Primatological Society and the 39th Meeting of the American Society of Primatologists, Chicago, IL, USA.

Dipa, A. 2016. Javan Gibbon returned to forest around West Java's Mount Tilu. *The Jakarta Post*, 25 April.

Java Primate Conservation Project Facebook page.

www.aspinallfoundation.org

White-handed Gibbon (*Hylobates lar*). C. R. Carpenter captured wild white-handed gibbons at an unknown location and released 14 on the island of Cayo Santiago in Puerto Rico in 1939, only months after hundreds of rhesus macaques had been released on the same island (see rhesus macaques, below). I assume that Carpenter was trying to establish a free-ranging colony to supply gibbons to laboratories and to support behavioral research in a naturalistic setting. The gibbons probably had access to the same provisioned vegetables as the macaques. The gibbons attacked the primate caretakers. The first gibbon infant that was born on the island was killed by rhesus macaques. This gibbon reintroduction was thus terminated, and the gibbons were ultimately relocated to zoos in the United States.

Commercial, Research

References

Kessler, M. J. and R. G. Rawlins. 2016. A 75-year pictorial history of the Cayo Santiago rhesus monkey colony. *American Journal of Primatology* 78: 6-43.

White-handed Gibbon (*Hylobates lar*). The US Armed Forces Research Institute of Medical Sciences, under the auspices of the former Southeast Asia Treaty Organization and in collaboration with the US Delta Regional Primate Research Center, established a free-ranging gibbon colony on Ko Klet Kaeo island in the Gulf of Thailand in 1966 and 1967 by reintroducing ten pairs (or 21 individuals; the sources vary) to the island. The island had 24 ha of secondary forest. There were no other gibbons on the island (but see below), but there were crab-eating macaques.

The gibbons had been paired in a captive colony prior to release, and were provisioned with food and water after release. There was extensive post-release monitoring. Some of the released gibbons were aggressive toward other gibbons and humans, and others spent most of their time on the ground. Many had to be returned to the captive colony. Twelve gibbons died, disappeared, or were returned to the colony by 1970. The surviving pairs of gibbons established territories that they advertised by morning inter-group calling. The project was terminated in 1970, at which time four pairs, each with one offspring, survived. Some of the survivors were returned to the captive colony from which they were acquired. Three individuals were released again in Saiyok, Thailand (see below).

Soave (1982) states that eight additional gibbons had been released on Ko Klet Kaeo in 1966, before the 20 (or 21) that are described above. They were not provisioned after release. Five disappeared and three survived as a group several months later. Two of these attacked men and were captured and returned to captivity. The third died.

Welfare (Rehabilitation), Research. (Conservation was claimed to be a purpose but this was an introduction and the numbers of gibbons and the size of the release area were too small to ever establish a self-sustaining population.)

References

Bennett, J. 1992. A glut of gibbons in Sarawak – is rehabilitation the answer? 1992. *Oryx* 26(3): 157-164.

Berkson, G., Ross, B.A., and S. Jatinandana. 1971. The social behavior of gibbons in relation to a conservation program. In: L.A. Rosenblum, ed., *Primate Behavior: Developments in Field and Laboratory Research*, pp. 225-255. New York, Academic Press.

Brockelman, W. Y., Ross, B.A., and S. Pantuwatana. 1973. Social correlates of reproduction in the gibbon colony on Ko Klet Kaeo, Thailand. *American Journal of Physical Anthropology* 38: 637-640.

Brockelman, W. Y., Ross, B.A., and S Pantuwatana. 1974. Social interactions of adult gibbons (Hylobates lar) in an experimental colony. In: D.M. Rumbaugh, ed. *Gibbon and Siamang, Volume 3*, pp. 137-156. Basel, S. Karger.

Soave, O. 1982. The rehabilitation of chimpanzees and other apes. *Laboratory Primate Newsletter* 21(3): 3-8.

White-handed Gibbon (*Hylobates lar*). The Yale University Medical School, the International Psychiatric Research Foundation, the Rockland (New York) State Hospital, and other collaborating organizations released ten subadult white-handed gibbons on Hall's Island, Bermuda (0.6 ha) in 1970 and 1971. The gibbons had been imported, apparently illegally, from Thailand and were probably all wild-born. The purpose of this release was to study the effects of intracranial brain stimulation on the behavior and activity cycles of free-ranging gibbons. Electrodes had been surgically implanted in the brains of the gibbons, and they wore backpacks with batteries and equipment that allowed remote electrical activation of the electrodes and measurement of activity cycles. There is no information about pre-release preparation or acclimation, but the gibbons were given chow and some fruits and vegetables after release. Five of the gibbons were known to have died, some after bouts of brain stimulation, and one was recaptured and euthanized. The fate of the other four is unknown to me.

C.R. Carpenter (see above) was involved in this project to advise on normal gibbon behavior, but became critical of the research design and implementation. Two of Carpenter's students, retained to study the post-release behavior of the gibbons, resigned for similar reasons. The reference in the *International Primate Protection League Newsletter* (see below), while not peer reviewed, provides credible information that indicates that this project was scientifically, legally, and ethically flawed. Despite my commitment to objectivity in these reports, I could not allow this program's alleged deficiencies to pass unnoticed.

Research

REFERENCES

Anon. 1976a. The Hall's Island gibbon project. *International Primate Protection League Newsletter* 3:1-7.

Baldwin, L.A. and G. Teleki. 1976. Patterns of gibbon behavior on Hall's Island, Bermuda. In D.M. Rumbaugh, ed. *Gibbon and Siamang Volume 4*, pp. 22-105. Basel, S. Karger.

Delgado, J.M.R., Del Pozo, F., Montero, P., Monteagudo, J.L., O'Keefe, T.O., and N.S. Kline. 1978. Behavioral rhythms of gibbons on Hall's Island. *Journal of Interdisciplinary Cycle Research* 9(3): 147-168.

Eudey, A.A. 1991-1992. Captive gibbons in Thailand and the option of reintroduction to the wild. *Primate Conservation* 12-13: 34-40.

White-handed Gibbon (*Hylobates lar*). The US Armed Forces Research Institute of Medical Sciences (see above) reintroduced 31 white-handed gibbons from a laboratory colony into 22,500 ha of mature forest in Amphoe Saiyok, Kanchanaburi Province, Thailand in 1976 and 1977. The purpose was to dispose of the gibbons, which were no longer required for research. The entire colony was being closed and all of the gibbons were released. The release also provided an opportunity to study whether "captive-raised" gibbons (really, "captive-kept"; only five had been captive-born and captive-raised) could survive in a natural habitat. Three of the 31 gibbons had previously been released on an island (see above), and had been captured and returned to the colony when the island reintroduction program was terminated. A habitat survey was conducted in Amphoe Saiyok, and four release sites were identified that were thought to have adequate food and water, a low density of wild gibbons, and an absence of hunting. The gibbons were given extensive pre-release physical examinations and were treated for any communicable diseases. Sixteen of the released gibbons were placed in acclimation cages at the release site, from which they were allowed to leave and re-enter at will. Food was provided in the cages for 14 days. The other 15 gibbons were released without acclimation cages. All of the gibbons were monitored irregularly for up to 17 months after release.

Two of the gibbons repeatedly returned to humans. One was removed from the program and given to a group of monks. The other disappeared after being re-released. Two others were known to have died. Twenty-three of the gibbons disappeared within eight days of release. Some of these had been observed eating natural foods before they disappeared. The remaining four gibbons (two adult pairs) survived. Two were integrated into one wild group, and each of the other two was integrated into different groups. These four survivors were all part of the soft release (acclimated) cohort. Many of the released gibbons were heard to call normally with wild gibbons. One surviving male suffered severe bite wounds, probably from intraspecific aggression. He was captured, treated, re-released, and was one of the four that joined a wild group. The authors feel that some of the other gibbons that disappeared likely survived.

The 26 adult gibbons that were released were between eight and 12 years of age and thus were probably wild-born founders of the colony. The other five were less than one year of age and thus were probably captive-born in the colony.

Welfare (Rehabilitation), Research

References

Marshall, J.T. 1992. Gibbon release in Thailand. *Asian Primates* 2(1): 4-5.

Tingpalapong, M., Watson, W.T., Whitmire, R.E., Chapple, F.E., and J.T. Marshall, Jr. 1981. Reactions of captive gibbons to natural habitat and wild conspecifics after release. *Natural History Bulletin of the Siam Society* 29: 31-40.

White-handed Gibbon (*Hylobates lar*). The Gibbon Rehabilitation Project of the Wild Animal Rescue Project of Thailand, in collaboration with the Wildlife Conservation Division of Thailand's Royal Forest Department, released 13 adult and immature white-handed gibbons into an unspecified forested area of the island of Phuket and on several smaller islands around Phuket between 1993 and 1995. The gibbons were confiscated or donated ex-pets, and were released as family groups or pairs. Because the islands were too small and remote to support a gibbon population, these releases were seen as a form of "training" for ultimate release into larger forested areas. There was little provisioning or other forms of post-release support. Twelve of the 13 gibbons disappeared and were thought to have been killed by local loggers and dogs.

Welfare (Rehabilitation)

References

Osterberg, P., Samphanthamit, P., Maprang, O., Punnadee, S. and W.Y. Brockelman. 2014. Population dynamics of a reintroduced population of captive-raised gibbons (*Hylobates lar*) on Phuket, Thailand. *Primate Conservation* 28: 179-188.

Osterberg, P., Samphanthamit, P., Maprang, O., Punnadee, S., and W.Y. Brockelman. 2015. Gibbon (*Hylobates lar*) reintroduction success in Phuket, Thailand, and its conservation benefits. *American Journal of Primatology* 77: 492-501.

White-handed Gibbon (*Hylobates lar*). The Gibbon Rehabilitation Project of the Wild Animal Rescue Project of Thailand, in collaboration with the Plant and Wildlife Department of Thailand's Department of National Parks, released 31 white-handed gibbons into the Khao Phra

Thaew non-hunting area on Phuket Island (2,228 ha of forest) in Thailand between 2002 and 2012. My reading of The Gibbon Rehabilitation Project's newsletters, which are posted on the Animal Rescue Project of Thailand's website, shows that six additional gibbons were released in the same area of Phuket Island between 2013 and 2016.

The releases of these 37 gibbons are a continuation of an earlier program that released white-handed gibbons on Phuket and other small islands in the 1990s by the same administrative and management authorities (see above), but the 2002-to-2016 releases were conducted with an entirely different, soft-release methodology that conformed to IUCN reintroduction guidelines. Indeed, this is an excellent example of adaptive reintroduction management in response to poor outcomes and professional criticism, e.g. Cheyne 2009b.

The released gibbons in the new program were confiscated or donated ex-pets and entertainment animals, and infants born to them in the Project's captive colony. The published scientific reports cover only the 30 or 31 gibbons (sources vary) that were released between 2002 and 2013, during which eight families, two subadult males, and one single adult female were released. Wild gibbons had been hunted to extinction on Phuket. Pig-tailed macaques still lived in the area. The purposes of the releases were to rehabilitate these former captive gibbons and to reintroduce the species to Phuket. The authors state that conservation was the primary purpose but the numbers of gibbons and the release area were too small to establish a self-sustaining population. There was an extensive habitat survey prior to the releases. The gibbons had been quarantined upon receipt at the Project's captive colony and were given pre-release veterinary examinations. Many of the project's captive gibbons were deemed unsuitable for release for veterinary or behavioral reasons. Each qualified individual was paired, and it was a requirement the pair must have raised at least one infant in the colony before they were eligible for release. Some of the family groups spent three to four months in an acclimation cage at the release site, and some spent only five to seven days in an acclimation cage. The gibbons were fed in elevated baskets for up to two years after release, and many have been monitored for years. Gibbons that were ill, injured, or not adjusting well in the wild were recaptured and returned to the captive colony. The releases appear to have complied fully with IUCN guidelines. Nine of the released gibbons had to be recaptured, some as long as ten years after release, and were either released at another site or returned to captivity. Five of the released gibbons have disappeared. Twenty-two gibbons (or 23) survived on Phuket in 2013, some for as long as 12 years. Included in this number are 12 infants that have been born (one was second-generation). There is peer-reviewed scientific documentation of space use, reproduction, and social behavior the reintroduced gibbons.

Welfare (Rehabilitation), Conservation

REFERENCES

Campbell, C.O., Cheyne, S.M., and B.M. Rawson. 2015. *Best Practice Guidelines for the Rehabilitation and Translocation of Gibbons*. Gland, IUCN/SSC Primate Specialist Group.

Cheyne, S.M. 2009b. The role of reintroduction in gibbon conservation: Opportunities and challenges. In S. Lappan and D.J. Whittaker, eds. *The Gibbons, Developments in Primatology: Progress and Prospects*, pp. 477-496. New York, Springer Science+Business Media.

Osterberg, P., Samphanthamit, P., Maprang, O., Punnadee, S. and W.Y. Brockelman. 2014. Population dynamics of a reintroduced population of captive-raised gibbons (*Hylobates lar*) on Phuket, Thailand. *Primate Conservation* 28: 179-188.

Osterberg, P., Samphanthamit, P., Maprang, O., Punnadee, S., and W.Y. Brockelman. 2015. Gibbon (*Hylobates lar*) reintroduction success in Phuket, Thailand, and its conservation benefits. *American Journal of Primatology* 77: 492-501.

Shanee S. and N. Shanee. 2007. The gibbon rehabilitation project in Phuket, Thailand. *Re-introduction News* 26: 48-49.

www.gibbonproject.org

White-handed Gibbon (*Hylobates lar*). The Gibbon Rehabilitation Project of the Wild Animal Rescue Project of Thailand, in collaboration with the Plant and Wildlife Department of Thailand's Department of National Parks, released white-handed gibbons into an 814-ha non-hunting conservation zone in the village of Baan Chum Pee in the province of Chiang Mai, Thailand between 2014 and 2016. These were the same management authorities that released gibbons in Thailand's Khao Phra Thaew non-hunting area on Phuket Island (see above). However, Khao Phra Thaew was thought to have reached its carrying capacity for gibbons, and the site in Chiang Mai was chosen for continued releases of confiscated or donated ex-pets and entertainment animals. The Chiang Mai forest site, which was community-managed, is connected to the much larger Mae On national reserve forest. Some of the released gibbons had originally been released on Phuket island (see above) and/or lived at the Project's captive colony there. The methodology appears to have been the same at that of the Phuket reintroduction.

My reading of the The Gibbon Rehabilitation Project's newsletters, which are posted on the Animal Rescue Project of Thailand's website, shows that 15 gibbons were released in Chiang Mai between 2014 and 2016. One died, three have disappeared, and two have been recaptured. There has been one birth. However, issue 3 of volume 15 of the newsletter states that seven were known to survive at Chiang Mai in 2016. The newsletters are written in narrative form for popular audiences, and I may have misunderstood some of the facts.

Welfare (Rehabilitation)

REFERENCES

www.gibbonproject.org

White-handed Gibbon (*Hylobates lar*). The Wildlife Friends Foundation Thailand, in collaboration with Thailand's Department of National Parks and Mahidol University, released four white-handed gibbons (two wild-born and two captive-born) in 2012 and three more (two wild-born, one captive-born) in 2013. The release sites were in the 118,100-ha Lum Nam Pai Wildlife Sanctuary in Mae Hong Son Province in northern Thailand. Some wild gibbons were present in the forest. The gibbons underwent a pre-release veterinary screening. The first group spent more than a year in a large acclimation cage at the release site. Wild fruits and leaves were added to their diet before release. No details are provided on the pre-release preparation of the second group, but I assume it was similar to that of the first group. Both groups have been monitored periodically since their release.

Shortly after the release of the first group, the adult female stopped using her left arm. The group was recaptured, and the female was found to have bone cancer in her arm, which was amputated. The group was re-released after her recovery. The group was thriving as of November 2014. The female was locomoting well. The second group also appeared to be thriving after a year.

Welfare (Rehabilitation)

REFERENCES

Wiek, E. 2014. An IPPL-sponsored gibbon release in Thailand. *International Primate Protection League News* 41(3): 14-15.

Chapter 5: Reintroduction of Gibbons and a Siamang

Agile Gibbon (*Hylobates agilis [albibarbis]*). The Kalaweit Gibbon Reintroduction Program reintroduced a pair of young adult agile gibbons into the 118,200-ha Bukit Baka Bukit Raya National Park in Indonesian Borneo in April, 2000. This is listed as a separate program from the Kalaweit Gibbon Reintroduction Program's releases on the island of Mintin (see below) because the area of release is different. The Program's rehabilitation center is within the Bukit Baka Bukit Raya National Park. Wild gibbons are common in the national park. The female of this pair, a confiscated ex-pet, escaped from the rehabilitation center while she was being introduced to a rehabilitant male. The male was apparently released shortly thereafter. Sometime after release, he was attacked and injured by a wild gibbon, and he had to be captured and returned to the center. The female disappeared but reappeared in 2002 with a wild male. She and the wild male were monitored systematically until 2004. The pair established a territory and was self-sufficient as of 2004.

Welfare (Rehabilitation), Accidental (Escape)

REFERENCES

Cheyne, S.M. and A. Brulé. 2004. Adaptation of a captive-raised gibbon to the wild. *Folia Primatologica* 75(1): 37-39.

Cheyne, S.M., Chivers, D.J., and J Sugardjito. 2008. Biology and behavior of reintroduced gibbons. *Biodiversity and Conservation* 17: 1741-1751.

Agile Gibbon (*Hylobates agilis [albibarbis]*). The Kalaweit Gibbon Reintroduction Program released an adult pair of agile gibbons onto the 100-ha island of Mintin in the Kapuas River in Central Kalimantan, Borneo in January, 2003 and another pair onto the same island in December 2004. A survey of potential food trees was conducted before the release. Local people agreed to stop hunting and logging on the island. The gibbons, which presumably were ex-pets, underwent quarantine and veterinary screening, and lived in cages that allowed some natural locomotion. Their diet was supplemented with leaves. There is no mention of acclimation or post-release support. There was daily post-release monitoring for up to eight months. There were no other gibbons on the island but the released gibbons interacted with proboscis monkeys and long-tailed macaques. Both pairs survived as of January, 2005, 24 and two months respectively after release. Cheyne and her colleagues collected systematic data on pre- and post-release behavior of one of these pairs and on the pair released in Bukit Baka Bukit Raya National Park (see above). Cheyne notes that the 2003 pair was not provisioned after release, and that both animals were alive but had not reproduced by 2007.

Cheyne, in these publications, provides a number of outcome- and science-based recommendations for gibbon rehabilitation and reintroduction that, with Bennett's seminal article (1992), appear to have stimulated the production of IUCN guidelines for gibbon reintroduction (Campbell et al 2015). There have been subsequent improvements in gibbon rehabilitation and reintroduction.

Welfare (Rehabilitation), Research

REFERENCES

Bennett, J. A glut of gibbons in Sarawak – is rehabilitation the answer? 1992. *Oryx* 26(3): 157-164.

Campbell, C.O., Cheyne, S.M., and B.M. Rawson. 2015. *Best Practice Guidelines for the Rehabilitation and Translocation of Gibbons.* Gland, IUCN/SSC Primate Specialist Group.

Cheyne, S.M. 2005. Re-introduction of captive-raised gibbons in Central Kalimantan, Indonesia. *Re-introduction News* 24: 22-25.

Cheyne, S.M. 2006. Wildlife reintroduction: considerations of habitat quality at the release site. *BMC Ecology* 6: 1-8.

Cheyne, S.M. 2009a. Challenges and opportunities of primate rehabilitation – gibbons as a case study. *Endangered Species Research* 9: 159-165.

Cheyne, S.M. 2009b. The role of reintroduction in gibbon conservation: Opportunities and challenges. In S. Lappan and D.J. Whittaker, eds. *The Gibbons, Developments in Primatology: Progress and Prospects*, pp 477-496. New York, Springer Science+Business Media.

Cheyne, S.M. and A. Brulé. 2004. Adaptation of a captive-raised gibbon to the wild. *Folia Primatologica* 75(1): 37-39.

Cheyne, S.M. and A. Brulé (Chanee). 2008. The Kalaweit Gibbon Re-habilitation Project: rescue, re-introduction, protection and conservation of Indonesia's gibbons. In P.S. Soorae, ed. *Global Re-introduction Perspectives: Re-introduction Case-Studies from Around the Globe*, pp. 202-206. Abu Dhabi, UAE, IUCN/SSC Re-introduction Specialist Group.

Cheyne, S.M., Chivers, D.J., and J Sugardjito. 2008. Biology and behavior of reintroduced gibbons. *Biodiversity and Conservation*, 17: 1741-1751.

Agile Gibbon (*Hylobates agilis [albibarbis]*). The Kalaweit Gibbon Reintroduction Program released two adult pairs of agile gibbons, each with a dependent infant (which I presume had been born in the sanctuary), into the 1,500-ha Hampapak Reserve in Central Kalimantan, Borneo in 2007. I assume that the methodology is the same as the Mintin Island releases (see above), including systematic post-release monitoring. The article specifies that these gibbons were not provisioned after release. The gibbons were said to be alive as of 2007, but they had not reproduced. I could find no publications or website information on additional gibbon reintroductions by the Kalaweit program after 2007.

Cheyne unexplainably does not mention in this article (2009b) the pair that was reintroduced in Bukit Baka Bukit Raya National Park in 2000 (see above) or the pair that was released on Mintin Island in 2004 (see above).

Welfare (Rehabilitation), Research

References

Cheyne, S.M. 2009b. The role of reintroduction in gibbon conservation: Opportunities and challenges. In S. Lappan and D.J. Whittaker, eds. *The Gibbons, Developments in Primatology: Progress and Prospects*, pp 477-496. New York, Springer Science+Business Media.

www.wildlifeextra.com

Eastern Hoolock Gibbon (*Hoolock leuconedys*). The Hoolock Gibbon Translocation Project of the Wildlife Trust of India captured and translocated eight groups (22 individuals) of wild eastern hoolock gibbons that were struggling to survive in an area of severe habitat conversion and degradation. The site of origin was Dello Village and the destination site was the 28,200-ha Mehao Wildlife Sanctuary in Arunachal Pradesh, India. The translocations took place between 2011 and 2014. The release site was surveyed for habitat suitability, food availability, and density of resident gibbons before the translocations. The translocated gibbons were trapped as entire groups in the field, underwent veterinary screening, and were quarantined and treated if necessary. They were transported to the release site, held overnight, and released early in the morning. The releases were conducted during the fruiting season to ensure availability of wild foods. There was no supplemental feeding or other forms of post-release support. All of the gibbons were alive as of 2015.

Welfare (Rescue)

REFERENCES

Campbell, C.O., Cheyne, S.M., and B.M. Rawson. 2015. *Best Practice Guidelines for the Rehabilitation and Translocation of Gibbons*. Gland, IUCN/SSC Primate Specialist Group.

Western Hoolock Gibbon (*Hoolock hoolock*). Programme HURO released a bonded pair of young adult hoolock gibbons in the 4,700-ha Nokrek National Park in India in 2016. The gibbons had been confiscated as infants in 2009 and kept at the Sonja Wildlife Rehabilitation Centre. They were kept in an enclosure that provided opportunities for brachiation and were fed natural foods. They received an extensive pre-release veterinary examination, and were kept in an acclimation cage for four days. They stayed together for at least two months after release and established a small territory. They interacted with wild gibbons.

Welfare (Rehabilitation)

REFERENCES

Programme HURO Facebook page

www.fondationlepalnature.org

"Gibbon". The Sumatra Rainforest Institute released three confiscated "gibbons" into the South Tapanuli Forest in North Sumatra. The species involved in this program is not identified. The one photo that is included in the source appears to be of a siamang (*Symphalangus syndactylus*), which does occur in northern Sumatra. The three individuals had been rehabilitated at the Pusat Transit Satwa (PTS) Wildlife Transit Centre. There are no details on pre-release management, acclimation, post-release management, or monitoring.

Welfare (Rehabilitation)

REFERENCES

Sumatra Rainforest Institute Facebook site, posted 25 September 2016

CHAPTER 6
REINTRODUCTIONS OF ASIAN MONKEYS AND BARBARY MACAQUES

Douc Langur (*Pygathrix nemaeus*). The Douc Langur Foundation is said to have released an unspecified number of confiscated and rescued douc langurs "back to nature" in Vietnam. No further details are provided.

Welfare (Rehabilitation)

REFERENCES

Lippold, L. K. and V. N. Thanh. 2015. Vietnam's civil war on primates: Douc langurs and gibbons at risk. *International Primate Protection League News* 42(3): 21-23.

Silver Leaf Monkey (*Trachypithecus villosus*). Wildlife Alliance, in collaboration with the Cambodian Forestry Administration and the Apsara Authority, released three silver leaf monkeys into the 40,000-ha Angkor Temple complex in 2015. No further details are provided.

Welfare (Rehabilitation)

REFERENCES

www.wildlifealliance.org

Black Leaf Monkey (Cat Ba Langur) (*Trachypithecus poliocephalus*). The Cat Ba Langur Conservation Project, which is supported by the Allwetterzoo (Münster Zoo), translocated two adult female Cat Ba langurs from an isolated islet to the 26,300-ha Cat Ba National Park on Vietnam's

Cat Ba island in 2012. The islet had been separated from the larger island and other langurs by excavation for construction of a shrimp farm. The females were the only two langurs on the islet and had no opportunity to reproduce. Because the species is critically endangered, with fewer than 100 left in the wild, the two stranded langurs were translocated to reinforce the main population in the national park. The two langurs were given a veterinary screening and fitted with radiocollars after their capture (see below). They were placed in an acclimation cage in the national park, but, when found to be in good condition, they were released immediately. At least one of the females was observed to have copulated with a wild male. There were plans to translocate another isolated group.

The capture of these two langurs is probably the most dramatic in this history. Cat Ba langurs sleep in caves. Cages had been constructed in caves on the islet to trap the langurs, and a cave watch was established to actually trap the langurs in the cages when they came in to sleep at dusk. When the females were finally captured, the watchers called the translocation team, who rushed to the islet by speedboat, then travelled in a canoe, and finally hiked to the capture site, all in the middle of the night. The veterinarians donned climbing harnesses and used ropes and and pre-constructed rope and bamboo ladders to climb up 15 m to the entrance of the cave. The langurs had climbed up a further 4 m into a "chimney" in the cave but were safely anesthetized and lowered from the cave mouth in baskets. The whole process was then reversed and the team and the langurs arrived at the release site at dawn.

Conservation (Reinforcement)

References

Passaro, R. 2012. New home for two Critically Endangered langurs. *The Babbler*, 44: 4-5.

Delacour's Leaf Monkey (Delacour's Langur) (*Trachypithecus delacouri*). The Endangered Primate Rescue Center in Cuc Phuong National Park, Vietnam released three captive-bred Delacour's leaf monkeys (an adult pair and their subadult son) into the 3,000-ha Van Long Nature Reserve in 2011, and an adult pair (captive-born in the center) in 2012. The 2012 pair had already sired two offspring at the center before release. The 2011 release was said to be a "pilot project". The 2012 release was intended to develop suitable post-release monitoring techniques and evaluate factors that contribute to reintroduction success. The releases were approved by the Van Long Nature Reserve management board and the Ninh Binh Forest Protection Department.

Chapter 6: Reintroduction of Asian Monkeys and Barbary Macaques

The rescue center was supported by the Frankfurt Zoological Society. The langurs underwent veterinary screening and quarantine before release. They had been raised in large naturalistic enclosures, and had been fed leaves from local native trees. They were fitted with lightweight GPS transmitters. The langurs were acclimated at the release site for two days, during which they were fed fresh leaves. They were offered leaves and water after release but did not eat the food or drink. They were monitored for between six months and a year after release. The langurs that were released in 2012 may have interacted with some of those that had been released in 2011, and all are thought to have interacted with wild langurs in the nature reserve. One of the langurs is known to have survived for 409 days, another for at least nine months, and the third for at least four months. They did not stay together and ranged widely in different areas before settling into normally-sized home ranges. Community-based rangers were hired for protection of the area and community education programs were established.

Research

REFERENCES

Agmen, F.L. 2014. Conservation strategies for Delacour's langur (*Trachypithecus delacouri*) in Vietnam: Behavioural comparisons and reviewing a release. PhD thesis, The Australian National University.

Elser, S.K., Chung, N.H. and C.A. Brühl. 2015. Reintroduction of the 'Critically Endangered' Delacour's langur (*Trachypithecus delacouri*) into Van Long Nature Reserve, Ninh Binh Province, Vietnam. *Vietnamese Journal of Primatology* 2(3): 1-13.

Nadler, T. 2012. Reintroduction of the 'Critically Endangered' Delacour's langur (*Trachypithecus delacouri*) – a preliminary report. *Vietnamese Journal of Primatology* 2: 67-72.

www.go-east.org

Javan Langur (Ebony Leaf Monkey, Silver Leaf Monkey) (*Trachypithecus auratus*). Balinese rajahs introduced an unknown number of silver leaf monkeys on 451,400-ha Lombok Island, probably between 1500 and 1800. There are no details on methodology. There may have been more than one cohort. The langurs were probably brought by boat from Bali as gifts or as pets. The population apparently still exists. Crab-eating macaques had also been reintroduced on Lombok (see below), and still exist there today. It's not clear if the two species share the same habitat.

Unspecified

References

Heinsohn, T. 2003. Animal translocation: long-term human influences on the vertebrate zoogeography of Australasia (natural dispersal versus ethnophoresy). *Australian Zoologist* 32(3): 351-376.

Javan Langur (Ebony Leaf Monkey) (*Trachypithecus auratus*). The Wild Animal Rescue Centre released 54 rescued or confiscated rehabilitated Javan langurs in three cohorts into forested areas on Mount Hyang and Mount Semeru in Java. No release dates or details are provided. Wild langurs were not present at the release sites. The langurs were monitored after release and they were said to be surviving and reproducing in 2006.

Welfare (Rehabilitation)

References

Wedana M., Kurniawan, I., Arsan, Z., Wawandono, N. B., Courage, A., and T. King. 2013. Reinforcing the Javan langur population in the Coban Talun Protected Forest, East Java, Indonesia. *Wild Conservation* 1: 31-39.

Javan Langur (Ebony Leaf Monkey) (*Trachypithecus auratus*). ProFauna, Indonesia is said to have released more than 50 confiscated Javan langurs. No details are provided.

Welfare (Rehabilitation)

References

Anon. 2015a. IPPL's "Small Grants Program" has big impact. 2015. *International Primate Protection League News* 42(3): 10-14.

Chapter 6: Reintroduction of Asian Monkeys and Barbary Macaques

Javan Langur (Ebony Leaf Monkey) (*Trachypithecus auratus*). The Aspinall Foundation Indonesia Programme and the Javan Langur Rehabilitation Centre, in collaboration with the Indonesian Ministry of Forestry, released eight confiscated or rescued rehabilitated wild-born Javan langurs, and five of their rescue center-born offspring in the Coban Talun Protected Forest in East Java, Indonesia in 2012. The area of the release is approximately 28,000 ha. The purpose of the release was to reinforce the wild population, which had decreased due to habitat conversion and hunting. The area was estimated to be able to support more langurs. The langurs underwent veterinary screening and quarantine before release. Pre-release preparation at the rescue center included feeding the langurs leaves from tree species that were present at the release site. The langurs were acclimated in a cage at the release site for one week. All of the langurs survived until at least February of 2015, and there were at least two births. Post-release monitoring included collection of data on survival, dispersal, and reproduction. Wedana et al (2013a, b) document the release of this cohort.

A JPCP Facebook post of 4 April 2015 stated that four groups of Javan langurs (24 individuals) had been successfully reintroduced by the Aspinall Foundation since 2012. I assume that the 24 include the first 13, described above. A JPCP Facebook post, dated 9 May 2015, reported the release of of eight Java langurs (two born at Howletts/Port Lympne Wild Animal parks in the U.K.) in "April-May" 2015. I will assume that these are also included in the 24, although my total comes to only 21. Of the 24, I'm assuming that 17 were wild-born, confiscated, and rehabilitated langurs, five were born in the rehabilitation station, and two were born in the UK.

Subsequent Javan Primate Conservation Project (JPCP) Facebook posts suggest that there have been at least six additional cohorts of Javan langurs that were released by the Aspinall Foundation in East Java at Coban Talun and another site, the Kondang Merak protected forest. A website, gettyimages.com, stated that nine rehabilitated Javan langurs had been released by the Aspinall Foundation in Kondang Merak on 27 April 2015. A JPCP Facebook post dated 11 November 2015 reported the release of an unspecified number of Javan langurs "this week". A JPCP Facebook post of 8 April 2016 noted that a group (number unspecified) of Javan langurs had been released in the Kondang Merak on 18 March 2016. A JPCP Facebook post of 25 October 2016 reports the release of two groups of Javan langurs (number of individuals unspecified) in East Java. A JPCP Facebook post of 22 April 2017 notes the release of two Javan langurs, and a JPCP Facebook post of 24 May 2017 notes the release of two more Javan langurs in East Java. Using my convention of using "one" as the number released when the actual number is not specified, these releases would add 17 langurs to the previous 24, bringing the count to 41, but JPCP states that a total of 37 is said to have been released through March 2016 (Facebook post, 11 November 2015); I use 37 as the current total of Javan langurs that have been reintroduced in this program. A JPCP Facebook post of 28 November 2017 noted the transfer of four groups of Javan langurs, comprising 14 individuals, to East Java, stating that they would be released "soon". I could find no subsequent report of the release of these monkeys. As noted, some of the 37 released langurs had been kept and/or born at Aspinall's Howlett's Zoo in the United Kingdom. The JPCF Facebook post dated 31 December 2015 stated that 57 "Javan primates" (not just Javan langurs) had been rehabilitated and released through the end of 2015, and a post of 12 December 2017 stated that 113 "Javan primates" had been released by the end of 2017.

The Javan Primates Conservation Project Facebook page provides a stream of posts about rescues, confiscations, rehabilitation, quarantine, transfers to release sites, releases, and post-release observations of Javan langurs in East Java, and Javan gibbons and grizzled langurs in West Java. Some of the posts refer only to "primates" and some only to "langurs". The posts are unsystematic and nonspecific. They report only positive events. They are not adequate substitutes for objective, accurate, and detailed reporting. I don't have much confidence in the dates and numbers that are derived from the facebook posts.

Conservation (Reinforcement), Welfare (Rehabilitation), Research

References

Javan Primates Conservation Project Facebook page.

Wedana M., Kurniawan, I., Arsan, Z., Wawandono, N. B., Courage, A., and T. King. 2013a. Lessons learned from Javan gibbon and langur rehabilitation and reintroduction project in Java: Reinforcing the isolated Javan langur population in Coban Talun Protected Forest, East Java, Indonesia. *Folia Primatologica* 84(3-5): 344. (Abstract of paper presented at the 5th Congress of the European Federation for Primatology, Antwerp, Belgium 2013).

Wedana M., Kurniawan, I., Arsan, Z., Wawandono, N. B., Courage, A., and T. King. 2013b. Reinforcing the Javan langur population in the Coban Talun Protected Forest, East Java, Indonesia. *Wild Conservation* 1: 31-39.

www.gettyimages.com

Javan Grizzled Leaf Monkey (Javan Surili) (*Presbytis comata*). The Aspinall Indonesia Programme and the Javan Primates Rehabilitation Centre in West Java, Indonesia released eight grizzled leaf monkeys in the Mount Tilu Nature Reserve in West Java in 2015 (Javan Primates Conservation Project [JPCF] Facebook posts, 1, 9 April and 4, 9 May 2015). An infant was born to the group in June 2016. One of the eight may have been born in the Howlett's Port Lympne Wild Animal Parks in the UK. The purpose of the release was said to give rehabilitated primates "a second chance for a normal life". No further details are available but it is assumed that the methodology is similar to that of the Aspinall Foundation's release of Javan langurs in East Java (see above). An additional seven grizzled leaf monkeys were shipped from Howlett's Port Lympne to Java later in 2015 (JPCF Facebook posts 19, 24 November 2015). Two more grizzled langurs were said to have been released into the Mount Tilu Nature Reserve in mid-2016 (JPCP Facebook post, 24 May 2016), and four more in late 2017 (JPCP Facebook post, 12 December 2017). It is not clear if these six were from the UK shipment. Other JCPF Facebook posts during this period mention births, long-term survival, and integration of and with wild conspecifics. The JPCF Facebook post dated 31 December 2015 stated that 57 "Javan primates" (not just grizzled leaf monkeys) had been rehabilitated and released through the end of 2015, and a post of 12 December 2017 stated that 113 "Javan primates" had been released by the end of 2017.

The only accessible source of information on these reintroductions is the Javan Primates Conservation Project Facebook page. There is a stream of posts about rescues, confiscations, rehabilitation, quarantine, transfers to release sites, releases, and post-release observations of grizzled leaf monkeys and Javan gibbons in West Java, and Javan langurs in East Java. Some of the posts refer only to "primates" and some only to "langurs". The posts are unsystematic and nonspecific. They report only positive events. They are not adequate substitutes for objective, accurate, and detailed reporting. I don't have much confidence in the above dates and numbers.

Welfare (Rehabilitation)

References

Javan Primates Conservation Project Facebook page.

Proboscis Monkey (*Nasalais larvatus*). A population of approximately 300 proboscis monkeys was living in the Palau Kaget Nature Reserve, South Kalimantan. The reserve, which was on an island, had been seriously degraded by human activity and the monkeys' food was depleted. They were "starving to death". Eighty-four were translocated in two cohorts to nearby, unprotected islets in 1997 and 1998. Proboscis monkeys already lived on the islets. There is no mention of any pre-release preparation, acclimation, or post-release support. There was said to be post-release monitoring of the first cohort for five months and of the second for 16 months, but the only published result is that "few monkeys were seen". Thirteen are known to have died. Other proboscis monkeys (61) from Palau Kaget were sent to the Surabaya Zoo, where few survived. Only nine proboscis monkeys were found on Palau Kaget in a 1999 survey.

Welfare (Rescue)

References

Mejaard, E. and V. Nijman. 2000. The local extinction of the proboscis monkey (*Nasalis larvatus*) in the Palau Kaget Nature Reserve, Indonesia. *Oryx* 34: 66-70.

Barbary Macaque (*Macaca sylvanus*). An unknown number of Barbary macaques have been reintroduced in an unknown number of cohorts from North Africa to the peninsula of Gibraltar, which is a British Overseas Territory. The dates of the reintroductions are not known with certainty. The earliest written description of macaques on Gibraltar is 1704, but macaques may have been brought as pets and food to Gibraltar by Moorish settlers as early as the 8th century. Long mentions that they may have been brought to Gibraltar even earlier by Phoenicians, Carthaginians, or Romans. Some were added during and after World War II to reinforce the population, which was said to be symbolic of British military superiority. Mitochondrial DNA studies confirm that macaques were introduced to Gibraltar more than once, from both Morocco and Algeria. The same work suggests that macaques may have been reintroduced *from* Gibraltar back to Algeria, perhaps to control the Gibraltar population.

The genus *Macaca* originated in Africa, but *Macaca sylvana* is the only macaque still living on the African continent. All other macaques now live in Asia, some 5,000 km away. *Macaca sylvana* was actually widely distributed in what is now western Europe during the Pleistocene. The species once occurred naturally on the Iberian Peninsula but became extinct there about 30,000 years ago. Gibraltar is thus within the species' historic range, making all of these releases Reintroductions *sensu strictu*.

The Gibraltar macaques were strictly protected and provisioned by the British military in 1856, but their numbers declined. The population was reinforced with additional wild-caught monkeys from northern Africa at least three times. The population numbered 40 in 1987, but grew to more than 200 by 2000. There has been culling to control the size of the population over the years, including a large and controversial removal (and presumed killing) in 2003. There are now between 200 and 250 macaques living in five or six groups on Gibraltar. They are a major tourist attraction but they also harass people and steal food and handbags. Tourists have provided food to the macaques for decades. The macaques are now managed by the Gibraltar Ornithological and Natural History Society, which provides food and veterinary care and uses "fertility regulation" to control the growing population. Each of the macaques is identified and marked. This population is probably now maintained because of commercial value as a tourist attraction.

Although the Gibraltar monkeys steal food and are given food by tourists and the management organization, some probably could survive without provisioning.

Other (Politically Symbolic), Conservation (Reintroduction), Commercial

References

Candland, D.K. and S.L. Bush. 1995. Primates and behavior. In: E.F. Gibbons, B.S. Durrant and J. Demarest, eds. *Conservation of Endangered Species in Captivity*, pp. 521-551. Albany, NY, State University of New York Press.

Dore, K.M. 2017b. Ethnophoresy. In A. Fuentes, B. Bezanson, C.J. Campbell, A.F. DiFiore, S. Elton, A. Estrada, L.E. Jones-Engel, K.C. MacKinnon, K.A.I. Nekaris, E. Riley, S. Ross, C. Sanz, R.W. Sussman, and B. Thierry, eds. *The International Encyclopedia of Primatology*. Hoboken, Wiley-Blackwell.

Fa, J. E. 1987. A park for the Barbary macaques of Gibraltar? *Oryx* 21: 242-245.

Long, J.L. 2003. *Introduced Mammals of the World*. Collingwood, Victoria, Australia, CSIRO Publishing.

Masseti, M. and E. Bruner. 2009. The primates of the Western Palearctic: A biogeographical, historical, and archeozoological review. *Journal of Antrhopological Sciences* 87: 33-91.

Modolo, L., Salzburger, W., and R.D. Martin. 2005. Phylogeography of Barbary macaques (*Macaca sylvanus*) and the origin of the Gibraltar colony. *Proceedings of the National Academy of Sciences* 102(20): 7392-7397.

Schiermeier, Q. 2003. Primatologist rocks Gibraltar by quitting over macaque cull. *Nature* 426 (13 November): 111.

www.gonhs.org

Barbary Macaque (*Macaca sylvanus*). The Affenberg Salem zoo in Germany reintroduced four intact groups of Barbary macaques (224 animals) to the Atlas Mountains of Morocco in 1980, and an additional seven groups (338 individuals) to the same region in 1986. Most of these animals had been born at the zoo, where they had been kept in large, naturalistic exhibits that allowed them to locomote in trees and eat a variety of natural plants and animals. Each of the 1980 groups had at least one old wild-born male. Both the 1980 and 1986 cohorts were released in May, well before the Moroccan winter. There are no details on acclimation or on the protocol for post-release monitoring, but at least one group from each cohort was followed for at least six months. The monkeys were given provisioned food (but not water) for at least six months. The 1986 animals were released in a national park that had leopards.

Twenty-three of the observed 1980 macaques (mostly infants) had disappeared, and 14 infants had been born during the first year. A wild male joined one of the 1980 groups. One of the observed 1986 macaques died in the first year. Nine infants were born but all of them died. The observed macaques of both cohorts settled into stable home ranges within a year, and they became less dependent on provisioned food. The wild-born individuals appeared to adapt better than the captive-borns. However, none of the 1986 macaques could be located after December 1986.

Angst stated that Reinforcement was a purpose of this reintroduction, but the wild population of Barbary macaques was not threatened at the time. I conclude that the primary purpose was to reduce the zoo population by non-lethal means. The Affenberg Salem zoo, and two other similar macaque zoos under the same ownership, still exist but it appears that reproduction is now controlled.

Welfare (Non-lethal control), Conservation (Reinforcement)

References

Angst, W. 1991, Personal communication.

Barbary Macaque (*Macaca sylvanus*). The Barbary Macaque Conservation and Awareness (BMCA) group rescued and released four (one male, three female) young macaques after they had been confiscated from private owners and entertainers in Tangier, Morocco. First, two female infants were released near a wild group in the Ifrane National Park in the Middle Atlas Mountains in 2013. The group was thought to have been the natal group from which the infants had been poached. Both infants fled on release. Only one was recovered; the other was not seen again. The surviving young female was fed and rehydrated and then re-released the next day in a "howdy cage" near the same group. Wild adult males showed considerable interest in the female, which is consistent with the high degree of male alloparental behavior that is seen in this species. The monkey was re-released on the fourth day, picked up by a subadult male, and ultimately integrated into the group. Her behavior was monitored for 16 months and she was known to have survived for at least 18 months. BMCA also released a confiscated eight month-old male and a confiscated 18 month-old female into two separate groups in the same area. No howdy cages were used in these releases. Each infant was picked up by males and each appeared to have been integrated into the groups.

BMAC rescued and released an additional two year-old female, an ex-pet, in 2014. The release site was "in a very remote part of the forest in Bouhachem". There was no pre-release preparation or acclimation; she was simply allowed to run toward a wild group. Observers heard "calls of greeting" and no aggressive vocalizations.

BMAC acknowledges that it lacked resources to properly quarantine and prepare these animals before release and to properly support and monitor them after release. They also note that some confiscated adults were not released because they were habituated to humans. These adults were transferred to the Rabat Zoo. The Rabat Zoo macaque colony became overcrowded and could not accommodate the rescued 2014 macaque.

Welfare (Rehabilitation) Note: the authors claim that the primary purpose of the release was public education.

References

www.barbarymacaque.org

Waters, S., El Harrad, A., Amhaouch, Z. and B. Kuběnová. 2016. Releasing confiscated Barbary macaques to improve national awareness of the illegal pet trade in Morocco. In P. S. Soorae, ed. *Global Reintroduction Perspectives 2016: Case-Studies From Around the Globe*, pp. 216-220. Gland, IUCN/SSC Re-introduction Specialist Group and Abu Dhabi, Environmental Agency of Abu Dhabi.

Tibetan Macaque (*Macaca thibetana*). An acrobatic troupe performed in Hong Kong in the 1960s. Their show included three Tibetan macaques, a mother, father, and one (presumably) captive-born offspring. The acrobats were prohibited from further travel with their monkeys. They released the monkeys in the Kowloon Hills of Hong Kong. Rhesus macaques had been reintroduced in the Hills in 1913, and crab-eating macaques had been released there in the 1950s (I regard the Hong Kong reintroductions of crab-eating macaques, Tibetan macaques, and rhesus macaques as separate programs, see below). There were probably between 50 and 100 macaques in the population at the time of the Tibetan macaque release. There are no details of pre- and post-release management of the Tibetan macaques, and their origin is unknown. They were probably brought from northern China.

The macaques were provisioned by local people and tourists. There are no reports that the Tibetan macaques ever reproduced. The last Tibetan macaque is said to have died in 1995 (or 2008, sources vary).

Welfare (Non-lethal control)

References

Cheng, W.W. 2014. *A review of the management measures of feral macaques in Hong Kong*. Master's thesis, Department of Environmental Management, The University of Hong Kong.

Gumert, M. D. 2011. "The common monkey of southeast Asia: Long-tailed macaque populations, ethnophoresy, and their occurrence in human environments. In M.D. Gumert, A. Fuentes, and L. Jones-Engel, eds. *Monkeys on the Edge: Ecology and Management of Long-Tailed Macaques and their Interface with Humans*, pp. 3-44. Cambridge, UK, Cambridge University Press.

Tibetan Macaque (*Macaca thibetana*). The local government in Anhui Province, China drove a troop of 43 Tibetan macaques 1 km from their natural home range on Mount Huangshan to the "Valley of Wild Monkeys", a site at which they could be viewed by tourists, in 1992. The macaques were driven by a team who shouted and threw stones at them. There were no other macaques at the destination site. The macaques were heavily provisioned at the destination site but they nevertheless attempted to return to the origin site several times in the year after their relocation. They were driven back to the destination site each time. Ten individuals formed a fission group and successfully returned to the origin site in 1993, and another fission group of seven returned to the origin site in 1996. There were 33 macaques in one group at the destination site in 1996, 46 in 1999, and 32 in 2012. The troop survives today and continues to be heavily provisioned to assure their visibility to tourists.

The demography and social behavior of the original macaque troop had been studied for six years before the translocation. Compared to this baseline, infant mortality increased for several years after the relocation, possibly due to infanticide by adult males in the troop. Frequent provisioning in limited feeding areas after the relocation appears to have led to increased intragroup aggression and fissioning for several years, after which social dynamics appear to have stabilized and reproductive success has increased.

Commercial

References

Berman, C.B. and J-H. Li. 2002. Impact of translocation, provisioning and range restriction on a group of *Macaca thibetana*. *International Journal of Primatology* 23(2): 383-397.

Usui, R., Sheeran, L.K., Li, J-H., Sun, L., Wang, X., and J.P. Pritchard. 2014. Park rangers' behaviors and their effects on tourists and Tibetan macaques (*Macaca thibetana*) at Mt. Huangshan, China. *Animals* 4: 546-561.

Lion-tailed Macaque (*Macaca silenus*). The New York Zoological Society released a small group of lion-tailed macaques into "semi-liberty" in a forested area in its sanctuary on St. Catherines Island (Georgia, USA) in 1991. I was unable to determine the exact number that was reintroduced.

The animals were captive-born. At least some of the macaques were radiocollared. The purpose was to study ranging, foraging and responses to radiocollars among captive-born lion-tailed macaques in a simulated reintroduction. Because there were no plans to reintroduce this specific group to the wild, this is categorized as an introduction for Research. There were six males and two females when the troop was studied in mid-1992, and five males and four females when it was studied in 1996-97. The macaques were being provisioned with primate biscuits, vegetables, and fruits during the latter study, and they were observed feeding on natural vegetation in approximately 20% of scan samples. At least two young were born during the course of the project.

This project was discontinued in 1997, when there were (I infer) 11 macaques in the group. Seven of the 11 had become infected with Chagas disease after they handled and ate assassin bugs (*Triatoma sanguisga*), which are vectors of the disease (Pung et al 1998). Eight of the 11 macaques were sent to two unspecified institutions in 1997. The remaining three males were implanted with deslorelin to decrease aggression (Norton et al 2000). One of these died; the other two lived on St Catherines until at least 2000 but I was unable to learn more about their outcomes.

Research

REFERENCES

Dierenfeld, E.S. and C.M. McCann. 1999. Nutrient composition of selected plant species consumed by semi free-ranging lion-tailed macaques (*Macaca silenus*) and ring-tailed lemurs (*Lemur catta*) on St. Catherines Island, Georgia, U.S.A. *Zoo Biology* 18: 481-494.

Fitch-Snyder, H. and J. Carter. 1993. Tool use to acquire drinking water by free-ranging lion-tailed macaques (*Macaca silenus*). *Laboratory Primate Newsletter* 32: 1-2.

Lindburg, D. G. and L. Gledhill. 1992. Captive breeding and conservation of lion-tailed macaques. *Endangered Species Update* 10(1): 1-4.

Norton, T.M., Penfold, L.M., Lessnau, B., Jochle, W., Staaden, S.L., Joliffe, A., Bauman, J.E., and J. Spratt. 2000. Long-acting deslorelin implants to control aggression in male lion-tailed macaques (*Macaca silenus*). Proceedings of the annual conference of the International Association for Aquatic Animal Medicine https://www.vin.com/apputil/content/defaultadv1.aspx?pId=11125

Pung, O.J., Spratt, J., Clark, C.G., Norton, T.M., and J. Carter. 1998. Trypanasoma cruzi infection of free-ranging lion-tailed macaques (Macaca silenus) and ring-tailed lemurs (Lemur catta) on St. Catherine's [sic] Island, Georgia, USA. *Journal of Zoo and Wildlife Medicine* 29(1): 25-30.

Bonnet Macaque (*Macaca radiata*). The Bangalore (India) City Corporation, the local forest department, the World Wildlife Fund, and the University of Agricultural Sciences in Bangalore translocated 718 bonnet macaques from Bangalore to the 647-ha Savandurga forest reserve, approximately 65 km away, in 1975. The monkeys had been trapped in residential areas of the city where they were eating cultivated fruits and vegetables. Citizens had begun to shoot the monkeys. Relocating the monkeys saved them from being shot and was a more religiously appropriate resolution. Trappers attempted to catch all or most members of a troop, and the monkeys were marked with indelible paint so that any that returned could be identified. Savandurga had a variety of trees that provided natural food for the monkeys, and there were only a few bonnet macaques there. None of the monkeys that were translocated to Savandurga returned to the capture sites, although some that had been moved earlier to a different destination site that was only 10 km did return. There was some post-release monitoring, although the duration and frequency are not specified.

Welfare (Non-lethal Control), Religious

References

Anon. 1976b. City monkeys moved. *The International Primate Protection League Newsletter* 3(1): 11.

Sulawesi (Crested) Black Macaque (*Macaca nigra*). Many sources, including the three cited here, conclude that an unknown number of black macaques were reintroduced onto Bacan (formerly Batchian, also Batjan) Island in Indonesia sometime before the 1830s. The island is approximately 300 km east of the main island of Sulawesi, which is presumed to be the site of origin. Examination of superficial morphological characteristics led Hamada et al (1994) to conclude that the Bacan macaques are descended from the Sulawesi population. It is assumed that traders, not conservationists, first brought the macaques to Bacan, probably as a source of food or as a gift to local political leaders. Thus, although black macaques are now classified as Endangered, I consider the purpose of this reintroduction to have been Commercial.

There have been rumors that black macaques were also introduced on the nearby island of Mandioli, but these could not be confirmed and there are no reports of monkeys on Mandioli now.

There is some conflict on Bacan between the monkeys and humans, but habitat conversion, mainly logging, is the chief threat to the macaques. A few are taken as pets. The highest-density population of black macaques on Bacan lives in the 23,000-ha Gunung Sibela Nature Reserve, where there may be as many as 40,000 individuals. Black macaques were thought to have once been more widely distributed on the 171,000-ha island.

We do not know the number(s), cohorts, or date(s) of this reintroduction. We are assuming that it was an Introduction, and that the monkeys were introduced as a food supply for traders plying the Spice Islands. This makes its purpose Commercial, although it may have been a political gift. There seems to be no question of its success.

Commercial

References

de Vos, A., Manville, R.H., and R.G. Van Gelder. 1956. Introduced mammals and their influence on native biota. *Zoologica* 41(4): 163-194.

Hamada, Y., Oi, T., and T. Watanabe. 1994. *Macaca nigra* on Bacan Island, Indonesia: Its morphology, distribution, and present habitat. *International Journal of Primatology* 15(3): 487-492.

Long, J.L. 2003. *Introduced Mammals of the World*. Collingwood, Victoria, Australia, CSIRO Publishing.

Rosenblum, B., O'Brien, T.C., Kinnaird, M., and J. Supriatna. 1998. Population densities of Sulawesi crested black macaques (*Macaca nigra*) on Bacan and Sulawesi, Indonesia: Effects of habitat disturbance and hunting. *American Journal of Primatology* 44: 89-106.

Pig-tailed Macaque (*Macaca nemestrina*). An unspecified organization(s) reintroduced an unspecified number of pig-tailed macaques in an unspecified number of cohorts to sites in the Andaman Islands. The date(s) and purpose(s) of these Introductions are unknown. Long states that the introduced macaques originated from India, but de Vos et al say Burma (now Myanmar).

Unspecified

References

de Vos, A., Manville, R.H., and R.G. Van Gelder. 1956. Introduced mammals and their influence on native biota. *Zoologica* 41(4): 163-194.

Long, J.L. 2003. *Introduced Mammals of the World*. Collingwood, Victoria, Australia, CSIRO Publishing.

Pig-tailed Macaque (*Macaca nemestrina*). An unspecified organization reintroduced an unspecified number of pig-tailed macaques in an unspecified number of cohorts to Cayo Cantiles, an island in the Canarreos Archipelago of Cuba in approximately 1984. The purpose of the reintroduction was to establish a free-ranging colony from which individuals could be removed for biomedical research. Dore cites Escobar ((1995) in saying that the site of origin was in Laos (I was unable to access the Escobar book). The macaques had been quarantined on Cayo Cantilles before release, and they were provisioned after release. Vervets were also reintroduced on the same island at approximately the same time (see below). Vervets, but not pig-tailed macaques were observed in a 1990 census (González et al 1994).

Commercial

REFERENCES

Borroto-Páez, R. 2009. Invasive mammals in Cuba: an overview. *Biological Invasions* 11: 2279-2290.

Dore, K.M. 2017b. Ethnophoresy. In A. Fuentes, B. Bezanson, C.J. Campbell, A.F. DiFiore, S. Elton, A. Estrada, L.E. Jones-Engel, K.C. MacKinnon, K.A.I. Nekaris, E. Riley, S. Ross, C. Sanz, R.W. Sussman, and B. Thierry, eds. *The International Encyclopedia of Primatology*. Hoboken, Wiley-Blackwell.

Escobar, T.R. 1995. *Isla de la Juventud: Introducidos por Causa Deliberadas*. Havana, Editorial Cientifico-Técnica.

González, A., Manójina, N. and A. Hernández. 1994. Mamíferos del Archipiélago de Camagüey, Cuba. *Avicennia* 1: 51-56.

Pig-tailed Macaque (*Macaca nemestrina*). The Pusat Penyelamatan Satwa, Lampung rescue center released an unspecified number of confiscated pig-tailed macaques into the 11,000-ha Batutegi Reserve in Sumatra, Indonesia in 2006. This is said to have been done to relieve overcrowding at the center, and to have been the organization's first release. No other details are available.

Welfare (Rehabilitation)

References

Collins, R. and K. A. I. Nekaris. 2008. Release of greater slow lorises, confiscated from the pet trade, to Batutegi Protected Forest, Sumatra, Indonesia. In P.S. Soorae, ed. *Global Re-introduction Perspectives: Re-introduction Case-Studies from Around the Globe*, pp.192-196. Abu Dhabi, UAE, IUCN/SSC Re-introduction Specialist Group.

Pig-tailed Macaque (*Macaca nemestrina*). The International Animal Rescue program (IAR) released six pig-tailed macaques in two groups in the 11,000-ha Batutegi Protected Forest in Sumatra in 2017. The forest had been surveyed to ensure that there would be enough suitable food for the monkeys. All of the macaques had been wild-born, captured for the pet trade, and then surrendered or confiscated. The macaques had been quarantined and rehabilitated in IAR's primate rehabilitation center in Bogor, West Java. During rehabilitation, the monkeys were provided with foods that they would find in their natural habitat, and allowed to locomote on natural vegetation in large enclosures. The monkeys were acclimated at the release site for three days. There was post-release monitoring of unspecified duration. The primary purpose of this reintroduction was to improve the welfare of the macaques, but a secondary purpose was to "restore their ecological functions in the natural habitat".

Welfare (Rehabilitation), Conservation

References

www.internationalanimalrescue.org

Rhesus Macaque (*Macaca mulatta*). The government of Hong Kong reintroduced an unspecified number of rhesus monkeys in an unspecified number of cohorts in the Kowloon Hills in 1913. The purpose of the reintroduction was to maintain the water quality of the newly opened Kowloon Reservoir. Specifically, authorities feared that the water could be poisoned by strychnos fruit, which is toxic to humans but eaten readily by rhesus macaques. Rhesus monkeys had lived

Chapter 6: Reintroduction of Asian Monkeys and Barbary Macaques

in Kowloon in the 1800s, making this a Reintroduction *sensu strictu*. There are no details of pre- and post-release management, and the origin of the macaques is unknown. They were probably brought from elsewhere in China.

The population grew quickly, to 100 in the 1980s, 113 in 1981, 72 in 1987, 600 in 1991, 690 in 1994, 700 in 2000, and 2000 in 2018. There are now approximately 2,000 monkeys in 30 polyspecific groups in Hong Kong. The population currently includes rhesus macaques (65.3%), crab-eating macaques (*M. fasicularis*) that were reintroduced in the 1950s (see below) (2.2%), and rhesus-crab-eater hybrids (32.3%). The Kowloon macaques live in the Kam Shan, Lion Rock, and Shing Mun Country Parks and the Tai Po Kai Nature Reserve. The four protected areas comprise approximately 2,530 connected hectares.

The macaques were heavily provisioned by local people and tourists, but a ban on public feeding was instituted in 1999. Cheng found that the number of people feeding macaques and the amount of provisioned food had decreased by approximately 90% by 2014. There have been ambitious and systematic attempts at contraception. Cheng found that abundance in heterosexual groups decreased by approximately 10% between 2010 and 2012, and that the birth rate decreased from 69% to 30% between 2008 and 2012. Some of the macaques are hunted and trapped for their meat.

Three Tibetan macaques (*M. thibetena*) were reintroduced in the 1960s (see above), but the last of these died in 1995 (or 2008, sources vary) without having interbred. There are unsubstantiated reports that Japanese macaques (*M. fuscata*), pig-tailed macaques (*M. nemestrina*), and Formosan macaques (*M. tonkeana*) were reintroduced in Hong Kong over the years. Southwick and Southwick reported that five Japanese macaques were present in 1981. I find it hard to believe that Charles Southwick would have misidentified macaques, but the Japaneses macaques may have been Tibetan macaques. Southwick and Manry did not see Japanese macaques in 1987, and Japanese macaques are not reported to be present in the Kowloon Hills today. I include the Hong Kong rhesus macaques, crab-eating macaques and Tibetan macaques, but not Japanese macaques, as separate reintroduction programs.

Commercial

REFERENCES

Cheng, W.W. 2014. *A review of the management measures of feral macaques in Hong Kong*. Master's thesis, Department of Environmental Management, The University of Hong Kong.

Dore, K.M. 2017b. Ethnophoresy. In A. Fuentes, B. Bezanson, C.J. Campbell, A.F. DiFiore, S. Elton, A. Estrada, L.E. Jones-Engel, K.C. MacKinnon, K.A.I. Nekaris, E. Riley, S. Ross, C. Sanz, R.W. Sussman, and B. Thierry, eds. *The International Encyclopedia of Primatology*. Hoboken, Wiley-Blackwell.

Gumert, M. D. 2011. "The common monkey of southeast Asia: Long-tailed macaque populations, ethnophoresy, and their occurrence in human environments. In M.D. Gumert, A. Fuentes, and L. Jones-Engel, eds. *Monkeys on the Edge: Ecology and Management of Long-Tailed Macaques and their Interface with Humans*, pp3-44. Cambridge, UK, Cambridge University Press.

Southwick, C.H. and K.L. Southwick. 1983. Polyspecific groups of macaques on the Kowloon Peninsula, New Territories, Hong Kong. *American Journal of Primatology* 5: 17-24.

Southwick, C.H. and D. Manry. 1987. Habitat and population changes for the Kowloon macaques. *Primate Conservation* 8: 48-49.

Wong, C.L. and I-H. Ni. 2000. Population dynamics of the feral macaques in the Kowloon Hills of Hong Kong. *American Journal of Primatology* 50: 53-66.

Wong, C.L. and G. Chow. 2004. Preliminary results of trial contraceptive treatment with SpayVac™ on wild monkeys in Hong Kong. *Hong Kong Biodiversity* 6: 13-16.

www.afcd.gov.hk

Rhesus Macaque (*Macaca mulatta*). In 1933 (or 1938, the cited dates vary), Colonel Tooey released four or six rhesus macaques (sources vary) on an island in the Lauderdale (Silver) River, near Ocala, Florida. Tooey (Colonel was his first name, not a title) had bought the monkeys from a New York animal dealer. The purpose of this reintroduction was to enhance a tourist attraction known as "Jungle Cruises". Tooey dredged the river to create an island on which he released the macaques, assuming that they could not swim to the mainland, which they did shortly after release. As Phoebus (1989, pg 158) later said, "rhesus monkeys are excellent swimmers". There were approximately ten macaques by the late 1940s. They were being provisioned to ensure that they would be visible to tourists. Tooey released an additional six macaques in 1948. There is also a report that six rhesus macaques that had escaped from a tourist attraction in Titusville, Florida were added to the Silver Springs population in the 1980s (see below). No details on the source of the 1948 macaques or on pre- or post-release management of the 1948 and 1980s cohorts are available, but I assume that all of these monkeys were provisioned and sighted frequently.

Chapter 6: Reintroduction of Asian Monkeys and Barbary Macaques

There were 78 macaques living in two groups on both sides of the Silver River in 1968, at least 170 in five groups in 1981, and more than 300 by 1984. Some of the macaques had moved downstream on the Silver River to the Ocklawaha River. Jungle Cruises was included into the Silver Springs State Park (1,889 ha) in 1985. There has been continuing tension regarding the likely ecological damage caused by the invasive omnivorous macaques. They also carry the Herpes B virus. The monkeys carry the virus nonsymptomatically, but bites, scratches, or body fluid splashes can cause fatal infections in humans. However, there has never been a documented case of Herpes B infection among staff or visitors to the park. Nonetheless, trapping began at Silver Springs in 1984. By 2012, trappers had removed more than 1,500 macaques, apparently with permission of the Florida Fish and Wildlife Conservation Commission. These monkeys were sold to dealers and laboratories for use in biomedical research. Some of the captured macaques were sent to a zoo. Some females were hysterectomized.

There were 66 macaques in four groups in Silver Springs State Park in 2011 (Gottschalk, in Riley and Wade 2016). By 2013, there were approximately 200 macaques living in four groups in forested areas of the state park, and others have been observed as far as 41 miles (64 km) away to the east, and more recently to the west, along the Gulf of Mexico coast, as far south as Sarasota. Macaques are sometimes killed crossing highways in the vicinity of the state park. I don't know if these are dispersing animals that are descended from Tooey's founders, or of rhesus that were introduced at other times and places. The Tooey release has resulted in a self-sustaining population of this exotic species that could exist without support by humans. Post-release provisioning has been systematic and heavy during some times and prohibited at others. In 2013, tourists were providing only small amounts of food on a regular basis. The small number of original founders suggests that there is little genetic variation in the population even with the release of the second cohort in 1948.

The Herpes B issue was reingnited by a paper published in 2018 (Wisely et al 2018) that recalled that blood samples that had been taken between 2000 and 2012 from macaques living along the Oklawaha River had indicated that 25% of the monkeys were infected with Herpes B. The paper also reported that saliva and fecal samples taken in the state park during the Fall reproductive season in 2015 indicated a shedding rate of 4% to 14%, but that the virus was not being shed during the following Spring and Summer. The authors hypothesized that the seasonal difference in the 2015-2016 sampling was due to stress related to the Fall reproductive competition. They reiterate that while humans have been bitten or scratched by the macaques, there have been no reported cases of humans being infected with Herpes B by the Silver Springs rhesus macaques, or by other wild rhesus monkeys worldwide (this could be due to under-reporting). The authors conclude that Herpes B in the Silver Springs monkeys "should be considered a low-incidence,

- 167 -

high-consequence risk, and adequate public health measures should be taken". A media storm followed, sensationalizing the public health hazards, and debating the logistical challenges and ethical considerations of removal of the macaques. Silver Springs park officials frequently close off parts of the park where people and monkeys can approach each other closely.

These rhesus monkeys are often seen diving from trees up to 10 m into the water, apparently in play and perhaps to cool themselves in hot temperatures. They also retrieve food from the river bottom by diving approximately a meter under water.

Commercial, Accidental (Escape)

REFERENCES

Anderson, C.J., Hostetler, M.E., Sieving, K.E., and S.A. Johnson. 2016a. Predation of artificial nests by introduced rhesus macaques (*Macaca mulatta*) in Florida, USA. *Biological Invasions*. Published online 10 June 2016

Anderson, C.J., Johnson, S.A., Hostetler, M.E., and M.G. Summers. 2016b. *History and Status of Introduced Rhesus Macaques (Macaca mulatta) in Silver Springs State Park, Florida*. Document # WEC367, Department of Wildlife Ecology and Conservation, UF/IFAS (University of Florida/Institute of Food and Agricultural Sciences) Extension Service.

Anderson, C.J., Hostetler, M.E., and S.A. Johnson. 2017. History and status of introduced non-human populations in Florida. *Southeastern Naturalist* 16(1): 19-36.

Floehe, S. 2010. Monkey business. *Ocala Style Magazine* 6 July 2010.

Florida Fish and Game Commission website: *myfwc.com/wildlifehabitats/nonnatives/mammals*

Gillespie, R. 2016. Monkeys continue to explore beyond state park near Ocala. *Orlando Sentinel*, 27 December 2015.

Maples, W.R., Brown, A.B., and P.M. Hutchens. 1976. Introduced monkey populations at Silver Springs, Florida. *Florida Anthropologist* 29(4): 133-136.

Phoebus, E.C. 1989. The FDA rhesus breeding colony at La Parguera, Puerto Rico. *Puerto Rico Health Sciences Journal*, 1989 8:157-158.

Riley, E.P. and T.W. Wade. 2016. Adapting to Florida's riverine woodlands: the population status and feeding ecology of the Silver River rhesus macaques and their interface with humans. *Primates* 57: 195-210.

Wisely, S.M., Sayler, K.A., Anderson. C., Boyce, C.L., Klegarth, A.R. and S.A. Johnson. 2018. Macacine

Herpesvirus 1 antibody prevalence and DNA shedding among invasive rhesus macaques, Silver Springs State Park, Florida, USA. *Emerging Infectious Diseases.* 2018: 24(2):345-351.

Wolfe, L.D. 2002. Rhesus macaques: A comparative study of two sites, Jaipur, India and Silver Springs, Florida. In A. Fuentes and L.D. Wolfe, eds. *Primates Face to Face: Conservation Implications of Human – Nonhuman Primate Interconnections*, pp. 310-330. Cambridge, UK, Cambridge University Press.

Wolfe, L.D. and E.H. Peters. 1987. History of the free-ranging rhesus monkeys (*Macaca mulatta*) of Silver Springs. *Florida Scientist* 50: 234-245.

www.baynews9.com Monkey spotted in Clearwater is latest animal sighting. 4 November 2016.

Rhesus Macaque (*Macaca mulatta*). The School of Tropical Medicine of the University of Puerto Rico reintroduced 409 Indian rhesus monkeys to Cayo Santiago island off the coast of Puerto Rico in 1938. This reintroduction is unique in many ways and was successful. It is well documented in the references cited below, from which this account has been derived.

A central figure in this reintroduction was Dr. C. Ray Carpenter, who was a founder of primatology (and one of my heroes as a graduate student). During his career, Carpenter studied the behavior and ecology of wild gibbons, orangutans, howler monkeys, and spider monkeys. He also became concerned about the use of Indian rhesus macaques in American biomedical laboratories. Approximately 13,000 rhesus macaques had been imported annually from India to the United States in 1936, 1937, and 1938 for biomedical research. Carpenter suspected that wild populations could not support such offtake. His hope was to establish a free-ranging rhesus population near the United States from which monkeys could be harvested for laboratory research, and would itself be large enough to support studies of sexual and social behavior. He also wanted to solve the ethical dilemma that the exportations created for Indian Hindus and Buddhists, who honor the monkeys. Finally, he was troubled by the inhumane methods of capture and transport, which had resulted in mortalities of up to 40%. He responded by publishing a set of importation guidelines, and by proposing to establish a rhesus breeding colony on Cayo Santiago, a 15-ha island that is approximately 1 km off the southeast coast of Puerto Rico. Candland and Bush (1995) also suggest that Carpenter was anticipating the "disruption of field research to be caused by WWII".

Carpenter oversaw the collection of approximately 500 rhesus monkeys near Lucknow, India, close to the Nepalese border. After tuberculosis testing in India, they were crated and shipped from Calcutta on the deck of an ocean liner. The ship detoured around the Cape of Good Hope and finally arrived in New York City, where Carpenter and the monkeys were transferred to another ocean liner and shipped to San Juan, Puerto Rico. The entire journey, on a route imperiled by German submarines, took 51 days and covered 14,000 miles, probably the greatest distance covered in any primate reintroduction in this history. The monkeys were kept for two weeks in their shipping crates on mainland Puerto Rico and were again tested for tuberculosis. They were finally rowed to the island and released. Carpenter personally cared for the monkeys during the entire trip. Of the 409 monkeys that were actually released, there were 40 adult males and 183 adult females. Because Cayo Santiago is only 15 ha in area, the monkeys destroyed much of the natural vegetation. Despite the presence of coconut palms, newly planted fruit and shade trees, and provisioning with local vegetables, the island could not sustain 400 macaques. There was considerable mortality in the first year, due largely to tuberculosis and fighting. There were a number of births on the island in ensuing years, but mortality was considerable as well. By 1940 there were 350 macaques in the colony (Carpenter 1942). By 1959 there were only 277. Several hundred had been removed for laboratory use. The United States National Institute of Neurological Diseases and Blindness assumed responsibility for the colony in 1956, and animal management and husbandry improved. Monkey chow was provisioned daily. The island population has exceeded 1,000 at times and has leveled off at about 400. The colony became the National Institute of Health's Caribbean Primate Research Center (CPRC). While the establishment of the colony did not entirely stem the importation of macaques for research, it did reduce importation. Thousands of monkeys have been removed from Cayo Santiago and sent to laboratories and other research colonies.

Cayo Santiago rhesus macaques have themselves been translocated to other islands off the coast of Puerto Rico. In the 1960s, an unspecified number of rhesus macaques from India, Cayo Santiago, and perhaps other locations were translocated in an unspecified number of cohorts to the islands of Cuerva (40 ha), Guayacán (40 ha), and Desecheo (152 ha). These three islands became known as the La Parguera Research Facility, which was managed by the CPRC to provide animals for polio research and vaccine testing. Vandenburg (1989) specifies that a total of 278 wild rhesus macaques were imported from India between 1961 and 1963 and released in "several waves" on Cuerva and Guayacán. These islands were drier than Cayo Santiago, and Vandenbergh states that the purpose of these introductions was to determine if the "breeding pattern and other ecological adaptations" would differ at sites at the same latitude as Cayo Santiago but with different habitats. The monkeys received veterinary screenings before release but there was no other form of pre-release preparation or acclimation. The Cuerva and Guayacán rhesus were provisioned indefinitely after release and were studied extensively (see below). The monkeys thrived, even on Desecheo, onto which 57 rhesus macaques were translocated from Cayo Santiago in 1966. The purpose of the Desecheo translocation was said to be the study the process of adaptation. The Desecheo animals were not provisioned with food or water, but nonetheless survived. There was no permanent water source on the island, but the macaques found moisture in the pulp of the almacigo tree. They ate birds' eggs and chicks. No birds, including endangered brown and red-footed boobies, nested on the island by 1970. Research ended on Desecheo in 1971. The island was declared a National Wildlife Refuge in 1976. A total of 119 macaques were trapped on Desecheo and taken to the Jardin Zoologico de Puerto Rico between 1977 and 1987. Despite numerous attempts to trap and remove all of the macaques, a remanant population still survives on Desecheo. The population may have been as large as 500 at one point.

Some of the rhesus macaques escaped from Cuerva and Guayacán to the Puerto Rican mainland, and a wild population became established on the mainland near Sierra Bermejam, Lajas, Cabo Rio, and San German. According to Phoebus (1989), the CPRC committed to increasing the La Parguera rhesus population to 2,000 by introducing large numbers of female and some male rhesus that had been obtained from "various commercial sources" in 1974 and 1975. At least 95 but probably many more were released. This stimulated the escapes because many of the escapees were driven off the islands to the mainland by resident groups. As Phoebus said, simply and prophetically, "rhesus monkeys are excellent swimmers" (pg 158). One estimate was that 175 rhesus monkeys were "missing" when the Cuerva and Guayacán island colonies were closed in 1982. As many as 500 rhesus macaques may still survive in the wild on the mainland, living sympatrically with the descendants of patas monkeys that also escaped to the mainland from Cuerva and Guayacán (see below). The two species occupied a range of 60,000 ha by 2006 and were causing approximately US$1.5 million in agricultural losses annually. The original escape of the rhesus macaques to the mainland and the subsequent discovery that some carried Herpes B virus led to the closing of La Parguera in 1982.

These many different intentional and accidental releases of rhesus macaques are not treated as separate reintroduction programs because they were a series of releases of the same species by the same organizational lineage in the same geographical area. However, a new program was initiated when the La Parguera rhesus macaques were translocated to Morgan Island in South Carolina (see below) in 1979.

Cayo Santiago has served as a convenient and safe venue for primate behavioral studies under semi-natural conditions for decades. Carpenter himself conducted an early study of rhesus sexual behavior on the island. After World War II, Stuart Altmann tattooed all of the macaques to facilitate observation and maintain known matrilines, and conducted a study of rhesus sociobiology. Altmann was the first of a long and distinguished series of investigators to conduct "field" work on the island (see Rawlins and Kessler 1986 and Kessler and Rawlins 2016). Hundreds of scientific papers on the Cayo Santiago macaques have been published. This is probably the most thoroughly documented reintroduction in this history. The Caribbean Primate Research Center thrives today, serving as the site for "studies of the entire life cycle of rhesus monkeys as a biological model for humans".

The introduction of rhesus macaques on Cayo Santiago demonstrated that a hardy, generalist, naturally-grouped, wild monkey species could be transported to and adapt quickly to a novel environment. The lesson would not go unnoticed. Reintroductions of large groups of baboons, macaques, howler monkeys, spider monkeys, and other monkeys for humane, commercial, and conservation purposes would become common in the 1980s and 1990s. Carpenter's original 1939 translocation of rhesus macaques from India to Puerto Rico may be the most successful primate reintroduction ever.

Commercial, Research, Religious, Welfare (Non-lethal control)

References

Carpenter, C.R. 1940. Rhesus monkeys for American laboratories. *Science* 92 (2387): 284-286.

Carpenter, C.R. 1942. Sexual behavior of free ranging rhesus monkeys. *Journal of Comparative Psychology* 33(1): 113-162.

Engeman, R.M., Laborde, J.E., Constatin, B.U., Shwiff, S.A., Hall, P., Duffiney, A., and F. Luciano. 2010. The economic impacts to commercial farms from invasive monkeys in Puerto Rico. *Crop Protection* 29: 401-405.

Evans, M.A. 1989. Ecology and removal of introduced rhesus monkeys: Desecheo Island National Wildlife Refuge, Puerto Rico. *Puerto Rico Health Sciences Journal* 8:139-156.

Jensen, K., Alvarado-Ramy, F., González-Martinez, J., Kraiselburd, E. and J. Rullán. 2004. B-Virus and free-ranging macaques, Puerto Rico. *Emerging Infectious Diseases* 10: 494-496.

Kessler, M. J. and R. G. Rawlins. 2016. A 75-year pictorial history of the Cayo Santiago rhesus monkey colony. *American Journal of Primatology* 78: 6-43.

Phoebus, E.C. 1989. The FDA rhesus breeding colony at La Parguera, Puerto Rico. *Puerto Rico Health Sciences Journal* 1989 8:157-158.

Rawlins, R.G. and M.J. Kessler. 1986. *The Cayo Santiago Macaques: History, Behavior and Biology*. Albany: State University of New York Press.

Vandenbergh, J.G. 1989. The La Parguera, Puerto Rico colony: Establishment and early studies. *Puerto Rico Health Sciences Journal* 8:117-119.

Rhesus Macaque (*Macaca mulatta*). The Instituto Oswaldo Cruz released approximately 300 rhesus macaques on Ilha de Pinheiro in the Guanabara Bay in Rio de Janeiro, Brazil in the 1940s. The purpose of this Introduction was to conduct research on yellow fever. I am not certain if research was actually conducted on the island, or if the intent was to breed monkeys on the island for laboratory research. The institute had been conducting laboratory studies on yellow fever using caged rhesus macaques since at least 1928. Caged monkeys may have been used to stock the island, or the founders may have been specifically imported for the Introduction. I could find no information about pre-release preparation, acclimation, or post-release monitoring. However, Hausfater and Walker reported that the monkeys were being fed and cared for by a full-time caretaker in 1974, at which time approximately 100 monkeys were living on the island. I have been unable to determine if and when the monkeys were removed from the island. They probably could not have survived on the island without supplemental feeding.

Research, Commercial

REFERENCES

Hausfater, G. and P. Walker. 1974. History of three little-known New World populations of macaques. *Laboratory Primate Newsletter* 13(1): 16-18.

Long, J.L. 2003. *Introduced Mammals of the World*. Collingwood, Victoria, Australia, CSIRO Publishing.

www.fiocruz.br

Rhesus Macaque (*Macaca mulatta*). Long (2003) records the release of "many" rhesus macaques on Morrillo del Diablo Key, near the Isle of Pines, Cuba, in the 1940s. The purpose was to conduct "pathological research". I don't know if the macaques were to be bred on the island for laboratory research, or if research was to be conducted in the free-ranging colony on the island. I could find no other details, except that some of the monkeys swam to the Isle of Pines when the project was abandoned in the 1950s. I have catalogued introductions of pig-tailed macaques, crab-eating macaques, stump-tail macaques, and vervets on Cuban islands in the 1980s (see above and below), but this rhesus reintroduction is not documented in any of my sources for these programs.

Research, Commercial

References

Long, J.L. 2003. *Introduced Mammals of the World.* Collingwood, Victoria, Australia, CSIRO Publishing.

Rhesus Macaque (*Macaca mulatta*). A "box load" of rhesus macaques were released in and around Bombay (now Mumbai), India in the early 1940s. The macaques were to be shipped by sea to biomedical laboratories in Europe or the United States, but they were regarded as "non-essential cargo" in a wartime shipping schedule and were therefore released. Bombay was south of the natural distribution of rhesus macaques at the time. I was unable to access the Serrao and Amladi paper; this account is taken from Radhakrishna and Sinha.

Commercial, Welfare (Non-lethal Control)

References

Radhakrishna, S. and A. Sinha. 2011. Less than wild? Commensal primates and wildlife conservation. *Journal of Bioscience* 36(5): 749-753.

Serrao, J.S. and S.R. Amladi. 1979. Of macaques-bonnet and rhesus. *Hornbill* 12: 29-32.

Rhesus Macaque (*Macaca mulatta*). An unknown number of rhesus macaques that had been imported from China escaped into surrounding forest from a tourist attraction in Japan's Chiba Prefecture in the 1960s. I was unable to access any further information about this program.

Accidental (Escape)

REFERENCES

Dore, K.M. 2017b. Ethnophoresy. In A. Fuentes, B. Bezanson, C.J. Campbell, A.F. DiFiore, S. Elton, A. Estrada, L.E. Jones-Engel, K.C. MacKinnon, K.A.I. Nekaris, E. Riley, S. Ross, C. Sanz, R.W. Sussman, and B. Thierry, eds. *The International Encyclopedia of Primatology.* Hoboken, Wiley-Blackwell.

National Institute for Environmental Studies. 2015a. *Macaca mulatta.* http://www.nies.go.jp/biodiversity/invasive/DB/detail/10390e.html

Rhesus Macaque (*Macaca mulatta*). Bausch and Lomb Inc. and its subsidiary Charles River Laboratories Inc., introduced 1,233 female and 176 male Indian rhesus macaques on Loggerhead (Lois) Key, Florida (40 ha, in the Atlantic Ocean) between 1973 and 1976. (A "key" is a small island.) The founding macaques were imported from Kashmir, India. They were quarantined for six months, screened for communicable diseases, vaccinated for measles, rabies, and tetanus, and tattooed for individual identification before release, and were provisioned with food and water after release. Between 1978 and 1980, approximately half (more than 500) of the Lois Key population, including some of the wild-born founders and some that had been born on Lois Key, were translocated to Raccoon Key (81 or 120 ha, estimates vary, probably due to tide cycles in the Gulf of Mexico). These were also provisioned with food and water. Both Lois and Raccoon Key are in the subtropical archipelago that extends off the southern tip of mainland Florida (the "Florida Keys").

The total population on both keys was estimated to have been 6,000 in 1983. There were 1,030 on Raccoon Key and 699 on Key Lois in 1991. Approximately 70 females were transferred from Lois Key to Raccoon Key in 1995, perhaps in anticipation of closure of the colonies. Many macaques survived on the keys until at least 1999, and most were finally removed between 1999 and 2000. The purpose of the original reintroduction was to produce monkeys to be sold for biomedical research, and many, probably thousands, were captured and removed from the islands and sent to biomedical research colonies between 1980 and 1999. Research on reproduction in the island colonies was conducted during the same period. Although the macaques were always provided with fresh water and food daily, they caused extensive damage to the keys' red and black mangroves and wildlife, and most of the macaques were confined in large cages before their eventual removal. The breeding farm operation was conducted under a permit issued by the Florida Game and Freshwater Fish Commission, despite the keys being located in a wildlife refuge. The Florida Audubon Society argued for the revocation of the permits. Although the commercial operation appears to have been discontinued, some monkeys may remain at large on Raccoon Key and perhaps other nearby islands.

After the two keys were vacated, Charles River Laboratories paid to revegetate the islands and to conduct research on possible water contamination. The company also made a large contribution to Florida's conservation trust.

Commercial

References

Anderson, C.J., Hostetler, M.E., and S.A. Johnson. 2017. History and status of introduced non-human populations in Florida. *Southeastern Naturalist* 16(1): 19-36.

Johnson, R. L. 1989. Live birthrates in two free-ranging rhesus breeding colonies in the Florida Keys. Primates 30: 433-437.

Johnson, R.L. and E. Kapsalis. 1995. Aging, infecundity, and reproductive senescence in free-ranging female rhesus monkeys. *Journal of Reproduction and Fertility* 105: 271–278.

Johnson, R.L. and E. Kapsalis. 1998. Menopause in free-ranging rhesus macaques: Estimated incidence, relation to body condition, and adaptive significance. *International Journal of Primatology* 19(4): 751–765.

Kleindienst, L. 1997. Florida at war against monkeys. articles.sun-sentinel.com

Kruer, C. 1996. The inside story on the monkey islands of the Florida Keys. *The Florida Naturalist* 69: 10.

Lehman, S.M., Taylor L.L., and S.P. Easley. 1994. Climate and reproductive seasonality in two free-ranging island populations of rhesus macaques (*Macaca mulatta*). *International Journal of Primatology* 15(1): 115-128.

Rhesus Macaque (*Macaca mulatta*). Between 40 and 50 rhesus macaques escaped from the failed tourist attraction known as Tropical Wonderland in Titusville, Florida, USA in 1976. They had lived on a moated island at the attraction since 1963 or 1964. Trees fell across the moat, which allowed the macaques to escape into a wooded area, and some eventually dispersed as many as three miles. Some were captured and removed, including approximately six that were released in Silver River State Park in the 1980s (see above). There were estimated to have been between 35 and 75 macaques in the feral Titusville colony in 1977, and they were reproducing. The colony survived at least until 1993 or 1994. They were fed by local residents of a trailer park.

Several "bob-tailed" (possibly pig-tailed) macaques escaped from the island at the same time as the rhesus, but these were apparently trapped quickly after escaping. A small group of squirrel monkeys were also among the escapees. The squirrel monkeys are included as a separate program (see below) but there is too little information about the "nonrhesus" macaques to include them here as a separate program.

Accidental (Escape)

References

Anderson, C.J., Hostetler, M.E., and S.A. Johnson. 2017. History and status of introduced non-human populations in Florida. *Southeastern Naturalist* 16(1): 19-36.

Layne, J.N. 1997. Nonindigenous mammals. In D. Simberloff, D.C. Schmitz, and T.C. Brown, eds. *Strangers in Paradise: Impact and Management of Nonindigenous Species in Florida*, pp 157-186. Washington DC, Island Press.

Rhesus Macaque (*Macaca mulatta*). The Caribbean Primate Research Center, the US Center for Disease Control, the US Food and Drug Administration, and the South Carolina Department of Natural Resources collaborated to translocate 1,396 rhesus monkeys in nine cohorts from La Parguera, Puerto Rico (see above) to Morgan Island, a 1,186-ha island (another source states 180 ha) off the coast of Beaufort, South Carolina, in 1979 and 1980. The monkeys were not shipped in intact social groups, but they re-established the groups themselves after release on the island. About half of Morgan Island is densely forested and half is marshland. The primary purpose of this reintroduction was to establish a colony to produce monkeys for biomedical research and pharmaceutical testing. However, another purpose may have been to prevent the macaques from being euthanized. Many of the La Parguera macaques were infected with Herpes B virus. Macaques were escaping regularly to the Puerto Rican mainland and there were cases of transmission of the virus to humans. The Puerto Rican government wanted the La Parguera colony to be closed. The South Carolina state government offered the island as a home for the animals. An additional 992 rhesus "from other US colonies" were added to the Morgan Island population by 1984.

The Morgan Island rhesus macaques, of which there were said to have been between 3,500 and

5,000 in 2016, are owned by the US National Institutes of Health and have been leased to various private corporations to manage them and remove animals for research. The South Carolina Department of Natural Resources leases the island to the management companies. The monkeys are given food and most likely water, and some veterinary care. Each is tattooed. They are presumed to have had some type of veterinary screening before they were moved, and because they were previously free-ranging on islands, they can be said to have had pre-release preparation. More than 4,000 infants had been born by 1989. Culling for biomedical research began in 1984; approximately 500 monkeys per year have been removed and sold from Morgan Island.

There have been environmental concerns about the impact of the macaques on the island's plants and animals, although one study concluded that the environmental impact of the macaques on water quality and tree cover was "localized and minimal" (Klopchin et al, 2008, pg. 311). Monkeys are reported to have escaped from Morgan Island periodically. Sixteen of the macaques escaped to the mainland in May 2016, but all were recaptured.

Commercial, Welfare (Non-lethal Control)

References

Davis, A. 2016. Monkeys back at Yemassee Lab. WSAV-TV website, 1 May 2016.

Jensen, K., Alvarado-Ramy, F., González-Martinez, J., Kraiselburd, E. and J. Rullán. 2004. B-Virus and free-ranging macaques, Puerto Rico. *Emerging Infectious Diseases* 10: 494-496.

Klopchin, J. L., Stewart, J. R., Webster, L. F., and P. A. Sandifer. 2008. Assessment of environmental impacts of a colony of free-ranging rhesus monkeys (*Macaca mulatta*) on Morgan Island, South Carolina. *Environmental Monitoring and Assessment* 137: 301-313.

Taub, D. M., and P. T. Mehlman. 1989. Development of the Morgan Island rhesus monkey colony. *Puerto Rico Health Sciences Journal* 8: 159-169.

Rhesus Macaque (*Macaca mulatta*). A cohort of 20 crop-raiding rhesus macaques were translocated to a site in Aligarh District in India in 1983. The macaques were provisioned after release and there was no observed mortality associated with the translocation. This reintroduced population numbered 105 within 14 years.

Welfare (Non-lethal Control)

REFERENCES

Southwick, C.H., Malik, I., and M. E. Siddiqi. 1998. Translocations of rhesus monkeys in India: Prospects and outcomes. *American Journal of Primatology* 45: 209-10. Abstract of presentation at the Twenty-first annual meeting of the American Society of Primatology.

Rhesus Macaque (*Macaca mulatta*). Two scientists, Iqual Malik and Rodney Johnson, presumably with the permission or at least knowledge of the Municipal Corporation of Delhi (India), translocated a group of 21 rhesus macaques in 1989 and another group of 13 macaques in 1990. The 1989 group was moved from the outskirts of New Delhi, India to Meetha Pur, a rural area, approximately 10 km away from the site of origin. The 1990 group was moved from a residential area of Old Delhi to the Lal Kuan public park. Both were intact social groups. Both were inevitably destined for relocation due to human/monkey conflict. There were resident macaque groups at both destination sites. Human residents at both sites were informed in advance of the releases and agreed to them. The macaques of each cohort were trapped and released on the same day. There was no veterinary screening or other pre-release preparation, but the macaques were fed for one month after release. A survey in late 1990 showed that both groups remained at the release sites and had reproduced well. One group had integrated with the resident group; the other had displaced the resident group from the area. The authors discuss the cost of translocating "problem" rhesus monkeys, compare translocation with other control options, and provide suggestions for rhesus translocation methodology.

Malik and Johnson mention that the Municipal Corporation of Delhi had trapped and relocated between 100 and 120 rhesus macaques in 1987 and 1988 respectively as a result of public complaints. These have been added to the program initiated by this government agency (see below). The same agency seems to have conducted many other, undocumented translocations of urban rhesus macaques.

Welfare (Non-lethal Control), Research

REFERENCES

Malik, I. and R. L. Johnson. 1994. Commensal rhesus in India: The need and cost of translocation. *Revue d'Ecologie* (*La Terre et La Vie*) 49: 233-243.

Rhesus Macaque (*Macaca mulatta*). Sambyal et al (2009) refer to a translocation of 40 rhesus monkeys from the National Zoological Park of India in New Delhi to the Tuglaqabad Fort in New Delhi. I could not access any details of this translocation.

Unspecified

REFERENCES

Sambyal, P., Kumar, S. and D. N. Sahi. 2009. Translocation of urban rhesus monkeys (*Macaca mulatta*) of Mubarak Mandi Jammu to forest areas of Nagrot. *Tigerpaper* 36: 1-3.

Rhesus Macaque (*Macaca mulatta*). Twelve groups, totaling 600 rhesus macaques, were reintroduced from the Vrindaban holy area in the city of Mathura, India to forested areas that were between 5 and 45 km outside of the city, in 1997. The macaques were part of a large urban population that was harassing people. Attempts were made to trap and release all members of a social group. The eight destination sites had no resident rhesus populations. The releases took place at night to avoid upsetting local people that were opposed to the translocations. The translocated macaques were monitored once per week for three months; the behavior of one of the groups was studied more intensively. A 2001 survey indicated that the translocated macaques were still present at the release sites and were behaving normally

Welfare (Non-lethal Control), Research

REFERENCES

Imam, E., Yahya, H. S. A., and I. Malik. 2002. A successful mass translocation of commensal rhesus monkeys *Macaca mulatta* in Vrindaban, India. *Oryx* 36: 87-93.

Southwick, C.H., Malik, I., and M. E. Siddiqi. 1998. Translocations of rhesus monkeys in India: Prospects and outcomes. *American Journal of Primatology*, 45: 209-10. Abstract of presentation at the Twenty-first annual meeting of the American Society of Primatology.

Rhesus Macaque (*Macaca mulatta*). The Guragon Air Force Station in India sponsored the translocation of 22 of a group of 28 wild rhesus macaques to a natural forest in Firozpur-Jhirka in 1998. There was no resident rhesus population at the release site. The animals were harassing staff at the air force station. The translocation took place in one day. The macaques were given food for one week after release. A group of 12 and another of eight were observed at the release site 20 months after the release.

Welfare (Non-lethal Control)

REFERENCES

Imam, E., Malik, I., and H. S. A. Yahya. 2001. Translocation of rhesus macaques from airforce station, Gurgaon (Haryana) to the natural forest of Firozpur Jhirka, Haryana, India. *Journal of The Bombay Natural History Society* 98: 355-359.

Rhesus Macaque (*Macaca mulatta*). The Delhi (India) Municipal Corporation translocated approximately 500 rhesus monkeys of several family groups from the city limits to the Pilibhut and Kuno National Parks in 2004. This is said to have been one of many translocations over decades that had been conducted by the Delhi government. One release was described by Lenin as dumping monkeys into the Asolo Batti Sanctuary. There was no medical screening, no acclimation and no post-release support or monitoring. The Kuno release was conducted in the month of June in the hot, dry season when natural plant foods were least abundant. There are no further details about the translocations, and the translocated macaques were probably not monitored systematically.

In India, monkeys are fed and protected for religious reasons and often harass people and steal food. Urban authorities are pressured to resolve the resulting monkey/human conflict, but they are prevented by wildlife law and custom from killing the monkeys and have lacked support for large-scale sterilization programs.

Malik and Johnson mention that the Municipal Corporation of Delhi had trapped and relocated between 100 and 120 rhesus macaques in 1987 and 1988 as a result of public complaints. The destination sites are unknown. The same government agency may have conducted many other, undocumented translocations of urban rhesus macaques (see, for example, Pirta et al 1997).

Welfare (Non-lethal control)

REFERENCES

Lenin, J. 2008. The business of monkey control. *Reintroduction Redux* 3: 14-15.

Malik, I. and R. L. Johnson. 1994. Commensal rhesus in India: The need and cost of translocation. *Revue d'Ecologie (La Terre et La Vie)* 49: 233-243.

Panwar, H. S. and M. K. Misra. 2004. Monkey and the lion. *Reintro Redux* 1: 3.

Pirta, R.S., Gadgil, M., and A.V. Kharshikar. 1997. Mangement of the rhesus monkey (*Macaca mulatta*) and Hanuman langur (*Presbytis entellus*) in Hinachal Pradesh, India. *Biological Conservation* 79(1): 97-106.

Rhesus Macaque (*Macaca mulatta*). The Department of Wildlife Conservation of Jammu (India) and the Heritage Society of Jammu collaborated to translocate 431 wild urban rhesus monkeys from Jammu District to five forested areas of Nagrota in 2008. The reason was to alleviate human/monkeys conflict without killing the monkeys. The macaques were live trapped and translocated over 20 days. There was no veterinary screening or other pre-release preparation, acclimation, or post-release support. There was a very short period of post-release monitoring, during which the macaques are said to have remained at the release sites and were behaving normally.

Welfare (Non-lethal Control)

REFERENCES

Sambyal, P., Kumar, S., and D. N. Sahi. 2009. Translocation of urban rhesus monkeys (*Macaca mulatta*) of Mubarak Mandi Jammu to forest areas of Nagrot. *Tigerpaper* 36: 1-3.

Japanese Macaque (*Macaca fuscata*). The Japan Monkey Centre released a total of 81 Japanese macaques in two cohorts on Ôhirayama Mountain, near the city of Inuyama in Aichi Prefecture, Japan in 1956 and 1957. Japanese macaques had lived previously in the area but were absent at the time of the reintroduction. The purposes of this Reintroduction were to conduct research on the process of group formation and to establish a breeding colony to produce monkeys for other research projects. The monkeys were collected by trappers at various locations in Yakushima in Kagoshima Prefecture, housed in small aggregations for short periods in a small cage at the primate center, and then formed into larger aggregations in a large outdoor corral that served as an acclimation cage near the release site. The monkeys did not initially know each other because they had been collected at various locations. The researchers "gathered them in a cage to unite them by enforcing a crowded life" (Furuya 1965, p 285). There is no mention of medical examination or other forms of pre-release preparation. The monkeys were fed at a fixed location in the acclimation cage to train them to return after they were released. The location of the acclimation cage was chosen to provide proximity to a good sleeping site and to be remote from people and dogs. Some monkeys were seriously wounded during the group formation process and had to be returned to colony cages. Significantly, Japanese macaques of a non-native subspecies and a single rhesus macaque, which had been included in group formation, were not released. The monkeys spent more than six months in the acclimation cage. The "group" splintered and separated after release, and the monkeys dispersed and were slow to return to the food provisioning site. Many of the monkeys died of malnutrition, pneumonia, and wounds. They failed to eat foods that had been eaten by macaques that had lived previously in the area, and they also ate inappropriate natural foods. Thirty-eight infants were born to the survivors over the next four years. The monkeys were studied intensively after release and the reintroduction did provide important early information on group formation, social organization, and rank. All of the macaques were removed from Ôhirayama in 1997 and transferred to the Japan Monkey Centre. Their descendants live in the Centre's popular Monkey Valley exhibit.

Research, Commercial

REFERENCES

Furuya, Y. 1965. Social organization of the crab-eating monkey. *Primates* 6 (3-4): 285-336.

Hirata, S. 2017. Personal communication (e-mail, 5 January).

Kawai, M. 1960. A field experiment on the process of group formation in the Japanese monkey (*Macaca fuscata*), and the releasing of the group at Ôhirayama. *Primates* 2: 181-255.

Japanese Macaque (*Macaca fuscata*). A wild group of Japanese macaques in Arashiyama, Japan split into two groups in 1966. All of the animals and their pedigrees were individually known, and Japanese and American scientists recognized an opportunity to study the social behavior of two genetically related troops in different environments with different scientific approaches. The Arashiyama A group (also known as the Arashiyama West group), with 98 monkeys, was shipped to a 17-ha enclosure that had been built on a ranch in the hot, arid desert near Laredo, Texas in 1972. The monkeys were initially provisioned with food and water, but later ate native plants, animals, and eggs. Some escaped from the corral, and some were culled and sent to zoos. They were studied intensively (social, cultural, cognitive, anatomical, and genetic research) for decades. One study found that the average body weight of the Texas macaques had decreased and that their surface-to-mass ratio had increased between their 1972 release and 1992. Laredo, at 28° North latitude, has a warmer, drier climate than that of the origin site in Japan, at 35° North. Paterson interprets these morphological changes as adaptation for heat tolerance in conformity with Bergmann's and Allen's Rules, although diet and activity could also have been responsible.

The monkeys have been relocated several times because of funding interruptions, and now (2018) reside at the Born Free USA Primate Sanctuary in Texas. There are now about 250 macaques in the group at the sanctuary. Although the macaques are now dependent on human support, they had established a self-sustaining population at the original reintroduction site. Some of the escaped Japanese macaques have established a feral population near Dilley, Texas.

This could be called a Research release (and much research has been done) but other sources suggest it was a Welfare release. Candland and Bush note that the A group had become agricultural pests. Gouzoules states clearly that they had become a "nuisance", damaging ornamental gardens, and that they "were to be captured for physiological and medical studies".

Welfare (Non-lethal control), Research

References

Candland, D.K. and S.L. Bush. 1995. Primates and behavior. In: E.F. Gibbons, B.S. Durrant and J. Demarest, eds. *Conservation of Endangered Species in Captivity*, pp. 521-551. Albany, State University of New York Press).

Fedigan, L.M. 1991. History of the Arashiyama West Japanese macaques in Texas. In L.M. Fedigan and P.J. Asquith (eds.), *The Monkeys of Arashiyama: Thirty-Five years of Research in Japan and the West*, pp. 140-154. Albany, State University of New York Press.

Gouzoules, H. 1977. Arashiyama West: A status report. *International Primate Protection League Newsletter* 4(2): 7.

Moore, Jr., C. 2017a. Feral monkeys in Texas (photo and more). *The Wildlife Journalist*, blog.wildlifejournalist.com 5 May 2017.

Moore, Jr. C. 2017b. More on Texas feral monkeys (photos and stories). *The Wildlife Journalist*, blog.wildlifejournalist.com 9 May 2017.

Paterson, J.D. 1996. Coming to America: Acclimation in macaque body structures and Bergmann's Rule. *International Journal of Primatology* 17(4): 585-611.

Crab-eating Macaque (*Macaca fascicularis*). An unknown party or parties reintroduced an unknown number of crab-eating macaques in an unknown number of cohorts on the 400,000-ha Sulawesian island of Kabaena at an unknown time, perhaps 10,000 years ago. The purpose of this Introduction is unspecified. The crab-eating macaque population is assumed to exist based on reports of citizens and examination of twelve pet monkeys on the islands. Only 100,000 ha of the island contain habit that is suitable for crab-eating macaques. Sulawesi macaques are absent on the island. Froelich et al speculate on the dynamics of establishment and maintenance of this population without observing a wild macaque on the island.

Unspecified.

References

Froehlich, J.W., Schillaci, M., Jones Engel, L., Froehlich, D.J. and B. Pullen. 2003. A Sulawesi beachhead by longtail monkeys (*Macaca fascicularis*) on Kabaena Island, Indonesia." *Anthropologie (Brno)* 41: 17–24.

Gummert, M. D. 2011. "The common monkey of southeast Asia: Long-tailed macaque populations, ethnophoresy, and their occurrence in human environments. In M.D. Gummert, A. Fuentes, and L. Jones-Engel, eds. *Monkeys on the Edge: Ecology and Management of Long-Tailed Macaques and their Interface with Humans*, pp3-44. Cambridge, UK, Cambridge University Press.

Crab-eating Macaque (*Macaca fascicularis*). In another prehistoric Introduction, an unknown party or parties released an unknown number of crab-eating macaques in an unknown number of cohorts on the 451,400-ha Indonesian island of Lombok, which is near Bali in the Lesser Sunda Islands. The macaques can be seen today in Pusuk Park. Silvered leaf monkeys have also been released on Lombok (see below), and apparently still exist there today. It's not clear if the two species share the same habitat.

Unspecified

REFERENCES

Dore, K.M. 2017b. Ethnophoresy. In A. Fuentes, B. Bezanson, C.J. Campbell, A.F. DiFiore, S. Elton, A. Estrada, L.E. Jones-Engel, K.C. MacKinnon, K.A.I. Nekaris, E. Riley, S. Ross, C. Sanz, R.W. Sussman, and B. Thierry, eds. *The International Encyclopedia of Primatology*. Hoboken, Wiley-Blackwell.

Crab-eating Macaque (*Macaca fascicularis*). Crab-eating macaques were released in unknown numbers and unknown cohorts, probably by Portuguese sailors, in the 16th and/or early 17th century on the island of Mauritius (1,865 km^2). The macaques were probably captured in Java and transported aboard ships as food and/or as pets. The population grew explosively. There were estimated to have been between 12,000 and 15,000 macaques on Mauritius in 1979 and between 25,000 and 35,000 in 1986. They are generally seen as destructive to the endemic plants and animals of Mauritius, although Sussman and Tattersall (1986) questioned this view. They also raid crops, causing millions of dollars in agricultural losses per year. The Mauritius macaque population has not (yet) contracted the Herpes B virus, which makes these monkeys especially attractive for biomedical research. As many as 10,000 macaques per year have been trapped and exported from Mauritius for supply to biomedical and pharmaceutical research laboratories and other "monkey farms". In 2016 alone, 8,245 were exported from Mauritius to the USA and Europe. Because many airlines are now refusing to transport commercially exported primates, the Mauritius government has recently approved construction and operation of biomedical research laboratories on the island.

Commercial

REFERENCES

Long, J.L. 2003. *Introduced Mammals of the World*. Collingwood, Victoria, Australia, CSIRO Publishing.

Gumert, M. D. 2011. "The common monkey of southeast Asia: Long-tailed macaque populations, ethnophoresy, and their occurrence in human environments. In M.D. Gumert, A. Fuentes, and L. Jones-Engel, eds. *Monkeys on the Edge: Ecology and Management of Long-Tailed Macaques and their Interface with Humans*, pp3-44. Cambridge, UK, Cambridge University Press.

Konstant, W.R. and R.A. Mittermeier. 1982. Introduction, reintroduction and translocation of Neotropical primates: Past experience and future possibilities. *International Zoo Yearbook* 22: 69-77.

Sussman, R. W. and I. Tattersall. 1981. Behavior and ecology of *Macaca fasicularis* in Mauritius: A preliminary study. *Primates* 22: 192-205.

Sussman, R. W. and I. Tattersall. 1986. Distribution, abundance and putative ecological strategy of *Macaca fasicularis* on the island of Mauritius, southwestern Indian Ocean. *Folia Primatologica* 46: 28-43.

Wadman, M. 2017. Mauritius invites primate research labs to set up shop. *Science* 356(6337): 472-473.

Crab-eating (Long-tailed) Macaque (*Macaca fascicularis*). German phosphate miners are said to have brought a pair of pet crab-eating macaques to Angaur (Ngeaur) Island (840 ha) in Micronesia in the early 1900s. They probably escaped. A 1973 survey estimated that there were 480 to 600 free-ranging macaques on the island. There were 825 to 900 in 1981, and 340 to 400 in 1999 (the decline was due to hunting and government "eradication" programs). There may have been subsequent reintroduction cohorts.

Accidental

References

Gumert, M. D. 2011. "The common monkey of southeast Asia: Long-tailed macaque populations, ethnophoresy, and their occurrence in human environments. In M.D. Gumert, A. Fuentes, and L. Jones-Engel, eds. *Monkeys on the Edge: Ecology and Management of Long-Tailed Macaques and their Interface with Humans*, pp3-44. Cambridge, UK, Cambridge University Press.

Poirier, F. E. and E. O. Smith. 1974. The crab-eating macaques (*Macaca fasicularis*) of Angaur Island, Palau, Micronesia. *Folia Primatologica* 22: 258-306.

Crab-eating (Long-tailed) Macaque (*Macaca fascicularis*). An unknown party or parties released an unknown number of crab-eating macaques in probably one cohort near the city of Jayapura in western Papua (formerly Irian Jaya), Indonesia (which is the western half of the island of New Guinea) between 1910 and 1980 (probably between 1940 and 1970). Kemp and Burnett (2003) review a number of scenarios for the establishment of this population, but there is no doubt that the macaques were introduced by humans. There were approximately 60 macaques living in six groups in 2007. It is notable that the population has not increased dramtically, as has the crab-eating macaque population on Mauritius.

Unspecified

REFERENCES

Kemp, N.J. and J.B. Burnett. 2003. Final report: A biodiversity risk assessment and recommendations for risk management of long-tailed macaques (*Maca fascicularis*) in New Guinea. Washington, DC, Indo-Pacific Conservation Alliance.

Gumert, M. D. 2011. "The common monkey of southeast Asia: Long-tailed macaque populations, ethnophoresy, and their occurrence in human environments. In M.D. Gumert, A. Fuentes, and L. Jones-Engel, eds. *Monkeys on the Edge: Ecology and Management of Long-Tailed Macaques and their Interface with Humans*, pp3-44. Cambridge, UK, Cambridge University Press.

ETHNOTRAMPS

Crab-eating macaques were brought over millennia, intentionally or unintentionally, to other islands that are east of Wallace's Line. One such destination in addition to Angaur is 451,400-ha Lombok Island, on which there is an established population today. There were probably many such releases of crab-eating macaques, some of which were ancient, even prehistoric. There is not sufficient data to list these releases as separate programs. People took crab-eating macaques on voyages as living food larders, pets, and gifts, and sometimes the macaques (and many other animals) simply hitchhiked on boats navigating the Greater and Lesser Sunda Islands. Heinsohn has written two brilliant, extraordinarily detailed papers that document dozens of introductions of mammals (especially marsupials), birds, reptiles, and amphibians across Wallace's Line within Australasia. He applied the charming term "ethnotramp" to crab-eating macaques (and a few other species, e.g. black rats) because of the ubiquity of their being transported by humans to areas that were outside of their native range and thriving there ("ethnophoresy"). Dore (2017) also provides a good summary of worldwide primate ethnophoresy.

References

Dore, K.M. 2017b. Ethnophoresy. In A. Fuentes, B. Bezanson, C.J. Campbell, A.F. DiFiore, S. Elton, A. Estrada, L.E. Jones-Engel, K.C. MacKinnon, K.A.I. Nekaris, E. Riley, S. Ross, C. Sanz, R.W. Sussman, and B. Thierry, eds. *The International Encyclopedia of Primatology*. Hoboken, Wiley-Blackwell.

Heinsohn, T. 2003. Animal translocation: long-term human influences on the vertebrate zoogeography of Australasia (natural dispersal versus ethnophoresy). *Australian Zoologist* 32(3): 351-376.

Heinsohn, T.E. 2010. Marsupials as introduced species: Long-term anthropogenic expansion of the marsupial frontier and its implications for zoogeographic interpretation. *Terra Australis* 32: 133-176.

Crab-eating Macaque (*Macaca fascicularis*). Joseph and Grace DuMond released six "Javan macaques" in a 12-ha tract of subtropical forest and marsh in South Florida, approximately 20 miles west of Miami, in 1933 to create an opportunity to conduct naturalistic behavioral and ecological research. Many local people stopped in to see the monkeys; the DuMonds began charging admission to finance the research operation, which was named Monkey Jungle. The release is said to have "signified the beginning" of Monkey Jungle's current free-ranging (but now fenced) group of more than 100 crab-eating macaques.

In perhaps the oddest form of pre-release preparation in this history, the DuMonds had allowed the macaques to roam at will from their Connecticut home during the preceding summer. There has been continuous post-release monitoring and provisioning at Monkey Jungle for over 80 years, and the colony has survived at least two devastating hurricanes. There continues to be a robust research program involving the macaques and other primates at Monkey Jungle and the

DuMond Conservancy.

This is the first Introduced free-ranging research colony of primates that is documented in this *History*.

Disclosure: I have served as an advisor to Monkey Jungle/DuMond Conservancy since 2016 and am currently (2018) acting chair of their Scientific Advisory Board.

Research, Commercial

References

DuMond, F.V. 1967. Semi-free-ranging colonies of monkeys at Goulds Monkey Jungle. *International Zoo Yearbook* 7: 202-207.

www.monkeyjungle.com

Crab-eating Macaque (*Macaca fasicularis*). An unknown party released five crab-eating macaques, presumably in one cohort, in the Kowloon Hills of Hong Kong in the 1950s. The purpose of the reintroduction was unspecified. Reintroduced rhesus monkeys had lived in the Kowloon Hills for 40 years (see above). There are no details of pre- and post-release management of the crab-eating macaques, and their origin is unknown.

The combined macaque population grew quickly, to 100 in the 1980s, 113 in 1981, 72 in 1987, 600 in 1991, 690 in 1994, 700 in 2000, and 2000 in 2018. Three Tibetan macaques (*M. thibetena*) were reintroduced in the 1960s (see above), but the last of these died in 1995 (or 2008, sources vary). I consider the crab-eating macaque, rhesus macaque, and Tibetan macaque reintroductions to be separate reintroduction programs.

There are now approximately 2,000 monkeys in 30 groups in Hong Kong, of which approximately 3% are crab-eating macaques, 32% are rhesus-crab-eater hybrids, and 65% are rhesus macaques. The Kowloon macaques live in polyspecific groups in the Kam Shan, Lion Rock, and Shing Mun Country Parks and the Tai Po Kai Nature Reserve. The four protected areas comprise approximately 2,530 hectares. The macaques are provisioned by local people and tourists, despite a ban that was passed in 1999. Cheng found that the number of people feeding macaques and the amount of provisioned food had decreased by approximately 90% by 2014. There have been attempts at contraception. Cheng found that abundance in heterosexual groups decreased by approximately 10% between 2010 and 2012, and that the birth rate decreased from 69% to 30% between 2008 and 2012. Some of the macaques are hunted and trapped for their meat.

Unspecified

REFERENCES

Cheng, W.W. 2014. *A review of the management measures of feral macaques in Hong Kong.* Master's thesis, Department of Environmental Management, The University of Hong Kong.

Dore, K.M. 2017b. Ethnophoresy. In A. Fuentes, B. Bezanson, C.J. Campbell, A.F. DiFiore, S. Elton, A. Estrada, L.E. Jones-Engel, K.C. MacKinnon, K.A.I. Nekaris, E. Riley, S. Ross, C. Sanz, R.W. Sussman, and B. Thierry, eds. *The International Encyclopedia of Primatology.* Hoboken, Wiley-Blackwell.

Gumert, M. D. 2011. "The common monkey of southeast Asia: Long-tailed macaque populations, ethnophoresy, and their occurrence in human environments. In M.D. Gumert, A. Fuentes, and L. Jones-Engel, eds. *Monkeys on the Edge: Ecology and Management of Long-Tailed Macaques and their Interface with Humans*, pp3-44. Cambridge, UK, Cambridge University Press.

Southwick, C.H. and K.L. Southwick. 1983. Polyspecific groups of macaques on the Kowloon Peninsula, New Territories, Hong Kong. *American Journal of Primatology* 5: 17-24.

Southwick, C.H. and D. Manry. 1987. Habitat and population changes for the Kowloon macaques. *Primate Conservation* 8: 48-49.

Wong, C.L. and I-H. Ni. 2000. Population dynamics of the feral macaques in the Kowloon Hills of Hong Kong. *American Journal of Primatology* 50: 53-66.

Wong, C.L. and G. Chow. 2004. Preliminary results of trial contraceptive treatment with SpayVac™ on wild monkeys in Hong Kong. *Hong Kong Biodiversity* 6: 13-16.

www.afcd.gov.hk

Crab-eating Macaque (*Macaca fasicularis*). The Japan Monkey Centre introduced 87 crab-eating macaques in seven cohorts on the 0.1-ha Kijima Island between 1958 and 1961. The purposes were to study the social organization and process of group formation of this species, and to develop a breeding colony from which monkeys could be harvested for other research programs. The monkeys had been acquired from a dealer in Singapore. Some appeared to know each other and others did not. They were probably trapped at various locations. There is no mention of medical examination or other forms of pre-release preparation. The monkeys were kept and socially integrated in a cage on the island. Some escaped from the cage within a month but they would have been introduced later. The remaining monkeys were provisioned in the cage and the escapees were provisioned outside the cage. Furuya mentions that white-handed gibbons that had been released previously on Kijima also visited the cage (this gibbon introduction is not included in this history because of lack of further information). The first cohort of crab-eating macaques was released in 1958 after having spent more than one year in the acclimation cage. They were provisioned daily after release and monitored for at least seven years. Copulations were observed within a month of release. Many died due to illness and exposure to cold weather at the end of 1958. Six additional cohorts were released over the following three years. Only 25 of the total of 87 introduced macaques survived in 1961. Many were driven by social aggression into the sea where they drowned. One monkey swam to the mainland and was returned to the island. One male had to be recaptured because he was aggressive toward researchers. Aggression among the macaques decreased and social organization largely stabilized by 1962. Forty-one infants had been born by 1965. The monkeys were removed from the island in approximately 1975, and most were probably transferred to the Japan Monkey Centre. There are no longer any monkeys on Kijima.

Research, Commercial

References

Furuya, Y. 1965. Social organization of the crab-eating monkey. *Primates* 6 (3-4): 285-336.

Hirata, S. 2017. Personal communication (e-mail 5 January).

Crab-eating (Long-tailed) Macaque (*Macaca fasicularis*). An unspecified organization reintroduced an unknown number of crab-eating macaques in an unknown number of cohorts on Cayo Campo, a 1,200-ha island in the Canarreos Archipelago of Cuba, in the early 1980s. The release was probably managed by the Cuban Ministerio de Ciencia, Tecnología y Medio Ambiente. The purpose of the reintroduction was to establish a free-ranging colony from which individuals could be removed for biomedical research. The number of founders is unspecified. Dore cites Escobar ((1995) in saying that the macaques had been imported from Vietnam (I was unable to access the Escobar book). The macaques may be being provisioned. Crab-eating macaques were seen on Cayo Campo in 1992.

Commercial

References

Borroto-Páez, R. 2009. Invasive mammals in Cuba: an overview. *Biological Invasions* 11: 2279-2290.

Dore, K.M. 2017b. Ethnophoresy. In A. Fuentes, B. Bezanson, C.J. Campbell, A.F. DiFiore, S. Elton, A. Estrada, L.E. Jones-Engel, K.C. MacKinnon, K.A.I. Nekaris, E. Riley, S. Ross, C. Sanz, R.W. Sussman, and B. Thierry, eds. *The International Encyclopedia of Primatology*. Hoboken, Wiley-Blackwell.

Escobar, T.R. 1995. *Isla de la Juventud: Introducidos por Causa Deliberadas*. Havana, Editorial Cientifico-Técnica.

González, A., Manójina, N. and A. Hernández. 1994. Mamíferos del Archipiélago de Camagüey, Cuba. *Avicennia* 1: 51-56.

Crab-eating (Long-tailed) Macaque (*Macaca fascicularis*). The Palau Natural Habitat Breeding Facility reintroduced 475 crab-eating macaques (58 males and 417 females) between 1988 and 1990. (Another source states that there were 58 males and 420 females, for a total of 478.) The reintroduction consisted of nine cohorts of crab-eating macaques from various locations in West Java and South Sumatra. The destination site was Tinjil Island (between 242 and 600 ha, sources vary), which is approximately 16 km off the coast of West Java, Indonesia. The purposes were to establish a "natural habitat breeding facility" to provide monkeys for biomedical research, and to "contribute to Indonesia's primate conservation efforts". The breeding facility was established by the University of Washington and the Oregon Regional Primate Research Centers, the Bowman Gray School of Medicine of Wake Forest University, and the Bogor Agricultural University, and was managed by Charles Darsono, a well-known animal trader. A pre-release botanical survey of the island indicated that there were many plant species that were edible to macaques. There were no native primates on the island.

The monkeys underwent veterinary screening and quarantine before release. They were given supplemental food and water after their release. A 1990 survey estimated that there were 760 macaques in 17 or 18 groups on the island, and that approximately 300 infants had been born. There were 540 macaques on Tinjil Island in 1994, and 1,550 in 18 to 20 groups in 1997. By 2002, at least 1,150 island-born juveniles had been removed for use in biomedical research and pharmaceutical testing. Nonetheless, the population had reached 2,000 by 2002 and was self-sustaining, with the number of macaques removed for export being balanced with the birth rate.

The assertion that the Tinjil colony was "contributing to Indonesia's primate conservation efforts" was based on the program's providing macaques for export for biomedical research without putting additional pressure on wild populations. Another option would have been to cease exportation of macaques entirely. However, the Bogor Agricultural University declared the island to be a primate research center, with funds from the sale of macaques being used to support university operations.

Bowden and Smith note that Darsono established a second colony on nearby Deli Island in the early 1990s with "thousands of breeders". Deli was reported to be 950 ha in area. We could find no further information about this effort except that Deli-born offspring began to be exported for biomedical research in 1992. I consider the Deli colony to be a component of the Tinjil Island program, but, in the absence of knowing the number of founders, I added 1,000 macaques to the Tinjil total and assumed that management techniques and methodology were the same.

Commercial, Conservation

References

Anon. Undated c. BUAV [The British Union for the Abolition of Vivisection] Briefing on Environment Protection and Biodiversity Conservation Amendment (Prohibition of Live Imports of Primates for Research), Bill 2015, Submission 48 - Attachment 3.

Bowden, D. M. and O. A. Smith. 1992. Conservationally sound assurance of primate supply and diversity. *Institute of Laboratory Animals Journal* 34: 53-56.

Crockett, C. M., Kyes, R. C., and D. Sajuthi. 1996. Modeling managed monkey populations: Sustainable harvest of longtailed macaques on a natural habitat island. *American Journal of Primatology* 40: 343-360.

Gumert, M. D. 2011. "The common monkey of southeast Asia: Long-tailed macaque populations, ethnophoresy, and their occurrence in human environments. In M.D. Gumert, A. Fuentes, and L. Jones-Engel, eds. *Monkeys on the Edge: Ecology and Management of Long-Tailed Macaques and their Interface with Humans*, pp3-44. Cambridge, UK, Cambridge University Press.

Kyes, R.C. 1993. Survey of long-tailed macaques introduced onto Tinjil Island, Indonesia. *American Journal of Primatology* 31: 77-83.

Crab-eating Macaque (*Macaca fasicularis*). Local government officials reintroduced an unknown number of crab-eating macaques from a recreational park in Wat Thammikaram Worawiharn in

Thailand's Prachuap Khirikhan province to the Nong Yai Water Reservoir in Chumphon province. The date of the translocation is not provided. The macaques had been fed by tourists at the Wat Thammikaram Worawiharn park and had become overpopulated. There were macaques at the destination site, and there was post-release competition between the resident and translocated groups. There are no details on pre- or post-release methods or management. There were at least 800 macaques at the reservoir destination site in 2005.

Welfare (Non-lethal Control)

REFERENCES

Malaivijitnond, S. and Y. Hamada. 2008. Current situation and status of long-tailed macaques (*Macaca fasicularis*) in Thailand. *The Natural History Journal of Chulalongkorn University* 8(2): 185-204.

Malaivijitnond, S., Vazquez, Y., and Y. Hamada. 2011. Human impact on long-tailed macaques in Thailand. In M.D. Gumert, A. Fuentes, and L. Jones Engel, eds. *Monkeys on the Edge: Ecology and Management of Long-tailed Macaques and their Interface with Humans*, pp 118-158. Cambridge, UK, Cambridge University Press.

Crab-eating Macaque (*Macaca fasicularis*). The head monk of the temple at Wat Pa Sila Wiwek in Thailand's Mukda Han province arranged for the reintroduction of an unknown number of crab-eating macaques from the Don Chao Poo Forest Park in Umnajjaroen province to the temple grounds. The translocation took place sometime between 2000 and 2004. The purpose of the translocation was to attract tourists to the temple. There are no details on pre- or post-release methods or management. One troop of 46 macaques was observed on the temple grounds in 2004, but I don't know if they were dependent on provisioning.

Commercial

REFERENCES

Malaivijitnond, S. and Y. Hamada. 2008. Current situation and status of long-tailed macaques (*Macaca fasicularis*) in Thailand. *The Natural History Journal of Chulalongkorn University* 8(2): 185-204.

Malaivijitnond, S., Vazquez, Y., and Y. Hamada. 2011. Human impact on long-tailed macaques in Thailand. In M.D. Gumert, A. Fuentes, and L. Jones Engel, eds. *Monkeys on the Edge: Ecology and Management of Long-tailed Macaques and their Interface with Humans*, pp 118-158. Cambridge, UK, Cambridge University Press.

Crab-eating Macaque (*Macaca fasicularis*). The International Animal Rescue program released 17 crab-eating macaques in four groups in the 11,000-ha Batutegi Protected Forest in Sumatra in 2017. The forest had been surveyed to ensure that there would be enough suitable food for the monkeys. All of the macaques had been wild-born, captured for the pet trade, and then surrendered or confiscated. The macaques were quarantined and rehabilitated in IAR's primate rehabilitation center in Bogor, West Java. During rehabilitation, the monkeys were provided with foods that they would find in their natural habitat, and allowed to locomote on natural vegetation in large enclosures. The monkeys were acclimated at the release site for three days. There was post-release monitoring of unspecified duration. The primary purpose of this reintroduction was to improve the welfare of the macaques, but a secondary purpose was to "restore their ecological functions in the natural habitat".

Welfare (Rehabilitation), Conservation

References

www.internationalanimalrescue.org 8 November 2017.

Taiwan (Formosan Rock) Macaque (*Macaca cyclopis*). An unknown number of Taiwan macaques were reintroduced on the Kii peninsula, Wakayama Prefecture, Japan in 1954 or 1955. They apparently escaped from a bankrupt zoo. The Taiwan macaques hybridized with resident Japanese macaques. The prefecture began to eliminate hybrid macaques in 2001.

The Japanese National Institute for Environmental Studies cites this reintroduction as one of four Taiwan macaque reintroductions that took place in southwestern Japan between the late 1940s and 1964. According to the NIES website, the 1940s reintroduction involved macaques that escaped from a zoo on Izushima. Other Taiwan macaques escaped from a zoo in Aomori Prefecture in 1952, and began to be "farmed" in 1971. There was also an intentional release on Onejima in 1964 to establish a tourist attraction. Long and de Vos et al cite an escape or release of Taiwan macaques from a zoo on Oshima Island in 1942 and subsequent years; this may be the same as the Izushima escape. The numbers of macaques and the numbers of cohorts for all of these releases are unspecificd, and current the current status of the 1940s, 1952, and 1964 groups are unspecified. By our definition, these Taiwan macaque reintroductions comprise five separate programs, but listing them as such inflates the number of programs without a concurrent increase in information. Because all five releases involve the same species in the same general part of the country, and because of the paucity of information, I list them here as one program.

Accidental (Escape), Commercial

REFERENCES

de Vos, A., Manville, R.H., and R.G. Van Gelder. 1956. Introduced mammals and their influence on native biota. *Zoologica* 41(4): 163-194.

Kawamoto, Y., Shirai, K., Araki, S., and K. Maeno. 1999. A case of hybridization between Japanaese macaques and Taiwanese macaques found in Wakayama Prefecture. *Primate Research* 15: 53-60. (English summary).

National Institute for Environmental Studies. 2015b. *Macaca cyclopis*. http://www.nies.go.jp/biodiversity/invasive/DB/detail/10030e.html

Taiwan (Formosan Rock) Macaque (*Macaca cyclopsis*). Both Kawai (1960) and Furuya (1965) mention that the Japan Monkey Centre introduced Formosan rock macaques onto Nojima Island in 1958. There are no further details about numbers or techniques of the release. I assume that the macaques were all wild-born, and that the purposes were the same as those of the reintroduction of Japanese macaques on Ôhirayama Mountain (see above) and the introduction of crab-eating macaques on Kijima Island (see above): to conduct research and establish a breeding colony. There were 51 macaques living in two groups on Nojima in 1962. At least four were subsequently removed for use in laboratory research. All of the monkeys were removed from the island in approximately 1975. Most were probably transferred to the Japan Monkey Centre. There are no longer any monkeys on Nojima, although there may be established introduced populations elsewhere in Japan.

Research, Commercial

REFERENCES

Furuya, Y. 1965. Social organization of the crab-eating monkey. *Primates* 6 (3-4): 285-336.

Hirata, S. 2017. Personal communication (e-mail 5 January).

Kawai, M. 1960. A field experiment on the process of group formation in the Japanese monkey (*Macaca fuscata*), and the releasing of the group at Ôhirayama. *Primates* 2: 181-255.

Kawai, M. and U. Mito. 1973. Quantitative study of activity patterns and postures of Formosan momkeys by the radio-telemetrical technique. *Primates* 14(2-3): 179-194.

Nishida, T. 1963. Intertroop relationships of the Formosan monkeys (*Macaca cyclopis*) relocated on Nojima Island. *Primates* 4(1): 121-122.

Stump-tail Macaque (*Macaca arctoides*). Twenty-four wild-born stump-tail macaques were reintroduced in two cohorts in Kao Tao, Thailand. Twenty were released in 1965 and four more were released sometime later. I have been unable to access Bertrand's (1969) extensive study of these animals and thus depend here on Hannah's (1989) summary. The first 20 macaques had been in captivity for 11 months. I have no details on pre-release preparation or post-release management or monitoring. There were 11 macaques at the destination site one year after the first cohort was released. Bertrand herself captured and released the four macaques in the second cohort and successfully integrated them into the group. The macaques were being trapped or shot at the sites of origin, which were apparently 700 km (the first cohort) and 200 km (the second cohort) away from the destination site, but they were protected at the destination site, which was a Buddhist temple.

Welfare (Rescue)

References

Bertrand, M. 1969. The Behavioural Repertoire of the Stumptail Macaque. *Bibliotheca Primatologica*, No. 11. Basel, S. Karger.

Hannah, A.C. 1989. *Rehabilitation of captive chimpanzees (Pan troglodytes verus)*. PhD Dissertation, University of Stirling.

Stump-tail Macaque (*Macaca arctoides*). The Behavioral Science Foundation, Rutgers University Medical School, the University of Veracruz, and the University of Mexico introduced 32 stump-tail macaques in two cohorts on the island of Totogochillo (0.4 ha) in Lake Catemaco, Veracruz, Mexico in 1974. The macaques were acquired from the Caribbean Primate Research Center in Sebana Seca, Puerto Rico. They were all taken from a single group of 56 that had lived in an outdoor corral at CPRC for four years. The purposes of this reintroduction were to establish a breeding colony and to conduct research on adaptation to a novel environment. There is no mention of medical examination, pre-release preparation, or acclimation.

The first cohort consisted of six wild-borns and 14 captive-borns (born at CPRC). I inferred from the sources that three of the second cohort were wild-born and nine were captive-born. The second cohort was released approximately three months after the first. There were four deaths and two births in the five months following the release of the first cohort, bringing total colony size to 30 by the end of 1974. Five animals were removed and sent to a neurological research colony in 1976. With additional births and only a few deaths, the colony had grown to 58 by 1984. The macaques were provisioned at least through 1983. Estrada and Estrada (1976) documented space use, activity cycles, diet, and responses to potential predators for 83 days following release of the first cohort. The monkeys' discovery and consumption of novel animal foods is also described. There was little serious aggression, probably because of the introduced monkeys had lived in a single group.

The group was moved to "a more natural environment" on the nearby Tanaxpillo and Tanaspi Islands in 1979.

Long (2003) reports that Rutgers University also introduced stump-tail macaques on Hall's Island, Bermuda. He adds that there were ten free-ranging stump-tail macaques on Hall's Island in 1989. I have been unable to verify the existence of this program or access any details. I mention it here because some of the Hall's Island monkeys may have come from Tanaxpillo or Tanaspi Islands in Mexico.

Commercial, Research

References

Brereton, A.R. 1994. Copulatory behavior in a free-ranging population of stumptail macaques (*Macaca arctoides*) in Mexico. *Primates* 35(2): 113-122.

Estrada, A. and R. Estrada. 1976. Establishment of a free-ranging colony of stumptail macaques (*Macaca arctoides*): Relations to the ecology I. *Primates* 17(3): 337-355.

Estrada A. and R. Estrada. 1981. Reproductive seasonality in a free-ranging troop of stumptail macaques

(*Macaca arctoides*): a five-year report. *Primates* 22(4): 503- 511.

Long, J.L. 2003. *Introduced Mammals of the World*. Collingwood, Victoria, Australia, CSIRO Publishing.

Rasmussen, D.R. 1991. Observer influence on range use of Macaca arctoides after 14 years of observation? *Laboratory Primate Newsletter* 30(3): 6-11.

Stump-tail Macaque (*Macaca arctoides*). Scientists from Stirling University in Scotland released three or four adult female colony-bred stump-tail macaques on Alloa Inch, an island in the River Forth in 1981. The island's area varied from as little as 5 ha to as much as 70 ha at times, depending on tides and flooding from storms; it was probably between 19 ha and 31 ha at the time of this reintroduction. The behavior of the Stirling University Primate Research Unit stump-tail macaques had for years been studied intensively and productively by Lecturer Arnold Chamove and his colleagues, including then-graduate student Jim Anderson.

When unit technicians became aware that macaques could carry Herpes B virus asymptomatically and transmit it to humans, in whom it can cause serious illness and death, the university ordered all of the stump-tail macaques in the colony to be euthanized. The macaques that were released had been separated from their mothers and hand-reared, and were found to be free of the virus. The purposes of the release were to spare the monkeys from euthanasia and determine if living in a naturalistic environment would reverse the self-abusive behavior that they had developed as a result of deprivation-rearing in captivity.

There was apparently no pre-release preparation (aside from veterinary examination and testing) or acclimation. Chamove, Anderson, and the island's owner rowed the macaques to the island in the early morning and released them in an abandoned barn. After release, the macaques had access to the barn and supplies of straw bedding and edible grain within. There was apparently no systematic post-release monitoring, although Chamove and Anderson did visit frequently and provided food to the monkeys. The island was uninhabited by people, and the owner, Mr. Gordon McGregor, had approved of the introduction. The local district council is said to have previously denied permission for the introduction, but McGregor, Chamove, and Anderson were unaware of the denial.

"After about a year, someone on the river heard the calls of the monkeys, which they reported sounded like a lost human baby. The council was called, and after speaking to the owner of the

Inch, Mr. McGregor, they contacted me and, based on veterinary recommendations the council said they had received, asked that the monkeys be removed immediately. Catching them was easily done as they well remembered Purina Lab Chow." (Chamove, personal communication). Three macaques were removed in 1982 and sent to the Edinburgh Zoo. One apparently had died during the year on the island.

By the criteria of this history, this was not a successful introduction. However, three monkeys were spared from euthanasia, which was Chamove and Anderson's purpose.

Welfare (Non-lethal Control), Research

References

Anderson, J. 2017. Personal communication (e-mail, 3 January).

Chamove, A. 2017. Personal communications (e-mails, 2, 3 January).

Sexton, R. and E. Stewart. 2005. Alloa Inch: The mudbank in the Forth that became an inhabited island. *Forth Naturalist and Historian* 28: 79-101.

Stump-tail Macaque (*Macaca arctoides*). An unspecified organization, probably the Cuban Ministerio de Ciencia, Tecnología y Medio Ambiente, reintroduced an unknown number of stump-tailed macaques in an unknown number of cohorts to Cayo Guajaba, a 1,830-ha island in the Camagüey Archipelago of Cuba, in approximately 1984. The purpose of the reintroduction was to establish a free-ranging colony from which individuals could be removed for biomedical research. The source of the macaques is unspecified. González et al found stump-tailed macaques on Guajaba in a 1992 census. They may have been provisioned at the time.

Commercial

References

Borroto-Páez, R. 2009. Invasive mammals in Cuba: an overview. *Biological Invasions* 11: 2279-2290.

Dore, K.M. 2017b. Ethnophoresy. In A. Fuentes, B. Bezanson, C.J. Campbell, A.F. DiFiore, S. Elton, A. Estrada, L.E. Jones-Engel, K.C. MacKinnon, K.A.I. Nekaris, E. Riley, S. Ross, C. Sanz, R.W. Sussman, and B. Thierry, eds. *The International Encyclopedia of Primatology*. Hoboken, Wiley-Blackwell.

González, A., Manójina, N. and A. Hernández. 1994. Mamíferos del Archipiélago de Camagüey, Cuba. *Avicennia* 1: 51-56.

Stump-tail Macaque (*Macaca arctoides*). Wildlife At Risk reintroduced four stump-tail macaques from the Hon Me rescue center to the "forested central highlands of southern Vietnam" in 2014. The adult male in the group was a confiscated ex-pet. He was paired with an adult female of unspecified origin at the rescue center, and they had two center-born offspring. There was veterinary screening but no acclimation, pre-release preparation, post-release support, or post-release monitoring.

Wildlife at Risk also relocated a total of eight pig-tailed and crab-eating macaques from a temple to a different forest area in Vietnam in 2016. The monkeys were harassing and biting people. These Translocations are not included in this *History* because they are described so briefly.

Welfare (Rehabilitation)

References

Khoi, N. V. 2014. WAR stories: Wildlife rehabilitation in Vietnam. *International Primate Protection League News* 41: 8-9.

www.wildlifeatrisk.org

CHAPTER 7
REINTRODUCTIONS OF AFRICAN MONKEYS

Kirk's (Zanzibar, Red Colobus) Monkey (*Procolobus kirkii*). The Zanzibar Forestry Department translocated 14 or 15 Zanzibar red colobus monkeys (the references disagree on the number; Butynski and de Jong specify that there were five males and ten females) in 1973 or 1974 from the Jozani Park on the island of Zanzibar (Unguja Island) to the Ngezi-Vumawimbi Forest Reserve (2,000 ha, with 500 to 1,000 ha of forest), which is on Pemba Island, approximately 50 km from the Tanzanian mainland and 150 km from the site of origin on Zanzibar. This was an attempt to establish a new population of this endangered species. Because red colobus monkeys were not known to occur previously on Pemba Island, this was an Assisted Colonization or Introduction. I could find no information on pre-release preparation or acclimation, but Butynski and de Jong assume there was none. There is also no information on immediate post-release monitoring but censuses in 1991 and 1992, 2000, 2005, and 2011 concluded that there were four small groups totaling between 15 and 40 individuals. Subsistence hunting by local residents may have limited population growth.

The Zanzibar Forestry Department conducted three additional translocations of Zanzibar red colobus monkeys in 1977, 1978, and 1981 (or 1982) on Unguja Island, the main island of the Zanzibar Archipelago. The destination sites were the Mayingini Forest Reserve (nine monkeys), the Masingini Forest Reserve (36, in four cohorts) and the Kichwele Forest Reserve (13, in one cohort). Note: Butynski and de Jong mention the destination site named "Mayangini", but Struhsaker and Siex do not. It may be that the nine noted to have been released at Mayangini are actually among the 36 that were released at Masangini.

Masingini had 556 ha of habitat that was suitable for the colobus monkeys. Vervets, Sykes' monkeys, and greater bushbabies were known to be present. Kichwele had 1,000 ha of suitable forest; vervets and probably bushbabies were present. As noted, these sites were on the island of Zanzibar itself. Because red colobus monkeys were present in low numbers at the sites or had occurred there historically, these releases were all Reintroductions or Reinforcements. Most of the monkeys that were destined for each site were trapped, moved, and released in one day, although one cohort of nine monkeys were kept in a cage at an unknown location for two months.

A 1994 census found a total of between 62 and 70 red colobus monkeys at the three sites. Only the Masingini population, with three groups totaling 56 to 64 individuals, appeared at that time to have the potential to be self-sustaining. A 2017 census (Davenport et al 2017) estimated that there were 309 at Masingini. A 1991 census found none, or perhaps very few, colobus at Kichwele; the 2017 census found none. The 2017 study does not include a site named "Mayingini".

The authors of this more recent and comprehensive distribution and abundance study (Davenport et al 2017) concluded that there are now 5,862 red colobus monkeys at all sites in Zanzibar, of which 4,042 live in protected areas. The population is large but recruitment appears to be low, and many forested areas are being developed for agriculture. The overall contribution of reintroduced individuals to the Zanzibar population is doubtlessly small, but the reintroduction at Masingini may have contributed to the growth of the population at the site. Davenport et al did not survey Pemba Island in this study, but they suggest that, as an exotic species, the red colobus monkeys on Pemba could be translocated back to a site on Unguja.

It should be noted that the entire Zanzibar red colobus population is itself most likely the result of one or more human-assisted introductions from mainland Tanzania, although the mainland and Zanzibar populations are now considered to be different species. The Zanzibar vervets were also introduced, probably intentionally or accidentally by pet owners, in the 1980s or 1990s. Historically, some of the colobus monkeys may have been translocated from Zanzibar back to the mainland. None of these hypothetical releases is included as a separate program in this history.

Conservation (Introduction), Research

References

Butynski, T. M. and Y. A. de Jong. 2011. Zanzibar red colobus on Pemba Island, Tanzania: Population status 38 years post-reintroduction. In Soorae, P. S., ed. *Global Re-introduction Perspectives: 2011. More Re-introduction Case-Studies from Around the Globe*, pp.168-174. Gland, Re-introduction Specialist Group and Abu Dhabi, Environment Agency – Abu Dhabi.

Camperio Ciani, A., Palentini, L. and E. Finotti. 2001. Survival of a small translocated Procolobus kirkii population on Pemba Island. *Animal Biodiversity and Conservation* 24: 15-18.

Davenport, T.R.B., Fakih, S.A., Kimiti, S.P., Kleine, L.U., Foley, L.S. and D.W. De Luca. 2017. Zanzibar's endemic red colobus Piliocolobus kirkii: first systematic and total assessment of population, demography and distribution. *Oryx* DOI: 10.1017/S003060531700148X

Silkiluwasha, F. 1981. The distribution and conservation status of the Zanzibar red colobus. *African Journal of Ecology* 19: 187-194.

Struhsaker, T.T. and K.S. Siex. 1998. Translocation and introduction of the Zanzibar red colobus monkey: success and failure with an endangered island endemic. *Oryx* 32: 277-284.

Black and White Colobus Monkey (*Colobus guereza*). A colleague, Rob Shumaker, visited the Mount Kenya Wildlife Conservancy and Orphanage in 1999. He was told by a staff member that the organization had successfully released at lease three intact groups of rescued and rehabilitated black and white colobus monkeys. The monkeys are said to have been fed leafy branches from native trees as preparation for release. I have not been able to find any other documentation for this program.

Welfare (Rehabilitation)

References

Shumaker, R. 1999. Personal communication (e-mail 11 January).

Black and White Colobus Monkey (*Colobus guereza*). Colobus Conservation, in conjunction with the Kenya Wildlife Service and Friends of the Karura Forest, has released at least 150 black and white colobus monkeys (in at least three intact groups) and several individual infants over unspecified years. The groups were released in the Karura Forest (1,063 ha) in Nairobi, Kenya.

A more recent description of this program (Fundi et al 2018a) states that 150 colobus monkeys in 22 groups were translocated from "agroecosystems of Kipipiri" to the Karura Forest between 2014 and 2016. The colobus monkeys had been crop-raiding. The purpose was to resolve conflicts with farmers and to conserve the monkeys. The release site was chosen for the availability of suitable food, water, and cover as well as low levels of agricultural development and low predator presence. There were three phases in this effort, involving 40, 60, and 50 monkeys respectively. Most of the reintroductions involved intact family units. The monkeys were held in acclimation cages for three to six days. They were not provisioned after release. Fundi et al (2018b) presumably refer to the same reintroductions, and note that five guerezas died due to falling from trees shortly after release, and 80% of the others locomoted on the ground following release.

The total of 150 released monkeys may not include some infant(s) that had become separated and were reunited with their mothers. The number of these infants is not specified; I have used the minium number (one) bringing the reintroduced total to 151. The success of the group releases and the reunification of infants is said to have been high. Colobus Conservation has also reintroduced vervets and Sykes monkeys (see below) and, according to the Colobus Conservation web site, bushbabies.

Welfare (Rehabilitation)

References

Donaldson, A. 2013. Reunited! A colobus monkey infant and his mum. *International Primate Protection League News* 40(1): 14-15.

Donaldson, A. 2016. Personal communication (e-mail 9 May).

Friends of Karura Forest. 2016. Facebook page, 7 March 2016.

Fundi, P., Kivai, S., Kariuki, T., and C. Mariotte. 2018a. Kenya guereza (*Colobus guereza kikuyensis*) reintroduction at Karura Forest Reserve. Abstract of a paper presented at the 27th Congress of the International Primatological Society, Nairobi, Kenya.

Fundi, P., Kivai, S., Kariuki, T., Mariotte, C., and H Croze. 2018b. Habituation, capture, release, and monitoring of Mount Kenya guerezas (*Colobus, guereza, kikuyuensis*) at Karura Forest. Abstract of a poster presented at the 27th Congress of the International Primatological Society, Nairobi, Kenya.

www.colobusconservation.org

Black and White Colobus Monkey (*Colobus guereza*). In a comment on a Facebook post by Andrea Donaldson (7 March 2016), A. B. Murage notes the translocation of four groups of black and white colobus monkeys from Kipiriri in Nyandarua, Kenya to Delamere Estates in Naivasha, Kenya. This is presumably a different destination site than the Karura Forest in the program above. These releases are said to have occurred over nine months but the year(s) of release, the total number of animals, and the purposes of the release are unspecified, and no further details are provided.

Unspecified

References

Murage, A. B. 2016. Comment on a Facebook post by Andrea Donaldson, 7 March 2016.

Chacma Baboon (*Papio ursinus*). The Centre for Animal Rehabilitation and Education in the Limpopo province of South Africa released 19 rescued and rehabilitated chacma baboons in or near Kruger National Park in 2014. Other than the release of the troop being gradual, i.e. just a few members at a time, I could find no information on veterinary examinations, pre-release preparation, acclimation, or post-release monitoring. The released animals apparently returned to the center periodically to visit the troop members that were awaiting release. The charismatic founder of the center, Rita Miljo, is said to have released "a number of" rehabilitant troops of chacma baboons since the center was founded in 1989, including two troops (a total of 35 baboons) into the Vredefort Dome conservation area in 2002. These groups were rescued and returned to captivity after members were poisoned or shot by landowners and hunters. Miljo died tragically in 2012, but the center's rehabilitation and release work appears to be continuing.

Welfare (Rehabilitation)

References

Anon. 2005. Baboons! *International Primate Protection League News* 32(1): 14-17.

Dewhirst, S. 2014. Thanks from the field: A baboon troop release. *International Primate Protection League News* 41(3): 7.

Chacma Baboon (*Papio ursinus*). The Riverside Wildlife Rehabilitation Centre released one troop of 24 rescued and confiscated chacma baboons on the Kondowe private game reserve in Limpopo, South Africa in 2011. The baboons were kept in large enclosures at the center for up to four years; some of the released monkeys were born during this time in captivity. I could find no information on veterinary examinations, pre-release preparation, acclimation, or post-release monitoring, except that some of the animals were sighted in 2013.

Welfare (Rehabilitation)

References

www.riversidewrc.com

Yellow and Olive (Anubis) Baboons (*Papio cynocephalus and P. anubis*). Both Kawai (1960) and Furuya (1965) mention that the Japan Monkey Centre introduced yellow and anubis baboons onto Tsukumijima (Tukumisima, the English spelling varies) Island in the late 1950s or early 1960s. There are no further details about numbers, techniques, or outcomes. I assume that the baboons were all wild-born, and that the purposes were the same as those of the reintroduction of Japanese macaques on Ôhirayama Mountain (see above) and the introduction of crab-eating macaques on Kijima Island (see above): to conduct research and establish a breeding colony. I visited these baboons on the island in 1974. The baboons were removed from the island in approximately 1975, and their descendants live in the Centre's Castle of Baboons exhibit. There are no longer any monkeys on Tsukumijima.

Research, Commercial

References

Furuya, Y. 1965. Social organization of the crab-eating monkey. *Primates* 6(3-4): 285-336.

Hirata, S. 2017. Personal communication (e-mail 5 January).

Kawai, M. 1960. A field experiment on the process of group formation in the Japanese monkey (Macaca fuscata), and the releasing of the group at Ôhirayama. *Primates* 2: 181-255.

Yellow Baboon (*Papio cynocephalus*). The Liongwe Wildlife Centre released a group of 25 rescued or confiscated, rehabilitated yellow baboons in the Kasungu National Park (231,500 ha) in Malawi in 2013. One additional group member was released several months after the original 25. There is no information on pre-release preparation other than that the baboons had been integrated into a single group. The baboons were acclimated in a cage at the release site for one week.

The adults were radiocollared, and the baboons were monitored for at least six months after release, when the report was written. The animals ranged widely, foraged for wild foods, withstood a leopard attack, reproduced, and dispersed normally. Several of the baboons became separated from the group after the leopard attack, and were led back to the group by observers. Data on social behavior that were collected before release were to be compared to post-release observations.

Welfare (Rehabilitation), Research

References

Ipema, J. 2013. Free at last! A troop of rescued baboons is released to a park in Malawi. *International Primate Protection League News* 40(1): 11-13.

Olive Baboon (*Papio anubis*). The Gilgil Baboon Project, under the direction of Professor Shirley Strum of the University of California, San Diego, translocated three groups of wild olive baboons (131 individuals) from the privately owned Kekopey Ranch in Kenya to two sites on the Laikipia Plateau (approximately 200 km away) in 1984. These baboons had become crop- and garden-raiders and were entering peoples' homes to steal food. Farmers and soldiers began to shoot them. Strum and her associates had studied the ecology, behavior, and reproduction of many of these baboons for 14 years. She knew the identity and history of every studied individual. She decided to save these baboons by moving them to a more remote site that had fewer human inhabitants and less agricultural activity. This was a welfare Translocation. The translocated groups survived and were spared what was likely to have been total extirpation or at least violent deaths and a lifetime of conflict with humans.

Two of the groups were released at one site, and the third group was released at a different site. Both sites were privately owned ranches and conservation areas. There was a resident baboon population and a full suite of predators at both sites. The translocated baboons were medically screened before translocation to reduce the possibility of transfer of communicable disease. Females were released while males were held in cages at the release site to increase the probability that the baboons would remain near the release site. The baboons were given some food supplementation for three weeks after release, and for 13 weeks during a drought in 1986. Eight of the released female baboons were given antibiotics for a bacterial infection in 1986

This reintroduction is unique and exemplary among all primate reintroductions for its meticulous planning and management and its degree of documentation. Strum was committed to a scientifically rigorous examination of the outcome of the translocations. She had documented the birth and death rates, mortality and survivorship, group sizes, body condition, and the occurrence of intestinal parasites of the baboon groups for years, and used this as a pre-release baseline for post-release comparisons for two of the groups. These two groups were observed with comparable methodology for 15 years after they were translocated. Strum also studied a wild, non-translocated group near the destination site as a "control" for further comparison. Although there was short-term variation, the long-term similarities in birth rates, death rates, survivorship, mortality, group sizes, and causes of death before and after translocation and between translocated and non-translocated groups provided compelling evidence for the success of the translocations.

Welfare (Non-lethal Control), Research

References

Strum, S. C. 2002. Translocation of three wild troops of baboons in Kenya. *Re-introduction News* 21: 12-15.

Strum, S. C. 2005. Measuring success in primate translocation: A baboon case study. *American Journal of Primatology* 65: 117-140.

Mandrill (*Mandrillus sphinx*). The Centre International de Recherches Medicales de Franceville (CIRMF) reintroduced 36 captive-born mandrills (16 males, 20 females; three female matrilines) into the Lékédi Park in Gabon in 2002. The park was privately owned by the Société du Développement du Parc de la Lékédi. The mandrills had been born and lived in a 6-ha forested enclosure at the center as part of a large colony that was maintained for noninvasive biomedical research. The colony had grown to more than 100 individuals; this reintroduction was conducted primarily to relieve crowding. A secondary purpose was to conduct research that would inform future mandrill reintroductions. The enclosure at the center presumably provided them with at least some experience foraging and locomoting on natural vegetation. The mandrills were treated for endoparasites and were genotyped before release. Six individuals were radiocollared.

The release site was a 1,750-ha fenced enclosure. Gorillas, chimpanzees, guenons, and a few mandrills were present. A vegetation survey showed that at least 50% of the plant species that are eaten by wild mandrills were present. The mandrills were acclimated in a 0.5-ha enclosure within the primary release area for two to five weeks. They received the same diet in the acclimation cages as they had at the center. Radio telemetry was used for post-release monitoring for the first eight weeks. Visual tracking was also used thereafter. Eight of ten infants died of malnutrition in the first eight weeks, and adults were emaciated, even though the release was timed to coincide with peak fruiting season. Supplemental feeding was initiated and was continued in diminishing amounts for more than two years. Four adults as well as the above eight infants died in the first year, but mortality decreased to 4% in the second year. Five infants were born in the second year.

Range use was limited, probably because of provisioning and lack of knowledge of seasonal habitat changes. The group numbered 22 in 2006, including 12 of the originally released mandrills. It is unclear if these mandrills could survive without supplemental feeding.

Welfare (Non-lethal Control), Research

References

Peignot, P., Charpentier, M. J. E., Bout, N., Bourry, O., Massima, U., Dosimont, O., Terramorsi, R. and E. J. Wickings. 2008. Learning from the first release project of captive-bred mandrills *Mandrillus sphinx* in Gabon. *Oryx* 42: 122-131.

Mandrill (*Mandrillus sphinx*). The Jane Goodall Foundation released 15 orphaned and confiscated, rehabilitated mandrills from the Tchimpounga Sanctuary into the 5,050-km^2 Conkouati Douli National Park in the Republic of Congo in 2015. The animals had been quarantined and had had extensive veterinary examinations before release. Some of the adults were radiocollared. The mandrills were released in two cohorts; a cohort of females and subadults and a subsequent cohort of males. The group had been formed on islands at the Tchimpounga Sanctuary, where they had access to natural vegetation and native foods. They were placed in an acclimation cage near the release site.

Three animals were returned to captivity because they were not thriving. One male died, possibly killed by a predator. Three females had given birth in the wild by mid-2016; all of the infants survived. Fecal glucocorticoid metabolites (FGCMs) were measured throughout the process. The FGCMs increased after the move to the acclimation cage and then again after the actual release. In each case, the FGCM levels returned to sanctuary levels within a month of being placed in the new environment. This is one of only a few studies of stress during the reintroduction process, and suggests that the animals' welfare was not permanently harmed by release to the wild.

Welfare (Rehabilitation), Research

REFERENCES

D. Cox, 2016. Personal communication (e-mail, 24 May 2016).

Woodruff, M. C., Lavin, S. R., Atencia, R., Woodruff, G. T., Lambert, F. N., Hill, R. A., Wheaton, C. J., and J. M. Setchell. 2016. Measuring fecal glucocorticoid metabolites during a reintroduction of mandrills (*Mandrillus sphinx*) in the Republic of Congo. Abstract of a paper presented at the joint meeting of the 26th Congress of the International Primatological Society and the 39th Meeting of the American Society of Primatologists, Chicago, IL, USA.

www.janegoodallinstitute.org

Drill (*Mandrillus leucophaeus*). The primary focus of Pandrillus, the Drill Rehabilitation and Breeding Center (also known as Drill Ranch), is to care for, rehabilitate, and reintroduce drills (*Mandrillus leucopheus*). Over the years the Center's managers, Liza Gadsby and Peter Jenkins, have rehabilitated orphaned wild drills and established the largest drill breeding colony in the world, now numbering more than 500 individuals. The center is located in Nigeria's 10,400-ha Afi Mountain Wildlife Sanctuary, in which wild populations of drills, chimpanzees, and gorillas survive despite considerable hunting pressure. Rescued chimpanzees also live at the center (see above).

I have been unable to locate any specific information about drill reintroduction, but the summary of a recent talk by Gadsby states: "In its 27-year history, Drill Ranch has rehabilitated over 86 orphaned drills and reintroduced them back into the wild."

Welfare (Rehabilitation)

REFERENCES

Anon. 2018. Drill Ranch: "The drill monkey". *IPPL News* 45(1): 5.

Patas Monkey (*Erythrocebus patas*). The Caribbean Primate Research Center (CPRC) captured an unknown number of patas monkeys in Nigeria in the late 1960s and early 1970s. They were apparently kept in a 0.2-ha corral(s) in Puerto Rico for some time, and then 46 patas monkeys were released on the islands of Guayacán and Cuerva, off the southwest coast of the Puerto Rican mainland, between 1971 and 1979. The islands were actually peninsulas, connected to the mainland at low tide by mangrove swamps. The monkeys were allowed to range freely on the islands. Previously introduced rhesus macaques also lived on the islands (see above). The islands were located in the Boqueron Commonwealth Forest, which is a marine protected area. An additional 85 patas monkeys were added to the free-ranging island population in 1981. This cohort consisted of 82 females and three males; 67 were wild-born from Nigeria and 18 had been born in National Institutes of Health laboratories. Thus the introduction to the island occurred in two cohorts with a total of 131 patas monkeys, of which 113 were wild-born and 18 were captive-born. They were medically examined and most were tattooed before release. They were provisioned after release. The colony was closed in 1982, and 106 patas monkeys were moved into corrals and cages at the CPRC mainland headquarters. In addition to the 106, 54 monkeys were unaccounted for when the colony was closed.

The primary purpose of this reintroduction was commercial, to provide subjects for biomedical research, mainly on communicable diseases, and for the production of vaccines. The hope was that the patas monkeys would use the dry interior of the islands that was unused by the rhesus monkeys, thereby increasing the effective carrying capacity of the islands.

Patas monkeys had been escaping from the islands to the mainland via the mangrove swamps since 1974. As noted, 54 of the patas monkeys were missing and had probably escaped to the mainland by crossing the mangrove swamp between 1974 and 1982. This is really a second reintroduction in our terms, but I have treated both as a single program. Escapes to the mainland peaked with the addition of the 85 patas monkeys to the islands in 1981, due to heightened aggression between the new and the established monkeys. The escaped monkeys settled in the Sierra Bermeja hills (approximately 22,000 ha) and surrounding area, and coexisted with escaped CPRC rhesus monkeys (see above). The size of the mainland population was estimated to have been 70 in 1984, and ultimately grew to between 400 and 600 individuals; one media account estimated a population size of more than 1,000. The behavioral ecology of one studied patas subpopulation of 120 individuals approximated that of wild patas monkeys.

The monkeys became agricultural pests. The descendants of the escaped patas and rhesus monkeys occupied a range of 60,000 ha by 2006 and were causing approximately US$1.5 million in agricultural losses annually. Extermination of the monkeys was begun in 2008. This second reintroduction was an accidental release.

Commercial, Accidental (Escape)

References

Anon. 2008b. Puerto Rico kills troublesome monkeys. *Associated Press article.*

Engeman, R.M., Laborde, J.E., Constatin, B.U., Shwiff, S.A., Hall, P., Duffiney, A., and F. Luciano. 2010. The economic impacts to commercial farms from invasive monkeys in Puerto Rico. *Crop Protection* 29: 401-405.

González-Martínez, J. 1998. The ecology of the introduced patas monkey (*Erythrocebus patas*) population of southwestern Puerto Rico. *American Journal of Primatology* 45: 351–365.

González-Martínez, J. 2004. The introduced free-ranging rhesus and patas monkey populations of southwestern Puerto Rico. *Puerto Rico Health Sciences Journal* 23:39–46.

Kessler, M. J. and R. G. Rawlins. 2016. A 75-year pictorial history of the Cayo Santiago rhesus monkey colony. *American Journal of Primatology* 78: 6-43.

Loy, J. 1989. Studies of free-ranging and corralled patas monkeys at La Parguera, Puerto Rico. *Puerto Rico Health Sciences Journal* 8: 129-131.

Mona Monkey (*Cercopithecus mona*). An unknown number of mona monkeys were released in an unknown number of cohorts by slave traders on the islands of São Tomé and Príncipe in the Gulf of Guinea, approximately 250 km off the coast of what is now Gabon. The first cohorts were probably released within years of the discovery of the islands in the late 15th century. The monkeys were carried on board ships as a live food supply. The site(s) of origin was probably in western Africa. The São Tomé and Príncipe mona monkey populations were probably the source of the reintroduced population on the Caribbean island of Grenada (see below). Mona monkeys survive in large numbers on São Tomé and Príncipe today.

Commercial

REFERENCES

Dore, K.M. 2017. Ethnophoresy. In A. Fuentes, B. Bezanson, C.J. Campbell, A.F. DiFiore, S. Elton, A. Estrada, L.E. Jones-Engel, K.C. MacKinnon, K.A.I. Nekaris, E. Riley, S. Ross, C. Sanz, R.W. Sussman, and B. Thierry, eds. *The International Encyclopedia of Primatology*. Hoboken, Wiley-Blackwell.

Glenn M.E. and K.J. Bensen. 2013. The mona monkeys of Grenada, São Tomé and Príncipe: Long-term persistence of a guenon in permanent fragments and implications for the survival of forest primates in protected areas. In L. Marsh and C. Chapman, eds. *Primates in Fragments. Developments in Primatology: Progress and Prospects*. New York, NY, Springer.

Glenn, M.E. and K.J. Bensen. 2016. Are small, isolated populations of forest monkeys worth saving? A 200+ year case study on mona monkeys (*Cercopithecus mona*) on the Caribbean island of Grenada. Abstract of a paper presented at the joint meeting of the 26th Congress of the International Primatological Society and the 39th Meeting of the American Society of Primatologists, Chicago, IL, USA.

Masseti, M. and E. Bruner. 2009. The primates of the Western Palearctic: A biogeographical, historical, and archeozoological review. *Journal of Antrhopological Sciences* 87: 33-91.

Mona Monkey (*Cercopithecus mona*). An unknown number of mona monkeys were released by slave traders on the island of Grenada between 1600 and 1800. There is no record of the number of releases or the number of founders, but genetic studies indicate that there may have been few or even only one founding female. The site of origin of the founder(s) was the island of São Tomé (see above) rather than from the African mainland. Lippold suggests that the mona monkeys may have been brought from Africa as "trade items", and we could also expect that traders brought the monkeys as a food supply for their voyage. de Vos et al claim that they had been brought to Grenada as pets. A recent survey found that the Grenada population had declined from more than 2,000 in 1995 to fewer than 300 in 2014 (Gunst et al), although Glenn and Bensen state that there are still "thousands" of mona monkeys living in the approximately 5,000 ha of suitable forest habitat on Grenada. Seasonal variation in numbers in the census area and use of non-forest, agricultural habitats may account for the difference in current population estimates. Hunting (monkey meat is regarded as a delicacy in Grenada), the pet trade, and Hurricane Ivan in 2004 caused the apparent population decline. Glenn and Bensen (2016) report: "(W)e have also not found other measurable change or negative inbreeding effects in gross morphology (sample n = 24) or vocal and social repertoire when compared to mona populations in Cameroon, Nigeria, Benin and São Tomé and Príncipe."

Commercial

References

de Vos, A., Manville, R.H., and R.G. Van Gelder. 1956. Introduced mammals and their influence on native biota. *Zoologica* 41(4): 163-194.

Glenn M.E. and K.J. Bensen. 2013. The mona monkeys of Grenada, São Tomé and Príncipe: Long-term persistence of a guenon in permanent fragments and implications for the survival of forest primates in protected areas. In L. Marsh and C. Chapman, eds. *Primates in Fragments. Developments in Primatology: Progress and Prospects*. New York, NY, Springer.

Glenn, M.E. and K.J. Bensen. 2016. Are small, isolated populations of forest monkeys worth saving? A 200+ year case study on mona monkeys (*Cercopithecus mona*) on the Caribbean island of Grenada. Abstract of a paper presented at the joint meeting of the 26th Congress of the International Primatological Society and the 39th Meeting of the American Society of Primatologists, Chicago, IL, USA.

Gunst, N., Forteau, A. M., Philbert, S., Vasey, P. L., and J-B Leca. 2016. Decline in population density and group size of mona monkeys in Grenada. *Primate Conservation* 30: 1-7.

Lippold, L.K. 1989. Mona monkeys of Grenada. *Primate Conservation* 10: 22-23.

Mona Monkey (*Caercopithecus mona*). The Centre for Education, Research and Conservation of Primates and Nature (CERCOPAN) released three (one male, two female) rescued and rehabilitated mona monkeys in 2007. The release took place in the 400-ha Iko Esai community forest in Nigeria. There was a resident population of mona monkeys and other *Cercopithecus* species in the area, but the numbers of all primates had been reduced by hunting. There was community support for the release; former hunters were hired to patrol and protect the forest. There was a vegetation survey of the area before release. The monkeys underwent quarantine and thorough veterinary screening before release. Some individuals were deemed unsuitable for release. The monkeys that were released were held in large forested enclosures in a sanctuary setting and were then acclimated in a large enclosure at the release site. They were given supplemental food after release. Two of the monkeys were radiocollared and there was intensive post-release monitoring. The reintroduction was terminated when the three monkeys returned to the acclimation enclosure and would not stay in the forest.

A Cercopan Facebook page post of 9 February 2017 states that two mona monkeys had been released in the Cross River National Park in Nigeria in 2017, and a post of 9 May 2017 states that a "final" group of mona monkeys had been released in the park. All of the releases were conducted in collaboration with the Nigeria National Park Service. Various other Cercopan posts note that there had been extensive veterinary screening, and that the monkeys had been held in acclimation cages at the release sites for varying periods.

I could document the release of only five mona monkeys by CERCOPAN, but the total was doubtlessly higher. More than 100 primates of all CERCOPAN species had been reintroduced by early 2017 (Facebook post dated 10 February 2017), and more were released subsequently.

There apparently was declining financial support for the sanctuary that led ultimately to a 2014 decision to close it. The sanctuary population had grown to approximately 143 monkeys of various species native to Nigeria, but a Cercopan Facebook post of 8 January 2017 states that all of the monkeys had been "saved", meaning that they had been released to the wild or re-homed to other sanctuaries for long-term captive care. Despite the seemingly desperate plight of the sanctuary, the managers maintained high reintroduction standards and appeared to proceed cautiously and responsibly. However, documentation of releases subsequent to the 2007 release is needed.

Welfare (Rehabilitation), Conservation (Reinforcement) (the small number of animals makes it unlikely that conservation can realistically be a primary goal).

References

Anon. 2008a. Primate conservation. *Cercopan Annual Report* 2008: 7-8.

Cercopan Facebook page

Tooze, Z. 2008. From the directors. *Cercopan Annual Report* 2008: 3.

Tooze, Z. J. and L. R. Baker. 2008. Re-introduction of mona monkeys to supplement a depleted population in community forest in southeast Nigeria. In P.S. Soorae, ed. *Global Re-introduction Perspectives: Re-introduction Case-Studies from Around the Globe*, pp. 207-212. IUCN/SSC Re-introduction Specialist Group, Abu Dhabi, UAE.

Blue Monkey (Samango) (*Cecopithecus mitis*). Ninety-five samango monkeys were translocated to the Pafuri area (24,000 ha) of Kruger National Park in South Africa between 1982 and 1988.

The monkeys were captured in the Entabeni state forests, where they had been stripping bark from and killing cultivated pine trees. There are no details on the number of cohorts or pre- or post-release methodology. The monkeys were said to have disappeared after a drought in 1991 and 1992, although there are reports of a recent sighting in the area.

Lawes, who was not associated with this reintroduction, noted that wild South African samangos persist in relatively large forest fragments but not in smaller ones. They appear to be constrained by diet (folivory) and social dynamics from crossing nonforested areas to nearby fragments. Lawes modeled the effects of building forest corridors between fragments and of translocation among fragments on metapopulation survival. Corridors would improve survival over several centuries but translocation would have no effect. This study reminds us that conclusions about reintroduction/translocation must consider species-specific behavioral and ecological characteristics.

Welfare (Non-lethal control)

References

Anon. undated a. Samango Monkeys. *Kruger Park Times*, www.krugerpark.co.za

Lawes, M.J. 2002. Conservation of fragmented populations of Cercopithecus mitis in South Africa: The role of reintroduction, corridors and metapopulation ecology. In M.E. Glenn and M. Cords, eds. *The Guenons: Diversity and Adaptation in African Monkeys*, pp. 367-384. New York, Kluwer Academic/Plenum Pubishers.

Blue (Sykes) Monkey (*Cercopithecus [mitis] albogularis*). The Institute of Primate Research in Nairobi, Kenya translocated 20 wild blue monkeys from one area in the Arabuko Sokoke National Forest to another area in the same forest where the density of the species was lower. The translocation, which took place in 1995, was conducted to study methodologies for conservation releases of endangered monkey species. "Biomedical samples" were taken before release but there is no mention of a veterinary examination. The monkeys were dye-marked and three were radiocollared. The monkeys were given one meal of cultivated fruits at the release site before being released. While post-release monitoring was planned to extend over 12 months, this unpublished report was written shortly after the release. The adult male of the group left the group and the remaining animals fissioned into two subgroups. One infant was rescued and integrated back into the group.

Research

REFERENCES

Stoinski, T. S., Moinde, N., Higashi, H., and T. L. Maple. 1996. Developing a translocation model for Kenyan forest primates. *American Zoo and Aquarium Association Annual Conference Proceedings*, September, 1996: 324-326.

Sykes Monkey (*Cercopithecus [mitis] albogularis*). Colobus Conservation released four Sykes monkeys in 2012 and eight in 2016 in Diani, a suburb near the southern coast Kenya. All were either rescued orphans or confiscated pets and had been rehabilitated. Data were collected on associations between individuals and on time budgets during rehabilitation and after release. Both cohorts were monitored for a year after release. I accessed only the abstract of this paper and therefore lack further details.

Welfare (Rehabilitation), Research

REFERENCES

Cunneyworth, P.M., Donaldson, A., and Z. Edwards. 2018. Using pre- and post-release assessments to evaluate a rehabilitation release of Sykes monkeys. Abstract of a paper presented at the 27th Congress of the International Primatological Society, Nairobi, Kenya.

Green Monkey (Grivet, Vervet) (*Cercopithecus aethiops [Chlorocebus sabeus]*). An unknown number of green monkeys were reintroducted in an unknown number of cohorts to the Cape Verde Islands, an archipelago of ten islands that lie approximately 500 km off the west coast of Senegal. They were reintroduced between 1462, when the islands were first discovered, and 1673, the date of the first written account of their presence. The site(s) of origin were probably in what is now Guinea and Guinea Bissau. They were probably brought as shipboard food reserves by Portuguese naval explorers. Green monkeys were once found on four of the ten islands but survive today only on Santiago and Fofo. Massetti and Bruner say that there are "plenty" of green monkeys on Santiago. The reintroduction of these green monkeys has probably impacted the native biodiversity of the Cape Verdes.

Commercial

REFERENCES

Dore, K.M. 2017b. Ethnophoresy. In A. Fuentes, B. Bezanson, C.J. Campbell, A.F. DiFiore, S. Elton, A. Estrada, L.E. Jones-Engel, K.C. MacKinnon, K.A.I. Nekaris, E. Riley, S. Ross, C. Sanz, R.W. Sussman, and B. Thierry, eds. *The International Encyclopedia of Primatology*. Hoboken, Wiley-Blackwell.

Masseti, M. and E. Bruner. 2009. The primates of the Western Palearctic: A biogeographical, historical, and archeozoological review. *Journal of Antrhopological Sciences* 87: 33-91.

Green Monkey (Grivet, Vervet) (*Cercopithecus aethiops*). An unknown number of vervets were released on the Caribbean islands of Barbados, Anguilla, St Kitts, and Nevis in the 17th century, or even as early as 1560. The vervets were introduced from western Africa, probably from Senegal, Gambia, Mauritania, Ghana, and/or Burkina Faso, by sailors who brought them aboard ship as pets, trade items, or, more likely, as food for the voyage. Some of the monkeys may also have come from the reintroduced population on the Cape Verde islands (see above). I am unable to find dates of releases or numbers introduced, but Dore concludes that thousands of vervets were probably released in hundreds of cohorts. The Barbados population was probably founded separately because Barbados is 600 km distant from the other vervet-populated islands in the Lesser Antilles. Denham believed that the Barbados reintroduction occurred earlier than the St Kitts, Anguilla, and Nevis reintroductions.

The descendants of these reintroduced vervets survive today and have become agricultural pests and are a threat to the islands' ecosystems. The monkeys on St Kitts may even outnumber the present human population of 35,000. There were more than 14,000 surviving in 1996 on Barbados alone, despite 2,000 having been shot for bounty and 8,000 having been trapped and exported for biomedical research between 1980 and 1994. Vervets are also being trapped and exported from Nevis and St Kitts for sale to biomedical research colonies. There are also trap, spay, and neuter programs to limit the population and crop-raiding on Nevis and St. Kitts.

Vervets were introduced to the Caribbean islands of St Martin/St Maarten and Tortola in the 1970s. They were probably brought as pets from St Kitts and Nevis, and then escaped or were released by their owners. There were approximately 50 on St Martin in 2007. A small population is also reported to live on the tiny island of Sint Eustatius, which is close to St Kitts.

Brown concludes his article with thoughts that pertain to many other introduced primate populations around the world: "With such a small population of monkeys on St. Martin, there is potential to successfully trap and remove all the monkeys from the island within a short period of time. If such a trapping effort is to take place, it should happen in the near future before the population gets too large for complete eradication. It is well understood that introduced mammals to island ecosystems are highly disruptive, however, it is difficult to explain to landowners and stakeholders that the removal of those species will be beneficial to the island.

Human empathy to protect animals such as monkeys, cats, and goats is strong, despite the ecological destruction that such species can cause on an island. Educating the public about island specific threats from introduced species is a necessary first step. Furthermore, promotion of the benefits resulting from prior eradication programs, even from other islands, would be beneficial. While immediate removal might not be practical for some introduced species, monitoring of their respective populations and ranges will be highly useful in further understanding the effects each species currently has on the native island biota." (pg. 17). Note: I do not personally support the wholesale removal of reintroduced primate populations unless they can be guaranteed lifelong quality care elsewhere.

These vervet reintroductions are all listed as one program because the dates and details of the many releases that must have occurred are unknown. Denham (1987) tries to unravel this history but a definitive reconstruction is still lacking.

Commercial, Recreational

REFERENCES

Boulton, A.M., Horrocks, J.A. and J. Baulu. 1996. The Barbados vervet monkey (Cercopithecus aethiops, sabeus): Changes in population size and crop damage, 1980-1994. *International Journal of Primatology* 17: 831-844.

Brown, A.C. 2008. Status and range of introduced mammals on St. Martin, Lesser Antilles. *Living World. Journal of the Trinidad and Tobago Field Naturalists' Club* 2008:14-18.

Denham, W.W. 1987. West Indian green monkeys: Problems in historical biogeography. In F.S. Szalay, ed. *Contributions to Primatology*, Vol. 24. Basel, Karger.

Dore, K. 2017a. Vervets in the Caribbean. In A. Fuentes, B. Bezanson, C.J. Campbell, A.F. DiFiore, S. Elton, A. Estrada, L.E. Jones-Engel, K.C. MacKinnon, K.A.I. Nekaris, E. Riley, S. Ross, C. Sanz, R.W. Sussman, and B. Thierry, eds. *The International Encyclopedia of Primatology*. Hoboken, Wiley-Blackwell.

Dore, K.M. 2017b. Ethnophoresy. In A. Fuentes, B. Bezanson, C.J. Campbell, A.F. DiFiore, S. Elton, A. Estrada, L.E. Jones-Engel, K.C. MacKinnon, K.A.I. Nekaris, E. Riley, S. Ross, C. Sanz, R.W. Sussman, and B. Thierry, eds. *The International Encyclopedia of Primatology*. Hoboken, Wiley-Blackwell.

Jasinska, A.J., Schmitt, C.A., Service, S.K., Cantor, R.M., Dewar, K., Jentsch, J.D., Kaplan, J.R., Turner, T.R., Warren, W.C., Weinstock, G.M., Woods, R.P. and N.B. Freimer. 2013. Systems biology of the vervet monkey. *ILAR Journal* 54(2): 122-143.

Konstant, W.R. and R.A. Mittermeier. 1982. Introduction, reintroduction and translocation of Neotropical primates: Past experience and future possibilities. *International Zoo Yearbook* 22: 69-77.

Long, J.L. 2003. *Introduced Mammals of the World*. Collingwood, Victoria, Australia, CSIRO Publishing.

Masseti, M. and E. Bruner. 2009. The primates of the Western Palearctic: A biogeographical, historical, and archeozoological review. *Journal of Antrhopological Sciences* 87: 33-91.

McGuire, M.T. 1974. The St. Kitts Vervet. *Contributions to Primatology* 1. Basel, S. Karger.

Vervet (Green) Monkey (*Cercopithecus [Chlorocebus] aethiops [sabaeus]*). At least 12 vervets escaped from The Anthropoid Ape Research Foundation (also known as the Dania Chimp Farm) in the late 1940s and established a population in the 3,700-ha Westlake (West Lake) Park in Dania Beach, Broward County, Florida, USA. Others may have escaped from or been intentionally released at the same site by unsuccessful tourist attractions, even as late as the 1970s. I assume that all of the released vervets were wild-born. The monkeys now use the mangrove areas of the park as well as adjacent private commercial and residential areas. They are provisioned by local people, who like the tradition of having the monkeys nearby. Williams (2016) found that 18% of area residents report that they actually feed the monkeys. Although the park is bounded by dense commercial and residential areas, roads, and waterways, two individuals dispersed in 2013; one was trapped more than 50 km away. "Mikey", an alpha male, was supplanted by another male in February 2018. Mikey left the park, traveled more than 10 km to the west through heavily developed and trafficked suburbs, and returned to the park, healthy and unharmed, in April 2018. His sojourn was a media and social media sensation, e.g. Block 2018, which confirms the public sentiment for these monkeys.

Population size appears to have varied between 20 and 120 over the years. Hyler (1995) reported that there were 36 vervets living in two groups at the site in 1992. Annual censuses between 2014 and 2016 have recorded between 36 and 44 individuals living in three groups (Williams 2016). At least seven of the vervets have been trapped since 1990, presumably for sale to biomedical laboratories or to the pet trade. The Florida Fish and Wildlife Conservation Commission does not plan to remove the vervets.

Accidental (Escape), Welfare (Non-lethal control)

References

Anderson, C.J., Hostetler, M.E., and S.A. Johnson. 2017. History and status of introduced non-human populations in Florida. *Southeastern Naturalist* 16(1): 19-36.

Block, E. 2018. Ousted colony monkey spotted in Cooper City. *Sun Sentinal*, 29 March.

Fleshler, D. 2015. Monkey business abounds at Dania Beach. *The Herald*, 4 September 2015, pg. 48.

Florida Fish and Game Commission website: *myfwc.com/wildlifehabitats/nonnatives/mammals*

Hyler, W.R. 1995. Vervet monkeys in the mangrove ecosystems of southeastern Florida: Preliminary census and ecological data. *The Florida Scientist* 58: 38-43.

Nolin, R. 2013. City of the apes: Monkey business haunts Dania Beach, Florida. *Florida Sun Sentinel*. 5 May 2013.

Williams, D. 2016. Census and local tolerance of *Chlorocebus sabeus* in Dania Beach, Florida. Abstract of a paper presented at the joint meeting of the 26th Congress of the International Primatological Society and the 39th Meeting of the American Society of Primatologists, Chicago, IL, USA.

Williams, D. 2018. Personal communication, e-mail 12 June.

Vervet Monkey (*Cercopithecus pygerythrus [aethiops]*). The Chipangali Wildlife Orphanage released a total of 17 former pet vervets and "several" infants that had been born to the ex-pets in the orphanage, on the 155-ha Zebra Island in Lake Kariba in what is today Zimbabwe in 1977. Zebra Island was only 1 km from the mainland and, when the lake level dropped, it was connected to the mainland. Elephants, lions, and leopards visited the island occasionally. Predatory birds and baboons lived there. There have been some human residents over the years.

While at the orphanage, the vervets were fed a variety of plant foods, bird eggs, insects, and mice. They were not fed on some days to "toughen" them. They were "introduced to" leopards, caracals, servals, predatory birds, and snakes. Contact with humans was decreased as the time for reintroduction approached.

The vervets were released directly from their shipping crates with no acclimation, provisioning, or systematic monitoring. Nine monkeys, including an infant, were seen on the island two months after reintroduction. They appeared to be traveling with a baboon group. Another visitor counted 19 vervets, including three infants, six months later. I could find no information on their present status.

Welfare (Rehabilitation)

References

Wilson, V. 1980. Operation monkey release. *International Primate Protection League Newsletter* 7(2): 12-13.

Vervet (Green) Monkey (*Cercopithecus [Chlorocebus] aethiops [sabaeus]*). An unspecified organization, probably the Cuban Ministerio de Ciencia, Tecnología y Medio Ambiente, reintroduced an unknown number of vervets in an unknown number of cohorts to Cayo Cantiles, a 3,400-ha island in the Canarreos Archipelago of Cuba, in approximately 1984. The purpose of the reintroduction was to establish a free-ranging colony from which individuals could be removed for biomedical research. The vervets came from St Kitts, which itself was the site of a much earlier reintroduction (see above). The vervets had been quarantined on Cayo Cantiles before release, and they were provisioned after release. Pig-tailed macaques were also reintroduced on the same island at approximately the same time (see above). Vervets, but not pig-tailed macaques were observed on Cayo Cantiles in a 1990 census, and were reported by Borroto-Páez to be present in 2009. They apparently are still being provisioned.

Vervets were alo released on the 77,700-ha Cayo Romano, an island in Cuba's Camagüey Archipelago, in the early 1980s. The purpose of the release was also to establish a free-ranging colony from which monkeys could be harvested for biomedical research. This release was managed by the Cuban Ministerio de Ciencia, Tecnología y Medio Ambiente. There were 50 founders, also from St Kitts. Vervets were still living on Romano in 1990 (González et al 1994), but were reported to be absent by Borroto-Páez in 2009.

The Canarreos Archipelago is to the south of Cuba and the Camagüey Archipelago is to the north. These were probably separate reintroductions but are listed here as one program.

Commercial

References

Borroto-Páez, R. 2009. Invasive mammals in Cuba: an overview. *Biological Invasions* 11: 2279-2290.

Dore, K.M. 2017b. Ethnophoresy. In A. Fuentes, B. Bezanson, C.J. Campbell, A.F. DiFiore, S. Elton, A. Estrada, L.E. Jones-Engel, K.C. MacKinnon, K.A.I. Nekaris, E. Riley, S. Ross, C. Sanz, R.W. Sussman, and B. Thierry, eds. *The International Encyclopedia of Primatology*. Hoboken, Wiley-Blackwell.

González, A., Manójina, N. and A. Hernández. 1994. Mamíferos del Archipiélago de Camagüey, Cuba. *Avicennia* 1: 51-56.

Vervet Monkey (Grivet) (*Cercopithecus [Chlorocebus] aethiops*). The Riverside Wildlife Rehabilitation Centre has released more than 462 rehabilitated, rescued, and confiscated vervet monkeys at various locations in South Africa. Nineteen established groups were released between 1994 and 2015. The monkeys were kept in large enclosures at the center for up to four years; some of the released monkeys were born during this time in captivity. I could find no information on veterinary examinations and pre-release preparation. The monkeys were kept in acclimation cages at the release sites for up to two weeks. I could find no information on post-release monitoring and long-term outcomes. Some of the releases occurred in protected areas and others on private land.

Welfare (Rehabilitation)

References

www.riversidewrc.com

Vervet Monkey (Grivet) (*Cercopithecus [Chlorocebus] aethiops*). Two groups of rescued vervets from the Centre for Rehabilitation of Wildlife (CROW) were released in the Duma Manzi Private Game Reserve, KwaZulu-Natal province of South Africa in 2007. There were 35 animals in one group and 24 in the other. Both groups had adults, subadults, and juveniles. Sexes are given for only the adults and subadults; there were a total of 15 males and 10 females. There appears to have been no pre-release preparation, but there was a short acclimation period at the release site, and food and water was provided after release for two months. The monkeys had colored ear tags, and adults and subadults were radiocollared. They were monitored for ten months after release. Six (17%) of the larger group and 12 (50%) of the smaller group survived for ten months. Losses were due to predation, conflict with humans, and conflict with resident vervets.

CROW released an additional three groups, apparently on private land, in KwaZulu-Natal in 2009. One of the troops had 39 vervets, and the others had 18 and 19. There is no breakdown of sexes or origins in the report but most were rescued and rehabilitated wild-borns. There was at least one infant that had been born in the center. There does not seem to have been pre-release preparation beyond formation of the groups. There was no veterinary screening. The vervets were held in acclimation cages for three to six days before release. None of the vervets was radiocollared. They received post-release supplemental feeding for one to three months and were monitored from two to six months. Wild vervets were present at the release sites. Survival was 10%, 39% and 10.5% in the three groups after six months. Guy et al (2012a) provide a thoughtful discussion of recommended methodologies for the release of rehabilitated vervets in South Africa.

Detailed data were collected on the post-release ranging, social behavior, and foraging of these groups.

Welfare (Rehabilitation), Research

References

Guy, A. J., Stone, O. M. L., and D. Curnoe. 2012a. Animal welfare considerations in primate rehabilitation: An assessment of three vervet monkey (*Chlorocebus aethiops*) releases in KwaZulu-Natal, South Africa. *Animal Welfare* 21: 511-515.

Wimberger, K. 2009. *Wildlife Rehabilitation in South Africa*. PhD Dissertation, University of KwaZulu-Natal.

Chapter 7: Reintroduction of African Monkeys

Wimberger, K., Downs, C. T., and M. R. Perrin. 2010. Postrelease success of two rehabilitated vervet monkey (Chlorocebus aethiops) troops in KwaZulu-Natal, South Africa. *Folia Primatologica* 81: 96-108.

Vervet Monkey (Grivet) (*Cercopithecus [Chlorocebus] aethiops*). The Wild Animal Trauma Centre and Haven (WATCH) released a troop of 16 vervets into the 5,250-ha Ntendeka Wilderness Area (part of a larger protected forest) in the KwaZulu-Natal province of South Africa in 2010. There were 11 males and 5 females that had been rescued and treated at a rehabilitation center. Some had been rescued as infants and had to be hand-reared. The group had been kept in a large enclosure at the WATCH rehabilitation center, where the monkeys encountered several types of predators and had some opportunity to locomote on natural vegetation. There was no pre-release veterinary examination. Patches of hair were snipped from their bodies to aid identification. Ten of the vervets were radiocollared but the batteries lasted only four months after release.

A plant survey showed that the release site had a number of species that were known to be eaten by wild vervets. A samango (blue monkey) troop lived within 1 km of the release site. The vervets were placed in an acclimation cage at the release site but escaped after one day, essentially releasing themselves. They were then provisioned daily for five weeks and occasionally thereafter to help locate them. They were monitored for six months. The vervets were seen to have foraged on natural foods from the second post-release day, showed strong group cohesion, and showed some predator awareness. Nonetheless, six vervets died of apparent predation and one was killed by hunters within five weeks. Additional individuals succumbed to predators and hunters, and others disappeared in succeeding months. Six of the original 16 vervets were known to be alive after six months.

WATCH released another troop of 29 vervets (18 males, 10 females, 1 unsexed infant) into the 30-km² Isishlengeni Game Farm, a privately owned plantation and conservation area in KwaZulu-Natal, in January 2008. The founders of this troop had all been rescued as infants and had been hand-reared at the center. Two of the 29 had been born into the group at the center. The group had lived in an enriched cage at the center but there was no specific pre-release preparation and no veterinary screening. None of the animals was radiocollared. They were acclimated at the release site for two days. They were monitored for six months after release and were given supplemental food for about two months. Wild vervets were present in the vicinity of the release. Hunters and hunting dogs were present, and they were known to have killed several of the released vervets. Eighteen of the 29 released vervets were known to be alive after six months.

WATCH released yet another group of 31 rescued and rehabilitated vervets (18 males, 12 females, 1 unsexed infant) on a different, 23,000-ha privately owned plantation and conservation area in KwaZulu-Natal in March 2009. They had lived in an enriched cage at the center but there was no specific pre-release preparation and no veterinary screening. Ten of the animals were radiocollared. They were acclimated at the release site for four days. They were monitored for more than six months after release and were given supplemental food for about two months. Wild vervets were not present at this release site, but wild blue monkeys were observed competing with the released vervets for the provisioned food. The dominant male of the released vervet group had to be recaptured three days after release because he behaved aggressively toward humans and entered homes. He was replaced by another male (which brought the total for this release to 32). Hunters were present; at least one of the monkeys was killed by a human. Ten of the released monkeys were known to be alive after one year.

Detailed data were collected on the post-release ranging, social behavior, and foraging of the latter two groups.

The authors of the articles referred to below, as well as Guy et al (2012a), noted that hundreds of wild vervets are rescued in South Africa each year and that there are 20 registered rehabilitation centers that care for them and try to reintroduce them back to the wild. These authors recognized the enormity of this challenge and provide thoughtful suggestions for vervet reintroduction in this context. This and the two previous programs have released almost 700 vervets in South Africa in two decades. Many others are likely unreported.

Guy and her colleagues strongly support the need for welfare-based primate reintroductions to follow IUCN primate reintroduction guidelines, but found that only 53% of practices derived from the guidelines were implemented in a sample of welfare-based primate reintroductions (Guy et al 2014).

Welfare (Rehabilitation), Research

References

Guy, A. 2013. Release of rehabilitated *Chlorocebus aethiops* to Isishlengeni Game farm in KwaZulu-Natal, South Africa. *Journal for Nature Conservation* 21: 214-216.

Guy, A. J., Stone, O. M. L., and D. Curnoe. 2011. The release of a troop of rehabilitated vervet monkeys (Chlorocebus aethiops) in KwaZulu-Natal, South Africa: Outcomes and Assessment. *Folia Primatologica* 82: 308-320.

Guy, A. J., Stone, O. M. L., and D. Curnoe. 2012b. Assessment of the release of rehabilitated vervet monkeys into the Ntendeka Wilderness Area, KwaZulu-Natal, South Africa: A case study. *Primates* 53: 171-179.

Guy, A.J., Curnoe, D., and P.B. Banks. 2014. Welfare based primate rehabilitation as a potential conservation strategy: Does it measure up? *Primates* 55: 139-147.

Vervet Monkey (Grivet) (*Cercopithecus aethiops*). Colobus Conservation, a primate and forest conservation organization, released a group of 12 rehabilitated, orphaned ex-pet vervet monkeys in 2012 in a suburban area (later described as an "anthropogenically modified landscape" by Andrea Donaldson) called Diani on the southern coast of Kenya.

According to Donaldson, who managed the release, "…the vervets are given pre-release training including wild food exposure and predator awareness training, and we ensure they are sleeping in groups, high in the pre-release enclosure. Once ready the group is released back in to the Diani environment. This is controversial as it is a human-populated area, but it is the location from which all of all the individuals originated. Should any individual display levels of pest behavior higher than those recorded in the wild troops, it is removed to undergo further rehabilitation. Released vervets are radiocollared, and monitored for one year post-release, collecting behavioral, feeding, proximity, and life history data. Our last release was in May 2012, when 12 individuals were released. Eight survived in the wild in 2014. Three wild males joined the troop at various points but two have since moved on. There have been four wild births in the troop, of which three infants survive. Baseline data on wild conspecifics were collected for one year prior to release and for 18 months post-release to provide a control within the same environment. Habitat assessments were also conducted to estimate any negative impact on the habitat." (edited for stylistic consistency). This data/research has formed the basis of Donaldson's PhD thesis at Durham University. At this writing (June 2018), the thesis is embargoed but the abstract is available and confirms Donaldson's account. "The release was deemed successful due to Release groups (sic) survivorship, activity budgets and general feeding ecology falling within the expected ranges set by the control groups."

Welfare (Rehabilitation), Research

References

Donaldson, A. 2013. Reunited! A colobus monkey infant and his mum. *International Primate Protection League News* 40(1): 14-15.

Donaldson, A. 2016. Personal communication (e-mail 15 June 2016).

Donaldson, A. 2017. Rehabilitation release of vervet monkeys (*Chlorocebus pygerythrus hilgerti*) in south coast Kenya: A Scientific Approach. PhD. thesis, Durham University. (Abstract only).

Red-capped Mangabey (*Cercocebus torquatus*). The Centre for Education, Research and Conservation of Primates and Nature (CERCOPAN), in collaboration with the Nigeria National Park Service, released at least two groups (numbers of individuals unspecified) into the 400,000-ha Cross River National Park in 2016 and 2017 (CERCOPAN Facebook posts dated 23 June and 16 July 2017).

Various other Cercopan posts note that there had been extensive veterinary screening, and that the managebeys had been held in acclimation cages at the release sites for varying periods.

I could not document the actual numbers of managbeys that have been released by CERCOPAN. A group of 41 had been transferred to an acclimation cage in Cross River National Park in early 2017 (CERCOPAN Facebook post dated 18 February 2017), but I don't know how many of these have actually been released. More than 100 primates of all CERCOPAN primate species is said to have been reintroduced by early 2017 (Facebook post dated 10 February 2017), and more were released subsequently.

A 26 August 2018 CERCOPAN Facebook post states that at least eight and perhaps as many as 20 red-capped mangabeys were seen in the national park in July 2018. The post does not claim that these were the mangabeys that were reintroduced.

There apparently was declining financial support for the CERCOPAN sanctuary that led ultimately to a 2014 decision to close it. The sanctuary population had grown to approximately 143 monkeys of various species native to Nigeria, but a Cercopan Facebook post of 8 January 2017 states that all of the monkeys had been "saved", meaning that they had been released to the wild or re-homed to other sanctuaries for long-term captive care. Despite the seemingly desperate plight of the sanctuary, the managers maintained high reintroduction standards and appeared to proceed cautiously and responsibly. However, documentation of releases subsequent to the 2007 release is needed.

Welfare (Rehabilitation)

REFERENCES

CERCOPAN Facebook page.

CHAPTER 8

REINTRODUCTIONS OF NEW WORLD MONKEYS

THE FIRST HISTORY OF PRIMATE REINTRODUCTION

William Konstant and Russell Mittermeier published the first comprehensive review of primate reintroductions in 1982. They focused on Neotropical primates but mention others as well, for a total of 18 reintroduction projects as defined in this history. Many are not documented anywhere else. Konstant and Mittermeier reviewed factors that contribute to primate reintroduction success, and provided recommendations that influenced the formulation of primate reintroduction guidelines. The paper also strongly influenced my and my colleagues' planning for the reintroduction of captive-born golden lion tamarins. Disclosure: Konstant served for a time as executive director of the Jersey Wildlife Preservation Trust International, which provided early support for the golden lion tamarin work.

References

Konstant, W.R. and R.A. Mittermeier. 1982. Introduction, reintroduction and translocation of Neotropical primates: Past experience and future possibilities. *International Zoo Yearbook* 22: 69-77.

Woolly Monkey (*Lagothrix lagotricha*). An unknown number of woolly monkeys were released on an island in the Rio Napo, Ecuador in the 1970s as a tourist attraction. There are no further details except for a second-hand report that there were between 20 and 30 woolly monkeys on the island by the early 1980s.

Commercial

References

Konstant, W.R. and R.A. Mittermeier. 1982. Introduction, reintroduction and translocation of Neotropical primates: Past experience and future possibilities. *International Zoo Yearbook* 22: 69-77.

Woolly Monkey (*Lagothrix lagothrica*). The staff of the Tahuayo Lodge and the people of the Peruvian village of San Pedro released five confiscated or surrendered former pet woolly monkeys in three cohorts into a small forest plot in a buffer zone just north of the 445,000-ha Area de Conservacion Regional Communal de Tamshiyacu-Tahuayo in Peru between 2005 and 2014. The monkeys of the first cohort, one male and two females, had lived on the grounds of the lodge between their confiscation in 2004 and their release. They were two to three years old at the time of release. I have no other details about pre-release preparation, the release itself, or post-release management. The villagers agreed not to hunt the monkeys.

The male was killed by a harpy eagle approximately one year after release. One of the females became ill and died in 2011. The surviving female, named "Dorilla", was groomed and fed by tourists thereafter. An additional male and female pet woolly monkey were acquired locally after their owners surrendered them to project staff. The female was treated by a veterinarian for infected wounds and was also found to be malnourished. She was released and initially avoided Dorilla. However, Dorilla approached her gently, gave her food, and eventually adopted her. The two females continued to approach the tourist boats for food. The male was released as the third cohort. He had been examined and treated for communicable diseases and parasites by a veterinarian. He integrated with the two females and sired an offspring with the older female in 2016. The mother became aggressively protective toward tourists and was re-released at a more remote location in the reserve. She and her infant joined a wild group.

When I visited the tourist lodge in 2017, there were two females and a juvenile ("Baby Mowgli") living in the forest across the river from the lodge. The oldest female was interacting with and was being fed by tourists. This was discontinued in 2018, and the monkeys are said to be spending more time deep in the forest and interacting with at least one wild wooly monkey.

Welfare (Rehabilitation)

References

Beaver, P. 2017. Personal communication (e-mail 29 January).

Woolly Monkey (*Lagothrix lagothrica*). Fundación Maikuchiga reintroduced eight confiscated and rehabilitated former pet woolly monkeys (two males, six females) in the 422,000-ha Amacayacu National Park in Colombia in 2010. The monkeys had lived in a "natural environment" at the Maikuchiga center for four years and had had veterinary support. There are no further details on pre-release preparation or veterinary screening. The oldest adult male and the two oldest females were acclimated at the release site for "a few days". The other five were then brought to the release site and all eight were released at the same time. The animals were given supplemental food for six months after release, and then during periods of food scarcity over the next two years. There was post-release monitoring at varying levels of intensity for two to three years.

The intent was to gradually reduce dependence on and contact with humans. There were six (one male, five females) living at liberty in 2011 when the Millán et al study began. The sources do not account for the two monkeys that were lost between 2010 and 2011. One of the five females that were alive in 2011 died between 2011 and 2012, another disappeared, and a third was rescued and returned to captivity. The three woolly monkeys (one male and two females) that survived in 2012 were apparently living independently. They had a home range of 350 ha and were eating a variety of natural foods. However, the male became ill and had to be rescued and returned to captivity. The females stopped foraging and returned to the base camp for food. Daily provisioning resumed.

Local communities had agreed to cease hunting woolly monkeys in the area before the release. No resident woolly monkey population was detected. The Colombian government later prohibited releases of confiscated wildlife of unknown origin. Bennett et al claim that conservation was the primary rationale for this reintroduction but the title and text of the article suggest that release of rehabilitants was primary. Millán et al's study compared the behavior, diet, ranging, and activity budgets of the reintroduced monkcys to those of captive and wild woolly monkeys.

Millán et al mention previous, undocumented reintroductions of an unknown number of woolly monkeys at the Caparú Biological Station in Vaupés, Colombia. Thomas Defler and Sara Bennett accepted a number of confiscated former pet woolly monkeys at Caparú during Defler's long-term field study of woolly monkeys there. They attempted to rehabilitate the woolly monkeys, which numbered as many as 15 over 25 or more years, by allowing them to range freely around the field station, feed on natural foods, locomote on natural vegetation, and encounter predators. They did likewise with unspecified numbers of squirrel monkeys, spider monkeys, uakaris, sakis, night monkeys, and other mammals and birds. Some of these were successfully reintroduced but the Caparú reintroductions are not included as separate programs in this history because of lack of documentation.

Welfare (Rehabilitation), Conservation

References

Bennett, S. E., Vásquez, J. J., Sánchez, L., Sinarahua, L., Murayari, A., Martinez, A., Peláez, L., and J. Millán. 2013. Preliminary observations from a welfare release of wooly monkeys in the Colombian Amazon. In P.S. Soorae, ed. *Global Re-introduction Perspectives: 2013. Further Case Studies from Around the Globe*, pp. 229-234. Gland, IUCN/SSC Re-introduction Specialist Group and Abu Dhabi, UAE, Environment Agency – Abu Dhabi.

Defler, T. 2017. Personal communication (e-mail and unpublished accounts, 27 January).

Millán, J.F., Bennett, S.E., and P.R. Stevenson. 2014. Notes on the behavior of captive and released woolly monkeys (*Lagothrix lagothrica*): Reintroduction as a conservation strategy in Colombian southern Amazon. In: T.R. Defler and P.R. Stevenson, eds. *The Woolly Monkey; Behavior, Ecology, Systematics, and Captive Research*, pp 249-266. New York, Springer.

Muriqui (Northern Muriqui) (*Brachyteles hypoxanthus*). Berger et al describe the release of one, presumably wild-born, female muriqui in a private reserve adjacent to Ibitipoca State Park in Minas Gerais, Brazil in 2017. The actual destination site, an isolated fragment known as the Mato dos Luna, had a very small isolated population of muriquis at the time. There were only two adult males, known to be brothers. The female was translocated to Mato dos Luna in the hope of "reinvigorating the local population". I was able to access only the abstract of this source and therefore can't provide further details. The private reserve is apparently being reforested and protected.

Conservation

References

Berger, B.C., Ferreira, A.I., Rodrigues de Melo, F., and F.P. Tabacow. 2018. The attempted reinvigoration of a population of Northern muriqui in Ibitipoca through reintroduction. Abstract of a paper presented at the 27th Congress of the International Primatological Society, Nairobi, Kenya.

Muriqui (*Brachyteles hypoxanthus*). Teixeira et al describe the release of four, presumably wild-born, muriquis (three females, one male) in unspecified locations in the states of Minas Gerais and Espirito Santo, Brazil. I had access only to the abstract of this presentation and thus lack details about the sites of origin and destination, pre- and post-release methodology, and outcomes. The monkeys did receive veterinary examinations and screenings.

Conservation

References

Teixeira, D.S., Vilela, D.A., Mangini, P., Lanna, A., Melos, F.R., and S. Lucena. 2018. Capture and translocation of muriquis (*Brachyteles sp.*) for the conservation of the species in Brazil. Abstract of a paper presented at the 27th Congress of the International Primatological Society, Nairobi, Kenya.

Muriqui (*Brachyteles arachnoides*). A wild female muriqui infant was rescued weak and cold from the ground in 1992 at the Caratinga Biological Station in Brazil. The infant was warmed, fed, and returned successfully to her mother within 27 hours.

Welfare (Rescue), Conservation

References

Nogueira, C.P., Carvalho, A.R.D., Oliveira, L.P., Veado, E.M., and K.B. Streier. 1994. Recovery and release of an infant muriqui (*Brachyteles arachnoides*) at the Caratinga Biological Station, Minas Gerais, Brazil. *Neotropical Primates* 2(1): 3-5.

Black (Red-faced) Spider Monkey (*Ateles paniscus*). The Faune Sauvage team of the Centre National de Equipement Hydraulique in French Guiana released one juvenile black spider monkey into a 15,000-ha portion of an unspecified forest in 1994. It was said to be an ex-pet but was included in an effort that released hundreds of other primates that were rescued from a forest that was being flooded by construction of a hydroelectric dam. There are no details about pre- or post-release management or the outcome for this monkey.

Welfare (Rehabilitation)

REFERENCES

Vié, J-C. and C. Richard-Hansen. 1997. Primate translocation in French Guiana – A preliminary report. *Neotropical Primates* 5(1): 1-3.

Black-handed (Black, Red-faced) Spider Monkey (*Ateles pigra, A. paniscus*). The Wildlife Care Center of Belize released three black-handed spider monkeys (two males, one female) into a "protected forest" of Belize in 2007. They were confiscated, rehabilitated monkeys. The release site was surveyed for other wildlife and plants before release. There was pre-release health screening, some pre-release exposure to natural food items, and post-release monitoring for 25 days. IUCN guidelines were followed. One of the monkeys was killed by a puma and one was injured by a wild male. The injured male and the female were returned to captivity after 25 days.

Welfare (Rehabilitation)

REFERENCES

Brockett, R. 2008. Designing a wildlife rehabilitation and release project – lessons learned. Poster presented at the First International Wildlife Reintroduction Conference, Lincoln Park Zoo, Chicago, IL, USA.

Geoffroy's Spider Monkey (*Ateles geoffroyi*). The Smithsonian Tropical Research Institute released 19 wild-born spider monkeys on Barro Colorado Island in Lake Gatun, Panama in several cohorts between 1959 and 1966. Spider monkeys had occurred naturally on Barro Colorado but had been hunted to extinction by 1912. The released monkeys were purchased as infants or juveniles from a market in Panama City. Some of the monkeys were released near the field station but others were released in more remote areas of the island. There is no account of their pre-release treatment but the ones near the field station were provisioned for a long time. The monkeys were monitored by a series of researchers until at least 2003. It is thought that only one male and four females survived the original reintroduction; they were the ones that had been released near the field station and had been regularly provisioned. The population had grown to 28 in 2003, and a demographic analysis suggested that it might be self-sustaining even though it had relatively low genetic heterozygosity due to the small number of founders.

Conservation (Reintroduction)

References

Eisenberg, J.F. and R.W. Kuehn. 1966. The behavior of *Ateles geoffroyi* and related species. *Smithsonian Miscellaneous Collections* 151(8): 1-63.

Konstant, W.R. and R.A. Mittermeier. 1982. Introduction, reintroduction and translocation of Neotropical primates: Past experience and future possibilities. *International Zoo Yearbook* 22: 69-77.

Milton, K. and M.E. Hopkins. 2006. Reintroduced spider monkey (*Ateles geoffroyi*) population on Barro Colorado, Panama. In: A. Estrada, P.A. Garber, M. Pavelka, and L. Luecke, eds. *New Perspectives in the Study of Mesoamerican Primates*, pp 417- 435. New York, Springer.

Geoffroy's Spider Monkey (*Ateles geoffroyi*). Perhaps to increase genetic diversity, an additional five spider monkeys were released into a forested area of Barro Colorado in 1991, some distance from the resident population that is described above. These monkeys had lived in a cage at a Panama City racetrack, and I infer that the primary reason for their reintroduction was to "dump" them as an alternative to killing them or keeping them at the track. Their history is unknown and their medical condition is assumed to have been compromised. There is no information about pre- and post-release management. They were monitored intermittently for less than a month. None is thought to have survived, and there was (thankfully) no interaction with the resident group. This is listed as a separate reintroduction program, given the dramatic differences in methodology between this effort and the previous one.

Welfare (Rescue), Conservation

REFERENCES

Milton, K. and M.E. Hopkins. 2006. Reintroduced spider monkey (*Ateles geoffroyi*) population on Barro Colorado, Panama. In: A. Estrada, P.A. Garber, M. Pavelka, and L. Luecke, eds. *New Perspectives in the Study of Mesoamerican Primates*, pp 417- 435. New York, Springer.

Black-faced Black Spider Monkey (*Ateles chamek*). The private primate rescue group "Ikamaperu" released nine spider monkeys (one group of two males, a female and an infant and another group of one male and four females) into the Pacaya Samiria National Reserve in the Amazon of northern Peru in 2012. All of the monkeys were confiscated wild-borns. The primary goal was to increase the wild population in this area, which had been reduced by illegal hunting. Protection had been increased in the area. The animals had lived for six years in a "free-ranging environment" in a sanctuary, and received pre-release veterinary screening. The females were radiocollared. The two groups were acclimated to the forest by being held in cages at the release site for two weeks. The monkeys were given supplemental food after release for an unknown time. The monkeys dispersed from the release site after six weeks. All of the monkeys were seen alive near a group of wild spider monkeys after four months.

Conservation (Reinforcement), Welfare (Rehabilitation)

REFERENCES

de Palomino, H.C. 2013. Rehabilitated spider monkeys successfully released in Peru. *International Primate Protection League News* 40(3): 16-18.

Black-faced Black Spider Monkey (*Ateles chamek*). The program for the Rehabilitation and Reintroduction of the Black-faced Spider Monkey in collaboration with the Taricaya Rescue Center, the Taricaya Ecological Reserve, and Projects Abroad, released at least 26 black-faced spider monkeys (in at least five groups) into the 476-ha Taricaya Ecological Reserve in Peru between 2010 and 2017. Spider monkeys had become extinct in the reserve due to hunting and offtake for the pet trade, until protection was re-established in 2009. The primary goal of this program was to re-establish a spider monkey population by reintroduction of confiscated wild-borns. The monkeys had rigorous veterinary screenings and treatment. They were fitted with radiocollars. They had been kept in cages at the rescue center, where they were fed some native fruits.

A total of eleven spider monkeys were released in the first three groups (cohorts). Four were released in 2010, six in 2011, and five in 2013. There was systematic daily monitoring for at least a year, with studies of behavior, activity cycles, diet, home range, and space use. Three of the 11 monkeys had to be rescued and returned to the rescue center; one was later re-released. There were four deaths, including three due to predation by a harpy eagle. Eight of the 15 monkeys in the first three groups survived in June 2014, including one wild-born offspring.

The fourth group (cohort), comprising six monkeys (counted among the overall total of 26), was released in October 2014. The fifth cohort comprised four females (counted among the total of 26) that were reintroduced in November 2016 in the hope that they would be assimilated into the previously reintroduced population.

The project website was taken down sometime between 2016 and June 2018. I had to reconstruct the reintroductions of the fourth and fifth groups from Spider Monkey Reintroduction Program – Peru Facebook posts of 18 April 2015, 17 November 2016, 22 March, and 5 December 2017, and 2 May 2018.

Monitoring appears to have been periodic and unsystematic since 2015. An 18 April 2015 Facebook post states that a group of ten monkeys was seen. There is little information on the outcomes of the fourth (2014) cohort. The four females in the 2017 cohort were not assimilated, and they were recaptured in March 2017. They were re-released with an adult male in December 2017. The male, and a female with a baby had to be recaptured after aggressive encounters with the resident population.

A 2 May 2018 Facebook post announced the birth of the seventh infant born in the wild to reintroduced parents. My rough calculation is that there were 20 to 25 monkeys surviving as a result of this reintroduction program as of May 2018.

Conservation (Reintroduction), Welfare (Rehabilitation)

References

Spider Monkey Reintroduction Program – Peru Facebook page, posts dated 12 and 14 February, 11 May, 20 June, 9 October 2014, 21 March, 18 April, 22 May 2015, 20 August, 17 November 2016, 22 March, 5

December 2017, 2 May 2018.

www.monosperu.com

Red Howler Monkey (*Alouatta seniculus*). "Operation Gwamba" rescued and translocated 479 red howler monkeys (and other monkeys) from flooding in the Brokopondo Valley due to the construction of the Afobaka Dam in Surinam in 1964. The monkeys were released in "unflooded forests". I could find no further details.

Welfare (Rescue)

References

Konstant, W.R. and R.A. Mittermeier. 1982. Introduction, reintroduction and translocation of Neotropical primates: Past experience and future possibilities. *International Zoo Yearbook* 22: 69-77.

Red Howler Monkey (*Alouatta seniculus*). "Operation Rescue" rescued and translocated "large numbers" of red howler monkeys from forest areas near Lake Guri, Venezuela to "the safety of surrounding forests" when the Guri Dam was constructed in the late 1960s. I could find no further details.

Welfare (Rescue)

References

Konstant, W.R. and R.A. Mittermeier. 1982. Introduction, reintroduction and translocation of Neotropical primates: Past experience and future possibilities. *International Zoo Yearbook* 22: 69-77.

Red Howler Monkey (*Alouatta seniculus*). Electricité de France, a corporation building the Petit Daut hydroelectric dam on the Sinnamary River in French Guiana, captured and released 124 red howler monkeys (29 groups) in 1994 and 1995. The monkeys were threatened by flooding of the forests behind the dam. The release area was a 15,000-ha forest that had been heavily hunted but received some protection for the reintroduction. Some of the monkeys were radiocollared and others were fitted with colored collars. The monkeys were medically screened and blood was taken for karyotypology. Two howler monkeys died as a result of irritation from fly larvae under the collars. Most of the howler monkeys established stable groups and home ranges after an initial period of dispersal and social instability. Reproduction and assimilation with the wild population was observed. There was post-release monitoring for at least six months.

Welfare (Rescue), Research

References

de Thoisy, B., Vogel, I., Reynes, J-M., Pouliquen, J-F., Carme, B., Kazanji, M., and J-C. Vie. 2001. Health evaluation of translocated free-ranging primates in French Guiana. *American Journal of Primatology* 54: 1-16.

Richard-Hansen, C., Vie, J-C., and B. deThoisy. 2000. Translocation of red howler monkeys (*Alouatta seniculus*) in French Guiana. *Biological Conservation* 93: 247-253.

Vié, J-C. and C. Richard-Hansen. 1997. Primate translocation in French Guiana – A preliminary report. *Neotropical Primates* 5(1): 1-3.

Red Howler Monkey (*Alouatta seniculus*). A wild-born juvenile female red howler monkey was reintroduced into a gallery forest at Hato Flores Moradas, Venezuela in 1989. The monkey had been kept as a house pet for 15 months and, after her surrender by the owner, she was kept for one year in a cage that was adjacent to a small captive howler monkey group that was the subject of a nutritional study. The female was provisioned with wild foods and was visited regularly by a wild howler monkey group during this time. The female was taken to Hato Flores Morados in a small cage four times a week for about six weeks, where she had a total of 11 hours of contact with a different wild howler monkey group that had been chosen to be the eventual release group. She had a veterinary examination and was marked with an ear notch before release. There was aggressive displaying by the female toward the wild group upon release, but she followed them as they moved away. She followed the group for several weeks after release and had joined the group after two months.

Welfare (Rehabilitation)

References

Agoramoorthy, G. 1995. Red howling monkey (*Alouatta seniculus*) reintroduction in a gallery forest of Hato Flores Moradas, Venezuela. *Neotropical Primates* 3(1): 9-10.

Black Howler Monkey (*Alouatta pigra*). Howlers Forever, The New York Zoological Society, and the Belize Audubon Society, in collaboration with the Belize Ministry of Natural Resources, established a population of black howler monkeys by translocating 62 wild-born individuals (19 adult males, 30 adult females, and 13 immatures) in three cohorts in 1992, 1993, and 1994. The destination site was the 51,800-ha protected forest in Belize that is known as the Cockscomb Basin Wildlife Sanctuary (the word "sanctuary" is usually used to describe a facility that rehabilitates animals in a captive setting, but here it means a "reserve"). Black howler monkeys had lived previously in the area, before it had been declared a sanctuary, but the species had been eradicated by the 1970s due to a combination of yellow fever, damage from Hurricane Hattie, and over-hunting. Hunting had been controlled at the time of the translocation, and there was community support for the conservation program. Phenology studies had indicated that there was sufficient and appropriate food for a self-sustaining howler monkey population in the reserve.

The first (1992) cohort comprised 14 individuals in three small groups. All of the adult monkeys carried individually- and group-marked ankle chains. Six females also carried radiocollars, and six other individuals had subcutaneous radiotransmittters. The monkeys were captured in the morning at the site of origin, given veterinary examinations (blood samples were drawn for later analysis), and then trucked or flown to the reserve. Acclimation cages were built at each of three release sites within the reserve. While in the acclimation cages, the monkeys were given leaves that were collected from the surrounding forest, and market fruits and vegetables. They were also given water. They were released after two or three days. There was no post-release support.

The monkeys were monitored every one to three days after release. One adult male and one juvenile disappeared after two months; the juvenile was believed to have died. The other 12 were alive after ten months, and four infants had been born by 1993.

The 1993 cohort consisted of 23 monkeys in five groups. The 1994 cohort consisted of 25 monkeys in six groups. Pre- and post-release methodology was similar to that of the 1992 cohort, except that three of these 11 groups were released on the day of capture and transport without having been held in an acclimation cage.

In all, 62 howler monkeys in 14 groups were translocated in 1992, 1993, and 1994. Two had died and an infant had been abandoned by its mother during capture. Forty-five of the 62 released monkeys were found in 1996 and 1997 censuses, and at least some of the 14 founders that had moved out of the study area were thought also to have been alive. Only three of the original founders were known to have died. There had been 34 births between 1992 and 1997 (including the four noted above). Six of the 42 infants died or disappeared. The population was estimated to have grown to between 300 and 500 by 2014 (R. Horwich, personal communication), and was independent of human support. A more systematic survey in 2017 estimated that there were at least 172 howler monkeys in 36 groups in the reserve. The population had spread as far as 20 km from the release sites.

Ostro et al studied group structure, dispersal, and feeding of the reintroduced howler monkeys for up to a year after release. Some of the groups disbanded immediately after release but the monkeys quickly established new groups or joined other groups. All of the resulting groups had established stable home ranges within six months of release. Silver et al studied the feeding behavior of four of the groups at the site of origin, the Community Baboon Sanctuary ("baboon" was the local name for "howler monkey"), which allowed Horwich et al (2002) to conclude that the reintroduced monkeys ate many plant species in the Cockscomb reserve that had not been available at the origin site.

Conservation (Reintroduction)

References

Cannon, J.C. 2017. Howler monkeys booming in Belize sanctuary 25 years after translocation. news.mongabey.com 10 May 2017.

Horwich, R.H., Koontz, F., Saqui, E., Saqui, H. and K. Glander. 1993. A reintroduction program for the conservation of the black howler monkey in Belize. *Endangered Species Update* 10(6): 1-6.

Horwich, R.H., Koontz, F., Saqui, E., Ostro, L., Silver, S., and K. Glander. 2002. Translocation of black howler monkeys in Belize. *Reintroduction News* 21: 10-12.

Horwich, R. Personal communication, 5 May 2014.

Ostro, L. E. T., Silver, S. C., Koontz, F. W., Young, T. P., and R. H. Horwich. 1999. Ranging behavior of translocated and established groups of black howler monkeys *Alouatta pigra* in Belize, Central America. *Biological Conservation* 87: 181-190.

Silver, S.C., Ostro, L.E.T., Yeager, C.P. and R.H. Horwich. 1998. Feeding ecology of the black howler monkey (*Alouatta pigra*) in northern Belize. *American Journal of Primatology* 45: 263-279.

Black Howler Monkey (*Alouatta pigra*). Two juveniles were secondarily noted to have escaped in Belize and lived and reproduced for at least two years in "not very favorable habitat".

Accidental (Escape)

REFERENCES

Horwich, R.H., Koontz, F., Saqui, E., Saqui, H. and K. Glander. 1993. A reintroduction program for the conservation of the black howler monkey in Belize. *Endangered Species Update* 10(6): 1-6.

Black Howler Monkey (*Alouatta pigra*). Two confiscated juvenile black howler monkeys (one male, one female) were released as a pair in the 859-ha Monkey Bay National Park in Belize in 1998. There was pre-release health screening, pre-release exposure to natural vegetation and foods, acclimation at the release site, "clicker" training to induce approach to humans, some post-release support, and two to six months of post-release monitoring. The two stayed together after release and joined a group of three wild howlers. IUCN guidelines were followed.

Welfare (Rehabilitation)

REFERENCES

Brockett, R.C. and B.C. Clark. 2000. Repatriation of two confiscated black howler monkeys (*Alouatta pigra*) in Belize. *Neotropical Primates* 8(3): 101-103.

Black Howler Monkey (*Alouatta pigra*). The Wildlife Care Center of Belize released 28 confiscated and rehabilitated black howler monkeys (14 males, 14 females) in "protected areas" of Belize from 1998 to 2008. They were released as six groups and six solitary individuals. The release sites were surveyed for other wildlife and plants before release. There was pre-release health screening, some pre-release exposure to natural food items, limited post-release provisioning, post-release monitoring for at least one year, and rescue of at least two of the released individuals. IUCN guidelines were followed. All of the groups and at least one solitary individual survived for at least one year, established home ranges, and interacted with wild howler monkeys.

Welfare (Rehabilitation)

References

Brockett, R. 2008. Designing a wildlife rehabilitation and release project – lessons learned. Poster presented at the First International Wildlife Reintroduction Conference, Lincoln Park Zoo, Chicago, IL, USA.

Mantled Howler Monkey (*Alouatta palliata*). As a pilot to develop methods for large-scale translocations of spider and howler monkeys, a group of seven mantled howler monkeys was translocated from an area slated for destruction to a 5-ha forest fragment in a public park in Mirador Pilapa, Mexico in the 1980s. The abstract provides no further details on methods or outcomes.

Welfare (Rescue), Research

References

Garcia-Orduna, F., Canales-Espinosa, D., Silva-Lopez, G., Jimenez-Huerta, J., Benitez-Rodriguez, J., and J. Hermida-Lagunes. 1987. Translocation program for the howler monkey (*Alouatta palliata*): A report. *American Journal of Primatology* 12: 363-364.

Horwich, R.H., Koontz, F., Saqui, E., Saqui, H. and K. Glander. 1993. A reintroduction program for the conservation of the black howler monkey in Belize. *Endangered Species Update* 10(6): 1-6.

Mantled Howler Monkey (*Alouatta palliata*). Two groups totaling 12 individuals were released on the 10-ha Agaltepec Island in Catemaco Lake in Veracruz, Mexico in 1988 and 1989. All of the monkeys had been born in the wild and captured shortly before release. The groups coalesced into one group of ten after the reintroduction, and then grew to 36. Females were marked with collars. There was extensive monitoring of births and deaths through 1994, and research was conducted on foraging strategies, food preferences, mother-infant relationships, and sexual behavior.

Research (to study the process of translocation)

References

Rodriguez-Luna, E. and L. Cortés-Ortiz. 1994. Translocacion y seguimiento de un grupo de monos *Alouatta palliata* liberado en una isla (1988-1994). *Neotropical Primates* 2(2): 1-5.

Serio-Silva, J. 1997. Studies of howler monkeys (*Alouatta palliata*) translocated to a neotropical forest fragment. *Laboratory Primate Newsletter* 36: 11-14.

Mantled Howler Monkey (*Alouatta palliata*). A group of four wild mantled howler monkeys (two male, two female) that had been captured and relocated specifically for this research project were released in a 90-ha privately owned forest with a palm plantation understory in the Flor de Catemaco near the Las Tuxtlas Biosphere Reserve in Veracruz, Mexico in the early 2000s. The monkeys were quarantined before release. Data were collected on feeding, resting, and movement for eight months after release. The group used only 5.5 ha as a home range of the 90 ha that were available. At least four births had been recorded by 2010.

A subsequent publication (Canales-Espinoza et al) reported the release of an additional eight mantled howler monkeys in 2012 in the same forest. These monkeys had been captured from forest fragments of 5 ha or less. They were quarantined. The authors report that the howler monkey population had grown to 25 in 2018, and that several births have been recorded; I don't know if the 25 include the four that were released previously or their four offspring. Six monkeys have emigrated to neighboring groups.

These releases appear to be parts of a single program managed by the University of Veracruz. The program demonstrates that wild primate populations can be established in forests that also support sustainable agricultural activities (in this case cultivation of ornamental plants) that provide economic opportunities for local residents.

Research, Welfare (Rescue)

References

Canales-Espinosa, D., Rangel-Negrin, A., Duarte Dias, P., Rodriguez-Luna, E., and A. Coyohua Fuentes. 2018. La Flor de Catemaco: Reintroduction Success in an agrosystem for howler monkeys. Abstract of a paper presented at the 27th Congress of the International Primatological Society, Nairobi, Kenya.

Shedden-Gonzalez, A. and E. Rodriguez-Luna. 2010. Responses of a translocated howler monkey (*Alouatta palliata*) group to new environmental conditions. *Endangered Species Research* 12: 25-30.

Mantled Howler Monkey (*Alouatta palliata*) and **Black Howler Monkey** (*Alouatta pigra*). This review documents the translocation of a total of 550 mantled and black howler monkeys in various locations of Mexico between approximately 1990 and 2015. The monkeys were rescued from areas that were "at imminent risk of disappearing." This number may include those documented in the three previous projects. There was assessment of physical condition, and blood was drawn before and after release; the animals were judged to be healthier after release. There are no further details in the abstract about release methodology, monitoring, and individual outcomes.

Welfare (Rescue), Research

References

Canales Espinosa, D., Rangel-Negrin A., and P.A. Dias. 2016. Translocation of Mexican primates: A critical analysis of past experiences and projection of future possibilities. Abstract of a paper presented at the joint meeting of the 26th Congress of the International Primatological Society and the 39th Meeting of the American Society of Primatologists, Chicago, IL, USA

Mantled Howler Monkey (*Alouatta palliata*). Thirteen mantled howler monkeys from two or three groups were rescued from flooding due to dam construction in Costa Rica in 1989. The monkeys were caged for one or two nights after their rescue. Three of the monkeys died between rescue and release. Ten were released in two groups in areas that were not occupied by resident howler monkeys, although some lived in adjacent areas. The released monkeys became solitary after release and they ranged widely. Some had to be captured and re-released. One died two months after release. Four were recaptured after six months, and the outcomes for the other five are unknown. This account was written from a secondary source (Horwich et al); I was unable to acquire de Vrie's thesis.

Welfare (Rescue), Research

References

de Vries, A. 1991. Translocation of mantled howling monkeys in Guanacaste, Costa Rica. M.A. Thesis, University of Calgary, Alberta.

Horwich, R.H., Koontz, F., Saqui, E., Saqui, H. and K. Glander. 1993. A reintroduction program for the conservation of the black howler monkey in Belize. *Endangered Species Update* 10(6): 1-6.

Mantled Howler Monkey (*Alouatta palliata*). The Refuge for Wildlife in Nosara, Costa Rica released five adult howler monkeys (two males, three females) in three cohorts in unspecified forest sites in Costa Rica in 2018. Howler monkeys are tragically electrocuted on uninsulated power lines in Costa Rica. The electrocuted monkey usually dies. Some infants carried by their mothers survive, and even a shocked adult can survive if it can be rescued and given prompt medical care by refuge personnel. The refuge also rescues howler monkeys that are savagely bitten by dogs.

The rescued howler monkeys are treated and screened and, when sufficiently recovered, are moved to outdoor enclosures and introduced to other howler monkeys. They are reintroduced as soon as their health permits. There is no post-release support or post-release monitoring. This information was taken from "news releases" posted on the International Animal Rescue website, dated 21 June, 27 July, and 15 August 2018.

Welfare (Rescue)

References

www.internationalanimalrescue.org

Brown Howler Monkey (*Alouatta guariba*). Biologists from the Federal University of Rio de Janeiro released two adult pairs of brown howler monkeys in the 39,500-ha Tijuca Forest in the city of Rio de Janeiro, Brazil in 2015. The release is said to be the first step in a program to re-establish howler monkeys in Tijuca as part of a program to restore the biodiversity of the forest itself. One of the male/female pairs came from a "private breeder" and the other from a government primate rescue center. All four had been rescued from animal traffickers. Both pairs were housed at the Rio de Janeiro Primate Center for nine months prior to release. They were fed native leaves at the center. They then spent 20 days in an acclimation cage in the forest. No details of post-release management were provided, but there has been post-release monitoring (the females wore radiocollars and the males wore neck bracelets). One infant was born but disappeared after six months.

Conservation, Welfare

References

de Oliveira Neto, C. 2015. Rio reintroduces howler monkeys after century's absence. www.physorg.com, 15 October 2015.

Escobar, H. 2016. Rewilding Rio. *Science* 353: 114-115.

Brown Howler Monkey (*Alouatta guariba*). Instituto Uriaçu reintroduced two brown howler monkeys (one male, one female) in the 2,500-ha Santa Bonita private forest reserve in Bahia, Brazil. The date was approximately 2016. One of the reintroduced howlers was an orphan subadult male that had been a pet of a human resident of the reserve since the monkey had been rescued as an infant. The female was a confiscated pet. Brown howler monkeys are native to the area but the Santa Bonita population had been extirpated in the 1960s by hunters and yellow fever. Hunting was controlled after the creation of the reserve. I was unable to find any details about pre- and post-release management. The release is said to have been successful, but there are no further details. It appears that the male, at least, was released because he was becoming a nuisance, and because the reserve's owner, Vitor Becker, wanted to re-establish the native fauna. However, in a later e-mail, Becker downplayed the reintroduction: "We did not have a proper reintroduction project. What we did have was a young male donated by a person who had this individual as a pet. He stayed with us free in the reserve (around the buildings), but one day disapeared in the forest and was never found again."

Welfare (Rehabilitation), Conservation (Reintroduction)

References

Becker, V. 2018. E-amil, 16 June.

Neves, L.G., Jerusalinsky, L., Melo, F.R., Rylands, A.B. and M. Talebi. 2017. Northern brown howler monkey. In C. Schwitzer, R.A. Mittermeier, A.B. Rylands, F. Chiozza, E.A. Williamson, E.J. Macfie, J. Wallis and A. Cotton, eds. *Primates in Peril; The World's 25 Most Endangered Primates, 2016-2018*, pp 96-99. Arlington, VA, IUCN SSC Primate Specialist Group (PSG), International Primatological Society (IPS), Conservation International (CI), and Bristol Zoological Society.

www.uriacu.org

Black-and-Gold (Black) Howler Monkey (*Alouatta caraya*). One group of seven and another group of an unspecified number of black-and-gold howler monkeys were reintroduced into the 35,000-ha Brasilia National Park in Brazil in 1983. The monkeys had been raised, free-ranging, in France by Scott Lindbergh and his wife. Some had been born in France. The sources provide no further details about pre- and post-release management. Most of the reintroduced howler monkeys survived and interacted with wild conspecifics. Santini studied feeding and daily activity for two months.

Welfare (Rehabilitation), Research

REFERENCES

Lindbergh, S.M. and M.E.L. Santini. 1984. A reintrodução do bugio preto (*Alouatta caraya*, Humboldt 1818 – Cebidae) no Parque Nacional de Brasília. *Brasil Florestal* 57: 35-53.

Santini, M.E.L. 1986. Modificações temporais na dieta de *Alouatta caraya* (Primates, Cebidae), reintroduzido no Parque Nacional de Brasília. *A Primatologia no Brasil* 2: 269-292.

Santini, M.E.L. 1986. Padrões de actividada de *Alouatta caraya* (Primates, Cebidae), reintroduzido no Parque Nacional de Brasília. *A Primatologia no Brasil* 2: 293-304.

Black (Black-and-Gold) Howler Monkey (*Alouatta caraya*). The Black Howler Monkey Rehabilitation Center released 26 confiscated pet howler monkeys and eight of their captive-born offspring in four groups into four small (0.18 ha) forest fragments in Cordoba, Argentina between

1994 and 2004. The release sites are on a private estate at the southern extreme of the natural distribution of the species. The monkeys were given complete veterinary examinations before release and they were given supplemental food and refuge boxes after release. They ate natural foods, used normal intergroup vocalizations, and showed natural social behaviors. These releases were said to demonstrate the feasibility of reintroducing black howler monkeys in larger natural forests in the future.

Welfare (Rehabilitation), Research

References

Bruno, G., Giudice, A. M., Nieves, M., and M. D. Mudry. 2005. Rehabilitación y reproducción de *Alouatta caraya* fuera de su area de distribución natural. *Neotropical Primates* 13: 21-22.

Squirrel Monkey (*Saimiri sciureus*). Two pairs of squirrel monkeys were released on the grounds of the 14-ha Bartlett Estate, also known as the Bonnet House, in the 1940s or the 1960s (sources vary). The estate is a forested "island" in the sea of high-rise condominiums, shopping centers, and roads that dominate the landscape of today's Fort Lauderdale, Florida.

The monkeys were released by a "social club" or bar that was adjacent to the estate. I could not determine the purpose of the release. There is no information on the origin of the monkeys; I assume they were wild-born. The population grew to 47 in 1988, and there were 39 in 1995. Some of the monkeys ranged into the nearby Hugh Taylor Birch State Park. Trappers periodically removed an unknown number of individuals from the Bonnet House property. The Bonnet House population declined to only three males by April 2017. Short periods of subfreezing temperatures are thought to have played a role in the group's decline. Bonnet House staff and tourists offer some food and water but the monkeys have always foraged extensively in the natural vegetation. Mangers of the estate are said to be committed to allowing the population to become extinct.

The Bartlett family, which was apparently not involved in the squirrel monkey reintroduction, had kept some pet monkeys of various species in the early 1900s. Some may have ranged in the estate's forests. One photo in the Bonnet House archives shows a caretaker with what appears to be a greater spot-nosed monkey, *Cecropithecus nictitans*, sitting, untethered, on his shoulder. There were no greater spot-nosed monkeys in the Caribbean, which suggests that this animal was imported from Africa. The property owner, Frederic Clay Bartlett, an artist, painted monkeys and collected monkey sculptures and other monkey-themed decorative art (personal observation).

Unspecified

References

Anderson, C.J., Hostetler, M.E., and S.A. Johnson. 2017. History and status of introduced non-human populations in Florida. *Southeastern Naturalist* 16(1): 19-36.

Layne, J.N. 1997. Nonindigenous mammals. In D. Simberloff, D.C. Schmitz, and T.C. Brown, eds. *Strangers in Paradise: Impact and Management of Nonindigenous Species in Florida*, pp 157-186. Washington DC, Island Press.

Taylor, L.L. and S.H. Lehman. 1997. Predation on an evening bat (*Nycticeius sp.*) by squirrel monkeys (*Saimiri scuireus*) in south Florida. *Florida Scientist* 60(2): 112-117.

Wheeler, R.J. 1990. Behavioral characteristics of squirrel monkeys at the Bartlett Estate, Ft. Lauderdale. *Florida Scientist* 53(4): 312-316.

Squirrel Monkey (*Saimiri sp*). An unknown number of squirrel monkeys were released at Silver Springs, Florida in approximately 1960. They were apparently introduced by the same tourist attraction that had earlier released rhesus macaques in the area (see above). The monkeys were caged at the site before release. There is no information on the origin of the monkeys; I assume they were wild-born. They presumably were fed and sighted after release. The squirrel monkeys left the release site and moved down the Silver River to the Ocklawaha River, as did some of the macaques. Between 12 and 15 squirrel monkeys were seen on the Ocklawaha in 1975. Their current status is unknown.

Commercial

References

Anderson, C.J., Hostetler, M.E., and S.A. Johnson. 2017. History and status of introduced non-human populations in Florida. *Southeastern Naturalist* 16(1): 19-36.

Layne, J.N. 1997. Nonindigenous mammals. In D. Simberloff, D.C. Schmitz, and T.C. Brown, eds. *Strangers in Paradise: Impact and Management of Nonindigenous Species in Florida*, pp 157-186. Washington DC,

Island Press.

Maples, W.R., Brown, A.B., and P.M. Hutchens. 1976. Introduced monkey populations at Silver Springs, Florida. *Florida Anthropologist*, 29(4): 133-136.

Squirrel Monkey (*Saimiri sp*). Long cites another, incompletely referenced, source stating that US Coast Guard personnel released a single squirrel monkey on Green Island in the Kure Atoll of Hawaii in 1961. The monkey lived "in a semi-wild state", which I assume to mean it was provisioned, until it disappeared in 1967. I was unable to access any other details.

Unspecified

References

Long, J.L. 2003. *Introduced Mammals of the World.* Collingwood, Victoria, Australia, CSIRO Publishing.

Squirrel Monkey (*Saimiri sp*). An unknown person or organization introduced an unknown number of squirrel monkeys in Masterpiece Gardens, a tourist attraction in Lake Wales, Florida, probably in the 1960s. The purpose is assumed to have been to enhance tourism. The techniques are unknown, but the monkeys were initially confined on a small island with some shelter. They escaped from the island sometime before 1980. There is no information on the origin of the monkeys; I assume they were wild-born. There were as many as 1,000 squirrel monkeys in the Gardens and the surrounding area in the 1980s. Masterpiece Gardens staff, visitors, and neighbors fed the monkeys at various times. Some were captured in 1981. The population is extinct.

Unspecified

References

Anderson, C.J., Hostetler, M.E., and S.A. Johnson. 2017. History and status of introduced non-human populations in Florida. *Southeastern Naturalist* 16(1): 19-36.

Bair, B. 1981. Masterpiece monkeys still driving Curtis bananas. Lakeland Ledger, 5 June 1981. https://news.google.com/newspapers?nid=1346&dat=19810605&id=348sAAAAIBAJ&sjid=MPsDAAAAIBAJ&pg=1743,1700939&hl=en.

Bair, B. 1983. Spider monkeys [sic] leaving like Masterpiece Gardens. Lakeland Ledger, 26 December 1983. https://news.google.com/newspapers?nid=1346&dat=19831226&id=E6lOAAAAIBAJ&sjid=afsDAAAAIBAJ&pg=2138,4090999&hl=en.

Layne, J.N. 1997. Nonindigenous mammals. In D. Simberloff, D.C. Schmitz, and T.C. Brown, eds. *Strangers in Paradise: Impact and Management of Nonindigenous Species in Florida*, pp 157-186. Washington DC, Island Press.

Squirrel Monkey (*Saimiri sciureus*). An unknown person or organization introduced an unknown number of squirrel monkeys along the Gordon River in Naples, Florida, probably in the 1960s. The purpose and techniques are unknown. There is no information on the origin of the monkeys; I assume they were wild-born. Some were subsequently trapped. Three squirrel monkeys remained in 2009, but none have been reported since.

Unspecified

References

Anderson, C.J., Hostetler, M.E., and S.A. Johnson. 2017. History and status of introduced non-human populations in Florida. *Southeastern Naturalist* 16(1): 19-36.

Squirrel Monkey (*Saimiri sciureus*). Animal welfare activists broke into an outdoor cage on the campus of Florida Atlantic University in the late 1960s or early 1970s and freed between 40 and 65 squirrel monkeys. The monkeys were being used in learning research by members of the psychology department. Thirteen monkeys in the colony remained in the cage. There is no information on the origin of the monkeys; I assume they were wild-born.

A popular source implies that the university made no attempt to recover them, although university employees did put out food and water for them and provided a heat lamp when the weather was cold. Members of the public may also have provided food. There were three animals remaining at liberty on the campus as of 1976. The population is thought to have gone extinct subsequently.

Those that freed the monkeys probably thought they were enhancing the monkeys' welfare, but the monkeys were not in imminent danger in the cage. By our definitions, the purpose of this release was Aesthetic.

Note: the Florida Game and Fish Commission website states that there have been at least six introductions of squirrel monkeys in Florida, but I have only been able to find documentation for the five listed above.

Aesthetic

REFERENCES

Anderson, C.J., Hostetler, M.E., and S.A. Johnson. 2017. History and status of introduced non-human populations in Florida. *Southeastern Naturalist* 16(1): 19-36.

Florida Fish and Game Commission website: *myfwc.com/wildlifehabitats/nonnatives/mammals*

Tarrant, B. 1976. Monkey see, monkey do...but FAU's monkey colony isn't do-ing (sic) too well. *Boca Raton News*, 6 December. Available online at https://news.google.com/newspapers?nid=1291&dat=19761206&id=IkBUAAAAIBAJ&sjid=V40DAAAAIBAJ&pg=1793,5241323&hl=en

Squirrel Monkey (*Saimiri sciureus*). "Operation Gwamba" rescued 32 squirrel monkeys (and other monkeys) from the Brokopondo Valley as it was being flooded by the construction of the Afobaka Dam in Surinam in 1964, and translocated them to "unflooded forests". There are no further details.

Welfare (Rescue).

REFERENCES

Konstant, W.R. and R.A. Mittermeier. 1982. Introduction, reintroduction and translocation of Neotropical primates: Past experience and future possibilities. *International Zoo Yearbook* 22: 69-77.

Squirrel Monkey (*Saimiri sciureus*). An animal dealer, Mike Tsalickis, released a total of 5,690 wild-born squirrel monkeys in 31 cohorts on Santa Sofia Island (405 ha) in the Colombian Amazon between 1967 and 1970. Santa Sofia was a newly formed island, and there were no conspecifics there. The purpose was to establish a "monkey farm" to produce a reliable supply of squirrel monkeys for export to primate biomedical laboratories. Tsalickis claimed that there were 20,000 in 1972 but Mittermeier et al and Bailey et al suggest that there were far fewer. There were between 850 and 966 in 1972 and 550 and 715 in 1977. These census outcomes led Hannah to suggest that the original number of reintroduced squirrel monkeys was far less than 5,690. There was no veterinary screening or other pre-release preparation, and no acclimation. There was some provisioning for an unspecified duration, and many fruit trees were planted to provide food. There was post-release monitoring of an unspecified duration, and there were informal population estimates for many years. There was protection against hunting on the island, but Hannah provides evidence that there was poaching over the years. The island currently has "several" species of monkeys, including squirrel monkeys, and is open to tourists.

Commercial

References

Bailey, R.C., Baker, R.S., Brown, D.S., Von Hildebrand, P., Mittermeier, R.A., Sponsel, L.D., and K.E. Wolf. 1974. Progress of a breeding project for non-human primates in Colombia. *Nature* 248: 453-455.

Hannah, A.C. 1989. *Rehabilitation of captive chimpanzees (Pan troglodytes verus)*. PhD. Dissertation, University of Stirling.

Jerkins, T. 1972. Free range breeding of squirrel monkeys on Santa Sofia Island, Colombia. In W. Beveridge, ed. *Breeding Primates*, pg. 144. Basel, Karger.

Konstant, W.R. and R.A. Mittermeier. 1982. Introduction, reintroduction and translocation of Neotropical primates: Past experience and future possibilities. *International Zoo Yearbook* 22: 69-77.

Mittermeier, R.A., Bailey, R.C., Sponsel, L.E., and K.E. Wolf. 1977. Primate Ranching – Results of an Experiment. *Oryx* 13: 449-453.

Sponsel, L.D., Slater Brown, D., Bailey, R.C., and R.A. Mitteremeier. 1974. Evaluation of squirrel monkey (*Saimiri sciureus*) ranching on Santa Sofia Island, Amazonas, Colombia. *International Zoo Yearbook* 14: 233-40.

Tsalickis, M. 1972. Trapping, husbandry and transport conditions of South American primates destined for research. *International Zoo Yearbook* 12: 23-6.

Squirrel Monkey (*Saimiri sciureus*). Two programs are described in this one textual description. The Pasteur Institute reintroduced 150 wild squirrel monkeys to a 56-ha offshore island (Ilet-la-Mère) in French Guiana in 1981 to establish a colony for the production of laboratory animals (Commercial) and to accommodate older and post-reproductive laboratory animals (Welfare, Non-lethal control) (Cohort I). An additional 14 post-experimental and old breeders were reintroduced to the island in 1999 (Cohort II). Five were captive-born and nine were wild-born. The purposes were to study the adaptation of these older animals and to study differences in post-release adaptation in captive-born and wild-born monkeys (Research).

There is some uncertainty about the overall number that were reintroduced; de Thoisy et al (2002) state that a total of 300 squirrel monkeys had been released on the island "over the years".

About 190 of the Cohort I animals and their descendants survived in four groups in 1997. One of the groups (n=90) was being provisioned. de Thoisy et al (2002) conducted an extensive behavioral ecology study in 1997.

Little is reported about how Cohort I was reintroduced. Cohort II was acclimated and trained before release. They had probably also undergone veterinary screening before release, and were provisioned after release. They were monitored for four months. The wild-born animals locomoted and adapted well but the captive-borns had to be removed after one month and brought back into captivity. One conclusion is that "…a captive existence in the infant and juvenile stages severely restricts the chances of learning to adapt fully to a free-ranging life". (Vogel et al 2002, pg. 149). The wild-borns integrated with the wild population.

These two cohorts are listed as two programs because of the different purposes and methods.

Cohort I: Commercial, Welfare (Non-lethal control)

Cohort II: Welfare (Non-lethal control), Research

References

de Thoisy, B., Contamin, H. 1998. The squirrel monkey breeding colony of the Pasteur Institute, Cayenne,

French Guiana. *Neotropical Primates* 6: 14-18.

de Thoisy, B., Loguet, O., Bayart, F., and H. Contamin. 2002. Behavior of squirrel monkeys (*Saimiri sciureus*) – 16 years on an island in French Guiana. *Neotropical Primates* 10: 73-6.

Vogel, I., Glöwing, B., Saint Pierre, I., Bayart, F., Contamin, H., and B. de Thoisy. 2002. Squirrel monkey (*Saimiri sciureus*) rehabilitation in French Guiana: A case study. *Neotropical Primates* 10: 147-149.

Squirrel Monkey (*Saimiri sciureus*). Authorities confiscated 25 squirrel monkeys that were being held illegally by traffickers, and released them into the 548-ha Saltinho Biological Reserve, in the state of Pernambuco, Brazil in 1987. Squirrel monkeys do not occur naturally in this area of Brazil. I could find no details of the release techniques, but in that era in Brazil, confiscated monkeys were usually just released with no veterinary screening, pre-release preparation, or post-release support or monitoring. Saltinho, which consists of secondary forest and is located within the Atlantic Coastal Forest, was occupied by a native species, the common marmoset (*Callithrix jacchus*) at the time.

The squirrel monkey population grew but no census figures could be found. However, the monkeys are reproducing and the population appears to have been established. The marmosets feed less when they encounter squirrel monkeys, and behave agonistically toward them. The two species do not form mixed-species groups or interact affiliatively.

Squirrel monkeys have been introduced elsewhere in Brazil but I could not find details of other releases.

Welfare (Non-lethal Control)

References

Camarotti, F.L.M., da Silva, V.L., and M.A. Borstelman de Oliveira. 2015. The effects of introducing the Amazonian squirrel monkey on the behavior of the northeast marmoset. *Acta Amazonica* 45(1): 29-34.

Oliveira, L.C. and C.E.V. Grelle. 2012. Introduced primate species of an Atlantic Forest region in Brazil: present and future implications for the native fauna. *Tropical Conservation Science* 5(1): 112-120.

Brown Capuchin Monkey (*Cebus apella*). The World Society for the Protection of Animals released a group of eight confiscated and rehabilitated brown capuchin monkeys in Los Llanos Orientales in Colombia. The monkeys were monitored for more than six months to determine their adaptation and survival after release. Data were collected on foraging, feeding, locomotion, sleeping, social interactions within the group and with other animals and species, predation, orientation, and establishment of a territory. At six and one-half months after release, five of the eight animals remained together, two were separated, and only one had been lost (during the first month).

Welfare (Rehabilitation), Research

References

Suarez, C. E., Gamboa, E. M., Claver, P. and F. Nassar-Montoya. 2001. Survival and adaptation of a released group of confiscated capuchin monkeys. *Animal Welfare* 10: 191-203.

White-Throated Capuchin Monkey (*Cebus capucinus*). "Operation Gwamba" rescued and translocated three white-throated capuchin monkeys (and other monkeys) from the Brokopondo Valley as it was being flooded by the construction of the Afobaka Dam in Surinam in 1964. I could find no further details.

Welfare (Rescue)

References

Konstant, W.R. and R.A. Mittermeier. 1982. Introduction, reintroduction and translocation of Neotropical primates: Past experience and future possibilities. *International Zoo Yearbook* 22: 69-77.

Saki Monkey (*Pithecia pithecia*). The Faune Sauvage team of the Centre National de Equipement Hydraulique in French Guiana arranged to translocate six saki monkeys (a group of three and three singletons) from a forest that was being flooded by construction of a hydroelectric dam into a 15,000-ha portion of a nearby forest in 1994 and 1995. Many other animals were translocated in the same operation. Five of the sakis were radiocollared and the other was ear-tagged. There was pre-release veterinary screening and a short pre-release acclimation period. The sakis were followed systematically for 287 days. They interacted and joined groups with wild residents. There was increased protection from hunting for some time at the release site.

Welfare (Rescue), Research

REFERENCES

de Thoisy, B., Vogel, I., Reynes, J-M., Pouliquen, J-F., Carme, B., Kazanji, M., and J-C. Vie. 2001. Health evaluation of translocated free-ranging primates in French Guiana. *American Journal of Primatology* 54: 1-16.

Vié, J-C., and C. Richard-Hansen. 1997. Primate translocation in French Guiana, a preliminary report. *Neotropical Primates* 5: 1-3.

Vié, J--C., Richard-Hansen, C. and C. Fournier-Chambrillon. 2001. Abundance, use of space, and activity patterns of white-faced sakis (Pithecia pithecia) in French Guinea. *American Journal of Primatology* 55: 203-221.

Cotton-top Tamarin (*Saguinus oedipus*). The National Institute of Renewable Natural Resources and Environment (INDERENA), the former environmental protection agency of Colombia, introduced approximately 30 cotton-top tamarins into the Tayrona National Natural Park in 1973 or 1974. The tamarins were said to have been former pets. I am assuming that all were wild-born, although some may have been born in captivity. Tayrona has an area of 19,257 ha, of which 12,692 are terrestrial. It is outside the normal range of cotton-top tamarins, and is drier that most cotton-top natural habitats. I could find no information about pre- or post-release management.

The population survives today and may number 5,000 or more. There is no systematic provisioning but some of the tamarins may be fed occasionally by tourists.

The sources mention other introductions of former pet cotton-tops by their owners in the Yotoco forest in Colombia, in small forest patches around Cali, and near Panama City, Panama. The Yotoco population may be extinct, but I could not find documentation of these releases or their outcomes.

Welfare (Rehabilitation).

References

Defler, T.R., Rodríguez, J.V., and J. I. Hernández-Camacho. 2003. Conservation priorities for Colombian primates. *Primate Conservation* 19: 10-18.

Mast, R. B., Rodríguez, J.V., and R. A. Mittermeier. 1993. The Colombian cotton-top tamarin in the wild. In: N.K. Clapp, ed. *A Primate Model for the Study of Colitis and Colonic Carcinoma: The Cotton-top Tamarin, Saguinus oedipus*, pp 3-43. Boca Raton, CRC Press.

Villarreal, S.G. 2010. Estudio poblacional del titi cabeciblanco (Saguinus oedipus) en el PNN Tayrona: Del mito a las oportunidades de conservacion. Thesis, Facultad de Estudios Ambientales y Rurales Carrera de Ecologia, Pontficia Universidad Javeriana, Bogota, Colombia.

Villarreal, S.G. and J.D. Amaya-Espinel. 2013. Densidad de una población del titi cabeciblanco (*Saguinus oedipus*) en el Parque Nacional Natural Tayrona y su relevancia en la conservación de la especie en Colombia. In: Defler, T.R., Stevenson, P.R., Bueno, M.L., and D.C. Guzmán-Caro, eds. *Primates Colombianos en Peligro de Extinción*, pp. 173-179. Bogota, Asociación Primatologica Colombiana

Cotton-top Tamarin (*Saguinus oedipus*). Investigators from the University of Cordoba and the Centro de Atención y Valoración de Fauna Silvestre (CAV) reintroduced a family group of five cotton-top tamarins in a small privately owned forest (Bosque La Montañita, Vereda Ceiba Pareja, Lorica Córdoba) in Colombia in 2009. The site was within the historic range of cotton-tops but none survived there at the time of the release. It appears that three were wild-born and two had been born in the center. The tamarins received extensive veterinary examinations and were individually marked while living in a large, enriched cage at the center. They were then moved to a similar cage in a wooded area for 45 days, and then to an acclimation cage at the La Montañita forest release site for 45 days. They were given fresh marketplace fruits and, increasingly, some natural foods in the cages, and had the opportunity to locomote on natural vegetation and forage for insects and small vertebrates and other natural foods. Their activity and behavior were documented in each of the cage settings, and for three weeks post-release. The tamarins expanded their range, slept outside the acclimation cage, and appeared to adapt well, but they were amply provisioned on platforms during the three post-release weeks in which they were studied.

Research (to develop techniques for reintroduction)

REFERENCES

Arango Guerra, H.L., Ballesteros Ruiz, S., Garcia Castillo, F., and S. Buritica. 2013.

Primer proceso de rehabilitación y reintroducción de un grupo de titís cabeciblancos (*Saguinus oedipus*). *Revista Lasallista de Investigación* 10(1): 49-61.

Moustached (Mustached) Tamarin (*Saguinus mystax*). The Peruvian Center for Reproduction and Conservation of Nonhuman Primates and the Ministry of Agriculture introduced 87 moustached tamarins to an 8,300-ha island (Padre Island), of which approximately 500 ha was forested, between 1977 and 1980. The population had increased by 36% by 1985 and was said to be self-sustaining. The animals were translocated wild-borns, and the primary purpose appears to have been commercial (offtake for primate research subjects). Hunting and habitat destruction were controlled, the animals were provisioned, and fruit production was "enhanced". There was long-term monitoring.

Commercial, Research

REFERENCES

Konstant, W.R. and R.A. Mittermeier. 1982. Introduction, reintroduction and translocation of Neotropical primates: Past experience and future possibilities. *International Zoo Yearbook* 22: 69-77.

Moya, L. and P. Soini. undated. Experimental introduction and management of the moustached tamarin (*Saguinus mystax*) in Padre Isla Island, Iquitos – Peru. Unattributed abstract.

Golden-Handed Tamarin (*Saguinus midas*). The Faune Sauvage team of the Centre National de Equipement Hydraulique in French Guiana arranged to translocate 98 golden-handed tamarins (22 groups) from a forest that was being flooded by construction of a hydroelectric dam into a

15,000-ha portion of a nearby forest in 1994 and 1995. Many other animals were translocated in the same operation. The tamarins were tattooed and fitted with collars with tags. There was pre-release veterinary screening. The tamarins were observed only opportunistically for the following 11 months. Some integrated with resident groups. There was increased protection from hunting for some time at the release site.

Welfare (Rescue), Research

REFERENCES

de Thoisy, B., Vogel, I., Reynes, J-M., Pouliquen, J-F., Carme, B., Kazanji, M., and J-C. Vie. 2001. Health evaluation of translocated free-ranging primates in French Guiana. *American Journal of Primatology* 54: 1-16.

Vie, J., and C. Richard-Hansen. 1997. Primate translocation in French Guiana, a preliminary report. *Neotropical Primates* 5: 1-3.

Golden-Handed (Red-Handed) Tamarin (*Saguinus m. midas*). "Operation Gwamba" rescued and translocated 14 red-handed tamarins (and other monkeys) from the Brokopondo Valley as it was being flooded by the construction of the Afobaka Dam in Surinam in 1964. I could find no further details.

Welfare (Rescue)

REFERENCES

Konstant, W.R. and R.A. Mittermeier. 1982. Introduction, reintroduction and translocation of Neotropical primates: Past experience and future possibilities. *International Zoo Yearbook* 22: 69-77. London.

Golden Lion Tamarin (*Leontopithecus rosalia*). A total of five golden lion tamarins escaped from the Tijuca Biological Bank breeding colony or the Rio de Janeiro Zoo into surrounding forests in the city of Rio de Janeiro in the 1970s. There were four escape events. A wild-caught tamarin (sex unspecified) that had been kept for several years at the zoo escaped and locomoted well in the trees until being captured several hours later. A wild-caught male escaped from the Tijuca Bank and was observed with a group of common marmosets in the forest one month later. He was never recaptured. A captive-born male escaped from the Tijuca Bank, locomoted well in the forest, and was recaptured when he returned to the breeding colony. A captive-born pair escaped from the zoo, locomoted poorly and were captured shortly after their escape. These escapes contributed to conclusion that wild-born primates are more likely to be reintroduced successfully than captive-born primates (see below).

Accidental (Escape)

References

Coimbra-Filho, A.F. and R.A. Mittermeier. 1978. Reintroduction and translocation of lion tamarins: A realistic appraisal. In: H. Rothe, H.J. Wolters and J.P. Hearn, eds. *Biology and Behaviour of Marmosets*, pp. 41-46. Göttingen, Eigenverlag Hartmut Rothe.

Golden Lion Tamarin (*Leontopithecus rosalia*). The Smithsonian National Zoological Park and the Rio de Janeiro Primate Center reintroduced 146 captive-born golden lion tamarins in ten cohorts into a single watershed in the state of Rio de Janeiro, Brazil between 1983 and 2000. The tamarins had been born at or lived at the National Zoo, the Rio de Janeiro Primate Center, a research colony at the University of Nebraska, Omaha, and 40 other North American and European zoos. The reintroductions were funded by the Smithsonian Institution, the Friends of the National Zoo, the Jersey Wildlife Preservation Trust, and the Frankfurt Zoological Society. Brazilian federal wildlife authorities granted permits for the work; during the years of the reintroductions the regulatory agency was known as the Instituto Brasiliero de Desenvolvimento Florestal and then as the Instituto Brasiliero do Meio Ambiente e Recursos Natureis. The destination sites for the reintroductions were within the historic range of the species, and were near but not fully connected with the range of a diminished, non-sustainable but legally protected wild golden lion tamarin population in the Poço das Antas Biological Reserve. Wild golden lion tamarins were absent from these destination sites at the time, making these releases Reintroductions *sensu strictu*.

The same administrative program (now the Associação Mico-Leao Dourado) also translocated 42 wild-born golden lion tamarins that had been rescued from isolated forest fragments that were slated for destruction. These tamarins were translocated in six cohorts (family groups) into the Fazenda União (now the União Biological Reserve) in 1994.

The captive-born tamarins received rigorous veterinary screening and quarantine before and after being shipped to Brazil. All had distinctive numerical tattoos, and dye marks for visual identification from a distance. Some (20) had received structured pre-release training in foraging and predator avoidance before reintroduction. Others (39) had been allowed to range freely in temperate forests in zoos before shipment to Brazil, and still others (81) had had no pre-release training or preparation at all. The pre-release environment of six of the released tamarins is unspecified.

Some (24) of these reintroduced tamarins had minimal post-release support with no provisioning after release. A few of these wore radiocollars, and survivors were monitored for at least six days per week. This "hard release" strategy was used in the initial years of the program. A "soft release" strategy was adopted later. These (116) captive-borns were provisioned with food and water for at least one year, provided with an artificial nest box, rescued when they were lost, and treated for illness or injury. A greater percentage wore radiocollars. This intensive post-release support and monitoring were provided daily for six months, and then reduced gradually as the tamarins adapted.

Only approximately 30% of all of the reintroduced captive-born tamarins survived for more than two years. Most of those that were lost simply disappeared. In a sample of 36 cases of loss where the cause was known, theft or shooting by people accounted for 21%, natural predation 15%, starvation 13%, lethargy/diarrhea, anorexia/dehydration 10%, hypothermia/exposure 10%, wounding in social conflict 8%, eating toxic fruit 5%, snakebite 5%, hemorrhage following abortion 3%, and head injury 3%. Approximately 70% of offspring born in the wild to captive-born reintroduced parents survived for more than two years. One captive-born reintroduced tamarin lived to be 18 years old in the wild.

The reintroduced captive-born population had grown to 359 by 2000. Most of these (341) had been born in the wild. A retrospective study found that intensive post-release support resulted in significantly higher survivorship than minimal post-release support in captive-born reintroduced golden lion tamarins. The same study showed that neither structured pre-release training in cages nor the opportunity range freely in temperate forests in zoos had provided any advantage in post-release survivorship.

The 42 rescued and translocated tamarins had no pre-release preparation, acclimation, or post-release support. Some were fitted with radiocollars and the groups were monitored regularly.

There were 120 golden lion tamarins in 16 family groups in the translocated União population by 2000. A total of 107 offspring were known to have been born at the site between 1994 and 2000; 79 (74%) of these survived to two years. The wild-born, rescued, and translocated tamarins had higher survival rates and reproduced more quickly than the reintroduced captive-borns, confirming Coimbra Filho's and Mittermeier's hypothesis (see above) that wild-borns would be more likely to be reintroduced succesfully. Reintroduction of captive-borns was far more costly than translocation of wild-borns.

Twenty-four captive-born golden lion tamarins were admitted into the program but, for various reasons, were not actually reintroduced. Some were disqualified before shipment to Brazil after an initial veterinary examination. One of these cases was particularly memorable. An adult male was found in a veterinary screening to be carrying antibodies to the callithrichid hepatitis virus, just days before he and his family were scheduled to be shipped to Brazil. Neither he nor his family showed any signs of active disease; the other family members were not even carrying antibodies because they had never even been exposed to the disease. Lemmon's unfortunate alarmist account claimed that the male was "carrying a lethal virus". This was never demonstrated, but the Smithsonian National Zoological Park's veterinarians and pathologists were concerned that the male could be sequestering active virus nonsymptomatically. If he were, the virus could have been introduced to the wild, with possible disastrous consequences for wild golden lion tamarins and other animals. The male was withdrawn from the reintroduction program and returned to captivity. Another young tamarin was euthanized after a heavy nestbox door dropped on and fractured his arm in quarantine. Six captive-borns died of suffocation and heat stress due to human error during transport within Brazil before they were released.

The total wild population of golden lion tamarins was estimated to exceed 3,000 in 2014 (J. Dietz, personal communication), a number that that would be self-sustaining if all of the habitat that they are occupying were protected and connected. Approximately 900 of these are thought to be descendants of captive-born reintroduced tamarins. All of the tamarins are independent of human support except that "mini-translocations" of individuals or families between isolated forest fragments are still conducted to maintain genetic diversity. Small amounts of food are also provided as bait for trapping individuals for attaching radiocollars and maintaining a census. These actions will no longer be necessary when the habitat is completely interconnected. Connection of forest fragments is now a major goal of the program (www.savetheliontamarin.org). The species has been downlisted from 'Critically Endangered' to 'Endangered'.

To my knowledge, the golden lion tamarin reintroduction program is the only program in this history that has served as the setting and basis for a novel, *Thirteen Gold Monkeys*, of which (full disclosure) I am the author.

An epidemic of yellow fever swept northeastern Brazil in 2017. Many unvaccinated people died. Howler monkey populations were wiped out in days. Some golden lion tamarins are known to have died of the disease, and a number of monitored groups have disappeared. As this account is being written (September 2018), the Associação Mico-Leao Dourado is conducting a range-wide census to determine the extent of yellow fever-caused losses in the wild golden lion tamarin population. A vaccine for nonhuman primates is being developed and tested at the Rio de Janeiro Primate Center, and plans are being discussed to vaccinate surviving wild golden lion tamarins. The carefully managed captive population is large and robust enough to provide founders for another reintroduction effort if that should prove necessary.

The yellow fever threat to Neotropical primates raises the question of how to define the long-term success of a reintroduction. Consider the case of a reintroduced primate population that has been thriving for decades, and thus has been judged to have been successful, and then is wiped out decades later by a virulent illness. Can the reintroduction still be said to have been successful even if the primates subsequently die of causes unrelated to the reintroduction?

Conservation (Reintroduction, Reinforcement), Research

References

Beck, B.B. 2013. *Thirteen Gold Monkeys*. Denver, Outskirts Press.

Beck, B.B., Kleiman, D.G., Dietz, J.M., Castro, I., Carvalho, C., Martins, A., and B. Rettberg-Beck. 1990. Losses and reproduction in reintroduced golden lion tamarins. *Dodo, Journal of the Jersey Wildlife Preservation Trust* 27: 50-61.

Beck, B.B., Castro, M.I., Stoinski, T.S., and J.D. Ballou. 2002. The effects of prerelease environments and postrelease management on survivorship in reintroduced golden lion tamarins. In: D.G. Kleiman and A.B. Rylands, eds. *Lion Tamarins: Biology and Conservation*, pp. 283-300. Washington, DC, Smithsonian Institution Press.

Kierulff, M.C.M and P.P. de Oliveira. 1994. Habitat preservation and the translocation of threatened groups of golden lion tamarins, *Leontopithecus rosalia. Neotropical Primates* 2 (suppl.): 15-18.

Kierulff, M.C.M., Beck, B.B., Kleiman, D.G., and P. Procopio. 2002a. Re-introduction and translocation as conservation tools for golden lion tamarins in Brazil. *Re-introduction News*, 21: 7-10.

Kierulff, M.C., Procopio de Oliveira, P., Beck, B.B., and A. Martins. 2002b. Reintroduction and translocation as conservation tools for golden lion tamarins. In D.G. Kleiman and A.B. Rylands, eds. *Lion Tamarins: Biology and Conservation*, pp. 271-82. Washington, DC, Smithsonian institution Press.

Kierulff, M.C.M., Ruiz-Miranda, C.R., Procópio de Oliveira, P., Beck, B.B., Martins, A., Dietz, J.M., Rambaldi, D.M. and A.J. Baker. 2012. The golden lion tamarin *Leontopithecus rosalia*: a conservation success story. *International Zoo Yearbook* 46 (1): 36–45.

Lemmon, T. 1991. Lion tamarin virus gives zoologists heart attack. *BBC Wildlife* 9(8): 527.

Montali, R.J., Scanga, C.A., Pernikoff, D., Wessner, D.R., Ward, R., and K.V. Holmes. 1993. A common-source outbreak of callithrichid hepatitis in captive tamarins and marmosets. *The Journal of Infectious Diseases* 167: 946-950.

Ruiz-Miranda, C.R., Beck, B.B., Kleiman, D.G., Martins, A., Dietz, J.M., Rambaldi, D.M., Kierulff, C., Procopio de Oliveira, P., and A.J. Baker. 2010 Re-introduction and translocation of golden lion tamarins, Atlantic Coastal Forest, Brazil: The creation of a metapopulation. In P.S. Soorae, ed. *Global Re-introduction Perspectives: Additional Case-Studies from Around the Globe*, pp. 225-230. Abu Dhabi, UAE, IUCN/SSC Re-introduction Specialist Group.

www.savetheliontamarin.org

Black Lion Tamarin (*Leontopithecis chrysopygus*). A male captive-born black lion tamarin escaped from a small cage at the Tijuca Biolgical Bank breeding colony into the surrounding Tijuca Forest within the city of Rio de Janeiro, Brazil in the 1970s. He did not climb trees and spent most of his time in low undergrowth. He did not defend himself when attacked by a nesting bird and did not avoid biting ants. He was apparently caught and returned to captivity. This escape contributed to conclusion that wild-born primates are more likely to be reintroduced successfully than captive-born primates (see above).

Accidental (Escape)

References

Coimbra-Filho, A.F. and R.A. Mittermeier. 1978. Reintroduction and translocation of lion tamarins: A realistic appraisal. In H. Rothe, H.J. Wolters, and J.P. Hearn, eds. *Biology and Behaviour of Marmosets*, pp. 41-46. Göttingen, Eigenverlag Hartmut Rothe.

Black Lion Tamarin (*Leontopithecus chrysopygus*). The Instituto de Pesquisas Ecológicas translocated a family group of four individuals (two males and two females) from one ranch to another (Mosquito Farm) in 1995, and translocated a second group of six (four adult males and two adult females) to the same ranch in 1999. The destination ranch was within the historic range of the species, making these Reintroductions *sensu strictu*. The destination ranch provided 1,344 ha of suitable forest habitat. Three additional groups comprising ten additional animals were reintroduced to the same ranch between 1999 and 2008; these would have been Reinforcements. The purposes of the reintroductions were to extend the area that was available to the species and to study the feasibility of reintroduction as a conservation tool for the species.

The adults of the first group were radiocollared. They were maintained in a cage at the release site for a day, during which they were given food and water. No post-release support was provided. There is no information on the pre-release management of the subsequent groups. The first two groups were monitored for 21 months, during which time the size of the group ranged between two and six as a result of births and deaths, some of which were due to predation. A male of the second group joined the first group. The second group was said to have "adapted well and reproduced normally". The first and fifth groups were monitored intensively in 2010 and 2011 and were reported to have expanded their home ranges significantly. Home range appeared to change seasonally depending on availability of resources. Neonates were observed in 2015. There are now attempts to interconnect all of the sites that are inhabited by black lion tamarins by means of forest corridors.

The same organization released one male captive-born black lion tamarin into the Morro do Diabo State Park in Sao Paulo, Brazil (36,000 ha) in 1999. He was released with two wild females. The male had had extensive free-ranging experience at the Jersey Zoo in the UK. There was quarantine, medical screening, post-release supplemental feeding and support, rescue and re-release, and monitoring with radiotelemetry and direct observation for three months, until he was killed by a predator. This was also a Reinforcement.

Conservation (Reinforcement, Reintroduction), Research

References

Medici, E.P., Valladares-Padua, C.B., Rylands, A.B., and C.S. Martins. 2003. Translocation as a metapopulation management tool for the black lion tamarin, *Leontopithecus chrysopygus*. *Primate Conservation* 19: 23-31.

Rezende, G.C. 2015. Updates from the BLT conservation program in Pontal do Paranapanema (2014-2015). *Tamarin Tales* 13: 12-13.

Rezende, G.C., Garbino, G.T., Jenkins, C.N., Martins, C.S., and C. Valladares-Padua. 2016. Home range of two translocated groups of black lion tamarins (*Leontopithecus chrysopygus*) and remarks on a 20-year population management program in Brazil. Abstract of a paper presented at the joint meeting of the 26th Congress of the International Primatological Society and the 39th Meeting of the American Society of Primatologists, Chicago, IL, USA.

Valladares-Padua, C., Martins, C.S., Wormell, D., and E.Z. Setz. 2000. Preliminary evaluation of the reintroduction of a mixed wild-captive group of black lion tamarins *Leontopithecus chrysopygus*. *Dodo* 36: 30-38.

Golden-Headed Lion Tamarin (*Leontopithecis chrysomelas*). Golden-headed lion tamarins have been successfully translocated from the Serra da Tiririca State Park and the Darcy Ribeiro Municipal Reserve within the city limits of Niteroi, in the state of Rio de Janeiro, Brazil. The founders of this population were released decades ago by a private collector. Golden-headed lion tamarins are not native to this area of Brazil, and conservationists feared that they might hybridize with the wild golden lion tamarins that live as close as 50 km away (see above). As of September 2016, 825 golden-headed lion tamarins had been captured. As of April 2015, when the total captured had been 741, 131 groups had been captured, of which 49 groups (293 individuals) had been translocated to destination sites in the state of Bahia, Brazil, within their historic range (C. Kierulff, personal communications). Most were released on the privately owned Fazenda Taquera. Some that were deemed unsuitable for release remain in captivity. More recently, all of the captured tamarins are being contracepted and placed in captivity because the destination sites are now at carrying capacity. There were still two golden-headed lion tamarin groups (one of six, another of two) and two lone individuals living in the parks in Niteroi in early 2017. These must be captured to completely eliminate the threat of hybridization with golden lion tamarins. This golden-headed lion tamarin population had an extraordinarily high density, most likely because they were being provisioned by people living near the parks and because they had overlapping home ranges. The human neighbors had been informed of the nature and reasons for the operation because the unauthorized capture of endangered animals is illegal in Brazil.

From the point of view of the golden-headed lion tamarins, this is a welfare translocation because it provides a non-lethal way to control animals that had become "problems", i.e., animals of an exotic species that were threatening to hybridize with a native endangered species. From the point of view of the golden lion tamarins, this was a conservation reintroduction. We are reminded that reintroductions can have multiple purposes.

I have counted this as only one reintroduction program, although the original reintroduction of golden-headed lion tamarins *to* Niteroi could also be counted as a program.

Welfare (Non-lethal control), Conservation (Protect another endangered species)

References

Kierulff, M.C.M. 2011. Invasive introduced golden-headed lion tamarins. *Tamarin Tales* 10: 5-7.

Kierulff, M.C. M. 2012. The removal of golden-headed lion tamarin invaders. *Tamarin Tales* 11: 2-3.

Kierulff, C. 2015. Golden-headed lion tamarin invaders in Niteroi. *Tamarin Tales* 13: 1-3.

Black Tufted-eared Marmoset (*Callithrix penicillata*). Many black tufted-eared marmosets have been released from the north of the state of Bahia in Brazil (where they are native) into the Atlantic Coastal Rainforest along the main highway that runs from the city of Rio de Janeiro to the state of Bahia. Many were released by truck drivers who bought them in Bahia as pets and grew tired of them by the time they reached Rio. Animal dealers may also have released them, and law enforcement officials have also released confiscated pets. Property owners released them as garden pets. They have a well-established population, and have hybridized with common marmosets (*Callithrix jacchus*). The marmosets compete with the naturally occurring endangered golden lion tamarins in the area.

Welfare (Non-lethal control), Aesthetic

References

de Morais Jr., M., Ruiz-Miranda, C.R.., Grativol, A.D., Caixeta de Andrade, C., Lima, C.S., and B.B. Beck. 2008. Os saguis, *Callithrix jacchus e penicillata*, como espécies invasoras na região de ocorrência do mico-leão dourado. In: P.P. de Oliveira, A.D. Grativol, and C.R. Ruiz-Miranda, eds. *Conservação do mico-leão dourado*, pp 86-117. Campos dos Goytacazes, Universidade Estadual do Norte Fluminense Darcy Ribeiro.

Ruiz-Miranda, C.R., Affonso, A.G., de Morais, M.M., Verona, C.E., Martins, A., and B. Beck. 2006. Behavioral and ecological interactions between reintroduced golden lion tamarins (*Leontopithecus rosalia*

Linnaeus 1766) and introduced marmosets (*Callithrix* spp, Linnaeus, 1758) in Brazil's Atlantic Coast forest fragments. *Brazilian Archives of Biology and Technology* 49: 99-109.

Ruiz-Miranda, C.R., de Morais Jr., M.M., Romana de Paula, V. Grativol, A.D., and D.M. Rambaldi. 2011. Vitimas e Vilões. *Ciencia Hoje* 48: 44-48.

Common Marmoset (*Callithrix jacchus*). The governor of Rio de Janeiro arranged to introduce many of these non-native marmosets to forested areas within the city of Rio de Janeiro in the early twentieth century. The animals are fed by citizens and are well established today.

Aesthetic

References

Konstant, W.R. and R.A. Mittermeier. 1982. Introduction, reintroduction and translocation of Neotropical primates: Past experience and future possibilities. *International Zoo Yearbook* 22: 69-77.

Common Marmoset (*Callithrix jacchus*). Many common marmosets (at least two releases of more than 60 individuals each in the 1980s) have been released from the northeast of the state of Bahia in Brazil (where they are native) into the Atlantic Coastal Rainforest along the main highway that runs from the city of Rio de Janeiro to the state of Bahia. Many were released by truck drivers who bought them in Bahia as pets and grew tired of them by the time they reached Rio. Animal dealers may also have released them, and law enforcement officials have also released confiscated pets. Property owners released them as garden pets. They have a well-established population, and have hybridized with black tufted-eared marmosets (*Callithrix penicillata*) whose introduction into the same area is described above. Both marmoset species and their hybrids compete with the naturally occurring endangered golden lion tamarins in the area.

Welfare (Non-lethal control), Aesthetic

References

Konstant, W.R. and R.A. Mittermeier. 1982. Introduction, reintroduction and translocation of Neotropical primates: Past experience and future possibilities. *International Zoo Yearbook* 22: 69-77.

de Morais Jr., M., Ruiz-Miranda, C.R.., Grativol, A.D., Caixeta de Andrade, C., Lima, C.S., and B.B. Beck. 2008. Os sagüis, *Callithrix jacchus e penicillata*, como espécies invasoras na região de ocorrência do mico-leão dourado. In: P.P. de Oliveira, A.D. Grativol, and C.R. Ruiz-Miranda, eds. *Conservação do mico-leão dourado*, pp 86-117. Campos dos Goytacazes, Universidade Estadual do Norte Fluminense Darcy Ribeiro.

Ruiz-Miranda, C.R., Affonso, A.G., de Morais, M.M., Verona, C.E., Martins, A., and B. Beck. 2006. Behavioral and ecological interactions between reintroduced golden lion tamarins (*Leontopithecus rosalia* Linnaeus 1766) and introduced marmosets (*Callithrix* spp, Linnaeus, 1758) in Brazil's Atlantic Coast forest fragments. *Brazilian Archives of Biology and Technology* 49: 99-109.

Ruiz-Miranda, C.R., de Morais Jr., M.M., Romana de Paula, V. Grativol, A.D., and D.M. Rambaldi. 2011. Vitimas e Vilões. *Ciencia Hoje* 48: 44-48.

Geoffroy's Marmoset (*Callithrix geoffroyi*). The Mello Leitão Museum of Biology, Aracruz Cellulose S.A., and the Rio de Janeiro Primate Center reintroduced seven groups of Geoffroy's marmosets (23 individuals, of which 16 were captive-born and 7 were wild-born) into a forest patch that was surrounded by eucalyptus on an Aracruz plantation (no size provided) in 1991. The sources do not state whether Geoffroy's marmosets had ever lived at the destination site. The reintroduced marmosets were given pre-release training, veterinary screening, acclimation, and post-release support, and were monitored with radiotelemetry and direct observation for 115 days, by which 13 had disappeared and six had died. One animal starved to death; small felid predation was suspected in some of the other losses. There may have been one birth to a reintroduced marmoset (Passamani pers. comm. 1993). Four survivors were recaptured and returned to captivity. None of the groups was successfully established in the wild and no individuals survived in the wild.

Conservation (Type Unspecified), Research

References

Chiarello, A., and M. Passamani. 1993. A reintroduction program of Geoffroy's marmoset, *Callithrix geoffroyi*. *Neotropical Primates* 1: 6-7.

Passamani, M. and J.A. Passamani. 1994. Losses of re-introduced Geoffroy's marmoset. *Re-introduction News* 8: 9-10.

CHAPTER 9
REINTRODUCTIONS OF LORISES AND LEMURS

Pygmy Loris (*Nycticebus pygmaeus*). The Endangered Species Rescue Center in Cuc Phuong National Park, Vietnam, released nine confiscated and rehabilitated adult pygmy lorises between 2000 and 2002. The purposes of the release were to study reintroduction methodology for this species and to reduce the rescue center population. It appears that each loris was released alone, but all were released in a 1,200-ha former botanical garden near the national park. The animals had been medically screened and quarantined. Five of the lorises were radiocollared. The lorises were acclimated in their home cages at the release site for several days before release. Food was provided after release for as long as the animals returned to the release area. The lorises were monitored until they died or disappeared. One was monitored for 134 days. Two of the lorises were killed by predators, two died of other causes, e.g. starvation, and the others disappeared, presumably deep into the national park. Data on ranging, feeding, and social behavior were collected. Streicher (2004b) refers to at least 35 pygmy lorises, probably many more, having been released previously in North Vietnam without adherence to guidelines and without documentation.

Research, Welfare (Rehabilitation).

REFERENCES

Kenyon, M., Streicher, U., Loung, H., Tran, T., Tran, M., Vo, B., and A. Cronin. 2014. Survival of released pygmy slow loris *Nycticebus pygmaeus* in South Vietnam. *Endangered Species Research* 25: 185-95.

Streicher, U. 2004a. Pygmy lorises re-introduction study in Vietnam. *Reintro Redux* 1: 5-10.

Streicher, U. 2004b. *Aspects of ecology and conservation of the pygmy loris Nycticebus pygmaeus in Vietnam*. PhD Thesis, Ludwig-Maximilians Universität München.

Streicher, U., and T. Nadler. 2003. Re-introduction of pygmy lorises in Vietnam. *Re-introduction News* 23: 37-40.

van der Sandt, C.M.G. 2016. Towards a successful translocation of captive slow lorises (*Nycticebus* spp.) in Borneo: a review and recommendations. Published online at http://dx.doi.org/10.1101/078535.

Pygmy Loris (*Nycticebus pygmaeus*). The Dao Tien Endangered Primate Species Rescue Centre in Vietnam's Cat Tien National Park released a total of 13 confiscated and rehabilitated adult pygmy lorises in Cat Tien and in the Vinh Cuu Biosphere Reserve in 2009, 2010, 2011, and 2012. Both areas are part of the 969,993-ha Dong Nai Biosphere Reserve in South Vietnam. A habitat assessment was conducted before the release; wild pygmy lorises were present at the release sites. The lorises underwent veterinary screening and quarantine at the rescue center. Some of them were deemed unfit for release, mainly because of clipped teeth, which is a common practice for pet lorises. Each of the released lorises was radiocollared. Pre-release preparation, acclimation, and post-release support were varied experimentally (Kenyon et al 2014). Some of the lorises lived in large, naturalistic enclosures at the center for a month. Some of the lorises were acclimated at the release site for days or months. Some were provided with food after release for as long as one month. Others received no post-release support. The lorises were monitored for up to 73 days after release. Four of the lorises survived for at least two months, until monitoring was discontinued. Four were killed by predators, three disappeared, one died of hyperthermia, and one was rescued and returned to captivity. The four survivors had been acclimated at the release site and had been given supplemental food after release. The authors conclude that "soft releases" were most successful for this species.

Welfare (Rehabilitation), Research

References

Kenyon, M., Streicher, U., Loung, H., Tran, T., Tran, M., Vo, B., and A. Cronin. 2014. Survival of released pygmy slow loris *Nycticebus pygmaeus* in South Vietnam. *Endangered Species Research* 25: 185-95.

van der Sandt, C.M.G. 2016. Towards a successful translocation of captive slow lorises (*Nycticebus* spp.) in Borneo: a review and recommendations. Published online at http://dx.doi.org/10.1101/078535

www.go-east.org

Sumatran Slow Loris (*Nycticebus c. coucang*). The Pusat Penyelamatan rehabilitation sanctuary released seven confiscated wild-born slow lorises into the 11,000-ha Batutegi Special Reserve in Sumatra in 2007. There were two groups. One was an adult female and two juveniles and the other was an adult female with three juveniles. Lorises were known to be present in the reserve but at low densities. The lorises were provided with natural foods and substrates in the center's enclosures before release and received veterinary examinations. They were studied intensively before release to ensure that they displayed natural behaviors. The lorises were acclimated in an enclosure at the release site for two days, and were monitored for one night after release.

Welfare (Rehabilitation)

REFERENCES

Collins, R. and K. A. I. Nekaris. 2008. Release of greater slow lorises, confiscated from the pet trade, to Batutegi Protected Forest, Sumatra, Indonesia. In P.S. Soorae, ed. *Global Re-introduction Perspectives: Re-introduction Case-Studies from Around the Globe*, pp. 192-196. IUCN/SSC Re-introduction Specialist Group, Abu Dhabi, UAE.

van der Sandt, C.M.G. 2016. Towards a successful translocation of captive slow lorises (*Nycticebus* spp.) in Borneo: a review and recommendations. Published online at http://dx.doi.org/10.1101/078535

Sumatran Slow Loris (*Nycticebus c. coucang*). The International Animal Rescue (IAR) program released 123 slow lorises in the 11,000-ha Batutegi reserve in Sumatra between 2009 and 2016 (13 October 2016 news story on the IAR website). IAR also released 15 Sumatran slow lorises (six males, nine females) in the nearby 356,800-ha Bukit Barisan National Park in Sumatra in 2017 (IAR news story, 15 August 2017). Releases at both sites are included in this same program.

International Animal Rescue has released hundreds of slow lorises at sites in Borneo, Sumatra, and Java between 2009 and 2017 (see below). The program maintains very high standards of pre-release preparation, and supports sound scientific post-release monitoring of many of the released lorises. However, the documentation of many of the releases is available only on the IAR website.

Even assuming that Sumatran, Bornean, and Javan slow lorises are different subspecies of one species (some would disagree and assign different species names), the reintroductions on Sumatra, Borneo, and Java are considered to be different programs in this history because they were conducted on different and distant islands.

IAR maintains two rehabilitation centers that care for confiscated, surrendered, or rescued lorises: The Ciapus Primate Rescue Center in Bogor, West Java, Indonesia and the Emergency

Rescue Center in Ketapang, West Kalimantan, Borneo. Lorises that have been confiscated in Java and rehabilitated at Ciapus have been reintroduced in Sumatra and Borneo as well as Java, depending on their subspecies. The same is true for lorises that have been confiscated in Borneo and rehabilitated at Ketapang. Reintroduction of primate species or subspecies at destination sites within their native range is, of course, recommended by all applicable guidelines, but can be logistically demanding. It also makes reconstruction of the various reintroduction efforts difficult.

Another difficulty is that two of the publications that best document IAR's slow loris reintroduction work include reintroductions in Sumatra and Java (Moore et al 2014) and in Java, Sumatra, and Borneo (Robitotul et al 2016). Moore et al clearly separate the two, but I was able to access only the abstract of the Robithoful et al presentation, and the abstract suggests that their results combine outcomes of reintroductions on all three islands.

There is some variation in pre- and post-release methodology, but all of the IAR lorises that were released in Sumatra were quarantined, medically screened and treated, provided with natural foods and locomotion substrates during rehabilitation, kept in large acclimation cages at the release sites where they could feed on natural foods, and then released. Those that were rehabilitated in West Java and reintroduced in Sumatra had to endure an overnight oceanic voyage. At least some wore radiocollars. There was post-release monitoring for up to a year. Additional details can be found in news stories on the IAR website, dated 9 June and 13 October 2016. Rehabilitation for those lorises that were eventually released in Sumatra required one to three years.

Procedures and outcomes for a subsample of five (two males, three females) of the slow lorises that were released in Batutegi between 2010 and 2014 are also described in detail in Moore et al (2014). It's not clear if these are among the ten lorises that were released in Batutegi that are described in Robithoful et al (2016).

Moore et al's five lorises had been confiscated or rescued in Java, rehabilitated at Ciapus, and ultimately released in Sumatra. Moore et al note that approximately 85% of the confiscated lorises that arrive at the center are judged to be physically unsuitable for reintroduction, mainly because their teeth had been extracted or cut down by traders and pet owners.

Habitat surveys had been conducted at the Sumatran release sites, and wild lorises were confirmed to have been present. The releases were described as "soft", which I infer to mean that some sort of post-release support was provided. The five Moore et al lorises that were released at Batuegi were able to return to their acclimation cages after release. They wore radiocollars, and were monitored for at least three months after release. One loris survived for 146 days, at which point its radiocollar battery failed and it was not detected again. The other four lorises died between nine and 287 days post-release. Two of these were killed by snakes, one was probably killed by a raptor, and one died of unknown causes. The loris that "survived" had been kept in a small habituation cage, and the four that died had been kept in large habituation cages. The sample sizes are small, but this outcome was contrary to the outcome regarding habituation cage size and survival for Javan slow lorises (see below).

Robithotul et al (2016) provided data on post-release ranging and habitat use on an unspecified subsample of radiocollared slow lorises that were released in Java, Sumatra, and Borneo between 2011 and 2015. Their behavior was compared with a sample of six radiocollared wild lorises. The released lorises were said to reach "behavioral stability" between three and six months. Robithoful et al stated that the "success rates" of loris reintroductions had increased by 60% between 2011 and 2015 due to improvements in pre- and post-release methods.

Moore et al and Van der Sandt provide many thoughtful and science-based suggestions for reintroducing lorises, foreshadowing Nekaris and Starr's and Nekaris and Nijman's later reservations about loris reintroduction (see comment box, below)

Conservation (Reinforcement), Welfare (Rehabilitation), Research

REFERENCES

Moore, R. 2012. Ethics, ecology and evolution of Indonesian slow lorises (*Nycticebus* spp.) rescued from the pet trade. PhD. Thesis, Oxford Brookes University.

Moore, R.S., Whihermonto, and K.A.I. Nekaris. 2014. Compassionate conservation, rehabilitation and translocation of Indonesian slow lorises. *Endangered Species Research* 26: 93-102.

Robithotul, H., Rattel, C., Anirudh, N. B., and K.L. Sanchez. 2016. Systematic reintroductions of Javan (*N. javanicus*), Sumatran (*N. coucang*) and Bornean (*N. menagensis*) slow lorises rescued from the illegal pet trade in Indonesia. Abstract of a paper presented at the joint meeting of the 26th Congress of the International Primatological Society and the 39th Meeting of the American Society of Primatologists, Chicago, IL, USA.

van der Sandt, C.M.G. 2016. Towards a successful translocation of captive slow lorises (*Nycticebus* spp.) in Borneo: a review and recommendations. Published online at http://dx.doi.org/10.1101/078535

www.internationalanimalrescue.org

Bornean Slow Loris (*Nycticebus coucang [menagensis]*). The International Animal Rescue (IAR) program has also released an unspecified number of slow lorises in Kalimantan, Borneo. News stories on the IAR website dated 7 November 2017 and 17 January 2018 state that nine rehabilitated Bornean slow lorises were released on Mount Tarak in West Kalimantan, Borneo in 2017. Eight had been confiscated by officials of the Centre for Natural Resources Conservation (BKSDA) and rehabilitated at IAR's Ketapang center. One had been born at the center. Three more slow lorises were said to have been released in Gunung Tarak National Park by IAR in June 2018, but the website "news story" (8 June 2018) says that the lorises had been introduced only to an acclimation cage, not to unbounded forest. They were to be kept in the acclimation cage for one month, but I have found no information about their reintroduction. Each of these rescued lorises (like so many others) had had their teeth clipped by traders and pet owners prior to their confiscation, but the IAR veterinary staff performed dental surgery during quarantine. The lorises could subsequently eat natural fruits and insects, but could not extract tree gum. Apparently this is sufficient for survival, and the surgery appears to represent a major advance in the reintroduction of rehabilitated lorises.

Anirudh et al (2018) studied a subsample of seven rehabilitated and reintroduced slow lorises in Gunung Tarak, and compared their behavior with that of a wild adult male. Each of these eight lorises was radiocollared and monitored for three months (the reintroduced lorises) or ten months (the wild loris). Five of the seven rehabilitants survived for at least three months. All of the lorises fed primarily on the fruit of an invasive plant. The authors claim that there are "close similarities" in behavior and space use of reintroduced and wild lorises, claiming that this is an indication of reintroduction success. I was able to access only the abstract of this presentation and thus lack further details. I am assuming that these seven rehabilitated lorises were among the nine noted above as having been reintroduced in Gunung Tarak by IAR in 2017.

As noted previously, Robithotul et al (2016) provided data on post-release ranging and habitat use on an unspecified subsample of radiocollared slow lorises that were released in Java, Sumatra, and Borneo between 2011 and 2015. Their behavior was compared with a sample of six radiocollared wild lorises. The released lorises were said to have reached "behavioral stability" between three and six months after release. Robithoful et al stated that the "success rates" of loris reintroductions had increased by 60% between 2011 and 2015 due to improvements in pre- and post-release methods.

International Animal Rescue has released hundreds of slow lorises in Borneo, Sumatra, and Java between 2010 and 2017. See the previous section on IAR's loris reintroductions in Sumatra for thoughts on the benefits and challenges presented by this ambitious effort.

Conservation (Reinforcement), Welfare (Rehabilitation), Research

References

Anirudh, N.B., Sanchez, K.L., Brown, E., and R. Saputra. 2018. Successes in releasing rescued and rehabilitated Bornean slow lorises (*Nycticebus menagensis*) in Gunung Tarak, West Kalimantan. Abstract of a paper presented at the 27th Congress of the International Primatological Society, Nairobi, Kenya.

Robithotul, H., Rattel, C., Anirudh, N. B., and K.L. Sanchez. 2016. Systematic reintroductions of Javan (*N. javanicus*), Sumatran (*N. coucang*) and Bornean (*N. menagensis*) slow lorises rescued from the illegal pet trade in Indonesia. Abstract of a paper presented at the joint meeting of the 26th Congress of the International Primatological Society and the 39th Meeting of the American Society of Primatologists, Chicago, IL, USA.

www.internationalanimalrescue.org

Javan Slow Loris (*Nycticebus coucang [javanicus]*). The International Animal Rescue (IAR) program, in collaboration with the Centre for Conservation of Natural Resources of West Java (BBKSDA), released 38 Javan slow lorises into the 40,000-ha Gunung (Mount) Halimun-Salak National Park in Java between 2010 and 2017 (IAR website news story, 10 February 2017). IAR also released 39 rehabilitated Javan slow lorises (one had been born in the rehabilitation center) in at least three cohorts in the 117-ha Mount Sawal Forest between 2014 and 2018, and 47 (28 males and 19 females) in at least two cohorts in the 15,500-hectare Mount Ciremai National Park in 2017. These sites are close to Halimun Salak, and thus all of these releases are included in the same program. The total number of slow lorises released by IAR in West Java is 124.

A "news release" on the IAR website (5 September 2018) claims that twenty more slow lorises were "translocated" or "released" in the 12,420-ha Masigit-Kareumbi Conservation Forest Area in Bandung, West Java in August 2017. There were seven males and 13 females; two of these 20 were infants that had presumably been born at the Ciapus rehabilitation center. The lorises had spent up to two years in the rehabilitation center, where they had been quarantined, medically screened, observed to assure that they were behaving normally, and fed natural foods. A careful reading of this news release, and of a coordinated media article (Grealish 2108), shows that these 20 had not actually been released to the wild but only moved to large acclimation cages, where they would be held for two to four weeks. They are therefore not counted as having been actually reintroduced by the IAR program in West Java.

Procedures and outcomes for a subsample of 18 (seven males, 11 females) of the slow lorises that were released in Halimun Salak are described in greater detail in Moore et al (2014). It's not clear if these 18 include the 11 released individuals that are described in Moore 2012 (cited in Kenyon et al 2014) or those described by Robithoful et al (2016). I'm assuming that they were among the 124.

All of these 18 lorises were confiscated or surrendered ex-pets that had been rehabilitated at IAR's Ciapus Primate Rescue Center in Bogor, West Java, Indonesia. They had been quarantined and given extensive veterinary screening and treatment at the center. They had been given "feed enrichment", which I assume to mean that they were fed with natural foods. They were acclimated at the release site for two to four weeks, some in large acclimation cages and some in small acclimation cages. At least some of the lorises had been fitted with radiocollars, and were monitored for up to one year after release. The release sites had been surveyed to assure their suitability for slow lorises, and there were apparently wild lorises present.

Seven of these lorises were known to have died, and one had to be recaptured within four months. Five were alive at the end of the study, several for nearly a year, and the outcomes for five were unknown although three of these had lived for more than a year in the wild. There was a statistically significant positive association between length of post-release survival and size of the acclimation cage: those that lived the longest had been kept in the larger acclimation cages. This was contrary to the outcome regarding cage size and survival for slow lorises that were released in Sumatra (see above), but samples sizes were small.

As noted previously, Robithotul et al (2016) provided data on post-release ranging and habitat use on an unspecified subsample of radiocollared slow lorises that were released in Java, Sumatra, and Borneo between 2011 and 2015. Their behavior was compared with a sample of six radiocollared wild lorises. The released lorises were said to have reached "behavioral stability" between three and six months after release. Robithoful et al stated that the "success rates" of loris reintroductions had increased by 60% between 2011 and 2015 due to improvements in pre- and post-release methods.

Wilcox et al (2018) compared the behavior of six lorises that had been reintroduced by IAR at

Mount Salak and Mount Sawal, with that of wild lorises as reported in the literature. The reintroduced lorises (which I'm assuming were among the 124 known to have been reintroduced by IAR in West Java) were studied for approximately eight weeks after release. The authors report that the released lorises traveled more and rested less than the wild lorises. They attribute this difference to differences in feeding behavior: the reintroduced lorises fed mainly on the nectar of flowers of one plant species, but the wild lorises fed on tree gum and sap. Recall that that rehabilitated lorises whose teeth had been cut, even when surgically repaired, are unable to aquire these tree exudates. I was able to access only the abstract of this presentation, which did not provide survivorship outcomes.

The news stories on the IAR website appear to carefully document the number of lorises (and other primates) that IAR has reintroduced. The stories state that there has been post-release monitoring, but outcomes are not provided, other than for a few cases of chance observation of previously released individuals. The reader is directed to the IAR website news stories of 29 July 2016, 10, 28 February, 12 May, 2 June, and 11 August, 2017, and 20 February, 4 April, and 5 September 2018 for additional details about the reintroductions of West Javan slow lorises. The latter three news releases appear to equate the lorises' being placed in acclimation cages in the forest with actual release to the wild, which may have caused the number said to have been released in Java to be inflated. An earlier IAR news release (8 June 2018) had similarly misrepresented a loris reintroduction in Borneo (see above). I don't know if the IAR managers simply use the term "release" differently than I do, if there may be some confusion in translation, or if there is an intentional attempt to exaggerate accomplishments.

As previously noted, International Animal Rescue has released hundreds of slow lorises in Borneo, Sumatra, and Java between 2009 and 2017. See the previous section on IAR's loris reintroductions in Sumatra for thoughts on the benefits and challenges presented by this ambitious effort.

Welfare (Rehabilitation), Conservation (Reinforcement), Research

References

Kenyon, M., Streicher, U, Loung, H., Tran, T., Tran, M., Vo, B., and A. Cronin. 2014. Survival of released pygmy slow loris *Nycticebus pygmaeus* in South Vietnam. *Endangered Species Research*, 25, 185-95.

Moore, R. 2012. *Ethics, ecology and evolution of Indonesian slow lorises (Nycticebus spp.) rescued from the pet trade*. PhD Thesis, Oxford Brookes University.

Moore, R.S., Whihermonto, and K.A.I. Nekaris. 2014. Compassionate conservation, rehabilitation and translocation of Indonesian slow lorises. *Endangered Species Research* 26: 93-102.

Grealish, R. 2018. Amazing moment 20 slow lorises are released into the wild for the first time. *LAD Bible News*, 7 September. www.ladbible.com (Accessed 9 September 2018).

Robithotul, H., Rattel, C., Anirudh, N. B., and K.L. Sanchez. 2016. Systematic reintroductions of Javan (*N. javanicus*), Sumatran (*N. coucang*) and Bornean (*N. menagensis*) slow lorises rescued from the illegal pet trade in Indonesia. Abstract of a paper presented at the joint meeting of the 26th Congress of the International Primatological Society and the 39th Meeting of the American Society of Primatologists, Chicago, IL, USA.

van der Sandt, C.M.G. 2016. Towards a successful translocation of captive slow lorises (*Nycticebus* spp.) in Borneo: a review and recommendations. Published online at http://dx.doi.org/10.1101/078535

Wilcox, C.H., Mubarok, H., Llano Sanchez, K., and N. Waran. 2018. A comparison of released and wild Javan slow loris behaviour. Abstract of a paper presented at the 27th Congress of the International Primatological Society, Nairobi, Kenya.

www.internationalanimalrescue.org

Javan Slow Loris (*Nycticebus coucang [javanicus]*). The Aspinall Foundation Indonesia Programme and the Javan Primate Conservation Project, in collaboration with the International Animal Rescue program and the East Javan Natural Resource Conservation Agency (BBKSDA), released eleven confiscated and rehabilitated Javan slow lorises in two cohorts in the Kondang Merak Protected Forest in East Java in April, 2017. A Javan Primates Conservation Project Facebook post of 22 April 2017 states that three had been released in Kondak Merak, and a newspaper story states that eight more lorises (four males and four females) were released in Kondang Merak on 8 November 2017. The release of the eight is said to have actually been conducted by IAR, which suggests that the pre- and post-release methodology that was used in the IAR Sumatran, Bornean, and West Javan programs (quarantine, some pre-release training, acclimation, post-release monitoring) were also used for the Kondak Merak lorises.

Welfare (Rehabilitation)

References

Javan Primate Conservation Project Facebook page.

Rochman, A. 2017. 8 Javan slow lorises released into natural habitat. *The Jakarta Post*, 9 November 2017.

A Note on Loris Reintroduction

Nekaris and Starr (2015) state that there have been many undocumented releases of lorises: "…hard releases of slow lorises are rampant. For example, the misconception that these animals are slow and solitary has led to their release in very small forest areas in large numbers, release with no monitoring, solitary release, release of non-endemic species, release into areas where no ecological assessment has been made, and/or release into areas where no health checks have been made of the releasees or of the wild slow lorises in the local area." (pg. 93). They urge that IUCN primate reintroduction guidelines be followed, which appears to be the case for International Animal Rescue and Javan Primate Conservation Project releases since 2014. However, there have been few reports of outcomes.

More recently, Nekaris and Nijman (2017) have written that "(R)eintroduction itself is a threat to the Javan slow loris" (pg 49). They observed that four of the six Indonesian loris species are traded in Java; confiscated lorises, if reintroduced, could result in hybridization or displacement of the native Javan loris. They cite Moore et al's (2014) finding that up to 90% of reintroduced Javan slow lorises die, but they concede that there have been improvements in reintroduction techniques that may result in higher survivorship. The same concerns may also apply to the reintroduction of Bornean and Sumatran slow lorises.

References

Nekaris, K.A.I. and C.R. Starr. 2015. Conservation and ecology of the neglected slow loris: priorities and prospects. *Endangered Species Research* 28: 87-95.

Nekaris, K.A.I. and V. Nijman. 2017. Javan slow loris. In C. Schwitzer, R.A. Mittermeier, A.B. Rylands, F. Chiozza, E.A. Williamson, E.J. Macfie, J. Wallis and A. Cotton, eds. *Primates in Peril; The World's 25 Most Endangered Primates, 2016-2018*, pp 48-51. Arlington, VA, IUCN SSC Primate Specialist Group (PSG), International Primatological Society (IPS), Conservation International (CI), and Bristol Zoological Society.

Aye-Aye (*Daubentonia madagascarensis*). Jean-Jacque Petter of the Museum of Natural History in Paris, in collaboration with the Madagascan Department de Eaux et Forêts and the (then) International Union for the Conservation of Nature, reintroduced nine aye-ayes (four females, five males) on Nosy Mangabe, a 520-ha island in Madagascar in 1967. The destination site had been designated a Special Reserve in 1966, and mango and coconut trees had been planted for the aye-ayes. The aye-ayes had been captured near coastal villages on the nearby mainland and they were released on a beach near Naroansetra in the Bay of Antogil. It is uncertain whether aye-ayes occurred on Nosy Mangabe at the time of the release.

Petter wanted to establish lemurs on Nosy Mangabe because they were highly endangered. The Mahombo Special Reserve on the mainland was being severely degraded and Petter doubted that aye-ayes could continue to survive there. Long (2003) states that there were only 12 aye-ayes remaining on the mainland at the time, of which nine were trapped for this reintroduction.

I was unable to access Petter et al (1977) and could find no further details about the release. I assume it was a hard release with no pre-release preparation, acclimation, post-release support, or post-release monitoring. Aye-ayes are common on Nosy Mangabe today.

Conservation (Probably Introduction)

REFERENCES

Constable, I.D., Pollock, J.I., Ratsirarson, J., and H. Simons. 1985. Sightings of aye-ayes and red ruffed lemurs on Nosy Mangabe and the Masoala Peninsula. *Primate Conservation* 5: 59-62.

Ganzhorn, J.U. and J. Rabesoa. 1986. The aye-aye (*Daubentonia madagascarensis*) found in the eastern rainforest of Madagascar. *Folia Primatologica* 46: 125-126.

Long, J.L. 2003. *Introduced Mammals of the World*. Collingwood, Victoria, Australia, CSIRO Publishing.

Mittermeier, R.A., Louis, E.E. Jr., Richardson, M., Schwitzer, C., Landgrand, O., Rylands, A.B., Hawkins, F., Rajaobelina, S., Ratsimbazafy, J., Rasoloarison, R., Roos, C., Kappeler, P.M., and J. MacKinnon. 2010. *Lemurs of Madagascar*, 3rd Edition. Arlington, Virginia, Conservation International.

Petter, J.-J., Albinac, R., and Y. Rumpler. 1977. *Mammifères Lemurièns (Primates, Prosimiens). Faunes de Madagascar*. Paris, ORSTROM/CNRS.

Pollock, J.I., Constable, I.D., Mittermeier, R.A., Ratsirarson, J., and H. Simons. 1985. A note on the diet and feeding behavior of the aye-aye *Daubentonia madagascarensis*. *International Journal of Primatology* 6(4): 435-447.

Diameded Sifaka (*Propithecus diadema*). The Madagascar Biodiversity and Biogeography Project of Henry Doorly Zoo in Omaha, Nebraska, in collaboration with the Madagascar National Parks department and the Ministère de l'Environnement, des Forêts et de Tourisme, reintroduced 27 wild-born diademed sifakas (six family groups) into the 810-ha Analamazaotra Special Reserve in Madagascar in 2006 and 2007. Four other lemur species lived in the reserve at the time of the release, but sifakas had been eliminated by hunting by 1973. The sites of origin had been degraded by hunting, agriculture, firewood collection, and mining. The lemurs were given two complete physical examinations, implanted subcutaneously with individually identifiable microchips, and fitted with radiocollars before release. The release is described as a "hard release", which I interpret as having no additional pre-release preparation other than the medical screenings, no acclimation, and no post-release support. The social behavior, ranging, and foraging behavior of the sifakas were studied for at least four years after release, and monitoring of survival and reproduction continued as of 2016. One of the sifakas had died of "natural causes" and another had disappeared by 2009. There had been seven births by 2009, of which three infants were killed infanticidally and two were killed by aerial predators.

This project occurred simultaneously with and in the same areas by the same organization as the reintroduction of black and white ruffed lemurs (see below) and is documented in the same publication (Day et al 2009). However, the two are treated as separate projects because of the two species that are involved.

Conservation (Reintroduction), Research

REFERENCES

Day, S.R., Ramarokono, R.E.A.F., Sitzmann, B.D., Randriamboahanginjatovo, R., Ramanankirija, H., Rence, V., Randrianindrina, A., Ravololonarivo, G. and E.E. Louis Jr. 2009. Re-introduction of diademed sifaka (*Propithecus diadema*) and black and white ruffed lemurs (*Varecia variegata editorum*) at Analamazaotra Special Reserve, eastern Madagascar. *Lemur News* 14: 32-37.

Louis, E.E. Jr., Rabetoandro, A.N., Rahajanirina, A.N., Hawkins, M.T., Randrianindrina, V.R., Lei, R., Bailey, J., Zaonarivelo, R., Andriantompohavana, R., and C.L. Frasier. 2016. Ten-year perspective of a reintroduction/translocation program for the diameded sifaka, *Propithecus diadema*, in Analamazaotra Special Reserve in Madagascar. Abstract of a paper presented at the joint meeting of the 26th Congress of the International Primatological Society and the 39th Meeting of the American Society of Primatologists, Chicago, IL, USA.

Black and White Ruffed Lemur (*Varecia variegata*). An unknown number of black and white ruffed lemurs were introduced on Nosy Mangabe, a 520-ha Madagascan island in the 1930s. No further details are provided (J-J. Petter, pers. comm in Constable et al 1985). Constable et al described the black and white ruffed lemur population on the island as "thriving" in 1984. They were still present on the island as of 1998 (Long 2003).

Unspecified

References

Constable, I.D., Pollock, J.I., Ratsirarson, J., and H. Simons. 1985. Sightings of aye-ayes and red ruffed lemurs on Nosy Mangabe and the Masoala Peninsula. *Primate Conservation* 5: 59-62.

Long, J.L. 2003. *Introduced Mammals of the World*. Collingwood, Victoria, Australia, CSIRO Publishing.

Black and White Ruffed Lemur (*Varecia variegata variegata*). The Madagascar Fauna Group released thirteen captive-born black and white ruffed lemurs in three cohorts in the Betampona Reserve in Madagascar between 1997 and 2001 to reinforce the reserve's diminished population of approximately 35 individuals (Britt et al. 2002, 2004 a, b). Betampona has a total area of 2,200 ha, of which approximately half is intact rainforest. There were ten other lemur species, and a number of rare, endemic birds, mammals, and plants living in the reserve. A systematic site evaluation and choice of release sites preceded the reintroduction. The 13 individuals met rigorous selection criteria, among which was being mother-reared. The lemurs all had pre-release experience in large forested enclosures, and were acclimated at or near the release sites for five days. Some of the lemurs were provided with food for an unspecified time after release. Three of the released males and one of the females joined the wild population and reproduced with wild mates. Three others survived at least until 2007. These seven became independent of post-release feeding. Six of the lemurs were killed by predators. The reintroduction was a component of a larger commitment by the Madagascar Fauna Group to the conservation of Betampona, which suggests that the conservation benefits of the reintroduction were greater than the reinforcement of the size and genetic diversity of the wild black and white ruffed lemur population (www.waza.org).

Conservation (Reinforcement), Research

References

Britt, A., Welch, C., and A. Katz. 2002. The release of captive-bred black and white ruffed lemurs into the Betampona Reserve, eastern Madagascar. *Re-introduction News* 21: 18-20.

Britt, A., Welch, C., Katz, A., Iambana, B., Porton, I., Junge, R., Crawford, C., Williams, C., and D. Haring. 2004a. The re-stocking of captive-bred ruffed lemurs (*Varecia variegata variegata*) into the Betampona Reserve, Madagascar. *Biodiversity and Conservation* 13: 635-57.

Britt, A., Welch, C., and A. Katz. 2004b. Can small, isolated primate populations be effectively reinforced through the release of individuals from a captive population? *Biological Conservation* 115: 319-27.

Britt, A., Welch, C. Katz, A. and K. Freeman. 2008. Supplementation of the black and white ruffed lemur population with captive-bred individuals in the Betampona Reserve, eastern Madagascar. In P.S. Soorae, ed. *Global Re-introduction Perspectives: Re-introduction Case-Studies from Around the Globe*, pp. 197-201. Abu Dhabi, UAE, IUCN/SSC Re-introduction Specialist Group.

Black-and-White Ruffed Lemur (*Varecia variegata*). The Madagascar Biodiversity and Biogeography Project of Henry Doorly Zoo in Omaha, Nebraska, in collaboration with the Madagascar National Parks department and the Ministère de l'Environnement, des Forêts et de Tourisme, reintroduced seven wild-born black and white ruffed lemurs (two family groups) into the 810-ha Analamazaotra Special Reserve in Madagascar in 2006 and 2007. Four other lemur species lived in the reserve at the time of the release, but there were no black and white ruffed lemurs at the time of the release. Some did live in nearby forest tracts. The site of origin of the released lemurs had been degraded by mining. The lemurs were given two complete physical examinations, implanted subcutaneously with individually identifiable microchips, and fitted with radiocollars before release. The release is described as a "hard release", which I interpret as having no additional pre-release preparation other than the medical screenings, no acclimation, and no post-release support. The social behavior, ranging, and foraging behavior of the lemurs were studied for at least four years after release. One of the lemurs had died of "natural causes" and another had disappeared by 2009. Two sets of twins had been born by 2009 (one set was a second-generation birth event). Two of the released lemurs disappeared and are thought to have been killed by hunters.

This project occurred simultaneously with and in the same areas by the same organization as the reintroduction of diameded sifakas (see above) and is documented in the same publication (Day et al 2009). However, the two are treated as separate projects because of the two species that are involved.

Conservation (Reintroduction), Research

References

Day, S.R., Ramarokono, R.E.A.F., Sitzmann, B.D., Randriamboahanginjatovo, R., Ramanankirija, H., Rence, V., Randrianindrina, A., Ravololonarivo, G., and E.E. Louis Jr. 2009. Re-introduction of diademed sifaka (*Propithecus diadema*) and black and white ruffed lemurs (*Varecia variegata editorum*) at Analamazaotra Special Reserve, eastern Madagascar. Lemur News 14: 32-37.

Red-fronted Brown Lemur (*Eulemur rufus, Eulemur fulvus rufus, Eulemur rufifrons*). Eight red-fronted brown lemurs escaped from cages during a cyclone in a 1,000-ha forested area of the Berenty private reserve in 1975. The lemurs had been captured in the coastal town of Morondava in western Madagascar. There are no further details about the release but there was apparently no pre-release preparation, acclimation, or post-release support. The lemurs reproduced successfully, and hybridized with collared brown lemurs (*Eulemur fulvus collaris, E. collaris*), some of which had been introduced to Berenty earlier and some later (see below). The hybrid population numbered 653 in 2007 and 596 in 2009.

Accidental (Escape)

References

Simmen, B., Hladik, A., and P. Ramasiarisoa. 2003. Food intake and dietary overlap in native *Lemur catta* and *Propithecus verrauxi* and introduced *Eulemur fulvus* at Berenty, southern Madagascar. *International Journal of Primatology* 24(5): 949-968.

Chapter 9: Reintroduction of Lorises and Lemurs

Mongoose Lemur (*Eulemur mongoz*). Mongoose lemurs are widely thought to have been reintroduced on the Union of the Comoros Islands of Grande Comore (Ngazidja, 102,500 ha), Anjouan (Ndzuwani or Nzwani, 42,400 ha), and Mohéli (Mwali, 29,000 ha). They were probably brought from the Madagascan mainland by seafaring traders and/or fishers, perhaps as early as the sixteenth century. The number of lemurs that were reintroduced and the number of reintroduction cohorts are undeterminable. They may have been transported as food for the voyage, pets, and/or trading items. Tattersall (1977a) raises the possibility that the lemurs may have rafted from Madagascar without human assistance, but thinks that human-mediated reintroduction is more likely. Mongoose lemurs occur endemically only in the northwest of Madagascar, so the responsible sailors would have sailed around to the southeast of Madagascar prior to releasing the lemurs in the Comoros.

Mongoose lemurs are one of only two lemur species that can be found outside of Madagascar (brown lemurs, also introduced in the Comoros, are the other, see below). The Anjouan and Mohéli populations of mongoose lemurs exist today. The Grande Comore population never exceeded a small number of individuals that escaped or were released from captivity. "Genetic data show no significant differentiation between Malagasy and Comorian populations of these species [mongoose and brown lemurs], supporting the interpretation that both were introduced only recently to the Comoro Islands." (Pastorini et al 2003, pg. 5879). These authors qualify "recently" as the "past several hundred years" (pg. 5883).

Unknown

REFERENCES

Long, J.L. 2003. *Introduced Mammals of the World.* Collingwood, Victoria, Australia, CSIRO Publishing.

Pastorini, J., Thalmann, U., and R.D. Martin. 2003. A molecular approach to comparative phylogeography of extant Malagasy lemurs. *Proceedings of the National Academy of Sciences* 100(10): 5879-5884.

Tattersall, I. 1977a. The lemurs of the Comoro Islands. *Oryx* 13(5): 445-448.

Brown Lemur (*Eulemur fulvus*). A subspecies of brown lemurs, *E. f. mayottensis*, was reintroduced to the island of Mayotte at about the same time under the same circumstances as mongoose lemurs were reintroduced to the Comoros (see above). Mayotte (37,400 ha), generally speaking, is part of the same Comoros archipelago but is in a portion of the archipelago that is the French External Department of Mayotte. The population of Mayotte lemurs exists today. Pastorini et al found that there is no significant genetic difference between the reintroduced brown lemurs of Mayotte and the endemic brown lemurs of northwestern Madagascar.

Unknown

References

Long, J.L. 2003. *Introduced Mammals of the World.* Collingwood, Victoria, Australia, CSIRO Publishing.

Pastorini, J., Thalmann, U., and R.D. Martin. 2003. A molecular approach to comparative phylogeography of extant Malagasy lemurs. *Proceedings of the National Academy of Sciences* 100(10): 5879-5884.

Tattersall, I. 1977a. The lemurs of the Comoro Islands. *Oryx* 13(5): 445-448.

Tattersall, I. 1977b. Ecology and behavior of *Lemur fulvus mayottensis* (Primates, Lemuriformes). *Anthropological papers of the American Museum of Natural History* 54(4): 425-482.

Crowned Lemur (*Eulemur coronatus*). Long reports that a teacher reintroduced an unspecified number of crowned lemurs in an unspecified number of cohorts at an unspecified time to the 320-ha island of Nosy Hara, off the northwest tip of Madagascar. The source population was probably from the island of Madagascar. There are no reports of crowned lemurs on Nosy Hara today, although there are some dwarf lemurs, which themselves may have been reintroduced.

Unspecified

References

Long, J.L. 2003. *Introduced Mammals of the World.* Collingwood, Victoria, Australia, CSIRO Publishing.

Marshall, M. 2015. New group of dwarf lemurs may be world's rarest primate. *BBC Earth*, April 2015. www.bbc.com Accessed 4 September 2018.

Collared (Red-collared) Brown Lemur (*Eulemur fulvus collaris, Eulemur collaris*). Two male red-collared brown lemurs were introduced into a 1,000-ha forested area of the Berenty private reserve prior to 1975, and the owners of the reserve, the de Heaulme family, added eight (or ten) pets and orphaned red-collared brown lemurs from markets in Fort Dauphin, in northern Madagascar. I could find no additional information about these releases. The introduced red-collared brown lemurs have reproduced successfully with introduced red-fronted brown lemurs (see below) despite having different numbers of chromosomes. The hybrid population numbered 653 in 2007 and 596 in 2009. The purposes are inferred from the sources.

Welfare (Rehabilitation), Recreational/Aesthetic

References

Jolly, A. 2012. Berenty Reserve, Madagascar: A long time in a small space. In P.M. Kappeler and D.P. Watts, eds. *Long-Term Field Studies of Primates*, pp 21-44. New York, Springer.

Simmen, B., Hladik, A., and P. Ramasiarisoa. 2003. Food intake and dietary overlap in native *Lemur catta* and *Propithecus verrauxi* and introduced *Eulemur fulvus* at Berenty, southern Madagascar. *International Journal of Primatology* 24(5): 949-968.

http://www-personal.umd.umich.edu/~fdolins/berenty/aboutberenty/fauna/lemurs/brownlemurs/index.html

Collared (Collared Brown, Red-Collared) Brown Lemur. (*Eulemur collaris*.). A scientific team headed by scientists from the University of Pisa, working in collaboration with the Department of Animal Biology and Anthropology of the University of Antananarivo, the Institute of Zoology of Hamburg University, QIT Madagascar Minerals (QMM), and the Malagasy Ministère des Eaux et Forèts, translocated 28 collared lemurs (six groups) from two forest tracts that were being cut and converted rapidly to two nearby tracts that had a total of 230 ha of secondary forest, in southeast Madagascar in 2000 and 2001. The lemurs were said to have been suffering severe malnutrition at the origin sites. Collared lemurs had lived previously in the destination forest tracts but had been exterminated by hunting. Hunting had been reduced at the time of the reintroductions, but the forests were degraded. The source provides no details on capture techniques, pre- or post-release management, or acclimation.

The lemurs were fitted with radiocollars and were monitored for four years after release. Data were collected initially on population dynamics, activity budgets, feeding behavior, home range, and habitat use, and comparisons were made between the translocated groups and a wild group of collared lemurs at another site. Group size among the translocated lemurs decreased after translocation and was less than that of the wild lemurs. Total population size among the translocated lemurs increased to 36 in the first two post-release years, despite the loss of two animals due to hunting, and then decreased in the following two years. The main reason for the decline was the immigration of predatory fossas into the areas. The fossas were trapped and were themselves translocated to another area. One of the translocated lemur groups traveled over 3 km of burned pasture to return to the site of origin; it was trapped and returned to the destination site. The translocation led to strong community support for conservation of the destination area.

Welfare (Rescue), Research

References

Donati, G., Ramanamanjato, J-B, Ravoahangy, A.M., and M. Vinclette. 2007. Translocation as a conservation measure for an endangered species in the littoral forest of southeastern Madagascar: the case of *Eulemur collaris*. In: J.U. Ganzhorn, S.M. Goodman, and M. Vinclette, eds. *Biodiversity, Ecology and Conservation of Littoral Forest Ecosystems on Southeastern Madagascar, Tolagnaro (Fort Dauphin)*, pp 237-245. Washington, DC, Smithsonian Institution Press.

Collared (Brown Ruffed-collared) Brown Lemur (*Eulemur collaris*). The Qit Minerals project captured and reintroduced 18 wild collared brown lemurs in an area of "high human pressure" to an unidentified area with no anthropogenic pressure in 2000 and 2001. The source does not say whether lemurs were living or ever had lived at the destination site. The purposes were to contribute to the conservation and protection of the species (Conservation), and to develop a new ecotourism program (Commercial). There was intermittent post-release monitoring for more than a year. Females gave birth at the new site in both years but may have been pregnant before capture. One group adapted to the release site and another returned to the site of origin. Two lemurs were killed by hunters. A small population was established at the new site.

Conservation (probably Introduction), Commercial

References

Andriamandranto, M.R. 2003. Post-release monitoring of brown-ruffed collared lemurs after translocation in the south-eastern forest of Madasgascar. *Re-introduction News* 23: 34-35.

White-fronted (Brown) Lemur (*Lemur fulvus albitrons, Lemur albifrons*). An unknown number of white-fronted brown lemurs were introduced on Nosy Mangabe, a 520-ha Madagascan island, in the 1930s. No further details are provided (J-J. Petter, personal communication in Constable et al 1985). Constable et al described the white-fronted lemur population as "thriving" in 1984.

Unspecified

References

Constable, I.D., Pollock, J.I., Ratsirarson, J., and H. Simons. 1985. Sightings of aye-ayes and red ruffed lemurs on Nosy Mangabe and the Masoala Peninsula. *Primate Conservation* 5: 59-62.

Ring-tailed Lemur (*Lemur catta*). The New York Zoological Society (now the Wildlife Conservation Society) and the Duke University Primate Center released twelve ring-tailed lemurs on the Society's 2,900-ha St Catherines Island in Georgia, USA in 1984 and 1986. Two males and four females were released in 1984 and five males and one female were released in 1986. All were captive-born. The NYZS lemurs had lived in a conventional zoo setting. The Duke animals had lived in a semi-free-ranging enclosure. All of the lemurs wore radio transmitter collars. They were provisioned daily with food and water and allowed access to heated enclosures in cold weather.

These first two cohorts were followed until 1992. Six of the original twelve died or disappeared by that date. One was hit by a truck, one was eaten by an alligator, two died of an illness, and two disappeared. Twenty-one lemurs that were born on the island and survived for more than one week were still alive in 1992, although some were among the twelve lemurs that had to be rescued and removed due to wounding during social conflict.

Twelve lemurs survived at liberty on St Catherines Island in 1992. The Island's website states that 83 lemurs survived in six groups in 2013. It is unlikely that these lemurs could survive without provisioned food and supplementary heat.

The purpose of this reintroduction was Research. Keith-Lukas et al provide extensive data on changes in body weight, locomotor agility, activity patterns, vocalizations, foraging, and social behavior and social organization during the first 22 months after release. The lemurs, most of which had been obese when released, attained more normal body weights, showed improved climbing and jumping, and a more complete vocal repertoire (including vocalizations that they apparently had not used or heard during their previous zoo and primate center lives). Ranging and the number of natural plant foods eaten increased. "The study group [eventually] resembled wild and semi-free-ranging conspecifics in aspects of their social organization, ranging, daily activity pattern … and vocalizations…" (Keith-Lucas et al 1999, pg .24).

Research

REFERENCES

Keith-Lucas, T., White, F.J., Keith-Lucas, L. and L.G. Vick. 1999. Changes in behavior in free-ranging *Lemur catta* following release in a natural habitat. *American Journal of Primatology* 47(1): 15-28.

www.stcatherinesisland.org

CHAPTER 10
TABULAR SUMMARY OF PRIMATE REINTRODUCTION PROGRAMS

For following tables, please note:

* The number of animals released is specified when it is provided or can be inferred from the source(s). The number is often stated in sources as the minimum number. In these cases, we show only the minimum number in the table. If no number of released primates is specified or can be inferred for a program in the source(s), "1" (in bold) is used in the table.

Unwitting Travelers: A History of Primate Reintroduction

	Common Name	Country	Release Site		Release Years	*Number and Source of Animals			Purpose		Pre-Release Preparation
			Name of Release Site	Size (ha)		Total Number of Animals	Number WB	Number CB	Primary	Secondary	
1	Chimpanzee	Tanzania	Rubondo Island	24,000	1966-1969	17	17	0	Conservation (Introduction)	Welfare (Non-lethal Control)	
2	Chimpanzee	Uganda	Kibale National Park	76,600	1994	1	1	0	Research	Welfare (Rehabilitation)	1
3	Chimpanzee	Uganda	Isinga Island, Queen Elizabeth National Park	5	1995	12	12	0	Welfare (Non-lethal Control, Rehabilitation)		
4	Chimpanzee	Republic of Gabon	Ipassa Island in Ipassa Makokou Biosphere Reserve	65	early 1970s	8	8	0	Unspecified		
5	Chimpanzee	Senegal	Nioloka Koba National Park	913,000	1973-1978	14	12	2	Welfare (Rehabilitation)		1
6	Chimpanzee	The Gambia	Small island (Island 2) in River Gambia National Park	77	1979	8	7	1	Welfare (Rehabilitation)		1
7	Chimpanzee	The Gambia	Baboon Island (Island 1), River Gambia National Park	435	1979	9	7	2	Welfare (Rehabilitation, Non-lethal Control)		1
8	Chimpanzee	The Gambia	Baboon Island and two other small islands (Islands 1, 2, and 3) in River Gambia National Park	565	1986-2005	33	33	0	Welfare (Rehabilitation)		1
9	Chimpanzee	Liberia	Five islands in the Little Bassa River	125	1976-2006	125	125	0	Welfare (Non-lethal Control, Rehabilitation)	Conservation (Reintroduction)	1
10	Chimpanzee	Ivory Coast	Island in Bandama River, Azagny National Park	169	1983	20	20	0	Welfare (Non-lethal Control, Rehabilitation)	Conservation (Reinforcement)	1
11	Chimpanzee	USA	Bear Island	10	1972, 1973	8	5	3	Commercial	Research	1
12	Chimpanzee	Republic of Congo	Conkouati-Douli National Park	505,000	1996-2012	53	53	0	Welfare (Rehabilitation)	Conservation (Reinforcement)	1
13	Chimpanzee	Republic of Guinea	Kerfalya Island	1	1992	12	12	0	Welfare (Rehabilitation)		
14	Chimpanzee	Nigeria	Afi Mountain Sanctuary	10,400	late 1990s	5	5	0	Other (Escape)		
15	Chimpanzee	Sierra Leone	Western Area Peninsula National Park	17,688	late 1990s?, 2006	36	32	4	Other (Escape)		
16	Chimpanzee	Senegal	along the Diarra River		2002	1	1	0	Welfare (Rescue)		

Chapter 10: Tabular Summary of Primate Reintroduction Programs

Acclimation			Post-Release Support			Post-Release Monitoring			Success A	Success B	References
Less Than One Month	One to Six Months	Greater Than Six Months	Less Than One Month	One to Six Months	Greater Than Six Months	Less Than One Month	One to Six Months	Greater Than Six Months			
				1			1		1		Borner 1985, Matsumota-Oda 2004, Moscovice et al 2007, Msindai 2015
1				1			1				Morell 1994, Treves and Naughton-Treves 1997
					1			1			Manning 1996
				1		1					Hannah 1989, Hannah and McGrew 1991, Hladik 1978
		1		1				1			Badham 1979, Brewer 1976, 1978, 1980, Brewer Marsden et al 2006, Carter 2003b, c, pers comm 2017, Carter et al 2003, Lemmon 1987
					1			1			Brewer 1976, 1980, Brewer Marsden et al 2006, Carter 1988, 2003b, c, pers comm 2017
		1		1				1			Carter 1981 a,b 1988, 2003b, c, pers comm 2017, Curtis pers comm 2017, Herzfeld 2017
1				1				1			Beck 2010, 2016, Brewer Marsden et al 2006, Carter 1988, 2003b, c, pers comm 2017, Hannah and McGrew 1991, Herzfeld 2017, www.friendsofanimals.org
1				1				1			Agoramoorthy and Hsu 1999, Carter 2003b, Clifton 2015, Conlee and Desmond 2015, Hannah 1989, Hannah and McGrew 1991, Prince 1985, 2005, Revkin 1996, www.humanesociety.org
				1				1			Carter 2003b, Clifton 2015, Hannah 1989, Koffi 2017, Prince 1985, Wanshel 2016
				1				1			McGrew 1983, Soave 1982, Wilson and Elicker 1976
				1				1	1		Aczel 1993, 1997, Beck et al 1994, Farmer 2000, 2002, Farmer and Jamart 2002, Farmer et al 2006, 2010, Goossens et al 2002, 2003, 2005, IUCN 1998, Karlowski 1996, Le Hallaye et al 2010, Renaud et al 2013, Tutin et al 2001
					1			1			Carter 2003b, Teleki 2001.
								1			Boki Blog 2018, Carter 2003b, Farmer 2002, Gadsby 2002, Pandrillus 2017
								1			Carter 2003b, Farmer 2002, Kabasawa et al 2008
						1					Carter 2003a, 2013-14

Unwitting Travelers: A History of Primate Reintroduction

	Common Name	Country	Release Site		Release Years	*Number and Source of Animals			Purpose		Pre-Release Preparation
			Name of Release Site	Size (ha)		Total Number of Animals	Number WB	Number CB	Primary	Secondary	
17	Chimpanzee	Guinea	Unspecified			2	2	0	Welfare (Rescue)		
18	Chimpanzee	Guinea	Mafour core area of Haut Niger National Park	55,400	2008, 2011	16	13	3	Conservation (Reinforcement)	Welfare (Rehabilitation)	1
19	Chimpanzee	Senegal	Fongoli	9,000	2009	1	1	0	Welfare (Rescue)		
20	Bonobo	Democratic Republic of Congo	Luo Scientific Reserve	15,000	1991	1	1	0	Welfare (Rehabilitation)		1
21	Bonobo	Democratic Republic of Congo	Maringa-Lopori-Wamba forest landscape	16,200	2009, 2011	16	14	2	Welfare (Rehabilitation)	Conservation (Reintroduction)	1
22	Lowland Gorilla	Republic of Gabon	Ipassa Makokou Biosphere Reserve	15,000	early 1970s	1	1	0	Unspecified		
23	Lowland Gorilla	Republic of Congo	Lefini Faunal Reserve (630,000 ha) and Lesio Louna Reserve (44,000 ha)	674,000	1996-2006	25	24	1	Conservation (Reintroduction)	Welfare (Rehabilitation)	1
24	Lowland Gorilla	Republic of Gabon	Batéké Plateau National Park	204,400	2001, 2004	26	17	9	Conservation (Reintroduction)	Welfare (Rehabilitation)	1
25	Lowland Gorilla	Republic of Gabon	Batéké Plateau National Park	204,400	2014-2016	10	1	9	Other (Aesthetic)	Conservation (Reinforcement)	1
26	Lowland Gorilla	Republic of Gabon	Petit Evengue Island	200	2001	4	2	2	Welfare (Rehabilitation)	Research	1
27	Grauer's Gorilla	Democratic Republic of Congo	Kahuzi Biega National Park	600,000	1973	1	1	0	Other (Accidental)	Conservation (Reinforcement)	1
28	Mountain Gorilla	Rwanda	Volcanoes National Park	600,000	1980	1	1	0	Welfare (Rehabilitation)	Conservation (Reinforcement)	1
29	Mountain Gorilla	Democratic Republic of Congo	Volcanoes National Park	600,000	1995	1	1	0	Welfare (Rehabilitation)	Conservation (Reinforcement)	
30	Grauer's Gorilla	Democratic Republic of Congo	Volcanoes National Park	600,000	2000	1	1	0	Welfare (Rehabilitation)	Conservation (Reinforcement)	1
31	Mountain Gorilla	Rwanda	Volcanoes National Park	600,000	2002, 2003	2	2	0	Welfare (Rehabilitation)	Conservation (Reinforcement)	1
32	Bornean Orangutan	Malaysia	Bako National Park	1,500	1962	3	3	0	Welfare (Rehabilitation	Research	1

Chapter 10: Tabular Summary of Primate Reintroduction Programs

Acclimation			Post-Release Support			Post-Release Monitoring			Success A	Success B	References
Less Than One Month	One to Six Months	Greater Than Six Months	Less Than One Month	One to Six Months	Greater Than Six Months	Less Than One Month	One to Six Months	Greater Than Six Months			
						1					Carter 2013-14
	1				1			1	1		Colin 2017, Humle et al 2011, 2013, 2018, Ongman et al 2013, Raballand 2008, Vanlangendonck et al 2013
								1	1		Carter 2013-14, Preutz 2011, Preutz and Kante 2010
	1						1				Idani 1993
1					1			1	1		Clay et al 2018, Morel 2017
											Hladik 1978
1					1			1	1	1	Anon undated c, Attwater 1999, Attwater 2001, Courage et al 2001, Farmer and Courage 2008, Hanlon 2007, King 2004, Ikoli 2012, King and Chamberlan 2007, King and Courage 2008, King et al 2005a, b, 2012, 2014, McRae 2000, Wells 1993
1					1			1	1	1	Beck et al 2007, King et al 2012, 2014, Le Flohic et al 2015, Pearson et al 2007
		1			1			1			Beck 2016, Jones 2014, Stahl 2015, www.aspinallfoundation.com
	1		1			1					Keizer and Keizer 2004, Projet Fernan-Vaz Facebook page 2018, www.gabongorillas.org
						1					Banes et al 2016, Buxton and Willock 1974, Heminway 1972, Lyon 1976, Williamson 2017
								1			Fossey 1983, Weber and Vedder 2001
											Morris 1995
						1					Morris 1995, Shalukoma 2000
								1			Anon 2002b, 2003, Childs 2006, Cress 2010, Kahlenberg et al 2018, Mudakikwa 2002, Sherman et al 2018, Smiley Evans et al 2018, Spelman 2007, Whittier and Fawcett 2006, www.gracegorillas.org
		1			1			1			Harrisson 1963, 1987

- 301 -

Unwitting Travelers: A History of Primate Reintroduction

	Common Name	Country	Release Site		Release Years	*Number and Source of Animals			Purpose		Pre-Release Preparation
			Name of Release Site	Size (ha)		Total Number of Animals	Number WB	Number CB	Primary	Secondary	
33	Bornean Orangutan	Malaysia	(Kabili) Sepilok Forest Reserve	4,294	1964-2002	409	409	0	Welfare (Rehabilitation)		1
34	Bornean Orangutan	Malaysia	Semenggoh Wildlife Reserve	640	1975-2000	32	32	0	Welfare (Rehabilitation)		1
35	Bornean Orangutan	Malaysia	Tabin Wildlife Reserve	120,000	1993, 1994	177	177	0	Welfare (Non-lethal control)		
36	Bornean Orangutan	Malaysia	Tabin Wildlife Reserve	120,000	2010, 2012, 2106	11	11	0	Research	Welfare (Rehabilitation)	1
37	Bornean Orangutan	Malaysia	Kubah or Batang Ai National Park	2,230	Late 1990s	3	3	0	Welfare (Rehabilitation)		
38	Bornean Orangutan	Indonesia	Tanjung Puting National Park and Lamandau Wildlife Reserve, 415,040 and 54,000 ha respectively	469,040	1971 to 2017	550	550	0	Welfare (Rehabilitation)	Research	1
39	Bornean Orangutan	Indonesia	East Kalimantan. Sungai Wain and Meratus Protected Forests, Kehje Sewen Forest, 9,783, 28,261, and 86,450 ha respectively.	124,494	1991-2018	566	562	4	Welfare (Rehabilitation)	Research	1
40	Bornean Orangutan	Indonesia	Central Kalimantan. Bukit Batikap Conervation Forest and Bukit Baka Bukit Raya National Park, 35,000 ha and 27,472 ha respectively. Bagantung, Mantangi River	62,472	2012-2018	364	328	36	Welfare (Rehabilitation, Rescue)	Research	1
41	Bornean Orangutan	Indonesia	Gunung Tarak Protected Forest, Gunung Palung National Park, and Bukit Baka Bukit Raya National Park, West Kalimantan	32,000	2010, 2013, 2014, 2016,2017, 2018	34	33	1	Welfare (Rehabilitation, Rescue)	Research	1
42	Sumatran Orangutan	Indonesia	Gunung Leuser National Park (Ketambe)	800,000	1971-1974	31	31	0	Welfare (Rehabilitation)	Research	1
43	Sumatran Orangutan	Indonesia	Gunung Leuser National Park (Bohorok)	800,000	1973-2007	177	177	0	Welfare (Rehabilitation)		1
44	Sumatran Orangutan	Indonesia	Bukit Tigapuluh National Park and Pinus Jantho Nature Reserve, 35,000 ha and 7,500 ha respectively	42,500	2003-2018	290	287	3	Conservation (Reintroduction *sensu strictu*)	Welfare (Rehabilitation)	1

Chapter 10: Tabular Summary of Primate Reintroduction Programs

Acclimation			Post-Release Support			Post-Release Monitoring			Success A	Success B	References
Less Than One Month	One to Six Months	Greater Than Six Months	Less Than One Month	One to Six Months	Greater Than Six Months	Less Than One Month	One to Six Months	Greater Than Six Months			
		1			1			1	1		Anon 2016, 2017, Agoramoorthy and Hsu 2006, Aveling and Mitchell 1981, de Silva 1971, Fernando 2000/2001, Kuze et al 2008, MacKinnon 1977, Mydans 1973, Palmer 2017, in press, Russon 2018, www.cleanmalaysia.com, www.orangutan-appeal.org.uk
	1			1				1	1		Commitante et al 2015, Mail 2013, www.sarawakforestry.com
											Andau et al 1994, Sale et al 1995
			1					1	1	1	Robins 2016, Robins et al 2013, Singleton et al 2004
											Commitante et al 2015, Mail 2013, Palmer 2017, www.sarawakforestry.com
		1	1					1	1	1	Aveling and Mitchell 1982, Banes et al 2016, Descovich et al 2011, Galdikas-Brindamour 1975, Palmer 2017, Russon 2004, Singleton et al 2004, Warren and Swan 2002, www.orangutan.org.uk, www.orangutan.org, Yeager 1997.
1				1				1	1		Anon 2015b, Commitante et al 2015, Grundmann 2005, Peters 1995, Russon 2002a, b, 2004, 2009, 2018, Siregar et al 2010, Smits 2001, Smits et al 1995, Sulistyo et al 2018, Warren and Swan 2002, www.orangutan.or.id, www.redapes.org, www.yorku.ca/arusson/rehab_sites.htm
			1					1	1		Commitante et al 2015, Husson et al 2014, 2016, 2018, Marzec et al 2018, Nugraha and Jacobson 2016, Russon et al 2007, Sulistyo et al 2018, www.orangutan.or.id, www.redapes.org
			1					1			Campbell-Smith et al 2016, Commitante et al 2015, Dasgupta 2016, www.internationalanimalrescue.org, www.orangutan.com
			1					1	1	1	MacKinnon 1977, Rijksen 1974, 1978, Rijksen and Rijksen-Graatsma 1978, Russon 2009
			1					1	1	1	Aveling and Mitchell 1981, Dellatore 2007, Frey 1978, Husson et al 2014, Kuze et al 2008, Singleton 2012, www.bukitlawang.com, www.orangutanrepublik.org
		1	1					1	1	1	Beck 2016, Cocks and Bullo 2008, Commitante et al 2015, McKelson and Singleton 2016, Riedler et al 2010, Sumatran Orangutan Conservation Programme Facebook page, Trayford et al 2010, www.iansingletonsocp.com, www.orangutan.org.au, www.paneco.ch, www.sumatranorangutan.org

Unwitting Travelers: A History of Primate Reintroduction

	Common Name	Country	Release Site		Release Years	*Number and Source of Animals			Purpose		Pre-Release Preparation
			Name of Release Site	Size (ha)		Total Number of Animals	Number WB	Number CB	Primary	Secondary	
45	Siamang	Indonesia	Marak Island, Sumatra and two unspecified locations in Sumatra	1,000	2006, 2014, 2015	10	10	0	Welfare (Rehabilitation)		1
46	Yellow- (Golden-) Cheeked Gibbon	Vietnam	Vinh Cuu Nature Reserve (adjacent to 970,000 Cat Tien National Park)	970,000	2011, 2012	8	6	2	Welfare (Rehabilitation)	Research	1
47	Pileated Gibbon	Thailand	Khao Kheio-Khao Chompoo Wildlife Sanctuary	14,500	2004-2006	6	6	0	Welfare (Rehabilitation)	Research	
48	Pileated Gibbon	Cambodia	Angkor Temple Complex	40,000	2012, 2015	4	4	0	Welfare (Rehabilitation)		1
49	Mueller's (Grey) Gibbon	Malaysia	Semengok Forest Reserve, Sarawak	650	1976-1988	87	87	0	Welfare (Rehabilitation)		
50	Javan Silvery Gibbon	Indonesia	Mount Puntang of Malabar	9,000	2009, 2013, 2014, 2015	12	10	2	Welfare (Rehabilitation)	Research	1
51	Javan Silvery Gibbon	Indonesia	Mount Tilu Nature Reserve	8,000	2014, 2015, 2016, 2017	12	10	2	Conservation (Reinforcement)	Research	1
52	White-handed Gibbon	Puerto Rico	Cayo Santiago	15	1939	14	14	0	Commercial	Research	
53	White-handed Gibbon	Thailand	Ko Klet Keao Island	24	1966-1967	28	28	0	Welfare (Rehabilitation)	Research	1
54	White-handed Gibbon	Bermuda	Hall's Island	0.6	1970-1971	10	10	0	Research		
55	White-handed Gibbon	Thailand	Saiyok	22,500	1976-1977	31	26	5	Welfare (Non-lethal Control)	Research	1
56	White-handed Gibbon	Thailand	Unspecified area of Phuket Island and surrounding islands		1993-1995	13	13	0	Welfare (Rehabilitation)		
57	White-handed Gibbon	Thailand	Khao Phra Thaew forest on Phuket Island	2,228	2002-2016	37	29	8	Welfare (Rehabilitation)	Conservation (Reintroduction)	1
58	White-handed Gibbon	Thailand	Non-hunting conservation zone in the village of Baan Chum Pee in the province of Chiang Mai	814	2014-2016	15	14	1	Welfare (Rehabilitation)		1
59	White-handed Gibbon	Thailand	Lum Nam Pai Wildlife Sanctuary	118,100	2012, 2013	7	4	3	Welfare (Rehabilitation		1
60	Agile Gibbon	Indonesia	Bukit Baka Bukit Raya National Park	118,200	2000	2	2	0	Welfare (Rehabilitation)	Other (Escape)	
61	Agile Gibbon	Indonesia	Mintin Island, Borneo	100	2003, 2004	4	4	0	Welfare (Rehabilitation)	Research	1
62	Agile Gibbon	Indonesia	Hampapak Reserve, Borneo	1,500	2007	6	4	2	Welfare (Rehabilitation)	Research	1

Chapter 10: Tabular Summary of Primate Reintroduction Programs

Acclimation			Post-Release Support			Post-Release Monitoring			Success A	Success B	References
Less Than One Month	One to Six Months	Greater Than Six Months	Less Than One Month	One to Six Months	Greater Than Six Months	Less Than One Month	One to Six Months	Greater Than Six Months			
	1		1					1	1		Brulé 2017, Cheyne 2009b, www.chaneekalaweit.blogspot.com, www.fondationlepalnature.org
1					1			1			Cronin 2011, Kenyon et al 2015
			1					1			Yatbantoong 2007
		1			1			1	1		www.wildlifealliance.org
											Bennett 1992, Campbell et al 2015, Ramlee 2006
1								1	1		Smith 2011, www.ekuatorial.com, www.silvery.org.au
1			1					1	1		Adiputra and Jeffery 2016, Dipa 2016, Java Primate Conservation Project Facebook page, www.aspinallfoundation.org
					1			1			Kessler and Rawlins 2016
					1			1	1		Bennett 1992, Berkson et al 1971, Brockelman et al 1973, 1974, Soave 1982.
				1			1				Anon. 1976a, Baldwin and Teleki 1976, Delgado et al 1978, Eudey 1991-1992
1			1					1	1		Tingpalapong et al 1981, Marshall 1992
			1					1			Osterberg et al 2014, 2015
1					1			1	1		Campbell et al 2015, Cheyne 2009b, Osterberg et al 2014, 2015, Shanee and Shanee 2007, www.gibbonproject.org
1					1			1			www.gibbonproject.org
		1	1					1	1		Wiek 2014
									1		Cheyne and Brulé 2004, Cheyne et al 2008
								1	1		Bennet 1992, Campbell et al 2015, Cheyne 2005, 2006, 2009a, b, Cheyne and Brulé 2004, 2008, Cheyne et al 2008
								1			Cheyne 2009b

Unwitting Travelers: A History of Primate Reintroduction

| | Common Name | Country | Release Site | | Release Years | *Number and Source of Animals | | | Purpose | | Pre-Release Preparation |
			Name of Release Site	Size (ha)		Total Number of Animals	Number WB	Number CB	Primary	Secondary	
63	Eastern Hoolock Gibbon	India	Mehao Wildlife Sanctuary	28,200	2011-2014	22	22	0	Welfare (Rescue)		1
64	Western Hoolock Gibbon	India	Nokrek National Park	4,700	2016	2	2	0	Welfare (Rehabilitation)		1
65	"Gibbon"	Indonesia	South Tapanuli Forest, Sumatra		2016	3	3	0	Welfare (Rehabilitation)		
66	Douc Langur	Vietnam	Unspecified		Unspecified	1	1	0	Welfare (Rehabilitation)		
67	Silver Leaf Monkey	Cambodia	Angkor Temple Complex	40,000	2015	3	3	0	Welfare (Rehabilitation)		
68	Cat Ba Langur	Vietnam	Cat Ba National Park	26,300	2012	2	2	0	Conservation (Reinforcement)		1
69	Delacour's Leaf Monkey	Vietnam	Van Long Nature Reserve	3,000	2011, 2012	5	0	5	Research	Welfare (Rehabilitation)	1
70	Javan Langur	Indonesia	Lombok Island	451,400	Probably 1500-1800	1	1	0	Unspecified		
71	Javan Langur	Indonesia	Mt. Hyang and Mt. Semeru, East Java		Unspecified	54	54	0	Welfare (Rehabilitation)		
72	Javan Langur	Indonesia	Unspecified		Unspecified	50	50	0	Welfare (Rehabilitation)		
73	Javan Langur	Indonesia	Coban Talun Protected Forest, Kondang Merak Protected Forest, East Java	28,000 (Coban Talun)	2012, 2015, 2016	37	30	7	Conservation (Reinforcement)	Welfare (Rehabilitation)	1
74	Javan Grizzled Leaf Monkey	Indonesia	Mount Tilu Nature Reserve in West Java		2015, 2016, 2107	14	8	6	Welfare (Rehabilitation		1
75	Proboscis Monkey	Indonesia	Unprotected islets near Palau Kaget Nature Reserve, East Kalimantan		1997, 1998	84	84	0	(Welfare (Rescue)		
76	Barbary Macaque	Gibralter (British Overseas Territory)	Rock of Gibraltar	200	Unspecified	1	1	0	Other (Politically Symbolic)	Conservation (Reintroduction)	
77	Barbary Macaque	Morocco	Unspecified site(s) in Atlas Mountains		1980, 1986	562	2	560	Welfare (Non-lethal Control)	Conservation (Reinforcement)	1
78	Barbary Macaque	Morocco	Ifrane National Park	50,000	2013-2014	5	5	0	Welfare (Rehabilitation)		
79	Tibetan Macaque	Peoples Republic of China	Kowloon Hills, Hong Kong, including Kam Shan, Lion Rock, and Shing Mun Country Parks and Tai Po Kai Nature Reserve	2,530	1960s	3	2	1	Welfare (Non-lethal control)		
80	Tibetan Macaque	China	Mt. Huangshan		1992	43	43	0	Commercial		
81	Lion-tailed Macaque	United States	St. Catherines Island, Georgia	5,900	1991	1	0	1	Research		
82	Bonnet Macaque	India	Savandurga forest reserve	647	1975	718	718	0	Welfare (Non-lethal control)	Other (Religious)	
83	Sulawesi Black Macaque	Indonesia	Bacan Island	171,000	Unspecified	1	1	0	Commercial		
84	Pig-tailed Macaque	India	Unspecified site(s) in the Andaman Islands		Unspecified	1	1	0	Unspecified		

Chapter 10: Tabular Summary of Primate Reintroduction Programs

Acclimation			Post-Release Support			Post-Release Monitoring			Success A	Success B	References
Less Than One Month	One to Six Months	Greater Than Six Months	Less Than One Month	One to Six Months	Greater Than Six Months	Less Than One Month	One to Six Months	Greater Than Six Months			
1								1	1		Campbell et al 2015.
1							1				Programme Huro Facebook page, www.fondationiepalnature.org
											Sumatra Rainforest Institute Facebook page 2016
											Lippold and Tranh 2015
											www.wildlifealliance.org
1								1			Passaro 2012
1			1					1	1		Agmen 2014, Elser et al 2015, Nadler 2012, www.go-east.org
									1		Heinsohn 2003
											Wedana et al 2013
											Anon 2015a
1								1	1		Javan Primates Conservation Project Facebook page, Wedana et al 2013a, b, www.gettyimages.com
1								1	1		Javan Primates Conservation Project Facebook page
							1				Mejaard and Nijman 2000
					1			1	1	1	Candland and Bush 1995, Dore 2017, Fa 1987, Masseti and Bruner 2009, Modolo et al 2003, Schiermeier 2003, www.gonhs.org
					1			1			Angst 1991
			1					1			Waters et al 2016
											Cheng 2014, Dore 2017b, Gumert, 2011, Southwick and Southwick 1983, Southwick and Manry 1987, Wong and Ni 2000, Wong and Chow 2004, www.afcd.gov.hk
				1			1				Berman and Li 2002, Usui et al 2014
				1			1				Dierenfeld and McCann 1999, Fitch-Snyder and Carter 1993, Lindberg and Gledhill 1992, Norton et al 2000, Pong et al 1998
						1					Anon1976b
									1	1	de Vos et al 1956, Hamada et al 1994, Long 2003, Rosenblum et al 1998
											de Vos et al 1956, Long 2003

Unwitting Travelers: A History of Primate Reintroduction

	Common Name	Country	Release Site		Release Years	*Number and Source of Animals			Purpose		Pre-Release Preparation
			Name of Release Site	Size (ha)		Total Number of Animals	Number WB	Number CB	Primary	Secondary	
85	Pig-tailed Macaque	Cuba	Cayo Cantiles	3,400	1984	1	1	0	Commercial		1
86	Pig-tailed Macaque	Indonesia (Sumatra)	Batutegi Reserve	11,000	2006	1	1	0	Welfare (Non-lethal control)		
87	Pig-tailed Macaque	Indonesia (Sumatra)	Batutegi protected forest	11,000	2017	6	6	0	Welfare (Rehabilitation)	Conservation	1
88	Rhesus Macaque	Peoples Republic of China	Kowloon Hills, Hong Kong, including Kam Shan, Lion Rock, and Shing Mun Country Parks and Tai Po Kai Nature Reserve	2,530	1913, 1960s	2	2	0	Commercial	Welfare (Non-lethal control)	
89	Rhesus Macaque	United States	Small island in Silver River, Florida		1938, 1948, 1980s	18	18	0	Commercial	Other (Escape)	
90	Rhesus Macaque	Puerto Rico, territory of the United States	Cayo Santiago (15 ha), Cuerva (40 ha), Guayacán (40 ha), and Desecheo (152 ha) Islands, and the Puerto Rican mainland	1,295	1938-1975	839	839	0	Commercial	Research	1
91	Rhesus Macaque	Brazil	Isla de Pinheiro	Unspecified	1940s	300	300	0	Research	Commercial	
92	Rhesus Macaque	Cuba	Morrillo del Diablo Key	Unspecified	1940s	1	1	0	Research	Commercial	
93	Rhesus Macaque	India	In and around Bombay (Mumbai)		early 1940s	1	1	0	Commercial	Welfare (Non-lethal Control)	
94	Rhesus Macaque	Japan	Chiba prefecture		1960s	1	1	0	Other (Escape)		
95	Rhesus Macaque	United States	Raccoon Key, 120 ha and Loggerhead (Lois) Key, 40 ha, in the Florida Keys	160	1973-1976	1409	1409	0	Commercial		1
96	Rhesus Macaque	United States	Wooded area in Titusville, Florida		1976	40	40	0	Welfare (non-lethal control)	Other (Escape)	
97	Rhesus Macaque	United States	Morgan Island, off Beaufort, South Carolina	1,186	1979-1984	2,388	2,388	0	Commercial	Welfare (Non-lethal Control)	1
98	Rhesus Macaque	India	Aligarh District		1983	20	20	0	Welfare (Non-lethal Control		
99	Rhesus Macaque	India	Meetha Pur (rural area), Lal Kuan public park		1989, 1990	34	34	0	Welfare (Non-lethal Control)	Research	
100	Rhesus Macaque	India	Tuglaqabad Fort, New Delhi		Unspecified	40	40	0	Welfare Non-lethal Control		
101	Rhesus Macaque	India	Forested areas near the Vrindaban holy area		1997	600	600	0	Welfare (Non-lethal control	Research	
102	Rhesus Macaque	India	Firozpur-Jhirka natural forest		1998	22	22	0	Welfare (Non-lethal Control)		
103	Rhesus Macaque	India	Pilibhut and Kuno National Parks, Asolo Batti Sanctuary; other unspecified destination sites		1987-1988, 2004	600	600	0	Welfare (Non-lethal Control)		
104	Rhesus Macaque	India	Five forested sites in Nagrota		2008	431	431	0	Welfare (Non-lethal Control)		

Chapter 10: Tabular Summary of Primate Reintroduction Programs

| Acclimation | | | Post-Release Support | | | Post-Release Monitoring | | | Success A | Success B | References |
Less Than One Month	One to Six Months	Greater Than Six Months	Less Than One Month	One to Six Months	Greater Than Six Months	Less Than One Month	One to Six Months	Greater Than Six Months			
			1								Borroto-Páez 2009, Dore 2017b, Escobar 1995, González et al 1994
											Collins and Nekaris 2008
1						1					www.internationalanimalrescue.org
									1		Cheng 2014, Dore 2017b, Gumert, 2011, Southwick and Southwick 1983, Southwick and Manry 1987, Wong and Ni 2000, Wong and Chow 2004, www.afcd.gov.hk
					1			1	1	1	Anderson et al 2016a, b, 2017, Floehe 2010, myfwc.com/wildlifehabitats/nonnatives/mammals, Gillespie 2016, Maples et al 1976, Phoebus 1989, Riley and Wade 2016, Wisely et al 2018, Wolfe, 2002, Wolfe and Peters 1987, www.baynews9.com
					1			1	1	1	Carpenter 1940, 1942, Engeman et al 2010, Evans 1989, Jensen et al 2004, Kessler and Rawlins 2016, Phoebus 1989, Rawlins and Kessler 1986, Vandenbergh 1989
											Hausfater and Walker 1974, Long 2003, www.fiocruz.br
											Long 2003
											Radhakrishna and Sinha 2011, Serrao and Amladi 1979
											Dore 2017b, National Institute for Environmental Studies 2015a
					1			1	1	1	Anderson et al 2017, Johnson 1989, Johnson and Kapsalis 1995, 1998, Kleindienst 1997, Kruer 1996, Lehman et al 1994
											Anderson et al 2017, Layne 1997
					1			1	1	1	Davis 2016, Jensen et al 2004, Klopchin et al 2008, Taub and Mehlman 1989
			1					1	1		Southwick et al 1998
			1					1	1		Malik and Johnson 1994
											Sambyal et al 2009
							1		1		Imam et al 2002, Southwick et al 1998
			1						1		Imam et al 2001.
											Lenin 2008, Malik and Johnson 1994, Panwar and Misra 2004, Pirta et al 1997
						1					Sambyal et al 2009

Unwitting Travelers: A History of Primate Reintroduction

	Common Name	Country	Release Site		Release Years	*Number and Source of Animals			Purpose		Pre-Release Preparation
			Name of Release Site	Size (ha)		Total Number of Animals	Number WB	Number CB	Primary	Secondary	
105	Japanese Macaque	Japan	Ōhirayama Mountain		1956, 1957	81	81	0	Research	Commercial	
106	Japanese Macaque	United States	Texas, enclosure	17	1972	98	98	0	Welfare (Non-lethal control)	Research	
107	Crab-eating Macaque	Indonesia	Kabaena Island	400,000 (100,000 suitable habitat)	Prehistoric?	1	1	0	Unspecified		
108	Crab-eating Macaque	Indonesia	Lombok Island	451,400	Prehistoric?	1	1	0	Unspecified		
109	Crab-eating Macaque	Mauritius	Island-wide	186,500	Late 16th and 17th centuries	1	1	0	Commercial		
110	Crab-eating Macaque	Palau	Angaur Island	800	early 1900s	2	2	0	Other (Escape)		
111	Crab-eating Macaque	Indonesia	West Papua, near the city of Jayapura		1910-1980	1	1	0	Unspecified		
112	Crab-eating Macaque	United States	Forested tract west of Miami, Florida	7	1933	6	6	0	Research	Commercial	1
113	Crab-eating Macaque	Peoples Republic of China	Kowloon Hills, Hong Kong, including Kam Shan, Lion Rock, and Shing Mun Country Parks and Tai Po Kai Nature Reserve	2,530	early 1950s	5	5	0	Unspecified		
114	Crab-eating Macaque	Japan	Kijima Island	0.1	1958, 1959, 1960, 1961	87	87	0	Research	Commercial	
115	Crab-eating Macaque	Cuba	Cayo Campo	1,200	early 1980s	1	1	0	Commercial		
116	Crab-eating Macaque	Indonesia	Tinjil Island (600 ha), Deli Island (950 ha)	1,550	1988-1992	1,540	1,540	0	Commercial	Conservation (Introduction)	1
117	Crab-eating Macaque	Thailand	Nong Yai Water Reservoir			1	1	0	Welfare (Non-lethal Control)		
118	Crab-eating Macaque	Thailand	Wat Pa Sila Wiwek		Between 2000 and 2004	1	1	0	Commercial		
119	Crab-eating Macaque	Indonesia (Sumatra)	Bututegi Protected Forest	11,000	2017	17	17	0	Welfare (Rehabilitation)	Conservation	1
120	Formosan Rock Macaque	Japan	Kii Peninsula, Wakayama Prefecture, Aomori, Izushima, Oneshima		late 1940s-1964	4	4	0	Other (Escape)	Commercial	
121	Formosan Rock Macaque	Japan	Nojima Island		1958	1	1	0	Research	Commercial	
122	Stump-tail Macaque	Thailand	Kao Tao		1965, 1966	24	24	0	Welfare (Rescue)		
123	Stump-tail Macaque	Mexico	Totogochillo Island	0.4	1974	32	9	23	Commercial	Research	
124	Stump-tail Macaque	Scotland	Alloa Inch (island)	19.0	1981	4	0	4	Welfare (Non-lethal control)	Research	

Chapter 10: Tabular Summary of Primate Reintroduction Programs

Acclimation			Post-Release Support			Post-Release Monitoring			Success A	Success B	References
Less Than One Month	One to Six Months	Greater Than Six Months	Less Than One Month	One to Six Months	Greater Than Six Months	Less Than One Month	One to Six Months	Greater Than Six Months			
		1			1			1	1		Furuya 1965, Hirata 2017, Kawai 1960
			1					1	1	1	Candland and Bush 1995, Fedigan 1991, Gouzoulez 1977, Moore 2017a, b, Paterson 1996
											Froelich et al 2003, Gummert 2011
									1		Dore 2017b, National Institute for Environmental Studies 2015a
									1	1	Gumert 2011, Konstant and Mittermeier 1982, Long 2003, Sussman and Tattersall 1981, 1986, Wadman 2017
									1	1	Gumert 2011, Poirier and Smith 1974
											Gumert 2011, Kemp and Burnett 2003
					1			1	1	1	DuMond 1967, www.monkeyjungle.org
											Cheng 2014, Dore 2017b, Gumert, 2011, Southwick and Southwick 1983, Southwick and Manry 1987, Wong and Ni 2000, Wong and Chow 2004, www.afcd.gov.hk
	1			1			1		1		Furuya 1965, Hirata 2017
											Borroto-Páez 2009, Dore 2017b, Escobar 1995, González et al 1994
					1			1	1	1	Anon undated d, Bowden and Smith 1992, Crockett et al 1996, Gumert 2011, Kyes 1993
									1		Malaivijitnond and Hamada 2008, Malaivijitnond et al 2011
											Malaivijitnond and Hamada 2008, Malaivijitnond et al 2011
1						1					www.internationalanimalrescue.org
											de Vos et al 1956, Kawamoto et al 1999, Long 2003, National Institute for Environmental Sciences 2015b
											Furuya 1965, Hirata 2107, Kawai 1960, Kawai and Mito 1973, Nishida 1963
											Bertrand 1969, Hannah 1989
							1		1		Brereton 1994, Estrada and Estrada 1976, 1981, Long 2003, Rasmussen 1991
					1		1				Anderson 2017, Chamove 2017, Sexton and Stewart 2005

Unwitting Travelers: A History of Primate Reintroduction

	Common Name	Country	Release Site		Release Years	*Number and Source of Animals			Purpose		Pre-Release Preparation
			Name of Release Site	Size (ha)		Total Number of Animals	Number WB	Number CB	Primary	Secondary	
125	Stump-tail Macaque	Cuba	Cayo Guajaba	1,830	1984	1	1	0	Commercial		
126	Stump-tail Macaque	Vietnam	"central highlands of southern Vietnam"		2014	4	2	2	Welfare (Rehabilitation)		1
127	Red Colobus Monkey	Tanzania	Ngezi-Vumawimbi Forest Reserve on Pemba Island, 1,000 ha and Mayingini, Masingini (556 ha), and Kichwele (1,000 ha) Forest Reserves on Unguja Island, all in the Zanzibar Archipelago	2,556	1974, 1977, 1978, 1982	63	63	0	Conservation (Reintroduction, 5 releases; Introduction, 1 release)	Research	
128	Black and White Colobus Monkey	Kenya	Unspecified		Unspecified	1	1	0	Welfare (Rehabilitation)		1
129	Black and White Colobus Monkey	Kenya	Karura Forest	1,063	Unspecified	151	151	0	Welfare (Non-lethal Control)	Welfare (Rehabilitation)	1
130	Black and White Colobus Monkey	Kenya	Delamere Estates, Naivasha		Unspecified	1	1	0	Unspecified		
131	Chacma Baboon	South Africa	Vredefort Dome and other sites in or near Kruger National Park		2002-2014	54	54	0	Welfare (Rehabilitation)		
132	Chacma Baboon	South Africa	Kondowe, Limpopo	4,000	2011	24	23	1	Welfare (Rehabilitation)		
133	Yellow and Anubis Baboons	Japan	Tsukumijima (Tukumisima) Island		Late 1950s/early 1960s	1	1	0	Research	Commercial	
134	Yellow Baboon	Malawi	Kasungu National Park	231,500	2013	26	26	0	Welfare (Rehabilitation)	Research	1
135	Olive Baboon	Kenya	Laikipia Plateau		1984	131	131	0	Welfare (Non-lethal Control)	Research	1
136	Mandrill	Gabon	Lékédi Park	1,750	2006	36	0	36	Welfare (Non-lethal Control)	Research	1
137	Mandrill	Republic of Congo	Conkouati-Douli National Park	505,000	2015	15	15	0	Welfare (Rehabilitation)	Research	1
138	Drill	Nigeria	Afi Mountain Wildlife Sanctuary	10,400	1990-2018	86	86	0	Welfare (Rehabilitation)		
139	Patas Monkey	Puerto Rico	Islands of Cuerva (22 ha) and El Guayacán (11 ha), Boqueron Community Forest, and Sierra Bermeja hills, approximately 22,000 ha, and surrounding area	22,033	1971-1979, 1981	131	113	18	Commercial	Other (Accidental)	1
140	Mona Monkey	Democratic Republic of São Tomé and Príncipe	Unspecified	Unspecified	Late 15th century, 16th century	1	1	0	Commercial		
141	Mona Monkey	Grenada	Unspecified	Unspecified	1600-1800	1	1	0	Commercial		
142	Mona Monkey	Nigeria	Iko Esai Community Forest (400 ha), Cross River National Park (400,000 ha)	400,400	2007, 2017	5	5	0	Welfare (Rehabilitation)	Conservation	1

Chapter 10: Tabular Summary of Primate Reintroduction Programs

Acclimation			Post-Release Support			Post-Release Monitoring			Success A	Success B	References
Less Than One Month	One to Six Months	Greater Than Six Months	Less Than One Month	One to Six Months	Greater Than Six Months	Less Than One Month	One to Six Months	Greater Than Six Months			
											Borroto-Páez 2009, Dore 2017b, González et al 1994
											Khoi 2014
								1	1		Butynski and de Jong 2011, Camperio et al 2001, Davenport et al 2017, Sikuluwasha 1981, Struhsaker and Siex 1998
											Shumaker 1999
1						1					Donaldson 2013, 2016, Friends of Karura Forest 2016, Fundi et al 2018a,b, www.colobusconservation.org
											Murage 2016
			1								Anon 2005, Dewhirst 2014
											www.riversidewrc.com
											Furuya 1965, Hirata 2017, Kawai 1960
1					1			1			Ipema 2013
1					1			1	1	1	Strum 2002, 2005
	1				1			1			Peignot et al 2008
1					1			1	1		Cox 2016, Woodruff et al 2016, www.janegoodallinstitute.org
											Anon 2018
					1			1	1	1	Anon 2008b, Engeman et al 2010, Gonzalez-Martinez 1998, 2004, Kessler and Rawlins 2016, Loy 1989
									1		Dore 2017b, Glenn and Bensen 2013, 2016, Masseti and Bruner 2009
									1	1	Glenn and Bensen 2013, 2016, Gunst et al 2016, Lippold 1989
1				1				1			Anon 2008a, CERCOPAN Facebook page, Tooze 2008, Tooze and Baker 2008

Unwitting Travelers: A History of Primate Reintroduction

	Common Name	Country	Release Site		Release Years	*Number and Source of Animals			Purpose		Pre-Release Preparation
			Name of Release Site	Size (ha)		Total Number of Animals	Number WB	Number CB	Primary	Secondary	
143	Blue Monkey	South Africa	Pafuri area of Kruger National Park	24,000	1982-1988	95	95	0	Welfare (Non-lethal Control)		
144	Blue (Sykes) Monkey	Kenya	Arabuko Sokoke National Forest	6,000	1995	20	20	0	Research		1
145	Sykes Monkey	Kenya	Diani		2012, 2016	12	12	0	Welfare (Rehabilitation)	Research	1
146	Vervet	Republic of Cabo Verde	Cape Verde Islands		Late 16th and 17th centuries	1	1	0	Commercial		
147	Vervet	Barbados, Federation of Saint Kitts and Nevis, Anguilla. Territories of the United Kingdom, France and the Netherlands	Caribbean islands of Barbados, Anguilla, St Kitts, Nevis, St Martin/St Maarten, Sint Eustatious, Tortola		1600s	1	1	0	Commercial	Other (Recreational)	
148	Vervet	United States	Westlake Park, Dania Beach, Florida	3,700	1950s	12	12	0	Other (Escape)	Welfare (Non-lethal Control)	
149	Vervet	Zimbabwe	Zebra Island in Lake Kariba	155	1977	18	17	1	Welfare (Rehabilitation)		1
150	Vervet	Cuba	Cayo Cantiles and Cayo Romano	3,400 (Cantiles), 77,700 (Romano)	early 1980s	51	51	0	Commercial		
151	Vervet	South Africa	Various locations in South Africa		1994-2015	462	461	1	Welfare (Rehabilitation)		1
152	Vervet	South Africa	Duma Manzi private Game Reserve and other private land in KwaZulu-Natal	5,000	2007, 2009	134	133	1	Welfare (Rehabilitation)	Research	1
153	Vervet	South Africa	Ntendeka Wilderness Area, 5,250 ha, Isishlengeni Game Farm, 3,000 ha private plantation, 23,000 ha	31,256	2008, 2009, 2010	77	74	3	Welfare (Rehabilitation)	Research	1
154	Vervet	Kenya	Diani		2012	12	12	0	Welfare (Rehabilitation)	Research	1
155	Red-capped Mangabey	Nigeria	Cross River National Park	400,000	2016, 2017	1	1	0	Welfare (Rehabilitation)		1
156	Woolly Monkey	Ecuador	Small island in Rio Napo		1970s	1	1	0	Commercial		
157	Woolly Monkey	Peru	Small forest plot in a buffer zone just north of the Area de Conservacion Regional Communal de Tamshiyacu-Tahuayo	445,000	2005-2014	5	5	0	Welfare (Rehabilitation)	Conservation	1
158	Woolly Monkey	Colombia	Amacayacu National Park	422,000	2010	8	8	0	Welfare (Rehabilitation)	Conservation	1
159	Muriqui	Brazil	Ibitipoca Private Reserve	2,500	2017	1	1	0	Conservation (Reinforcement)		
160	Muriqui	Brazil	Unspecified sites in Minas Gerais and Espirito Santo		Unspecified	4	4	0	Conservation		
161	Muriqui	Brazil	Caratinga Biological Station		1992	1	1	0	Welfare (Rescue)	Conservation	
162	Black Spider Monkey	French Guiana	"forest"	15,000	1994	1	1	0	Welfare (Rehabilitation)		

Chapter 10: Tabular Summary of Primate Reintroduction Programs

| Acclimation | | | Post-Release Support | | | Post-Release Monitoring | | | Success A | Success B | References |
Less Than One Month	One to Six Months	Greater Than Six Months	Less Than One Month	One to Six Months	Greater Than Six Months	Less Than One Month	One to Six Months	Greater Than Six Months			
											Anon undated a, Lawes 2002
						1					Stoinski et al 1996
								1			Cunneyworth et al 2018
									1		Dore 2017b, Masseti and Bruner 2009
									1	1	Boulton et al 1996, Brown 2008, Denham 1987, Dore 2017a, Jansinska et al 2013, Konstant and Mittermeier 1982, Masseti and Bruner 2009, McGuire 1974
										1	Anderson et al 2017, Block 2018, Fleshler 2015, myfwc.com/wildlifehabitats/nonnatives/mammals, Hyler 1995, Nolin 2013, Williams 2016, 2018
											Wilson 1980
											Borroto-Páez 2009, Dore 2017b, González et al 1994
1											www.riversidewrc.com
1			1					1	1		Guy et al 2012a, Wimburger 2009, Wimburger et al 2010.
1			1				1		1		Guy 2013, Guy et al 2011, 2012b, 2014
1								1	1		Donaldson 2013, 2016
1											CERCOPAN Facebook page
									1		Konstant and Mittermeier 1982
					1			1			Beaver 2017
1				1				1			Bennett et al 2013, Defler 2017, Millán et al 2014
											Berger et al 2018
											Teixeira et al 2018
								1	1		Nogueira et al 1994
											Vié and Richard-Hansen 1997.

Unwitting Travelers: A History of Primate Reintroduction

	Common Name	Country	Release Site		Release Years	*Number and Source of Animals			Purpose		Pre-Release Preparation
			Name of Release Site	Size (ha)		Total Number of Animals	Number WB	Number CB	Primary	Secondary	
163	Black Spider Monkey	Belize	"protected forest"		2007	3	3	0	Welfare (Rehabilitation)		1
164	Geoffroy's Spider Monkey	Panama	Barro Colorado Island	15,600	1959-1966	19	19	0	Conservation (Reintroduction)		
165	Geoffroy's Spider Monkey	Panama	Barro Colorado Island	15,600	1991	5	5	0	Welfare (Non-lethal Control)	Conservation (Reinforcement)	
166	Black-faced Spider Monkey	Peru	Pacaya Samiria National Reserve	2,000,000	2012	9	9	0	Conservation (Reinforcement)	Welfare (Rehabilitation)	1
167	Black-faced Spider Monkey	Peru	Taricaya Ecological Reserve	476	2010-2014	26	26	0	Conservation (Reintroduction)	Welfare (Rehabilitation)	1
168	Red Howler Monkey	Surinam	Unspecified forests		1964	479	479	0	Welfare (Rescue)		
169	Red Howler Monkey	Venezuela	Unspecified forests		Late 1960s	1	1	0	Welfare (Rescue)		
170	Red Howler Monkey	French Guiana	Unspecified forests	15,000	1994-1995	124	124	0	Welfare (Rescue)	Research	1
171	Red Howler Monkey	Venezuela	Hato Flores Moradas		1989	1	1	0	Welfare (Rehabilitation)		1
172	Black Howler Monkey	Belize	Cockscomb Basin Wildlife Sanctuary	51,800 ha	1992, 1993,1994	62	62	0	Conservation (Reintroduction)		1
173	Black Howler Monkey	Belize	Unspecified		Unspecified	2	2	0	Other (Escape)		
174	Black Howler Monkey	Belize	Monkey Bay National Park	859	1998	2	2	0	Welfare (Rehabilitation)		1
175	Black Howler Monkey	Belize	Unspecified protected areas		1998-2008	28	28	0	Welfare (Rehabilitation)		1
176	Mantled Howler Monkey	Mexico	Mirador Pilapa Park	5	1980s	7	7	0	Welfare (Rescue)	Research	
177	Mantled Howler Monkey	Mexico	Agaltepec Island, Lake Catemaco	10	1988, 1989	12	12	0	Research		1
178	Mantled Howler Monkey	Mexico	Flor de Catemaco	90	early 2000s, 2012	12	12	0	Research	Welfare (Rescue)	1
179	Mantled Howler Monkey, Black Howler Monkey	Mexico	Various		1990 to 2015	550	550	0	Welfare (Rescue)	Research	1
180	Mantled Howler Monkey	Costa Rica	Unspecified		1989	10	10	0	Welfare (Rescue)	Research	
181	Mantled Howler Monkey	Costa Rica	Unspecified		2018	5	5	0	Welfare (Rescue)		1
182	Brown Howler Monkey	Brazil	Tijuca Forest	39,500	2015	4	4	0	Conservation	Welfare (Rehabilitation)	1
183	Brown Howler Monkey	Brazil	Santa Bonita private forest reserve	2,500	2016	2	2	0	Welfare (Rehabilitation)	Conservation (Reintroduction)	
184	Black-and-Gold Howler Monkey	Brazil	Brasilia National Park	35,000	1983	7	0	7	Welfare (Rehabilitation)	Research	1
185	Black-and-Gold Howler Monkey	Argentina	Four 0.18-ha fragments on a private estate in Cordoba	0.72	1994-2004	34	26	8	Welfare (Rehabilitation)	Research	1
186	Squirrel Monkey	United States	Bartlett Estate (Bonnet House), Ft. Lauderdale, Florida	14	1940s or 1960s	4	4	0	Unspecified		

Chapter 10: Tabular Summary of Primate Reintroduction Programs

Acclimation			Post-Release Support			Post-Release Monitoring			Success A	Success B	References
Less Than One Month	One to Six Months	Greater Than Six Months	Less Than One Month	One to Six Months	Greater Than Six Months	Less Than One Month	One to Six Months	Greater Than Six Months			
			1			1					Brockett 2008
					1			1	1	1	Eisenberg and Kuehn 1966, Konstant and Mittermeier 1982, Milton and Hopkins 2006
						1					Milton and Hopkins 2006
1			1				1				De Palomino 2013
			1					1			Spider Monkey Rehabilitation Program - Peru Facebook page, www.monosperu.com
											Konstant and Mittermeier 1982
											Konstant and Mittermeier 1982
								1	1		de Thoisy et al 2001, Richard-Hansen et al 2000, Vié and Richard-Hansen 1997
	1					1					Agoramoorthy 1995
1								1	1		Cannon 2017, Horwich et al 1993, 2002, Horwich pers comm 2014, Ostro et al 1999, Silver et al 1998
								1	1		Horwich et al. 1993
1			1			1			1		Brockett and Clark 2000
			1					1	1		Brockett 2008
											Garcia-Orduna et al. 1987, Horwich et al 1993
								1	1		Rodriguez-Luna and Cortés-Ortiz 1994, Serio-Silva 1997
								1	1		Canales-Espinosa et al 2018, Shedden-Gonzalez and Rodriguez-Luna 2010
								1	1		Canales Espinosa et al 2016
								1			de Vries 1991, Horwich et al 1993
											www.internationalanimalrescue.org
1							1				de Oliveira Neto 2015, Escobar 2016
											Neves et al 2017, www.uriacu.org
							1		1		Lindbergh and Santini 1984, Santini 1986a, b
					1			1			Bruno et al 2005
					1			1			Anderson et al 2017, Layne 1997, Taylor and Lehman 1997, Wheeler 1990

Unwitting Travelers: A History of Primate Reintroduction

	Common Name	Country	Release Site		Release Years	*Number and Source of Animals			Purpose		Pre-Release Preparation
			Name of Release Site	Size (ha)		Total Number of Animals	Number WB	Number CB	Primary	Secondary	
187	Squirrel Monkey	United States	Silver River, Florida		1960	1	1	0	Commercial		
188	Squirrel Monkey	United States	Green Island, Kure Atoll	78	1961	1	1	0	Unspecified		
189	Squirrel Monkey	United States	Masterpiece Gardens, Lake Wales, Florida		1960s	1	1	0	Commercial		
190	Squirrel Monkey	United States	Gordon River, Naples, Florida		1960s	1	1	0	Unspecified		
191	Squirrel Monkey	United States	Florida Atlantic University campus		late 1960s or early 1970s	40	40	0	Other (Aesthetic)		
192	Squirrel Monkey	Surinam	Unspecified		1964	32	32	0	Welfare (Rescue)		
193	Squirrel Monkey	Colombia	Santa Sofia Island	405	1967-1970	5,690	5,690	0	Commercial		
194	Squirrel Monkey	French Guiana	Ile-de-Mère	56	1981 (Cohort I)	300	300	0	Commercial	Welfare (Non-lethal Control)	
195	Squirrel Monkey	French Guiana	Ile-de-Mère	56	1999 (Cohort II)	14	9	5	Welfare (Non-lethal Control)	Research	1
196	Squirrel Monkey	Brazil	Saltinho Biological Reserve	548	1987	25	25	0	Welfare Non-lethal Control		
197	Brown Capuchin Monkey	Colombia	Los Llanos Orientales		1999	8	8	0	Welfare (Rehabilitation)	Research	
198	White-Throated Capuchin Monkey	Surinam	Surinam River		1964	3	3	0	Welfare (Rescue)		
199	Saki Monkey	French Guiana	Forests on the Sinnamary River	15,000	1994-1995	6	6	0	Welfare (Rescue)	Research	1
200	Cotton-top Tamarin	Colombia	Tayrona National Natural Park	12,692	1973 or 1974	30	30	0	Welfare (Rehabilitation)		
201	Cotton-top Tamarin	Colombia	Bosque La Montañita		2009	5	3	2	Research		1
202	Moustached Tamarin	Peru	Padre Isla Island	8,300	1977-1980	87	87	0	Commercial	Research	
203	Golden-Handed Tamarin	French Guiana	Forests on the Sinnamary River	15,000	1994, 1995	98	98	0	Welfare (Rescue)		1
204	Red-Handed Tamarin	Surinam	Surinam River		1964	14	14	0	Welfare (Rescue)		
205	Golden Lion Tamarin	Brazil	Tijuca National Park, and forested areas of the Rio de Janeiro Zoo, City of Rio de Janeiro	32,000	1970s	5	2	3	Other (Escape)		
206	Golden Lion Tamarin	Brazil	Poço das Antas Reserve, União Reserve and surrounding privately owned ranches	Poço das Antas=5,000 ha, União Reserve=3,200 ha, ranches=3,200 ha	1983-2000	188	42	146	Conservation (Reinforcement, Reintroduction)	Research	1
207	Black Lion Tamarin	Brazil	Tijuca National Park, City of Rio de Janeiro	32,000	1970s	1	0	1	Other (Escape)		
208	Black Lion Tamarin	Brazil	Fazenda Mosquito, Morro do Diabo State Park	1,344	1995-2008	21	20	1	Conservation (Reintroduction, Reinforcement)	Research	1

Chapter 10: Tabular Summary of Primate Reintroduction Programs

Acclimation			Post-Release Support			Post-Release Monitoring			Success A	Success B	References
Less Than One Month	One to Six Months	Greater Than Six Months	Less Than One Month	One to Six Months	Greater Than Six Months	Less Than One Month	One to Six Months	Greater Than Six Months			
1											Anderson et al 2017, Layne 1997, Maples et al 1976
								1			Long 2003
					1						Anderson et al 2017, Bair 1981, 1983, Layne 1997
											Anderson et al 2017
					1						Anderson et al 2017, Florida Fish and Game Commission website: myfwc.com/wildlifehabitats/nonnatives/mammals, Tarrant 1976
											Konstant and Mittermeier 1982
			1			1			1	1	Bailey et al 1974, Hannah 1989, Jerkins 1972, Konstant and Mittermeier 1982, Mittermeier et al 1977, Sponsel et al 1974, Tsalickis 1972
					1			1	1		De Thoisy and Contamin 1998, de Thoisy et al 2002
1			1			1			1		Vogel et al 2002
								1			Camarotti et al 2015, Oliveira and Grelle 2012
								1			Suarez et al 2001
											Konstant and Mittermeier 1982
1								1			de Thoisy et al 2001, Vié and Richard Hansen 1997, Vié et al 2001
								1	1		Defler et al 2003, Mast et al 1993, Villarreal 2010, Villarreal and Amaya-Espinel 2013
	1		1			1					Arango Guerra et al 2013
					1			1	1	1	Konstant and Mittermeir 1982, Moya and Soini undated
								1	1		Vie and Richard-Hensen 1997, de Thoisy 2001
											Konstant and Mittermeier 1982
						1					Coimbra-Filho and Mitteremeier 1978
1					1			1	1	1	Beck 2013, Beck et al 1990, 2002, Kierulff and de Oliveira 1994, Kierulff et al 2002a, 2002b, 2012, Lemmon 1991, Montali et al 1993, Ruiz-Miranda et al 2012, www.savetheliontamarin.org
						1					Coimbra-Filho and Mittermeier 1978
1								1	1		Medici et al 2003, Rezende 2015, Rezende et al 2016, Valladares-Padua et al 2000

Unwitting Travelers: A History of Primate Reintroduction

	Common Name	Country	Release Site		Release Years	*Number and Source of Animals			Purpose		Pre-Release Preparation
			Name of Release Site	Size (ha)		Total Number of Animals	Number WB	Number CB	Primary	Secondary	
209	Golden-Headed Lion Tamarin	Brazil	Fazenda Taquera		2012 to present (ongoing)	293	293	0	Welfare (Non-lethal Control)	Conservation	
210	Black Tufted-eared Marmoset	Brazil	Forests northeast of city of Rio de Janeiro along main highway BR101		1970 - present	1	1	0	Welfare (Non-lethal Control)	Other (Aesthetic)	
211	Common Marmoset	Brazil	City of Rio de Janeiro		1900s	1	1	0	Other (Aesthetic)		
212	Common Marmoset	Brazil	Forests northeast of city of Rio de Janeiro along main highway BR101		1970 - present	120	120	0	Welfare (Non-lethal Control)	Other (Aesthetic)	
213	Geoffroy's Marmoset	Brazil	Private plantation of Aracruz Cellulose		1992-1993	23	7	16	Conservation (Type unspecified)	Research	1
214	Pygmy Loris	Vietnam	Botanical garden near Cuc Phuong National Park	1,200	2000-2002	9	9	0	Research	Welfare (Rehabilitation)	1
215	Pygmy Loris	Vietnam	Cat Tien National Park and Vinh Cuu Biosphere Reserve in Dong Nai Biosphere Reserve	97,000	2009, 2010, 2011, 2012	13	13	0	Welfare (Rehabilitation)	Research	1
216	Slow Loris	Indonesia (Sumatra)	Batutegi Special Reserve	11,000	2007	7	7	0	Welfare (Rehabilitation)		1
217	Slow Loris	Indonesia (Sumatra)	Batutegi Special Reserve	11,000	2009-2016	138	138	0	Welfare (Rehabilitation)	Conservation (Reinforcement)	1
218	Slow Loris	Indonesia (Borneo)	Kalimantan, site unspecified, Mount Tarak		2010-2017	9	8	1	Conservation (Reinforcement)	Welfare (Rehabilitation)	1
219	Slow Loris	Indonesia (Java)	Gunung (Mount) Halimun National Park, Mount Sawal forest, Mount Ciremai National Park	40,000 (Mount Halimun, 117 (Mount Sawal), 15,500 (Mount Ciremai)	2010-2017	124	123	1	Welfare (Rehabilitation)	Conservation (Reinforcement)	1
220	Slow Loris	Indonesia (Java)	Kondang Merak Protected Forest		2017	11	11	0	Welfare (Rehabilitation)		1
221	Aye-Aye	Madagascar	Nosy Mangabe	510	1967	9	9	0	Conservation (Introduction?)		
222	Diameded Sifaka	Madagascar	Analamazaotra Special Reserve	810	2006, 2007	27	27	0	Conservation (Reintroduction)	Research	1
223	Black-and-White Ruffed Lemur	Madagascar	Nosy Mangabe island	520	1930s	1	1	0	Unspecified		
224	Black-and-White Ruffed Lemur	Madagascar	Betampona Reserve	2,200	1997-2001	13	0	13	Conservation (Reinforcement)	Research	1
225	Black-and-White Ruffed Lemur	Madagascar	Analamazaotra Special Reserve	810	2006, 2007	7	7	0	Conservation (Reintroduction)	Research	1
226	Red-fronted Brown Lemur	Madagascar	Berenty private reserve	1,000	1975	8	8	0	Other (Escape)		

Chapter 10: Tabular Summary of Primate Reintroduction Programs

| Acclimation | | | Post-Release Support | | | Post-Release Monitoring | | | Success A | Success B | References |
Less Than One Month	One to Six Months	Greater Than Six Months	Less Than One Month	One to Six Months	Greater Than Six Months	Less Than One Month	One to Six Months	Greater Than Six Months			
								1	1	1	Kierulff 2011, 2012, 2015
									1	1	de Morais Jr. et al 2008, Ruiz-Miranda et al 2006, 2011
									1	1	Konstant and Mittermeier 1982
									1	1	Konstant and Mittermeir 1982, de Morais Jr. et al 2008, Ruiz-Miranda et al 2006, 2011
1			1				1				Chiarello and Passamani 1993, Passamani and Passamani 1994
1			1				1				Kenyon et al 2014, Streicher 2004a, b, Streicher and Nadler 2003, van der Sandt 2016
1			1				1				Kenyon et al 2014, van der Sandt 2016, www.go-east.org
1						1					Collins and Nekaris 2008, van der Sandt 2016
	1		1					1			Moore 2012, Moore et al 2014, Robithoful 2016, van der Sandt 2016, www.internationalanimalrescue.org
1			1				1				Anirudh et al 2018, Robithoful et al 2016, www.internationalanimalrescue.org
1			1				1				Kenyon et al 2014, Moore 2012, Moore et al 2014, Robithoful et al 2016, van der Sandt 2016, www.internationalanimalrescue.org
1			1								Rochman 2017, Javan Primate Conservation Project Facebook page
									1		Constable et al 1985, Ganzhorn and Rabesoa 1986, Long 2003, Mittermeier et al 2010, Petter et al 1977, Pollock et al 1985
								1	1		Day et al 2003, Louis et al 2016
									1		Constable et al 1985, Long 2003
1			1					1	1		Britt et al 2002, 2004a, b, 2008
								1	1		Day et al 2009
									1		Simmen et al 2003

Unwitting Travelers: A History of Primate Reintroduction

	Common Name	Country	Release Site		Release Years	*Number and Source of Animals			Purpose		Pre-Release Preparation
			Name of Release Site	Size (ha)		Total Number of Animals	Number WB	Number CB	Primary	Secondary	
227	Mongoose Lemur	Union of the Comoros Islands	Islands of Grand Comore, Anjouan, and Mohéli	102,500, 42,400, and 29,000 respectively	16th century?	**1**	**1**	0	Unknown		
228	Mayotte Brown Lemur	France (External Department of Mayotte)	Mayotte island	37,400	16th century?	**1**	**1**	0	Unknown		
229	Crowned Lemur	Madagascar	Nosy Hara	320	Unspecified	**1**	**1**	0	Unspecified		
230	Collared Brown Lemur	Madagascar	Berenty private reserve	1,000	1975 and later	10	10	0	Welfare (Rehabilitation)	Other (Recreational / Aesthetic)	
231	Collared Brown Lemur	Madagascar	Unpsecified	230	2000, 2001	28	28	0	Welfare (Rescue)	Research	
232	Collared Brown Lemur	Madagascar	Unspecified		2000-2001	18	18	0	Conservation (Introduction?)	Commercial	
233	White-fronted Brown Lemur	Madagascar	Nosy Mangabe island	520	1930s	**1**	**1**	0	Unspecified		
234	Ring-tailed Lemur	United States	St Catherines island	2,900	1984, 1986	12	0	12	Research		

For following tables, please note:

* The number of animals released is specified when it is provided or can be inferred from the source(s). The number is often stated in sources as the minimum number. In these cases, we show only the minimum number in the table. If no number of released primates is specified or can be inferred for a program in the source(s), "1" (in bold) is used in the table.

Chapter 10: Tabular Summary of Primate Reintroduction Programs

Acclimation			Post-Release Support			Post-Release Monitoring			Success A	Success B	References
Less Than One Month	One to Six Months	Greater Than Six Months	Less Than One Month	One to Six Months	Greater Than Six Months	Less Than One Month	One to Six Months	Greater Than Six Months			
									1		Long 2003, Pastorini et al 2003, Tattersall 1977a
									1		Long 2003, Pastorini 2003, Tattersall 1977a, b
											Long 2003, Marshall 2015
									1		Jolly et al 2012, Simmen et al 2003, http://www-personal.umd.umich.edu/~fdolins/berenty/aboutberenty/fauna/lemurs/brownlemurs/index.html
				1				1	1		Donati et al 2007
							1		1		Andriamandranto 2003
									1		Constable et al 1985
					1			1			Keith-Lucas et al 1999, www.stcatherinesisland.org

BIBLIOGRAPHY

Actman, J. 2017. A Buddhist tradition to save animals has taken an ugly turn. news.nationalgeographic.com 23 January 2017.

Aczel, P. 1993. Pointe-Noire zoo chimpanzees rescued. *International Primate Protection League News* 20(2): 15-16.

Aczel, P. 1997. Encounter between a group of ex-captive chimpanzees and a group of lowland gorillas in the forest of the Conkouati Reserve, Congo. *Gorilla Gazette* 11(1): 5-6.

Adiputra, M.W. and S. Jeffery. 2016. Reinforcing the Javan silvery gibbon population in the Mount Tilu Nature Reserve, West Java Indonesia. Abstract of a paper presented at the joint meeting of the 26th Congress of the International Primatological Society and the 39th Meeting of the American Society of Primatologists, Chicago, IL, USA.

Agmen, F.L. 2014. Conservation strategies for Delacour's langur (*Trachypithecus delacouri*) in Vietnam: Behavioural comparisons and reviewing a release. PhD thesis, The Australian National University.

Agoramoorthy, G. 1995. Red howling monkey (*Alouatta seniculus*) reintroduction in a gallery forest of Hato Flores Moradas, Venezuela. *Neotropical Primates* 3(1): 9-10.

Agoramoorthy, G. and M.J. Hsu. 1999. Rehabilitation and release of chimpanzees on a natural island. *Journal of Wildlife Rehabilitation* 22(1): 3-7.

Agoramoorthy, G. and M.J. Hsu. 2006. Rehabilitation and release of orangutans in northern Borneo. *Journal of Wildlife Rehabilitation* 28(3): 10-17.

Andau, P.M., Hiong, L.K., and J.B. Sale. 1994. Translocation of pocketed orang-utans in Sabah. *Oryx* 28: 263-268.

Anderson, C.J., Hostetler, M.E., Sieving, K.E., and S.A. Johnson. 2016a. Predation of artificial nests by introduced rhesus macaques (*Macaca mulatta*) in Florida, USA. *Biological Invasions*. Published online 10 June 2016.

Anderson, C.J., Johnson, S.A., Hostetler, M.E., and M.G. Summers. 2016b. *History and Status of Introduced Rhesus Macaques (Macaca mulatta) in Silver Springs State Park, Florida*. Document # WEC367, Department of Wildlife Ecology and Conservation, UF/IFAS (University of Florida/Institute of Food and Agricultural Sciences) Extension Service.

Bibliography

Anderson, C.J., Hostetler, M.E., and S.A. Johnson. 2017. History and status of introduced non-human populations in Florida. *Southeastern Naturalist* 16(1): 19-36.

Anderson, J. Personal communication (e-mail, 3 January 2017).

Andriamandranto, M.R. 2003. Post-release monitoring of brown-ruffed collared lemurs after translocation in the south eastern forest of Madasgascar. *Re-introduction News* 23: 34-5.

Angst, W. 1991, Personal communication.

Anirudh, N.B., Sanchez, K.L., Brown, E., and R. Saputra. 2018. Successes in releasing rescued and rehabilitated Bornean slow lorises (*Nycticebus menagensis*) in Gunung Tarak, West Kalimantan. Abstract of a paper presented at the 27th Congress of the International Primatological Society, Nairobi, Kenya.

Anon. undated a. Samango Monkeys. *Kruger Park Times*, www.krugerpark.co.za

Anon. undated b. Draft Project Proposal, Lesio-Louna Site, Lefini Reserve, Republic of Congo. Unpublished.

Anon undated c. BUAV (The British Union for the Abolition of Vivisection) Briefing on Environment Protection and Biodiversity Conservation Amendment (Prohibition of Live Imports of Primates for Research), Bill 2015, Submission 48 - Attachment 3.

Anon. 1976a. The Hall's Island gibbon project. *The International Primate Protection League Newsletter* 3: 1-7.

Anon. 1976b. City monkeys moved. *The International Primate Protection League Newsletter* 3(1): 11.

Anon. 2002a. *Guidelines for the Placement of Confiscated Live Animals*. Gland, International Union for the Conservation of Nature and Natural Resources.

Anon. 2002b. Poachers kill mountain gorilla and steal a baby. *Gorilla Journal* 24: 11.

Anon. 2003. First attempt made at mountain gorilla reintroduction. *Communique, Newsletter of the American Zoo and Aquarium Association*, February, 2003: 42.

Anon. 2005. Baboons! *International Primate Protection League News* 32(1): 14-17.

Anon. 2008a. Primate conservation. *Cercopan Annual Report* 2008: 7-8.

Anon. 2008b. Puerto Rico kills troublesome monkeys. Associated Press article.

Anon. 2015a. IPPL's "Small Grants Program" has big impact. *International Primate Protection League News* 42(3): 10-14.

Anon. 2015b. Indonesia: Rescued orangutans returned to the forest. *AP Archive*, 21 July 2015. (Accessed on Youtube.com).

Anon. 2016. Orangutan care program nearly completed at Rasa Ria Resort. *BorneoPostonline*. 1 February 2016.

Anon. 2017. Tiger release. *Orangutan Appeal UK News* 33: 3.

Anon. 2018. Drill Ranch: "The drill monkey". *IPPL News* 45(1): 5.

Arango Guerra, H.L., Ballesteros Ruiz, S., Garcia Castillo, F., and S. Buritica. 2013. Primer proceso de rehabilitación y reintroducción de un grupo de titís cabeciblancos (*Saguinus oedipus*). *Revista Lasallista de Investigación* 10(1): 49-61.

Attwater, H. 1999. *My Gorilla Journey: Living With the Orphans of the Rainforest*. London, Sidgwick & Jackson.

Attwater, M. 2001. Challenging developments in primate rehabilitation programs, Africa. *Re-introduction News* 20: 12-13.

Aveling, R. and A. Mitchell. 1981. Is rehabilitating orang utans worthwhile? *Oryx* 16: 263-271.

Badham, M. 1979. *Chimps with Everything*. London, W.H. Allen/Virgin Books.

Bailey, R.C., Baker, R.S., Brown, D.S., Von Hildebrand, P., Mittermeier, R.A., Sponsel, L.D., and K.E. Wolf. 1974. Progress of a breeding project for non-human primates in Colombia. *Nature* 248: 453-455.

Bair, B. 1981. Masterpiece monkeys still driving Curtis bananas. *Lakeland Ledger*, 5 June 1981. https://news.google.com/newspapers?nid=1346&dat=19810605&id=348sAAAAIBAJ&sjid=MPsDAAAAIBAJ&pg=1743,1700939&hl=en.

Bair, B. 1983. Spider [sic] monkeys leaving like Masterpiece Gardens. *Lakeland Ledger*, 26 December 1983. https://news.google.com/newspapers?nid=1346&dat=19831226&id=E6lOAAAAIBAJ&sjid=afsDAAAAIBAJ&pg=2138,4090999&hl=en.

Baldwin, L.A. and G. Teleki. 1976. Patterns of gibbon behavior on Hall's Island, Bermuda. In D.M. Rumbaugh, ed. *Gibbon and Siamang Volume 4*, pp. 22-105. Basel, S. Karger.

Banerjee, D.P. 2015. *Population Assessment of the Common Squirrel Monkey (*Saimiri sciureus*) on Sumak Allpa, Ecuador*. Undergraduate thesis, Environmental Studies, University of Delaware.

Banes, G.L., Galdikas, B.M.F., and L. Vigilant. 2016. Reintroduction of confiscated and displaced mammals risks outbreeding and introgression in natural populations, as evidenced by orang-utans of divergent subspecies. *Scientific Reports* 6, 22026; doi: 10.1038/srep22026.

Basalamah, F., Atmoto, S.S.U., Perwitasari-Farajallah, D., Qayim, I., Sihite, J., Van Noordwijk, M., Willems, E., and Van Schaik, C.P. 2018. Monitoring orangutan reintroduction: Results of activity budgets, diets, vertical use and associations during the first year post-release in Kehje Sewen forest, East Kalimantan, Indonesia. Biodiversitas 19(2): 609-620.

Beaver, P. 2017. Personal communication, e-mail 29 January.

Beck, B.B. 2010. Chimpanzee orphans: Sanctuaries, reintroduction, and cognition. In E.V. Lonsdorf, S.R. Ross, and T. Matsuzawa, eds. *The Mind of the Chimpanzee*, pp. 332-346. Chicago, University of Chicago Press.

Beck, B.B. 2013. *Thirteen Gold Monkeys*. Denver, Outskirts Press.

Beck, B. 2015. *Ape*. Berlin, MD USA, Salt Water Media.

Beck, B.B. 2016. The role of translocation in primate conservation. In S.A. Wich and A.J. Marshall, eds. *An Introduction to Primate Conservation*, pp. 241-255. Oxford, UK, Oxford University Press.

Beck, B.B. 2017. *A History of Primate Reintroduction*. Accessed at www.drbenjaminbeck.com

Beck, B.B. and D.M. Rambaldi. 2006 Reintroduction of golden lion tamarins (*Leontopithecus r. rosalia*): Implications for African great apes. Paper presented at the XXIst Congress of the International Primatological Society; Entebbe, Uganda.

Beck, B.B., Kleiman, D.G., Dietz, J.M., Castro, I., Carvalho, C., Martins, A., and B. Rettberg-Beck. 1990. Losses and reproduction in reintroduced golden lion tamarins. *Dodo, Journal of the Jersey Wildlife Preservation Trust* 27: 50-61.

Beck, B.B., Rapaport, L.G., Stanley Price, M.R., and A.C. Wilson. 1994. Reintroduction of captive-born animals. In P.J.S. Olney, G.M. Mace, and A.T.C. Feistner, eds. *Creative Conservation: Interactive Management of Wild and Captive Animals*, pp. 265-286. London, Chapman & Hall.

Beck, B.B., Castro, M.I., Stoinski, T.S., and J.D. Ballou. 2002. The effects of prerelease environments and postrelease management on survivorship in reintroduced golden lion tamarins. In: D.G. Kleiman and A.B. Rylands, eds. *Lion Tamarins: Biology and Conservation*, pp. 283-300. Washington, DC, Smithsonian Institution Press.

Beck, B.B., Walkup, K., Rodrigues, M., Unwin, S., Travis, D., and T. Stoinski. 2007. *Best Practice Guidelines for the Re-introduction of Great Apes*. Gland, IUCN/SSC Primate Specialist Group.

Becker, V. 2018. E-amil, 16 June.

Bennett, J. 1992. A glut of gibbons in Sarawak – is rehabilitation the answer? *Oryx* 26(3): 157-164.

Bennett, S. E., Vásquez, J. J., Sánchez, L., Sinarahua, L., Murayari, A., Martinez, A., Peláez, L., and J. Millán. 2013. Preliminary observations from a welfare release of wooly monkeys in the Colombian Amazon. In P.S. Soorae, ed. *Global Re-introduction Perspectives: 2013. Further Case Studies from Around the Globe*, pp. 229-234. Gland, IUCN/SSC Re-introduction Specialist Group and Abu Dhabi, UAE, Environment Agency – Abu Dhabi.

Berger, B.C., Ferreira, A.I., Rodrigues de Melo, F., and F.P. Tabacow. 2018. The attempted reinvigoration of a population of Northern muriqui in Ibitipoca through reintroduction. Abstract of a paper presented at the 27th Congress of the International Primatological Society, Nairobi, Kenya.

Berkson, G., Ross, B.A., and S. Jatinandana. 1971. The social behavior of gibbons in relation to a conservation program. In: L.A. Rosenblum, ed., *Primate Behavior: Developments in Field and Laboratory Research*, pp. 225-255. New York, Academic Press.

Berman, C.B. and J-H. Li. 2002. Impact of translocation, provisioning and range restriction on a group of *Macaca thibetana*. *International Journal of Primatology* 23(2): 383-397.

Bertrand, M. 1969. The Behavioural Repertoire of the Stumptail Macaque. *Bibliotheca Primatologica*, No. 11. Basel, S. Karger.

Block, E. 2018. Ousted colony monkey spotted in Cooper City. *Sun Sentinal*, 29 March.

Bock, K. 2018. Personal communication (e-mail, 26 June).

Boki Blog Facebook page, 4 and 7 May 2018.

Borner, M. 1985. The rehabilitated chimpanzees of Rubondo Island. *Oryx* 19: 151–154.

Borroto-Páez, R. 2009. Invasive mammals in Cuba: an overview. *Biological Invasions* 11: 2279-2290.

Boulton, A.M., Horrocks, J.A. and J. Baulu. 1996. The Barbados vervet monkey (*Cercopithecus aethiops, sabeus*): Changes in population size and crop damage, 1980-1994. *International Journal of Primatology* 17: 831-844.

Bowden, D. M. and O. A. Smith. 1992. Conservationally sound assurance of primate supply and diversity. *Institute of Laboratory Animals Journal* 34: 53-56.

Brereton, A.R. 1994. Copulatory behavior in a free-ranging population of stumptail macaques (*Macaca arctoides*) in Mexico. *Primates* 35(2): 113-122.

Brewer, S. 1976. Chimpanzee rehabilitation. *International Primate Protection League Special Report*, December 1976: 1-10.

Brewer, S. 1978. *The Chimps of Mt. Asserik*. New York, Alfred A. Knopf.

Brewer, S. 1980. Chimpanzee rehabilitation, why and how? *International Primate Protection League Newsletter* 7(2): 1-5.

Brewer Marsden, S., Marsden, D., and M.E. Thompson. 2006. Demographic and female life history parameters of free-ranging chimpanzees at the Chimpanzee Rehabilitation Project, River Gambia National Park. *International Journal of Primatology* 27(2): 391-410.

Britt, A., Welch, C., and A. Katz. 2002. The release of captive-bred black and white ruffed lemurs into the Betampona Reserve, eastern Madagascar. *Re-introduction News* 21: 18-20.

Britt, A., Welch, C., Katz, A., Iambana, B., Porton, I., Junge, R., Crawford, C., Williams, C., and D. Haring. 2004a. The re-stocking of captive-bred ruffed lemurs (*Varecia variegata variegata*) into the Betampona Reserve, Madagascar. *Biodiversity and Conservation* 13: 635-57.

Britt, A., Welch, C., and A. Katz. 2004b. Can small, isolated primate populations be effectively reinforced through the release of individuals from a captive population? *Biological Conservation* 115, 319-27.

Britt, A., Welch, C. Katz, A. and K. Freeman. 2008. Supplementation of the black and white ruffed lemur population with captive-bred individuals in the Betampona Reserve, eastern Madagascar. In P.S. Soorae, ed. *Global Re-introduction Perspectives: Re-introduction Case-Studies from Around the Globe*, pp. 197-201. Abu Dhabi, UAE, IUCN/SSC Re-introduction Specialist Group.

Brockelman, W. Y., Ross, B.A., and S. Pantuwatana. 1973. Social correlates of reproduction in the gibbon colony on Ko Klet Kaeo, Thailand. *American Journal of Physical Anthropology* 38: 637-640.

Brockelman, W. Y., Ross, B.A., and S Pantuwatana. 1974. Social interactions of adult gibbons (*Hylobates lar*) in an experimental colony. In: D.M. Rumbaugh, ed. *Gibbon and Siamang, Volume 3*, pp. 137-156. Basel, Karger.

Brockett, R.C. and B.C. Clark. 2000. Repatriation of two confiscated black howler monkeys (*Alouatta pigra*) in Belize. *Neotropical Primates* 8(3): 101-103.

Brockett, R. 2008. Designing a wildlife rehabilitation and release project – lessons learned. Poster presented at the First International Wildlife Reintroduction Conference, Lincoln Park Zoo, Chicago, IL, USA.

Brown, A.C. 2008. Status and range of introduced mammals on St. Martin, Lesser Antilles. *Living World. Journal of the Trinidad and Tobago Field Naturalists' Club* 2008:14-18.

Brulé, A. 2017. Kalaweit – The Founder's Dream. *IPPL News* 44(2): 22-23.

Bruno, G., Giudice, A. M., Nieves, M., and M. D. Mudry. 2005. Rehabilitación y reproducción de *Alouatta caraya* fuera de su area de distribución natural. *Neotropical Primates* 13: 21-22.

Butynski, T. M. and Y. A. de Jong. 2011. Zanzibar red colobus on Pemba Island, Tanzania: Population status 38 years post-reintroduction. In Soorae, P. S., ed. *Global Re-introduction Perspectives: 2011. More Re-introduction Case-Studies from Around the Globe*, pp.168-174. Gland, Re-introduction Specialist Group and Abu Dhabi, Environment Agency – Abu Dhabi.

Buxton, A. (producer) and C. Willock (writer). 1974. *Gorilla* (documentary film). UK: Survival Anglia Ltd.

Camarotti, F.L.M., da Silva, V.L., and M.A. Borstelman de Oliveira. 2015. The effects of introducing the Amazonian squirrel monkey on the behavior of the northeast marmoset. *Acta Amazonica* 45(1): 29-34.

Campbel-Smith, G., Sanchez, K.L., and A.A. Jabbar. 2016. Long-term post-release monitoring of three female orangutans (*Pongo pygmaeus*) in Gunung Tarak Nature Reserve, West Kalimantan, Indonesia. Abstract of a paper presented at the joint meeting of the 26th Congress of the International Primatological Society and the 39th Meeting of the American Society of Primatologists, Chicago, IL, USA.

Campbell, C.O., Cheyne, S.M., and B.M. Rawson. 2015. *Best Practice Guidelines for the Rehabilitation and Translocation of Gibbons*. Gland, IUCN/SSC Primate Specialist Group.

Camperio Ciani, A., Palentini, L. and E. Finotti. 2001. Survival of a small translocated *Procolobus kirkii* population on Pemba Island. *Animal Biodiversity and Conservation* 24: 15-18.

Bibliography

Canales Espinosa, D., Rangel-Negrin A., and P.A. Dias. 2016. Translocation of Mexican primates: A critical analysis of past experiences and projection of future possibilities. Abstract of a paper presented at the joint meeting of the 26th Congress of the International Primatological Society and the 39th Meeting of the American Society of Primatologists, Chicago, IL, USA.

Canales-Espinosa, D., Rangel-Negrin, A., Duarte Dias, P., Rodriguez-Luna, E., and A. Coyohua Fuentes. 2018. La Flor de Catemaco: Reintroduction Success in an agrosystem for howler monkeys. Abstract of a paper presented at the 27th Congress of the International Primatological Society, Nairobi, Kenya.

Candland, D.K. and S. L. Bush. 1995. Primates and behavior. In E.F. Gibbons, B.S. Durrant and J. Demarest, eds. *Conservation of Endangered Species in Captivity*, pp. 521-551. Albany, State University of New York Press.

Cannon, J.C. 2017. Howler monkeys booming in Belize sanctuary 25 years after translocation. news.mongabey.com 10 May 2017.

Carpenter, C.R. 1940. Rhesus monkeys for American laboratories. *Science* 92: 284-86.

Carpenter, C.R. 1942. Sexual behavior of free ranging rhesus monkeys. *Journal of Comparative Psychology* 33: 113-162.

Carter, J. 1981a. A journey to freedom. *Smithsonian* 12(1): 90-101.

Carter, J. 1981b. Free again. *International Primate Protection League Newsletter* 8(1): 2-4.

Carter, J. 1988. Freed from keepers and cages, chimps come of age on Baboon Island. *Smithsonian* 19(3): 36-49.

Carter, J. 2003a. Tama and the baby. *Friends of Animal Action Line*, Autumn 2003: 5-7.

Carter, J. 2003b. Orphan chimpanzees in West Africa: Experiences and prospects for viability in chimpanzee rehabilitation. In R. Kormos, C. Boesch, M.I. Bakarr, and T.M. Butynski, eds. *West African Chimpanzees. Status Survey and Conservation Action Plan*, pp. 157-167. Gland, IUCN.

Carter, J. 2003c. The Gambia. In R. Kormos, C. Boesch, M.I. Bakarr, and T.M. Butynski, eds. *West African Chimpanzees. Status Survey and Conservation Action Plan*, pp. 51-53. Gland, IUCN.

Carter, J. 2013-14. Toto orphaned chimpanzee. *Friends of Animals Action Line*, Winter 2013-14: 1-3.

Carter, J. Personal communications (e-mails, 9-17 May 2017).

Carter, J., Ndiaye, S., Preutz, J., and W.C. McGrew. 2003. Senegal. In R. Kormos, C. Boesch, M.I. Bakarr, and T.M. Butynski, eds. *West African Chimpanzees. Status Survey and Conservation Action Plan*, pp. 31-39. Gland, IUCN.

Chamove, A. Personal communications (e-mails, 2, 3 January 2017).

Cheng, W.W. 2014. *A review of the management measures of feral macaques in Hong Kong*. Master's thesis, Department of Environmental Management, The University of Hong Kong.

Cheyne, S.M. 2005. Re-introduction of captive-raised gibbons in Central Kalimantan, Indonesia. *Re-introduction News* 24: 22-25.

Cheyne, S.M. 2006. Wildlife reintroduction: considerations of habitat quality at the release site. *BMC Ecology* 6: 1-8.

Cheyne, S.M. 2009a. Challenges and opportunities of primate rehabilitation – gibbons as a case study. *Endangered Species Research* 9: 159-165.

Cheyne, S.M. 2009b. The role of reintroduction in gibbon conservation: Opportunities and challenges. In S. Lappan and D.J. Whittaker, eds. *The Gibbons, Developments in Primatology: Progress and Prospects*, pp. 477-496. New York, Springer Science+Business Media.

Cheyne, S.M. and A. Brulé. 2004. Adaptation of a captive-raised gibbon to the wild. *Folia Primatologica* 75(1): 37-39.

Cheyne, S.M. and A. Brulé (Chanee). 2008. The Kalaweit Gibbon Re-habilitation Project: rescue, re-introduction, protection and conservation of Indonesia's gibbons. In P.S. Soorae, ed. *Global Re-introduction Perspectives: Re-introduction Case-Studies from Around the Globe*, pp. 202-206. Abu Dhabi, UAE, IUCN/SSC Re-introduction Specialist Group.

Cheyne, S.M., Chivers, D.J., and J Sugardjito. 2008. Biology and behavior of reintroduced gibbons. *Biodiversity and Conservation* 17: 1741-1751.

Chiarello, A., and M. Passamani. 1993. A reintroduction program of Geoffroy's marmoset, *Callithrix geoffroyi*. *Neotropical Primates* 1: 6-7.

Childs, S. 2006. Caring for confiscated gorillas: Making decisions, learning, teaching. *The Gorilla Journal*, Fall 2006: 2-4.

Clay, Z., Garai, C., André, C., Minesi-André, F., and R. Belais. 2018. Reintroducing bonobos (*Pan paniscus*) into the wild – insights and outlooks from the Ekolo Ya Bonobo Project. Abstract of a paper presented at the 27th Congress of the International Primatological Society, Nairobi, Kenya.

Clifton, M. 2015. Abandoning ViLab II chimps in Liberia, New York Blood Center did it before in Ivory Coast, SAEN charges. *Animals 24-7*. 12 August 2015. www.animals24-7.org

Cocks, L. and K. Bullo. 2008. The processes of releasing a zoo-bred Sumatran orang-utan (*Pongo abelli*) at Bukit Tigapuluh National Park, Jambi, Sumatra. *International Zoo Yearbook* 42: 183-189.

Coimbra-Filho, A.F. and R.A. Mittermeier. 1978. Reintroduction and translocation of lion tamarins: A realistic appraisal. In H. Rothe, H.J. Wolters, and J.P. Hearn, eds. *Biology and Behaviour of Marmosets*, pp. 41-46. Göttingen, Eigenverlag Hartmut Rothe.

Colin, C. 2017. Saving chimps in Guinea. *International Primate Protection League News* 44(3): 10-11.

Collins, R. and K. A. I. Nekaris. 2008. Release of greater slow lorises, confiscated from the pet trade, to Batuegi Protected Forest, Sumatra, Indonesia. In P.S. Soorae, ed. *Global Re-introduction Perspectives: Re-introduction Case-Studies from Around the Globe*, pp. 192-196. Abu Dhabi, UAE, IUCN/SSC Re-introduction Specialist Group.

Commitante, R., Unwin, S., Jaya, R., Saraswati, Y., Sulistyo, F. and C. Nente (eds.). 2015. *Orangutan Conservancy 2015 Orangutan Veterinary Advisory Group Workshop Report*. wwww.orangutan.com

Conlee, K. and J.A.Z. Desmond. 2015. Liberian chimpanzees abandoned by New York Blood Center. *African Primates* 10: 57-58.

Constable, I.D., Pollock, J.I., Ratsirarson, J., and H. Simons. 1985. Sightings of aye-ayes and red ruffed lemurs on Nosy Mangabe and the Masoala Peninsula. *Primate Conservation* 5: 59-62.

Courage, A., Henderson, I., and J. Watkin. 2001. Orphan gorilla reintroduction: Lesio-Louna and Mpassa. *Gorilla Journal* 22: 33-35.

Cox, D. 2016. Personal communication (e-mail, 24 May 2016).

Cronin, A. 2011. Rescued, rehabilitated, and released. *Ape Rescue Chronicle* Summer, 2011: 2-3. (Retrieved from www.go-east.org).

Cress, D. 2010. Gorilla Rehabilitation and Conservation Education (GRACE) Center. *Gorilla Journal* 40: 7-9.

Crockett, C. M., Kyes, R. C., and D. Sajuthi. 1996. Modeling managed monkey populations: Sustainable harvest of longtailed macaques on a natural habitat island. *American Journal of Primatology* 40: 343-360.

Cunneyworth, P.M., Donaldson, A., and Z. Edwards. 2018. Using pre- and post-release assessments to evaluate a rehabilitation release of Sykes monkeys. Abstract of a paper presented at the 27th Congress of the International Primatological Society, Nairobi, Kenya.

Curtis, L. 2017. Personal communication (letter, 13 July).

Dasgupta, S. 2016. Video: Two rescued pet orangutans return to the wild. *Mongabay* 21 December 2016.

Davenport, T.R.B., Fakih, S.A., Kimiti, S.P., Kleine, L.U., Foley, L.S. and D.W. De Luca. 2017. Zanzibar's endemic red colobus Piliocolobus kirkii: first systematic and total assessment of population, demography and distribution. *Oryx* DOI: 10.1017/S003060531700148X

Davis, A. 2016. Monkeys back at Yemassee Lab. WSAV-TV website, 1 May 2016.

Day, S.R., Ramarokono, R.E.A.F., Sitzmann, B.D., Randriamboahanginjatovo, R., Ramanankirija, H., Rence, V., Randrianindrina, A., Ravololonarivo, G. and E.E. Louis Jr. 2009. Re-introduction of diademed sifaka (*Propithecus diadema*) and black and white ruffed lemurs (*Varecia variegata editorum*) at Analamazaotra Special Reserve, eastern Madagascar. *Lemur News* 14: 32-37.

Defler, T. 2017. Personal communication (e-mail and unpublished accounts, 27 January).

Defler, T.R., Rodríguez, J.V., and J. I. Hernández-Camacho. 2003. Conservation priorities for Colombian primates. *Primate Conservation* 19: 10-18.

Delgado, J.M.R., Del Pozo, F., Montero, P., Monteagudo, J.L., O'Keefe, T.O., and N.S. Kline. 1978. Behavioral rhythms of gibbons on Hall's Island. *Journal of Interdisciplinary Cycle Research* 9(3): 147-168.

Dellatore, D.F. 2007. *Behavioural Health of Reintroduced Orangutans (*Pongo abelii*) in Bukit Lawang, Sumatra, Indonesia*. Master's Thesis, Oxford Brookes University.

de Morais Jr., M., Ruiz-Miranda, C.R.., Grativol, A.D., Caixeta de Andrade, C., Lima, C.S., and B.B. Beck. 2008. Os sagüis, Callithrix jacchus e penicillata, como espécies invasoras na região de ocorrência do mico-leão dourado. In: P.P. de Oliveira, A.D. Grativol, and C.R. Ruiz-Miranda, eds. *Conservação do mico-leão dourado*. pp 86-117. Campos dos Goytacazes, Universidade Estadual do Norte Fluminense Darcy Ribeiro.

Denham, W.W. 1987. West Indian green monkeys: Problems in historical biogeography. In F.S. Szalay, ed. *Contributions to Primatology*, Vol. 24. Basel, Karger.

de Oliveira Neto, C. 2015. Rio reintroduces howler monkeys after century's absence. www.physorg.com, 15 October 2015.

de Palomino, H.C. 2013. Rehabilitated spider monkeys successfully released in Peru. *International Primate Protection League News* 40(3): 6-18.

Descovich, K.A., Galdikas, B.M., Tribe, A., Lisle, A. and C.J. Phillips. 2011. Fostering appropriate behavior in rehabilitant orangutans (*Pongo pygmaeus*). *International Journal of Primatology* 32(3): 616-633.

de Silva, G.S. 1971. Notes on the orang-utan rehabilitation project in Sabah. *Malayan Nature Journal* 24: 50-77.

de Thoisy, B. and H. Contamin. 1998. The squirrel monkey breeding colony of the Pasteur Institute, Cayenne, French Guiana. *Neotropical Primates* 6: 14-18.

de Thoisy, B., Vogel, I., Reynes, J-M., Pouliquen, J-F., Carme, B., Kazanji, M., and J-C. Vie. 2001. Health evaluation of translocated free-ranging primates in French Guiana. *American Journal of Primatology* 54: 1-16.

de Thoisy, B., Loguet, O., Bayart, F., and H. Contamin. 2002. Behavior of squirrel monkeys (*Saimiri sciureus*) – 16 years on an island in French Guiana. *Neotropical Primates* 10: 73-6.

de Vos, A., Manville, R.H., and R.G. Van Gelder. 1956. Introduced mammals and their influence on native biota. *Zoologica* 41(4): 163-194.

de Vries, A. 1991. Translocation of mantled howling monkeys in Guanacaste, Costa Rica. M.A. Thesis, University of Calgary, Alberta.

Dewhirst, S. 2014. Thanks from the field: A baboon troop release. *International Primate Protection League News* 41(3): 7.

Dierenfeld, E.S. and C.M. McCann. 1999. Nutrient composition of selected plant species consumed by semi free-ranging lion-tailed macaques (*Macaca silenus*) and ring-tailed lemurs (*Lemur catta*) on St. Catherines Island, Georgia, U.S.A. *Zoo Biology* 18: 481-494.

Dipa, A. 2016. Javan Gibbon returned to forest around West Java's Mount Tilu. *The Jakarta Post*, 25 April.

Donaldson, A. 2013. Reunited! A colobus monkey infant and his mum. *International Primate Protection League News* 40(1): 14-15.

Donaldson, A. Personal communication 15 June 2016.

Donaldson, A. 2017. Rehabilitation release of vervet monkeys (*Chlorocebus pygerythrus hilgerti*) in south coast Kenya: A Scientific Approach. PhD. thesis, Durham University. (Abstract only).

Donati, G., Ramanamanjato, J-B, Ravoahangy, A.M., and M. Vinclette. 2007. Translocation as a conservation measure for an endangered species in the littoral forest of southeastern Madagascar: the case of *Eulemur collaris*. In: J.U. Ganzhorn, S.M. Goodman, and M. Vinclette, eds. *Biodiversity, Ecology and Conservation of Littoral Forest Ecosystems on Southeastern Madagascar, Tolagnaro (Fort Dauphin)*, pp 237-245. Washington, DC, Smithsonian Institution Press.

Dore, K. 2017a. Vervets in the Caribbean. In A. Fuentes, B. Bezanson, C.J. Campbell, A.F. DiFiore, S. Elton, A. Estrada, L.E. Jones-Engel, K.C. MacKinnon, K.A.I. Nekaris, E. Riley, S. Ross, C. Sanz, R.W. Sussman, and B. Thierry, eds. *The International Encyclopedia of Primatology*. Hoboken, Wiley-Blackwell.

Dore, K.M. 2017b. Ethnophoresy. In A. Fuentes, B. Bezanson, C.J. Campbell, A.F. DiFiore, S. Elton, A. Estrada, L.E. Jones-Engel, K.C. MacKinnon, K.A.I. Nekaris, E. Riley, S. Ross, C. Sanz, R.W. Sussman, and B. Thierry, eds. *The International Encyclopedia of Primatology*. Hoboken, Wiley-Blackwell.

DuMond, F.V. 1967. Semi-free-ranging colonies of monkeys at Goulds Monkey Jungle. *International Zoo Yearbook* 7: 202-207.

Eisenberg, J.F. and R.W. Kuehn. 1966. The behavior of *Ateles geoffroyi* and related species. *Smithsonian Miscellaneous Collections* 151(8): 1-63.

Elser, S.K., Chung, N.H., and C.A. Brühl. 2015. Reintroduction of the 'Critically Endangered' Delacour's langur (*Trachypithecus delacourai*) into Van Long Nature Reserve, Ninh Binh Province, Vietnam. *Vietnamese Journal of Primatology* 2(3): 1-13.

Engeman, R.M., Laborde, J.E., Constatin, B.U., Shwiff, S.A., Hall, P., Duffiney, A., and F. Luciano. 2010. The economic impacts to commercial farms from invasive monkeys in Puerto Rico. *Crop Protection* 29: 401-405.

Escobar, H. 2016. Rewilding Rio. *Science* 353: 114-115.

Escobar, T.R. 1995. *Isla de la Juventud: Introducidos por Causa Deliberadas*. Havana, Editorial Cientifico-Técnica.

Estrada, A. and R. Estrada. 1976. Establishment of a free-ranging colony of stumptail macaques (*Macaca arctoides*): Relations to the ecology I. *Primates* 17(3): 337-355.

Estrada A. and R. Estrada. 1981. Reproductive seasonality in a free-ranging troop of stumptail macaques (*Macaca arctoides*): a five-year report. *Primates* 22 (4): 503- 511.

Eudey, A.A. 1991-1992. Captive gibbons in Thailand and the option of reintroduction to the wild. *Primate Conservation* 12-13: 34-40.

Evans, M.A. 1989. Ecology and removal of introduced rhesus monkeys: Desecheo Island National Wildlife Refuge, Puerto Rico. *Puerto Rico Health Sciences Journal* 1989 8:139-156.

Fa, J. E. 1987. A park for the Barbary macaques of Gibraltar? *Oryx* 21: 242-245.

Farmer, K.H. 2000. The final step to freedom. Conkouati chimpanzees returned to the wild. *International Primate Protection League News* 27(2): 17-20.

Farmer, K.H. 2002. *The Behaviour and Adapation of Reintroduced Chimpanzees (*Pan troglodytes troglodytes*) in the Republic of Congo*. PhD Dissertation, University of Stirling.

Farmer, K.H., and A. Jamart. 2002. Habitat Ecologique et Liberté des Primates: A case study of chimpanzee re-introduction in the Republic of Congo. *Re-introduction News* 21: 16-18.

Farmer, K.H., and A. Courage. 2008. Sanctuaries and reintroduction: A role in gorilla conservation? In T.S. Stoinski, H.D. Steklis, and P. Mehlman, eds. *Conservation in the 21st century: Gorillas as a case study*, pp. 79–106. New York, Springer.

Farmer, K.H., Buchanan-Smith, H.M., and A. Jamart. 2006. Behavioural adaptation of *Pan troglodytes troglodytes*. *International Journal of Primatology* 27(3): 747-765.

Farmer, K.H., Honig, N., Goossens, B., and A. Jamart. 2010. Habitat Ecologique et Liberté des Primates: re-introduction of central chimpanzees to the Conkouati-Douli National Park, Republic of Congo. In P.S. Soorae, ed. *Global Re-introduction Perspectives 2010: Additional Case-Studies from Around the Globe*, pp 231-237. Abu Dhabi, UAE, IUCN/SSC Re-introduction Specialist Group.

Faust, L.J., Cress, D., Farmer, K.H., Ross, S.R., and B.B. Beck. 2011. Predicting capacity demand on sanctuaries for African chimpanzees. *International Journal of Primatology* 32(4): 849-864.

Fedigan, L.M. 1991. History of the Arashiyama West Japanese macaques in Texas. In L.M. Fedigan and P.J. Asquith, eds. *The Monkeys of Arashiyama: Thirty-Five Years of Research in Japan and the West*, pp. 140-54. Albany, State University of New York Press.

Fernando, R. 2000/2001. Rehabilitating orphaned orang-utans in North Borneo. *Asian Primates* 7(3/4): 20-21.

Fitch-Snyder, H. and J. Carter. 1993. Tool use to acquire drinking water by free-ranging lion-tailed macaques (*Macaca silenus*). *Laboratory Primate Newsletter* 32: 1-2.

Fleshler, D. 2015. Monkey business abounds at Dania Beach. *The Herald*, 4 September 2015, pg. 48.

Floehe, S. 2010. Monkey business. *Ocala Style Magazine*, 6 July 2010.

Florida Fish and Game Commission website: *myfwc.com/wildlifehabitats/nonnatives/mammals*

Fossey, D. 1983. *Gorillas in the Mist*. Boston, Houghton Mifflin.

Frey, R. 1978. Management of orangutans. In J.A. McNeely, D.S. Rabor, and E.A. Sumardja, eds. *Wildlife Management in Southeast Asia*, pp 199-215. Bogor, SEAMO Regional Center for Tropical Biology.

Friends of Karura Forest. 2016. Facebook post, 7 March 2016.

Froehlich, J.W., Schillaci, M., Jones Engel, L., Froehlich, D.J. and B. Pullen. 2003. A Sulawesi beachhead by longtail monkeys (*Macaca fascicularis*) on Kabaena Island, Indonesia." *Anthropologie (Brno)* 41: 17–24.

Fundi, P., Kivai, S., Kariuki, T., and C. Mariotte. 2018a. Kenya guereza (*Colobus guereza kikuyensis*) reintroduction at Karura Forest Reserve. Abstract of a paper presented at the 27th Congress of the International Primatological Society, Nairobi, Kenya.

Fundi, P., Kivai, S., Kariuki, T., Mariotte, C., and H Croze. 2018b. Habituation, capture, release, and monitoring of Mount Kenya guerezas (*Colobus, guereza, kikuyuensis*) at Karura Forest. Abstract of a poster presented at the 27th Congress of the International Primatological Society, Nairobi, Kenya.

Furuya, Y. 1965. Social organization of the crab-eating monkey. *Primates* 6(3-4): 285-336.

Gadsby, E.L. 2002. Planning for re-introduction: 10 years of planning for drills in Nigeria. *Re-introduction News* 21: 20-23.

Galdikas-Brindamour, B. 1975. Orangutans, Indonesia's "People of the Forest". *National Geographic* 148: 444-473.

Ganzhorn, J.U. and J. Rabesoa. 1986. The aye-aye (*Daubentonia madagascarensis*) found in the eastern rainforest of Madagascar. *Folia Primatologica* 46: 125-126.

Garcia-Orduna, F., Canales-Espinosa, D., Silva-Lopez, G., Jimenez-Huerta, J., Benitez-Rodriguez, J., and J. Hermida-Lagunes. 1987. Translocation program for the howler monkey (*Alouatta palliata*): A report. *American Journal of Primatology* 12: 363-364.

Gillespie, R. 2016. Monkeys continue to explore beyond state park near Ocala. *Orlando Sentinel*, 27 December 2015.

Glenn M.E. and K.J. Bensen. 2013. The mona monkeys of Grenada, São Tomé and Príncipe: Long-term persistence of a guenon in permanent fragments and implications for the survival of forest primates in protected areas. In L. Marsh and C. Chapman, eds. *Primates in Fragments. Developments in Primatology: Progress and Prospects*. New York, NY, Springer.

Glenn, M.E. and K.J. Bensen. 2016. Are small, isolated populations of forest monkeys worth saving? A 200+ year case study on mona monkeys (*Cercopithecus mona*) on the Caribbean island of Grenada. Abstract of a paper presented at the joint meeting of the 26th Congress of the International Primatological Society and the 39th Meeting of the American Society of Primatologists, Chicago, IL, USA.

González, A., Manójina, N. and A. Hernández. 1994. Mamíferos del Archipiélago de Camagüey, Cuba. *Avicennia* 1: 51-56.

Gonzalez-Martinez, J. 1998. The ecology of the introduced patas monkey (*Erythrocebus patas*) population of southwestern Puerto Rico. *American Journal of Primatology* 45: 351-365.

Gonzales-Martinez, J. 2004. The introduced free-ranging rhesus and patas monkey populations of southwestern Puerto Rico. *Puerto Rico Health Sciences Journal* 23: 39-46.

Goossens, B., Funk, S.M., Vidal, C., Latour, S., Jamart, A., Ancrenaz, M., Wickings, E.J., Tutin, C.E.G., and M.W. Bruford. 2002. Measuring genetic diversity in translocation programmes: principles and application to a chimpanzee release project. *Animal Conservation* 5: 225-236.

Goossens, B., Setchell, J.M., Vidal, C., Dilambaka, E., and A. Jamart. 2003. Successful reproduction in wild released orphan chimpanzees (*Pan troglodytes troglodytes*). *Primates* 44: 67-69.

Goossens, B., Setchell, J.M., Tchidongo, E., Dilambaka, E., Vidal, C., Ancrenaz, M., and A. Jamart. 2005. Survival, interactions with con-specifics and reproduction in 37 chimpanzees released into the wild. *Biological Conservation* 123: 461–475.

Gouzoules, H. 1977. Arashiyama West: A status report. *International Primate Protection League Newsletter* 4(2): 7.

Grealish, R. 2018. Amazing moment 20 slow lorises are released into the wild for the first time. *LAD Bible News*, 7 September. www.ladbible.com (Accessed 9 September 2018).

Grundmann, E. 2005. Will re-introduction and rehabilitation help the long-term conservation of orangutans in Indonesia? *Re-introduction News* 24: 26-27.

Gumert, M. D. 2011. "The common monkey of southeast Asia: Long-tailed macaque populations, ethnophoresy, and their occurrence in human environments. In M.D. Gumert, A. Fuentes, and L. Jones-Engel, eds. *Monkeys on the Edge: Ecology and Management of Long-Tailed Macaques and their Interface with Humans*, pp. 3-44. Cambridge, UK, Cambridge University Press.

Gunst, N., Forteau, A. M., Philbert, S., Vasey, P. L., and J-B Leca. 2016. Decline in population density and group size of mona monkeys in Grenada. *Primate Conservation* 30: 1-7.

Gupta, A.K. (2002) Release of golden langurs in Tripura, India. *Re-introduction News*, 21, 26-28.

Guy, A. 2013. Release of rehabilitated *Chlorocebus aethiops* to Isishlengeni Game farm in KwaZulu-Natal, South Africa. *Journal for Nature Conservation* 21: 214-216.

Guy, A. J., Stone, O. M. L., and D. Curnoe. 2011. The release of a troop of rehabilitated vervet monkeys (*Chlorocebus aethiops*) in KwaZulu-Natal, South Africa: Outcomes and Assessment. *Folia Primatologica* 82: 308-320.

Guy, A. J., Stone, O. M. L., and D. Curnoe. 2012a. Animal welfare considerations in primate rehabilitation: An assessment of three vervet monkey (*Chlorocebus aethiops*) releases in KwaZulu-Natal, South Africa. *Animal Welfare* 21: 511-515.

Guy, A. J., Stone, O. M. L., and D. Curnoe. 2012b. Assessment of the release of rehabilitated vervet monkeys into the Ntendeka Wilderness Area, KwaZulu-Natal, South Africa: A case study. *Primates* 53: 171-179.

Hamada, Y., Oi, T., and T. Watanabe. 1994. *Macaca nigra* on Bacan Island, Indonesia: Its morphology, distribution, and present habitat. *International Journal of Primatology* 15(3): 487-492.

Hanlon, M. 2007. ASBO gorillas: How delinquent gorillas were given a second chance. www.dailymail.co.uk

Hannah, A.C. 1989. *Rehabilitation of Captive Chimpanzees (Pan troglodytes verus)*. PhD Dissertation, University of Stirling.

Hannah, A.C. and W.C. McGrew. 1991. Rehabilitation of captive chimpanzees. In: H.O. Box, ed. *Primate Response to Environmental Change*, pp. 167-86. London, Chapman and Hall.

Harcourt, A.H. 1987. Options for unwanted or confiscated primates. *Primate Conservation* 8: 111-113.

Harcourt, A.H. 1993. Options for confiscated infant gorilla, Amahoro. Unpublished report to the International Gorilla Conservation Programme.

Harrisson, B. 1963. Education to wild living of young orangutans at Bako National Park. *Sarawak Museum Journal* 11: 222-258.

Harrisson, B. 1987. *Orang-Utan*. New York, Oxford University Press.

Hausfater, G. and P. Walker. 1974. History of three little-known New World populations of macaques. *Laboratory Primate Newsletter* 13(1): 16-18.

Heinsohn, T. 2003. Animal translocation: long-term human influences on the vertebrate zoogeography of Australasia (natural dispersal versus ethnophoresy). *Australian Zoologist* 32(3): 351-376.

Heinsohn, T.E. 2010. Marsupials as introduced species: Long-term anthropogenic expansion of the marsupial frontier and its implications for zoogeographic interpretation. *Terra Australis* 32: 133-176.

Heminway, J. 1972. A walk with the gorillas. *Africana* 4(11): 11, 22-23, 26.

Herzfeld, C. 2017. *The Great Apes*. New Haven, Yale University Press (originally published in French in 2012 by Editions du Seuil).

Hirata, S. Personal communication (e-mail, 5 January 2017).

Hladik, C.M. 1978. Adaptive strategies of primates in relation to leaf-eating. In G.G. Montgomery, ed. *The Ecology of Arboreal Folivores*, pp. 373-395. Washington, DC, Smithsonian Institution Press.

Horwich, R. Personal communication, 5 May 2014.

Horwich, R.H., Koontz, F., Saqui, E., Saqui, H. and K. Glander. 1993. A reintroduction program for the conservation of the black howler monkey in Belize. *Endangered Species Update* 10(6): 1-6.

Horwich, R.H., Koontz, F., Saqui, E., Ostro, L., Silver, S., and K. Glander. 2002. Translocation of black howler monkeys in Belize. *Re-introduction News* 21: 10-12.

Humle, T., Colin, C., Laurans, M., and E. Raballand. 2011. Group release of sanctuary chimpanzees (*Pan troglodytes*) in the Haut Niger National Park, Guinea, West Africa: Ranging patterns and lessons so far. *International Journal of Primatology* 32(2): 456-473.

Humle, T., Colin, C., Laurans, M., Danaud, C., and E. Raballand. 2013. Release of the western subspecies of chimpanzees in Guinea, West Africa. In P. S. Soorae, ed. *Global Re-introduction Perspectives: 2013. Further Case Studies from Around the Globe*, pp. 222-228. Gland, IUCN/SSC Re-introduction Specialist Group and Abu Dhabi, UAE Environment Agency.

Humle, T., Legras, J., Kalyongo, P.S., Raballand, E., and C. Colin. 2018. Releasing chimpanzees back to the wild: Lesson learnt and challenges ahead. Abstract of a paper presented at the 27th Congress of the International Primatological Society, Nairobi, Kenya.

HURO Programme Facebook page.

Husson, S., Nayasilana, I., Maruly, A., Purnomo, Suyoko, A., and D. Kurniawan. 2014. *Progress Report #4. Orangutan Reintroduction and Post-release Monitoring in Bukit Batikap Conservation Forest, Murung Raya*. BOS Foundation.

Husson, S.J., Kurniawan, D., Purnomo, P., Boyd, N., Suyoko, A., Sunderland-Groves, J., and J. Sihite. 2016. The survival and adaptation of reintroduced ex-captive orangutans in Central Kalimantan, Indonesia. Abstract of a paper presented at the joint meeting of the 26th Congress of the International Primatological Society and the 39th Meeting of the American Society of Primatologists, Chicago, IL, USA.

Husson, S.J., Suyoko, A., Kurnianwan, D., Sunderland-Groves, J., and J. Sihite. 2018. Factors affecting the successful reintroduction of Bornean orangutans (*Pongo pygmaeus*). Abstract of a paper presented at the 27th Congress of the International Primatological Society, Nairobi, Kenya.

Hyler, W.R. 1995. Vervet monkeys in the mangrove ecosystems of southeastern Florida: Preliminary census and ecological data. *The Florida Scientist* 58: 38-43.

Idani, G. 1993. (A bonobo orphan who became a member of the wild group). *Primate Research* 9(2): 97-106. Note: Title is taken from an English summary of the article, which was published in Japanese.

Imam, E., Malik, I., and H. S. A. Yahya. 2001. Translocation of rhesus macaques from airforce station, Gurgaon (Haryana) to the natural forest of Firozpur Jhirka, Haryana, India. *Journal of The Bombay Natural History Society* 98: 355-359.

Imam, E., Yaha, H.S.A., and I. Malik. 2002. A successful mass translocation of commensal rhesus monkeys *Macaca mulatta* in Vrindaban, India. *Oryx* 36: 87-93.

Ipema, J. 2013. Free at last! A troop of rescued baboons is released to a park in Malawi. *International Primate Protection League News* 40(1): 11-13.

IUCN. 1998. *Re-introduction Specialist Group: Guidelines for Reintroduction*. Gland, International Union for the Conservation of Nature.

Jasinska, A.J., Schmitt, C.A., Service, S.K., Cantor, R.M., Dewar, K., Jentsch, J.D., Kaplan, J.R., Turner, T.R., Warren, W.C., Weinstock, G.M., Woods, R.P. and N.B. Freimer. 2013. Systems biology of the vervet monkey. *ILAR Journal* 54(2): 122-143.

Javan Primates Conservation Project Facebook page.

Jensen, K., Alvarado-Ramy, F., González-Martinez, J., Kraiselburd, E. and J. Rullán. 2004. B-Virus and free-ranging macaques, Puerto Rico. *Emerging Infectious Diseases* 10: 494-496.

Jerkins, T. 1972. Free range breeding of squirrel monkeys on Santa Sofia Island, Colombia. In W. Beveridge, ed. *Breeding Primates*, pg. 144. Basel, Karger.

Johnson, R. L. 1989. Live birthrates in two free-ranging rhesus breeding colonies in the Florida Keys. *Primates* 30: 433-437.

Johnson, R.L. and E. Kapsalis. 1995. Aging, infecundity, and reproductive senescence in free-ranging female rhesus monkeys. *Journal of Reproduction and Fertility* 105: 271–278.

Johnson, R.L. and E. Kapsalis. 1998. Menopause in free-ranging rhesus macaques: Estimated incidence, relation to body condition, and adaptive significance. *International Journal of Primatology* 19(4): 751–765.

Jolly, A. 2012. Berenty Reserve, Madagascar: A long time in a small space. In P.M. Kappeler and D.P. Watts, eds. *Long-Term Field Studies of Primates*, pp 21-44. New York, Springer.

Jones, D. 2014. Who murdered my gorillas? Heartache for the man who returned his family of primates to African jungle as his experiment end in a bloodbath – and the prime suspect is a jealous ape. www.KentOnline.co.uk, 6 September 2014.

Junker, J., Kühl, H.S., Orth, L., Smith, K., Petrovan, S.O., and W.J. Sutherland. 2017. *Primate Conservation: Global Evidence for the Effects of Interventions*. Cambridge, UK, University of Cambridge.

Kabasawa, A., Garriga, R.M., and B. Amarasekeran. 2008. Human fatality by escaped *Pan troglodytes* in Sierra Leone. *International Journal of Primatology* 29: 1671-1685.

Kahlenberg, S.M., Williamson, E.A., Mbeke, J.K., Syahula, E.K., Cranfield, M., de Merode, E., Caillaud, D., Farmer, K.H., Iyer, N., Kyungu, J., and J. Sherman. 2018. Reinforcement for imperiled Grauer's gorilla population in Democratic Republic of Congo: Prospects, preparation, and remaining obstacles. Abstract of a paper presented at the 27th Congress of the International Primatological Society, Nairobi, Kenya.

Kalpers, J. 1993. Long-term future for Amahoro: Summary of possible options. Unpublished working paper, International Gorilla Conservation Programme.

Karlowski, U. 1996. The Conkouati Chimpanzee Refuge – a new chance for orphans. *Gorilla Journal* 12(June): 20.

Kavanagh, K. and J.O. Caldecott. 2013. Strategic guidelines for the translocation of primates and other animals. *The Raffles Bulletin of Zoology*, Supplement 29: 203-209.

Kawai, M. 1960. A field experiment on the process of group formation in the Japanese monkey (*Macaca fuscata*), and the releasing of the group at Ôhirayama. *Primates* 2: 181-255.

Kawai, M. and U. Mito. 1973. Quantitative study of activity patterns and postures of Formosan momkeys by the radio-telemetrical technique. *Primates* 14(2-3): 179-194.

Kawamoto, Y., Shirai, K., Araki, S., and K. Maeno. 1999. A case of hybridization between Japanaese macaques and Taiwanese macaques found in Wakayama Prefecture. *Primate Research* 15: 53-60. (English summary).

Keith-Lucas, T., White, F.J., Keith-Lucas, L. and L.G. Vick. 1999. Changes in behavior in free-ranging Lemur catta following release in a natural habitat. *American Journal of Primatology* 47(1): 15-28.

Keizer, F. and M. Keizer. 2004. The gorillas of "Petit Evengue". *Gorilla Journal* 29: 28-30.

Kemp, N.J. and J.B. Burnett. 2003. Final report: A biodiversity risk assessment and recommendations for risk management of long-tailed macaques (*Maca fascicularis*) in New Guinea. Washington, DC, Indo-Pacific Conservation Alliance.

Kenyon, M., Streicher, U., Loung, H., Tran, T., Tran, M., Vo, B., and A. Cronin. 2014. Survival of released pygmy slow loris *Nycticebus pygmaeus* in South Vietnam. *Endangered Species Research* 25, 185-95.

Kenyon, M., Streicher, U., Jai-Chyu Peil, K., Cronin, A., van Dien, N., van Mui, T., and L. van Hien. 2015. Experiences using VHF and VHF/GPS-GSM radio transmitters on released southern yellow-cheeked gibbons (*Nomascus gabriellae*) in South Vietnam. *Vietnamese Journal of Primatology* 2(3): 15-27.

Kessler, M. J. and R. G. Rawlins. 2016. A 75-year pictorial history of the Cayo Santiago rhesus monkey colony. *American Journal of Primatology* 78: 6-43.

Khoi, N. V. 2014. WAR stories: Wildlife rehabilitation in Vietnam. *International Primate Protection League News* 41: 8-9.

Kierulff, M.C.M. 2011. Invasive introduced golden-headed lion tamarins. *Tamarin Tales* 10: 5-7.

Kierulff, M.C.M. 2012 The removal of golden-headed lion tamarin invaders. *Tamarin Tales* 11: 2-3.

Kierulff, C. 2015. Golden-headed lion tamarin invaders in Niteroi. *Tamarin Tales* 13: 1-3.

Kierulff, M.C.M and de Oliveira, P.P. 1994. Habitat preservation and the translocation of threatened groups of golden lion tamarins, *Leontopithecus rosalia*. *Neotropical Primates* 2 (suppl.): 15-18.

Kierulff, M.C.M., Beck, B.B., Kleiman, D.G., and P. Procopio. 2002a. Re-introduction and translocation as conservation tools for golden lion tamarins in Brazil. *Re-introduction News*, 21: 7-10.

Kierulff, M.C., Procopio de Oliveira, P., Beck, B.B., and A. Martins. 2002b. Reintroduction and translocation as conservation tools for golden lion tamarins. In D.G. Kleiman and A.B. Rylands, eds. *Lion Tamarins: Biology and Conservation*, pp. 271-82. Washington, DC, Smithsonian institution Press.

Kierulff, M.C.M., Ruiz-Miranda, C.R., Procópio de Oliveira, P., Beck, B.B., Martins, A., Dietz, J.M., Rambaldi, D.M. and A. J. Baker. 2012. The golden lion tamarin *Leontopithecus rosalia*: a conservation success story. *International Zoo Yearbook* 46 (1): 36–45.

King, T. 2004. Reintroduced western gorillas reproduce for the first time. *Oryx* 38(3): 251-252.

King, T. and C. Chamberlan. 2007. Orphan gorilla management and reintroduction: Progress and perspectives. *Gorilla Journal* 34: 21-25.

King, T. and A. Courage. 2008. Western gorilla re-introduction to the Batéké Plateau region of Congo and Gabon. In P.S. Soorae, ed. *Global Re-introduction Perspectives: Re-introduction Case-Studies from Around the Globe*, pp. 217-210. Abu Dhabi, UAE IUCN/SSC Re-introduction Specialist Group,

King, T., Chamberlan, C., and A. Courage. 2005a. Rehabilitation of orphan gorillas and bonobos in the Congo. *Oryx* 52(4): 198-209.

King, T., Chamberlan, C., and A. Courage. 2005b. Reintroduced gorillas: Reproduction, ranging and unresolved issues. *Gorilla Journal* 32: 30-32.

King, T., Chamberlan, C., and A. Courage. 2012. Assessing initial reintroduction success in long-lived primates by quantifying survival, reproduction, and dispersal parameters: Western lowland gorillas (*Gorilla gorilla gorilla*) in Congo and Gabon. *International Journal of Primatology* 33: 134-149.

King, T., Chamberlan, C., and A. Courage. 2014. Assessing reintroduction success in long-lived primates through population viability analysis: western lowland gorillas *Gorilla gorilla gorilla* in Central Africa. *Oryx* 48: 294-303.

Kleindienst, L. 1997. Florida at war against monkeys. articles.sun-sentinel.com

Klopchin, J. L., Stewart, J. R., Webster, L. F., and P. A. Sandifer. 2008. Assessment of environmental impacts of a colony of free-ranging rhesus monkeys (*Macaca mulatta*) on Morgan Island, South Carolina. *Environmental Monitoring and Assessment* 137: 301-313.

Koffi, C. 2017. Helping Ponso, sole survivor of 'Chimapnzee Island', I. Coast. www.phys.org 24 September.

Konstant, W.R. and R.A. Mittermeier. 1982. Introduction, reintroduction and translocation of Neotropical primates: Past experience and future possibilities. *International Zoo Yearbook* 22: 69-77.

Kruer, C. 1996. The inside story on the monkey islands of the Florida Keys. *The Florida Naturalist* 69: 10.

Kuze, N., Sipangkui, S., Malim, T.P., Bernard, H., Ambu, L.N., and S. Kohshima. 2008. Reproductive parameters over a 37-year period of free-ranging Borneo orangutans at Sepilok Orangutan Rehabilitation Centre. *Primates* 49: 126-134.

Kyes, R.C. 1993. Survey of long-tailed macaques introduced onto Tinjil Island, Indonesia. *American Journal of Primatology* 31, 77-83.

Lawes, M.J. 2002. Conservation of fragmented populations of *Cercopithecus mitis* in South Africa: The role of reintroduction, corridors and metapopulation ecology. In M.E. Glenn and M. Cords, eds. *The Guenons: Diversity and Adaptation in African Monkeys*, pp. 367-384. New York, Kluwer Academic/Plenum Publishers.

Layne, J.N. 1997. Nonindigenous mammals. In D. Simberloff, D.C. Schmitz, and T.C. Brown, eds. *Strangers in Paradise: Impact and Management of Nonindigenous Species in Florida*, pp 157-186. Washington DC, Island Press.

Leclere, M. 2017. Port Lympne gorilla brothers heading to Congo in Back to the Wild initiative. *KentOnline*, 6 October 2017.

Le Flohic, G., Motsch, P., DeNys, H., Childs, S., Courage, A. and T. King. 2015. Behavioural ecology and group cohesion of juvenile western lowland gorillas (*Gorilla g. gorilla*) during rehabilitation in the Batéké Plateaux National Park, Gabon. *PLoS ONE* 10(3): e0119609.

Le Hallaye, Y., Goossens, B., Jamart, A., and D.J. Curtis. 2010. Acquisition of fission-fusion social organization in a chimpanzee (*Pan troglodytes troglodytes*) community released into the wild. *Behavioral Ecology and Sociobiology* 64(3): 349-360.

Lehman, S.M., Taylor L.L., and S.P. Easley. 1994. Climate and reproductive seasonality in two free-ranging island populations of rhesus macaques (*Macaca mulatta*). *International Journal of Primatology* 15(1): 115-128.

Lemmon, T. 1987. The long way back to nature. *BBC Wildlife* 5(2): 172-175.

Lemmon, T. 1991. Lion tamarin virus gives zoologists heart attack. *BBC Wildlife* 9(8): 527.

Lenin, J. 2008. The business of monkey control. *Reintroduction Redux* 3: 14-15.

Lindbergh, S.M. and M.E.L. Santini. 1984. A reintrodução do bugio preto (*Alouatta caraya*, Humboldt 1818 – Cebidae) no Parque Nacional de Brasília. *Brasil Florestal* 57: 35-53.

Lindburg, D. G. and L. Gledhill. 1992. Captive breeding and conservation of lion-tailed macaques. *Endangered Species Update* 10(1): 1-4.

Lippold, L.K. 1989. Mona monkeys of Grenada. *Primate Conservation* 10: 22-23.

Lippold, L. K. and V. N. Thanh. 2015. Vietnam's civil war on primates: Douc langurs and gibbons at risk. *International Primate Protection League News* 42(3): 21-23.

Long, J.L. 2003. *Introduced Mammals of the World*. Collingwood, Victoria, Australia, CSIRO Publishing.

Louis, E.E. Jr., Rabetoandro, A.N., Rahajanirina, A.N., Hawkins, M.T., Randrianindrina, V.R., Lei, R., Bailey, J., Zaonarivelo, R., Andriantompohavana, R., and C.L. Frasier. 2016. Ten-year perspective of a reintroduction/translocation program for the diameded sifaka, *Propithecus diadema*, in Analamazaotra Special Reserve in Madagascar. Abstract of a paper presented at the joint meeting of the 26th Congress of the International Primatological Society and the 39th Meeting of the American Society of Primatologists, Chicago, IL, USA.

Loy, J. 1989. Studies of free-ranging and corralled patas monkeys at La Parguera, Puerto Rico. *Puerto Rico Health Sciences Journal* 8: 129-131.

Lyon, L. 1976. The saving of the gorilla. *Africana* 5(9): 11-13, 23.

MacKinnon, J. 1977. The future of orang-utans. *New Scientist* 74: 697-699.

Mail, R. 2013. Orangutan population looking good but wildlife centre runs out of space. *The Star, Malaysia* 26 July 2013.

Malaivijitnond, S. and Y. Hamada. 2008. Current situation and status of long-tailed macaques (*Macaca fasicularis*) in Thailand. *The Natural History Journal of Chulalongkorn University* 8(2): 185-204.

Malaivijitnond, S., Vazquez, Y., and Y. Hamada. 2011. Human impact on long-tailed macaques in Thailand. In M.D. Gumert, A. Fuentes, and L. Jones Engel, eds. *Monkeys on the Edge: Ecology and Management of Long-tailed Macaques and their Interface with Humans*, pp 118-158. Cambridge, UK, Cambridge University Press.

Malik, I. and R. L. Johnson. 1994. Commensal rhesus in India: The need and cost of translocation. *Revue d'Ecologie (La Terre et La Vie)* 49: 233-243.

Manning, C. 1996. The Lake Edward Chimpanzee Sanctuary. *IPPL News*, 23(2): 25-28.

Maples, W.R., Brown, A.B., and P.M. Hutchens. 1976. Introduced monkey populations at Silver Springs, Florida. *Florida Anthropologist* 29(4): 133-136.

Marshall, J.T. 1992. Gibbon release in Thailand. *Asian Primates* 2(1): 4-5.

Marshall, M. 2015. New group of dwarf lemurs may be world's rarest primate. *BBC Earth*, April 2015. www.bbc.com Accessed 4 September 2018.

Marzec, A., Laubi, B., Kumiawan, D., Utami-Atmoko, S., van Noordwijk, M., Willems, E., and C. van Schaik. 2018. Can necessity be the mother of invention? How do Bornean orangutans (*Pongo pygmaeus*) adjust to a new environment? Abstract of a paper presented at the 27th Congress of the International Primatological Society, Nairobi, Kenya.

Masseti, M. and E. Bruner. 2009. The primates of the Western Palearctic: A biogeographical, historical, and archeozoological review. *Journal of Antrhopological Sciences* 87: 33-91.

Mast, R. B., Rodríguez, J.V., and R. A. Mittermeier. 1993. The Colombian cotton-top tamarin in the wild. In: N.K. Clapp, ed. *A Primate Model for the Study of Colitis and Colonic Carcinoma: The Cotton-top Tamarin*, Saguinus oedipus, pp 3-43. Boca Raton, CRC Press.

Matsumoto-Oda, A. 2004. Chimpanzees in the Rubondo National Park, Tanzania. http://mahale.web.infoseek.co.jp/PAN/7_2/7(2)-02.html

McGrew, W.C. 1983. Chimpanzees can be rehabilitated. *Laboratory Primate Newsletter* 22(2): 2-3.

McGuire, M.T. 1974. The St. Kitts Vervet. *Contributions to Primatology* 1. Basel, S. Karger.

McKelson, J., UNU, M., and I. Singleton. 2016. Training ex-captive orangutans within the Jantho Reintroduction Station Aceh, Indonesia. Abstract of a paper presented at the joint meeting of the 26th Congress of the International Primatological Society and the 39th Meeting of the American Society of Primatologists, Chicago, IL, USA.

McRae, M. 2000. Central Africa's orphan gorillas. *National Geographic*, February 2000: 84-97.

Medici, E.P., Valladares-Padua, C.B., Rylands, A.B., and C.S. Martins. 2003. Translocation as a metapopulation management tool for the black lion tamarin, *Leontopithecus chrysopygus*. *Primate Conservation* 19: 23-31.

Mejaard, E. and V. Nijman. 2000. The local extinction of the proboscis monkey (*Nasalis larvatus*) in the Palau Kaget Nature Reserve, Indonesia. *Oryx* 34: 66-70.

Mensink, M. 1986. Julia: A gorilla with an identity crisis. *New Scientist* 19 June: 68-69.

Millán, J.F., Bennett, S.E., and P.R. Stevenson. 2014. Notes on the behavior of captive and released woolly monkeys (*Lagothrix lagothrica*): Reintroduction as a conservation strategy in Colombian southern Amazon. In: T.R. Defler and P.R. Stevenson, eds. *The Wooly Monkey; Behavior, Ecology, Systematics, and Captive Research*, pp 249-266. New York, Springer.

Milton, K. and M.E. Hopkins. 2006. Reintroduced spider monkey (*Ateles geoffroyi*) population on Barro Colorado, Panama. In: A. Estrada, P.A. Garber, M. Pavelka, and L. Luecke, eds. *New Perspectives in the Study of Mesoamerican Primates*, pp 417- 435. New York, Springer.

Mittermeier, R.A., Bailey, R.C., Sponsel L.E., and K.E. Wolf. 1977. Primate ranching – Results of an experiment. *Oryx* 13: 449-453.

Mittermeier, R.A., Louis, E.E. Jr., Richardson, M., Schwitzer, C., Landgrand, O., Rylands, A.B., Hawkins, F., Rajaobelina, S., Ratsimbazafy, J., Rasoloarison, R., Roos, C., Kappeler, P.M., and J. MacKinnon. 2010. *Lemurs of Madagascar*, 3rd Edition. Arlington, Virginia, Conservation International.

Modolo, L., Salzburger, W., and R.D. Martin. 2005. Phylogeography of Barbary macaques (*Macaca sylvanus*) and the origin of the Gibraltar colony. *Proceedings of the National Academy of Sciences* 102(20): 7392-7397.

Montali, R.J., Scanga, C.A., Pernikoff, D., Wessner, D.R., Ward, R., and K.V. Holmes. 1993. A common-source outbreak of callithrichid hepatitis in captive tamarins and marmosets. *The Journal of Infectious Diseases* 167: 946-950.

Moore, R. 2012. *Ethics, Ecology and Evolution of Indonesian Slow Lorises (Nycticebus spp.) Rescued from the Pet Trade*. PhD Thesis, Oxford Brookes University.

Moore, R.S., Whihermonto, and K.A.I. Nekaris. 2014. Compassionate conservation, rehabilitation and translocation of Indonesian slow lorises. *Endangered Species Research* 26: 93-102.

Moore, Jr., C. 2017a. Feral monkeys in Texas (photo and more). *The Wildlife Journalist*, blog.wildlifejournalist.com 5 May 2017.

Moore, Jr. C. 2017b. More on Texas feral monkeys (photos and stories). *The Wildlife Journalist*, blog.wildlifejournalist.com 9 May 2017.

Morel, D. 2017. Personal communication (e-mail 11 January 2017, with numerous attachments of unpublished quarterly reports to the World Society for the Protection of Animals in 2009, 2010, and 2011, proposals and reports to the Great Ape Conservation Fund of the US Fish and Wildlife Service, and presentations to the Pan African Sanctuary Alliance in 2009 and 2013 by Claudine André).

Morell, V. 1994. Orphan chimps won't go back to nature. *Science* 265: 312.

Morris, J. 1995. Gorilla conservation program suffers setback. *Oryx* 29(4): 219.

Moscovice, L. R., Issa, M.H., Petrzelkova, K.J., Keuler, N.S., Snowdon, C.T., and M.A. Huffman. 2007. Fruit availability, chimpanzee diet, and grouping patterns on Rubondo Island, Tanzania. *American Journal of Primatology* 69: 487–502.

Moya, L. and P. Soini. undated. Experimental introduction and management of the moustached tamarin (*Saguinus mystax*) in Padre Isla Island, Iquitos – Peru. Unattributed abstract.

Msindai, N.J., Sommer, V., and C. Roos. 2015. The chimpanzees of Rubondo Island: Genetic data reveal their origin. *Folia Primatologica* 86(4): 327.

Mudakikwa, A. 2002. Ubuzima, a 13-month-old re-introduced to her group. *Gorilla Journal* 25: 8.

Murage, A. B. 2016. Comment on a Facebook post by Andrea Donaldson, 7 March 2016.

Mydans, C. 1973. Orangutans can return to the wild with some help. *Smithsonian* 4(8): 26-33.

Nadler, T. 2012. Reintroduction of the 'Critically Endangered' Delacour's langur (*Trachypithecus delacouri*) – a preliminary report. *Vietnamese Journal of Primatology* 2: 67-72.

Nadler, T. 2015. A center for primate conservation in Vietnam. *International Primate Protection League News* 42(1): 18-22.

National Institute for Environmental Studies. 2015a. *Macaca mulatta*. http://www.nies.go.jp/biodiversity/invasive/DB/detail/10390e.html

National Institute for Environmental Studies. 2015b. *Macaca cyclopis*. http://www.nies.go.jp/biodiversity/invasive/DB/detail/10030e.html

Nekaris, K.A.I. and C.R. Starr. 2015. Conservation and ecology of the neglected slow loris: priorities and prospects. *Endangered Species Research* 28: 87-95.

Nekaris, K.A.I. and V. Nijman. 2017. Javan slow loris. In C. Schwitzer, R.A. Mittermeier, A.B. Rylands, F. Chiozza, E.A. Williamson, E.J. Macfie, J. Wallis and A. Cotton, eds. *Primates in Peril; The World's 25 Most Endangered Primates, 2016-2018*, pp 48-51. Arlington, VA, IUCN SSC Primate Specialist Group (PSG), International Primatological Society (IPS), Conservation International (CI), and Bristol Zoological Society.

Neves, L.G., Jerusalinsky, L., Melo, F.R., Rylands, A.B. and M. Talebi. 2017. Northern brown howler monkey. In C. Schwitzer, R.A. Mittermeier, A.B. Rylands, F. Chiozza, E.A. Williamson, E.J. Macfie, J. Wallis and A. Cotton, eds. *Primates in Peril; The World's 25 Most Endangered Primates, 2016-2018*, pp 96-99. Arlington, VA, IUCN SSC Primate Specialist Group (PSG), International Primatological Society (IPS), Conservation International (CI), and Bristol Zoological Society.

Nishida, T. 1963. Intertroop relationships of the Formosan monkeys (*Macaca cyclopis*) relocated on Nojima Island. *Primates* 4(1): 121-122.

Nogueira, C.P., Carvalho, A.R.D., Oliveira, L.P., Veado, E.M., and K.B. Streier. 1994. Recovery and release of an infant muriqui (*Brachyteles arachnoides*) at the Nolin, Caratinga Biological Station, Minas Gerais, Brazil. *Neotropical Primates* 2(1): 3-5.

Nolin, R. 2013. City of the apes: Monkey business haunts Dania Beach, Florida. *Florida Sun Sentinel*. 5 May 2013.

Norton, T.M., Penfold, L.M., Lessnau, B., Jochle, W., Staaden, S.L., Joliffe, A., Bauman, J.E., and J. Spratt. 2000. Long-acting deslorelin implants to control aggression in male lion-tailed macaques (*Macaca silenus*). Proceedings of the annual conference of the International Association for Aquatic Animal Medicine. https://www.vin.com/apputil/content/defaultadv1.aspx?pId=11125

Nugraha, I. and P. Jacobson. 2016. 10 orangutans released into the wild in Borneo. www.news.mongabey.com 15 August.

Oliveira, L.C. and C.E.V. Grelle. 2012. Introduced primate species of an Atlantic Forest region in Brazil: present and future implications for the native fauna. *Tropical Conservation Science* 5(1): 112-120.

Ongman, L., Colin, C., Raballand, E., and T. Humle. 2013. The "super chimpanzee": The ecological dimensions of rehabilitation of orphan chimpanzees in Guinea, West Africa. *Animals* 3: 109-126.

Osterberg, P., Samphanthamit, P., Maprang, O., Punnadee, S. and W.Y. Brockelman. 2014. Population dynamics of a reintroduced population of captive-raised gibbons (*Hylobates lar*) on Phuket, Thailand. *Primate Conservation* 28: 179-188.

Osterberg, P., Samphanthamit, P., Maprang, O., Punnadee, S., and W.Y. Brockelman. 2015. Gibbon (*Hylobates lar*) reintroduction success in Phuket, Thailand, and its conservation benefits. *American Journal of Primatology* 77: 492-501.

Ostro, L. E. T., Silver, S. C., Koontz, F. W., Young, T. P., and R. H. Horwich. 1999. Ranging behavior of translocated and established groups of black howler monkeys *Alouatta pigra* in Belize, Central America. *Biological Conservation* 87: 181-190.

Palmer, A. 2017. Personal communication; e-mail 4 November.

Palmer, A. In press. Kill, incarcerate, or liberate? Ethics and alternatives to orangutan rehabilitation. *Biological Conservation*.

Pandrillus Facebook page, 1 and 3 May 2017, 30 May 2018.

Panwar, H. S. and M. K. Misra. 2004. Monkey and the lion. *Reintro Redux* 1: 3.

Passamani, M. and J.A. Passamani. 1994. Losses of re-introduced Geoffroy's marmoset. *Re-introduction News* 8: 9-10.

Passaro, R. 2012. New home for two Critically Endangered langurs. *The Babbler*, 44: 4-5.

Pastorini, J., Thalmann, U., and R.D. Martin. 2003. A molecular approach to comparative phylogeography of extant Malagasy lemurs. *Proceedings of the National Academy of Sciences* 100(10): 5879-5884.

Paterson, J.D. 1996. Coming to America: Acclimation in macaque body structures and Bergmann's Rule. *International Journal of Primatology* 17(4): 585-611.

Pearson, L., Aczel, P., Mahé, S., Courage, A., and T. King. 2007. Gorilla reintroduction to the Batéké Plateau National Park, Gabon: An analysis of the preparations and initial results with reference to the IUCN guidelines for the re-introduction of Great Apes. Franceville, Gabon, PPG-Gabon/The Aspinall Foundation and Hythe, Kent, UK, The Aspinall Foundation.

Peignot, P., Charpentier, M. J. E., Bout, N., Bourry, O., Massima, U., Dosimont, O., Terramorsi, R. and E. J. Wickings. 2008. Learning from the first release project of captive-bred mandrills *Mandrillus sphinx* in Gabon. Oryx 42: 122-131.

Peters, H.H. 1995. *Orangutan reintroduction? Development, use and evaluation of a new method: reintroduction.* MSc dissertation, University of Groningen, The Netherlands.

Petter, J.-J., Albinac, R., and Y. Rumpler. 1977. *Mammifères Lemuriëns (Primates, Prosimiens). Faunes de Madagascar.* Paris, ORSTROM/CNRS.

Phoebus, E.C. 1989. The FDA rhesus breeding colony at La Parguera, Puerto Rico. *Puerto Rico Health Sciences Journal* 1989 8:157-158.

Pirta, R.S., Gadgil, M., and A.V. Kharshikar. 1997. Mangement of the rhesus monkey *Macaca mulatta* and Hanuman langur *Presbytis entellus* in Himachal Pradesh, India. *Biological Conservation* 79(1): 97-106.

Poirier, F. E. and E. O. Smith. 1974. The crab-eating macaques (*Macaca fasicularis*) of Angaur Island, Palau, Micronesia. *Folia Primatologica* 22: 258-306.

Pollock, J.I., Constable, I.D., Mittermeier, R.A., Ratsirarson, J., and H. Simons. 1985. A note on the diet and feeding behavior of the aye-aye *Daubentonia madagascarensis*. *International Journal of Primatology* 6(4): 435-447.

Preutz, J.D. 2011. Targeted helping by a wild adolescent male chimpanzee (*Pan troglodytes*): evidence for empathy? *Journal of Ethology* 29(2): 365-368.

Preutz, J.D. and D. Kante. 2010. Successful return of an infant chimpanzee to its natal group after a poaching incident. *African Primates* 7: 35-41.

Prince, A.M. 1985. Rehabilitation and release program for chimpanzees. *Primate Conservation* 5: 33.

Prince, A.M. 2005. Leadership sought for chimpanzee sanctuary in Liberia. *ASP Bulletin* 29(4): 15.

Pung, O.J., Spratt, J., Clark, C.G., Norton, T.M., and J. Carter. 1998. Trypanasoma cruzi infection of free-ranging lion-tailed macaques (*Macaca silenus*) and ring-tailed lemurs (*Lemur catta*) on St. Catherine's [sic] Island, Georgia, USA. *Journal of Zoo and Wildlife Medicine* 29(1): 25-30.

Raballand, E. 2008. Annual Report, Chimpanzee Conservation Center, 2008.

Radhakrishna, S. and A. Sinha. 2011. Less than wild? Commensal primates and wildlife conservation. *Journal of Bioscience* 36(5): 749-753.

Ramlee, H. 2006. Re-introduction of gibbons in Sarawak, Malaysia. *Re-introduction News* 25: 41-43.

Rasmussen, D.R. 1991. Observer influence on range use of *Macaca arctoides* after 14 years of observation? *Laboratory Primate Newsletter* 30(3): 6-11.

Rawlins, R.G. and M.J. Kessler. 1986. *The Cayo Santiago Macaques: History, Behavior and Biology*. Albany: State University of New York Press.

Renaud, A., Jamart, A., Goossens, B., and C. Ross. 2013. A longitudinal study on feeding behavior and activity patterns of released chimpanzees in Conkouati-Douli National Park, Republic of Congo. *Animals* 3(2): 532-550.

Revkin, A. C. 1996. A life's work disrupted in Liberia; Newark native hopes to return to her study of chimps. *The New York Times*, 1 May 1996.

Rezende, G.C. 2015. Updates from the BLT conservation program in Pontal do Paranapanema (2014-2015). *Tamarin Tales* 13: 12-13.

Rezende, G.C., Garbino, G.T., Jenkins, C.N., Martins, C.S., and C. Valladares-Padua. 2016. Home range of two translocated groups of black lion tamarins (*Leontopithecus chrysopygus*) and remarks on a 20-year population management program in Brazil. Abstract of a paper presented at the joint meeting of the 26th Congress of the International Primatological Society and the 39th Meeting of the American Society of Primatologists, Chicago, IL, USA.

Richard-Hansen, C., Vie, J-C., and B. deThoisy. 2000. Translocation of red howler monkeys (*Alouatta seniculus*) in French Guiana. *Biological Conservation* 93: 247-253.

Riedler, B., Millesi, E., P.H. Pratje. (2010) Adaptation to forest life during the reintroduction process of immature Pongo abelii. *International Journal of Primatology* 31(4): 647-663.

Rijksen, H.D. 1974. Orang-utan conservation and rehabilitation in Sumatra. *Biological Conservation* 6(1): 20-25.

Rijksen, H.D. 1978. *A Field Study of Sumatran Orang Utans (Pongo pygmaeus abelli, Lesson 1872), Ecology, Behavior and Conservation.* Wageningen, the Netherlands, Mededlingen Landbouwhogeschool: H Veerman and Zonen B.V.

Rijksen, H.D. and A.G. Rijksen-Graatsma. 1975. Orang utan rescue work In North Sumatra. *Oryx* 13: 63-73.

Riley, E.P. and T.W. Wade. 2016. Adapting to Florida's riverine woodlands: the population status and feeding ecology of the Silver River rhesus macaques and their interface with humans. *Primates* 57: 195-210.

Robins, J. 2016. Post release monitoring project. *Orangutan Appeal UK News* 31: unpaginated.

Robins, J.G., Ancrenz, M., Parker, J. Goossens, B., Ambu, L., and C. Walzer. 2013. The release of northeast Bornean orangutans to Tabin Wildlife Reserve, Sabah, Malaysia. In P.S. Soorae, ed. *Global Re-introduction Perspectives: 2013. Further Case Studies from Around the Globe*, pp. 215-221. Gland, IUCN/SSC Re-introduction Specialist Group and Abu Dhabi, UAE, Environment Agency – Abu Dhabi.

Robithotul, H., Rattel, C., Anirudh, N. B., and K.L. Sanchez. 2016. Systematic reintroductions of Javan (*N. javanicus*), Sumatran (*N. coucang*) and Bornean (*N. menagensis*) slow lorises rescued from the illegal pet trade in Indonesia. Abstract of a paper presented at the joint meeting of the 26th Congress of the International Primatological Society and the 39th Meeting of the American Society of Primatologists, Chicago, IL, USA.

Rochman, A. 2017. 8 Javan slow lorises released into natural habitat. *The Jakarta Post*, 9 November 2017.

Rodriguez-Luna, E. and L. Cortés-Ortiz. 1994. Translocacion y seguimiento de un grupo de monos *Alouatta palliata* liberado en una isla (1988-1994). *Neotropical Primates* 2(2): 1-5.

Rosenblum, B., O'Brien, T.C., Kinnaird, M., and J. Supriatna. 1998. Population densities of Sulawesi crested black macaques (*Macaca nigra*) on Bacan and Sulawesi, Indonesia: Effects of habitat disturbance and hunting. *American Journal of Primatology* 44: 89-106.

Ruiz-Miranda, C.R., Affonso, A.G., de Morais, M.M., Verona, C.E., Martins, A., and B. Beck. 2006. Behavioral and ecological interactions between reintroduced golden lion tamarins (*Leontopithecus rosalia* Linnaeus 1766) and introduced marmosets (*Callithrix* spp, Linnaeus, 1758) in Brazil's Atlantic Coast forest fragments. *Brazilian Archives of Biology and Technology* 49: 99-109.

Ruiz-Miranda, C.R., Beck, B.B., Kleiman, D.G., Martins, A., Dietz, J.M., Rambaldi, D.M., Kierulff, C., Procopio de Oliveira, P., and A.J. Baker. 2010 Re-introduction and translocation of golden lion tamarins, Atlantic Coastal Forest, Brazil: The creation of a metapopulation. In P.S. Soorae, ed. *Global Re-introduction Perspectives: Additional Case-Studies from Around the Globe*, pp. 225-230. Abu Dhabi, UAE, IUCN/SSC Re-introduction Specialist Group.

Ruiz-Miranda, C.R., de Morais Jr., M.M., Romana de Paula, V. Grativol, A.D., and D.M. Rambaldi. 2011. Vitimas e Vilões. *Ciencia Hoje* 48: 44-48.

Russon, A. 2002a. Activities in Kalimantan focus on orangutan reintroduction & environmental protection. *Voices from the Wilderness* (Newsletter of the Balikpapan Orangutan Society/USA) 5(1): 1-2.

Russon, A.E. 2002b. Return of the native: Cognition and site-specific expertise in orangutan rehabilitation. *International Journal of Primatology* 23(3): 461-477.

Russon, A.E. 2004. *Orangutans: Wizards of the Rainforest*. Firefly Books, Buffalo, NY.

Russon, A.E. 2009. Orangutan rehabilitation and reintroduction. In S.A. Wich, S.S. Utami Atmoko, T. Mitra Setia, and C.P. van Schaik, eds. *Orangutans: Geographic Variation in Behavioural Ecology and Conservation*, pp. 327-350. Oxford, UK, Oxford University Press.

Russon, A. 2018. Personal communication; e-mail 7 March.

Russon, A.E., Handayani, D.P., Kuncoro, P., and A. Ferisa. 2007. Orangutan leaf-carrying for nest-building: Toward unraveling cultural processes. *Animal Cognition* 10: 189-202.

Sale, J.B., Andau, P.M., and L.K. Hiong. 1995. The capture and translocation of orang-utans in Sabah, Malaysia. *Re-introduction News* 10: 12-14.

Sambyal, P., Kumar, S., and D. N. Sahi. 2009. Translocation of urban rhesus monkeys (*Macaca mulatta*) of Mubarak Mandi Jammu to forest areas of Nagrot. *Tigerpaper* 36: 1-3.

Santini, M.E.L. 1986a. Modificações temporais na dieta de *Alouatta caraya* (Primates, Cebidae), reintroduzido no Parque Nacional de Brasília. *A Primatologia no Brasil* 2: 269-292.

Santini, M.E.L. 1986b. Padrões de actividada de *Alouatta caraya* (Primates, Cebidae), reintroduzido no Parque Nacional de Brasília. *A Primatologia no Brasil* 2: 293-304.

Schiermeier, Q. 2003. Primatologist rocks Gibraltar by quitting over macaque cull. *Nature* 426 (13 November): 111.

Serio-Silva, J. 1997. Studies of howler monkeys (*Alouatta palliata*) translocated to a neotropical forest fragment. *Laboratory Primate Newsletter* 36: 11-14.

Serrao, J.S. and S.R. Amladi. 1979. Of macaques-bonnet and rhesus. *Hornbill* 12: 29-32.

Sexton, R. and E. Stewart. 2005. Alloa Inch: The mudbank in the Forth that became an inhabited island. *Forth Naturalist and Historian* 28: 79-101.

Shalukoma, C. 2000. Attempt to re-introduce a young gorilla to the Kahuzi-Biega forest. *Gorilla Journal* 21: 3-4.

Shanee S. and N. Shanee. 2007. The gibbon rehabilitation project in Phuket, Thailand. *Re-introduction News* 26: 48-49.

Shedden-Gonzalez, A. and E. Rodriguez-Luna. 2010. Responses of a translocated howler monkey (*Alouatta palliata*) group to new environmental conditions. *Endangered Species Research* 12: 25-30.

Sherman, J., Farmer, K.H., Williamson, E.A., Unwin, S., Kahlenberg, S.M., Russon, A.E., Cheyne, S.M., Humle, T., Mylniczenko, N., Macfie, E., and S. Wich. 2018. Methodology and technical advisory resources for ape reintroductions to natural habitats. Abstract of a paper presented at the 27th Congress of the International Primatological Society, Nairobi, Kenya.

Shumaker, R. Personal communication (e-mail 11 January 1999).

Silkiluwasha, F. 1981. The distribution and conservation status of the Zanzibar red colobus. *African Journal of Ecology* 19: 187-194.

Silver, S.C., Ostro, L.E.T., Yeager, C.P. and R.H. Horwich. 1998. Feeding ecology of the black howler monkey (*Alouatta pigra*) in northern Belize. *American Journal of Primatology* 45(3): 263-279.

Simmen, B., Hladik, A., and P. Ramasiarisoa. 2003. Food intake and dietary overlap in native *Lemur catta* and *Propithecus verrauxi* and introduced *Eulemur fulvus* at Berenty, southern Madagascar. *International Journal of Primatology* 24(5): 949-968.

Singleton, I. 2012. Stasiun pengamatan orangutan semi liar dan tantanganya: Orangutan tourism case study. *Proceedings of the Africa-Asia Ape Conservation and Poverty Alleviation Learning Exchange*, Bogor, Indonesia, 11-15 January. Retrieved from www.povertyandconservation.info/node/7916

Singleton, I., Wich, S., Husson, S., Stephens, S., Utami Atmoko, S., Leighton, M., Rosen, N., Traylor-Holzer, K., Lacy, R., and O. Byers. 2004. *Orangutan Population and Habitat Viability Assessment: Final Report*. Apple Valley, MN, IUCN/SSC Conservation Breeding Specialist Group.

Siregar, R.S.E., Farmer, K.H., Chivers, D., and B. Saragih. 2010. Re-introduction of Bornean orang-utans to Meratus protected forest, East Kalimantan, Indonesia. In: P.S. Soorae, ed. *Global Re-introduction Perspectives 2010: Additional Case-Studies from Around the Globe*, pp. 243-48. Abu Dhabi, UAE, IUCN/SSC Re-introduction Specialist Group.

Smiley Evans, T., Gilardi, K., Lowenstine, L., Ssebide, B., Nizeyimana, F., Noheri, J., Kinani, J., Syahula, E., Cranfield, M., Mazet, J., and C. Johnson. 2018. Human herpes simplex virus 1 (HSV-1) and reintroduction risks for free-ranging mountain gorillas in the Virunga Massif. Abstract of a paper presented at the 27th Congress of the International Primatological Society, Nairobi, Kenya.

Smith, J.H. 2011. *Reintroducing Javan Gibbons (Hylobates moloch): An Assessment of Behavior Preparedness*. MA Thesis, Department of Anthropology, San Diego State University.

Smits, W. 2001. From the desk of Dr. Willie Smits. *Voices from the Wilderness* (Newsletter of the Balikpapan Orangutan Society/USA) 4(1): 12-15.

Smits, W.T.M., Heriyanto, and W. Ramono. 1995. A new method for rehabilitation of orang-utans in Indonesia: A first overview. In: R.D. Nadler, B.M.F. Galdikas, L.K. Sheeran, and N. Rosen, eds. *The Neglected Ape*, pp. 23-27. New York and London, Plenum Press.

Soave, O. 1982. The rehabilitation of chimpanzees and other apes. *Laboratory Primate Newsletter* 21(4): 3-8.

Southwick, C.H. and K.L. Southwick. 1983. Polyspecific groups of macaques on the Kowloon Peninsula, New Territories, Hong Kong. *American Journal of Primatology* 5: 17-24.

Southwick, C.H. and D. Manry. 1987. Habitat and population changes for the Kowloon macaques. *Primate Conservation* 8: 48-49.

Southwick, C.H., Malik, I., and M. E. Siddiqi. 1998. Translocations of rhesus monkeys in India: Prospects and outcomes. *American Journal of Primatology* 45: 209-10. Abstract of presentation at the Twenty-first annual meeting of the American Society of Primatology.

Spehar, S.N., Sheil, D., Harrison, T., Louys, J., Ancrenaz, M., Marshall, A.J., Wich, S.A., Bruford, M.W., and E. Meijaard. 2018. Orangutans venture out of the rainforest and into the Anthropocene. *Science Advances* 4: e1701422.

Spelman, L. 2007. Eastern gorilla orphans: Update. *Gorilla Journal* 35: 8.

Spider Monkey Reintroduction Program – Peru Facebook page, posts dated 12 and 14 February, 11 May, 20 June, 9 October 2014, 21 March, 18 April, 22 May 2015, 20 August, 17 November 2016, 22 March, 5 December 2017, 2 May 2018.

Sponsel, L.D., Slater Brown, D., Bailey, R.C., and R. A. Mitteremeier. 1974. Evaluation of squirrel monkey (*Saimiri sciureus*) ranching on Santa Sofia Island, Amazonas, Colombia. *International Zoo Yearbook* 14: 233-40.

Stahl, L. 2015. Back to the wild. http://www.cbsnews.com/news/zoo-gorilla-family-freed-to-wild-60-minutes 15 March 2015.

Stiles, D., Redmond, I., Cress, D., Nellemann, C., and R.K. Formo. 2013. *Stolen Apes: The illicit Trade in Chimpanzees, Gorillas, Bonobos and Orangutans*. GRID-Arendal.

Stoinski, T. S., Moinde, N., Higashi, H., and T. L. Maple. 1996. Developing a translocation model for Kenyan forest primates. *American Zoo and Aquarium Association Annual Conference Proceedings*, September, 1996: 324-326.

Streicher, U. 2004a. Pygmy lorises re-introduction study in Vietnam. *Reintro Redux* 1, 5-10.

Streicher, U. 2004b. *Aspects of ecology and conservation of the pygmy loris Nycticebus pygmaeus in Vietnam*. PhD Thesis, Ludwig-Maximilians Universität München.

Streciher, U., and T. Nadler. 2003. Re-introduction of pygmy lorises in Vietnam. *Re-introduction News* 23: 37-40.

Struhsaker, T.T. and K.S. Siex. 1998. Translocation and introduction of the Zanzibar red colobus monkey: success and failure with an endangered island endemic. *Oryx* 32: 277-284.

Strum, S. C. 2002. Translocation of three wild troops of baboons in Kenya. *Re-introduction News* 21: 12-15.

Strum, S. C. 2005. Measuring success in primate translocation: A baboon case study. *American Journal of Primatology* 65: 117-140.

Suarez, C. E., Gamboa, E. M., Claver, P. and F. Nassar-Montoya. 2001. Survival and adaptation of a released group of confiscated capuchin monkeys. *Animal Welfare* 10: 191-203.

Sulistyo, F., Fahroni, A., Sriningsih, A.P., Sunderland-Groves, J. and J. Sihite. 2018. Overview of medical interventions in Bornean orangutan reintroduction sites in Kalimantan, Indonesia. Abstract of a paper presented at the 27th Congress of the International Primatological Society, Nairobi, Kenya.

Sumatra Rainforest Institute Facebook page.

Sumatran Orangutan Conservation Programme Facebook page.

Sussman, R. W. and I. Tattersall. 1981. Behavior and ecology of *Macaca fasicularis* in Mauritius: A preliminary study. *Primates* 22: 192-205.

Sussman, R. W. and I. Tattersall. 1986. Distribution, abundance and putative ecological strategy of *Macaca fasicularis* on the island of Mauritius, southwestern Indian Ocean. *Folia Primatologica* 46: 28-43.

Tarrant, B. 1976. Monkey see, monkey do…but FAU's monkey colony isn't do-ing (sic) too well. *Boca Raton News*, 6 December. Available online at https://news.google.com/newspapers?nid=1291&dat=19761206&id=IkBUAAAAIBAJ&sjid=V40DAAAAIBAJ&pg=1793,5241323&hl=en

Tattersall, I. 1977a. The lemurs of the Comoro Islands. *Oryx* 13(5): 445-448.

Tattersall, I. 1977b. Ecology and behavior of *Lemur fulvus mayottensis* (Primates, Lemuriformes). A*nthropological papers of the American Museum of Natural History* 54(4): 425-482.

Taub, D.M. and P. T. Mehlman. 1989. Development of the Morgan Island rhesus monkey colony. *Puerto Rico Health Sciences Journal* 8: 159-169.

Taylor, L.L. and S.H. Lehman. 1997. Predation on an evening bat (*Nycticeius* sp.) by squirrel monkeys (*Saimiri scuireus*) in south Florida. *Florida Scientist* 60(2): 112-117.

Teleki, G. 2001. Sanctuaries for ape refugees. In B.B. Beck, T.S. Stoinski, M. Hutchins, T.L. Maple, B. Norton, A. Rowan, E.F. Stevens, and A. Arluke, eds. *Great Apes and Humans: The Ethics of Coexistence*, pp. 133-149. Washington, DC, Smithsonian Institution Press.

Tingpalapong, M., Watson, W.T., Whitmire, R.E., Chapple, F.E., and J.T. Marshall, Jr. 1981. Reactions of captive gibbons to natural habitat and wild conspecifics after release. *Natural History Bulletin of the Siam Society* 29: 31-40.

Tooze, Z. 2008. From the directors. *Cercopan Annual Report* 2008: 3.

Tooze, Z. J. and L. R. Baker. 2008. Re-introduction of mona monkeys to supplement a depleted population in community forest in southeast Nigeria. In P.S. Soorae, ed. *Global Re-introduction Perspectives: Re-introduction Case-Studies from Around the Globe*, pp. 207-212. Abu Dhabi, UAE, IUCN/SSC Re-introduction Specialist Group.

Trayford, H., Pratje, P., and I. Singleton. (2010) Re-introduction of the Sumatran orangutan in Sumatra, Indonesia. In: P.S. Soorae, ed. *Global Re-introduction Perspectives: Additional Case-Studies from Around the Globe*, pp. 238-242. Abu Dhabi, UAE, IUCN/SSC Re-introduction Specialist Group.

Treves, A. and L. Naughton-Treves. 1997. Case study of a chimpanzee recovered from poachers and temporarily released with wild conspecifics. *Primates* 38(3): 315-324.

Tsalickis, M. 1972. Trapping, husbandry and transport conditions of South American primates destined for research. *International Zoo Yearbook* 12: 23-26.

Tutin, C., Ancrenaz, M., Paredes, J., Vacher-Vallas, M., Vidal, C., Goosens, B., Bruford, M., and A. Jamart. 2001. Conservation biology framework for the release of wild-born orphaned chimpanzees into the Conkouati Reserve, Congo. *Conservation Biology* 15(5): 1247–1257.

Usui, R., Sheeran, L.K., Li, J-H., Sun, L., Wang, X., and J.P. Pritchard. 2014. Park rangers' behaviors and their effects on tourists and Tibetan macaques (*Macaca thibetana*) at Mt. Huangshan, China. *Animals* 4: 546-561.

Valladares-Padua, C., Martins, C.S., Wormell, D., and E.Z. Setz. 2000. Preliminary evaluation of the reintroduction of a mixed wild-captive group of black lion tamarins *Leontopithecus chrysopygus*. *Dodo* 36: 30-38.

Vandenbergh, J.G. 1989. The La Parguera, Puerto Rico colony: Establishment and early studies. *Puerto Rico Health Sciences Journal* 8:117-119.

van der Sandt, C.M.G. 2016. Towards a successful translocation of captive slow lorises (*Nycticebus* spp.) in Borneo: a review and recommendations. Published online at http://dx.doi.org/10.1101/078535

Vanlangendonck, N., Colin, C., Laurans, M., Raballand, E., and T. Humle. 2013. The socio-ecological adaptation of released chimpanzees in Guinea, West Africa. Abstract of a paper presented at the 5th Congress of the European Federation of Primatology, Antwerp, 10-13 September 2013. *Folia Primatologica* 84: 341.

Vié, J-C., and C. Richard-Hansen. 1997. Primate translocation in French Guiana, a preliminary report. *Neotropical Primates* 5: 1-3.

Vié, J--C., Richard-Hansen, C. and C. Fournier-Chambrillon. 2001. Abundance, use of space, and activity patterns of white-faced sakis (*Pithecia pithecia*) in French Guinea. *American Journal of Primatology* 55: 203-221.

Villarreal, S.G. 2010. Estudio poblacional del titi cabeciblanco (*Saguinus oedipus*) en el PNN Tayrona: Del mito a las oportunidades de conservacion. Thesis, Facultad de Estudios Ambientales y Rurales Carrera de Ecologia, Pontficia Universidad Javeriana, Bogota, Colombia.

Villarreal, S.G. and J.D. Amaya-Espinel. 2013. Densidad de una población del titi cabeciblanco (*Saguinus oedipus*) en el Parque Nacional Natural Tayrona y su relevancia en la conservación de la especie en Colombia. In: Defler, T.R., Stevenson, P.R., Bueno, M.L., and D.C. Guzmán-Caro, eds. *Primates Colombianos en Peligre de Extinción*, pp. 173-179. Bogota, Asociación Primatologica Colombiana

Vogel, I., Glöwing, B., Saint Pierre, I., Bayart, F., Contamin, H., and B. de Thoisy. 2002. Squirrel monkey (*Saimiri sciureus*) rehabilitation in French Guiana: A case study. *Neotropical Primates* 10: 147-49.

Voigt, M., Wich, S.A., Ancrenaz, M., Meijaard, E., Abram, N., Banes, G.L., Campbell-Smith, G., d'Arcy, L.J., Delgado, R.A., Erman, A., Gaveau, D., Goossens, B., Heinicke, S., Houghton, M., Husson, S.J., Leiman, A., Sanchez, K.L., Makinuddin, N., Marshall, A.J., Meididit, A., Miettinen, J., Mundry, R., Nardiyono, M., Nurcahyo, A., Odom, K., Panda, A., Prasetyo, D., Priadjati, A., Purnomo, Rafiastanto, A., Russon, A.E., Santika, T., Sihite, J., Spehar, S., Struebig, M., Sulbaran-Romero, E., Tjiu, A., Wells, J., Wilson, K.A., and H. S. Kühl. 2018. Global demand for natural resources eliminated more than 100,000 Bornean orangutans. *Current Biology* 28(5): 761-769.

Wadman, M. 2017. Mauritius invites primate research labs to set up shop. *Science* 356(6337): 472-473.

Walder, C. 2014. *Rehabilitation Assessment of a Juvenile Woolly Monkey (Lagothrix lagothrica poeppigii) Troop on Sumak Allpa Island, Ecuador*. Report submitted for Bowdoin College's Comparative Ecology and Conservation SIT Study Abroad Program.

Wanshel, E. 2016. "World's loneliest chimp, Abandoned on a small island, gets cuddly teddy bear". *Huffington Post*, 9 March 2016.

Ward, M. and A. Nelving. 1999. Island home for chimps. *Sanctuary* 1(1): 56-61.

Warren, K.S. and R.A. Swan. 2002. Re-introduction of orang-utans in Indonesia. *Re-introduction News* 21: 24-26.

Waters, S., El Harrad, A., Amhaouch, Z. and B. Kuběnová. 2016. Releasing confiscated Barbary macaques to improve national awareness of the illegal pet trade in Morocco. In P. S. Soorae, ed. *Global Reintroduction Perspectives 2016: Case-Studies From Around the Globe*, pp. 216-220. Gland, IUCN/SSC Re-introduction Specialist Group and Abu Dhabi, Environmental Agency of Abu Dhabi.

Weber, B. and A. Vedder. 2001. *In the Kingdom of Gorillas*. New York, Simon & Schuster.

Wedana M., Kurniawan, I., Arsan, Z., Wawandono, N. B., Courage, A., and T. King. 2013a. Lessons learned from Javan gibbon and langur rehabilitation and reintroduction project in Java: Reinforcing the isolated Javan langur population in Coban Talun Protected Forest, East Java, Indonesia. *Folia Primatologica* 84(3-5): 344. (Abstract of paper presented at the 5th Congress of the European Federation for Primatology, Antwerp, Belgium 2013).

Wedana M., Kurniawan, I., Arsan, Z., Wawandono, N. B., Courage, A., and T. King. 2013b. Reinforcing the Javan langur population in the Coban Talun Protected Forest, East Java, Indonesia. *Wild Conservation* 1: 31-39.

Wells, K. 1993. This mom teaches her young to walk on the wild side. *The Wall Street Journal*, 22 March 1993: A1, A6.

Wheeler, R.J. 1990. Behavioral characteristics of squirrel monkeys at the Bartlett Estate, Ft. Lauderdale. *Florida Scientist* 53(4): 312-316.

Whittier, C. and K. Fawcett. 2006. Application of the RSG Guidelines in the case of confiscated mountain gorillas, Virunga Massif: Rwanda, Uganda & DRC. *Re-introduction News* 25: 40-41.

Wiek, E. 2014. An IPPL-sponsored gibbon release in Thailand. *International Primate Protection League News* 41(3): 14-15.

Wilcox, C.H., Mubarok, H., Llano Sanchez, K., and N. Waran. 2018. A comparison of released and wild Javan slow loris behaviour. Abstract of a paper presented at the 27th Congress of the International Primatological Society, Nairobi, Kenya.

Williams, D. 2016. Census and local tolerance of *Chlorocebus sabeus* in Dania Beach, Florida. Abstract of a paper presented at the joint meeting of the 26th Congress of the International Primatological Society and the 39th Meeting of the American Society of Primatologists, Chicago, IL, USA.

Williams, D. 2018. Personal communication, e-mail 12 June.

Williamson, E.A. 2017. Personal communication, e-mail 23 July.

Wilson, M.L. and J.G. Elicker. 1976. Establishment, maintenance, and behavior of free-ranging chimpanzees on Ossabaw Island, Georgia, U.S.A. *Primates* 17(4): 451-473.

Wilson, V. 1980. Operation monkey release. *International Primate Protection League Newsletter* 7(2): 12-13.

Wimberger, K. 2009. *Wildlife Rehabilitation in South Africa*. PhD Dissertation, University of KwaZulu-Natal.

Wimberger, K., Downs, C. T., and M. R. Perrin. 2010. Postrelease success of two rehabilitated vervet monkey (*Chlorocebus aethiops*) troops in KwaZulu-Natal, South Africa. *Folia Primatologica* 81: 96-108.

Wisely, S.M., Sayler, K.A., Anderson. C., Boyce, C.L., Klegarth, A.R. and S.A. Johnson. 2018. Macacine Herpesvirus 1 antibody prevalence and DNA shedding among invasive rhesus macaques, Silver Springs State Park, Florida, USA. *Emerging Infectious Diseases*. 2018: 24(2):345-351.

Wolfe, L.D. 2002. Rhesus macaques: A comparative study of two sites, Jaipur, India and Silver Springs, Florida. In A. Fuentes and L.D. Wolfe, eds. *Primates Face to Face: Conservation Implications of Human – Nonhuman Primate Interconnections*, pp. 310-330. Cambridge, UK, Cambridge University Press.

Wolfe, L.D. and E.H. Peters. 1987. History of the free-ranging rhesus monkeys (*Macaca mulatta*) of Silver Springs. *Florida Scientist* 50: 234-245.

Wong, C.L. and I-H. Ni. 2000. Population dynamics of the feral macaques in the Kowloon Hills of Hong Kong. *American Journal of Primatology* 50: 53-66.

Wong, C.L. and G. Chow. 2004. Preliminary results of trial contraceptive treatment with SpayVac™ on wild monkeys in Hong Kong. *Hong Kong Biodiversity* 6: 13-16.

Woodruff, M. C., Lavin, S. R., Atencia, R., Woodruff, G. T., Lambert, F. N., Hill, R. A., Wheaton, C. J., and J. M. Setchell. 2016. Measuring fecal glucocorticoid metabolites during a reintroduction of mandrills (*Mandrillus sphinx*) in the Republic of Congo. Abstract of a paper presented at the joint meeting of the 26th Congress of the International Primatological Society and the 39th Meeting of the American Society of Primatologists, Chicago, IL, USA.

www.afcd.gov.hk

www.aspinallfoundation.org

www.barbarymacaque.org

www.baynews9.com

www.bukitlawang.com

www.chaneekalaweit.blogspot.com

www.cleanmalaysia.com

www.colobusconservation.org

www.ekuatorial.com

www.fiocruz.br

www.fondationlepalnature.org

www.friendsofanimals.org

www.gettyimages.com

www.gibbonproject.org

www.go-east.org

www.gonhs.org

www.gorillasgabon.org

www.gracegorillas.org

www.humanesociety.org

www.iansingletonsocp.com

www.internationalanimalrescue.org

www.janegoodllinstitute.org

www.monkeyjungle.com

www.monosperu.com

www.ngambaisland.org

www.orangutan.org

www.orangutan.or.id

www.orangutan-appeal.org.uk

www.orangutanrepublik.org

www.pan.eco.ch

www.riversidewrc.com

www.sarawakforestry.com

www.savetheliontamarin.org

www.silvery.org.au

www.stcatherinesisland.org

www.sumatranorangutan.org

www.uriacu.org

www.wildlifealliance.org

www.wildlifeatrisk.org

www.wildlifextra.com

www.yorku.ca/arusson/rehab_sites.htm

Yatbantoong, N. 2007. Reintroduction of pileated gibbons (*Hylobates pileatus*): A study in southeastern Thailand. MSc Thesis, Department of Environmental Biology, Mahidol University.

Yeager, C.P. 1997. Orangutan rehabilitation in Tanjung Puting National Park, Indonesia. *Conservation Biology* 11(3): 802-805.

REFERENCES, GENERAL

Anon undated c. BUAV (The British Union for the Abolition of Vivisection) Briefing on Environment Protection and Biodiversity Conservation Amendment (Prohibition of Live Imports of Primates for Research), Bill 2015, Submission 48 - Attachment 3.

Anon. 1998. IUCN Guidelines for Re-introductions. Gland, IUCN/SSC Re-introduction Specialist Group.

Anon. 2002a. *Guidelines for the Placement of Confiscated Live Animals*. Gland, International Union for the Conservation of Nature and Natural Resources.

Baker, L.R. 2002. IUCN/SSC Re-introduction Specialist Group: Guidelines for nonhuman primate re-introductions. *Re-introduction News* 21: 29-57. (Cross-listed as IUCN/SSC 2002).

Beck, B.B. 2016. The role of translocation in primate conservation. In S.A. Wich and A.J. Marshall, eds. *An Introduction to Primate Conservation*, pp. 241-255. Oxford, UK, Oxford University Press.

Beck, B.B. 2017. *A History of Primate Reintroduction*. Accessed at www.drbenjaminbeck.com

Beck, B.B., Rapaport, L.G., Stanley Price, M.R. and A.C. Wilson. 1994. Reintroduction of captive-born mammals. In: P.J.S. Olney, G.M. Mace, and A.T.C. Feistner, eds. *Creative Conservation: Interactive Management of Wild and Captive Animals*, pp. 265-286. London, Chapman and Hall.

Beck, B.B., Walkup, K., Rodrigues, M., Unwin, S., Travis, D., and T. Stoinski. 2007. *Best Practice Guidelines for the Re-introduction of Great Apes*. Gland, IUCN/SSC Primate Specialist Group.

Caldecott, J. and M. Kavanaugh. 1983. Can translocation help wild primates? *Oryx* 17: 135-139.

Campbell, C.O., Cheyne, S.M., and B.M. Rawson. 2015. *Best Practice Guidelines for the Rehabilitation and Translocation of Gibbons*. Gland, IUCN/SSC Primate Specialist Group.

Cheyne, S.M. 2009. The role of reintroduction in gibbon conservation: Opportunities and challenges. In S. Lappan and D.J. Whittaker, eds. *The Gibbons, Developments in Primatology: Progress and Prospects*, pp. 477-496. New York, Springer.

Chivers, D. 1991. Guidelines for re-introductions: procedures and problems. *Symposium of the Zoological Society of London* 62: 88-89.

Custance, D.M., Whiten, A., and T. Fredman. 2002. Social learning and primate reintroduction. *International Journal of Primatology* 23(3): 479-499.

Ewen, J.G., Armstrong, D.P., Parker, K.A., and P.J. Seddon. 2013. *Reintroduction Biology: Integrating Science and Management*. London, Wiley-Blackwell.

Fischer, J. and D.B. Lindenmeyer. 2000. An assessment of the published results of animal relocations. *Biological Conservation* 96: 1-11.

Germano, J.M., Field, K.J., Griffiths, R.A., Clulow, S., Foster, J., Harding, G., and R.R. Swaisgood. 2015. Mitigation-driven translocations: are we moving wildlife in the right direction? *Frontiers in Ecology and the Environment* 13(2): 100-105.

Griffith, B., Scott, M., Carpenter, J.W., and C. Reed. 1989. Translocation as a species conservation tool: Status and strategy. *Science* 24: 477-80.

Bibliography

Guy, A.J., Curnoe, D., and P.B. Banks. 2014. Welfare based primate rehabilitation as a potential conservation strategy: Does it measure up? *Primates* 55: 139-147.

Harcourt, A.H. 1987. Options for unwanted or confiscated primates. *Primate Conservation* 8: 111-113.

Harrington, L.A., Moehrenschlager, A., Gelling, M., Atkinson, R.P.D., Hughes, J., and D.W. Macdonald. 2013. Conflicting and complementary ethics of animal welfare considerations in reintroductions. *Conservation Biology* 27(3): 486-500.

Hockings, K., and T. Humle. 2009. *Best Practice Guidelines for the Prevention and Mitigation of Conflict Between Humans and Great Apes.* Gland, IUCN/SSC Primate Specialist Group.

IUCN. 1998. *Re-introduction Specialist Group: Guidelines for Reintroduction.* Gland, International Union for the Conservation of Nature.

IUCN/SSC. 2002. Re-introduction Specialist Group: Guidelines for nonhuman primate re-introductions. *Re-introduction News* 21: 29-57. (Cross-listed as Baker 2002)

IUCN/SSC. 2013. *Guidelines for Reintroductions and Other Conservation Translocations. Version 1.0.* Gland, IUCN Species Survival Commission.

Junker, J., Kühl, H.S., Orth, L. Smith, R.K., Petrovan, S.O., and W.J. Sutherland. 2017. *Primate Conservation; Global Evidence for the Effects of Interventions.* Cambridge, UK, University of Cambridge.

Kavanagh, M. and J.O. Caldecott. 2013. Strategic guidelines for the translocation of primates and other animals. *The Raffles Bulletin of Zoology*, Supplement 29: 203-209.

Kleiman, D.G. 1989. Reintroduction of captive mammals for conservation. *BioScience* 39: 14-16.

Long, J.L. 2003. *Introduced Mammals of the World.* Collingwood, Victoria, Australia, CSIRO.

Pérez, I., Anadón, J.D., Díaz, M., Nicola, G.G., Tella, J.L. and A. Giménez. 2012. What is wrong with current translocations? A review and a decision-making proposal. *Frontiers in Ecology and the Environment* 10(9): 494-501.

Streier, K.B. 2007. *Primate Behavioral Ecology.* Boston, Allyn and Bacon.

INDEX

Index does not include bibliography, references, or scientific names of animals.

Purposes (of Reintroduction)

Accidental (not including Escape, see Escape below) 5, 73, 187, 300, 312

Aesthetic 5, 71, 256, 272, 273, 293, 300, 318, 320, 322

Commercial iii, vii, 5, 42, 72, 131, 135, 155, 159, 162, 163, 165, 168, 172, 173, 174, 176, 178, 183, 186, 190, 192, 194, 195, 197, 199, 201, 208, 213, 214, 216, 219, 221, 225, 233, 252, 257, 258, 262, 294, 298, 304, 306, 308, 310, 312, 314, 318, 320

Conservation iii, 4, 12, 38, 40, 46, 54, 59, 65, 69, 71, 81, 82, 84, 123, 136, 140, 148, 152, 155, 156, 164, 194, 196, 204, 217, 235, 236, 238, 239, 240, 243, 244, 249, 268, 270, 272, 274, 279, 281, 283, 286, 287, 289, 290, 294, 298, 300, 302, 304, 306, 308, 310, 312, 314, 316, 318, 320, 322

Escape 5, 48, 49, 50, 143, 168, 174, 177, 197, 213, 223, 245, 265, 269, 290, 298, 304, 308, 310, 316, 320

Politically Symbolic 155, 306

Recreational 5, 221, 293, 314, 322

Religious 5, 131, 135, 161, 172, 181, 306

Research iii, vii, 5, 14, 42, 72, 87, 95, 101, 107, 113, 118, 130, 133, 134, 136, 137, 144, 145, 149, 152, 159, 172, 173, 174, 179, 180, 183, 184, 190, 192, 197, 198, 199, 201, 204, 208, 209, 210, 211, 212, 219, 226, 228, 229, 242, 246, 247, 248, 251, 252, 258, 260, 261, 262, 264, 268, 270, 274, 275, 276, 279, 281, 283, 287, 289, 290, 294, 296, 298, 300, 302, 304, 306, 308, 310, 312, 314, 316, 318, 320, 322

Unspecified/Unknown 5, 21, 61, 149, 162, 180, 185, 186, 188, 191, 206, 253, 254, 255, 288, 291, 292, 295, 298, 300, 306, 310, 312, 316, 318, 320

Welfare iii, 4, 12, 14, 19, 25, 27, 29, 33, 38, 40, 46, 48, 51, 54, 55, 57, 59, 65, 69, 72, 76, 81, 82, 84, 87, 91, 93, 94, 95, 96, 101, 107, 113, 115, 118, 120, 123, 128, 130, 131, 132, 133, 134, 136, 139, 140, 142, 143, 144, 145, 146, 147, 150, 152, 153, 154, 156, 157, 158, 161, 163, 164, 172, 174, 178, 179, 180, 181, 182, 184, 195, 196, 198, 201, 202, 205, 206, 207, 208, 209, 210, 211, 212, 217, 218, 219, 223, 224, 225, 226, 228, 229, 231, 234, 235, 236, 237, 239, 240, 241, 245, 246, 247, 248, 249, 250, 251, 252, 256, 258, 259, 260, 261, 262, 264, 272, 273, 275, 276, 277, 279, 281, 283, 284, 293, 294, 298, 300, 302, 304, 306, 308, 310, 312, 314, 316, 318, 320, 322

Nonhuman Primates Mentioned by Personal Name in Text

Aimee 55,

Amahoro 77, 78, 79

Arthur 87, 89, 90

Baby Mowgli 233

Bahati 13-15

Bee (fictional) 55

Bitorwa 81, 82

Bob 86

Bonne Année 74-76, 78, 84

Boubane 51

Casimir 73

Cynthia 87, 89

Djala 70

Dorilla 233

Julia 78, 79

Julie 72, 73, 78, 82

Lucy 28- 32

Marianne 28, 29, 30

Mikey 222

Mvuyekure 83, 84

Ponso 40

Robert 53

Shirley 15, 49

Sunday 18

Tia 55

Toto 55

Ubuzima 82-84

William 24, 25

People Mentioned by Name in Text (exclusive of references and bibliography)

Altmann, Stuart 171, 172

Anderson, Jim vii, 200

Andre, Claudine vii, 59

Angst, Walter vii

Aspinall, Damian 62, 70

Aspinall, John 62

Attwater, Helen 62

Attwater, Mark 62

Aveling, Conrad 118

Aveling, Rosalind 118

Bartlett, Frederic Clay 252

Beaver, Paul vii

Becker, Vitor 250

Bennett, Sara 235

Bock, Kaitlyn vii

Boerner, Monica 118

Bonang, Rene 30

Boubane, Bruno 30

Brewer, Eddie 24

Brewer Marsden, Stella 23, 24-28, 30-33

Brindamour, Rod 96, 97

Brotman, Betsy 34, 37, 38

Carpenter, C. R. 137, 169-172

Carter, Janis vii, 22, 26-33, 48, 51, 55

Chamove, Arnold vii, 200

Cocks, Leif vii, 123

Coimbra Filho, Adelmar 267

Courage, Amos 62

Cox, Debbie vii

Curtis, Larry vii, 28

Darsono, Charles 193, 194

Davenport, R.K. 89

Davenport, Tim viii

Defler, Thomas viii, 235

Deschryver, Adrian 72, 73

De Silva, G.S. 97, 117

Donaldson, Andrea viii, 206, 229

Dorkenoo, Helen 47

DuMond, Grace 189

DuMond, Joseph 189

Evans, Sian vii

Farmer, Kay 22, 48

Fossey, Dian 74-76, 78, 84, 96

Fowler, Stephanie viii

Frey, Regina 118

Gadsby, Liza 48, 212

Galdikas, Birute 96, 97

Goodall, Jane 96

Gregorio, Patty viii

Hannah, Alison 22, 31

Harcourt, Alexander 77-79

Hare, Brian viii

Harrisson, Barbara 86-89, 97, 116, 117

Harrisson, Tom 86

Herzfeld, Chris viii, 31

Hirata, Satoshi viii

Horr, David 89

Horwich, Rob viii, 244

Idani, Gen'ichi 57

Jamart, Aliette 42, 43

Jenkins, Peter 48, 212

Index

Johnson, Rodney 179

Kalpers, José 78

Kierulff, Cecilia viii

King, Tony viii

Leakey, Louis 96

Leroy, Yvette 61, 62

Lindbergh, Scott 251

Koidja, Germaine Djenemaya 40

Konstant, William 232

MacKinnon, John 89

Malik, Iqual 179

Marshall, Andy ii

McGregor, Gordon 200, 201

McGrew, Bill viii, 22, 31

Mensink, M. 79

Miljo, Rita 207

Mittermeier, Russell viii, 232, 267

Morel, Dominique viii

Msindai, Nadezda viii

Murage, A.B.

Nekaris, Anna 285

Noell, Anna Mae 28

Noell, Bob 28

Palmer, Alexandra viii, 89, 90

Petter, Jean-Jacque 286

Preutz, Jill 54, 55

Prince, Alfred 34, 38

Raballand, Estelle 53

Rettberg-Beck, Beate viii

Rijksen, Herman 103, 116, 117, 120

Rijksen-Grattsma, Ans 116

Ruiz-Miranda, Carlos viii

Russon, Anne viii, 92

Rylands, Anthony viii

Shumaker, Rob viii, 205

Smits, Willie 103

Southwick, Charles 165

Stoinski, Tara viii

Streier, Karen 2

Strum, Shirley 209, 210

Tooey, Colonel 166, 167

Tsalickis, Mike 257

Tutin, Caroline viii

Uetz, Peter viii

von der Becke, Jean-Pierre 74, 75

Wich, Serge ii,

Williams, Missy viii

Williamson, Liz viii

Wrangham, Richard 14, 15

Yoshiba, Kenji 89

Common Names of Animals Mentioned in Text

Agile Gibbon 143-145, 304

Alligator 295

Ant 36, 269

Antelope 26

Anubis Baboon 208, 312

Assassin bug 160

Aye-Aye 286, 320

Baboon 26, 27, 53, 172, 207-210, 223, 312

Baboon, Anubis 208, 312

Baboon, Chacma 207, 208, 312

Baboon, Olive 208-210, 312

Baboon, Yellow 208, 209, 312

Barbary Macaque 2, 154-157, 306

Black and White Colobus Monkey 205, 206, 312

Black and White Ruffed Lemur 287-290, 320

Black-and-Gold Howler Monkey 251, 316

Black-faced Spider Monkey 239, 240, 316

Black-handed Spider Monkey 237

Black Howler Monkey 243-246, 248, 251, 252, 316

Black Leaf Monkey 147

Black Lion Tamarin 269, 270, 318

Black Spider Monkey 237-240, 314, 316

Black-handed Spider Monkey 237

Black Tufted-eared Marmoset 272, 273, 320

Blue Monkey 217, 218, 227, 228, 314

Bonnet Macaque 161, 306

Bonobo 57-60, 62, 63, 125, 300

Boobies 171

Bornean Orangutan 86-115, 300, 302

Brown Capuchin Monkey 260, 318

Brown Howler Monkey 250, 316

Brown Lemur 292, 293, 322

Bushbaby 203, 206

Index

Caracal 224

Cat Ba Langur 147, 306

Chacma Baboon 207, 208, 312

Chimpanzee 2, 11-59, 61, 63, 67, 69, 79, 125, 210, 212, 298, 300

Collared Brown Lemur 290, 293, 294, 322

Colobus Monkey 26, 29, 203-206, 312

Common Marmoset 259, 265, 272, 273, 320

Cotton-top Tamarin 261, 262, 318

Crab-eating Macaque (see also Long-tailed Macaque) vii, 135, 149, 158, 165, 174, 184-196, 197, 202, 208, 310

Crowned Lemur 292, 322

Crocodile 26

Delacour's Langur 148

Delacour's Leaf Monkey 148, 306

Diamedled Sifaka 287, 290, 320

Douc Langur 147, 306

Drill 48, 49, 212, 312

Dwarf Lemur 292

Ebony Leaf Monkey 149-152

Eel 59

Elephant 223

Felid, Feline 26, 274

Formosan Rock Macaque 165, 196-198, 310

Fossa 294

Genet 26

Geoffroy's Marmoset 274, 320

Geoffroy's Spider Monkey 237, 238, 316

Gibbon 2, 101, 116, 128-146, 152, 153, 169, 304, 306

Gibbon, Agile 143-145, 304

Gibbon, Hoolock 145, 146, 306

Gibbon, Mueller's 132, 304

Gibbon, Pileated 130, 304

Gibbon, Silvery 133, 134, 304

Gibbon, White-handed 135-142, 192, 304

Gibbon, Yellow-cheeked Crested 129, 304

Golden-handed Tamarin 263, 264, 318

Golden-headed Lion Tamarin 271, 272, 320

Golden Lion Tamarin 232, 264-269, 271-273, 318

Gorilla 43, 44, 48, 61-85, 125, 210, 212, 300

Gorilla, Grauer's 2, 72-82, 300

Gorilla, Lowland 61-72, 300

Gorilla, Mountain 2, 82-85, 300

Grauer's Gorilla 2, 72-82, 300

Green Monkey (see also Vervet, Grivet) 219-229

Grivet (see also Green Monkey, Vervet) 219-229

Guenon 210, 216

Harpy Eagle 233, 240

Hippopotamus 18, 26

Hoolock 145, 146, 306

Howler Monkey 172, 246-249, 251, 252, 268

Hyena 26

Japanese Macaque 165, 182-184, 197, 208, 310

Javan Grizzled Leaf Monkey 152, 153, 306

Kirk's Monkey 203, 204

Javan Langur 149-153, 306

Langur, Cat Ba, 147, 306

Langur, Delacour's 148, 306

Langur, Douc 147, 306

Langur, Javan 149-153, 306

Lemur, Black and White Ruffed 287-290, 320

Lemur, Brown 292, 293, 322

Lemur, Collared Brown 290, 293, 294, 322

Lemur, Crowned 292, 322

Lemur, Dwarf 292

Lemur, Mongoose 291, 322

Lemur, Red-collared Brown 293, 322

Lemur, Red-fronted Brown 290, 320

Lemur, Ring-tailed 295, 322

Lemur, White-fronted 295, 322

Leopard 26, 117, 156, 209, 223, 224

Lion 223

Lion-tailed Macaque 159, 306

Long-tailed Macaque (see also Crab-eating Macaque) vii, 132, 143, 174, 184-196

Loris 2, 101, 275-285, 320

Loris, Pygmy 275, 276, 320

Loris, Slow 276-285, 320

Lowland Gorilla 61-72, 300

Macaque, Barbary 2, 147, 154, 155, 156, 157, 306

Macaque, Bonnet 161, 306

Macaque, Crab-eating (see also Macaque, Long-tailed) vii, 135, 149, 158, 165, 185-196, 197, 202, 310

Macaque, Formosan Rock 165, 196-198, 310

Macaque, Japanese 165, 182-184, 197, 208, 310

Macaque, Lion-tailed 159, 306

Index

Macaque, Long-tailed (see also Macaque, Crab-eating) vii, 132, 143, 185-196, 208, 310

Macaque, Pig-tailed 140, 162-165, 174, 177, 202, 224, 306, 308

Macaque, Rhesus vii, 2, 134, 135, 158, 164-183, 190, 213, 253, 308

Macaque, Stump-tail 174, 198-202, 310, 312

Macaque, Sulawesi Black 161, 185, 306

Macaque, Taiwan 196-198, 310

Macaque, Tibetan 158, 159, 165, 190, 306

Manatee 26

Mandrill 57, 210, 211, 312

Mangabey, Red-capped 230, 314

Mantled Howler Monkey 246-249, 316

Marmoset, Black Tufted-eared 272, 273, 320

Marmoset, Common 259, 265, 272, 273, 320

Marmoset, Geoffroy's 274, 320

Marsupial 188

Mona Monkey 214-217, 312

Mongoose Lemur 291, 322

Monitor Lizard 26

Monkey, Black-and-Gold Howler 251, 316

Monkey, Black and White Colobus 205, 206, 312

Monkey, Black Howler 243-246, 248, 251, 252, 316

Monkey, Black Leaf 147

Monkey, Black Spider 237-240, 314, 316

Monkey, Black-faced Spider 239-240, 316

Monkey, Black-handed Spider 237

Monkey, Blue 217, 218, 227, 228, 314

Monkey, Brown Capuchin 260, 318

Monkey, Brown Howler 250, 316

Monkey, Colobus 26, 29

Monkey, Delacour's Langur 148

Monkey, Delacour's Leaf 148, 306

Monkey, Ebony Leaf 149-152

Monkey, Geoffroy's Spider 237, 238, 316

Monkey, Green (see also Vervet, Grivet) 219-229

Monkey, Howler 172, 241-252, 268, 316

Monkey, Javan Grizzled Leaf 152, 153, 306

Monkey, Kirk's 203, 204

Monkey, Mantled Howler 246-249, 316

Monkey, Mona 214-217, 312

Monkey, Night (see also Monkey, Owl) 235

Monkey, Owl (see also Monkey, Night) 235

Monkey, Patas 171, 213, 214, 312

Monkey, Proboscis 143, 154, 306

Monkey, Red Colobus 203, 204, 312

Monkey, Red Howler 241-243, 316

Monkey, Red-faced Spider 237

Monkey, Saki 235, 261, 318

Monkey, Silver Leaf 147, 306

Monkey, Spider 169, 172, 235, 237-240, 246

Monkey, Spot-nosed 252

Monkey, Squirrel 2, 177, 235, 253-259, 316, 318

Monkey, Sykes 218, 219, 314

Monkey, White-throated Capuchin 260, 318

Monkey, Woolly 233-235

Mountain Gorilla 2, 82-85, 300

Moustached Tamarin 263, 318

Mueller's Gibbon 132, 304

Muriqui 235, 236, 314

Night Monkey (see also Owl Monkey) 235

Olive Baboon 208-210, 312

Orangutan ii, 2, 86-127, 169, 300, 302

Orangutan, Bornean 2, 86-115, 300, 302

Orangutan, Sumatran 2, 89, 116-127, 302

Otter 26

Owl Monkey (see also Night Monkey) 235

Patas Monkey 171, 213, 214, 312

Pig-tailed Macaque 140, 162-165, 174, 177, 202, 223, 306, 308

Pileated Gibbon 130, 304

Porcupine 26

Proboscis Monkey 143, 154, 306

Puma 237

Pygmy Loris 275, 276, 320

Python 26

Rat 189

Red Colobus Monkey 203, 204, 312

Red Howler Monkey 241-243, 316

Red-capped Mangabey 230, 314

Red-collared Brown Lemur 293

Red-faced Spider Monkey 237

Red-fronted Brown Lemur 290

Red-handed Tamarin 264, 318

Reptile 26, 188

Rhesus Macaque vii, 134, 135, 158, 164-183, 190,

213, 253, 308

Ring-tailed Lemur 295, 322

Saki Monkey 235, 261, 310

Samango 217, 227

Serval 224

Siamang 128, 146, 304

Sifaka 287, 290, 320

Silver Leaf Monkey 147, 149, 186, 306

Silvery Gibbon 133, 134, 304

Slow Loris 276-285, 320

Snake 15, 26, 29, 55, 58, 224, 279

Spider Monkey 169, 172, 235, 237-240, 246

Spot-nosed Monkey 252

Squirrel Monkey 2, 177, 235, 253-259, 316, 318

Stump-tail Macaque 174, 198-202, 310, 312

Sulawesi Black Macaque 161, 185, 306

Sumatran Orangutan 116-127, 302

Surili 153

Sykes Monkey 203, 206, 218, 219, 314

Taiwan Macaque 196-198, 310

Tamarin, Black Lion 269, 270, 318

Tamarin, Cotton-top 261, 262, 318

Tamarin, Golden-handed 263, 264, 318

Tamarin, Golden-headed 271, 272, 320

Tamarin, Golden Lion 232, 264-269, 271-273, 318

Tamarin, Moustached 263, 318

Tamarin, Red-handed 264, 318

Tibetan Macaque 158, 159, 165, 190, 306

Tick 41

Uakari 235

Vervet (see also Green Monkey, Grivet) vii, 2, 26, 163, 174, 203, 204, 206, 219-229, 314

Warthog 26

Western Lowland Gorilla (see Lowland Gorilla or Gorilla, Lowland)

White-fronted Lemur 295, 322

White-handed Gibbon 135-142, 192, 304

White-throated Capuchin Monkey 260, 318

Woolly Monkey 233-235, 314

Yellow Baboon 208, 209, 312

Yellow-cheeked Crested Gibbon 129, 304

Places

Abuko Nature Reserve 22, 28, 31

Aceh 121

Afi Mountain Wildlife Sanctuary 48, 49, 212, 298, 312

Africa 15, 17, 22, 79, 81, 125, 126, 154, 155, 214, 215, 220, 252

Agaltepec Island 246, 316

Aichi Prefecture 182

Algeria 154

Aligarh 178, 308

Alloa Inch 200, 201, 310

Amacayacu National Park 234, 314

Amazon River 239, 257

Amphoe Saiyok 136, 138

Analamazaotra Special Reserve 287, 289, 322

Andaman Islands 162, 306

Angkor Temple 131, 147, 304, 306

Angaur Island 187, 188, 310

Anguilla 220, 314

Anhui Province 159

Anjouan 291, 322

Aomori Prefecture 196, 310

Arabuko Sokoke National Forest 218, 314

Arashiyama 184

Area de Conservacion Regional Communal de Tamshiyacu-Tahuayo 233, 314

Argentina 251, 316

Arunachal Pradesh 146

Asia 125, 126, 147, 154

Asolo Batti 181, 308

Atlantic Coastal Forest, 259, 272, 273

Atlantic Ocean 175

Atlas Mountains 156, 157, 306

Australasia 189

Australia 79, 121, 123, 134

Azagny National Park 39, 298

Baan Chum Pee 141, 304

Baboon Island 26, 27, 30, 31, 298

Bacan Island 161, 306

Bahia 250, 271, 272, 273

Bako National Park 86, 87, 97, 300

Bali 103, 149, 186

Bandama River 39, 40, 298

Bandung 281

Bangalore 161

Barbados vii, 220, 314

Barro Colorado 237, 238, 316

Bartlett Estate 252, 316

Batang Ai National Park 96, 302

Batéké Plateau National Park 66, 67, 70, 71, 300

Batutegi Protected Forest/Reserve 163, 164, 196, 276-278, 308, 310, 320

Bay of Antogil 286

Bear Island 41, 298

Beaufort 177, 308

Belgium 78, 79

Belize 237, 243, 245, 316

Benin 215

Berenty Private Reserve 290, 293, 320, 322

Bermuda 137, 199

Betampona Reserve 288, 289, 320

Bogor 164, 196, 277, 282

Bohorok 118-120, 302

Bombay 174, 308

Boqueron Commonwealth Forest 213, 312

Borneo 2, 86, 87, 96, 102, 103, 116, 122, 125, 126, 128, 143, 145, 277, 278, 279, 280, 281, 282, 283, 284, 285, 304, 320

Bosque La Montañita 262, 318

Brasilia National Park 251, 316

Brazil 173, 235, 236, 249, 250, 251, 259, 264-273, 308, 314, 316, 318, 320

Brazzaville 63, 65

Brokopondo Valley 241, 256, 260, 264

Bukit Baka Bukit Raya National Park 109, 110, 114, 115, 143, 144, 302, 304

Bukit Barisan National Park 277

Bukit Batikap Bukit Raya Conservation Forest 109, 110, 112, 302

Bukit Tigapuluh National Park 121, 122, 302

Burkina Faso 220

Burma 162

Burundi 77

Cabo Rio 171

Cairo 83

Calcutta 170

Cali 262

Camagüey Archipelago 201, 224, 225

Cambodia 130, 304, 306

Cameroon 215

Canarreos Archipelago 163, 192, 224, 225

Cape of Good Hope 170

Cape Verde Islands 219, 220, 314

Caribbean 214, 220, 252

Cat Ba National Park/Island 147, 148, 306

Cat Tien National Park 129, 276, 304, 320

Cayo Campo 192, 310

Cayo Cantiles 163, 224, 308, 314

Cayo Guajaba 201, 312

Cayo Romano 224, 314

Cayo Santiago vii, 134, 135, 169-173, 304, 308

Central Kalimantan 96, 103, 105, 107, 109, 110, 112, 143, 145, 302

Chiang Mai Province 141, 142, 304

Chiba Prefecture 174, 308

China 158, 159, 174, 306, 308, 310

Chumphon Province 195

Coban Talun Protected Forest 152, 306

Cockscomb Basin Wildlife Sanctuary 243, 244, 316

Colombia 234, 235, 257, 260-262, 314, 318

Comoros Islands 291, 292, 322

Congo (see Republic of Congo)

Congo River 65

Conkouati-Douli Reserve/National Park 42, 43, 45, 57, 211, 298, 312

Connecticut 189

Cordoba 251, 262, 316

Costa Rica 248, 249, 316

Côte d'Ivoire (see Ivory Coast)

Cross River National Park 217, 230, 312, 314

Cuba 163, 173, 174, 192, 201, 224, 225, 308, 310, 312, 314

Cuc Phuong National Park 148, 275, 320

Cuerva Island 170, 171, 213, 308, 312

Dania Beach 222, 314

Darcy Ribeiro Municipal Reserve 271

Delamere Estates 206, 312

Delhi 179, 180, 181

Deli Island 194, 310

Democratic Republic of Congo 57, 58, 63, 72, 77, 80, 81, 83, 84, 300

Democratic Republic of São Tomé and Príncipe (see São Tomé, Príncipe) 312

Desecheo Island 170, 171, 308

Diani 219, 229, 314

Index

Diarra River 51, 298

Dilley 184

Don Chao Poo Forest Park 195

Dong Nai Biosphere Reserve 276, 318

Duma Manzi Game Reserve 226, 314

East Java 151-153, 284, 306

East Kalimantan 102, 103, 105, 107, 109, 112, 302, 306

Ecuador 2, 233, 314

Egypt 83

England (see also UK) 62

Entabeni State Forest 218

Espiritu Santo 236, 314

External Department of Mayotte (see Mayotte)

Fazenda Mosquito (see Mosquito Farm)

Fazenda Taquera 271, 320

Fazenda União 266

Federation of St Kitts and Nevis 314

Firozpur-Jhirka 181, 308

Flor de Catemaco 247, 316

Florida 2, 28, 166, 175, 176, 189, 222, 252-256, 308, 310, 314, 316, 318

Florida Keys vii, 175, 308

Fofo 219

Fongoli 54, 300

Fort Dauphin 293

Fort Lauderdale 252, 316

France 251, 314, 322

French External Department of Mayotte (see Mayotte)

French Guiana 237, 241, 258, 261, 263, 314, 316, 318

Gabon (see Republic of Gabon)

Gambia (see also The Gambia) 22, 24, 25, 28, 32, 79, 220, 298

Georgia 41, 159, 295

Germany 156

Ghana 220

Gibraltar 2, 154, 155, 306

Gordon River 255, 318

Grande Comore 291, 322

Greater Sunda Islands 188

Green Island 254, 318

Grenada 214, 215, 312

Guanabara Bay 173

Guayacán Island 170, 171, 213, 312

Guinea 47, 48, 51, 52, 55, 219, 298

Guinea Bissau 219

Gulf of Guinea 214

Gulf of Mexico 167, 175

Gulf of Thailand 135

Gunung Gede-Pangrango National Park 133

Gunung Leuser National Park 116, 117, 118, 122, 302

Gunung Palung National Park 114, 302

Gunung Sibela Nature Reserve 162

Gunung Tarak Protected Forest/National Park 114, 280, 302

Hall's Island 137, 199, 304

Hampapak Reserve 145, 304

Hato Flores Moradas 242, 316

Haut Niger National Park 52, 300

Hawaii 254

Hong Kong 158, 164, 165, 306, 308, 310

Hugh Taylor Birch State Park 252

Iberian Peninsula 155

Ibitipoca State Park/Private Reserve 235, 314

Ifrane National Park 157, 306

Iko Esai 216, 312

Ilet-la-Mère 258, 318

Ilha de Pinheiro 173, 174, 308

India 145, 146, 161, 162, 169, 170, 172, 174, 175, 178-181, 182, 306, 308

Indonesia 99, 102, 133, 134, 143, 150, 151, 153, 161, 163, 188, 193, 277, 282, 302, 304, 306, 308, 310, 320

Inuyuama 182

Ipassa Island 21, 298

Ipassa Makokou Biosphere Reserve 21, 61, 298, 300

Irian Jaya 188

Isinga Island 17, 20, 298

Isishlengeni Game Farm 227, 314

Isle of Pines 173, 174, 308

Ivindo River 21, 61

Ivory Coast 38, 39, 40, 298

Izushima Island 196, 310

Jambi 121

Jammu 182

Japan 103, 174, 182, 184, 196, 308, 310, 312

Index

Java 2, 103, 122, 150, 186, 277-283, 285, 320

Jayapura 188, 310

Jozani Park 203

Kabaena Island 185, 310

Kabili Sepilok Forest Reserve 91, 302

Kagoshima Prefecture 183

Kahuzi-Biega National Park 72, 73, 77, 81, 300

Kaja Island 111

Kalimantan (see also East Kalimantan, Central Kalimantan, West Kalimantan) 280, 320

Kam Shan Country Park 165, 190, 306, 308, 310

Kao Tao 198, 310

Kapuas River 143

Karura Forest 205, 206, 312

Kashmir 175

Kasungu National Park 208, 312

Kehje Sewen Forest 102, 105-107, 302

Kekopey Ranch 209

Kenya 205, 206, 209, 218, 219, 229, 312, 314

Kerfalya Island 47, 298

Ketapang 114, 115, 278, 280

Khao Kheio-Khao Chompoo Wildlife Sanctuary 130, 304

Khao Phra Thaew 139, 141, 304

Kibale Forest/National Park 13, 15, 298

Kichwele Forest Reserve 203, 204, 312

Kigali 77

Kii Peninsula 196, 310

Kijima Island 191, 192, 197, 208, 310

Kipiriri 205, 206

Ko Klet Kaeo Island 135, 136, 304

Kondang Merak Protected Forest 151, 284, 306, 320

Kondowe 207, 312

Konkoure River 47

Kouilou River 56

Kowloon Hills/County Parks 158, 164, 165, 190, 306, 308, 310

Kowloon Reservoir 164

Kruger National Park 207, 217, 312, 314

Kubah National Park 96, 302

Kuching 86, 87

Kuno National Park 181, 308

Kure Atoll 254, 318

KwaZulu-Natal Province 226, 227, 228, 314

Laikipia Plateau 209, 312

Lajas 171

Lake Catemaco 199, 246, 316

Lake Edward 17

Lake Gatun 237

Lake Guri 241

Lake Kariba 223, 314

Lake Victoria 11, 19

Lake Wales 254, 318

Lal Kuan Public Park 179, 308

Lamandau Wildlife Reserve 98, 99, 302

Laos 163

Laredo 184

Las Tuxtlas Biosphere Reserve 247

Lefini Faunal Reserve 63, 64, 67, 300

Lékédi Park 70, 210, 312

Lesio-Louna Reserve/Sanctuary 63, 64, 65, 300

Lesser Antilles 220

Lesser Sunda Islands 186, 188

Liberia 22, 34, 37, 39, 298

Limpopo Province 207, 312

Lion Rock Country Park 165, 190, 306, 308, 310

Little Bassa Island 36

Little Bassa River 34, 35, 298

Loango National Park 71, 72

Loggerhead Key 175, 308

Lois Key 175, 308

Lombok Island 149, 186, 188, 306, 310

Lorica 262

Los Llanos Orientales 260, 318

Louna River 63

Lucknow 169

Luo Scientific Reserve 58, 300

Madagascar 286-295, 320, 322

Mae Hong Son Province 142

Mae On National Reserve Forest 141

Mahombo Special Reserve 286

Malawi 208, 312

Malaysia 86, 87, 88, 116, 300, 302, 304

Mandioli Island 161

Mantangi River 109

Marak Island 128, 304

Maringa-Lopori-Wamba 58, 300

Masigit-Kareumbi Conservation Forest 281

Masingini Forest Reserve 203, 204, 312

Mathura 180

Mato dos Luna 235

Mauritania 220

Mauritius vii, 186, 310

Mayingini Forest Reserve 203, 312

Mayotte 292, 322

Medan 122

Meetha Pur 179, 308

Mehao Wildlife Sanctuary 145, 306

Meratus Protection Forest 102, 104, 106, 107, 109, 302

Mexico 199, 246-248, 310, 316

Miami 189, 310

Micronesia 187

Minas Gerais 235, 236, 314

Mintin Island 143, 145, 304

Mirador Pilapa 246, 316

Mohéli 291, 322

Monkey Bay National Park 245, 316

Morgan Island vii, 171, 177, 178, 308

Morocco 154, 156, 157, 306

Morondava 290

Morrillo del Diablo Key 173, 308

Morro do Diabo State Park 270, 318

Mosquito Farm 270, 318

Mount Asserik 24

Mount Ciremai National Park 281, 320

Mount Halimun-Salak National Park 281, 283, 320

Mount Huangshan 159, 306

Mount Hyang 150, 306

Mount Puntang of Malabar 133, 304

Mount Sawal Forest 281, 283, 320

Mount Semeru 150, 306

Mount Tarak 280, 320

Mount Tilu Nature Reserve 134, 153, 304, 306

Mpassa Reserve 66, 67

Mukda Han Province 195

Mumbai 174, 308

Myanmar 162

Nagrota 182, 308

Nairobi 205, 218

Naivasha 206, 312

Naples 255, 318

Naroansetra 286

Ndouna Island 65

Nebraska 287, 289

Nepal 170

Netherlands 28, 314

Nevis vii, 220, 314

New Delhi 308

New Guinea 188

New World/Neotropical (Primates) 232-274

New York 170

Ngamba Island 19, 57

Ngombe 56

Ngezi-Vumawimbi Forest Reserve 203, 312

Nigeria 15, 48, 212, 213, 215-217, 230, 298, 312, 314

Niokola Koba National Park 23-28, 30, 298

Niteroi 271, 272

Nojima Island 197, 310

Nokrek National Park 146, 306

Nong Yai Water Reservoir 195, 310

North Sumatra 122, 146

Nosara 249

Nosy Hara 292, 322

Nosy Mangabe 286, 287, 295, 320

Ntendeka Wilderness Area 227, 314

Nyandarua 206

Ocala 166

Ocklawaha River 167, 253

Ôhirayama Mountain 182, 197, 208, 310

Omaha 265, 287, 289

Onejima Island 196, 310

Orique Island 72

Oshima Island 196

Ossabaw Island 41

Pacaya Samiria National Reserve 239, 316

Padre Island 263, 318

Pafuri 217, 314

Palau 310

Palau Kaget Nature Reserve 154, 306

Index

Panama 237, 262, 316

Panama City 238, 262

Papua 188

Parc de la Lékédi 70

Parc National des Volcans (see Volcanoes National Park)

Pemba Island 203, 204, 312

Peoples Republic of China (see China)

Pernambuco 259

Peru 233, 239, 263, 314, 316, 318

Petit Evengue 71, 72, 300

Phuket Island 139-141, 304

Pilibhut National Park 181, 308

Pinus Jantho Nature Reserve 121, 302

Poço das Antas Biological Reserve 265, 318

Pointe Noir 42, 43, 56, 63

Prachuap Khirikhan Province 195

Príncipe 214, 215, 312

Puerto Rico 2, 135, 169-173, 177, 199, 213, 304, 308, 312

Pusuk Park 186

Raccoon Key 174-176

Republic of Cabo Verde 314

Republic of Congo 42, 43, 56, 61-63, 66, 67, 69, 70, 211, 298, 312

Republic of Gabon 21, 61, 62, 66, 67, 69-72, 210, 214, 298, 300, 312

Rimba Raya Biodiversity Reserve 98

Rio de Janeiro 173, 249, 264, 265, 269-273, 318, 320

Rio Napo 233, 314

River Forth 200

River Gambia 26, 27, 31, 32

River Gambia National Park 25-27, 298

Robertsfield (Liberia) 34

Rubondo Island 11, 12, 298

Rungan River 111

Rwanda 74, 77, 81-84, 300

Sabah 88

Saint/St Catherines Island 159, 295, 306, 322

Saiyok 136, 188, 304

Saltinho Biological Reserve 259, 318

Sandakan 89

San German, 171

San Juan 170

- 387 -

San Pedro 233

Santa Bonita Reserve 250, 316

Santa Sofia Island 257, 318

Santiago 219

Sao Paulo 270

São Tomé 214, 215, 312

Sarasota 167

Savandurga Forest Reserve 161, 306

Scotland 200, 310

Sebana Seco 199

Semenggoh/Semengok Forest Reserve 93, 132, 302, 304

Senegal 23, 24, 51, 54, 219, 220, 298, 300

Sepilok Forest Reserve 88-91, 302

Serra da Tiririca State Park 271

Shing Mun Country Park 165, 190, 306, 308, 310

Sierra Bermeja 171, 213, 312

Sierra Leone 49, 298

Silver River 166, 167, 253, 308, 318

Silver Springs vii, 166, 253

Silver Springs State Park 167, 176

Singapore 191

Sinnamary River 241, 318

Sint Eustatius 220, 314

South Africa 207, 217, 225-228, 228, 312, 314

South Carolina 171, 177, 308

South Kalimantan 154

South Tapanuli Forest 146, 306

Spice Islands 162

St Kitts vii, 220, 224, 314

St Martin/St Maarten 220, 221, 314

Sulawesi 161, 185

Sumak Allpa 3

Sumatra 2, 86, 116, 121, 125, 126, 128, 132, 163, 164, 193, 196, 276-285, 304, 308, 310, 320

Sunda Islands 188

Sungai Wain Protection Forest 102-107, 109, 302

Surinam 241, 256, 260, 264, 316, 318

Surinam River 318

Tabin Wildlife Reserve 90, 93-95, 302

Taiwan 103

Tai Po Kai Nature Reserve 165, 190, 306, 308, 310

Tamshiyacu-Tahuayo 233

Tanaspi Island 199

Index

Tanaxpillo Island 199

Tangier 157

Tanjung Puting Wildlife Reserve 96-101, 103, 116, 302

Tanzania 11, 203, 204, 298, 312

Taricaya Ecological Reserve 239, 316

Tayrona National Park 261, 318

Tchiebebe 56

Tchindzoulou 56

Texas 184, 310

Thailand 110, 130, 135-142, 195, 198, 304, 310

The Gambia (see Gambia)

The Triangle (Conkouati-Douli National Park): 43, 45

Tijuca Forest/Tijuca National Park 249, 269, 316, 318

Tinjil Island vii, 193, 194, 310

Titusville 166, 176, 177, 308

Tortola 220, 314

Totogochillo Island 199, 310

Tsukumijima Island 208, 312

Uganda 13, 15, 17, 57, 298

UK (see also England) 23, 62, 65, 67, 69, 70, 151, 152, 153, 270, 314

Umnajjaroen Province 195

Unguja 203, 204, 312

União Biological Reserve 266, 267, 318

Union of the Comoros Islands 291, 322

USA/United States 41, 34, 159, 174, 176, 177, 186, 222, 295, 298, 306, 308, 310, 314, 316, 318

Van Long Nature Reserve 148, 306

Vaupés 235

Venezuela 241, 242, 316

Veracruz 199, 246, 247

Vietnam 129, 147, 148, 192, 202, 275, 276, 304, 306, 312, 320

Vinh Cuu Nature Reserve 129, 276, 303, 320

Virunga 83, 84

Volcanoes National Park 74, 82, 300

Vredefort Dome 207, 312

Vrindaban 180, 308

Wakayama Prefecture 196, 310

Wat Pa Sila Wiwek 195, 310

Wat Thammikaram Worawiharn 194, 195

West Java 133, 134, 152, 153, 164, 193, 196, 277, 278, 281-284, 306

West Kalimantan 114, 278, 280, 302

West Papua 310

Westlake Park 222, 314

Western Area Peninsula National Park 49, 198

Yakushima Prefecture 183

Yotoco Forest 262

Zaire 28, 57, 72, 77-79

Zanzibar 203, 204, 312

Zebra Island 223, 314

Zimbabwe 223, 314

Institutions, Organizations, Topics, Other

Acclimation vi, 2, 6, 11, 28, 36, 45, 52, 56, 57, 58, 59, 64, 65, 68, 70, 71, 72, 78, 82, 87, 88, 94, 95, 99, 103, 104, 106, 112, 115, 128, 129, 131, 133, 134, 137, 138, 140, 142, 143, 146, 148, 149, 151, 154, 156, 164, 170, 173, 181, 183, 192, 196, 199, 200, 202, 203, 205, 207, 208, 210, 211, 216, 217, 224, 225, 226, 227, 228, 229, 234, 239, 243, 245, 250, 257, 258, 261, 262, 263, 266, 270, 274, 275, 276, 277, 278, 280, 282, 283, 284, 286, 287, 289, 290, 294, 299, 301, 303, 305, 307, 309, 311, 313, 315, 317, 319, 321, 323

Affenberg Salem Zoo 156

African Primate Reintroduction Workshop iv

Africa's Eden 71

Aggression/Aggressive vi, 7, 11, 14, 15, 16, 18, 24, 25, 28, 31, 35, 36, 37, 41, 44, 45, 50, 53, 58, 59, 69, 70, 72, 73, 74, 75, 90, 100, 122, 132, 135, 136, 138, 139, 143, 159, 160, 170, 183, 192, 199, 202, 213, 226, 228, 233, 240, 242, 259

Allen's Rule 184

All-male Group (see also Bachelor Group) 64

Allwetter Zoo (see also Münster Zoo) 147

American Sign Language 28

Anesthetize/Anesthesia 30, 53, 148

Angkor Temple 131, 147, 304, 306

Anthropoid Ape Research Foundation 222

Antibiotic 32, 43, 52, 209

Antwerp Zoo 78

Ape (a novel) 55

Apenheul Primate Park iv

Appendicitis 68

Apsara Authority 130, 147

Aracruz Cellulose S.A. 274, 320

Aspinall Foundation (John Aspinall Foundation) 62, 63, 65, 69, 70

Aspinall Foundation Indonesia Programme 134, 151, 153, 284

Assisted Colonization 4, 203

Associação Mico-Leão Dourado 265, 268

Index

Bachelor/Bachelor Group (see also All-male Group) 64

Bacteria 39, 209

Bahati Principle vi, 15, 16, 76

Balinese Rajah 149

Bangalore City Corporation 161

Bangalore University of Agricultural Sciences 161

Barbary Macaque Conservation and Awareness 157

Batu Mbelin Quarantine Station 122

Bausch and Lomb 175

Behave/Behavior/Behavioral Ecology 7, 13, 14, 22, 29, 32, 42, 43, 44, 45, 52, 53, 54, 58, 62, 68, 77, 89, 95, 100, 101, 104, 105, 106, 107, 110, 112, 116, 117, 122, 126, 137, 140, 143, 159, 169, 171, 180, 182, 184, 189, 200, 209, 213, 218, 229, 234, 240, 252, 258, 262, 275, 277, 279, 280, 281, 282, 287, 289, 294, 296

Behavioral Science Foundation 198

Belize Audubon Society 243

Belize Ministry of Natural Resources 243

Berggorilla & Regenwald Direkthilfe 85

Bergmann's Rule 184

Biomedicine/Biomedical vii, 5, 21, 34, 38, 39, 41, 61, 71, 163, 167, 169, 174, 175, 177, 178, 184, 186, 192, 193, 194, 201, 210, 213, 220, 223, 224, 257

Birth/Birth Rate/Born vi, 20, 24, 26, 29, 30, 31, 32, 37, 38, 40, 41, 44, 45, 53, 58, 59, 63, 65, 68, 72, 90, 95, 100, 101, 102, 104, 105, 106, 110, 112, 121, 128, 131, 134, 135, 142, 153, 156, 160, 165, 170, 175, 178, 183, 191, 192, 193, 199, 204, 210, 211, 229, 240, 243, 244, 246, 247, 250, 267, 270, 274, 287, 290, 294, 295

Black Howler Monkey Rehabilitation Center 251

Blood Test: 43, 52, 58, 94, 243, 248

Boat/Ship/Voyage i, 18, 56, 59, 64, 106, 111, 115, 148, 149, 170, 186, 188, 200, 214, 219, 220, 278

Bogor Agricultural University 193

Bohorok Orangutan Rehabilitation Program 117-120

Bonnet House 252, 316

Born Free/Born Free Foundation 19

Born Free USA Primate Sanctuary 184

Bornean Orangutan Conservation Foundation/ Bornean Orangutan Conservation Society/ Balikpapan Orangutan Survival Foundation (BOS, BOSF) v, 102-112

Bowman Gray School of Medicine 193

Brain Stimulation 137

Brazzaville Zoo 61, 62

Breeding Colony i, 5, 41, 42, 163, 169, 170, 173, 175, 177, 183, 191-194, 197, 199, 201, 208, 210, 212, 213, 224, 258, 263, 265

Bridge 43, 70

British Union for the Abolition of Vivisection 3

Buddhism/Buddhist 132, 169

Bukit Lawang Orangutan Rehabilitation Program 118, 119

Bushmeat 61

Callithrichid Hepatitis Virus 267

Cambodian Forestry Administration 130, 147

Camp Filomena 98

Camp Kerantungan 98

Camp Rendell 98

Camp Seluang 98

Cancer 142

Canoe 58, 148

Caparú Biological Station 235

Captive-born/Captive-bred/Captivity (see also Zoo-born) ii, iii, 3, 4, 23, 28, 29, 31, 41, 50, 52, 53, 58, 62, 65, 67, 68, 70, 71, 102, 105, 110, 121, 123, 129, 133, 134, 138, 142, 145, 148, 151, 158, 160, 199, 200, 202, 207, 210, 213, 223, 225, 226, 232, 251, 258, 262, 265, 266, 267, 268, 274, 280, 281, 295, 298, 300, 302, 304, 306, 308, 310, 312, 314, 316, 318, 320, 322

Captive Breeding Specialist Group iv

Caratinga Biological Station 236, 314

Caribbean Primate Research Center (CPRC) 170-172, 177, 199, 213

Carrying Capacity 123, 151, 170, 195, 213, 271

Carthage/Carthaginian 154

Castle of Baboons 208

Cat Ba Langur Conservation Project 147

Cave 148

Census (see Survey)

Central Kalimantan Conservation and Natural Resources Authority 109, 110

Centre for Animal Rehabilitation and Education 207

Centre for Conservation of Natural Resources of West Java (BBKSDA) 281

Centre for Education, Research and Conservation of Primates and Nature (CERCOPAN) 216, 217, 230, 231

Centre for Natural Resources Conservation, West Kalimantan, Borneo (BKSDA) 280

Centre for Rehabilitation of Wildlife (CROW) 226

Centre International de Recherches Medicales de Franceville 71, 210

Centre National de Equipement Hydraulique 237, 261, 263

Centro de Atención y Valoración de Fauna Silvestre 262

Chagas Disease 160

Charles River Laboratories 175, 176

Chimpanzee Conservation Centre 52, 53, 55

Chimpanzee Rehabilitation Project (Program) 26, 30, 32

Chimpanzee Sanctuary and Wildlife Conservation Trust 19

Chipangali Wildlife Orphanage 223

Chromosome 293

Ciapus Primate Rescue Center 277, 281, 282

Circus 11, 12, 17, 158

CITES/Convention on International Trade in Endangered Species 3

Cognition/Cognitive 20, 31, 58, 92, 101, 104, 105, 184

Colobus Conservation 205, 206, 219

Communicable Disease (see also Disease) 34, 209, 213, 233

Community Baboon Sanctuary 244

Confiscate/Confiscated/ Confiscation 15, 17, 20, 28, 42, 48, 49, 52, 55, 67, 72, 74, 77, 81, 83, 86, 89, 90, 93, 97, 102, 109, 110, 111, 116, 121, 122, 124, 129, 130, 132, 133, 134, 139, 140, 141, 146, 147, 150, 152, 153, 157, 163, 164, 196, 202, 207, 208, 211, 219, 225, 233, 234, 235, 237, 239, 240, 245, 250, 251, 259, 260, 272, 273, 275, 276, 277, 278, 280, 282, 284, 285

Congolese Ministry of Economics and Forestry 62

Conseil National des Parcs Nationaux du Gabon 71

Conservation ii, iii, iv, v, 1, 12, 16, 88, 92, 123, 124, 132, 136, 140, 161, 172, 176, 193, 194, 205, 209, 218, 227, 228, 229, 243, 270, 271, 289, 294

Consilience 31

Contraception/Contracepted 16, 20, 21, 32, 38, 52, 155, 160, 165, 167, 190, 220, 271

Convention on International Trade in Endangered Species (CITES) 3

Copulation/Copulate 148, 192

Corridor/Connection (of Habitat) 218, 265, 268, 270

Crop-raiding 48, 64, 93, 161, 171, 178, 184, 186, 205, 209, 214, 218, 220

Cruelty Free International 2

Cuban Ministerio de Ciencia, Tecnología y Medio Ambiente 192, 201, 224

Dam 5, 237, 241, 242, 248, 256, 260, 261, 263, 264

Dania Chimp Farm 222

Dao Tien Endangered Primate Species Rescue Centre 129, 276

Dealer/Trader (Wildlife) 162, 166, 167, 191, 193, 249, 257, 259, 272, 273, 278, 280, 291

Dehydration 24, 41, 62, 74, 266

Delta Regional Primate Research Center 135

Department de Eaux and Forets (Senegal) 54

Department of Wildlife Conservation of Jammu 182

Dependency, Infant 145

Dian Fossey Gorilla Fund International 82, 84, 85

Diarrhea 266

Die/Death/Kill vi, 7, 13, 18, 23, 25, 26, 31, 32, 35, 36, 39, 40, 41, 44, 45, 47, 49, 53, 64, 68, 69, 70, 72, 75, 80, 81, 83, 90, 100, 107, 109, 110, 112, 117, 119, 135, 136, 137, 138, 139, 142, 154, 156, 158, 160, 167, 183, 190, 192, 199, 201, 205, 209, 210, 211, 227, 228, 233, 234, 237, 240, 242, 243, 244, 246, 248, 249, 266, 268, 270, 274, 275, 276, 278, 282, 284, 287, 289, 290, 294, 295

Disappear/Disappearance vi, 3, 7, 25, 31, 44, 45, 47, 53, 64, 68, 70, 82, 90, 107, 114, 134, 136, 138, 139, 140, 142, 143, 156, 213, 218, 234, 243, 244, 250, 254, 266, 268, 274, 275, 276, 287, 289, 290, 295

Disease 39, 55, 62, 63, 67, 76, 79, 83, 84, 103, 111, 116, 117, 118, 133, 138, 167, 168, 175, 266, 267, 268, 295

Disney Conservation Fund 84

DNA 11, 43, 154

Dog (Predation by) 55, 139, 227, 249

Douc Langur Foundation 147

Drill Rehabilitation and Breeding Center 48, 212

Duke University Primate Center 295

DuMond Conservancy vii, 190

East Javan Natural Resource Conservation Agency (BBKSDA) 284

East Kalimantan Natural Resources Conservation Agency 102

Ecological Replacement 4

Ecosystem iv, 3, 205, 220, 221

Ecotourism (see Tourism)

Edinburgh Zoo 201

Ekolo ya Bonobo 58

Electricité de France 241

Electrocution 6, 249

Emergency Rescue Center 277

Endangered Asian Species Trust 129

Endangered Primate Rescue Center 148

Endangered Species Rescue Center 275

Endoparasite/Endoparasitism (see also Parasite) 28, 29, 32, 36, 52, 95, 116, 210, 233

Entebbe Zoo 14, 15, 17, 19

Environmental Impact 171, 178, 186

Escape/Escaped 21, 35, 49, 50, 52, 58, 143, 168, 174, 176, 177, 178, 184, 187, 197, 213, 220, 222, 227, 245, 254, 264, 265, 269, 290, 291, 298, 304, 308, 310, 316, 318

Ethnotramp 188, 189

Ethnophoresy 189

Euthanize/Euthanasia 77, 79, 83, 94, 137, 155, 177, 181, 182, 200, 201, 214, 221, 267

Exposure (see also Hypothermia) 42, 73, 192, 252, 266

Extinction 4, 35, 38, 128, 140, 238, 239, 243, 250, 252, 254, 255, 262, 287, 293

Fauna Conservation Ordinance (Sabah) 88

Faune Savage 237, 261, 263

Fecal Glucocorticoid Metabolites vi, 211

Feces/Fecal Examination 43, 94, 167, 211

Federal University of Rio de Janeiro 249

Fernan-Vaz Gorilla Project 72

Filovirus 43

Florida Atlantic University 255, 318

Florida Audubon Society 176

Florida Game and Freshwater Fish Commission/Florida Fish and Wildlife Conservation Commission 167, 175, 223, 256

Fondation Le Pal Nature 128

Foraging/Feeding 6, 7, 43, 58, 62, 68, 70, 86, 99, 105, 106, 112, 114, 115, 116, 119, 122, 129, 160, 199, 210, 227, 229, 234, 240, 244, 246, 247, 251, 260, 262, 266, 275, 283, 287, 289, 294, 296

Founder (of Population) 11, 167, 175, 192, 215, 227, 238, 268, 271

Fragment (of Habitat) 218, 247, 252, 265, 267

Frankfurt Zoological Society/Frankfurt Zoo 11, 118, 121, 149, 265

Friends of Animals 33

Friends of Orangutans Malaysia 91

Friends of the Karura Forest 205

Friends of the National Zoo 265

Fundación Maikuchiga 234

Gabonese Department of Eaux and Forêts 66

Gambia Wildlife Conservation Department (Department of Parks and Wildlife Management) 24, 26, 30

Genetic Diversity/Inbreeding ii, 117, 167, 215, 238, 267, 289

Genetic Screening 11, 28, 32, 43, 45, 52, 58, 94, 100, 111, 122, 154, 210, 215, 242, 291, 292

Gibbon Rehabilitation Project 139-141

Gibbon Translocation Project of the Wildlife Trust of India 145

Gibraltar Ornithological and Natural History Society 155

Gift i, 149, 161, 162, 188

Gilgil Baboon Project 209, 210

Gorilla Rehabilitation and Conservation Education Center (GRACE) 84

GPS 44

Grooming 13, 14, 15, 41

Guidelines iv, v, vi, 3, 45, 52, 58, 67, 79, 123, 132, 140, 144, 169, 228, 232, 237, 245, 246, 275, 278, 285

Guragon Air Force Station 181

Habitat Ecologique et Liberté des Primates (HELP) 42, 43

Hamburg University 293

Hammer 24

Hand (Human)-rearing/Hand (Human)-reared (see also Nursery-rearing) 23, 28, 29, 30, 31, 41, 67, 72, 200, 227

Hard Release 5, 78, 82, 95, 266, 285, 286, 287, 289

Helicopter 103, 120

Help Guinea 47

Henry Doorly Zoo 287, 289

Hepatitis A/Hepatitis B/Hepatitis C Virus 34, 35, 36, 43, 52

Heritage Society of Jammu 182

Herpes B Virus 167, 171, 177, 186, 200

Hindu 169

Historic Range/Native Range 4, 11, 39, 174, 188, 238, 243, 252, 259, 261, 262, 265, 270, 271, 272, 273, 278, 285

Home Range 7, 59, 68, 69, 87, 106, 114, 119, 122, 149, 156, 211, 221, 234, 240, 242, 244, 246, 247, 263, 270, 271, 275, 279, 280, 282, 287, 289, 294, 296

Hon Me Rescue Center 202

Hoolock Gibbon Translocation Project 145

Howlers Forever 243

Howletts Animal Park 62, 65, 69, 70, 134, 151, 152, 153

Humane/Inhumane 88, 132, 169, 172

Humane Society International 84

Humane Society of the United States 38

Hunter/Hunting 48, 54, 55, 58, 63, 67, 126, 128, 131, 138, 140, 151, 165, 187, 191, 203, 207, 212, 215, 216, 227, 228, 233, 234, 238, 239, 242, 243, 250, 257, 261, 263, 264, 287, 290, 293, 294

Hurricane/Cyclone 189, 215, 243, 290

Hybridize/Hybrid/Hybridization 11, 21, 28, 32, 48, 73, 76, 100, 111, 165, 190, 196, 271, 272, 273, 284, 290, 293

Hyperthermia 83, 267, 276

Hypothermia 24, 252, 266

Ikamaperu 239

Ilonga-Pôo Community 58

Imitate/Imitation (see also Social Learning) 24, 36, 53, 89, 97

Immunize, Immunization, Immunity 5, 43, 58, 62, 63, 67, 70, 123

Indonesian Directorate of Wildlife Conservation 118

Indonesian Department of Forestry/Indonesian Ministry of Forestry/ Indonesian Department of Forest Protection and Nature Conservation/ Indonesian Directorate-General of Forestry/ Indonesian Forestry Department/Indonesian Forestry Service 97, 98, 99, 102, 109, 116, 121, 133, 151

Indonesian Orangutan Action Plan and Conservation Strategy 111

Infant Mortality (see also Mortality) 44, 53, 90, 119, 135, 159, 211, 244, 266, 287

Infinite EARTH 98

Innate Behavior/Instinct 88

Institut Congolais pour la Conservation de la Nature 81, 84

Institut Zairois pour la Conservation de la Nature 81

Institute of Primate Research 218

Instituto Brasiliero de Desenvolvimento Florestal 265

Instituto Brasiliero do Meio Ambiente e Recursos Natureis 265

Instituto de Pesquisas Ecológicas (IPE) 270

Instituto Oswaldo Cruz 173

Instituto Uriaçu 250

International Animal Rescue (IAR) 114, 115, 164, 196, 249, 277, 278, 280-285

International Fund for Animal Welfare 19, 84

International Gorilla Conservation Programme 77, 78, 81, 82, 84

International Primate Protection League 137

International Psychiatric Research Foundation 137

Introduction (of Primates) ii, 4, 160, 162, 173, 174, 175, 185, 188, 190, 191, 192, 197, 199, 201, 203, 204, 261, 286, 288, 290, 291, 292, 294, 298, 310, 312, 320, 322

Island/Islet (not as part of a place name) i, 2, 3, 11, 16, 17, 18, 19, 21, 26, 27, 31, 32, 34, 35, 36, 37, 38, 39, 40, 42, 43, 44, 47, 56, 57, 61, 64, 65, 70, 71, 72, 87, 106, 107, 111, 115, 122, 129, 135, 138, 139, 140, 147, 148, 149, 154, 159, 160, 161, 166, 167, 169, 170, 171, 173, 174, 175, 176, 177, 178, 188, 194, 199, 200, 201, 211, 213, 214, 219, 220, 221, 224, 233, 238, 254, 257, 258, 263, 288, 291, 292, 295

IUCN Re-introduction Specialist Group iv, 45

IUCN/World Conservation Union iv, v, vi, 3, 58, 67, 79, 84, 123, 132, 140, 144, 228, 237, 245, 246, 285, 286

Jambi Reintroduction Station 121, 122

Jane Goodall Institute/Foundation 17, 19, 56, 63, 77, 211

Jantho Reintroduction Station 121, 122

Japan Monkey Centre 182, 183, 191, 192, 197, 208

Japanese National Institute for Environmental Studies 196

Jardin Zoologico de Puerto Rico 171

Javan Gibbon Centre 133

Javan Gibbon Foundation 133

Javan Langur Rehabilitation Centre 151

Javan Primate Conservation Project/ Javan Primate Rehabilitation Centre 134, 151, 152, 153, 284, 285

Jersey Wildlife Preservation Trust International 232, 265

Jersey Zoo 270

Jungle Cruises 166, 167

Kalaweit Gibbon Reintroduction Program 128, 143, 145

Kanyawara 13

Kariosoke 74, 75

Kenya Wildlife Service 205

Ketambe 116-120

Kibale Forest Chimpanzee Project 13, 14

Krabok Koo Wildlife Breeding Center 130

Kyoto University 57

Laboratory i, vii, 23, 34, 35, 36, 37, 39, 41, 42, 135, 138, 167, 169, 170, 172, 174, 186, 197, 199, 200, 213, 223, 257, 258

La Parguera Research Facility 170, 171, 177

Les Amis de Ponso 40

Les Amis des Bonobos du Congo 58

Liberian Institute for Biomedical Research 34, 38

Lifetime Care 16, 38, 49, 101, 107, 109, 111, 122, 221

Liongwe Wildlife Centre 208

Locomote/Locomotion 6, 13, 14, 15, 41, 43, 52, 58, 62, 68, 70, 71, 86, 87, 89, 93, 97, 99, 103, 105, 115, 122, 123, 129, 132, 133, 143, 146, 156, 164, 196, 205, 210, 227, 235, 258, 260, 262, 264, 265, 269, 278, 296

Lola ya Bonobo Sanctuary 58, 63

London Zoo 23

Lum Nam Pai Wildlife Sanctuary 142, 304

Madagascan/Malagasy Department de Eaux et Forèts 286, 293

Madagascar Biodiversity and Biogeography Project 287, 289

Madagascar Fauna Group 288, 289

Madagascar National Parks Department 287, 289

Mahidol University 130, 142

Malnutrition (see Starvation)

Masterpiece Gardens 254, 318

Matang Wildlife Centre 93, 96

Mate Choice 3

Measles 175

Melbourne Zoo 79

Mello Leitão Museum of Biology 274

Mercy Release 131

Ministère de l'Environnement, des Forêts et de Tourisme (of Madagascar) 287, 289

Ministry of Agriculture (Peru) 263

Ministry of the Environment (Democratic Republic of Congo) 58

Monkey Farm/Monkey Farming vii, 186, 196, 257

Monkey Jungle 189

Monkey Valley 183

Moor/Moorish 154

Mortality (see also Infant Mortality) 26, 62, 65, 69, 122, 169, 170, 178, 210, 211, 277, 278, 285

Mother-reared: 288

Mount Kenya Wildlife Conservancy and Orphanage 205

Mountain Gorilla Project 74

Mountain Gorilla Veterinary Project 82, 84

Municipal Corporation of Delhi 179, 181

Münster Zoo (see also Allwetter Zoo) 147

Natal Group 13, 51, 55, 81, 83, 157

National Institute of Renewable Natural Resources and Environment (INDERENA) 261

National Parks and Wildlife Office of the Sarawak Forest Department 93, 132

National Zoological Park of India 180

Natural Foods 3, 6, 11, 12, 13, 14, 15, 19, 20, 21, 24, 28, 36, 37, 41, 43, 44, 45, 52, 59, 62, 67, 70, 71, 73, 74, 81, 82, 83, 87, 89, 90, 93, 97, 99, 101, 103, 104, 111, 116, 119, 122, 129, 132, 133, 134, 138, 142, 143, 145, 146, 151, 156, 160, 161, 164, 171, 181, 183, 184, 193, 196, 199, 205, 209, 210, 211, 224, 227, 229, 234, 235, 237, 240, 243, 245, 246, 250, 252, 262, 277, 278, 280, 281, 282, 296

Natural Resources Conservation Office of Aceh 121

Natural Vegetation 41, 52, 57, 58, 61, 62, 70, 71, 93, 97, 111, 115, 122, 129, 132, 143, 164, 170, 196, 210, 211, 227, 235, 245, 252, 262, 277, 278, 288

Nest/Nest-building 7, 11, 12, 13, 21, 24, 28, 36, 37, 41, 43, 44, 52, 57, 59, 62, 72, 74, 87, 89, 99, 101, 103, 104, 105, 106, 111, 113, 115, 122, 123

Nest Box 266, 267

New York Blood Center 34, 38, 39

New York Zoological Society 243, 295

Ngamba Island Chimpanzee Sanctuary 14, 15, 18, 19, 20, 57

Nigeria National Park Service 217, 230

Ninh Binh Forest Protection Department 148

Noell's Chimp Farm 28

Non-lethal Control ii, 5, 12, 19, 29, 38, 40, 94, 138, 154, 156, 158, 161, 163, 172, 174, 178, 179, 180, 181, 182, 184, 195, 201, 210, 211, 218, 223, 238, 258, 259, 271, 272, 273, 298, 302, 304, 306, 308, 310, 312, 314, 316, 318, 320

Nursery-rearing/Nursery-reared (see Hand-rearing)

Nyaru Mentang Orangutan Reintroduction Project 109-113, 114

Office Rwandais du Tourisme et des Parc Nationaux (ORTPN) 74, 81, 82, 83

Oklahoma City Zoo 28

Operant Conditioning 122

Operation Gwamba 241, 256, 260, 264

Operation Loango 71

Operation Rescue 241

Orangutan Appeal UK 94

Orangutan Care Centre and Quarantine 98, 99

Orangutan Foundation International (OFI) 97, 98

Orangutan Foundation of the United Kingdom (OFI-UK) 98, 99, 100, 101

Orangutan Haven 122

Orangutan Rehabilitation Center 97

Orangutan Research and Conservation Program 97

Order of the British Empire 33

Oregon Regional Primate Research Center 3, 193

Orientation/Navigation (by primates): 7, 43

Orphan/Orphaned v, vi, 13, 15, 17, 34, 38, 51, 52, 55, 56, 57, 58, 61, 62, 67, 72, 73, 77, 81, 82, 83, 84, 91, 101, 121, 125, 126, 211, 212, 219, 223, 229, 250, 293

Outbreeding 100

Palau Natural Habitat Breeding Facility 193

Pan African Sanctuary Alliance iv, 125

Pandrillus 15, 48, 49, 212

PanEco Foundation 121, 122

Parasite/Parasitism (see also Endoparasite) 41, 43, 58

Paris Museum of Natural History 286

Pasteur Institute 258

Peritonitis 68

Personhood 40

Perth Zoo 121, 123, 134

Peruvian Center for Reproduction and Conservation of Nonhuman Primates 263

Pet/Ex-pet i, 23, 28, 34, 35, 36, 37, 77, 97, 129, 130, 132, 133, 139, 141, 143, 149, 154, 157, 162, 164,

186, 188, 196, 202, 204, 215, 219, 220, 223, 229, 233, 234, 235, 237, 239, 242, 250, 251, 252, 261, 272, 273, 276, 278, 280, 282, 291, 293

Phoenician 154

Plant and Wildlife Department of Thailand's Department of National Parks 139, 141

Play 14, 15, 68, 69, 72, 75, 132, 167

Pleistocene 155

Pneumonia 41, 75, 76, 183

Poacher/Poaching 13, 15, 20, 46, 54, 57, 59, 72, 74, 79, 80, 81, 82, 257

Pointe Noire Zoo 43

Poison 207, 266

Polio 43, 58, 170

Pondak Tanggui 97

Population and Habitat Viability Analysis 8, 64, 69, 90, 101

Port Lympne Animal Park 62, 65, 67, 69, 70, 151, 153

Portuguese Sailors/Explorers (see also Sailors) 186, 219

Post-release Monitoring v, vi, 7, 11, 12, 26, 32, 35, 36, 39, 41, 44, 46, 57, 58, 59, 64, 68, 78, 81, 90, 94, 95, 100, 101, 104, 106, 110, 111, 112, 114, 115, 116, 120, 121, 122, 123, 128, 129, 130, 133, 134, 136, 140, 142, 143, 145, 146, 148, 149, 150, 151, 152, 153, 154, 156, 157, 161, 164, 180, 181, 182, 189, 192, 196, 198, 200, 202, 203, 207, 209, 210, 211, 216, 217, 218, 219, 221, 224, 225, 226, 227, 228, 229, 234, 236, 237, 238, 240, 242, 243, 245, 246, 248, 249, 250, 251, 257, 258, 259, 260, 263, 264, 266, 268, 270, 274, 275, 276, 277, 278, 280, 282, 283, 284, 285, 286, 287, 288, 289, 294, 299, 301, 303, 305, 307, 309, 311, 313, 315, 317, 319, 321, 323

Post-release Support/Post-release Management vii, 6, 7, 8, 11, 12, 24, 30, 31, 35, 68, 82, 89, 94, 97, 99, 101, 103, 105, 106, 112, 114, 115, 119, 128, 129, 139, 143, 145, 146, 154, 158, 165, 166, 173, 181, 182, 190, 195, 198, 202, 207, 209, 226, 233, 237, 238, 243, 245, 249, 250, 251, 259, 261, 266, 270, 274, 275, 276, 278, 279, 282, 284, 286, 287, 288, 289, 290, 294, 299, 301, 303, 305, 307, 309, 311, 313, 315, 317, 319, 321, 323

Predation/Predator 3, 6, 7, 15, 28, 73, 117, 199, 205, 209, 211, 223, 224, 226, 227, 229, 233, 237, 240, 260, 266, 270, 274, 275, 276, 279, 280, 287, 288, 294

Pregnant/Pregnancy 41, 45, 294

Prehistoric/Prehistory 126, 185, 188

Pre-release Preparation/Pre-release Management v, vii, 2, 3, 5, 6, 11, 13, 24, 31, 36, 39, 45, 56, 57, 63, 64, 65, 68, 70, 73, 78, 82, 94, 97, 99, 103, 105, 106, 111, 114, 119, 128, 129, 131, 132, 137, 142, 146, 151, 154, 157, 158, 165, 166, 170, 173, 178, 179, 182, 183, 189, 190, 191, 195, 196, 198, 199, 200, 202, 203, 205, 207, 208, 210, 218, 224, 225, 226, 227, 228, 229, 233, 234, 236, 237, 238, 243, 246, 250, 251, 257, 259, 261, 262, 266, 270, 276, 277, 278, 279, 280, 282, 284, 286, 287, 288, 289, 290, 293, 298, 300, 302, 304, 306, 308, 310, 312, 314, 316, 318, 320, 322

ProFauna, Indonesia 150

Program for the Rehabilitation and Reintroduction of the Black-faced Spider Monkey 239

Programme HURO 146

Projects Abroad 239

Projet de Conservation des Chimpanzés en Guinée 48, 52

Projet de Protection des Gorilles (PPG) 62, 66, 67, 69, 70

Provisioning/Provisioned (see also Supplemental Feeding) v, 5, 7, 8, 11, 13, 18, 19, 20, 21, 22, 24, 26, 29, 31, 32, 35, 36, 37, 39, 40, 41, 48, 52, 53, 56, 57, 59, 63, 64, 89, 101, 116, 117, 119, 128, 132, 135, 136, 137, 138, 139, 144, 145, 149, 155, 156, 158, 159, 160, 163, 165, 166, 167, 170, 171, 175, 177, 178, 179, 181, 184, 189, 190, 192, 193, 195, 199, 200, 201, 205, 213, 222, 224, 226, 227, 228, 234, 238, 246, 252, 253, 254, 255, 257, 258, 261, 263, 266, 267, 271, 273, 275, 276, 288, 295

Purpose (of reintroduction) iii, iv, 1, 4, 5, 21, 61, 62, 70, 71, 82, 172, 183, 197, 199, 201, 206, 208, 213, 224, 239, 255, 256, 258, 263, 272, 275, 293, 296, 298, 300, 302, 304, 306, 308, 310, 312, 314, 316, 318, 320, 322

Pusat Penyelamatan Rehabilitation Sanctuary/ Pusat Penyelamatan Satwa Rescue Center/ Pusat Transit Satwa (PTS) Wildlife Transit Centre 146, 163, 276

QIT Madagascar Minerals 293, 294

Quarantine 5, 45, 58, 70, 72, 82, 83, 89, 97, 98, 103, 111, 119, 121, 122, 123, 129, 132, 133, 134, 140, 143, 145, 149, 151, 152, 153, 157, 163, 164, 175, 193, 196, 211, 216, 224, 247, 266, 267, 270, 275, 276, 278, 280, 281, 282, 284

Rabat Zoo 157

Rabies 175

Radio/Radiotelemetry/Radio Collar v, 7, 35, 36, 44, 52, 53, 56, 59, 95, 105, 106, 110, 111, 114, 122, 129, 134, 148, 149, 160, 209, 210, 211, 216, 226, 227, 228, 229, 239, 240, 242, 243, 250, 261, 266, 267, 270, 274, 275, 276, 278, 279, 280, 282, 287, 289, 294, 295

Recapture 7, 23, 34, 35, 36, 37, 44, 50, 52, 100, 104, 110, 114, 129, 130, 136, 137, 138, 140, 142, 143, 192, 207, 211, 213, 216, 218, 228, 229, 235, 237, 240, 246, 248, 258, 265, 269, 270, 274, 276, 282, 294, 295

Record-keeping 100, 104, 210

Refuge for Wildlife 249

Rehabilitate/Rehabilitation ii, 4, 13, 16, 19, 27, 29, 33, 38, 40, 42, 46, 48, 49, 54, 57, 58, 59, 61, 62, 63, 65, 69, 70, 72, 76, 77, 79, 81, 82, 84, 86, 87, 88, 90, 91, 92, 93, 94, 95, 96, 97, 98, 99, 100, 101, 102, 103, 104, 105, 106, 107, 109, 110, 111, 112, 113, 114, 115, 116, 118, 120, 121, 124, 125, 128, 130, 131, 132, 133, 134, 136, 138, 139 140, 142, 143, 144, 145, 146, 147, 150, 151, 152, 153, 164, 165, 196, 202, 205, 206, 207, 208, 209, 211, 212, 216, 217, 219, 224, 225, 226, 227, 228, 229, 231, 234, 235, 237, 239, 240, 242, 245, 246, 250, 251, 252, 260, 262, 275, 276, 277, 278, 279, 280, 281, 282, 283, 284, 293, 298, 300, 302, 304, 306, 308, 310, 312, 314, 316, 318, 320, 322

Reinforce/Reinforcement 4, 40, 46, 52, 54, 59, 71, 81, 82, 84, 134, 148, 151, 152, 154, 155, 156, 203, 217, 219, 239, 268, 270, 279, 281, 283, 289, 298, 300, 302, 306, 312, 314, 320

Reintroduction sensu strictu ii, 1, 4, 7, 59, 65, 66,

69, 70, 124, 140, 155, 165, 203, 238, 240, 243, 249, 265, 268, 270, 287, 290, 293, 298, 300, 302, 304, 306, 312, 316, 318, 320

Reproduce, Reproduction v, 7, 8, 12, 32, 43, 88, 90, 100, 101, 106, 122, 128, 140, 145, 148, 150, 151, 158, 159, 167, 175, 177, 179, 209, 233, 242, 245, 246, 258, 259, 267, 270, 287, 288, 290

Re-release 7, 14, 23, 36, 37, 44, 52, 72, 83, 100, 104, 105, 106, 110, 114, 130, 138, 140, 142, 157, 207, 233, 240, 248, 270, 294

Rescue ii, v, vi, 5, 7, 15, 23, 34, 42, 44, 48, 49, 51, 52, 55, 56, 58, 61, 62, 75, 77, 86, 93, 97, 98, 99, 101, 107, 109, 111, 113, 114, 115, 121, 123, 125, 126, 146, 147, 150, 151, 152, 153, 154, 157, 198, 205, 207, 208, 209, 212, 216, 218, 219, 225, 226, 227, 236, 237, 239, 240, 241, 242, 246, 247, 248, 249, 250, 256, 260, 261, 264, 265, 266, 267, 270, 276, 277, 294, 295, 298, 300, 302, 304, 306, 310, 314, 316, 318, 322

Restocking 1

Restorasi Habitat Orangutan Indonesia (PT RHOI) 105, 106

Retrovirus 43

Rewilding 1

Rifle (Gun, Gunshot, Shoot) 11, 15, 59, 72, 74, 80, 81, 82, 90, 101, 110, 111, 115, 161, 198, 207, 209, 220, 266

Rio de Janeiro Primate Center 250, 265, 268, 274

Rio de Janeiro Zoo 264, 265, 318

River Blindness 34

Riverside Wildlife Rehabilitation Centre 207

Rockland State Hospital 137

Rock of Gibraltar 306

Rome/Roman 154

Rutgers University Medical School 198

Sabah Wildlife Department 91, 93-95

Sailors (see also Portuguese Sailors/Explorers) i, 149, 161, 185, 186, 188, 214, 215, 220, 291

Salt Water Media viii

Samboja Lestari Center 103, 105, 106, 107, 109, 111, 114

Sanctuary/Rehabilitation Center/Rescue Center (not as part of an institutional name) v, vi, 4, 5, 15, 16, 19, 38, 40, 42, 43, 44, 48, 52, 53, 57, 58, 61, 63, 66, 67, 77, 79, 83, 125, 126, 130, 159, 184, 211, 216, 217, 223, 227, 228, 230, 231, 239, 240, 276, 277, 280, 281

San Diego Zoo 86

Sarawak Forestry Department 96

Sarawak Museum of Natural History 86

School of Tropical Medicine 169

Self-sustaining (Population) iv, v, 3, 7, 8, 107, 140. 167, 184, 193, 204, 238, 243, 263, 267

Semengok Wildlife Rehabilitation Centre 93, 96

Senegal Direction de Parcs Nationaux, 23

Sepilok Orangutan Rehabilitation Centre/Sepilok 87-90, 91, 94, 95

Sex Ratio 44, 90

Shangri-La Rasa Ria Resort and Spa 91

Sheraton Kampala Hotel 17

Silvery Gibbon Project 133

Smithsonian Institution 265

Smithsonian National Zoological Park 265, 267

Smithsonian Tropical Research Institute 237

Smuggle, Smuggler 28, 137

Snakebite 55, 58, 123, 268

Social Learning/Observational Learning (see also Imitate/Imitation) 6, 36, 62, 87, 89, 105, 112, 113, 117, 122

Société du Développement du Parc de la Lékédi 210

Société pour la Conservation et le Development 71

Soft Release 5, 24, 67, 100, 101, 106, 111, 138, 140 266, 276, 278

Sonja Wildlife Rehabilitation Centre 146

SOS Ponso 40

South Carolina Department of Natural Resources 177, 178

Southeast Asia Treaty Organization 135

Starvation/Malnutrition 73, 109, 112, 114, 117, 154, 183, 211, 233, 266, 274, 275, 293

Stereotypic Behavior 36, 37, 200

Sterilization/Sterilize (see also Contraception) 167, 181, 220

Stirling University/Stirling University Primate Research Unit 200

Strychnos Fruit 164

Success/Successful v, vi, vii, 7, 8, 12, 14, 31, 32, 42, 90, 100, 101, 107, 112, 113, 123, 148, 162, 169, 206, 210, 229, 232, 250, 265, 267, 268, 269, 279, 280, 299, 301, 303, 305, 307, 309, 311, 313, 315, 317, 319, 321, 323

Suffocation 267

Sumatra Rainforest Institute 146

Sumatran Orangutan Conservation Program (SOCP) 67, 121-123

Supplemental Feeding (see also Provisioning) 7, 18, 28, 44, 59, 64, 68, 70, 93, 94, 95, 100, 104, 106, 110, 112, 122, 128, 129, 130, 131, 134, 140, 145, 173, 209, 211, 216, 226, 227, 228, 234, 239, 252, 270, 286

Surabaya Zoo 154

Surface-to-Mass Ratio 184

Survey/Census 20, 41, 46, 58, 63, 90, 94, 102, 104, 122, 132, 138, 140, 143, 145, 163, 164, 179, 187, 193, 196, 201, 203, 204, 210, 215, 216, 222, 224, 227, 244, 245, 259, 267, 276, 278, 282, 285, 288

Survival-critical Skills 5, 6, 24, 28, 53, 88, 89, 90,

97, 99, 101, 105, 111, 113, 117

Survive/Survival/Survivorship v, vi, 12, 25, 32, 36, 37, 40, 44, 46, 48, 49, 58, 64, 69, 75, 100, 106, 107, 110, 112, 120, 121, 136, 138, 140, 142, 143, 149, 150, 151, 153, 154, 157, 171, 173, 175, 177, 189, 192, 209, 210, 211, 212, 218, 220, 226, 229, 238, 240, 246, 251, 258, 260, 261, 266, 267, 274, 276, 282, 285, 286, 287, 288, 295

Sustainable Ecosystem Foundation (YEL) 121, 122

Tacugama Chimpanzee Sanctuary 49

Tahuayo Lodge 233

Tanjung Harapan 97

Taricaya Rescue Center 239

Tattoo/Tattooed 122, 171, 175, 178, 213, 264, 266

Tchimpounga Sanctuary/ Tchimpounga Chimpanzee Rehabilitation Centre 56, 57, 63, 211

Temple 131, 147, 195, 198, 202

Territory 136, 143, 146, 260

Tetanus 43, 58, 175

Thailand Department of National Parks 142

Theft (of Primates) (see also Poaching) 266

Thirteen Gold Monkeys 267, 268

Tijuca Biological Bank 264, 265, 269

Tool/Tool-using 24, 28, 35, 37, 50, 53, 87, 117

Tourism/Tourist/Ecotourist 11, 13, 17, 18, 20, 23, 32, 56, 64, 65, 71, 72, 79, 81, 83, 87, 90, 93, 94, 97, 100, 104, 118, 119, 131, 155, 158, 159, 166, 167, 195, 196, 222, 233, 234, 252, 253, 254, 257, 261, 294

Train/Training 6, 7, 24, 28, 45, 56, 57, 64, 70, 78, 87, 89, 106, 139, 183, 245, 258, 266, 274, 284

Translocate/Translocation ii, 1, 92, 93, 94, 98, 99, 102, 103, 104, 110, 114, 121, 145, 147, 148, 154, 159, 161, 170, 171, 172, 175, 177, 178, 179, 180, 181, 182, 195, 202, 203, 204, 209, 217, 218, 218, 235, 241, 243, 244, 246, 247, 256, 260, 261, 263, 265, 266, 267, 270, 271, 281, 293, 294

Trap/Trapper/Trapping 161, 167, 171, 179, 180, 182, 183, 186, 191, 198, 203, 220, 221, 223, 252, 255, 267, 286, 294

Tropical Wonderland 176

Truck 17, 24, 58, 64, 94, 103, 106, 111, 243, 272, 273, 295

Tuberculosis 13, 36, 43, 52, 170

Tuglaqabad Fort 180, 308

Tumor 68

Twycross Zoo 23, 24

Uganda Wildlife Research and Education Center 17, 18, 19

Ugandan Wildlife Authority 13, 19

University of Agricultural Sciences 161

University of Antananarivo 293

University of California, San Diego 209

University of Cordoba 262

University of Mexico 198

University of Nebraska 265

University of Pisa 293

University of Puerto Rico 169

University of Veracruz 198, 247

University of Wageningen 116

University of Washington Regional Primate Research Center 193

US Agency for International Development 17

US Armed Forces Research Institute of Medical Sciences 135, 138

US Center for Disease Control 177

US Coast Guard 254

US Fish and Wildlife Service 84

US Food and Drug Administration 177

US National Institute of Neurological Diseases and Blindness 170

US National Institutes of Health 170, 178, 213

Vaccinate/Vaccination/Vaccine 43, 63, 119, 122, 170, 175, 213, 268

Valley of Wild Monkeys 159

Vasectomize/Vasectomy 17, 18, 19, 20

Veterinarian/Veterinary/Animal Health/Medical 5, 7, 13, 17, 18, 20, 21, 28, 32, 40, 41, 42, 43, 44, 45, 56, 58, 59, 63, 64, 67, 68, 70, 73, 76, 78, 79, 81, 82, 83, 86, 89, 93, 94, 95, 99, 101, 103, 106, 107, 111, 115, 119, 121, 122, 129, 131, 132, 133, 134, 138, 140, 142, 143, 145, 146, 148, 149, 151, 155, 170, 178, 179, 181, 182, 183, 191, 193, 199, 200, 201, 202, 207, 209, 211, 213, 216, 217, 218, 225, 226, 227, 228, 230, 233, 234, 236, 237, 238, 239, 240, 242, 243, 245, 246, 249, 252, 257, 258, 259, 261, 262, 264, 266, 267, 270, 274, 275, 276, 277, 278, 280, 281, 282, 285, 287, 289

Vietnam Forestry Protection Department 129

VILAB (ViLab, VILAB II) 22, 34, 35, 37, 38, 39, 40

Virus/Viral 34, 35, 36, 43, 52, 167, 171, 177, 186, 200, 267

Vocalization 7, 28, 29, 73, 75, 129, 136, 138, 157, 200, 252, 296

Wake Forest University 193

Wallace's Line 188, 189

Wanariset Orangutan Reintroduction Project 102, 103, 104, 105, 109

Weight 184, 296

Welfare ii, iii, iv, 13, 19, 34, 39, 57, 77, 124, 131, 209, 211, 255, 256

Wellbeing ii, vi, 15, 16, 28, 42

Whiskey/Scotch Whiskey 11, 28

Index

Wild Animal Rescue Centre 150

Wild Animal Rescue Project of Thailand 139-141

Wild Animal Trauma Centre and Haven (WATCH) 227, 228

Wild-born ii, iii, 3, 4, 17, 20, 21, 23, 24, 28, 31, 35, 36, 41, 42, 50, 52, 67, 68, 70, 71, 102, 105, 110, 121, 123, 130, 133, 138, 142, 151, 156, 164, 196, 197, 198, 199, 208, 213, 222, 226, 235, 236, 239, 240, 242, 246, 252, 253, 254, 255, 258, 262, 263, 264, 265, 266, 267, 269, 274, 289, 298, 300, 302, 304, 306, 308, 310, 312, 314, 316, 318, 320, 322

Wildlife Alliance 130, 147

Wildlife At Risk 202

Wildlife Care Center of Belize 237, 245

Wildlife Conservation Division of Thailand's Royal Forest Department 139

Wildlife Conservation Society 295

Wildlife Friends Foundation Thailand 142

Wildlife Trust of India 145

World Society for the Protection of Animals 260

World War II 154, 169, 170, 171, 174

World Wildlife Fund 116, 118, 161

Wound/Wounding 15, 24, 30, 55, 183, 233, 266, 295

Xenophobia/Xenophobic 44, 75

Yale University Medical School 137

Yellow Fever 173, 243, 250, 268

Yerkes Regional Primate Research Center 41

Zanzibar Forestry Department 203

Zoo iii, 3, 4, 11, 12, 14, 15, 17, 23, 29, 61, 62, 65, 67, 70, 71, 72, 76, 77, 78, 79, 87, 88, 123, 135, 151, 153, 156, 184, 196, 201, 264, 265, 266, 295, 296

Zoo-born (see also Captive/Captive-born) 29, 62, 65, 67, 70, 121, 123, 124, 134, 151, 156, 265, 295

Zoological Parks Board of New South Wales 19